HAND-BOOK

OF THE

MANUFACTURES AND ARTS

OF THE

PUNJAB

HAND-BOOK

OF THE

MANUFACTURES AND ARTS

OF THE

PUNJAB,

WITH A COMBINED GLOSSARY AND INDEX OF VERNACULAR TRADES AND TECHNICAL TERMS, &c., &c.

IN TWO VOLUMES

VOL. II.

FORMING

TO THE "HAND-BOOK OF THE ECONOMIC PRODUCTS OF THE PUNJAB."

BY

B. H. BADEN POWELL,

H. M. BENGAL CIVIL SERVICE

GYAN

Published by

Gyan Publishing House
5, Ansari Road
Daryaganj, New Delhi-110002
Phone: 011-47034999, 9811692060
E-mail: books@gyanbooks.com

Distribution Network
gyanbooks.com
India, USA, Canada, UK, Australia, France

ISBN: 978-81-212-8180-5 (Set)
978-81-212-8178-2 (PB)
First Published, 1872

2nd Impression 2023

Printed at: Gyan Press, Delhi.

HAND-BOOK OF THE MANUFACTURES AND ARTS OF THE PUNJAB, VOL. II. (FORMING)
Author: B. H. BADEN POWELL

HAND-BOOK

OF THE

MANUFACTURES AND ARTS

OF THE

PUNJAB,

WITH A COMBINED GLOSSARY AND INDEX OF VERNACULAR TRADES AND TECHNICAL TERMS, &c., &c.

FORMING VOL. II
TO THE "HAND-BOOK OF THE
ECONOMIC PRODUCTS OF THE PUNJAB."

PREPARED UNDER THE ORDERS OF GOVERNMENT,

BY

B. H. BADEN POWELL,

H. M. BENGAL CIVIL SERVICE.

LAHORE:

PUNJAB PRINTING COMPANY,

1872.

NOTICE.

It is necessary that a word or two should be said in explanation of the system of spelling adopted in this book.

From typographical and other difficulties, the varieties of consonants in the vernacular, have not been distinguished by the diacritical points sometimes adopted. To this, indeed, an exception is to be found in the nasal "n" which often closes Punjabí words, this is represented by "ṅ."

The vowels in all purely vernacular words are either accented or unaccented. Of the accented vowels—

á is always broad, as in the French "gâteau."

e is always pronounced "ay," or as "é" in French.

í is long, as "ee."

o is long, like "ó" in depôt.

ú is long, as "oo."

y is a consonant, as in "yes."

The unaccented vowels are—

a always like the "a" in "organ."

i like "i" in "pit."

u like the "u" in "full."

The varieties of consonants need not, for the mere understanding of the terms in this book, be nicely attended to.

Indeed, in any case, it is rare to find an European who really distinguishes between the س and the ص; or between ض, ظ, ذ, ز.

The only thing I could have wished would have been to distinguish the guttural غ ghain, and the khe خ; but this was impracticable for want of type.

I may add in the āin ع is represented by an apostrophe (') before the vowel to which it is attached.

Any reader who will remember the vowel list, just given, will find no difficulty in correctly pronouncing the vernacular words in the book.

I have not, however, thought it necessary to alter the received spelling of such common words as "Calcutta," "Punjab," "Lahore;" but in the case of the technical names of fabrics, tools, &c., every one's experience of the defects of such an uncertain method as that formerly in use will tell him that there is no other system which secures accuracy but the "letter for letter" system.

CONTENTS.

CLASS XII. METAL MANUFACTURES.

CLASS XIII. JEWELLERY, ... 175

CLASS XIV. ARTICLES OF VERTU, ... 202

CLASS XV. WOOD MANUFACTURES, ... 203

CLASS XVI. IVORY CARVING, ... 214

CLASS XVII. PAPIER MACHE AND PAINTED WARE, ... 218

CLASS XVIII. POTTERY, ... 220

SECTION C. MACHINERY.

ERRATA.

Please to correct your book or you may be misled as to Vernacular terms.

Page vii, line 14 from top, *for* " Bishahr, " *read* " Basáhir."
„ viii, (p. 3), *for* " coarse blankets called *bórá* and mats for the floor called *ásan*," *read* " coarse blankets and mats for the floor called " bhúrá."
„ 7, No. 70, *for* " Kálábágh," *read* " from Kálábágh."
„ 11, line 15, and throughout the page, *for* " gori," *read* " ghori."
„ 13, No. 197, *for* " in shamyána," *read* " a shamyána."
„ 25-28, and *passim*, *for* " lohí," *read* " loí."
„ 28, line 14 from the bottom, *for* " Bishair," *read* " Basáhir."
„ 29, the heading " GALIM," should be *read* galím.
„ 30, No. 279, *for* " a thick rug," *read* " a thick ring."
„ 34, line 8 from the top, *for* " Un Rampúri," *read* " U'n Rampúri."
„ 47, No. 392, *for* ' úrmuk,' read ' urmak,' and *for* " camel's hair," *read* " sheep's wool roughly embroidered."
„ 61, lines 8 and 11 from the bottom } *for* " treddles," *read* heddles.
„ 62, line 6 from the top }
„ 71, „ 538, *for* ' sash,' *read* ' leash.'
„ 72, „ 545, *for* " bamchí," *read* " penchí."
„ 73, (Prize list), *for* ' twilled silk,' *read* " twisted silk."
„ 74, line 4 from bottom, *for* " course," *read* " coarse."
„ 98, line 7 from bottom, *for* " one," *read* " some."
„ 99 No. 602, *for* chabbadár, *read* " jhabbadár."
„ 111, line 13 from bottom, *for* ' strap or tape,' *read* " strip of paper."
„ 117, No. 668, *for* " kufshi," *read* " kafshi."
„ 118, line 8 from bottom, *for* " stationery," *read* " stationary."
„ 130, line 8 from top, *for* " integrument," *read* " integument."
„ 130, last line but one, *for* " tasse," *read* " tassel."
„ 132, last line, *for* " brought, " *read* " wrought."
„ 139, line 12 from bottom, *for* " karáhí, a flat iron, &c.," *read* " karáhí an open cauldron, see p. 143."
„ 142, last line, *for* " bindlí," *read* " jagjagán."
„ 145, No. 735, *for* " mottled brass, " *read* " mottled brown."
„ 162, line 8 from top, *for* " treddles, " *read* " heddles."
„ 164, line 6 from bottom, *for* " chán," *read* " chín."
„ 180, line 10 from top, *for* " broad thin rings, " *read* " broad plain rings."
„ 181, No. 29, *for* " durichah," *read* " bunda " or " bundela," (being most worn by Bundelas or people of Bundelkand).
„ 181, No. 32, *for* " pipal-watta, " *read* " pipal-watra."
„ 181, „ 34, (last line from bottom), *for* " fig. 18," *read* " fig. 17."
„ 182, „ 43, *for* " cartilidge," *read* " cartilage," and at No. 52, *for* " fig. 1." *read* " fig. 12."
„ 187, line 9 from bottom. *for* " military metal," *read* " military medal."
„ 188, last line, for " engraves, " *read* " polishes."
„ 194, line 11 from top, *for* " náth " *read* " nath."
„ 197, last foot note, *for* " kair," *read* " kán."
„ 199, line 9 from bottom, *for* " set out from, " *read* " set out for."
„ 215, line 12 from top, *for* " should," *read* " show."
„ 222, line 8 from top, *for* " is," *read* " are."
„ 237, No. 839, *for* " course blown," *read* " coarse blown."
„ 244, line 2 from top, *for* " lás," *read* " láo,"
„ 276, line 2 from bottom, *for* " parkar," *read* " parkár."
„ 292, line 3 from top, } *for* " babúdí " *read* " bihbúdí."
„ 294, line 4 from top, }
„ 300, line 16 from bottom, *for* " nímgáz " *read* " nímgaz."
„ 304, (2nd heading), *for* " JILD SAZ," *read* " Jild sáz."
„ 307, (3rd „), Bhárpunja, the second time should be without the accent (Bharpunja).
„ 327, line 13 from top, *for* " curves," *read* " eaves."
„ 331, foot note, *for* " p. VIII," *read* " Vol. VIII."
„ 333, line 10 from bottom, *for* " for either," *read* " from either."

LIST OF PLATES AND SKETCH DIAGRAMS.

Those marked with an asterisk (*) are replaced in the 'presentation copies' by the original photographs.

SECTION B.

MANUFACTURES.

INTRODUCTION.

In the first volume of this work, the products described were only those which are utilized in the state in which nature produces them, or which, though subjected to various processes of manipulation, alteration or refinement, are still considered as raw material,—being destined for further treatment, either to be dressed as food, woven up to form clothing, or wrought, adapted and blended together to form other objects of use or ornament.

Accordingly, in the first volume we passed in review the metallic ores and crude metals, the stones, the earths, the grains, the timbers and the fibres, which are either found in the Panjab and its adjacent countries, or else are imported to meet the wants of its population. In this the second volume we have to observe the results of these crude substances, and to see how they are turned to account and used for manufacturing the various articles which are demanded by the habits and customs of the several classes of people inhabiting the provinces.

The interest which attaches to the study of the manufactures of a country is widely different in kind from that which attaches to the contemplation of its natural products. In the latter we see only the results of physical conditions of soil and climate, more or less modified by cultivation, and by the amount of skill (itself indicative of civilization) with which the valued plants of other countries have been introduced and naturalized; and our throughts are carried away to the study of their botany and chemistry in an economic point of view, while the ultimate practical result attained is the development of produce that is valuable commercially or excellent for local consumption. But when, among the manufactures, we see the hand of man brought to bear on the raw material, and can notice how far he has rendered it subservient to his purposes, we are at once in possession of a standard by which to mark the degree of skill which the people possess; while by observing the classes of articles made, and how far the wants of civilized life are supplied by them, we are enabled to fix the degree of civilization to which they have advanced; lastly, the form of the objects made, the colour and the pattern worked out, give us insight into the æsthetic peculiarities of the manufacturers,—their perception of beauty, their appreciation of colour, —their inventive faculty and other similar powers, which may help us, even though it be only partially and to a limited extent, to fix the place which the producers should hold in the ranks of the intellectual creation.

Separated from the manufactures only for the convenience of classification, is the division which embraces machinery, tools and implements—the aids which man has invented, and gradually improved on and elaborated, with a view to reduce his labour, to save time, and, in not a few instances, to do for him what his own hands are unable to accomplish.

In this department still more may be learnt and inferred as to the state of progress in which the people are, and also the inventive and reasoning faculties they are capable of exercising.

Lastly, and appropriately concluding the collection, as summing up what we can learn of the mind from the works of the hand, comes the department of fine arts. I cannot here dwell on the indications afforded by this department; indeed it would be unnecessary, for though I have not yet applied these principles of examination to the collection which has to be described, yet, with regard to fine arts, every one must feel before approaching this section, that these indications are of a mind and a power which has scarcely yet taken the first steps in progress and cultivation. Among a highly civilized people, as the eye wanders over their art productions, we read the workings, not only of the general but of the individual mind; we trace in one, the grand aspiring mind that has grasped and rendered in its work the noblest ideal of form; in another we see the loving spirit dwelling in ecstasy on the calm beauties of nature,—the gleaming lights, the soft shades, the clear blue skies and the sunny foliage of the homestead and the winding lane; in another we feel the sanctity of hallowed conception and of the spirit heavenward tending in its flight ; in another the sympathies of human suffering and the touch of tenderness that never fails to awake its response in the gazer's heart ;—in all, the aim at what is capable of calling forth the best feelings of human nature, be it the deeper affections and emotions of the heart, or the happy spirit and the harmless mirth of its lighter hours ; but in a country like this, we must not expect to find anything that appeals to mind or to deep feeling ; delicacy of finish, beauty of colour, wonderful imitation, all are to be met with, and these said, we have concluded the enumeration of what the art of the period can furnish.

How far education, the diffusion of European knowledge, and above all the spread of a purer faith, will expand, improve, and exalt, it is for coming years to show, and will be for the exhibitions of future time to display to public notice.

But we must pass on to the consideration of the classes before us, and the application to their study, of such principles as have been above indicated.

I shall deal at present only with the 1st section—that containing manufactured articles, reserving any comment that may be offered to illustrate the others for the appropriate places which they occupy.

The manufactures present themselves under the following classes :—

CLASS V.

Cotton Manufactures.

These consist of native cloths worked with native thread, both coloured and plain. The coloured cloths are generally either striped and check goods, with or without borders, such as "*lúnghía*" and "*súsís*," or fabrics woven in a pecular diagonal method and called "*khes*." Coarse cloths dyed red, called "*sálú*," and "*khárwá*," and the same dyed with indigo called "*nílah*," are much in use. Of course other coloured cloths are used in all shades and varieties, but are not distinguished as *kinds of cloth*, as "*níla*" and "*khárwá*" are.

Of white cloths : there are, 1st, damask cloth, principally made at Jálandhar, Hushyarpúr, Patyála, and also at Lúdhiána. This fabric is about the best of all the thicker cotton fabrics, and shows the

Another cotton manufacture is broad tape, or "*newár,*" made exactly on the same principle as the durree, only varying in width from 1 inch to 2½; it is also applied to the manufacture of horse girths.

Cotton rope, coloured and plain, horse nets, fringe for a horse's head to keep off flies, and narrow tape called "*fíta,*" are also among the manufactures of this class. All the above are made with native thread.

The next class is of articles made with European thread, and consists of finer white fabrics, such as the richer classes wear. The great bulk of the white cloth used for turbans and for dresses, is Glasgow or Manchester cambric, and fine linen occasionally is to be met with.

There is no difference in form of the articles made with English thread, and the loom is the same,—only the cloth is finer.

Lastly, there are the jail manufactures of table cloths (*damask*), table napkins and towels of all sorts, fine and rough (Turkish towels), which are made principally by the convicts, with the native looom, and native or English thread, according as the fabric is to be of finer or coarser sort.

I cannot here enter into a description of the looms employed for weaving; this belongs to the section devoted to machinery and implements;—I may mention here however that the loom is of one universal construction and entirely of hand power.

Much improvement has been effected in jails as to the fabric produced, by greater attention to the preparation and evenness of the threads, by the more regular working of the shuttle and the compacting together of the threads of the woof, and the skilful joining of the ends of the threads;—but nothing has been done to improve the loom itself. It is not often that the excellent weaving thus learnt in the jail is turned to account on the release of the prisoner, though to this there are some exceptions, one of which is noticed by Mr. Cowan in his report on Kachí in the old Leia district, where the manufacture of the blanket had flourished, consequent on the exertions of a man who had learnt in jail. As a rule, however, the natives are so attached to the custom of their family, that if a man should happen to be in a butcher's family, he will not leave the occupation. I once asked a man of this class who had attained great excellence in weaving while in jail, what he would do when he was released, and reminded him that he might be the best weaver in his village; but he remarked that his caste or business was "*kasai*" (butcher's) and he should return to that occupation. I believe this is very much the case with other trades, even with those who learn to perfection in the Lahore Central Jail the somewhat high art of manufacturing Turkey carpets.

To turn, therefore, to account the manufacturing skill that can be acquired in the best of our jails, such as Lahore and Gujrat, the officers in charge should endeavour to apportion to the various works, men of such castes (or rather hereditary occupations, for this kind of distinction is hardly a religious caste so much as customary prejudice) as will be likely to carry away with them and put into practice, on their release, the knowledge they have acquired.

CLASS VI.

The next fabrics of textile manufacture are those made of wool.

In this province woollen manufactures are either of (1) "*pashmína*," Thibet goat hair, (the process of preparing and collecting which has already been described under Class II in Section A), and of Kirmání wool and Rampúr wool; or (2) country sheep's wool; or (3) goat and camel hair.

Of "*pashmína*" there is plain "*pashmína pattú*," i. e., woven cloth, which has been felted; it is made of various degrees of fineness, and in colour generally black, white, grey, and shades of brown or drab. Pashmína is also woven into a fine class of coloured, black or white fabrics, which are afterwards richly embroidered round the edge with silk of the same colour; this class of manufacture is more recent, and articles of European clothing and shawls are the principal manufactures.

The next class of pashmína goods are the "*alwán*" and "*sáda*" shawls, being fine pashmína fabrics coloured and woven into a long oblong shawl without pattern or embroidery; they are much esteemed for softness and texture.

Lastly, come that wonderful class of manufactures which are known as Kashmír shawls. They are of two kinds, loom wove, where the whole pattern is wrought in the loom, with an endless series of threads of all colours,—the other "*amlikár*," where a foundation is made of a plain fabric, or a fabric in portions of different colours, the surface of which is then minutely worked over by hand with a pattern embroidered in fine pashm thread or sometimes silk. For this class of work only the finest pashmína is used, the threads are fine twined and do not "felt."

In other pashmína goods there are qualities of softness and fineness dependent on the wool used, for the same animals yield a fleece which has to be separated into qualities—of the inner wool or pashm, which is the finest, and then the second and third and the outer hair, which is coarse. The fine wool of the sheep of Kirmán is largely imported, and second class pashmína goods are made of it, but Kirmání wool is also largely used to adulterate real pashmína, being mixed with it. The subject will be noticed when we come to the class of shawls. At Rámpúr, the chief town of Bishahr, the wool is of such exquisite softness, almost like Kirmání, that it is largely imported and made up at Lúdhiána and other places into plain shawls or wrappers of great softness and durability called "Rámpúr chaddars."

2. *Country wool.*—This is the wool of the "*dúmba,*" or flat tailed sheep of the Salt Range and of Peshávar, and black and white wool of the common sheep. From these the "*kambal*" or blanket is made. The best come from Rohtak, Sirsa, Gugaira and Leịa, and good blankets are also made in the hills ;—very good blankets are made in the Lahore district, but the thread employed is twisted too hard, and this deprives it of the property of felting, and produces a more open texture and a harsher feel.* In many places they are also finished without subjecting them to any process of rubbing and working in with any softening agent such as European fabrics are treated with. In some places they are softened by men's feet repeatedly treading them, after saturation with the liquor of the soap nut ("*ríta*").

Beyond blankets made in the plains and a coarse flannel or pattú in the hills, very few other woollen fabrics are seen. The climate of the plains

* The property of *felting* which wool possesses is dependent on the structure of the wool fibres. Under the microscope they are found to consist of a series of rings or joints fitting one into the other, like the joints of the well known marestail plant (Equisetum); the edges of the jointed rings are serrated, and when a number of fibres are rubbed or pressed together, the serratures become entangled and felt together. Excessive twisting of woollen threads or passing the fibres over a heated iron comb,—as is done in Europe for worsted—destroys the felting property.

does not demand the use of wool for warmth during several months, and when the winter does set in, either pashmína or European flannel is used, or more commonly the ordinary cotton cloth made double and padded with cotton wool. In some of the jails attempts have been made to make plaids and coarse cloth. The Kashmíris also make woollen cloth something like our tweeds.

One other class of fabric remains to be noticed, viz., pile or Turkey carpets. A number of these are made of great excellence at Multán, while others are imported, chiefly of small size, from Bukhára, Yarkand, and Kashmír—for which latter carpets pashmína is employed. The Lahore Central Jail produces very fine samples, manufactured by the convicts whose term of imprisonment is sufficiently long to admit of their learning to perfection the art, which requires much more skill than the ordinary mechanical operations of the loom.

3. *Goat hair* &c. This is principally used for making coarse bags in which grain and other burdens are carried on the backs of cattle and camels. Coarse blankets called "*bora*" and mats for the floor called "*asan*" are also made of goat's hair. In some places ropes are also made of hair but are not strong.

There is in Peshávar a fine kind of goat hair worked into a pattú or cloth.

Camel hair. The soft inner wool is woven into chogahs, (long overcoats,) and some kinds of cloth. But these are mostly made in the Kábul, Bukhára and Kohkan states.

CLASS VII. Silks.

This class embraces a very important article of manufacture, which has been for ages carried on in the Panjab, though it is said that at present the silks made at Multán and Lahore are of less value and excellence than they formerly were.

In the exhibition of 1864, however, an Amritsar firm, Messrs. Devi Sahai and Chumba Mull, by reviving expressly the manufacture, and making up silks of the fine old qualities, demonstrated that the art is not lost, but that there is no longer that demand for the better made and more expensive class of fabric which there was in the days of native rule, when the court patronized the manufacture and required the richest products of the loom for its wear.

At present the best silks are made at Multán, Lahore and Baháwalpúr. The former are principally plain, striped, or shot silks. Silk pieces made plain or unicolourous are called "*daryai*;" if they have a metallic texture or "shot," produced by the silk of warp and woof being different colours—the silk is called "*daryai dhúpchán̄.*"

Neat check silks are also made; these find the readiest sale among European ladies; and as they will wash and wear well they are really valuable and useful articles; they are called "*daryai chárkhánah.*"

When the silk pieces have a plain ground colour, but variegated by stripes of a second colour in the direction of the length, the fabric is called "*gúlbadan.*" Large silk scarves, generally square, with a rich gold border, are called "*Sáfá.*" Turbans and waistbelts are also made of long pieces of silk with silver gold thread borders and fringes.

The Baháwalpúr silks are remarkable for their design; they often have patterns in two or three colours or variegated by the introduction of gold or silver thread, and sometimes are unicolourous, the pattern being of the nature of a damask produced by the arrangement of the threads. These fabrics also are often varied by the intermixture of satin or glossy portions with the plain silk. Regular satin is called "*atlas,*" and is not produced at Lahore or Multán, or even Baháwalpúr. That which is sold in shops is imported from Europe, or more rarely from Bukhára, Yarkand and China. Russian satin also is sometimes met with. A kind of striped satin is brought from Hindustán and Bombay, and is called "*mashrú.*"

There is another curious fabric produced in the Baháwalpúr territory; this is generally made striped as a gúlbadan, and is a very close woven silk, or a mixture of silk and cotton artifically glazed. In fact, these fabrics look exactly like a piece of common glazed furniture chintz, and to our European ideas it seems a great waste of silk to make such fabrics out of it.

Notwithstanding the local manufactures, silk "*dopattas,*" or scarves worked with gold, are largely imported from Benares, which latter place supplies the silk "*dhotís,*" (large silk sheets, worn by Hindús in lieu of the "*paijáma,*" or loose trowsers of the Musulmans) and spotted handkerchiefs called "*búndí.*"

Silk fabrics, very thin, almost like muslin, and inwoven with gold thread, are also used in various parts of the Panjab, both as "*dopattas*" or scarves, and as "*mandils*," which when twisted up into narrow rolls, like a rope, are worn coiled round the head for a turban.

Kamkháb ("kincob") a rich silk fabric worked all over with patterns in gold thread (something like the cloth of gold of ancient days in Europe), is not made in the Panjab except perhaps at a few places, as Nabha, and a little at Amritsar; it is principally imported from Benares, or from Ahmadabad (Bombay).

Occasionally the silk "*khes*" and "*sárí*," or thick silk scarves of the Dakhan and Central India, find their way up to the Panjab from Jhánsi, Gwalior, and *via* Delhi.

Velvet, called "*makhmal*," is not made, as far as I know, in any part of India, and certainly not in the Panjab. It is in demand for native saddles and saddle cloths, which are made of velvet richly embroidered with gold. It is also used for "*masnads*," the small carpet on which kings and great dignitaries sit, and for cushions, and for the covering of sword scabbards. It used to be imported from Russia *viá* Bukhára, and was of a thin quality; but the superior velvets of France and England have driven out the trade, and the imports are from Calcutta and Bombay. Russian velvet is still to be seen on the scabbards of Irán or Persian and Bukhára swords. Cotton velvet is imported also, none is made in the Panjab.

The fancy articles in silk, that is, articles made without the aid of the loom, are more numerous than those of the cotton or wool classes. First there are the "*ízárband*," or netted sashes: these are universally employed as a string or girdle by which the paíjámas are fastened round the waist, they are made of silk netted, either plain or coloured, and the long ends of silk are knotted off and end in tassels, which are sometimes ornamented with gold thread and beads &c. The making of these articles is a trade by itself called "*patholi*" or "*ilákabandi*." Various head ornaments are made of silk; among them the female "*paránda*," which consists of long skeins of crimson silk, which are not plaited or twisted but left loose, only secured at each end by being bound up and the lower end being formed into a long tag ending with a tassel, generally highly ornamented with gold thread tinsel &c. This long tail of silk is plaited by the women into their hair and hangs down their back, the tassels of the "*paránda*" giving a finish to the plait.

Horse trappings of all kinds, fringes for the nose, the long tassels that ornament the trappings of the saddle, and leading ropes, called "*bagdaur,*" are also made of silk.

Another kind of fancy manufacture is curious, and confined chiefly to one or two men resident of the Gújranwalla district, who also visit Lahore :—it consists in working pieces of coloured chenille (or piping of long piled velvet) side by side on to any cloth, in such a way as to form patterns or designs in leaves and flowers ; the cloth so worked in is made up into cushions &c.,—or else the chenille is neatly glued on to the surface of a glove box or trinket case ; these present a very pleasing appearance when well made.

CLASS VIII.

Fibrous Manufactures.

This class gradually takes us out of the division of "Textile Manufactures." Its first division is intended for fabrics not included in the previous three classes.

The necessity for such a division is almost exclusively of European creation ; it will contain the canvas woven of the flax grown at Sealkot, and also some linen fabrics of European manufacture but from Indian fibre.

One indigenous fabric of this class is the coarse sacking or "*tát,*" answering to the "*gunny*" of Bengal : it is used for packing, or for a floor cloth, or for making sacks and bags for grain, &c., &c.

The second division of this class contains ropes of all kinds. The commonest forms of these are the ropes of "*bán múnj,*" or the sheaths of the flower stalks of the *Saccharum múnja* already described ; ropes of hemp, and of "*san,*" and also of the "*sankokra*" or Rozelle plant are commonly used. The coarser kinds of grass rope used as make-shifts by the villagers for agricultural purposes, are hardly to be classed as manufactures, and are exhibited with the fibrous products of Section A.

The next division contains native paper, either plain or colored; it differs not in kind, like European note paper, foolscap, tissue paper, printing paper, &c., but only in quality and excellence of manufacture and in the size of the sheets.

The paper of Kashmír is however different in kind, and is superior yet to anything produced in this province.

Sealkot is or was the famous place for paper,—but the jails now all produce paper, and that (in some of them) of excellent quality. In the jails also was originated the paper made of "*madár*" fibre, of *daphne* and *desmodium* bark, of plantain fibre, of flax tow, and of "*dhák*" bark and other materials. Old *tát* chopped into pieces is the ordinary paper material, not old rags.

The last division in this class comprises a series of mats, of baskets, and of chicks or light screens for doors, which keep flies and birds out without excluding the light and air. Punkahs and hand fans and mats manufactured from the tough fibrous pieces of the palm leaves, and also of the "*patha,*" or *Chamærops Ritchiana*, are very common, and are imported largely from Pesháwar. There are also baskets and screens of the culm of the "*sirkí*" or *Saccharum múnja*, ornamented with patterns, &c., of woollen thread.

CLASS IX.

In this class more perhaps than in any other is the special skill of the native artizans displayed. It includes embroidery of all kinds, the rich gold embroideries of saddles, '*masnads,*' and '*chogahs,*' the beautiful silk needlework in pashmína, cotton, and net,—and lastly the wonderful Kashmír "*amlikar*" or needle-worked goods, consisting of shawls, caps, coats, and chogas, whose substance is pashmína, but the pattern is worked by hand stitching to a degree of fineness that is perfectly marvellous.

In these works, the great patience and extreme delicacy of finger of the workman is exhibited to the utmost. Many of the embroidered specimens must have required the patient minute labour of consecutive months,—and the beautiful arrangement of colour, and great variety and elegance of design in pattern are very striking.

The perception of colour appears purely intuitive; they have an empiric knowledge of what the complementary colours are, and know that setting one beside its complementary throws out both to the greatest effect,—or gives them "*zeb*"—as the native phrase is. It is however needless to observe that they have no knowledge of the principles of colouring, and hence it not seldom happens that their colour degenerates into glare, and their contrasts into gaudiness. Much might be done by educated supervision, in leading and restraining this natural impulse, so valuable in itself as a foundation in design art.

The elegance in pattern of these embroideries as also in the woven shawls, is scarcely less remarkable than the selection and arrangement of colour; and this is a very noteworthy circumstance, because it shows that the power of design in tracing patterns, whether it be on a shawl, or on an enamelled cup, or on a gold inlaid shield, is a different power from designing in solid. In the late exhibition for instance, on all sides we could see beautiful patterns;—there were enamelled wares from Multán, chased silver from Kashmír, glazed tiles from Multán again, embroideries from Delhi, Lahore, Amritsar, Kashmír and Lúdiána, elaborate borders and illuminated titles to manuscripts,—all covered with designs as beautiful in conception as they were faultless in execution, but for beauty of *form* we looked in vain. The few articles that had anything like elegant shape were almost entirely copied or made to order, and under supervision. But take any purely native article, say one of the carved marble chairs figured in Class XV. The back and sides are covered with tracery in pattern most beautiful, but the general *form* of the chair is hideous and clumsy to a degree. The same thing perpetually appears also in native drawings: I have before me as I write a native portrait of His Highness the Maharajah of Kashmír and Jamú; the figure is seated resting against a velvet cushion, which is placed in the centre of a carpet, with an attendant behind: in the first place the paper is bordered round with an edging of flower tracery, very beautifully complete; as to the picture itself, the velvet cushion on which the king reposes is wrought out with all its little pattern of gold embroidery, and the blue carpet on which the masnad is placed shows a miracle of tracery in gold and white,—but the figure itself, the '*form*' part of the picture, is contorted, and the graceful folds which the soft muslin in which he is clothed would naturally assume are represented by lines conventional, stiff and utterly impossible, drawn without a thought of the original. The explanation is easy: the artist had the oriental perception of tracery and flat designing,—of solid form he had none.

It is not a little remarkable that the countries where *form* has been most appreciated have been less prolific in *patterns,* or traced design. In ancient Greece and Rome, for instance, where grandeur of form and severe truth of outline, coupled however with the most perfect grace, are pre-eminent in every sculpture and building, we see comparatively little of fine pattern design. We have, no doubt, tesselated pavements, and Etruscan and Greek borders, but the patterns are few, and constantly repeated, rigidly simple, and always occupy a place entirely secondary and subservient.

It may be objected to this depreciation of the native perception of form, that considerable elegance is displayed in their vessels and vases, but this is not a fair test; for when the clay is placed on the wheel there is a tendency in the gyrations of the wheel to produce certain forms in themselves elegant. When the first potters pressed their hands on the clay and the vessel came forth of a shape that was elegant, it was a chance: the potter had no design to make it with the particular curve that gives grace and beauty. But when once the vessel was made, and beautiful or not answered the purpose for which it was intended, whether a long necked "*surahí*" or water bottle, or a "*hándi*" or a "*chátti,*" it became an established form, and was copied ever after, and copied not only in pottery, but in metal; hence the elegance of a few of the suráhís and cups in silver is easily explained, and in no way militates against the general principle that traced design is separate from form design.

I have extended this notice beyond the limits of a preliminary sketch; but the class of embroidery is one so remarkable, and the subject of pattern in general is forced on our notice by the whole collection so strongly, that it is impossible to avoid devoting some pages to it. Form and design in pictures and in architecture have been excluded from this place, but I shall recur to this interesting subject when we come to the fine art collection in Section D.

CLASS X.

This class gives an opportunity for the display of the peculiarities of dress to be found within the varied districts of the province. The wild marauding tribes of the hills and Pesháwar and down to the Derajat, the inhabitants of the peaceful and settled plains, in their several occupations or castes, Hindu and Mussulman, Jat, Arain, Banya, Khatri, Brahmin, Munshi, the hill people of the Kangra and Simla States, as far as to the borders of Thibet, of Ladak and Spiti, of Kashmír and Kábul,—all are represented in the province in one part or another; and their distinctive dresses, turbans, or shoes, &c. &c., form interesting articles for exhibition. Under the same class are also included the articles of clothing which are exhibited as specimens of work, and not for the sake of the form of the dress. Also all articles which illustrate ethnographic peculiarities, or have reference to particular customs, ceremonies and superstitions, are here included.

CLASS XI.

This class is for Leather Goods. The original native manufactures of leather are not extensive. Common shoes, saddlery, book-binding, water-bags and buckets, are almost the only leather articles in common use; but the intestinal skin of various animals is made by moulding when wet into bottles or jars for holding oil &c. and camel hide is occasionally employed for the dishes of weighing scales &c. The more promising kinds of leather manufacture in this class are the result of European demand on the one hand, and European instruction on the other, and now superior book-binding, saddlery, harness, and English boots and shoes, very well made, form a part of the collection.

CLASS XII.

This is a large and important class, embracing all manufactures in metal. The class is sub-divided according to the metal employed, and primarily into the two main divisions of work in the precious and non precious metals.

The sub-classes A and B contain samples of the work in copper, brass and bell metal, chiefly in the form of vessels for cooking, drinking and holding water. Such vessels are always used wherever the people are rich enough to have them, it is only the very poorest that are confined entirely to earthenware pots. Rough iron-work was included in the exhibition; bolts, screws, nails, iron pans, and implements, were shewn, but formed neither a large nor an important collection, but one in which there was very great room for improvement; it is possible however that many exhibitors were deterred from sending specimens by the great weight and consequent cost of carriage, and also by the unsightliness of the objects themselves. The exhibition prize for the best piece of rough filed iron-work could not be awarded. Sub-class C contains cutlery, the best samples of which are the manufacture of table knives from Shahpúr, and of various articles from Gujrat and Sealkot, but all on the European model, some of the latter under European superintendence also. A portion of the large collection of swords and daggers exhibited for the sake of their blades came under this class. It may be added that there is some difficulty in classifying these articles, and a number will be found in this class, some more among the works in the precious metals, a few under jewellery, and a number in section C, in the class XXVIII—devoted to arms. The principle of classification is derived from a consideration of the prominent characteristics of the specimen. If a weapon exhibits a peculiar form and name,—as the long juggling sword, the twisted bichwá or dagger, or the katár, it is included in the proper class as a weapon; but if the form presents nothing remarkable, but the blade is of beautiful metal, or finely tempered and watered, it is shown as a sample of steel under the present class; if it is inlaid with gold the specimen will consort with "*koftgari*" or inland gold work,—if the handle and scabbard are richly jewelled or enamelled, it forms part of the jewellery collection. In one instance daggers, whose handles and sheaths were of finely carved ivory, and the blades quite ordinary both as to shape and metal, have been included as "ivory carvings."

The next great division of this class contains work in the precious metals. In the exhibition there was a collection of considerable beauty. The first sub-class is divided to illustrate the manufactures of gold wire, such as gold thread, and spangles, gold military lace, gold edgings and ribbands, &c., called "*kalabatún*" "*mukesh*," "*laus*," "*anchal*," *&c.*

In the next class the gold thread and fine flattened wires of the former are found woven into gold cloth by the aid of a silk warp and forming the rich patterns of a Benares kimkháb, or the golden sheen of a "*mandíl*" or "*dopatta*."

Leaving these light fabrics of gold, illustrating the wonderful malleability and ductility of the precious metals, we come to another class, where the same metals are exhibited in a more solid form, in cups and vessels both plain and ornamental, or chased over with the beautiful flower work in relief as in the Kashmír silver.

In this class are also included a multitude of trinkets whose endless shapes and names are as curious as they are puzzling; several of these are local, and worn only by certain tribes, and will receive full notice in their proper place.

Next come the beautiful koftgari work, arms and shields, pen-boxes and caskets, combs, buttons, paper-knives, letter weights and many other articles of iron, polished and wrought all over with curious devices in gold lines made by hammering in gold wire.

Last in this class, is a sub-division to receive a few samples of plating, both water and electro-plate. The former has been done for years in the cities of this province by overlaying with thin gold,—but the latter is quite new, and has been practised by a few workmen with fair success.

CLASS XIII.

Contains the samples of native jewellery and enamelling. The latter is noticable chiefly on the backs of set jewels, many rings and bracelets being finished with enamelling in this way; but the most showy pieces of enamelling are the silver vases from Kashmír and Múltán and the enamelled jewellery of Kangra;—a pattern is formed on the silver in high relief and the lower parts filled up with coloured enamel, so that the surface presented is that of a coloured ground, with silver leaves, and flowers, delineated upon it.

The jewellery, properly so called, consists of gems cut and set in gold for rings, necklaces, armlets, &c. The native names and varieties of jewels are perfectly endless, and vary in different districts. Trinkets and ornaments in silver and gold, all included under the general term "*zewarát*" are worn by both sexes, but especially by women.

Almost the only gems esteemed by natives for their finest ornaments are rubies, emeralds, diamonds and pearls; all the others are despised, and sapphires are quite uncommon, and only worn in the "*nau ratn*," or armlet with nine gems.* The lower order of jewels, such as agates and cornelians are condemned to the rank of "*nagínahs*" or "*mankas*," stones for signet rings or beads for rosaries. The gems are all imported;—rubies from Ceylon and Burmah, diamonds from Central India, but many from Calcutta, from Brazil, &c.; emeralds are not found anywhere in India, but stones of immense size are to be met with, filled however with flaws;—they are all imported. An account of these gems will be found in section A, under the class devoted to minerals used for ornament, at page 49 of vol. I.

There is another class of jewellery which deserves notice, viz., that of Delhi made in European fashion, with stones cut as in Europe, which latter are chiefly brought from Calcutta. Very good native work in imitation of European also done at Kangra—but principally in gold and enamel not with stones.

CLASS XIV.

Is a class designed to include rock crystal cups, and handles, agate bowls, jade vases, and other articles of vertu not strictly to be classed with gems.

CLASS XV.

We pass on to a different series of manufactures, viz., those in which wood and ivory are the chief materials.

First comes furniture. This is principally by European hands in the regimental workshops, or by natives under European superintendence.

Natives use so little furniture beyond chairs, beds and boxes, that there is no scope for a native collection of furniture.

The second division of the class contains all the wood carvings, some in the form of articles of funiture, such as legs of beds, boxes,

* The Raja of Chambah has an immense sapphire for a head jewel: stones of this size are very rare among native jewellery.

walking sticks and other articles. A few articles are of wood inlaid with ivory with great neatness and skill.

The third division is expressly for the turned wood ware of Pàk Pattan and other places; the turned vases, boxes, &c., being afterwards covered with variegated lacquer and polished.

CLASS XVI.

Contains all the delicate ivory carving of Delhi and Amritsar.

CLASS XVII.

Almost specially constructed for the wares of Kashmír; for beyond a rude papier maché from Muzaffargarh, there is hardly any made in the province. The Kashmír boxes, pen-trays, card cases, &c., are some of them of wood, and some of papier maché—the pulp of old paper, moulded, pressed and dried into the desired form. The surface of these articles is most beautifully and delicately painted over in gold, or colours, or both, on a ground of some colour previously laid on. Nothing can exceed the delicacy of the flower patterns or the shawl patterns which are delineated on them; the gloss is given by a varnish of copal.

CLASS XVIII.

Includes all the ceramic art of the province.

Generally speaking, nothing is made but rude porous earthern vessels of the various forms of water bottles, cups, pans, and "*degchis*" or "*chattis*" (cooking pots); but several districts have produced beautiful thin paper pottery, unglazed, and the Rohtak district has a very pleasing variety formed of brownish clay, the surface of which is ribbed or marked and indented with patterns, and then has a pearly lustre given to it by the addition of finely powdered talc.

Some of the pottery is of a pale yellow, and a little of a black colour; the latter is exhibited with a pattern worked in on it with quicksilver and tin leaf, which is not permanent but to look at has a sufficiently pleasing effect. There are a few specimens of pottery painted over, and of pottery to which the lacquer of the turned wood has been applied, the latter is very fairly durable when well made.

Some of the jails exhibited glazed pottery, which shows great progress, both as to form, colour, and quality of glaze; but still the art is rude and imperfect, and the apparatus and substances employed need improvement.

From Ludhiána the exhibition had a large series of ceramic vases made on classical or quasi-classical models. The glazed tiles under this class are some of them very good and of brilliant colour, being both ancient and of modern manufacture.

CLASS XIX.

This represents the attempts of the province at glass making.

The crude glass is a thick greenish material from which bulbous bottles are blown, but no advance in this has hitherto been made; the tools, the furnace and the annealing are all on the smallest scale, and of the rudest and most unsatisfactory kind. The few white glass articles that are made, are made of broken European articles melted down. The best glass is made at Pánipat and Karnál, they there also silver glass with some success. Some tolerable white glass candle shadles were sent from Patyálá, and some fancy articles from Lahore. As yet glass is not used for drinking out of by natives, and that employed by Europeans is imported, as is also window glass; hence there is no stimulus given to the manufacture.

CLASS XX.

Which concludes the section, is designed for the few articles of ornament or of fancy work that could not be conveniently included in any of the regular classes. Native ingenuity is often and not altogether unsuccessfully exercised in producing fancy or ornamental goods.

In the foregoing sketch it is hoped the reader will have gained some idea of what he may expect to find detailed under the various classes. He will see there, the result of patient industry struggling with rude materials, imperfect tools, and ignorance of any principles by which to learn to improve them, and opposed, albeit unconsciously, by that apathy and dislike for change which produces an almost insurmountable obstacle to the introduction of new methods, even when their superiority, actually exhibited, cannot be denied.

In other branches of manufacture, where the material is more pliant and seems dependent on patient delicate handling, combined with a power of pattern making and colour arranging,—we see all the excellencies of the best manufacture displayed at once; the embroideries, the shawls, the inlaid work are without rival. It only remains to ask could not this excellence be produced with less labour, less time and less expense?

Notwithstanding the general backwardness of maunfacturing skill, the commencement of European influence of the best kind on the manufactures is clearly perceptible. New materials are being turned to account, better tools are being tried, in spite of the apathy and dislike just alluded to; better form and better finish is already discernible in the articles of furniture, cutlery, jewellery and many others; while even in the exclusively native art of shawl making, the value of European design and colour teaching is to be traced in several of the productions of Amritsar looms.

The survey of the manufactures is on the whole an encouraging one; advance though very slow is being made in almost every department. Our jails introduce better styles of work, and should be encouraged to go still further, and with still greater care and attention to see that the skill acquired is not thrown away or lost; private manufacturers, regimental workshops, railway industrial workshops and mission industrial schools are all tending to give the onward impulse.

The establishment of good industrial and design-art schools is now a desideratum; in many places the people are ripe for them and would gladly learn. The establishment of such a school at Lahore has been determined on, and will no doubt become the centre of improvement on all hands. Not a little will be gained if we can succeed in teaching the manufacturers the principles on which the processes of dyeing, metal working, weaving and the like depend; guided by such knowledge, it is possible to effect those improvements which are urgently required both in material and implements; mere empiric knowledge of certain rude processes can be handed down as in this country from father to son, but never can lead to any advance or improvement. A very important point which should occupy the attention of the educational authorities is the necessity of teaching and spreading a knowledge of the elements of natural science, especially Chemistry, Botany, Electricity, Hydrostatics and Mechanics. Almost every process of art or manufacture is dependent on one or other of these sciences; and if a knowledge of them were to begin to prevail among the educated classes, improvement would gradually spread as it has in Europe to the masses, and the result would be that every manufacture in the country would eventually be benefitted ; we would then see improvement carried into paper making, cutlery, pottery, glass blowing, in which it is most required, and even the old cotton and silk weaving loom might give way before a simple, cheap and improved substitute.

SECTION C.

MACHINERY.

INTRODUCTION.

This Section is at present destined to occupy but a small space in the account of the Products of the Punjab. The distribution of Classes under it, given at page xxxiii of Volume I, is rather intended for an Exhibition where both native and imported machinery is displayed, than a scheme of classification adaptable to the actually existing indigenous machinery of the Punjab. Accordingly, these Classes in the scheme that are noted below as containing nothing, will be omitted in the descriptive catalogue which follows :—

CLASS XXI.—*Prime movers,* &c. This class is blank.

CLASS XXII.—Distributed under four divisions : we have a few samples thus :—

DIVISION I.—*Machines for raising water.*—There is the Persian wheel, the "Lao-charas" the "Dhanklí" and the "Chalâr."

DIVISION II.—Machines for raising weights ;—is blank.

DIVISION III.—*Carriages.*—There is no great variety, but the indigenous carriages are admirably adapted for the purposes they are built to serve ; and the "Ekka," being built on the very principle adopted some years back in the Hansom cab, will deserve notice.

DIVISION IV.—*Railway Plant.*—Although under effective supervision native workmen are able to build railway carriages, and to do a great deal of useful metal and other work in repairing and fitting machinery, all the specimens in such a division being purely of European origin, will have no place in this book.

Division V.—*Models of Boats.*—This Section will contain an account of the boats that have been in use on the Punjab rivers from time immemorial. Like almost everything else the art of boat building is stationary; and I doubt not that traces of Alexander's boat building may still be found in the Jhelum boat of to-day.

CLASS XXIII.—*Instruments for weighing and registering*:—is separated into two divisions :—

Division I.—***Horological instruments,*** which is a blank, except in the remarkable instance to be noted in its proper place.

Division II.—***Weighing Instruments*** are represented only by the common *tarázu* or scale, with the suspended trays at either end of the beam. It is generally made of wood and with leather and basket work for larger work, while for jewellers and others a small steel beam carrying little hemispherical brass cups hung on with three silk threads is used. The balance is indicated by the pointed tongue "kantha" of the beam, just as in European scales. They are always fitted into a little wooden case, in which one cup lies over the other, and the case is shaped thus

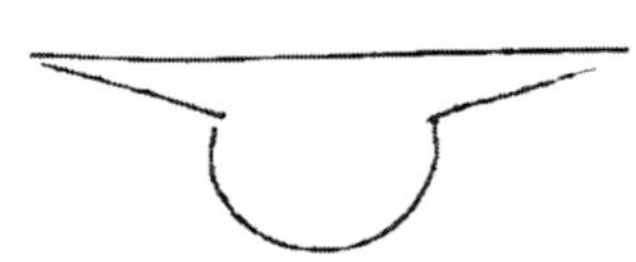

The steel-yard is unkown.

CLASS XXIV.—Contains *Mathematical and Philosophical instruments,* and is unrepresented, save by the instruments (still to be found) used by native astrologers, including the astrolabe, and instruments for determining latitude and longitude, the equation of time, and so forth.

CLASS XXV.—(*Surgical instruments*) will present a small, but somewhat curious collection, showing how far the surgical art has gone among a people who consider the noble art—one of the great powers whereby we contend against the host of suffering and misery in the world—as only fit for barbers and blacksmiths; and who found their surgery, like their medicine, on a purely empirical basis. The patience of the native character, however, is admirably exhibited by the known surgical processes, most of them being as slow and tedious for the operator, as they require patience and determined submission in the subject. The delicacy of handling and skill in using rough weapons, which natives undoubtedly possess, will further appear in their operations for cataract, and for restoring the cartilage of the nose.

CLASS XXVI.—(*Musical instruments*) will contain a series which is certainly curious and interesting, however unmelodious to European ears the twang of the "*madham*" or guitar may be.

CLASS XXVII.—*Locks and small machines.*—This Class is represented by a few small articles, which show however an embryo ingenuity which might receive great development in future, and under suitable guidance.

CLASS XXVIII.—Contains specimens of *Arms and Ordnance.*

CLASS XXIX.—*Machinery and Trade Implements.*

DIVISION I.—*Used in Manual trades.*—A great many of the implements which are required for various manufactures have already been described in Section B. of this Volume. I use this Division to contain a variety of miscellaneous information as to Tools and Trades which I could not include elsewhere.

DIVISION II.—*Agricultural Instruments,* are represented by the somewhat rude, but by no means inefficient implements used all over the country. They have at least the merit of extreme cheapness. The common cultivator would be almost ruined by the price of an English plough ; at least by what it would cost out here.

DIVISION III.—Shews a similar series of tools used in horticulture.

CLASS XXX.—(*Photographic Apparatus*) is blank.

CLASS XXXI.—*Contrivances used in architecture.* Under this Class will be given some notes on the houses built in various parts of the Punjab, and some remarks also on the construction of wells.

The Class Machinery, which occupies a large portion of the great European Exhibition Catalogues, is thus reduced in the Punjab to very narrow limits. All the progress that has been made in the introduction of machinery is of European origin. Nor is this to be wondered at, for the manufacture of machinery demands many aids which the Punjab at present has not. First, there must be the inventive mind long trained by close study of the successive processes which one by one have perfected the construction of machines in Europe. Next there must be large foundries, and abundant supply of fuel for large and powerful furnaces ; metallurgy must be brought to a high degree of perfection; fine and malleable iron, pure and even tempered steel, well compounded metals, must be produced in abundance. Again, the making of one machine requires the aid of many others. All the machinery requisite for casting metal, all the contrivances for turning, planing, boring, and shaping metal, that are now seen in the great engine factories of Europe, must be brought into play. Still, the day is perhaps not far distant when we may have machinery of native manufacture. Already the workshops of Rurki, Madhopur, and of the great railway stations, employ hundreds of native artisans, who are thus becoming familiarized with the arts of forging and casting metal, and with the control of powerful engines and prime movers, whether worked by water power as at Madhopore and Rurki, or by steam as at the Lahore and other railway workshops. These abundantly prove that the native workman is not wanting either in sagacity or in power; and these works under European supervision are but the first step towards works where the learners have become teachers, and whence the arts imported from abroad have gradually become naturalized and familiar.

CLASS V.

COTTON MANUFACTURES.

To trace the process of manufacture upwards from the first gathering of the cotton pods to the final egress from the loom of the woven fabric, we must refer to the class of fibres where, under the head of raw cotton, the first part of the story has been told; suffice it here to say that the native cotton fibre is of much shorter staple than the American varieties, and that even the latter when acclimatized shew, except under very favorable circumstances, a tendency to shorten also.

When the cotton is gathered and separated from the husks of the pod, the first step is to separate the fibre from the seed to which it is attached. This is effected by the "*belna,*" a very simple little apparatus, consisting of a pair of rollers, supported between two uprights fixed on to a wooden stand: the rollers are just sufficiently far apart to allow the cotton but not the seed to pass between. The ends of the rollers are cut into wormed screws, which work one into the other and cause both rollers to revolve, when force is applied to a wooden lever handle attached to the upper one.

The cotton having passed through this process, is cleaned from broken bits of seed and dirt, and also frayed out and separated, by a very simple apparatus called a "*pinjan.*" This is little more than a bow loosely strung and suspended from the ceiling of the room. The operator sits on the ground, and the bow lies nearly on the ground; the operator twists a little stick round the string in the centre, and placing the bow-string over a little heap of cotton, by the aid of the little stick, twangs the string against the cotton, which is frayed out and cleaned simply by the vibration of the string; the passer by can constantly hear the twanging of this bow as he approaches the shop.

When the cotton is thus cleaned, it is formed into spindle shaped lumps or balls, called "puni" from which thread is drawn out and twisted. This is done by the aid of a "*charka,*" a very simple instrument, consisting of a large lantern wheel* about a foot or eighteen inches in diameter, which turned by hand communicates by a band with a very small reel-like wheel which revolves rapidly; from the side of the reel or small wheel an iron spike projects, over which a hollow grass straw is slipped and on which the cotton thread is wound as fast as it is spun.

The thread being thus obtained, it is wound off from the reels of the charkha and converted into the form of large skeins by winding it over a wooden frame called "*áteran.*" In this state it is put into the weaver's hands. The weaver opens out the skein into a circle which he then places on a sort of skeleton cylinder, or rather pyramid shaped wheel, from which, while revolving, the thread is again wound off on bits of reed for use. Next, the web of the fabric has to be prepared, which is of course double. In order to do this, a smooth piece of clean ground is selected, and pairs of pegs are set up, at intervals of two yards or less, in two paralled rows. A person then takes in each hand a stick, at the bottom of which is a revolving reel charged with thread; he fixes to the first peg one end of the thread on the reel, and then walks along the pegs, first down one row and up the next, and so the thread unwinds as he goes, and he takes care to let the thread fall alternately outside and inside each peg :—thus

* The wheel consists of two discs of wood separated by pieces of wood to the distance of 2 or 3 inches; the edge of the wheel is formed by a net work of string stretched between the two discs, over this surface the band revolves.

a number of threads are deposited on the ground over the pegs, and the workman goes on unwinding till there are threads enough for his purpose. The requisite number of threads is calculated according to the breadth of the intended fabric; the threads are then carefully taken up off the ground. The double rows of pegs having served to keep the two sets of threads apart, sticks of "sarkand" grass are also inserted breadthwise to keep them from becoming re-entangled. The workman next spread out the threads to the breadth of the intended web; one end of the web is then tied to a stick fixed in the ground and the other held by another man and stretched out to its full length, when it is well brushed with a broad brush (called "*kúch*") to cleanse the threads from the little particles of cotton seed and other impurities that invariably stick to the thread. It is now ready to be transferred to the loom.

All native cotton fabrics are made in one or other of four styles:—

1st. These are plain cloths, either wove with a single thread or with two or three or four threads, according to the required stoutness of the fabric, from the thinnest "*malmal*" or "*eksúti*" to the thickest "*durree*;" for all these the web is unicolorous.

2nd. Are cloths with a longitudinal stripe, of which the type is the *susí*; or with a check pattern as the "*lungí*;" the web here has coloured threads introduced at intervals for the stripe. "Jabbalpúri" durrees are also made on this principle. Both these kinds are wove plain and called "sádábáfí."

3rd. Are cloths with various diagonal patterns, such as the "*khes*," and are woven on a different principle and called "khesbáfí."

4th. Are those fabrics which are not woven merely by passing the shuttle across and across in a straight line, but which exhibit in their texture a damask or pattern, generally in diamond shapes, and fantastically called "*Bulbul chashm*" or "Nightinale's eye." This is commonly seen in the "*ghátí*" and in the "*chádar*" worn as wrappers or cloths.

The weaving of towels, table linen and the like, is of purely European origin, and is only practised in jails, &c., under European supervision. Such cannot be counted as a class of native indigenous manufactures.

Notwithstanding the simplicity of the cotton manufacture, the varieties of the cloth are numerous, as the following list of names of cloths met with in the Punjab will testify. The names sometimes indicate the number of threads constituting the breadth of the web, and sometimes the number of threads, whether single, double, &c., with which the shuttle is charged. Sometimes the colour gives a name, sometimes the pattern. Besides these general names there are varieties of fabrics known locally by peculiar names. These are not given here, but will be found in the catalogue which follows. The Gúgaira lists will furnish a good example of this. Foreign piece goods, whether European, or imported from Kábul and Túrkistán, or from India, have also distinctive titles: all such are indicated in the sequel.

With regard to the distribution of cotton manufacture in various districts of the Punjab,—it is, of course, scarcely possible to exclude any city or town from the list of cotton manufacturing localities. In every place will be found shops of weavers employed in producing at least the coarser cloths required in quantity by all classes.

In the large cities, as Lahore, Amritsar, Múltán, Lúdhiána and others, every kind of fabric almost is woven. Lúdhiána has a special notoriety for drills, check cloths, and other fabrics resembling European, as well as for "*lúnghís*" and other native fabrics.

Múltán is noted for cotton pile carpets, and for printed and painted calicos or chintzes, called "chit," and for "dhotis" with a red printed border.

But the most important seat of all the finer cotton weaving was and still is the Doábah, or districts of Húshyárpúr, Jálandhar and Kangra. It is true indeed, that the excellence and cheapness of European fabrics has almost caused the manufacture of the finer cottons to cease, but still the "ghátis" of Rahún and the muslin turbans of Bajwára are celebrated even to Hindústán.

Coarse cloth, which is generically called "*kadha*," (which literally means "woven," just like the Persian "*báfta*,") is also largely manufactured in the Doábah, and is exported to the hills beyond Kúlú and Spití.

In other parts of the Punjab there is equally a demand for this kind of fabric for export to Kábul and Túrkistán, in those towns through which the Parácha merchants pass when they return to their own country after disposing of their goods in Hindústán and Bengal.

In this way it is that the districts of Jhung and Shahpúr, the latter especially in the town of Khusháb, have a considerable trade in coarse cloth. Chintzes or printed fabrics are also much in demand, and are largely exported; Múltán, which is a great rendezvous of Povinda merchants, has a considerable trade in them, as indeed in all the articles that constitute the export trade to the Western frontier.

Gúgaira, and especially the towns of Syadwálla and Pákpattan, are noted for the weaving of an improved variety of "lúnghi" and "khes."

Khusháb in Shahpúr is also noted for its lúnghis, both silk and cotton. The lúnghis of Pesháwar are also famous, and the dark blue scarf with its crimson edge, woven in the Kohat district, is quite characteristic. A similar kind of scarf is largely manufactured in Hazára, both plain and ornamented with a border of gold. The Deputy Commissioner informs me that of the plain kind universally worn by zemindars, from 5 to 6000 are made yearly, and valued from 2 to 15 rupees each. Of the gold bordered kinds worn by Kháns and the better classes, and valuing from 10 to 70 rupees, about fifteen hundred or two thousand are annually woven.

The Panjáb districts bordering on Hindústán are principally remarkable for muslin. Turbans of this fabric are largely manufactured at Delhi. In the Sirsa district, the principal manufactures are coarse cloths called "*gazi*" and "*painsi*" and "*dabba khes*" or khes of two colours.

It must be remarked generally with reference to the *prices* attached to articles in the following list, that they are not constant. The price of durres and all cotton goods alters with the price of raw cotton :—

"LUNGHI."

The first class of cotton fabrics to be noticed is the "lúnghi." This is a long scarf. They are made everywhere, but especially in the Pesháwar division, where they are woven of exquisite fineness, and with most beautiful borders, in which coloured silk and gold thread are often tastefully introduced. The lúnghi is universally worn by the inhabitant of the Pesháwar and Deraját divisions. The long ends with the coloured borders hanging down, present a very elegant and picturesque appearance. When the lúnghi is not worn as a turban it is used as a scarf, being cut in half and the two pieces sown together. A lúnghi is either plain cloth of any colour, oftenest white or dark blue, or else a small check like the Pesháwar lúnghi. The exhibited samples were as follows :—

1.—[5736.] Yellow and black check lúnghi with silk borders, by Wazir.

Sirsa.

2.—[3737]. Another, black and blue.

3.—[5763-4]. Check lúnghi (charkhána) by Muhammad Baksh.

Ambala.

4.—[5765-8]. Four lúnghis by Habib-ullah, valuing Rs. 4, 17, 25 and 27, respectively.

5.—[5820]. Three lúnghis by Nathu of Kánpúr.

Hushyarpur.

6.—[5823-43]. Lúnghis, value Rs. 15 and 35, with borders.

Amritsar.

7.—[5881]. "Lúnghi Fakíri," an excessively cheap kind of cloth, worn by Fakírs or beggars, its value is 9 annas.

Lahore.

8.—[5889]. Is an orange coloured lúnghi by Thakur Das of Lahore.

9.—[5899]. Is a lúnghi by the Superintendent of the Central Jail.

10.—[5935]. One from Gujranwálla.

11.—[6002]. One from the Jihlam jail

12.—[6027-31]. Are various coloured lúnghis made at Khusháb in Shahpúr (which is celebrated for them) by Ahmad Din and Pir Bakhsh.

13.—[6147]. Is a lúnghi from Jhung.

14.—[6165]. A lúnghi from Dera Ismail Khán.

15.—[ ]. Check lúnghi called "Sirdár Khori," which means "check for the chieftain," said to be so called because when first invented the new fabric was presented to a certain Sirdár whose name, however, is not remembered, value Rs. 4-8.

Gugaira.

16.—[6064]. "Lúnghi Chautání," so called because the warp (tání) is divided into four (chau) breadths, each of which is of different coloured threads, red, yellow, green, and white.

17.—[6087]. "Lúnghi tirtání," similar to the preceding. except that the warp is divided into three parts instead of four, each being a different colour.

18.—[6065]. "Lúnghi tirkandí," called from 'three threads' (tirkandí) of red. green and yellow color being employed in weaving it.

19.—[6066]. "Lúnghi safid reshami manchawálí." Of this fabric 10 parts are cotton and one part (mancha) is silk (reshami).

20.—[6067]. "Aláchá úda." Purple coloured (úda) check. The check is so very small that the marks are like the seeds of cardamoms (iláchi).

21.—[6068]. "Chak-lá." 'Chak' means a piece—and 'lá' a kind of cloth.

22.—[6069]. "Lúnghi chaugarri," a check of two colors, generally worn by women.

23.—[6070]. Lúnghi chirwín." This is a plain unicolorous fabric except that at regular intervals a single thread of another color is woven in.

24.—[6072]. "Lunghi safed." A plain white scarf.

25.—[6073]. "Lúnghi Jallá khoriwallá." A check with three colors in it, first made by a weaver named "Jallá."

26.—[6074]. Lúnghi Sáví." Made of five parts green thread and one white.

27.—[6075]. "Alácha Siyah" by Bhanimal of Pák Pattan, black small check, (see No. 6067 above).

28.—[6184]. Is a green lúnghi by Kamaliya.

29.—[6085]. "Lúnghi Khesí," as its name implies, a lúnghi made like "a khes."

30.—[6088]. "Lunghi anárdáni." A check, but not a square check; the marks of the check are elongated like the grains of pomegranate fruit (anárdána).

31.—[6173]. **Peshawar.** Lúnghi with silk borders, value Rs. 8-8, by MIYAN NIZAM-UD-DIN.

These lúnghis are of extreme fineness of texture and great beauty. They are universally worn by Afgháns; some further account of them will be found under the head of articles of clothing. There is one kind of lúnghi which is chiefly worn by the agricultural population, it is of a uniform dark blue color with a border of crimson and yellow silk; the best of these are made at Hangú in Kohat, and can be made of any value up to Rs. 100.

32.—[6174]. "Lúnghi langotah," value Rs. 60. 'Langotah' means waistcloth or girdle, indicating the use to which this kind of lúnghi is put.

33.—[6175]. Lúnghi Hindwáni, value Rs. 25, for Hindús' wear.

34.—[ ]. A small check lúnghi, fine wove, with deep border in stripes of black and turquoise blue silk alternating with broad stripes of twilled gold thread, value Rs. 190.

35.—[6176-8]. Three lúnghis, used either as head dresses or scarves, called "chaddar chamkáni" and "purra."

KHES.

This fabric is generally woven in pieces, which are sown together to make a square "chaddar" or upper wrapper, worn by all classes that can afford it. The fabric is remarkable chiefly as exhibiting a different kind of weaving to the others. The natives acknowledge three kinds of weaving: "Sádá báfi," commencing when the pattern is all in lines or checks and runs either straight down or straight across the webs. "Khes báfi," where the pattern may be either plain or check, but the thread of the weft entwined alternately with those of the warp that the make of the fabric appears to be diagonal or cornerwise across the fabric, instead of the threads crossing at right angles. The looms for this kind of weaving are more complicated than the other, having a greater number of treddles &c., and the shuttle being differently employed; the looms will be fully described under section C. Machinery. The third kind or "Bulbul chashm báfi" is where the fabric is damasked with a pattern of diamond shapes produced by interweaving the threads of warp and weft. The khes báfí includes two kinds of coverlets called "dotahi and chautahi," white sheets with a red or dark blue edging. Sometimes however the chautahis are made with a large check pattern. Occasionally cotton kheses are made with a silk edging.

The exhibited samples were as follows :—

36.—[5731]. **Sirsa.** Black and yellow plaid, half silk and half cotton, made by WAZIR of Ranea, Sirsa district.

Two coloured kheses are in this district called "dabba khes."

37.—[5732]. Red and yellow plaid by FATTEH.

38.—[5733]. Black and white plaid with silk border, by WAZIR.

39.—[5734]. Red and white plaid with red edge, by JIWAN RAM.

40.—[5735]. Coarse khes made at Sahowala.

There were also kheses exhibited from the following districts :—

[5729], Rohtak. [5733], Ludhiána, by KANHYA LAL. [5890], Lahore. [4918], Chúnian, in Lahore district, a plain white khes, worth Rs. 7. [5948-51], Rawal Pindi Jail, and also [5951-2], Checks value Rs. 2-10 and 10 respectively. [6158-61], Leia (Dera Ismail Khan.) [6033], Shahpúr, by MUHAMMAD BAKHSH of Bhera. [6168], Dera Ghází Khan, from Dújal. [6200], Patyála. [6214], Maler Kotla.

A special collection deserves notice from Gúgaria.

41.—[6077]. "Khes Bulbul chashm," a white damasked wrapper with red edge.

These are worn by the better classes, who can afford them. A very good specimen of the fabric is sent by the Tehsildar of Chúnián (Lahore district) valued at Rs. 10, (No. 59-9) under the name of chautahi. (See explanation of term "chautahi" lower down.) Another khes called chautahi of this pattern with a red edge is sent from Nábha (No. 6199); this is smooth and glazed exactly like the "gháti;" a similar one comes from Jhínd (No. 6196), and one also from Patyála (No. 6201).

42.—[6078]. "Khes chándana." Black and white khes, by BHANI MAL of Pák Pattan.

The pattern is of alternate diamond shapes of black and white.

43.—[6079]. "Khes Gadrá." A khes in which thread of two colors is woven together into a large check like a plaid shawl.

44.—[6080]. "Khes charkhána." Common check khes.

45.—[6082]. White khes.

46.—[6094]. "Khes nila." Dark blue ditto.

The remaining specimens under this head are exhibited as "chautahi" and "dotahi." These are made on the same principle as the khes, but with this difference that they are used only for bedding and coverlets, except perhaps in the neighbourhood of the Jhung and Gúgaria districts, where they are occasionally worn as wrappers by the zemindars.

The terms chautahi and dotahi have reference to the size.

They are always made to fit an ordinary sized "charpoy" or bed; if by folding (tahi) in two, or once across, (do) they fit the bed, they are called "dotahi," if the piece is so large as to require to be folded in four (char) to make it the size of the bed it is called "chautahi."

They are made of various qualities and thickness, from a value of a little more than a rupee, up to 10 or 12 rupees.

47.—[5887]. "Dotahi kanni siyah," or a "dotahi" with a black border of the common quality, and worth Rs. 1-5, by THAKUR DAS of Lahore.

48.—[6076]. Is a chautahi with silk border from Gugaria.

49.—[6213]. One from Maler Kotla.

GHATI.

This fabric is either plain or else damasked or diapered with the "Bulbul chasm" or diamond pattern.

Both fabrics are highly glazed; the manufacture is almost confined to the Jalandhar Doab, including Kangra.

There are however specimens of the work from Patyála and Nábha, and the Ambala district.

The exhibited samples are—

50.—[5804-7]. Ghátí from Rahún, Jalandhar district.

51.—[5807]. "Do-lúnghi," Jalandhar.

52.—[5815 and 16] Khes of two qualities, made like white ghâti, by ABDULLA of Kangra.

SUSI.

This is a narrow cotton fabric, universally used for making pyjamas or trowsers, especially the large loose garments worn by females. The fabric is also occasionally worn round the waist. It is distinguished by having stripes lengthwise down the piece, of a different color from the ground work;—dark blue with white stripe, blue and red stripe, green and white stripe, are the patterns most commonly seen, but other varieties are made. This fabric is plain woven or made by *Sáda báfi.*

Ludhiana.

53.—[5774]. 5 yards of "Dorya" by MUHAMMAD BAKSH, worth Rs. 4-6 a yard.

54.—[5775]. Dorya of coarse quality by NATHA MALL.

55.—[5776]. Black susí, at 4 annas six pies a yard, by DESU MALL.

56.—[5777]. Pink susí, at the same price, by GOBIND LAL.

Lahore.

57.—[5896]. Green susí, by THAKUR DAS, value 12 annas for 6¼ yards.

58.—[5897]. "Susí" chaukánni, value Rs. 1-8 for the piece of 9¼ yards.

The terms "chaukánni" &c., refer to the breadth

of the coloured stripe on the piece, a chaukánni súsí has the stripes four threads broad, a "dokánni" has it two threads broad, and so on.

59.—[5898]. "Súsí dokánni," value Rs. 1-4 per piece of 6⅞ yards.

60.—[5899]. "Súsí sandali," value Rs. 1-4 for 7¼ yards.

'Sandali' refers to the drab or brown color.

61.—[5886]. "Dosíla," blue and orange stripe, 10 yards worth Rs. 2-8.

The other "Súsis" exhibited were from the Jhung Jail (Nos. 6137 and 6149), Dera Ghazi Khán (Dosila No. 6167), Peshawar (6179.) Agra Jail, one of English thread fine woven (6255) and one of Dacca thread (6256).

DOSUTI, GARHA, GAZZI, and other plain cloths.

These are a series of coarse woven cloths differing in thickness, according as single, double, or treble thread is employed in weaving them; the coarsest and loosest textured is "gazzi," then comes "garha," and eksúti, and then dosúti, and the thicker sorts, tinsúti, chausúti, &c.

These cloths receive different names when dyed. There are a few such samples, which are given at the end of the list.

DOSUTI.

Is a thick cloth much used for dusters, it is also used for clothing by the poorer population, also for bedding and other general purposes. As its name implies, the thread is double (do-sút) with which it is woven.

The samples sent were from—

62.—[5717]. The Jail of Delhi.

63.—[5723]. Karnál, value 8 yards for Rs. 1-4.

64.—[5741]. Sirsa Jail, 4 ans. per yard.

65.—[5780]. Ludhiána, by Mehtab, at 3½ ans. per yard. Also an inferior quality at 2½ ans. per yard. Also from the Jail (5799) at 4 ans. per yard.

66.—[5868]. Lahore, by Haku, at 10 yards the rupee; there is also another piece (5881) value 11 annas for 8½ yards, and a sample from the Central Jail (5495).

67.—[5934]. From Gujranwálla.

68.—[5953]. Ráwalpindí.

69.—[5138 and 39]. Jhung Jail, both white and dyed, "kháki" or grey.

70.—[6169 and 70]. "Kalabágh."

71.—[6181]. Kohat.

72.—[6218 and 19]. Maler Kotla.

When the threads of the cloth are doubled, trebled or quadrupled the cloth is called tinsúti, charsúti, &c.

73.—[6240]. Chausúti. Agra jail.

74.—[6241]. Tinsúti, ditto.

75.—[6242]. Dosúti, ditto.

There remain to be mentioned a few varieties of this cloth under the names painsi, chaunsi, &c. These refer to the breadth of the cloth, indicating that there are 500, or 400, &c. threads in the warp. The reader should remember the difference between chau*súti* and chau*si*; the former refers to the thickness of the weaving thread, the latter to the breadth of the warp.

The specimens are—

76.—[5738]. "Painsadi" cloth, value 3 annas 1 pic per yard, made at Ranea, Sirsa.

77.—[5739]. "Rethi" by Jewan Ram of Sahowala, Sirsa; the value of this 2½ annas per yard.

78.—[5885]. "Painsi" cloth, Lahore, value 5½ yards for 9 annas.

79.—[6203]. "Chausi" cloth, Patyála.

EKSUTI.

Is a cloth similar to the last, but woven with only one thread, as its name implies. A sample is sent from Amritsar [5824], by Gulasar Husain.

Many of the following specimens are hardly distinguishable from eksúti.

GARHA.

Is a cheap and thin fabric, woven with one thread; it is used for the common purposes to which cloth is applied. It can be very well made however, as is the sample [No. 6245].

Samples of this cloth were sent from—

80.—[5718]. Delhi jail.

81.—[5800]. Ludhiána jail, value 2¼ ans. a yard.

82.—[5898]. Lahore Central Jail.

83.—[6032]. Shahpúr.

84.—[6141-2-3]. Jhung Jail. Three qualities.

The trade of this jail is wonderfully great; the merchants from the North West returning from Calcutta and Hindustán readily purchase at the jail quantities of coarse cotton cloth; hence the manufacture thrives.

85.—[6245]. Agra jail, fine quality.

"GAZZI."

Is also a thin cloth, somewhat inferior to "gárha;" the specimens are from the following districts:—

86.—[5744]. Sirsa jail, value 2 annas 10 pies per yard.

87.—[5782]. Ludhiána, value 1 anna 6 pies per yard, by MEHTAB.

88.—[5954]. Rawalpindí.

89.—[6192-3 and 4]. Jhung jail, three qualities of coarse white cloth.

90.—[6583]. "Kadak," (equivalent to "báftah,") Kashmír. This is the Kashmíri name for a soft kind of cloth, like gazzi.

"DARI."

Is a useful cotton fabric, being a kind of drill, made exactly on the same principle as the cotton carpet, also called darri, but not to be confounded with it.

The specimens are from—

91.—[5778 and 5779]. Ludhiána, one sample value 7 ans. a yard by MUHAMMAD BAKHSH, and the other worth 5¼ ans. a yard.

92.—[5792-5]. Ludhiána Jail, 3 samples valuing 5 annas ten pies, 4 annas five pies, and 4 annas a yard respectively.

93.—[5817]. Hushyarpúr, value Rs. 7 for 18 yards, made at Bassí by ALLADAYA.

The remaining samples of cloths of this kind are miscellaneous, as follows:—

94.—[5878]. "Kora Kapra," coarse cloth; Lahore.

95.—[5580]. Another quality, valuing 6 annas for 5½ yards.

96.—[5873]. Piece of "Níla," dark blue cloth worn as a turban, worth Rs. 1-10-0.

97.—[5867]. "Sálu," cloth dyed with madder, Lahore, (European turkey red cloth is also called "Salu or alwán").

98.—[ ]. "Khárwa," coarse cloth dyed with madder, is known by a black stamp always impressed on it; it is used chiefly to make bags and coarse covering for property, also for screens or purdahs.

99.—[5875-76]. "Kapra Majíthi," Lahore. Madder dyed cloth as its name imports.

TURBANS AND "DHOTIS."

The next series of cloths are generally light in texture and soft: they are of very different qualities, and made for turbans, both the "sáfa" or under turban and the "dastár" or upper turban. In the Panjab, both are usually worn and of different colours, which has a pleasing appearance, but some castes wear only the sáfa. The "pagri" is a peculiar kind of head dress worn by itself, and different from either of the foregoing. Of a similar fabric are also the "dhotis" or sheets worn round the waist by Hindus.

The exhibited samples are as follows:—

100.—[5719]. Dhoti from Delhi Jail.

Samples are also sent from Amritsar (No. 5825) by GULABAR HUSAIN, who also sends a variety of cloth called "Goripat" similarly worn. (5826) is from Lahore, (No. 5879) by THAKUR DAS, who also exhibited a dhoti 10 yards in length.

The turbans exhibited are as follows :—

101.—[5724-26]. Three turbans (pagri) of cotton thread, Rohtak.

102.—[5759]. Black Dastár, (outer turban) worth Rs. 10, by GHULAM KADIR of Lúdhiána.

103.—[5760]. A white Dastár, by the same.

104.—[5761]. Check Dastar, worth Rs. 1-8-0, by MUHAMMAD BUKSH of Lúdhiána.

105.—[5762]. Unbleached (korhi) turban, worth 1 rupee, by KIRPA RAM of Lúdhiána.

106.—[5883.] Coarse "pagri," worth 9 annas, Lahore.

107.—[5975-76]. Two "pagris" made with English thread, in the Gújrát Jail, (one of them has a gold border).

108.—[6121]. Pagri from Gúgaira Jail.

109.—[6120]. Is a "chaddar," made at the same place.

110.—[6215-26]. Two turbans from Maler Kotla.

MUSLINS.

The samples are very few, and the manufacture does not appear to flourish in the Punjab. The best muslins come from Delhi, there are also some of tolerable fineness from Hushyárpúr and the Doábah, and Lúdhiána exhibits one or two of good quality. None are however equal to the Dacca and Hindustan muslins.

111.—[5715]. Six specimens of muslins, Delhi.

These muslin turbans are manufactured in great quantities of Chinese cotton; about two lakhs of rupees worth are annually exported.

112.—[5819-20-21]. Three turbans of white muslin by NATHU of Khanpúr—Húshyárpúr.

113.—[ ]. "Dhotar" coarse muslin of narrow width, by THAKUR DAS of Lahore.

114.—[ ]. "Silára," muslin with coloured stripe used for women's dress and for a lining to other garments.

N. B.—Some specimens of muslins are included as "Pagrís" in the foregoing list; such are those from Roktak, which gained one of the special prizes for muslin.

FANCY CLOTHS.

Principally in the European style.

This class of fabric has been kept separate since they are all either made at jails under European supervision or else have been made from European patterns.

115.—[5772]. "Gambroon," worth 0-5-4 per yard, by MUHAMMAD BAKSH, Lúdhiána.

116.—[5818]. Búrdán or "Ticken," at 1 rupee per yard.

A thick striped cloth like English bed-ticken: made by ALLADYA of Bassi in the Húshyárpúr district.

117.—[5819]. "Lachak" or drill, at Rs. 2 per yard, by the same.

118.—[5897]. Drill, at 8 annas a yard, by the Lahore Central Jail.

119.—[5916]. American drill, at 2 rupees a yard, by the Gújranwálla Jail.

120.—[5917]. Double drill cloth, at 10 annas a yard, by the Gújrát Jail.

121.—[6005]. Jean, at 6¼ annas a yard, by the Jhilam Jail.

122.—[6007]. "Gumti," by the Jihlam Jail.

The following are "checks" :—

123.—[5766]. Blue check, 1 rupee per yard, by the Sirsa Jail.

124.—[5773]. Check cloth, at 12 annas a yard, by MUHAMMAD BAKSH of Lúdhiána.

125.—[5174]. Blue check, Lahore.

126.—[6046]. Lady's check dress, Múltán Jail, value Rs. 3.

127.—[6047]. Black and white ditto.

128.—[6048]. Striped ditto.

129.—[6234-35]. Check cloth made with English thread, Agra Jail.

130.—[6236]. Green cloth made with English thread, Agra Jail.

131.—[6250-51]. Check cloth and check horse clothing made with Dacca thread, Agra Jail.

TABLE AND HOUSE LINEN.

This series is exclusively the product of the various jails in the Punjab. Many of the articles are made with English fine thread, especially the table linen;—but the dusters, towels, &c. are usually made with the best class of native thread. It is scarcely necessary to remark that all these fabrics are of English patterns.

132.—[5770]. One dozen Handkerchiefs, value Rs. 2-4, by Muhammad Baksh, of Lúdhiána.

133.—[5841-52]. Handkerchiefs, by the Amritsar Jail.

134.—[5813]. Table cloth, value Rs. 32, by the Jalandhar Jail.

135.—[5901]. White damask table cloth, at Rs. 1-4-0 per yard, by the Lahore Central Jail.

136.—[5902]. Fancy table cover, Rs. 2, Lahore Central Jail.

137.—[5896]. Table cloth, made with cotton grown in the Jail garden, Gújrát, with sample (5888-89) of thread used in making them.

Table cloths are also sent from Ferozpúr, value Rs. 9-12-0, from Rawalpindi (5956), Gújrát Jail, accompanied by a sample of the English thread from which they are made (Nos. 5971, 73, 93, & 5985), from Jhilam (5996), and from Agra (6237) where the damask for table cloth is called white "Mashajú."

138.—[5987]. One dozen table napkins, made from cotton grown in the Jail garden, Gújrát.

Table napkins are also sent from Lahore Central Jail (5902). From Gújrát (various qualities 5972, 41, & 94). From Jihlam (6002). From Múltan, value Rs. 4 a dozen, (6056).

139.—[5771]. Towels, by Muhammad Baksh of Lúdhiána.

Towels are also exhibited in great variety, as follows :—

140.—[4795-8]. Lúdhiána Jail, samples of towelling at 0-6-8, 0-5-4, 0-4-8, and 0-4-0 each piece.

141.—[5900]. Lahore Central Jail, seventeen samples of towels, plain pattern, 'honey comb,' 'Baden-baden,' 'Pile,' 'Turkish,' &c., &c.

Besides there are towels made at all the jails of the Punjab.

142.—[5720]. Dusters, Delhi jail.

143.—[5741]. Do., black bordered, worth 3½ annas each. Sirsa.

144.—[5756]. Do., worth Rs. 3 a dozen. Amballa jail.

145.—[5896]. Do., value 3 annas each. Lahore Central Jail.

(All the Jails exhibited dusters.)

146. [5977]. Diaper cloth, Gújrát jail, value annas 5-4 per yard.

147 —[6057-8]. Napkins, (Diaper) Multan jail.

148.—[6231-2-3]. Colored table covers, woven with English thread, on the principle of a fine "durree." Agra jail.

149.—[6244]. Screen or curtain for a door, of English thread, Agra jail.

COTTON CARPETS.

These are in universal use in India. They are variously called "dari" or "satranji," according to the size: satranji being a large carpet, and dari a narrow piece just big enough for a bed to stand on, (which is what natives generally use them for,) but Europeans call all sizes indifferently by the name "durree." In pattern they are usually striped with bands of several colours, arranged according to taste; but a clever workman can produce various patterns in a durree, such as squares, diamond shapes, &c., provided only that the figures of the pattern be not too complicated, and are made up wholly of straight lines.

The method of manufacture is very simple.

All that is requisite is a flat smooth space of ground as large as the intended durree. At either end of this a long roller is set up, and to either roller the ends of the web are attached just as in an ordinary loom. When the web is properly stretched out, it only remains to provide a simple agency for crossing and recrossing the threads of the warp in the usual way, as the thread of the woof is passed across and across.

This is effected by placing a long pole supported at either end by two legs, trestle fashion, across the whole width of the warp. This pole is called a "gori" (which literally means "mare," and so called from its rude resemblance to a quadruped), from the "gori" are hung two bamboos, each of which carry a number of threads, which are attached to the under and upper threads of the web respectively. When it is desired to cross the threads of the warp, it is simply necessary to pull up one of the bamboos and lower the other: as the bamboos are merely hung to the "gori" by ropes at each end, the raising and lowering is easily done by tightening or loosening the suspending string by means of a stick attached. No regular shuttle is used. A number of workmen sit in a row, on that part of the durree which has already been completed, and pass the thread along between the lines of the warp, from hand to hand. The thread is wound in a long egg shape on an iron skewer or needle.

If the pattern is elaborate there will be a considerable number of these thread shuttles at work: each workmen has charge of his own, and passes it along according to the pattern, taking the thread out and allowing the next workman to insert and withdraw his shuttle in the same manner, and so on; the threads as they are passed through the threads of the warp, are kept close together and the work is rendered compact and even by striking between the lines of the warp with a kind of fork, having a wooden handle and iron teeth and called a "kangi." The "gori" above described, with its bamboos and threads for raising and changing the lines of the warp, can be shifted down the web as the work progresses.

I have seen a large durree worked with at both ends simultaneously, with 2 "goris," the workmen approaching each other till they finish in the middle. The simple apparatus for durree making can be taken up and put down anywhere.

Samples of durrees were exhibited from most of the Jails.

There is also a special kind of ribbed durree called Jabbalpúrí (because first made at the Jabbalpúr School of Industry), it is made on the Kidderminister carpet principle, the coloured lines being longitudinal (made in the web), and not transverse in the woof as ordinary durrees are. They have also a peculiar wavy or corrugated texture.

Common durrees are made not only in jails but in the cities and bazars. I never saw the Jabbalpúrí durree made elsewhere but in jails.

It is only necessary to notice two samples which are specialties in this kind of manufacture: they are as fallows:—

150.—[5927]. A fancy "durree" from Baháwulpúr (Lahore Museum). This is made in white red and blue, and has a cleverly designed border.

151.—[5980]. Durree from the Gújrát jail.

This was the most elegant durree exhibited, the pattern consisted of plain stripes of white, grey, black and turquoise blue, with an occasionally thin line of red against the black. It was very neat in style, and peculiarly regular and well finished in make.

152.—[5981]. A sample of the thread used in the manufacture accompanied it.

PILE CARPETS.

A few specimens of Kálín or soft pile carpeting, made of cotton instead of wool, were exhibited. Múltán jail is noted for the manufacture.

153.—[5730]. Kálín from Rohtak jail.

154.—[5755]. Soft carpeting, Amballa jail.

155.—[5970]. "Kálín súti," value Rs. 59, Gújrát jail.

156.—[6034]. Cotton carpet, Múltán, value Rs. 29-8.

157.—[6281]. Cotton rug, Agra jail.

Tape, String and Miscellaneous Cotton Manufactures.

These articles are much manufactured at jails, they require no remark ; the most useful of them is the broad coarse tape called "newar," this is always used to form the webbing of beds: the charpoy being a mere oblong frame supported on four feet, the centre is filled in with this broad tape, put on lengthwise and then interwoven crosswise, thus forming a firm and elastic web on which the bedding is placed.

The poorer people who cannot afford newár of cotton, use string for the same purpose.

158.—[5748]. Newár, broad coarse tape, Sirsa jail, value Rs. 2 a seer (2Ibs).

It is also exhibited from various other jails.

159.—[6051-53]. White, red, and black tape, value 1½ annas to 2 annas a yard, from Múltán jail.

160.—[6140]. Red tape from Jhung jail.

161.—[6055]. Lamp wicks, 6 annas a yard, from Múltán jail, also from Rawalpindi (5966), and from Jihlam jail (6004).

162.—[6135]. Wax cloth, Jhung jail.

163.—[6172]. "Izárband" or cotton sash, Peshawar.

164.—[6209-10-12]. Cotton rope, and fine twine called "dori patang," (or string for flying a kite) from Patyála.

165.—[5828], Cotton rope, Amritsar.

166.—[5926]. Various colours and patterns of cotton rope, Lahore Central Jail.

167.—[5914], Cotton tassels, Lahore.

168.—[5905]. Pairs of cotton socks made by the prisoners in the Female Penitentiary Lahore.

169.—[6126]. Various coloured threads, prepared at Gúgaira jail.

170.—[5928]. Common native spun thread from Lahore.

HORSE CLOTHING.

171.—[6249]. Horse net, Agra jail.

172.—[6236]. Rollers and surcingle of English thread.

6252 is one of Dacca thread.

173.—[6254]. Double net for horse rollers.

174.—[6125]. Horse's head frings, Gúgaira jail.

175.—[5130]. "Bágdaur," horse-halters and girths, Amritsar.

176.—[ ]. Several patterns of horse-girths, Lahore Central Jail.

COTTON PRINTS.

The last remaining specimens in the class of cotton fabrics are more specimens of dyeing and printing art than of cotton manufacture.

For the various names descriptive of the sorts of printing, see the report of the jury at the end of the class.

Almost any kind of light cloth is used for the purpose of printing. These fabrics are used for bed covers, for furniture covers, or for floor cloths.

Coarse stout cloth is often stamped and printed in this way and used to line tents with.

The process of calico printing has already been noticed in the Raw Produce section under the head of dyeing.

Generally speaking, the prints are not permanent and will not wash.

Sometimes they are effected by dipping the cloth in boiling solutions of dyes which take on certain portions of the cloth but do not affect others which have been previously prepared by stamping with a block charged with some resisting material. A good instance of this kind of printing, resulting in a pattern in shades of red and black, is exhibited from Muzaffargarh and has been described under the head of Dyes.

The other kind of calico printing is done without immersing the cloth in any colouring solution at all. The colour is simply applied by wooden blocks, of hard dark wood, on which the pattern projects in strong relief; the blocks are charged with colour and then pressed down on the cloth previously damped and stretched out.

The exhibited samples of this work were as follows :—

177.—[5784-85]. Bed covers, "palang-posh," value Rs. 2 and 1-8 each, by Hukmi and Dasi of Lúdhiána.

178.—[5861-62]. Printed cotton carpets, Kasúr (Lahore district) worth Rs. 15 each.

179.—[5863-67]. Coarse printed cloths used as coverings, Lahore, value 13 annas to Rs. 1-4 each.

180.—[5916]. Dosúti printed in yellow and black, for tents. Thuggee School of Industry Lahore.

181.—[6035]. Floor cloth, value Rs. 25, Multán. This is a very elaborate and elegant design and introduces a great variety of colour.

182.—[6036-37]. Bed covers from Multán.

183.—[6038-39]. 'Chintz,'(print) Multán.

184.—[6182]. "Thán chet," piece of chintz or print from Sultánpur, Kapurthala

'Abrah' means coloured or marbled pattern.

186.—[6184]. "Toshak-chet," printed coverlet, Kapurthala

187.—[6185]. "Palang posh," bed cover, Kapurthala.

188. [6187-71]. 4 patterns of "chet" or print, Kapurthala.

189.—[6099]. "Angocha," small printed sheet, worth Rs. 1-4, made at Kamalia, Gúgaira district.

190.—[6100]. "Gilaf takya," pillow-cases, from the same place.

191.—[6104]. Printed counterpane, from the same place.

192.—[6105]. Printed floor cloth, called jájam. From Kamalia, Gúgaira.

193. –[6118]. "Thán chet," piece of print.

194.—[6119].—"Nainú," from Gúgaira.

195.—[6114]. "Liháf," counterpane. Gúgaira.

Before closing the list of cotton prints, it should be remarked that English and Russian glazed chintzes, chiefly of gaudy patterns, are much valued for sale across the frontier, in Kábul, Bukhárá, and Turkistán, generally; the varieties are known by different names, as "Nasrkháni," "Lálgeri," Shakarkuzi," &c.

196.—[ ]. Dhoti from Multán.

This is a white soft cloth worn either as a dhoti or for a scarf or even for a pagri; its distinguishing characteristic is that it is white with a crimson printed border. This article is commonly worn.

TENTS.

Some tents being entirely of cotton are included in this class.

197. –[6040 to 6045]. Large tent of coloured cloth including a "shamyána" or canopy, with "kanats" or side screens of varigated cloth and richly embroidered, from Múltán.

198.—[6221]. Small model of tent in white and red cotton cloth. Maler Kotla.

MIXED FABRICS.

Then follow also same fabrics which as being made of both cotton and wool come between class V and VI.

199.—[6191]. Striped sheet made of mixed cotton and wool, value Rs. 3. Kashmír.

200.—[6192]. Is another variety of the same material.

201.—[6194]. Flannel made of cotton and wool, value Rs. 3-8.

202.—[6194]. Is another specimen of the same, but of slightly better quality.

The Jury's report on this large and important class now follows :—

REPORT ON COTTON FABRICS.

The Jury for this class consisted of:—

Mr. D. F. Macleod, C. B.
Mr. F. E. Moore.
Major Farrington.
Mr. Coldstream, Reporter.
Diwán Rattan Chand.

It is unnecessary here to dwell upon the great importance of cotton fabrics to the world generally, or to the natives of India in particular. It would be difficult to name a manufacture on which the latter are more dependent. From the highest to the lowest, all classes employ it for the commonest articles of their clothing. Everywhere, from the hills of Kábul to the swamps of Burmah, the cotton plant is cultivated. In every age, from the earliest historic times down to the present, the Hindu has gone clad in cotton cloth.

These manufactures are effected without any exception by hand looms of the simplest and rudest construction, and there is no reason to believe that any, the slightest alteration or improvement has taken place in the form of the loom for centuries past. Notwithstanding this, many of the fabrics produced are conspicuous for their regularity of workmanship, for durability, and in some instances for extreme softness and fineness of texture.

The muslins of Dháka long outrivalled the fabrics of European looms, and till very lately held the highest place in the markets of the West. In fact, in particular places in India, and with regard to particular fabrics, cotton manufactures have probably attained as high an excellence as is possible without the aid of intricate machinery. Yet this superiority is confined to a few fabrics, and to a few places : and very much remains to be done in most localities to encourge the cotton weaver to do the best with the means at his disposal.

The Government Jails doubtless contribute much to this end throughout the country : their produce (as will be seen in the sequel) being superior, to the unguided native manufacture.

What effect a great increase in the growth and exports of an improved staple will have on Indian manufactures on the one hand, and on the import of English piece goods on the other, it would be difficult to predict. Certain it is that the extended cultivation of improved cotton must eventually influence the quality of native manufactures.

Indications of this may be seen in the collection under report. There are several specimens of fabrics woven in jails from cotton raised experimentally from the imported seed, and the samples of the thread used in the manufacture and spun from the foreign cotton shew to what a degree of excellence we may hope to attain.

Hence the importance of giving to *cotton fabrics* a prominent place in the Punjab Exhibition.

A separate court in the north-west corner of the building was allotted to the display of articles in this class. The specimens were numerous, and more than occupied the space assigned to them. Fifty shares of the Prize Fund, (one-twentieth of the whole,) were at the disposal of the Jury. Its distribution will be recorded at the close of this report.

In describing the various kinds of cotton manufactures which came under the notice of the Jury, the order of *texture* will as much as possible be followed—the finer varieties being described first.

Muslin. Native name "Malmal."

Muslin in the shape of pagris was exhibited from Delhi, and the adjacent district of Rohtak, and from Húshyárpúr very fine specimens were exhibited, by the Municipal Commissioners of Delhi; to one of these, as also to a Rohtak pagri, a prize was awarded. It would seem that as far as the Punjab is concerned the manufacture of the finer muslins is carried on only in Delhi and the adjacent districts, and in the Doábah or country about Húshyárpúr. The manufacture in the latter place is very old.* A very fine piece of *Doria* (or muslin with stripes of a thicker texture at regular intervals) was exhibited from the Government Toshakhanah; but it appeared that this was a Dháka fabric. A coarse kind of Doria is made in the Doábah.

Dhotar.

Coarse muslin of narrow width, called *Dhotar*, was exhibited from Lahore: its manufacture is largely carried on throughout the Punjab. It is commonly used for coats, dopattahs, &c.: when shot with coloured lines it is called *Silára,* and is used for women's clothes.

Gazi.

A still coarser fabric of the same make is *gazi.* It is much used by the poor for clothing: and by the richer classes for lining coats &c.: also as the middle ply in tent cloth. The several kinds of *gazi* are distinguished by various names; as hazári, áthsi, chísi, painsi, chausi, &c. These have reference to the number of threads in the than or warp, thus painsi has 500 threads, chausi 400, &c. It is commonly made all over the Punjab. Specimens were exhibited from Sirsa, Rawal-Pindi and other places.

Garha.

Very coarse gazi is called *garha.* It is much used as tent-cloth; its manufacture is not confined to any particular district. *Gazi* or *garha,* dyed red, if narrow, is called *sálú*: if broad, *khárwá*: sálú with embroidered edge, and used for a woman's shawl, is called *chob.*

Lúngi.

The *lúngi*, perhaps the commonest and most universal article of clothing with the natives, was exhibited in great variety. It is usually made of fine stuff: but stout warm ones are common. The 'lúngi' is 'dopat' or 'tínpat,' according as it has to be cut and joined in two or three parts before it is worn. It is usually less than two feet in breadth, and the ends are adorned with a border and fringe (háshya) often wrought in gold or silver thread. The kinds of lungi are very numerous, often taking their names from the place where they are manufactured. Thus, there is the *Mánjha* lungi, the pattern of which is a check in light and dark blue: or a plain dark blue like the "Battála lungi;" another kind is checked *red*: these are worn by Hindus only: blue being the distinctive colour of the Mussulman lúngi. Lúdhiána manufactures blue check lungis in immense quantities, and of late large consignments of them have been annually sent to Peshawar.

Lúngis are also much manufactured in the Peshawár and Derajat divisions, always either a dark blue plain or blue check, being blue upon black or blue on white; in these districts the lungi is worn as a turban, as indeed it generally is by the Pathán and Wazírí tribes.

The Peshawár lungis are generally of fine texture, and have silk or gold thread borders at either end.

* The old Doábah muslins were of two kinds.—*Sirisáf,* and *Adras.*

The most handsome lúngi that came under the notice of the Jury was a Peshawár fabric, exhibited by Kazi Nazirullah Ján (No. 7659). It was upwards of 2 feet broad, and nearly 6 yards long, the ends consisting of a border in which stripes of black silk alternated with torquoise blue, between which again was a very rich broad stripe of gold twilled thread (kalabatun), of about 2 feet in depth. The colour of the scarf itself was a very light blue checked with a darker shade. The texture was remarkably fine. The value of this one scarf was Rs. 190, shewing what value can be given to fabrics of this class; it was made expressly for the Exhibition, and was considered at Peshawar as a master-piece. To this handsome specimen the Jury awarded a prize of two shares.

The Jury also took particular notice of the lúngi from Hazara (No. 7333) of stouter texture and a uniform dark blue colour, also adorned with a gold embroidered 'háshya.'

Khes.

The word 'khes' includes a great variety of fabrics; and is the name given to a kind of shawl or upper garment worn by all classes in the Punjab; in equal favor with the Sikh Sirdar, and the Mussulman Jat. "Khes patpatti" is the name applied to the white and red checks of the Mánjah. "Khes tukridár" to the white and blue checks of Pákpattan. For the finer white cloths (used as 'khes') the Doábah has long been famous, especially the towns of Rahún and Kangra.

Cloth used for 'khes' is usually woven so as to shew lines running diagonally, hence this particular mode of weaving is called *khesbáf.* Khes of all kinds were exhibited. To a khes from Kangra (5815), (white 'bulbul chashm' pattern) a prize was awarded; also to a specimen (No. 6077) from Pák Pattan in the Gúgaira district.

Ghúti.

Among the most excellent of the native fabrics exhibited were the specimens of the *gháti* of Rahún and the Doábah generally. This is a fine white cloth, of strong texture and highly glazed, not unlike English diaper. It is used for sheets, pyjama, *angarkahs*, &c., and is in great repute. They are several varieties of it. If very fine and plain, it is called *báftah*: wrought in rhomboidal check, it is *bulbul chashm*: with diagonal lines it is *khesbáf*: if very coarse it degenerates into *khaddar.* The Jury awarded two prizes for ghάti: one to Jhínd and one to Patyála.

'Dotahi' 'Chautahi.'

Dotahi, is a sheet usually used for a bed cover. It is generally of fine white cloth, resembling coarse gháti. If it has to be folded four times before being used, it is called *chautahi.* A beautiful *chautahi* with gold embroidered edging was exhibited by the Raja of Nabha (7396 D). To this the Jury awarded a prize.

Súsi.

Another excellent fabric of purely native manufacture is *Súsi*: a fine colored cloth, and striped in the direction of the warp with silk or cotton lines of a different colour. Battala and Sealkot are famous for its manufacture, and export it to other parts of the Punjab; to a specimen from the former place a prize was awarded.

It is now chiefly used as a material for women's pyjama: Mussulman women of the lower class usually wearing a black 'susi' shot with red lines. If the stripe has two lines in it, the fabric is called *dokanni,* if three *tinkanni,* and so on. Susi was formerly used by men also for the tight fitting trowsers of the Punjab, but since English goods have been largely imported, it has gone out of fashion, and except at Multan, no men but those too old to change with the *mode* of the day wear 'susi.'

There are several varieties of cotton cloth, which although unknown before the English rule was extended to the province, have since become widely manufactured, and as it were naturalized. Such are the Lúdiána *durris*, a stout closely woven fabric like a 'twill,' much used by Europeans for clothing: *dosúti, tinsúti, chausúti*, coarse cloths of great strength, used principally for tent cloths and dusters, and 'gambroons' or 'dabbis,' fancy clothes woven in checks, lines, &c. in various colours and patterns. All these are chiefly manufactured in our jails: but excellent 'dosutis' and 'gambroons' were exhibited by private manufacturers in Lúdiána.

Durri cloth (Lúdiána.)

A piece of drill, and blue striped ticking after European patterns were exhibited by Allah Dya of Bassya, Húshyárpúr, and were deemed worthy by the Jury of the award of a medal and 3 shares of the Prize Fund;—such manufactures being in the opinion of the Jury deserving of encouragement.

Goods manufactured after European patterns.

It is needless here to enter into detail regarding the various Jail manufactures on English models. Their general appearances and uses are known to all. Suffice it to say, that the Jails of Gújrát, Lahore, Rawalpindi, Jihlam, Dera Ismail Khan, Fírozpúr, Lúdiána, Múltán, Sirsa, Gujráwalah,* Ambála, and the Lahore Thuggee School of Industry, are all represented in the Prize List: the excellence of the table cloths, napkins, towelling, dusters, and a large durri contributed by the Gújrát Jail being very conspicuous.

Before the English occupation of the country, thick durri carpets were not largely manufactured in the province (of old, Ambála and Bareilly appear to have been particularly famous for them). Now they are produced in every Jail, and here and there by private manufacturers. Very beautiful specimens of plain durri and Kidderminster carpet were exhibited, the latter is called Jabbalpúri durri as having been made at the Jabbalpúr School; they are of narrow-breadth like a stair carpet, and their texture is waved or slightly quilled on the surface: the coloured longitudinal stripes are produced by introducing coloured threads into the warp, not like other durris in which the warp is white and the colour only is the woof.

The colours of a very large and fine durri from Gújrát Jail, noted above, were much admired, consisting of a well arranged alteration of white, grey, turquoise-blue and black.

A variety of durri, a large cotton carpet with a 'chaupar' board woven in the centre, and used for playing that game, is called *Shahnashín*: one specimen of this was exhibited.

The above noted varieties of cotton fabrics include almost all those represented in the Exhibition which come directly within the scope of the Jury. But a prize was also awarded for a handsome 'sozni,' or quilted bed-cover, embroidered in a shawl pattern, the contribution of the Maharaja of Kashmir (exhibited in the cotton court), and the Jury especially noticed some printed cloths of fair design and colour.

Sozni.

Printed cloths, if the pattern be continuous are called *chail*: if composed of separate designs, flowers, &c., they are called *chít*. Dyed cloths with spots of a different colour are called *bhându*. They are principally used for women's clothing, for floor cloths and for bed covers; and some large print floor cloths of this kind were exhibited from Kasúr and Múltán, and Kapúrthala, and also a number of liháf or "plang posh," bed covers. As the excellence of

* Gujránwalah obtained prizes for dusters and dosúti. It is presumed they are from the Jail, although not so marked in the list.

these consisted solely in the process of printing in the colours with blocks, the examination of them was made over to the Jury on the processes of dyeing &c.

Two collections to which by the rules of the Exhibition shares of the Prize Fund could not be awarded deserve especial notice, viz., that sent by the Government of Bombay, and that from the Central Prison, Agra. These did not come into competition with the Punjab contributions, but the Jury feel it their duty here to record their appreciation of the great excellence of the collections as wholes, and the high merits of many of the individual specimens, and beg to recommend to the General Committee, in the event of medals being available, that one be awarded to Dr. Birdwood, Curator of the Bombay Government Museum, through whose agency the Bombay articles were forwarded, and one to the Superintendent of the Central Prison, Agra.

The following is a list of the prizes awarded by the Jury,

Award of Special Prizes.

	I. 1.	Gújrát Jail for excellent quality of its table and house linen,	Mr. Scarlett's special prize, Rs. 25.
	2.	Muslin pagris from Delhi (No. 7430-1) and Rhotak,	Municipal Committee Delhi, special prize Rs. 25. Rs. 15 to Delhi and Rs. 10 to Rohtak.

N. B. For special prizes offered for fire-proof durree or tarpaulin, no competition.

Award of Shares of General Prize Fund.

	II.	To Gújrát Jail for the excellent quality of its *towellings, table-cloths, table-napkins, dimity, and jean and drill,*	A silver medal and 5 shares of fund.
		Nos. 5995, 5996, 5984, 5992, and 5993. These articles also gained the special prize, see No. 1.	
	III.	To Alla-Dya, Húshiárpúr, for the excellence of his duck or drill and ticken (Nos. 5818, 5819),	A silver medal and 3 shares of general fund.
Towelling.	IV.	(1.) Vide No. 1.	
		(2.) For a piece of superior towelling from Dera Ismail Khan, (6163),	1 share.
	V.	For Turkish towelling from Fírozpúr Jail, (5945),	2 shares.
Dusters.	VI.	For close textured thick dusters, Lahore (5596),	1 share.
		Ditto ditto Gújránwalla (5933),	1 share.
Chautahi.	VII.	For fine textured *chautahi,* (No. 7396) from Nábha,	2 shares.
Gháti.	VIII.	For very fine *gháti,* 1 Patyála, 2 Jhínd (7394),	2 shares, certificate.
Lúngi.	IX.	(1.) For broad, fine textured, ornamented lungi (No. 7659) Peshawar, Kazi Nazirúllah Ján,	2 shares.
		(2.) For lúngi (No. 6178) by Local Committee of Peshawar,	1 share.
		(3.) For fine textured lúngi, Jálándhar, (No. 61 District List.)	1 share.
		(4.) For Amritsar lúngi (No. 5823),	1 share.
		(5.) „ Hazára, embroidered (7333),	1 share.
		(6.) „ brown „ (supposed to be Sirsa),	1 share.

Súsi. X. Batálah Local Committee, Gúrdaspúr (5858), 1 share.

Khes. XI. (1.) For khes red border (6077) Pák Pattan, 1 share.

(2.) „ white (5815) Kangra, 1 share.

Darri. XII. Lúdiána (5792) Superintendent of Jail, 2 shares.

Dosúti. XIII. Gújránwalla (5934) do., 1 share.

Jean. XIV. (1.) Gújrát (vide No. 1), (2.) Lahore Jail (5897), } 2 shares.

Garha. XV. Lahore Jail (5898), 1 share.

Malmal Dhotar. } XVI. Thakur Dass, Lahore, Certificate.

Tickin. XVII. (Vide No. 2).

Printed Cloth. } XVIII. For excellence of dye and pattern.

1. Hukmi of Rahún, 1 share.

2. Gúgaira (6104), 1 share.

Sozni. XIX. Embroidered from Kashmír (6195), 1 share.

Miscellaneous Cloths. XX. For striped sheeting, mixture of cotton and wool, (6193-4), His Highness the Maharajah of Kashmír, } 1 share.

To Mahammad Bakhsh of Lúdhiána for Gambroon (5772) 1 share.

Superintendent Rawal Pindi Jail for ditto (6453), 2 shares.

Ditto ditto check cloth for horse clothing, (5952), } 2 shares.

Múltán Jail for Gambroons, 2 shares.

Kallah of Lúdhiána for ditto, 1 share.

Sirsa district, check cloth, 1 share.

Pák Pattan in Gúgaira, do. for coverlets, 1 share.

Local Exhibition Committee Ambála, for embroidered red cloth (No. 5747), } 1 share.

Ditto ditto Gúgaira for ditto ditto (6083), 1 share.

Carpets. XXI. Superintendent Jail, Sirsa, for thick white carpeting (5746), } 1 share.

Gújrát Jail for elegant durri in white, grey, black and blue, of good design and excellent work, } 3 shares.

Ditto ditto for another durree, 2 shares.

Jihlam Jail, for a durri, 2 shares.

Ditto for Kidderminster carpeting, 1 share.

Ambála Jail, ditto ditto, 1 share.

Lahore Central Jail, ditto ditto, 1 share.

Múltán Jail, for rich cotton rug, 2 shares.

Rawal Pindi Jail, for durree, Certificate of merit.

Tapes, rope, &c. } XXII. His Highness Maharajah of Patyála, for fine cotton twine, } Certificate of merit.

His Highness Maharajah of Patyála for "Newár,"	1 share.
Lahore Thuggee School of Industry for ditto,	½ share.
Lahore Central Jail, cotton ropes of sorts,	½ share.

Múltán for large tent and embroidered kanáts,	3 shares and a silver medal.

W. COLDSTREAM,
Reporter.

☞ For convenience of reference I have added, at the end of each of the classes devoted to fabrics in cotton, silk and wool, a list of the fabrics commonly met with. I take the opportunity also of reminding the reader that special information about the looms and machinery for weaving will be found in the sequel under Section C.

LIST OF COTTON FABRICS MET WITH IN THE PUNJAB.

I. EUROPEAN IMPORTED GOODS.

WHITE CLOTHS.

Lathá, long cloth.
Khásá or Nainsúk, (a soft white cloth, 'nainsook,' used for all white garments worn by the more respectable classes of servants, Moonshees, Clerks, &c.
Malmal, (muslin).
Sítan, (corruption of 'sheeting.')
Jín or Zín, (jean, the word being corrupted.)
Dabal Jín, (double jean, thick white jean.)
Makkan Jín, ('Duck,' has a sort of nap on the surface.)
Kamrak, (corruption of 'cambric.')
Pauní, (a coarse long cloth or calico in one quarter the length of 'lathá.')
Sáltín, not now in use—a fabric resembling very fine long cloth.
Khes-báft, called also túl (twill) is ribbed diagonally.
Gumtí, diaper, either of linen or imitated in cotton.
Mezposh, table linen.
Rumál, handkerchiefs.
Chíkan, any white figured or embroidered muslin (also applied to edging, 'insertion work' &c., &c.)
Jálí, plain net.
Nainú, a sprigged or figured net or muslin ; all white.
Sénú, the same but having the worked sprig or pattern in colored thread on the white ground.
Alwán, (Turkey red cloth in several qualities.)
Khásá rangín, (same as Khásá but colored and glazed ; glazed calico.)
Malmal rangín, (colored muslin.)
Drés, (I expect this is our word 'dress piece' ; it is applied to all figured muslins, used among Europeans only for female garments, but among natives largely used for chogahs and light outer coats for summer wear.)
Chít, (chintz or calico print). The varieties are—
Chít, Gulánár, red print ; colored flowers on a red ground.
Do. Do. naklí (imitation of European red print.)
Do. Safed, (white ground and printed pattern on it.)
Do. Bundri (spotted).
Do. Márpech (striped) with a sort of corkscrew pattern or "serpent fold."
Do. Ráhdár, with a wavy line.
Do. Kalamkár, lined with fine stripes.
Do. Bútídár (sprigged with flowers).
Do. Nakl-íráni, (*lit.* 'imitation Persian' has an arabesque or shawl pattern.)
Do. Khám rang, (inferior print, the colors not being fast.)
Do. Shikárgáh, (has figures of animal, &c., on it).

II. FABRICS OF INDIAN MANUFACTURE.

WHITE GOODS.

From Dháká.
Malmal, (muslin.)
Dastár, (muslin turbans.)
Rumál, (kerchiefs.)

WHITE GOODS.—*Continued.*

From Rádhá Nagar.

Dopatta (scarf).
Dhotí máre dár (waistcloth worn by Hindús).
Doryá, (striped muslin all white.)
Chárkhána, (check).

From Banáras.

White dopatta or scarf.
Dhotí, waistcloth worn by Hindús.

From Farkhábád.

Abra liháf, (calico print for bed covers, &c.).
Chít, (chintz or print).
Jájam (floor cloth) a kind of coarse red cloth used for flooring, and is generally stamped with a pattern in black on the red ground.
Saláthi.

From Agra.

Darí (" Durrees," cotton carpets.)
Shatranjí, (carpets).
Kálín sútí (pile carpets in cotton).

(*The following have been nearly all described in the text, hence no explanation is added.*)

From Delhi.

Malmal pagrí, (muslin turban).
Dosútí, tinsútí, chaustúí, &c., &c., (p. 7.)
Gambroon, (p. 9.)
Sírí sáf (a kind of muslin).
Gárhá, (thin cloth, p. 8.)

From various places, Lahore, &c.

Plain or sádá báfí.

Adhotar (coarse muslin).
Khadar (coarse thin cloth.)
Chaunsí, painsí, áthsí, chísí, &c. } *All very much alike in quality.*
Hazárí (broad white cloth). }
Gazzí (thin cloth). }
Dhotí, a cloth woven of a size for wear round the loins.
Ghátí, (stiff glazed white cloth, p. 6.)
Doryá, muslin striped with two lines together, all white.
Silaí Khatá, plain striped muslin (stripes close together.)
Chárkhána, check muslin.
Táftá, a fabric of 'tafta' (twisted thread, made both in silk and cotton.
Mahmúdí, (a fabric which used to be made as long cloth, but is superseded by imported 'lathá;' it was made of cotton and also of silk.

Khes báfí.

Dotáhí, (pages 5, 6.)
Chautáhí.
Palang posh.
Khes.
Lungí, (p. 3.)

COLORED GOODS.

Khes báfí.

Khes sádá, (p. 5.)
Khes dabba (check large).
Khes tukrídár showing pieces of different colours joined together.
Khes dorukha (different coloured plaid on either side).
Khes Jat ká, (jat or villager's khes).

Súsí sádí, (page 6.)
Do. dokanní.
Do. chaukanní.

COLORED GOODS.—*Continued*

Súsí panjkanní.
Do. satkanní.
Do. salái khattí, a súsí with five lines; the field and the stripes being equal thickness.
Do. súfiyaná, a súsí partly of silk and partly of cotton, so as to be lawful for Mohamadans to wear.
Salárí, a thin cloth with double stripe used as a scarf or as a "tahband" by boys.
Lúngí, (all the varieties are not here given, many have been named in the foregoing descriptive lists).
Do. Fakiráná, a scarf with white ground and a large check pattern on it in red, black or blue.
Shamlá, (a scarf for winding into a loose turban, three yards long.)
Lúngí Charkhána (check).
Do. Safed kináradár (white with coloured border).
Tahband or Lúng, (waistcloth).
Lúngí Peshawrí sádá, (plain check lungí.)
Do. Amírána. The Peshawar lungí with gold border, &c.

Printed or Stamped.
Sámbá Chít, (print made at Sámbá in Jummoo, generally flowered on a green ground.)
Chít Múltaní (Múltan prints.)
Búgcha (a square piece of print used for packing up bundles, &c.
Abra, (a printed piece) an upper bed cover.
Tolái, (a printed piece for an under sheet.)
Jájam, (printed floor cloth).

Miscellaneous.
Sálú, (red dyed cloth.)
Band, (a cloth with a pattern made by tying up tight, little knots in the cloth, so that when the whole is dyed, the parts remain uncolored.
Chogulá, the same, only the uncolored spots are again dyed a different color from the ground.
Bánnú—a woman's veil,—coarse, dyed with madder with a pattern made the same way as 'Band.'
Dotiya—the same ; met with in Kábul, Peshawur, &c.
Makhí—a red veil, stamped with a black pattern like 'flies' (Makhí.)
Cháskú, stamped pattern on a red ground (Kussumbhá red.)
Jálandharí chunniá, a sort of fabric stamped; is fine cloth and dyed with 'Kussumbhá.'
Khárwá, coarse red cloth or printed in black.
Phúlkárí, a coarse red cloth worn as a veil by peasant women, it is lightly embroidered in green and yellow silk, and costs from 8 to 12 annas.
Bág, a similar veil, but heavily embroidered and costing 4 or 5 rupees.
Chop, a similar veil embroidered at the edges only.
Sirgá, a kind of "chop."
Bund, a spotted sheet worn by women.
Dopatta, a scarf of cotton, (two breadths sown together.)

III. FABRICS FROM THE ADJACENT PROVINCES.

From Kashmír.
Kadak or báfta, cheap and very coarse cloth.
Chúnní, (from Bombay) a kind of spotted cloth.

From Turkistán, &c.
Sámsún, cotton cloth 8 yards long, and 10 girahs broad.
Dokh, ditto 4 yards long, and 10 girahs broad.

CLASS VI.

WOOLEN FABRICS.

This class is subdivided into three "Divisions," on account of the exceedingly diverse nature of the trade and manufacture under each division.

The first division comprises such fabrics as are made of sheep's wool. They are few in number, though useful and traded in to a considerable extent. As in the plains, the season when warm garments are requisite is limited, it is natural that this class of manufacture should not have received anything like the attention it has in the more rigorous climates of northern Europe.

In the plains no great care is taken of wool, and all that is woven from it is blanketing, generally coarse and hard: a finer kind of woolen wrapper called "lohi," and occasionally a coarse cloth or "pattu." Nothing like the fine broad cloths and tweeds, the soft wool shawls, the lambs' wool clothing, and countless other woolen fabrics of England, are known here.

One class of woolen fabrics however deserves to be added to the list; but this is principally carried on in the jails and is the result of European supervision. I allude to the manufacture of pile or "Turkey" carpets. These carpets are produced, in a great degree of excellence, and some of them have been sent to Europe, where they have fetched high prices.

To the statement that woolen manufactures receive but little attention in the Punjab one general exception must be made in favor of the Hill districts. In these the climate is most rigorous, and the dress of the people consists almost wholly of wool, both sheep's and goat's, hence from the districts of Kangra and Simla, including as they do Spiti, Lahaul and Kanawar, the collection contains many specimens of stout and well fulled woolen cloths and blankets. The Kashmír territories also exemplify this class to a considerable extent.

The second division contains a very different class of articles: the fabrics in this division are wholly woven of the wool of the Thibetan shawl goat, known as "pashmína." In it will be found the celebrated shawls of Kashmír, all of which are woven with the finest varieties of this wool. In it also will be found the shawls woven by the Kashmírí colonies, who have settled at Núrpúr, Amritsur, Gujrát, Jelálpúr, and other places, who can only get the second best wool from the districts of Chángthán and Rodok (since the Maharajah of Kashmír holds the strictest monopoly of all the finest class of wool that comes from the frontier districts of Turfan and Kúchár) and who strive in vain to equal the bright tints and delicate weaving of the genuine Kashmír Shawl.

In this division will be found all the series of plain pashmína piece goods, such as Puttu or cloth, Malída, and Alwán, which also furnishes the ground work of the beautiful silk embroidered articles of dress, which are produced so plentifully in Kashmír, Amritsar, and Lúdhiána. In this division have further been included the well known Rámpore Chaddur, which from the soft fine texture resemble the real pashmína, though in reality they are made of Rámpore wool. Many fabrics made of this wool and of the Kirmáni wool are called at Lúdhiána and elsewhere "nakli-pashmína" imitation pashm.

The third and last division of the class contains all the fabrics made of goat's hair, and camel's hair,—the coarse ropes so much in use about the Deraját,—the huge bags in which merchandise is loaded on to camels,—the 'khoorjas' or sacks in which the farmers carry their grain to market,—the coarse cloths or mats which they spread out to winnow and clean their grain on,—and, lastly, the camel hair chogas, and the "bark" or camel hair cloth, imported from Kábul and Túrkistán.

Taking these divisions in this order we have.

DIVISION I.

Fabrics made of Sheep's Wool.

SUB-CLASS V.—CARPETS.

Carpets are called "Kálín" and "Kálícha." The method of manufacturing the "Kálín" or pile carpet is characterized by that simplicity which is observable in all native loom work. The foundation for the carpet is a warp of the requisite number of strong cotton threads according to the breadth of the carpet. The warp is however not placed flat on the ground, but is worked erect, being attached at either end to two rollers, which are supported between the extremities of two upright posts, the lower roller is below the surface of the ground in a pit or trench dug out for the purpose, the threads of the warp are passed over this, and reach to the upper roller, which is about 5 feet above it, all the superfluous web is wound round the upper roller, and as the carpet gets done, the finished work is wound on to the lower roller, and more web is unwound from the upper one. The workmen sit in front of the warp on the ground with their feet in the tench or pit above alluded to. The process of weaving consists in dexterously twisting short lengths of coloured wool into each of the threads of the warp in a straight line, so that the two ends of the wool stick out in front. When a whole line is completed the (colours chosen being of course regulated by the pattern) the projecting ends of wool are clipped to a uniform length, and a single thread of wool is run across the breadth of the carpet, between the threads of the warp, just as in ordinary weaving, and the threads of the warp are crossed as usual: then another row of ends of wool is put in the same manner, another line of wool passed between the threads of the warp to keep the woollen tags in their places, and so on. The lines of work are compacted together by stricking them with a blunt fork or "kangí" in the manner described in the manufacture of "durrees." Line after line is thus completed, the workmen putting in the proper colours, either by their own knowledge if they are very skilful, or at the word of command of one who 'reads out' the pattern. When the whole is completed, the surface is clipped or sheared all over, to reduce the pile to a uniform length and smoothness, and the carpet is complete.

Cotton rugs are sometimes made in this way, especially at Múltán. A little bunch of cotton thread being substituted for the pieces of wool, in the process. Perhaps the best carpets of any are made at the Lahore Central Jail. The prisoners here recently succeeded in producing pictures of birds, dogs, &c. in the carpet work, almost like the beautiful pictures that are so often seen on Brussels and pile rugs in England.

The exhibited specimens of carpeting are as follows :—

203.—[6259-60]. 2 carpets, Delhie Jail.

204.—[5262]. Woolen carpet from Hansi—Hissar.

205.—[6263]. Carpet from the Hissar Jail.

206.—[6350]. Rugs from Núrpúr, worth Rs. 7.

The following series are from Lahore Central Jail :—

207.—[6409]. Large carpet in the pattern called "Kandahárí," which consists of large squares placed diagonally and woven in consecutive shades of colour,—it has a very rich and pleasing effect, value Rs. 313-5-4.

208.—[6410]. A carpet in the "new shawl" pattern. This was the pattern sent to the International Exhibition of 1862, where it gained a prize.

209.—[6411]. Carpet bag, the pattern being pictures of dogs, hawks, &c.

210.—[6413]. A rug, "shawl" pattern.

211.—[6414]. Two small carriage rugs.

212.—[6415]. Seven samples of various patterns in Turkey carpeting: some of them are European, others native patterns: among the samples are also designs of birds, dogs, &c., in carpet work, also a new style of carpeting in black and white wool.

213.—[5809]. Large carpet, Brussels flower pattern, value Rs. 216, JALANDHAR JAIL.

214.—[5810-11]. Are rugs in Persian and English pattern by the same jail.

215.—[6432]. Woolen rugs made by the prisoners in the Female Penitentiary Lahore.

216.—[6416]. Turkey carpet, in soft wool from Yarkand. Exhibited by T. D. FORSYTH, ESQ., C. B.

217.—[6448]. A carpet from Khuttan imported *viâ* Yarkand, exhibited by PUNDIT MUNPHOOL.

218.—[6432]. Woolen "durrees" from Baháwalpúr, (Lahore Central Museum).

These carpets are made precisely like the cotton 'durree,' but are of stout woolen thread. There is a very cleverly wrought border and fringe to each carpet.

219.—[6452]. A woolen "durree" by the Rawalpindí Jail.

220.—[6454, 5, 6, 7, 8]. Five carpets by the Rawalpindí Jail.

221.—[6463, 4]. Two hearth-rugs, of various patterns, by the Gújrát Jail.

222.—[6465-6]. Small rugs for carriage use, by the Gújrát Jail.

These are accompanied by a sample of the woolen thread used in the manufacture (No. 6471) and of the raw wool before it is spun into thread (6472). The District Jails of Jihlam and Múltán also sent carpets and rugs. The Múltán carpets are of great excellence and regularity of make.

The following District Jails also exhibit carpets and rugs:—

223.—[6506-7 and 6509]. Carpets from Barkhan, exhibited by JAMAL KHAN,—Dera Ghazi Khan.

No. 6506 is called 'Lunga,' value Rs. 24.
„ 6507 a rug, "Galícha," valuing Rs. 12.
„ 6509 is called Garíri, valuing Rs. 15.

224.—[6508]. Is a carpet from Bartí, sent by the Lúnd chief.

225.—[6509-10]. Woolen durrees, locally called "Phalási," value Rs. 4 each, from Barti and Rajhan, sent by the Lúnd chief and Imám Bakhsh Khán.

226.—[6523]. Rug from Marwat and (6226) carpet from Waziri Hills.—DEPUTY COMMISSIONER OF BANNU.

227.—[6538]. Persian carpet, value Rs. 60, sent by KAZI NASR-ULLAH JAN of Peshawar.

SUB-CLASS B.

WOOLEN FABRICS OTHER THAN CARPETS.

As before remarked, the districts of the plains have not attained any great excellence in the manufacture of woolen articles, nor are there any variety in the manufactures. The collection however represents very well what the present state of the manufacture is. The jails will often be found in this, as in the last class, to take the lead in excellence.

It is certainly a remarkable fact, that in the plains during the cold weather natives do not like woolen goods, it is only the poorer classes who resort to the kambal or blanket. Every one who can afford it, much prefers wearing several thicknesses of cotton cloth, and coats padded with cotton wool are universally worn. Of course, pashmína shawls and fine woolen "lohis" are much used for wrappers, but for all kinds of made up articles of clothing, cotton &c., and padded cloths are preferred. The same is observable in the bedding: natives seldom if ever use blankets, but prefer the "razai," or quilt padded with cotton wool. This preference for cotton is quite remarkable; perhaps it may be due to some extent to the extreme liability of woolen goods to destruction in the rainy season from the attacks of moths and insects: the most vigilant care will scarcely preserve cloth goods from being pierced with holes, while an article of cloth left to itself in a box, and not exposed to the sun, will be totally destroyed before the winter comes round. These facts should not be overlooked is estimating the causes of the low state of woolen manufactures in the plains, but these remarks apply to the districts of the plains only.

The places most noted for woolen manufacture are Sirsa and Rohtak, and also Leia for blankets. At these places thick and well felted blankets are made. In general native blankets are hard and coarse, the woolen thread is too tightly twisted; and also the manufacturers take no pains when the blanket is made to cause the wool to felt, that is to make the fibres combine together (which they do by virtue of microscopic serratures on the joints of the fibres). In Scotland the blankets are felted and softened by a sufficiently disagreeable process, which consists in working and rubbing them with putrid urine. In this country the method adopted is to spread the blanket on a previously smoothed and prepared piece of ground, and then to moisten them with soap and water and "ríta" (the soapnut): when the mixture is poured on, men tread on and work about the fabric with their feet. This has the desired effect, but unless very carefully done, is apt to make holes in the blanket.

Lúdhiána may also be mentioned as the seat of a considerable wool manufacture, apart from its well known trade in the plain shawls known to Europeans as "Rámpur Chaddars." From information recently received from the district, I find that the annual import of sheep's wool from Rámpur (Bishair) is 250 maunds, worth Rs. 10,000: this fine quality of wool is worked into "doshálas" or chaddurs and passes as an imitation of pashmína. The annual import of common country wool amounts to 500 maunds, worth also about 10,000 rupees. Out of these imports goods to the value of 1,30,000 rupees are yearly manufactured, and also stockings, and "pattu" or cloth, to the yearly value of Rs. 20,000. There are about 500 shops of wool manufacturers in the city, in which no less than 2,000 persons are employed.

The large cities of Lahore and Amritsar also have considerable woolen manufactures besides their trade in pashmína. Lahore has a special manufacture of Kábuli pashm or Kábul wool, which is woven into "Lahori Cháddars."

It will be seen however on a mere glance at the lists, that the hill districts of Kangra and Simla, and the Kashmír valley, produce the greatest variety of woolen fabrics. The rigorous climate of these more northern districts demands this class of fabric, and moreover the extreme scarcity of cotton prevents recourse being had to those kinds of clothing which are more in favor on the plains.

From the districts of Kangra and Simla we have not only blankets of various degrees of fineness, but series of stout woollen cloths, or flannels termed "pattú," and these in several varieties. The trade in wool and woollen articles is one of the most important among the hill people.

The woollen fabrics of Kashmír are remarkable for their variety, as well as for the closeness of texture. From these territories there are striped and checked woollen pieces, imitations of European plaids and checks, flannels and other fabrics, as well as several varieties of "pattú."

It is now time to enumerate the samples exhibited under the class, giving the various kinds of articles, as they are most conveniently grouped together.

BLANKET, "KAMBHAL" OR "GALIM."

They are generally made either of the natural brownish black colour of the wool, or else in a check pattern, sometimes but rarely they are white.

None of them are anything like the Witney blankets of English make; but they make tolerable horse clothing, for which purpose the European community chiefly employ them, while the poorer classes of natives wear them as wrappers.

The specimens were :—

228.—[6261]. Blankets from Delhi Jail, value Rs. 1-8.

229.—[6264]. Black, white and check blankets from Rohtak.

Two check blankets of superior quality Rs. 7 each.
Four others at Rs. 6 each.
White blanket at Rs. 5.
Check blanket at Rs. 4.
The checks are large, in black and white, black and red, and black and orange color.

230.—[6278]. Check blanketing at 4 annas per yard from Sirsa Jail.

231.—[6421]. Blanket, Lahore city, by Thakur Das, (coarse, worth Rs. 2].

232.—[6422]. Another, inferior, worth 1 rupee, by Jawinda Mal.

233.—[6244]. Striped blanket, by the same.

234.—[6425]. Blanket from Kasúr, black and white.

235.—[6426 & 27]. Check blankets with crimson border, worth Rs. 6, 7 and 9 each.

236.—[6442]. Lahore coarse blankets for use in the Female Penitentiary, made by the prisoners.

237.—[6450]. Ferozpúr Jail, horse blanket with rollers and surcingle.

238.—[6374]. Blanket by Radha of Haryánah, Hushyarpúr, worth Rs. 1-14.

239.—[6460]. Do. from Rawulpindi Jail, worth Rs. 5, other specimens were sent from the Gujranwálla and Gujrát Jails.

240.—[6474-47]. Jihlam Jail: horse cloth and blanket, also white blanket at 9 as. a yard, check blanket at 12 as. and black ditto at 9 as. a yard.

241.—[6482]. Blanket, worth Rs. 3, by Harbans Singh of Núrpúr (Shahpúr district).

242.—[6595 & 96]. Pattyala, black and white blankets.

LOI.

The finer woven woollen wrapper or covering, was exhibited in the following varieties :—

243.—[6274, 75 & 76]. Lois by Zalim Chund and Fattih Chund of Sirsa.

244.—[6429]. Lois, worth Rs. 3-8 each, by Rahim Buksh of Lahore.

245.—[6500]. Loi, worth Rs. 2-4, from Kamalia, Gugaira.

246.—[6531]. "Loi Kashgarí," value Rs. 5, imported from Kashgar, Peshawar Committee.

247.—[6532]. "Loi Peshawarí," value Rs. 7.

248.—[6540]. "Black loi," of Kághán, Hazara, worth Rs. 4.

249.—[6541]. "White do.," of Pakli, worth Rs. 3-8.

Miscellaneous Woollen Manufactures.

These present a variety of work, including some goods machine made (for the first time) at Sealkote, including also the woollen knitted work of various schools and orphanages, and other miscellaneous woollen manufactures of the plains.

The various fabrics of the hills and the Kashmir valley present so distinct a character, that it appeared proper to separate them and bring to an end first the list of goods made in the plains.

250.—[6272]. Sample of woollen thread, Sirsa, by FATTIH CHUND.

251.—[6320 & 21]. Gloves by AHSAN SHAH of Ludhiana.

252.—[6310—]. Knitted work in Berlin wool and worsted, by the pupils of the MISSION ORPHAN SCHOOL, Ludhiana.

Neckties (various colors).

Baby's jackets.

Gaiters, brown, snuff-colored, blue and white.

Riding gloves.

Baby's socks, (various colors).

Baby's hoods, (various colors).

Lamp mat.

253.—[6389—6396]. Knitted wool work by the AMRITSAR FEMALE ORPHANAGE.

254.—[6304]. Red pattú at Rs. 2 per yard, by KALA.

255.—[6305]. White check pattú, at Rs. 1-12 per yard.

256.—[6306]. Pattú with long stripes, at Rs. 1-4 per yard.

257.—[6308]. Blue check, at Rs. 1-8.

258.—[6309]. Black check, at Rs. 1-8.

259.—[6428]. Sample of tweed or woollen cloth made at the LAHORE CENTRAL JAIL.

260.—[6430 & 31]. Knitted wool work by the prisoners of the FEMALE PENITENTIARY Lahore, viz., 4 pairs colored wool socks, 2 pairs knitted wool cuffs.

261.—[6444]. Scarlet wool tassel, by AZIMULLAH, Lahore.

262.—[6453]. Gambroon, woollen, Rawalpindi jail.

263.—[6477]. Sample of woollen thread, Jihlam jail.

264.—[6481]. Is a sample of dyed thread (woollen).

265.—[6483 and 45]. Thick felt rugs, felt coat and felt saddle cloth, by AHMAD DIN, of Bhera, Shahpúr.

This is a thick white felt made in the district and a few other places—is a very useful article, and shows that the felting properties of wool are well understood.

The following woollen articles are from Gugaira:—

266.—[6492]. Pair of "Khosa," or mufflers for cattla, from Hujra.

This district being great in the cattle stealing line, (vast herds of both buffaloes and oxen being fed in the "Bar" tracts), the thieves employ woollen mufflers to put over the feet of the cattle, which prevents the impression of the hoofs in the ground, and thus foils the utmost skill of the tracker or "khoji."

267.—[6494] Namda, or felt for saddle cloth, from Syadwalla.

268.—[6495]. "Khojar," or saddle pad used with native saddle, and made of felt.

269.—[6496]. "Indawájat," a thick rug or coil of wool worn like a porter's pack to assist carrying a burden on the head.

270.—[6497]. "Tang," or saddle-girth.

271.—[6501 &c.]. Colored woollen threads from Hujra.

272.—[6505]. White woollen thread, made in the jail.

273.—[6601]. Red braid of English wool. AGRA JAIL.

274.—[6591]. Socks and gloves, exhibited by His Highness the Maharajah of Patyála.

275.—[6520]. Woollen bag, Dera Ghazi Khan.

276.—[6521]. Samples of woollen thread, Dera Ghazi Khan.

HILL MANUFACTURES IN WOOL.

The fabrics manufactured in the hill states or imported from Kabul and Turkistan, &c. are now enumerated:—

As the term "pattú" frequently occurs in the following list, it will be proper to explain that woollen cloth is usually woven in pieces about ½ a yard broad, and only a few yards long: such a piece is called "pattí;" when 4 or more of these pattís are joined together, making a large piece, perhaps 2½ or 3 yards broad and from 10 to 12 yards long, such a piece is called "pattú." The "pattú" is folded as often as may be convenient and used as a wrapper.

The following collection is from SIMLA:—

277.—[6339]. "Kaddma," a kind of blanket from Basáhair, by the RAJAH OF BASAHIR.

278.—[6340]. "Dûra," a woollen cloth of a whitish color, Basáhir.

279.—[6647]. Blanket from Barmaur, by the RAJAH OF CHAMBAH.

Pattú is largely imported from Changthán and Rodokh, from Ghar or Garo, through Leh, and thence by Rampúr, especially a kind of pattú called "Thirma" or Balmor.*

The next series is from KANGRA, KULU AND SPITI:—

* See Mr. Davies' report on the Trade of the North West Frontier, page CCXXXII, Appendix XXIV.

280.—[6344]. Blanket from Kulu, value Rs. 3.

281.—[6345]. "Pattú" woollen cloth, piece of natural color of the wool from Kulu.

282.—[6346]. Black pattí, from Kulu.

283.—[6348 & 49]. 2 samples of pattís, Kulu.

284.—[6347]. Pattú from Palách, [BY THE KANGRA LOCAL COMMITTEE.)

285.—[6350 & 51]. "Doran," woollen cloth, from Kulu.

The wollen cloths of Kulu are all home-made, by the zemindars, who rear vast flocks of sheep. These are taken over the snowy range during the hot season to pasture in the mild regions of Spiti, Ladákh and Changthán. They are shorn twice a year. The cloth when made is sold by weight.

The pattú is worn round the shoulders, and is fastened there by two pins forming a kind of brooch, not unlike those worn by the Highlanders of Scotland.

286.—[6352].— White pattí, Kulu.

287.—6353]. "Pattú Dháridár," (striped wrapper), from Palách.

288.—[6354]. White pattú, from Sukait.

289.—[6355]. "Safed châdar," white wrapper or loi, from Kulu.

The following are made in the DHARMSALA JAIL:—

290.—[6360]. Pattí, "khud-rang," *i. e.* natural color of the wool, 1st sort, value 1 rupee for 2 yards.

291.—[6361]. Do. second sort, value 12 annas for 2 yards.

292.—[6362.] White pattí, 1st sort, value 14 annas for 2 yards; and

293.—[6363]. Do. 2nd sort, value 11 as. for 2 yards.

294.—[6364]. "Pattú Gadiyán or Gadíná," value Rs. 6.

295.—[6365]. "Pattú Garú or Garúá.

The following are from SPITI, exhibited by PHILIP EGERTON ESQR.

296.—[6369]. Yellow cloth called "Nimbú Sarpú," value Rs. 2-12 for the piece of 7 yards.

297.—[6370]. Red cloth, "Sarpú Marbú."

298.--[6371]. Black cloth, "Sarpú Nakpú."

299.—[6372]. Cloth of the natural color of the wool (khud-rang) "Thirine" (*sic in original catalogue*)

The following fabrics are imported and exhibited from the PESHAWAR District :—

300.—[6527]. "Pattú safed," from Kábul.

A large quantity of wool is imported from Kábul. In Lahore there is a regular manufacture of chadars made of "Kábul pashm," a very soft wool of a brownish color, which is however not sheep's wool, but of a goat, resembling the shawl wool. Kábul is also celebrated for its postína, or coats lined with the skins of young lambs, which are reared in the province of Karákul to the south of Bukhárá.

301.—[6528]. "Pattú nabâtì," value Rs. 60, from Kábul, by KAZI AMIR JAN.

302.—[7646]. "Choga pattú nakhúdi, or cloak made of pattú (color of nakhúd or gram), value Rs. 30.

303.—[7647]. "Choga pattú, khud-rang," cloak of natural colored woollen cloth, Peshawar, by the MUNICIPAL COMMITTEE, value Rs. 25.

304.—[7649]. "Choga Káshgari," by KAZI NISR-ULLAH JAN, imported from Káshgar, as its name indicates.

305.—[7650]. "Kosa Kandáhári," cloak of white felt of Kandáhár.

306.—[6531]. Loi Káshgari wrapper, from Káshgar.

Of other Imported Woollen Fabrics.

307.—[6532]. Loi Peshawuri, Rs. 7, of local manufacture.

308.—[6539]. Pattú from Kághán, Hazára, value Rs. 6.

The wool of Kághán has always been of excellent quality, recently attempts have been made to further improve it by the introduction of the 'Merino' breed of sheep, (see chapter on Wool in Vol. I).

The following is the collection from KASHMIR, contributed by His Highness the Maharajah of Kashmír.

309.—[6565]. "Salang" (blue or lájwardi color).

A very coarse tough cloth made into coats worn by Patháns ; it is also much used by the natives of the Thibet and provinces of Ladákh, Balkh, &c.

310.—[6566]. Another piece of a lilac color.

311.—[6570]. "Namda," felt.

Felt is largely produced in Elchi of Khotan, where they also make felt caps, which are used by Europeans. The import is by Leh. Of other imported fabrics several are mentioned as imported from Yarkund, though they do not reach the Punjab : these are called "Shirn" and "Garn," fabric of sheep and goat's wool mixed together, another is called "Khojá." These articles derive their names from the places of manufacture, (see Mr. Davies' Report, Appendix XXIV page CCXXIX.)

312.—[6573]. "Pattú, khud-rang," retaining the brownish color of the natural hair.

313.—[6574]. Pattú chárkhána, checked cloth, value Rs. 4-8.

314.—[6575]. White pattú, value Rs. 6-4. No. 6580 is another sample.

315.—[6576]. Khákí, or grey pattú striped with a very fine stripe called "Kalam kár" from "Kalam," a straight reed to which the stripe is likened, see (No. 6597), No. 6578 is another sample of this.

316.—[6577]. Woollen cloth printed like a chintz, called "pattú chhet."

This fabric consists of the ordinary woollen pattú but stamped or printed with a very small uniform pattern.

It is in general use for making the "fíran" or long coat worn by Kashmírís, value Rs. 5-4.

317.—[6579]. "Pattú Abshár." Common striped woollen cloth or flannel.

The stripe is in the fabric, like that of the "súsí" in cotton, it is a straight plain line, while the "Kalam kár" stripe is much finer, and the stripe being differently inwoven into the material is not a continous line but appears like a fine waved line or succession of little marks, forming a stripe thus :—

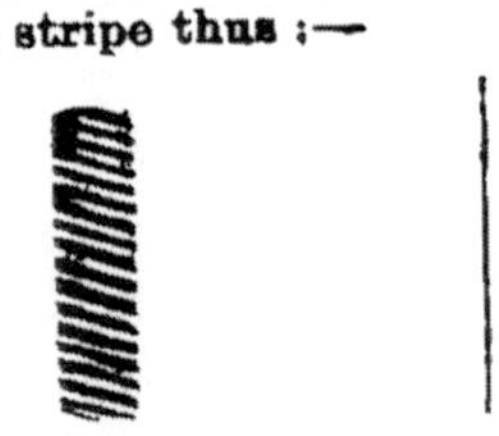

Kalam kár. Abshár.

DIVISION II.

Pashmina Goods.

SUB-CLASS A.—SHAWLS.

(*Loom woven.*)

Both sub-classes of this division are distinguished from the first and the third by the fact that they are manufactured from the "Pashmína" or wool of the shawl goat of Thibet.

For a minute account of the production of and trade in this wool I must refer the reader to the division which treats of wools, under "Animal substances used in manufactures," in volume I.

It may however be advisable to recapitulate so far as to remind the reader, that the Thibetan shawl wool varies in quality according to the districts it is produced in. There is also a difference between the wool from the domesticated goat and the wool from the animal in its wild state: the latter is called "Asli tus." That, the best, which comes from Turfán, Kuchár, Ukturfán, Aksu, Khutan, Yarkand and Káshgar, is strictly monopolized by the Maharajah of Kashmír: it is imported from Yarkand via Leh. Indeed, the Maharajah has the monopoly of the wool of Changthán and Rodokh in Thibet. It is exported from Garo and goes via Leh to Balti, Kishtwar and Kashmír; a portion of it however is brought down by the traders of Rampúr Basáhir, and also by the merchants of British Lahaul through Ladákh,* and thus the Kashmíri shawl weaving colonies in the Punjab (of whom more hereafter) are supplied.

Pashmína in its natural state, *i. e.* before dyeing, when clean, is white, but there is also a sort which is comparatively rare, and is of a grey color called "Tús," or "Túsha." This is highly esteemed as of exquisite softness.

The Changthán pashmína is of two sorts, 'Khulchak' and 'Ralchak,' being first and second qualities, this is ordinarily white in color.

A good deal of confusion results from the miscellaneous use of the term "Pashm" as applied to shawl wool: it will be advisable on first starting to describe the different kinds of soft wool that are in use.

1. There is the genuine Thibet shawl wool of Kashmír, of its two kinds, white and tús.

2. The very rare Ibex wool, which is also of "tús color." The costly Ibex shawls of Thibet and China are made of this; this wool is never seen in the Punjab, probably rarely seen even in Kashmír. A small sample sent to the Exhibition was obtained from Zangskár.

3. The Changtháni wool, of 2 or 3 qualities, being real shawl wool used by the shawl weavers of Amritsar and other places.

4. The Kirmáni wool, a very soft white wool, which is imported from Kirmán, a province of Persia: it is used to adulterate Pashmína at Amritsar and other places.

5. "Kábuli Pashm," a very soft hair of a goat, not unlike the Thibet shawl wool only not so fine; it is principally in Lahore, where it is used for making the "Lahori chadar" or soft wool wrapper.

* All the wool that comes from the Chinese provinces of Eastern Turkistan and the Pamer steppes is called in Kashmír, Turfáni and Kúchari.

I have obtained it of two or three qualities, some of them white, other a brownish grey, with the ends of the hairs a darker color than the rest, giving it a varigated appearance. They call this "Khud-rang" or "Túsha."

It appears that this wool is produced in the mountainous portions of Kandáhár and Herat. Khelat also produces a fine wool from the fat tailed variety of sheep.

Also a shawl wool called pat is obtained from Kokán through Bukhára.

The Kábuli pashm appears to be a goat's wool and not a sheep's.

6. "Un Rampuri." A very fine wool is obtained from Rampur probably from Changthán and Rodokh, which is worked at Ludhiana as the Kirmáni wool is at Amritsar, to produce an adulterated or "nakli pashmína," in imitation of real pashmína.

We are at present to consider the fabrics woven of real shawl wool.

The fabrics may be generally stated to be of two sorts :—

1st, regular shawls.—The material used for these fabrics is thread very finely spun of pashmína, and dyed of various shades ; the weaving is effected in a rude kind of upright loom, more like the carpet loom than the ordinary loom for piece goods, but it is distinct from either : no shuttle is employed, but the different kinds of colored thread required in the pattern hang down on as many little reels or bobbins, and the pattern of the shawl is indicated on paper, by a regular pattern alphabet or "*memoria technica*" of written signs.

The other class of pashmína goods are plain and woven in the ordinary way. Fine pashmína cloth is called "Alwán ;" this is used for shawls or chadars, plain and dyed of various colours, but the same all over. When pashmína cloth is carefully felted and softened by repeated working and treading with water and "rita" or soap-nut, it shrinks, felts, and softens, and is called "Malida" (literally "rubbed fabric") ; this is used for a variety of articles and forms the ground-work of the silk embroidered chogahs, capes, jackets, neckties and other embroidered fabrics so common in Kashmír, Amritsar and Ludhiana. Thin pashmína "Alwán," generally unprepared, is also the ground-work for the beautiful "Amlikár" work of Kashmír, which consists in elaborate patterns and devices in colored silks executed on shawl borders, chogahs and other articles ; this Amlikár is quite distinct from the embroidered fabrics previously described, on which the pattern of the silk is always of one color, generally the same color as the pashmína or else white or black on a colored pashmína ground. The art of this last, rich and beautiful as it is, is utterly inferior to the renowned Amlikár, which is unique, and which is practised in Kashmír itself in a style so much superior to any other place, that an experienced eye can detect in a moment the genuine work of Kashmír.

These articles however do not come into this class, but are reckoned as embroidery; it is only with shawls woven in a loom that Sub-class A has to do, and only with plain pashmína goods exhibited for the sake of the *fabric* that Sub-class B contains.

There are a few miscellaneous fabrics woven of pashmína in Kashmír, such as "paripurz" and some varieties of pashmína cloth introducing checks, and other patterns, but this will be noted *in situ*.

It only remains to add that the pashmína is the *inner* wool of the goat. At the commencement of summer the animal is shorn with a knife in the direction of the growth of the hair, *i, e.* from head to tail. When this is done the wool is combed down in a *reverse* direction, and this separates almost entirely the upper hair from the wool underneath, the hair is soft and is wrought up into coarser fabrics. The wool is cleaned in the first instance by washing with lime-water.

THE SHAWL-LOOM.

In the Punjab, when the pashmína is first imported, it is bought up by the wool-pickers, who separate the various qualities, the finest wool, the second, and the goat hair, and sell these sorted wools to the Kashmíri shawl weavers, who spin it into thread for the different kinds of manufactures.

In the following list the genuine loom-woven shawls of Kashmír are first enumerated.

Shawls besides having a very considerable number of varieties in form, size, pattern, &c., &c., are mainly divided into two classes.

1st.—Shawls loom-woven, called Tiliwalla, "Tíli kár" or "Káni kár," whereof the pattern is produced in the loom. They are sometimes woven all in one piece, but oftener are woven in distinct portions, which are afterwards most skilfully joined together by hand; the suture is so delicate as to be quite imperceptible except on minute inspection, and then with difficulty.

2nd.—Shawls "Amlikár," wherein the ground work is a plain pashmína piece, and the pattern is entirely due to minute and most elaborate needlework in pashmína thread all over the whole surface. Borders which are always made on a warp of silk, are attached to loom-woven shawls; the stiff edging serves to spread out the shawl and make it set properly when worn. Shawl borders are made quite separate from shawls and at different localities: no shawls, for instance, are made at Sealkote, but shawl borders are.

This second sort of shawl is not included in this class, which is solely concerned with *loom-woven fabrics*. There is a separate class for needlework done by hand and embroidery. It has been remarked that the shawls of Kashmír have never been equalled by the colonies of Kashmíris who have settled in the Punjab; not only is the Kashmír shawl wool finer and purer in thread, but the workmen pretend that there is something in the nature of the air and the water of Kashmír which allows of brighter and purer dyeing for the thread; and also the process of washing the shawls, which is quite an art of itself, is always better done in Kashmír.

The very high price of Kashmír shawls even at the places where they are made, has often excited wonder * since the actual cost of the raw wool necessary to make a shawl is only a few rupees. But it must be remembered, that the wool has to be sorted by hand with great labor, and the fineness of the shawl subsequently will much depend on the care bestowed on this operation; next, the fine thread has to be spun with great delicacy: this is done with the aid of a common 'Charkha,' as used for cotton, but requires great nicety of work. The thread is extremely fine. A pound weight of first class thread will sell as high as 25 rupees. The thread has now to be dyed, which is a difficult operation, and some of the colors are costly (they are all made permanent); and then the weaving process begins: this is slow and indefinitely elaborate and difficult in proportion to the intricacy of the pattern. The wages of the skilled labor for such work are extremely high.

Years of patient toil have to be passed by the apprentice before he is perfect in any one branch of the art; when therefore he does become a practised artizan, his wages must remunerate him for the expense and long delay of his education. It is no wonder therefore that shawls should be costly. On to the price that they command when exported, we must add

* A first rate woven shawl, weighing 7lbs. will fetch in Kashmír as much as £300,
which price is made up of, £ 30, the cost of material.
150, the wages of labor.
70, Duty.
50, Miscellaneous expenses.

Total, ... 300

to original cost, the customs duties, the cost of carriage, the risk of robbery—which by some routes is great, the risk of the bales damping and becoming mildewed inside, the cost of the commission charged by brokers who manage the export and sales, besides various other incidental charges that occur between the workshop of the shawl weaver and the market of final sale.

Before entering on the list of shawls exhibited, it will be necessary to present the reader with an account of the process of shawl weaving. This has been already so well done by Moorcroft that it would be hopeless to attempt a better description. As Moorcroft's work is now scarce and inaccessible to the general reader, I shall make no apology for extracting his account in extenso:—

"The first task of the spinner is to separate the different materials of which the fleece consists, usually in about the following proportions:—

Coarse hair, ...	1⅛	seers.
Seconds, or Phiri, ...	0⅝	,,
Dust and foreign substances,	2¼	,,
Fine wool, ...	2	,,
	6 seers, or 1 tark.	

Much attention is required to free the wool from the hair, and the process is a tedious one. The next step is cleaning and separating the wool. A quantity of husked rice is steeped in clean cold water, for a day and a night, or longer, until it becomes soft, when it is ground or bruised upon a stone slab to fine flour. Thin layers of this and of the picked wool are laid alternately, and squeezed with the hand until they are completely intermixed. A little water may be occasionally sprinkled over the heap, if the weather is hot and dry, else it is not necessary. Soap is never used, as it makes the wool harsh; and its employment in Hindustan being communicated to the Kashmírians, induced them to boast that in this matter at least they were more knowing than Europeans. After being thus treated for about an hour, the flour is shaken out, the wool opened and torn to pieces, chiefly by the nails, and made into somewhat square, thin, elastic pads, called Tumbu. In this process the Phiri, or second shool, is extricated. Though too coarse for fine shawls, it is used in the manufacture of those of inferior quality, and of a strong shawl cloth called pattú. The tumbu is then worked out into a thin flat roving, about half a yard long, which is called a mála. The mála is folded up to the size of the tumbu, and deposited in a deep pot of red earthenware, called a taskas, to be out of the way of dust or accident till required for the spinning wheel.

The wheel is constructed on the same principle as that used in Hindustan, but varying in neatness of form and finish, according to its price; the rudest, the Takhtidar, or Pachindar, costs a half rupee; the Katzker, which is the most serviceable, three or four rupees; and the Pakchedar, which is used by those who spin for amusement only, costs from six to sixteen rupees. The iron spindle is enclosed in a cylindrical tube of straw or reed grass, and instead of one line of radii or spokes, supporting a continued circular wooden rim, there are two circular and parallel walls of flat spokes in contact at their edges, leaving between them at their outer circumference an empty space. A hair cord fastened to the loose end of the one spoke, is carried across the space or trough, to the end of the next spoke but one on the opposite side, and having been passed round, it returns to a spoke on the side from which it began. By a continuation of this process a rim is formed of a surface of hair cord, over which runs a small band, that is said seldom to be cut by the friction to which it is exposed. The principle kept in view by this arrangement of spindle and of rim, is to produce a continuance of soft elastic movements without jerk or stiffness, to prevent the yarn breaking on the occurrence of any slight interruption in drawing it out.

Women begin to work at daybreak, continue with little interruption the whole day, if not taken off by other domestic affairs, and extend their labor until very late in the night, spinning by moon-light when available, and when they cannot afford to purchase oil for a lamp. The fine wool is spun commonly into about seven hundred gaz, each gaz consisting of sixteen girahs, about equal to two nails. This yarn is doubled and formed into twist, which is cut into two hundred lengths, each length of three gaz and a half; this measure being suited to the length of the warp for a shawl. From the Phiri, or seconds wool, about one hundred gaz of yarn are also produced. The yarn of the fine wool is sold sometimes by measure and sometimes by weight. A hundred lengths of yarn of fine wool doubled, and each three gaz and a half, bring ordinarily seven tangas, or about seven-pence. But if the same kind of yarn be sold without being doubled and twisted, the price is regulated by weight, a "pal" bringing from twelve annas to one rupee four annas, according to the demands of the market. The yarn from Phiri, or seconds wool, is sold only by measure, but the gaz employed consists of no more than twelve girahs, or nails, that is, of four girahs less than the gaz in ordinary use. A hundred yards of Phiri twist, and each of two short gaz, or of twenty four girahs, sell for one and a half tanga, three pice, or about three half-pence. Although calculations upon this matter can be little more than approximations, yet three pence or three pence-half penny a day, or from three rupees to three rupees eight annas, or from six to seven shillings a month, may be taken as the general earnings of an industrious and expert spinner in Kashmír, out of which, however, must be subtracted the price of the wool,* leaving only one rupee eight annas for her labor.

If shawl-wool be furnished to a spinner to clean and to spin, eight annas are paid for spinning one pal, or three and one third rupees weight of yarn of

* Thirty two Tanga or annas, equal two rupees.

the requisite quality for shawls. Sheep's wool, spun by contract, is paid for by the pao, or quarter of a seer, at the rate of from two tangas. or four pice, to twelve annas per pao, according to the fineness of the yarn; and the spinning of this quantity into yarn suited for shawls will occupy a woman for eight days. There are several varieties of thread, distinguished by different degrees of fineness. From one pao of clean fine shawl wool a spinner will draw from a hundred to a thousand threads of three and a half gaz each. There is not such a difference between the price of coarse and of fine yarn as might be expected, owing to the greater expenditure on the former of a material that is dear, and on the latter of labor that is cheap. Shawl wool is sometimes spun by men, with a loose spindle like that used in Ladakh. These men are called Trakhans, and the yarn thus spun is finest, but very little of it is now made. Girls begin to spin at the age of ten, and a hundred thousand females are employed in this occupation in Kashmír. About one-tenth of this number are supposed to spin for the purpose of obtaining shawls for themselves, or for other members of their families, and nine tenths to earn their livelihood.

The Puimangu keeps a shop for the purchase of yarn, but also sends people to collect it from the houses of the spinners, who give notice of their approach by ringing a bell. The yarn is sold to the weavers at a profit of from one pice to a tanga in the rupee. As a large stamp duty is levied on shawl-goods when finished, the exportation of the yarn is forbidden, and prohibition is enforced by heavy fine and imprisonment. Much of it is, nevertheless, exported to those places in the Punjab where the expatriated weavers have settled.

Having ascertained the kind of pattern most likely to suit the market, the weaver applies to persons whose business it is to apportion the yarn according to the colors required; and when this is settled, he takes it to another, whose function it is to divide the yarn into skeins accordingly, and each skein is delivered to the Rangrez, or dyer. When the body of the cloth is to be left plain, the Phiri, or seconds yarn, is alone given to be dyed. This is generally about the thickness of common cotton sewing thread, is loosely twisted, of a coarser quality than the yarn used for the cloth, and is preferred for employment in flowers, or other ornaments, from its standing higher, and being, as it were, embossed upon the ground.

The dyer prepares the yarn by steeping in clean cold water. He professes to be able to give it sixty-four tints, most of which are permanent. Each has a separate denomination, as for instance: the crimson is termed Gulanar (pomegranate flower); the best kind is derived from cohineal, imported from Hindustan; inferior tints are from Lac and Kirmis (Chermes), distinguished as Kirmisi, Kirmdana, and Kirmisi lac, or cochineal and lac chermes: log wood is used for other red dyes; blues and greens are dyed with indigo, or colouring matter extracted by boiling from European broad cloth. Logwood is imported from Multan and Indigo from India. Carthamus and Saffron, growing in the province, furnish means of various tints of orange, yellow, &c. The occupation of a dyer is invariably hereditary. The whiter and finer the fibre of the wool, and the finer the yarn into which it is made, the more capable it is said to be of receiving a brilliant dye; and this is one reason why the fine white wool of the goat is preferred to that of the sheep.

The Nakatu adjusts the yarn for the warp and for the weft. That intended for the former is double, and is cut into lengths of three gaz and a half, any thing short of that measure being considered fraudulent. The number of these lengths varies from two thousand to three thousand, according to the closeness or openness of texture proposed, and the fineness or coarseness of the yarn.

The weft is made of yarn which is single, but a little thicker than the double yarn or twist of the warp. The weight of the weft is estimated at a half more than that of the warp. The Nakatu receives the yarn in hunks, but returns it in balls: he can prepare in one day the warp and weft for two shawls.

The Pennakamguru, or warp dresser, takes from the weaver the yarn which has been cut and reeled, and stretching the lengths by means of sticks into a band of which the threads are slightly separate, dresses the whole by dipping it into thick boiled rice water. After this the skein is slightly squeezed and again stretched into a band, which is brushed and suffered to dry: by this process each length becomes stiffened and set apart from the rest.

Silk is generally used for the warp on the border of the shawl, and has the advantage of showing the darker colors of the dyed wool more prominently than a warp of yarn, as well as hardening and strengthening, and giving more body to the edge of the cloth. When the border is very narrow it is woven with the body of the shawl; but when broader, it is worked on a different loom, and afterwards sown on the edge of the shawl by the "rafugar," or fine drawer, with such nicety that the union can scarcely be detected. The silk is twisted for the border warp by the "tabgar." The warp differs in breadth, the narrowest consisting of twenty, and the broadest of a hundred threads. From the tabgar the silk is handed to the "Alakaband," who reels it, and cuts it into the proper lengths.

The operation of drawing or of passing the yarns of the warp through the heddles, is performed precisely in the same way as in Europe, and the warp is then taken by the shal-baf, or weaver, to the loom. The weavers are all males, commencing to learn the art at the age of ten years. In all transactions there are two parties, the Master, or Ustad, and the scholar, or Shagird, the former being the capitalist, the latter the mechanic. Work is executed under four different conditions. First, for wages, when it almost always happens that a system of advances has occurred, by which the workman is so deeply indebted to his employer that he may, in some sort, be considered as his bond-slave. Secondly, upon contract, of which the common term is, that one pice is paid for every hundred needles carrying colored yarn that shall have been each once passed round as many yarns of the warp. Third, a sort of partnership, in which the Ustad finds all the materials, and the workmen give their labour. When a shawl is sold the outlay of the Ustad is deducted from the price, and the remainder is divided into five shares, of which one goes to the master, and the other four to the workmen. The fourth mode is an equal division of the proceeds; in which case the master not only finds the materials, but feeds the workmen. Three men are employed upon an embroidered shawl of an ordinary pattern for three months, but a very rich pair will occupy a shop for eighteen months.

The loom differs not in principle from that of Europe, but is of inferior workmanship. An Ustad has from three to three hundred in his establishment, and they are generally crowded together in long low apartments. When the warp is fixed in the loom, the nakásh, or pattern drawer, and the tarah-guru, and talím-guru, or persons who determine the proportion of yarn of different colors to be employed, are again consulted, The first brings the drawing of the pattern, in black and white. The tarah-guru, having well considered it, points out the disposition of the colors, beginning at the foot of the pattern and calling out the color, the number of threads to which it is to extend, that by which it is to be followed, and so on in succession, until the whole pattern has been described. From his dictation, the talim-guru writes down the particulars in a kind of character or short hand, and delivers a copy of the document to the weavers.

The workmen prepare the tojis, or needles, by arming each with colored yarn of the weight of about four grains; these needles, without eyes, are made of light, smooth wood, and have both their sharp ends slightly charred, to prevent their becoming rough or jagged through working. Under the superintendence of tarah-guru, the weavers knot the yarn of the tuji to the warp. The face or right side of the cloth is placed next to the ground, the work being carried on at the back or reverse, on which hang the needles in row, and differing in number from four hundred to fifteen hundred, according to the lightness or heaviness of the embroidery. As soon as the Ustad is satisfied that the work of one line or woof is completed, the comb is brought down upon it with a vigour and repetition apparently very disproportionate to the delicacy of the materials.

The cloth of shawls, generally, is of two kinds, one plain, or of two threads, one twilled, or of four. The former was, in past times, wrought to a great degree of fineness, but it has been of late less in demand. The various twilled cloths are usually from five to twelve girahs, or nails wide. shawls are twilled, and are commonly about twenty-four nails broad and differ in their extent of field. Two persons are employed in weaving a cloth of this breadth. One throws the shuttle from the edge as far as he can across the warp, which is usually about half way. It is there seized by the second weaver, who throws it onwards to the opposite edge, and then returns it to his companion, who, in his turn, introducing his fingers into the warp, forwards the shuttle to the edge whence it started, and then recommences the operation. The cloth thus made is frequently irregular, the threads of some parts of the woof being driven up tightly, and in others left open, from which results a succession of bands, sufficiently distinguishable whilst without colour, but still more obvious when dyed. The open texture is in a degree remediable by the introduction of fresh threads; but there is no sufficient cure for that which has been much compacted. One might be led to suspect that there existed some radical defectiveness in the principle of this mode of weaving not readily mastered, were not pieces of cloth found occasionally of an almost perfect regularity of texture. But the greatest irregularity is discoverable in those shawls which have the deepest and heaviest borders, and a further examination compels me to retract an observation somewhere made, of the artist being so much engrossed by attention to the work of the pattern as to neglect the structure of the field. The edge of the warp in the loom is filled with the heavy thread of the phiri, or seconds yarn, charged also with colour, so that in a few lines the front of the worked part advances beyond that of the plain part or field, and an endeavour to equalize this betrays the weaver into a work which proves fruitless; and, in general, the heavier the embroidery on the border, and, of course, the higher the price of the shawl, the less regular is the structure of the cloth.

Such, indeed, in some instances, is the degradation of the cloth in the field, as to induce some foreign merchants to cause it to be removed, and another piece to be engrafted within the edge of the border. But in this case there is no other remedy than in a judicious selection of a sheet of the same breadth and fineness; for, although two breadths of the narrow cloth might fit the vacant space, yet these must be joined by the refugar in the middle; and although this can be so done that the band differs not in thickness from the rest of the cloth, yet the joint is discernible when held between the eye and the light, from the threads in the joined breadth being not continuous in the same line, whereas any irregularity of this nature is drowned in the edge of the border. The best practice to ensure a good field seems to consist in weaving the border, in every case, separately, and inserting the field by the refugar.

When finished, the shawls are submitted to the purusgar or cleaner, whose business it is to free the shawl from discoloured hairs or yarn, and from ends or knots: he either pulls them out severally with a pair of tweezers, or shaves the reverse face of the cloth with a sharp knife: any defects arising from either operation are immedately repaired by the refugar. At this stage of the manufacture the shawls are sent to the Collector of the stamp duties, by whom an ad valorem duty of twenty-six per cent is levied, and each piece is then stamped and registered.

The goods are now handed over to the wafarosh, or person who has advanced money on them to the manufacturer, and to the mokkim, or broker, and these two fix the price, and effect the sale to the merchant; the former charges interest on his advances, the latter a commission, varying from two to five per cent. The purchaser takes the goods unwashed, and often in pieces, and the fine drawer and washerman have still to do their part.

When partly washed the dhobi brings the shawls to the merchant, that they may be examined for any holes or imperfections; should such occur, they are remedied at the expense of the seller: if there are none, the washing is completed. This is done with clear cold water, using soap very cautiously, to white parts alone, and never to embroidery: coloured shawls are dried in the shade; white ones are bleached in the open air, and their colour is improved by exposure to fumes of sulphur. After being washed, the shawls are stretched in a manner which answers in some degree to calendering: a wooden cylinder in two parts is employed for this purpose, round which the shawl, folded so as not to be quite as broad as the cylinder is long, is carefully wrapped, being occasionally damped to make it fold tighter; the end is sewn down: two wedges are then gradually driven between the two parts of the cylinder at the open extremities, so as to force them asunder, and the surrounding folds of the shawl are thus stretched to as great an extent as is consistent with its texture. The piece remains in this state for two days, when it is removed to be packed. The packages are of various dimensions, but they are formed on one principle: the shawls are separated by sheets of smooth glazed, and coloured paper, and they are placed between two smooth planks of wood, with exterior transverse bars, which, projecting beyond the planks, offer a purchase for cords to tie them together: the whole is then placed in a press, or under heavy weights for some days, when the planks are withdrawn, the bale is sewed up in strong cloth, and the whole is sewed up as smoothly and tightly as possible in a raw hide, which, contracting in drawing, gives to the contents of the package a remarkable degree of compactness and protection.

An immense variety of articles of shawl stuff are manufactured in Kashmír, besides the shawls themselves: of them also there are two chief varieties, those made in the manner described, and the worked shawl (doshálí amli), in which the whole of the embroidery is worked on the cloth, with needles having eyes, and with a particular kind of woollen thread, instead of the silk employed in the usual embroidered work. In the amli shawl the pattern, which is in every case delineated, but which at the loom is read off in certain technical terms from a book, is covered with transparent paper, upon which the outlines of the composition are slightly traced with a charcoal twig and the traced lines are permanently defined by being pricked through with a small needle. The cloth intended to receive the pattern is rubbed strongly upon a smooth plank, with a piece of highly polished agate or cornelian, until it is perfectly even and regular. The pricked pattern is then stretched upon the cloth, and some fine colored powder, charcoal, or chalk, is passed slightly over the paper, which penetrating through the holes, transfers the outline to the cloth underneath. This is next more accurately delineated with some coloured powder rendered tenacious by mucilage of gum arabic, which, when the work is completed, is readily detached in dust by the hand.

The use of patterns by the chain stitch embroiderer, and the carpet weaver of Kashmir, is more restricted to a confined number of forms, by being transferred from a wooden block to the cloth, in regard to the former, and to paper in respect to the latter.

The following are the chief articles of this manufacture, with their usual prices.

Shawls in pairs form the principal article of this manufacture, and have different names, according to their nature and quality, as plain white coloured, embroidered in the loom, or by the hand with the needle: viz:—

Pattú Pashmini, sometimes made of 'Asal tús,' but more frequently of the coarse kinds of shawl wool, is in length four gaz, and in breadth one and half gaz. This is thick, and used as a blanket, or for outer clothing. Price from 5 to 6 rupees per gaz.

Shala phiri, as its name denotes, is made of phiri, or of seconds wool. Its length is from three and a half to four gaz, and breadth one and a half gaz. Price from 20 to 30 per piece.

Alwán, or plain white cloth, of fine shawl-wool, without flower, border, or other ornament, differs in length, but is twelve girahs in breadth, and is used for turbans and for dyeing. Price from 3 to 6 rupees per gaz.

Jowhar Shala Sadu, or shawl with a narrow edging of colored yarn, is from three and a half to three and three quarters gaz in length, and one and a half in breadth, price from 50 to 60 rupees per piece.

As all the following shawls are of the same dimensions, viz., three and a half gaz in length, and one and a half gaz in breadth, it is unnecessary to affix the measures to their several names.

Shala hashiadar, is edged by a single border, 60 to 70 rupees.

Shala dohashiadar, has a double border, 40 to 70 rupees.

Shala chahar hashiadar, has four borders, 60 to 70 rupees.

Hashiadar Khosar, or Khalil Khani, has two borders and two tanga, sometimes with, at others without, a flower in the corners, 40 to 50 rupees.

Hashiadar kiungreedar. This has a border of the usual form with another within side, or nearer to the middle, resembling the crest of the wall of Asiatic forts furnished with narrow niches or embrasures for walls pieces, or matchlocks, whence its name; 100 to 150 rupees.

Dhourdar, has an ornament running all round the shawl, between the border and the field, 200 to 2,000 rupees per pair.

Mathandar has flowers or decorations in the middle of the field; 300 to 1,800 rupees per pair.

Chanddar, has a circular ornament or moon in the centre of the field; 500 to 1,500 rupees per pair.

Chantahidar has four half moons, 300 to 1,500 rupees per pair.

Kunjbuthadar, has a group of flowers at each corner, 200 to 900 rupees per pair.

Alifdar, has green sprigs without any other colour, on a white ground or field; 120 to 1,150 rupees per pair.

Kaddar, has larger groups of flowers somewhat in the form of the cone of a pine, with the ends or points straight, or curved downwards.

Dokaddar, has two heights of such groups; Sekaddar has three rows; and so on to five and upwards: in the latter case, however, the cones are somewhat small; 100 to 800 rupees per pair.

The ornaments of shawls are distinguished by different names, as Pala, Hashia, Zanjir, Dhour, &c., and these are divided into different parts. By the term Pala is meant the whole of the embroidery at the two ends, or, as they are technically called, the heads of the shawl.

The Hashia, or border, is disposed commonly one at each side in the whole length, and if double or triple, gives particular denominations to the shawl.

The Zanjir, or chain, runs above and also below the principal mass of the Pala, and as it were confines it.

The Dhour, or running ornament, is situated to the inside in regard to the Hashia and the Zanjir, enveloping immediately the whole of the field.

The Kunjbutha, is a corner ornament, or clustering of flowers.

The Mattan, is the decorated part of the field or ground.

Butha, is the generic term for flowers, but is specifically applied, when used alone, to the large cone like ornament which forms the most prominent feature of the Pala. Sometimes there is only one line of these ornaments, extending from the lower Zanjir to the upper one. When there is a double row, one above the other, the Butha is called Dokad, Sehkad, up to five, after which it takes the name of Tukadar.

Each Butha consists of three parts; viz. the pai or foot, or pediment of leaves generally; the shikam or belly, and the sir or head. The head is either erect, or straight, or inclined. If the butha slope generally, it is named butha kaj. The shal or net, is the work which separates the different buthas, but sometimes the interstice is without ornament.

Jamawar, signifies literally a gown piece. The length of this cloth is three and three quarter gaz, and the breadth one and a half gaz.

This article branches into many varieties, as Khirkhabutha, large compound flowers, consisting of groups of smaller ones. It is used by the Persians and Afghans.

	Rs. per piece.
Rezabutha, small flowers thickly set,...	200 to 700
Shaldar, net work, ...	500 to 1,700
Islimi, ...	250 to 400
Mehramat, ...	150 to 300
Khatherest, ...	150 to 750
Marpech, ...	200 to 350
Kahnkar, ...	300 to 1,000
Laklie Angur, ...	300 to 500
Chaporast, ...	300 to 7,000
Dogul, Sehgul, Chahargul, &c., ...	500 to 1,000
Barghebed,* ...	250 to 400
Gulisaut, ...	200 to 900
Duazdhekhat, ...	700 to 1,500
Duazdehrang, ...	800 to 1,400
Guleparwane, ...	300 to 450
Kaddhar, ...	300 to 2,000
Kayhama, Subzkar Safed, ...	120 to 130

These are made by the shawl weaver alone, and largely into Hindustan, where they are dyed, the small green flowers being previously tied up in hard small knots, so as to be protected from the action of the dye, and are of course, when united, each surrounded by a small white field. Small eyes of spots of yellow, red, and of other colours, are supposed to harmonize with the green flowers and the new ground, and these are added by embroiderers or Chikandoz.

Kasaboh, or rumál, women's veils, square shawls. These are from one and a half to two and a half gaz square and are called:—

Khathdar, ...	Rs. 300 to 500
Mehramat, ...	,, 150 to 300
Islimi, with the thirteen other patterns of the Jamawars; and in addition there are,	
Chaharbágh, ...	,, 300 to 350
Hashia, ...	,, 100 to 175
Chánd, ..	,, 50 to 200
Chautahi, ...	,, 150 to 400
Shash Mantahi, ...	,, 250 to 200
Feringi, ...	,, 100 to 500

Exported chiefly to Russia,

Tara Armeni, 100 to 250 rupees; exported chiefly to Armenia, and Persia.

Tara Rumi, 120 to 300 rupees; exported chiefly to Turkey.

Sada, 12 to 15 rupees; for domestic use.

Shamlas, or girdles for the waist, worn by the Asiatics, are eight gaz in length, and one and a half gaz broad, and of various colours and patterns, and vary from 50 to 2,000 rupees a piece, according to the richness of the work.

Doshala, or shawls, which contain three palas instead go only to Tibet, and sell for 100 to 150 rupees.

Goshpech, or patka or turbans, are in length from eight to ten gaz, breadth one gaz, and of all colours; one variety has two palas, two zanjirs, and two hashias, 150 to 800 rupees.

Mandila, another variety, sometimes has a zanjir, and sometimes is without this ornament. This latter is from eight to ten gaz in length, and about twelve giras broad, 45 to 70 rupees.

Khalín Pashmina, shawl carpet. This is sold at 20 to 40 rupees the square gaz of only three quarters, and is made of any size in a single piece.

Nakash, trowsers. Some are with, others without, seams. The former are made of two pieces, which are sewn together by the refugar, the latter by the jaráb sáz, or stocking maker; 200 to 500 rupees a pair.

Chaharkhána, check cloth. Length indefinite; breadth one and a half gaz, used by women; 5 to 10 rupees per gaz.

Lungi, girdles, length three and a half gaz, breadth one and a half gaz. These differ from Shamlas by being in narrow check and bordered by lines of different colours; 50 to 70 rupees.

Takhin, caps, 8 annas to 4 rupees.

Jarâb, short stockings. Guldar and Mehramat, flowered and striped; 1 to 5 rupees.

Moze Pashmina, long stockings, 5 to 25 rupees.

Sakab Posh, canopies, 300 to 1,500 rupees.

Dárparda, curtains for doors and windows. Same price as Jamawar by measure.

Kajjari Asp, saddle-cloths, by measure.

Kajjari Fil, elephant's housing, ditto.

Bálaposh, Palang Posh, quilt or coverlet, 300 to 1,000 rupees.

Guluband, cravat, 12 to 300 rupees.

Pistanband, neckerchief, 5 to 15 rupees.

Langota, waist-belts, 15 to 30 rupees.

Postin, cloths left long in the nap to line pelisses, 500 to 1,000 rupees.

Paipech, leggings. Length two gaz, breadth one gira, of all colours, 2 to 10 rupees.

Yezar, or Izarband, waist strings, 1 to 15 rupees.

Takkia, pillow bier. Same price as Jamawar.

Khalíta, bags or purses, 8 annas to 2 rupees.

Kabbar Posh, shrouds or covers for tombstones. Same price as Jamawar.

Takposh, covers or hangings in front of recesses or cupboards.

Aukhwânposh, dish covers or napkins, of various qualities and patterns, from from 30 to 500 rupees a piece.

The following were imported from Kashmir by Messrs. Devi Saha and Chamba Mal of Amritsar :—

318.—[7141 & 42]. Long shawls.

319.—[7143 & 74]. Square shawls.

320.—[6402-6405]. Shawls, long and square, Kashmír, by Government Toshakhana.

The series exhibited by His Highness the Maharajah of Kashmír, were as follows :—

321.—[7347]. Shawl of colour called Múshki, a kind of maroon, worth Rs. 1,250.

322.—[7348]. Shawl, " Shál khardár," value Rs 1,000.

323.—[7349]. Shawl, " Suráhí dár," value Rs. 1,000.

324.—[7350]. Shawl, rose color ground, value Rs. 725.

325.—[7351]. Dark brown shawl, (Múshki), value Rs. 845.

326.—[7352]. Shawl in turquoise blue, (zangári), value Rs. 945.

327.—[7353]. Another worth Rs. 950.

328.—[7354]. Another, "Mûshki" color, value Rs. 800.

329.—[7355]. White Jámawár or long piece of shawl stuff, striped in the " Kalamkár " style, value Rs. 1,109.

330.—[7357]. " Jorah Sháh Pasand," Gulánár, pair of scarlet long shawls, value Rs. 900.

331.—[7358]. Pair of grey do., value Rs. 256.

332.—[7359]. Pair of scarlet do., háshiya-dár, *i. e.* with worked border, value Rs. 210.

333.—[7361]. Pair of scarlet shawls called "kad-dár," value Rs. 87-8.

334.—[7632]. Pair with scarlet borders on all four sides, " chárháshiya gulánár, " value Rs. 134.

335.—[7633]. Rumal or square shawl, color "Mushki," value Rs. 825.

336.—[7634]. Another, worth Bs. 850.

337.—[7635]. "Rúmál safed khardár," with white edging, value Rs. 700.

338.—[7638]. White Rúmál, worth Rs. 600.

339.—[7369]. Rúmál, rose color, worked with gold, "Zarkár," worth Rs. 250.

340.—[7370]. Rúmál, rose colored, of the sort called "Mûkhtár sháhi," worth Rs. 200.

341.—[7373]. White Rúmál, with edging "Kinára dár," value Rs. 100.

SHAWLS WOVEN IN THE PUNJAB.

In turning next to the samples of shawl weaving in the Punjab it will be interesting to offer a few remarks on the colonies of Kashmíris who have emigrated from their home and settled in the great cities of Amritsar, Ludianah, Jalálpur in the Gújrát district, Dínanagar—(Gurdaspúr district), Núrpúr and Tiloknáth (Kangra district), and a few other places where small bodies of Kashmíris are to be met with, as in Lahore.

These people are known by their fair complexion, their peculiar dialect, their way of closely shaving the head and wearing small skull caps.

In Núrpúr especially, they are quite the characteristic feature of the place.

These people have emigrated at various times from Kashmír, but especially in the time when General Mihán Singh was Governor of Kashmír under Maharaja Ranjít Singh, between thirty and forty years ago, at which time a fearful famine raged in Kashmír and numbers of the people emigrated to the Punjab.

The following extract from Mr. Barnes' report on Kangra, is primarily applicable to the colonies in that district, at Tiloknáth and Núrpúr, but the author's remarks are equally true of Kashmír colonists generally. They maintain their distinctive habits wherever they go.

"The Kashmíris reside almost exclusively in Núrpúr and Tiloknáth There are a few scattered families in other parts of the district, but not exceeding a hundred together. The total number of Kashmíris is 6,656. They are divided among themselves into several gradations, and like all Musulman races have no restrictions on marriage, except immediate relations, marriages with first cousins are not only allowable, but frequently occur. They are almost exclusively employed in the shawl trade. There are two classes in the profession, the master workmen, or "Ustáds," and the apprentices or "Shagirds." The former supply the capital, and the apprentices earn their livelihood by task work. The more opulent Kashmíris not only keep large manufactories for shawls, but trade in wool and other produce of Ladakh and Chinese Tartary. The rooms devoted to the workmen, are long apartments with looms placed in the centre, and benches ranged parallel for the weavers; they are well lighted and airy. The workmen, all males, sit hard employed the whole day, and sometimes enliven the labor by singing choruses. They are a discontented and quarrelsome race, very deficient in personal courage, but so litigious, that their disposition for law has become a proverb. It is a common saying that two old women will wrangle all day till night sets in; they will then call a truce, and put a stone down in token of the armistice, next morning the stone is removed and the dispute is renewed with double acrimony. The men fight with each other, and it is not uncommon for one to bite off the ear or nose of his antagonist. The apprentices will often receive advances and abscond, and the master workman cheats his labourers by withholding their just dues. They are remarkable for their dirty and immodest habits. The women wear a wadded red cap, and a loose linen frock, quite open to the wind, filthy, and unbecoming. The men wear better clothes and are remarkable for high foreheads and jewish features. They speak a dialect intelligible only to themselves, though they are also conversant with the vernacular. The shawls of Núrpúr and Tiloknáth are not much prized; the work is inferior, but the great cause of inferiority is the hardness of the water, which communicates a roughness to the shawls, greatly detracting from their marketable value.* The Kashmíris themselves say that there is no water like the river Jhelum, and that the superiority of the shawls of the valley is mainly ascribable to the virtue of the water. The weavers of Kashmír possess also greater artistic qualifications, since none but the worst, who fail to get a livelihood in their native country, would consent to leave the charming valley for the heats of the Punjab and the discomforts of a strange country. The present population consists almost entirely of the descendants of original emigrants, and are now acclimated. They still retain the dress and dialect of Kashmír, and are constantly reinforced by new arrivals from the valley. In the cold winter months, the women adopt a peculiar custom of carrying under their frocks little pans of heated charcoal over which they warm their hands, and maintain the circulation like English ladies with their muffs."

* This at least is *said* to be the cause. B. P.

The shawls of Núrpúr are scarcely ever found in the foreign market, while those of Amritsar and Gújrát are sold in London and in France in considerable numbers: recently however they have fallen somewhat into disrepute.

In the case of Amritsar this is said to be owing to the adulteration of the wool, of which I shall speak presently.

In Gújrát it is partly owing to this cause and partly to that inferiority which the shawls markedly display in contrast with those from Srinagar.

The Deputy Commissioner of Gújrát, writing in August 1864, informed me that the weavers of Gújrát and Jalálpúr were in a very depressed state; at the last sale in London, the Gújrát shawls had sold at a loss of four ans. in the rupee, and those of Amritsar at a loss of 8 ans. or 50 per cent., the Kashmírí genuine shawls realizing a profit of 25 per cent.

In Ludhiana there are as many as 500 shops of pashmína workers, giving occupation to more than a thousand persons; the regular pattern shawl is much less woven than plain pashmina alwán, gloves and stockings, &c. of pashmina thread. Of these fabrics about Rs. 70,000 worth are annually exported, but by far the largest manufacture is that of the shawls and chadars made of soft *Rámpúri* wool, and which is often passed off as pashmina or genuine shawl wool. Of these fabrics no less than 1,30,000 rupees worth are annually made and exported. The import of real pashmina wool from Rámpúr amounts to about 30 or 40,000 rupees a year, that of Rámpúri wool about 20,000 rupees. A number of "Rámpúr Chadars" are however made of real Kashmír pashm.

The Amritsar shawl weaving approaches nearest in excellence to the Kashmír valley.

In this city also several European merchants and agents have done much in supervising the manufacture and in furnishing designs.

Some of the shawls exhibited in the collection were of great beauty, very far superior to many of the samples from other cities.

The number of Kashmírís in the Amritsar district is large. According to Mr. Cust,* the total number of *houses* of Kashmírís or Shál báf, is 6,493, of which 5,111 are in the city itself.

Amritsar besides being the seat of manufacture is also an emporium of the Kashmírí shawl trade. Of late years the shawl manufacture of Amritsar had deteriorated so from the use of mixed or adulterated pashm, that the trade was threatened with extinction in Europe ; large meetings were accordingly held at Amritsar with a view to the adoption of measures to prevent adulteration. It is proposed to effect this by a provision of contract law, which should compel persons under contract to furnish only genuine wool. It was also proposed to establish a guild or trade company, who should have a stamp or mark to be affixed as a warrant in all genuine pashmina articles. The Indian Penal Code would then become usefully operative, inasmuch as it provides for the punishment of persons who affix a false trade mark, or a mark indicative of an article being of a certain quality when in reality it was inferior or adulterated.

I here extract a portion of the proceedings of one of these great meetings held in 1861, which contains an extract from the remarks made by the London Brokers, Messrs. Brown, Buckley & Co. of Great Tower St. London, on the adulteration of Amritsar shawls :—

* Statistical Report of Amritsar Division, 1861, Appendix VIII.

" Never has been so large a proportion of coarse and defective shawls ; and in addition to the former irregularity in the work, manufacturers are now making use of a coarse sort of sheep's wool, which they work up with the pashm ; the effect of all this has at length paralysed the trade, buyers viewed these shawls as altogether unmerchantable, only to be purchased at an enormous reduction from their former rates.

"The fact of the deterioration of the trade, especially as regards the Umritsur manufactures, being established beyond the shadow of a cavil, the question of the alleged and actual cause of this deterioration was entered into at considerable length by the meeting, and while it was admitted that some amount of over-trading and haste in making up goods to be in time for the recent auctions had probably affected the later sales in London, it must be conceded that there is too much reason for agreeing with the brokers that a considerable and fraudulent admixture of coarse sheep's wool, such as Kirmanee (Persian) Thibet, and even country lamb's wool had taken place. On the other hand it was maintained that there are two material obstacles in the way of correcting the evil. These the meeting deemed it right to place in a most prominent point of view. They are :—First the difficulty of ascertaining even by the most experienced judges before shawl goods are washed and exposed for a while to the action of the air, the amount of admixture if any that may have taken place in the weaving of shawls ; —and it may be here mentioned that the length of the staples of sheep's wool offering great facilities in spinning the thread is the chief inducement to its being used, the pashm being very short and consequently more difficult to spin :—secondly, the total indifference and worse than indifference of the manufacturers (notwithstanding the promises of amendment and positive contracts to the contrary) to the frequent and urgent remonstrances of the dealers against practices which they are assured would lead as they now have done to the discovery of frauds that must affect all interested in the trade and manufacture of shawl wool goods.

The beauty of the shawl, whether Umritsur or Kashmír, depends as much on the brilliancy and durability of its unrivalled colours, and their being carefully harmonized, and the material of which it is made, as on the quality of the workmanship. The sheep's wool however fine, never will assume that permanent brilliancy of color which is the peculiar character of the pashm, and the meeting were fully alive to the reasonableness of the brokers' assurances, that unless remedial and repressive measures be adopted to check the evil, the trade will dwindle to insignificance and perhaps be lost altogether to the Punjab. There are the numerous weavers of the raw material in the hills far north, the carriers to the plains who purchase return produce, the dealers and brokers concerned in the buying and selling of this produce, the numerous hands engaged in picking, cleaning, spinning and dyeing the wool, amounting in Amritsar alone to from 18 to 20,000 hands of all ages and both sexes, all these are dependent on the trade for their subsistence. The weavers cannot be less than from 7 to 8,000 in number, after whom come the washers, the fullers, tailors, darners and workers of needle-made shawls."

The principal kind of wool used in adulteration was a soft white wool imported from Kirman, a province of Persia. The following table prepared for the meeting alluded to shows the rates at which real pashm and Kirmani wool were sold at respectively for the years 1850 to 1861 in the city of Amritsar; the gradual increase in the price of genuine pashm and decrease on that of Kirmani is no less remarkable in itself than indicative of the state of the import trade of both articles and of the increasing facility for and temptation to the adulterative use of the wool of Kirmani.

Real Pashm.			
Year in which sold.	Rate per rattí, i. e., 2 Srs. 2 Ch.		
1850-51	3	...	...
	3	8	...
1851-52	3	4	...
	3	8	...
	5	8	...
1852-53	4	...	...
	3	14	...
1853-54	5	5	...
	6	4	...
	5	8	...
	5	12	...
1854-55	5	14	...
	6	4	...
	7	1	..
1855-56	5	5	...
	5	8	...
	5	12	...
1856-57	4	8	...
	5	7	...
	4	15	...
	3	8	..
1857-58	5	8	..
	3	10	...
1858-59	3	5	...
	3	8	...
	3	4	...
1859-60	3	..	...
	2	8	...
	2	12	...
1860-61	5	...	...
	4	...	...
	3	4	...
	4	10	...
1861	4	5	6
	4	3	...
	4	...	...

Kirmani Wool.			
Year in which sold.	Rate per rattí, i. e., 2 Srs. 2 Ch.		
1850-51	7	...	...
	8	8	...
1851-52	9	..	...
	9	8	...
1852-53	9	...	...
	10	8	...
1853-54	11	...	...
	12	...	...
1854-55	9	4	...
	9	8	...
1855-56	6	...	...
1856-57	6	4	...
	6	...	...
	4	8	...
1857-58	6	4	...
	6	...	...
	5	12	...
	5	10	...
1858-59	6	...	...
	5	8	...
	5	5	...
1859-60	4	12	...
	4	10	...
1860-61	4	10	...
	4	8	...
	4	7	...
1861	3	14	...
	4	...	...
	3	12	...

With regard to the export of shawls from Amritsar to Europe, the following information was obligingly furnished to me by Mr. Richard Chapman of Amritsar, Agent to the firms of Messrs. Les Fils De. C. Oulman, of Paris. He writes :

" About the time of the arrival of the first French Agent in India, in 1850, the total yearly value of shawls exported to Europe was £85,00 to £100,000, sterling; since that time the trade has steadily increased, and may do so still more. The amount realized by public sale in London is shown in the following table. Mr. Chapman observes that, justly to estimate the trade, we must take into consideration the shawls that are exported direct to Paris and other places by the agents of European firms in India, the value of which exports is very considerable. In 1853, shawls were sold in London to the value of £ 104,000

,, 1854,	,,	,,	£ 106,500
,, 1855,	,,	,,	£ 173,900
,, 1856,	,,	,,	& 250,600
,, 1857,	,,	,,	£ 147,900
,, 1858,	,,	,,	£ 247,600
,, 1859,	,,	,,	£ 217,500
,, 1860,	,,	,,	£ 264,586
,, 1861,	,,	,,	£ 222,360
,, 1862,	,,	,,	£ 272,784
,, 1863,	,,	,,	£ 226,279

Since the European agents settled in the country considerable improvement has taken place in the patterns. It is to this fact that the increase of the trade is in a great measure to be attributed. At first (and in fact until within a few years) much difficulty was experienced in persuading the native designers to alter or amend their patterns.

They were attached to their old style and would not accept an alteration; but now this difficulty has been overcome and the weavers are willing to adopt hints, in fact they now seldom begin to work till the pattern has been inspected or approved by the agent for whom they work.

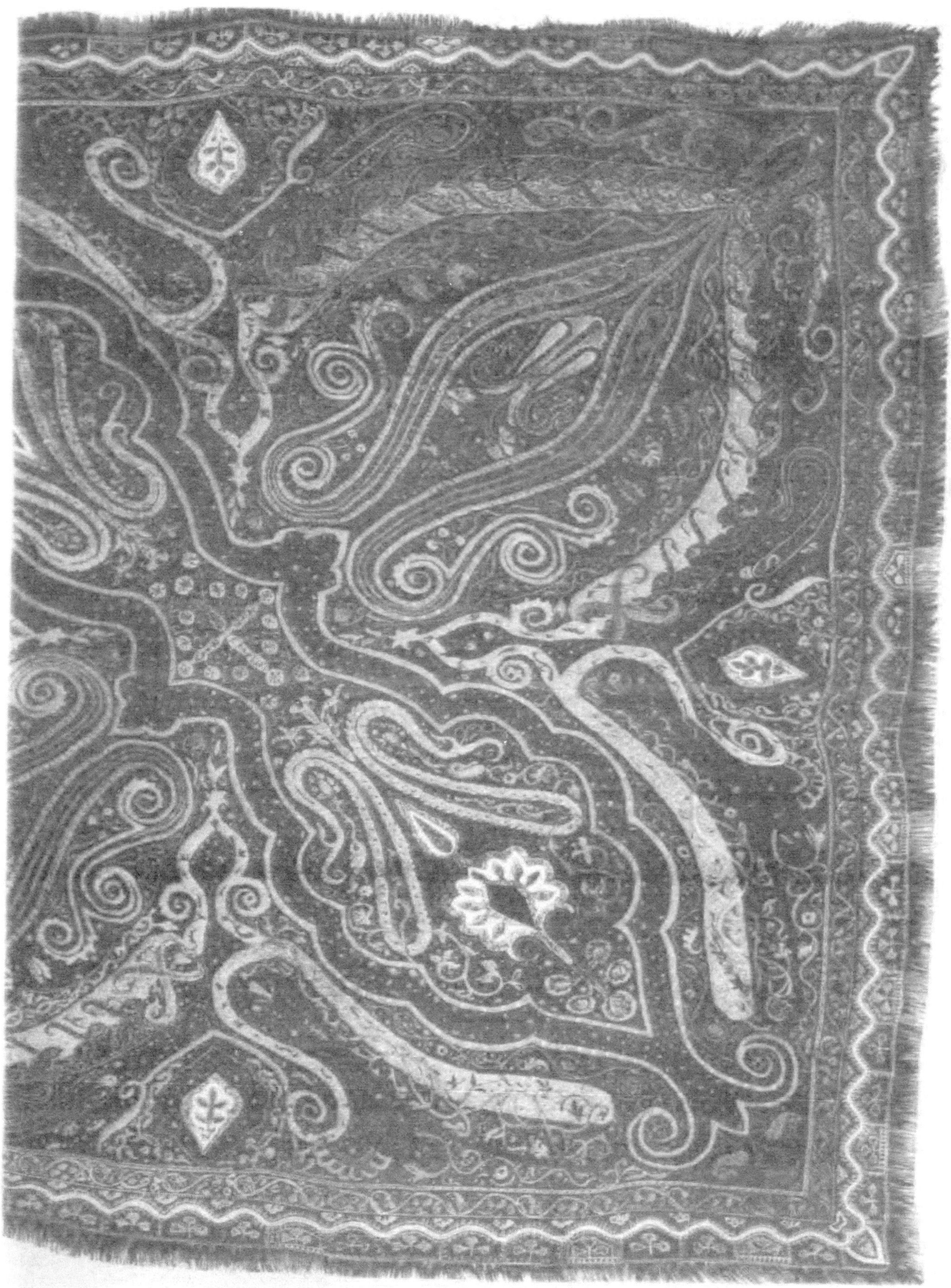

Mr. Chapman remarks that the people do not understand the loss that occurs by adulterating the wool, although there is hope that they will amend when they find the shawls selling at an actual loss in Europe.

A shawl even of adulterated pashm, still sells for double what a shawl of sheep's wool would, though the work be otherwise the same.

The samples of Punjab woven shawls were as follows :—

From LUDHIANA :—

342.—[6281]. Jámawár, worth Rs. 30, by AHSAN SHAH.

343.—[7082]. 'Patká,' or scarf, by the same.

344.—[7083 & 84]. White shawls and rúmáls (pashmina), by AZIZ of Ludhiana.

345.—[7085]. Black shawl, called "tíkáh."

346.—[7086]. Red shawls, do.

347.—[7087]. Red shawl, (tíkáh,) by KASHI RAM.

The following series is from AMRITSAR :—

348.—[7119]. Long shawl (woven), value Rs. 400, by DAYA SHANKAR.

349.—[7120 & 21]. Two others, same value, by ABDULLAH KHAN.

350.—[7122]. Another, of same value, by LASJU.

351.—[7124]. Square shawl, rúmál, by LASJU, value Rs. 315.

352.—[7125]. Jámawár, shawl piece (pattern in stripe), worth Rs. 125, by GHULAM HUSAIN.

353.—[7126]. Another, value Rs. 100, by MUHAMMAD SHAH.

354.—[7127]. Square shawl, by MUHAMMAD SHAH.

355.—[7128-32]. Square shawls, worth Rs. 85 each, by MUHAMMAD SHAH.

The following series were made expressly for dna on the original designs of R. W. CHAPMAN ESQR. of Amritsar, and under his superintendence they gained the first prize for the best Shawls in the Punjab.

356.—[7133 & 34]. Two long shawls, each value of Rs. 400.

357.—[7135]. Another, value Rs. 380.

358.—[7136]. Another, value Rs. 370.

359.—[7137]. Another, value Rs. 350.

360.—[7138]. Another, value Rs. 375.

361.—[7139]. Another, value Rs. 350.

362.—[7140]. Square shawl, Rs. 375

Two of the long shawls are made on a plan now for the first time produced by Mr. Chapman, on his own design. The shawl is so woven as to have two distinct patterns in it,—when folded it can be worn to shew either pattern, and thus appears as if there were two different shawls.*

The next series was exhibited by the firm of DEVI SAHA AND CHAMBA MAL.

363.—[7145 & 46]. Two long shawls, woven at Amritsar.

364.—[7147 & 48]. Two square shawls woven at Amritsar.

365.—[6434-5-6]. 3 "Jámawárs," worth Rs. 60 and 70, by GHULAM NABI, of Lahore.

366.—[7188]. Striped shawl (Jámawár), value Rs. 40, from Pathánkot, Gurdáspúr district.

367.—[7189]. A jámawár, value Rs. 85, by GHULAM MURTAZA, of Batálah.

368.—[7191-95]. Pashmina shawl edging or kináru (woven). several specimens by BUTAH, SUBHAN, MIR KAMALDAR, and PIRA of Syalkot.

369.—[7198 & 99]. Two pieces of shawl woven "kínára" or bordering, from the LAHORE CENTRAL JAIL.

* Four of these long shawls were exhibited in the case occupying the centre of the Exhibition building : the case was constructed in the shape of a four pointed star, each ray having 2 faces, and one shawl being hung from the top of each, the two halves of a long shawl were displayed half in each face, to great advantage.

370.—[7219]. "Chárbágh pashmina," exhibited by Harsahaimal, Lahore, a shawl divided into 4 parts, each of a different color, value Rs. 32.

371.—[7221]. "Doshála," by the same, called "Doshála tilawála."

372.—[7273]. Shawl borders from Gujranwálla.

The following are from Gujrat :—

373.—[7286, 87 & 88]. Three scarf shawls, "Dopatta Shál," value Rs. 200, by Sadik, of Jalálpúr.

374.—[7289]. Patka, or scarf of blue shawl work, value Rs. 13, by the same.

375.—[7290]. Another, grey.

376.—[7291]. Another, white.

377.—[7292 & 93]. Two others, scarlet.

In concluding the list of Shawls, I take occasion to notice the practice of skilful merchants as to altering Shawls. It has before been remarked that many shawls are made up of pieces sewn together by a "rafúgar" with such delicacy that the suture is imperceptible. Merchants take advantage of this. When they buy a shawl which they think only partly good, they cut out of it such parts as displease them. They then draw on paper a design for a new piece to fill up the gap, and give it to a shawl weaver to execute. As soon as the new piece is completed, it is sewn into the shawl, which is entirely changed in appearance, and often immensely increased in value by the process. Shawls are often purchased with indifferent borders and improved by putting new ones on. The border is always worked on a web of silk, as this gives it weight and solidity and causes the whole fabric to set well. In Paris and other places, the merchants frequently exchange shawls for parties who are tired of or otherwise displeased with their own: the shawl so taken will be washed, and parts taken out and replaced by new pieces, so that eventually it comes out like a new article.

I should also add that, in Kashmír, when a shawl is about to be made, a small square piece shewing the design, by way of pattern, is made and carried to the Maharaja's Inspector. On approval, a duty according to the quality of the future shawl (as indicated by the pattern) is taken, and a seal mark impressed in token of such payment. The piece is afterwards worked into the shawl and the seal or stamp disappears when the fabric is washed.

SUB-CLASS B.

PASHMINA FABRICS OTHER THAN SHAWLS.

This division includes the various species of plain pashmina cloth, malída and alwán exhibited, it also includes many articles made of Rámpúrí wool called "Naklí Pashmina," or wool resembling the real Thibetan pashm in softness and fine texture ;—the principal of these being the Rámpúrí Châdar already alluded to.

For the rest, knitted fabrics, such as stockings, are often made of pashmina thread ; and there is the plain woven cloth called alwán. When this has been pulled, shrunk and softened by soaking in a mixture of water and soap-nut (ritá), and then by treading by men with bare feet, it is called malídá.

The specimens were as follows :—

FROM LUDHIANA :—

378.—[6282]. Rámpúrí shawl, value Rs. 80, by AHSAN SHAH.

379.—[6301]. Another white châdar, by the same, and worth Rs. 35.

380.—[6283 to 6300]. 19 specimens of Rámpúrí Châdar, in green, orange, white, brown, red, blue, pink, crimson, and grey colors. at prices from Rs. 24 to Rs. 26-8 each, by BHIR BHAN, merchant.

381.—[6330, 31 & 32]. Pairs of men's and children's socks of Pashmina, made by MANOWAR.

382.—[5802]. Châdar, from Basáhir, contributed by the RAJA OF BASAHIR.

The following are from AMRITSAR :—

383.—[6357-8]. Colored "Alwán," or plain woven pashmina pieces, by MESSRS. DEVI SAHAI AND CHAMBA MAL.

384.—[6379-388]. Pieces of Malídá or shrunk and pulled pashmina cloth, MESSRS. DEVI SAHAI AND CHAMBA MAL.

Some of these were imported from Kashmír and some made at Amritsar, without specification in the original lists.

385.—[6412]. Plain shawl, made up in the style of a European travelling shawl, of pashmina, made at the Lahore Central Jail, exhibited by DR. PENNY.

386.—[6443]. Pashmina pattú, by NIZAMUDDIN, Lahore, worth Rs. 35.

A good deal of cloth and material for wrappers is made at Lahore from the Kábul goat's wool called "Kabulí pashm."

387.—[6444]. Another, "khud-rang," by the same, worth Rs. 25.

N. B.—The term "pattú" is not *properly* applied to pashmina articles : "pattús" are made of sheep's and goats' hair.

388.—[5859]. Comforters or neck-ties, made of pashmina and wool, machine wove, by MR. SPENCE, Sealkote.

389.—[6445-47]. Three pieces of Malidá, worth Rs. 13-2, 24-9 and 17-4 each respectively, by KARM CHAND, of Lahore.

390.—[6544]. Rúmál, woven (full doz) by HIS HIGHNESS THE RAJAH OF KAPURTHALA.

The following collection was from KASHMIR:

391.—[6408]. 3 pieces of pashmina cloth, woven in imitation of European plaid patterns. (GOVERNMENT TOSHAKHANA).

392.—[6548]. Pink "úrmuk" of pashmina, worth Rs. 42, (by HIS HIGHNESS THE MAHARAJH OF KASHMIR).

"Urmuk" is a cloth usually woven of camels' hair, the fabric here mentioned is woven in the same style, only of pashmina ; it is stout and thick and used as a saddle-cloth.

393.—[6549]. Check lúngí of pashmina, worth Rs. 24.

394.—[6550]. Pink colored 'Dorya,' or striped cloth, worth Rs. 49.

395.—[6551]. "Par-i-taús" safed (káníkár, or loom wove).

Par-i-taús or Peacock's feather, is applied to silk or pashmina goods which are "shot" with a different color, and so have a changeful lustre like the peacock's feather. Scarlet and green are the two colors usually woven together, but in the sample the ground is white, shot red, value Rs. 450.

396.—[6552]. "Par-i-purz, zangárí zanjírídár," *i. e.* light blue par-i-purz with a fringe or edging, value Rs. 53-1-3.

The fabric called "par-i-purz" ("Purz" means a shred or fragment) has a pile or nap like coarse velvet, except that the pile consists of innumerable little loops of the thread; this piece has a border fringe or zanjír (*Angl*: chain) sown on to it, hence its name.

397.—[6553]. Gulbadan of pashmina.

This is a red striped piece made exactly like the 'gulbadan,' which properly is always silk. Value Rs. 22.

398.—[6554]. 'Alwán,' shot with two colors (par-i-taús).

399.—[6555]. "Alwán, yak tára safed," value Rs. 28-7-6.

"Alwán" is called either "yak tára" or "do tára" according as a single or double line or thread (tár) is used in weaving, just like the 'eksútí' and 'dosútí' of cotton weavers.

400.—[6536 & 57 as also 6561 & 62]. Are similar pieces of scarlet, green, white and lilac colors.

401.—[6558]. "Alwán dotárah" rose colored.

402.—[6559, 60 & 63]. Are also double thread alwán, of lilac, blue and grey colors.

403.—[6564]. Malidá alwán "asl tús," value Rs. 43-10, that is, of the finest and rarest kind of pashm, which is of a grey colour (see Vol. I, page 180) but wool dyed to this color is called also "Tús."

404.—[6555]. A large carpet in the Pile or Turkey Carpet style, all of pashmina, with occasional introduction of silk for flowerings and patterns, value Rs. 3,000.

This was a very beautiful sample of the style of carpeting and of extraordinarily fine workmanship and design.

405.—[6571]. Pashmina 'ním tús.'

That is, cloth dyed grey of a color resembling the natural "tús" above alluded to, hence called 'half' (ním) tús color.

406.—[6581]. Pashmina pattú, worth Rs. 26-13-6.

407.—[6593]. A specimen of pashmina carpet, Pattyála, (by HIS HIGHNESS THE MAHARAJAH).

....

DIVISION III.

This last division of the class of woollen fabrics comprises articles that are made of goats' hair and camels' hair, &c., they are not many in number, but are useful and highly characteristic of different parts of the province.

Nose bags for horses,—huge bags for carrying grain on the backs of cattle (called jhúl), stout pattú or matting, and occasionally rope, are the principal manufactures to which the people of the plains apply goat hair.

In the Deraját, in Sirsa and Gugaira, where camels are much used, goat's hair is employed for the large bags or (khûrjas) in which merchandize is carried, and for the various fantastic ornaments with which in these places both camels and horses are decorated. Such ornaments are made of plaits and tassels, &c., of goat hair, wrought with crimson wool, and white cowry shells sown on: they are quite characteristic of these districts.

In the hills, waist ropes or girdles are made of goat hair, as also bags, and many other articles.

The collection exhibited the following specimens:—

408.—[6273]. " Tang," horse girth, by JIWAN RAM of KOTAKH.

409.—[6277]. Girth for camel-saddle, made at the Fazilka jail, Sirsa.

410.—[6279]. Goat hair waist-girdle, Basáhir.

This rope is a collection of strings untwisted and of a dark brown color; it is universally worn in the hills together with the thick woollen tunic.

411.—[6341]. Cloth made of black goat's hair at Kannaum, in Kanáwar, exhibited by CAPT. HOUCHEN.

412.—[6342]. Round rope made of the hair of the ' Yak ' (Bos grunniens) at Shyálkar, Kanáwar (CAPT. HOUCHEN).

This rope is made by placing the wool in position and working it with hand and foot till it 'felts' together as wool does; (See Vol. I,—" Wools.")

413.—[6343]. Flat rope of goat hair, red, white and black, made at Chiní.

414.—[6365]. Goat hair cloth bag, from Kulu.

415.—[6367]. Goat's hair rope, Lahaul, by TARA CHAND.

416.—[6368]. Rope of yak hair, Lahaul, by TARA CHAND.

417.—[6373]. Twine made of goat hair, at Spítí, exhibited by P. EGERTON ESQR.

418.—[6418, 19 & 20]. Set of ' Khúrjas' or camel bags, ornamented with tassels, fringe and cowry shells, made at Baháwalpúr, (LAHORE CENTRAL MUSEUM).

419.—[6423]. " Tát pattí," of goat's wool, a sacking cloth used for bags and also for floor cloth, LAHORE CENTRAL JAIL.

420.—[6443]. Rope of goat's hair, by CHAUDRI IMAM BAKSH.

421.—[6462]. Bag made of goat's hair, GUJRAT JAIL.

422.—[6486]. Rope of goat's hair, made at Shahpúr, value 4 ans. a seer.

423.—[6487]. Rope of camel's hair made at Khúsháb in Shahpúr, value 4 ans. a seer.

The following are from GUGAIRA :—

424.—[6497]. Saddle girth, made at Syadwalla in Gugaira.

425.—[6498]. Ornament for camel's neck.

426.—[6499]. Ornament for horse's neck, called " Sailí."

427.—[6504]. Bag for grain, called " Chatti " or " Gún."

The next series represents the DERAJAT :—

428.—[6512-15]. Saddle bags or "khorjín," value from Rs. 5 to 9 each, made at various places, as Tibli, Lúndí, Barkhan (capital of the chief Jamal Khan) Bartí and Rájhanpúr.

429.—[6616-20]. Horse's nose-bags, (Tobra) value Re. 1-2 each, made at various places, as above.

430.—[6524]. Grain bag, 'chat,' from the Waziri hills, Bunnú, made of camel and goat's hair.

431.—[6529]. Camel hair cloth, "Bark Shutri," value Rs. 30, imported from Kabul by Kazi Nasr-ullah Jan, of Peshawur.

432.—[6530]. 'Bark Dahzangí' another kind of camel hair cloth from Kabul, sent by Kazi Amir Jan.

433.—[6542]. Goat's hair cloth, and hair from which it is made, value Re. 1-0-6 per foot, by the Kohat Jail.

434.—[6582]. "Zangoz Khatái," from Yarkand, by His Highness the Maharajah of Kashmir.

This is a coarse floor cloth imported from the Chinese provinces by Yarkand, hence its name of "Khatái."

435.—[6592]. A "Jhûl Bailí" or grain bag used for loading on cattle. Patyala, by His Highness the Maharajah.

436.—[6594]. "Pattú Khár," goat's hair sack cloth, Patyala.

437.—[6595]. A 'Charna,' Patyala.

The Charna is a long narrow open bag of goat's hair set out with pegs stuck into the ground, by way of a pocket or trough, out of which cattle are given their grain.

438.—[6597]. Travelling bag, for horse or camel, Patyala.

The following is a list of all the woollen and pashmíná manufactures used in the Punjab :—

I. EUROPEAN GOODS.

Banát (broad cloth).
Merino (Marína).
Pashmíná Naklí.
Alpaca (Alpáka).
Chintz.
Kashmírá.
Carpets.
Gloves and Stockings.

II. INDIAN MANUFACTURES.

Punjab and its Dependencies, together with hill territories :—

Kashmír.

Shál Pashmíná.
Do. Sádá.
Do. Kaní kár.
Do. Amlí kár.
Do. Dorí dár.
Do. Kitání kár. (Twisted thread.)
Fard shál.
Doshalá.
Rúmál.
Jámawár.
Shamlá.
Lúngí.
Gulbadan.
Alwán.
Do. Yak tárá.
Do. Dó tárá.
Par-i-purz.
Par-i-taús.
Caps.
Stockings.
Gloves.
Loí.
Do. Yak arz.
Do. Dó arz,
Do. Tín arz.
Do. Lahorí.
Do. Kinará dár.
Do. Sádá.
Pattí.
Pattú.
Pattú Túsh.
Do. Khudrang.
Do. Abshár.
Do. Khat dár.
Do. Chárkháná.
Chint Pattú.
Gabba.
Urmak.

Kángrá.

Pattú Garrú.
Do. Gúdmá.

Kashmir.

Pattú Malidá—a soft or felted (*lit* "rubbed") woollen fabric.

Pattú Fodak or Fruk: a pattú made in Ladákh.

Do. Rámnagari: made at Rámnagar, Jamú.

'Parm-narm'—a name given by AKBAR to the soft fine and rare fabric of Ibex wool.

Lahore and Amritsar.

Bhúra;—a coarse blanketing.

Táni:—a long piece of 'bhúra.'

Loi:—a fine blanket or woollen shawl.

Kálin: a pile or 'Turkey' carpet.

Asan: a small carpet used by Mussulmans to kneel on at prayer time.

Khah: tough cloth of asses' hair.

Javál: or Chhat: bags of do.

Namad: felt.

Toshá: double felt.

Multán.

Shatranjí: a large pile carpet.

Kalín and Asan as before.

III. MANUFACTURES FROM OTHER PARTS OF ASIA.

Chánthán.

Pattú Chánthání. } Kinds of woollen cloth.
Do. Durma.
Do. Zangoz Khatai.
Takya, bádshahi.

Yarkand.

Saling—(pashmína) a cloth 22 yards in length, 6 girahs broad, price 35 rupees a piece.

Kálín and Kalímcha, Yarkand carpets.

Kálanamd, black felt.

Khosá: a thick felt.

Káshgar.

Loi Káshgari—a kind of loi.

Persia.

Pashmína Irani.

Kálín Iráni, Persian carpets.

Kábul.

Khosá: thick felt cloth.

Dhúsá—coarse woollen cloth.

Namd: felt.

Bark: cloth of camel hair used for chogahs.

Kark: cloth of sheep's wool.

Patti Shutri, fine camel hair cloth.

Urmak; a coarse cloth of sheeps' wool, roughly embroidered, used as a mat or as a saddle cloth.

Pattú Dahzangi: a soft cloth made at Dahzang near Ghazni.

Bard Yamání: a green sheep's wool cloth made like those of Yamán.

Kúrat: a cloth of goat's hair.

Kagmak: a cloth of camels' hair.

To this notice may be added that in the Deraját, carpets of several kinds are made. The names appear to indicate carpets of different sizes. A caste of people called "Chinál" are the principal manufacturers, and the carpets are made either out of wool from the hills on the frontier or of the wool of the plains of the Deraját.

These carpets are of the descriptions called "farsh," "galím," "falási," "langa," "gharári," "kamal," "chhul chamba dar," (flowered), "falási reta," and "falási pateli," the last four kinds are made by Bilúchis.

NOTE.

The juries for silk and woollen fabrics in the exhibition of 1864 met several times, and awarded the prizes noted below. The Reporter to the Jury, Mr. Henry Cope, whose great experience and knowledge would have made his report on these subjects peculiarly valuable, did not send in any report on either class.

VI. WOOLLEN MANUFACTURES.

District or Locality.	Prize taker.	Description of articles.	Medal.	Certificate.
Kashmír, ...	H. H. the Mahárájáh,	Carpet, ...	1	1
Jalandhar, ...	Darogah of the Jail, ...	Woollen Manufactures, ...	...	1
Rawalpindi, ...	Do., ...	Do., Carpets, ...	...	2
Gujrát, ...	Do., ...	Rugs, &c., ...	...	1
Multán, ...	Local Exhibition Comt.,	Woollen Carpet, (No. 6489), ...	...	1
Kangra, ...	Do., ...	Núrpúr worked Rug (No. 6358),	...	1
Lahore, ...	Supdt. Central Jail, ...	Carpet of Kandahárí pattern, ...	1	1
Do., ...	Darogah, ...	Collection generally, ...	...	1
Do., ...	Nizám-ud-dín, ...	Pattú, (pashmína fine quality) No. 6433, ...	...	1
Shahpúr (Bhaira),	Amír-ud-dín, ...	Hearth rugs, (No. 6484), ...	...	1
Kashmír, ...	H. H. the Mahárájah,	Felt, (Nos. 6570 and 6571), ...	...	1

In concluding this class, it is necessary to remark, that the shawls, both loom-woven and needle-worked, were submitted for inspection to the same Jury which examined the Embroidery class. As most of their report relates to shawls, it is annexed to this class. I have already called attention to the impossibility of retaining the old classification in the original catalogue : not only were woven and worked shawls indiscriminately admitted with "embroidery," but plain Rampúrí chaddars and alwans, because they were denominated 'shawls,' went thither also.

REPORT ON SHAWLS AND EMBROIDERY.

Major Farrington.
Captain Pollock.
G. R. Elsmie, Esquire.
Babu Mohan Lal.
Lallá Dúni Chand.
Thakurdas. (Toshakhánah.)
Kunya Lál, son of the Vakíl of the Maharajah of Kashmir.

The class on which this Jury had to form their opinion is very important and extensive; the articles were chiefly contributed from Delhi, Ludhiana, Amritsar, Lahore, Kashmir, Jhínd, Nabha, Patiala. Other districts of the Punjab also contributed to this class, but it is one in which Kashmir, Amritsar and Delhi must necessarily take the lead.

The Jury had under their inspection shawls woven and worked with the needle, embroidery with silk-braid, gold and silver thread, tinsel embroidery, plain pashmina pieces &c.

Owing to the articles belonging to this class having been laid out in several different parts of the building, considerable delay occurred before they could be arranged so as to ensure a satisfactory inspection.

The Jury have decided in awarding prizes in shares as noted in the accompanying list; they wish it to be understood they have allotted the full number of shares, the money value of each must therefore be raised to correspond with the number of shares recorded.

The remarks are sufficiently full to obviate the necessity of entering at any length into the merits of the articles that have obtained prizes.

There were many articles for which probably the Jury might have been inclined to award shares, but the amount of money at their disposal was too limited.

The Amritsar shawls can never compete with those of Kashmir, but the Jury consider those for which prizes have been given are very good of their kind. It is well known that the Amritsar shawls do not go beyond a certain price, the wool is not so pure, and therefore they cannot bear comparison in texture with the fabrics of Kashmir.

The shawl trade has not decreased; on the contrary, there is every reason to believe it has increased, but its character has changed considerably; formerly, the trade was limited to a certain number of well known firms. There used to be a large demand for shawl fabrics at the Courts of Delhi, Lucknow, Sindh, &c.; now, numbers have embarked in the trade, and amongst them many are mere speculators: this is shown by the result of the half yearly sales that take place in London. The appointment of gentlemen from England and France, as agents of large firms in those countries, has brought about a considerable change in the designs and patterns; these are of course a matter of taste, and there are many purchasers who still wish to see a considerable amount of the Oriental characteristics in the patterns. The careful supervision exercised by these European agents has caused an improvement in the work, those who export *direct* to Europe still endeavour to throw inferior articles into the markets. It is believed the Maharajah has this year set on foot some arrangements for checking this.

The collection exhibited by the Maharajah of Kashmir deserves mention. The Jury feel they cannot, with reference to the funds at their disposal, award many prizes. The collection from the Maharajah is large and valuable. The would award a medal for the whole.

Next to this, the collection contributed by the firm of Devee Sahai and Chumba Mull of Amritsar, is the most worthy of notice; this firm has shown great interest and zeal in adding to the success of the Exhibition; the articles displayed are numerous and of superior quality. The Jury award a medal to this firm.

The Jury are led to understand that certain gold medals are at the disposal of the General Committee for distribution to contributors in the Punjab territories; the Jury would bring prominently to the notice of the General Committee, the claim of the firm of Devee Sahai Chumba Mull to so valuable a mark of the appreciation of their services.

It is now requisite to report regarding the special prizes. To Mr. R. Chapman of Amritsar, it will be observed, has been awarded Lady Montgomery's prize for the best long shawl made in the Punjab. This gentleman has exhibited 6 or 8 other shawls of superior quality. Owing to some misunderstanding, they were withdrawn before the Jury had arrived at a final decision, others were presented in their stead; the Jury consider them of superior quality, and award a silver medal for the collection.

The Jury have awarded Lady Rundheer Singh's shawl prize for No. 7085, of Class IX, B Section: they consider it meets the stipulations in preference to any other of the same sort.

The competition for Mr. Chapman's prize for the best Jamewar of certain dimensions manufactured in the Punjab was very limited. The Jury award the prize for No. 7106. The Catalogue shows this article was manufactured at Amritsar, but they are of opinion it was made at Núrpúr.

O. J. McL. FARRINGTON,
Reporter to the Jury.

AWARD OF THE JURY APPOINTED TO ALLOT PRIZES UNDER CLASS IX SECTION B.

No.	No of Catalogue.	Description of Articles.	No. of Shares allotted.	REMARKS.
1	7355	White Jámawar, ...	7	The texture of this is very fine, worked all over, the design new.
2	7142	Black Shawl, ...	6	A long woven shawl, fine texture, pattern in good taste.
3	7164	A Chogah, ...	6	A red woven chogah, work of fine texture.
4	7163	Ditto, ...	5	A puce colored dressing gown, extensively embroidered with needle-work, the peculiarity of which is, that the stitches are not carried through the other side.
5	7363	A Square Shawl, ...	2	Color black, pattern and work good.
6	7343	A Long Shawl, ...	5	The price of this is Rs. 1200. A beautiful specimen of needle-work.
7	7352	A Square Shawl, ...	4	Color black, pattern and work good.
8	7370	A Square Shawl, ...	3	Rose color, work fine.
9	7144	A Do. Do., ...	3	Black ground.
10	7366	A Do. Do., ...	3	A turquoise blue, needle-work.
11	7149	A Do. Do., ...	2	Needle-work.
12	7856	A Pair of Red Shawls, ...	3	Embroidered with gold and silk thread needle-work, borders embroidered with figures of men and animals.
13	7369	A Square Shawl, ...	2	Richly embroidered with gold.
14	7377	A Square Shawl, white ...	1	Pattern and work good.
15	7171	A Red Cap, ...	1	Embroidered needle-work,
16	7120	A Long Shawl (woven),	6	Good pattern and work, Amritsar manufacture.
17	7124	A Square Shawl, ...	3	Ditto ditto.
18	7051	A Red Lace Scarf, ...	4	Black lace scarf for a native lady, embroidered with gold and silk, Delhi, } Very pretty
19	7053	Ditto, ...	4	A Red ditto ditto. } Very pretty
20	7155	A Velvet Masnad, ...	4	Handsome velvet masnad with a deep embroidered border of gold, pattern bold.
21	7046	A Green Scarf, ...	2	This is handsomely embroidered with gold.
22	7156	An embroidered Chogah,	1	Handsomely embroidered with gold throughout.
23	7182	Red Scarf, ...	1	Fine material, needle-work border.
24	7058	A piece of Lace with Gold embroidery, ...	1	A piece for a native lady's bodice, fine work.
25	7199	Embroidered edging, ...	1	Shawl pattern, worked by prisoners in the Lahore Jail.
26	7170	A Rampur Chaddur, ...	1	Fine texture.
27	...	A Masnad and pillow case,	4	A handsome amber colored velvet masnad and pillow case, from Nabha, handsomely embroidered with gold and silver and also beads.
28	7392	Green Velvet Saddle cloth (or Charjáma), ...	2	Handsomely embroidered : this deserves honorable mention.

SPECIAL PRIZES.

Serial number.	Catalogue No.	Name of article.	The prize awarded.	REMARKS.
1	7136	A Long Shawl, contributed by R. Chapman, Esquire, ...	Lady Montgomery's prize, ...	Amritsar work, first rate work for that place considered the best coming within the terms on which this prize is given.
2	7126	Jámawar, Mahomed Shah of Amritsar,	Mr. Chapman's prize,	This article comes within the terms for the prize, in the catalogue. It is recorded as the manufacture of Amritsar, the native members pronounce it from Núrpúr, the prize however is open to the Punjab.
4	7085	A Square Shawl, ...	Lady Rundheer Singh's prize, ...	This shawl is the best of the description for which the prize was offered.
	Medals	To the Maharajah of Kashmir. ,, R. Chapman, Esquire, ,, Davee Sahai Chumba Mull.		The articles under this class are many of them very fine, and equally deserving of notice.

CLASS VII.

MANUFACTURES IN SILK.

For the history of silk in its raw state, as well as for an account of the localities of its production, and the details of its trade, the reader is referred once more to the first volume. It will be ever thus as we come to class after class of manufactured products. The substances described in volume I are applied to use in volume II.

I shall therefore at once commence the class with a sketch of the method in which the manufacture of silk is conducted, and then pass on to notice the various kinds of silken fabrics which the province and its adjacent countries produce, and the particular localities which are famous for the production of them.

The silk most commonly used by manufacturers and by them esteemed best, (although by Europeans it would be considered inferior to Chinese or Italian silk) is that from Bukhára and Khorásán. The silk is of two descriptions, called respectively "Khora Khúndadár" and "Khora Singal." The first named, though to ordinary eyes the same as the second, is really superior and contains a less quantity of refuse.

Amritsar and Múltan are the principal marts for raw silk.

It appears that silk now commands a much less price in the market than formerly, though the manufacture has not diminished, at any rate in total quantity.*

Although the large demand for fine silk has passed away with the Sikh Durbar, yet there is still a large quantity consumed by the people, and the progressive wealth of the community of late years has increased the general use of silk, while the facilities of trade under British rule have also opened the gates of external commerce.

Silk, the produce of the Punjab, is also beginning to enter the market, and the result of present experiments is to shew that silk can be produced which will sell quite as well as the Bukhara silk, though often from defective manipulation and other causes the indigenous silk sells somewhat cheaper.

Mr. Cope (writing in 1858) remarks that the price of silk is generally from Rs. 11 to 13; that is also approximately true now. He adds that 18 to 20 rupees was formerly the value. The weight by which silk is purchased is calculated at 105 rupees Nának Sháhi.†

The Hindú caste of 'Khatris' are the principal silk holders; they furnish the weavers with the raw material throguh the hands of brokers ("dalál"); the finished fabric again returns to their hands for sale to the public.

The raw silk as imported is found to be so badly wound as to require that operation to be done over again in order to separate the fine silk from the coarse and from the refuse.

The first workman therefore to whom the silk goes is the 'Pat-phéra' or winder. Some of them only wind on behalf of the merchant, receiving payment according to the weight wound off, and others (a less numerous kind) purchase silk on their own account, which they then wind and retail.

---

* See Mr. Cope's valuable paper on Silk in the Journal of the Agri-Horticultural Society of India, volume X. part. 2, and at page 4 of the reprint circulated in the Punjab.

† The "Nának Sháhi" rupee of the Sikh time weighs half a másha, *i. e.* 7¼ grains less than the Government rupee, which is 180 grains.

The first thing the winder does is to open out the large skein or hank in which the silk comes to him, and to divide it into two or more parts according to its size. These are stretched tight over two reels called "úri" or "charkha," one at each end of the skein :—the upper reel is then fixed against the wall about 8 or 10 feet high, and the lower one is fixed close to the ground, so far away from the wall as to incline the whole skein at an angle of about 45°.

The winder sits on the ground in front of the lower reel, being furnished with 3 or even 4 little reels or "úras" on which to wind the silk as it comes off the skein. These reels revolve on a stick called "gaz," being made to spin round by the workman continuously giving light jerks to the end of the "gaz". Having found the end of the thread on the skein, he fixes it to the first little reel, and then begins rapidly winding. The silk thread passes through his left hand, the stick with the reels being held and kept revolving with the right hand and against the right side. The winder's hand being delicately experienced, he feels the quality of the thread as it passes through his left hand: as soon as he perceives a change in its fineness he stops the reel, bites off the silk with his teeth, and winds this new quality of silk on to the next reel, and so on.

When the winding reels are already charged with a certain portion of silk, the end on the reel is joined to end on the skein with the utmost adroitness with the tongue, and the knot is so fine that the joint becomes imperceptible after the silk has been dyed.

Three qualities are usually obtained on three different reels in this way.*

The first is fine and regular, and is twisted to form the threads of the warp (táni) of the intended fabric, the second quality is used for the weft or shoot, called "vána" and "peta." The third kind is a coarse refuse called "kachar."

Mr. Cope mentions that a seer of raw silk or "khora" yields from 2 to 3 tolahs of refuse silk; the smaller the quantity of refuse the higher the price of the silk. The "kachar" is however by no means useless: it is dyed, converted into thread, and used for embroidery and other purposes.

The wages of the winder are Re. 1-8 per seer of raw silk. He can wind a seer of silk in from 8 to 12 days, and the merchant gives him about 3 or 4 seers of silk at a time to wind.

The second and third qualities are made into skeins and given to the "rangrez" or dyer.

The first quality kept for the warp, passes on the reel as it is to the "todi," who twists the thread to make it strong for the warp: he answers to the "thrower" of the European loom, who makes the silk into "organzine." This consists of two threads, which are first separately twisted in one direction, and then the two are twisted together in the *reverse* direction: this is effected by considerable art,—it was long unknown in England, and organzine ready twisted was imported from Italy in the early days of England silk manufacture, until at last the art of "throwing" was spied out and brought over.

The native process of twisting does not appear to compass the double twist, which is the peculiarity of the organzine; the process simply causes two lines of the táni silk to twist together into one thread.

It will be easiest to describe the 'todi's' apparatus first, and then say what he does with it.

He works under a long open shed with a smooth clean floor of the bare ground: on this a number of little frames (called 'khána') made of four pieces of 'sarkanda' (the culm of

* A fourth called 'Pumbi' which is very soft, is rarely obtained.

the Munj grass) are erected. They are arranged in two parallel rows, consisting each of 16 frames, each placed one behind the other, and at two yards interval ; each frame carries on it a small ring or "chúri" made of 'lac.'

The 'todi' now takes two reels just as they come from the 'patphera,' charged with first quality silk for the 'táni ;' he sticks them into the ground, and then finding the end of each reel's thread, he puts them together and with his hand passes the united threads successively through the little rings on the frames, taking the threads down one row of the frames and up the other. When the two threads emerge from the last frame and ring they are attached to a simple arrangement called the "dúkh :" this is nothing more than a bit of thin bamboo 4 inches long, with a little ball of clay fastened to the lower end, which swings about 3 feet above the ground. When the two threads are attached to the bamboo piece, it is given a sharp turn between the hands of the operator (like spinning a "teetotum") : the result of this is, that the two threads as they lie along in the rings and frames are twisted together into one, through the whole length. As fast as they are twisted, the thread is wound off on a reel revolving on a "gaz," just like the original process of winding, but the action of the reel in this case is so much more violent, owing to the strength of the double twisted line, that the winder has to put a pad of cloth against his right side on the place where he rests the end of the "gaz" or reel stick as it revolves. The silk loses weight in twisting, owing to the friction of the rings, to the extent of one tolah per seer.

As soon as two reels are charged with twisted thread, they are given to the "táni wallah" to prepare the warp of the fabric to be. He does this just like the cotton weaver; he has two long light sticks of the sarkanda grass stalk, one for each hand; at the end of each stick is an iron wire upon which the reel is placed and can revolve easily : the reel is kept on to the wire by the aid of a little knob carrying a ring, the thread on the reel as it unwinds has to pass through this ring. The warp maker now sets upon the ground two parallel rows of sarkanda sticks ; the rows are at a sufficient distance apart to allow the warp man to pass with a stick and reel in each hand between them. The upright sticks in each row are placed two and two, each pair being two yards distant from the next, and the pairs of sticks in one row are of course exactly opposite to those in the other.

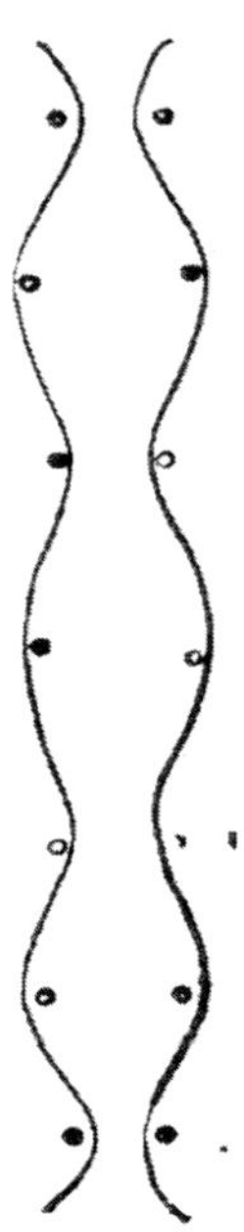

The workman now fixes the ends of his thread on the two reels, one to each of the first pair of sticks on the 1st row, and then walking up the row passes the threads as they run off the reels held downwards, inside one stick and outside the next, each hand having one reel : two threads are thrown down at once in this way over the pairs of sticks. As soon as the workman, throwing down silk as he goes, reaches the end of the first row of pairs of sticks he turns round and walks down the next, or parallel row, setting out the silk alternately inside and outside the sticks as before described ; the whole length of the two threads, thus put down in and out of the pairs of sticks both on the up-row and down-row is 108 yards.

The next process is to fasten a tie wherever the threads of the warp cross each other, so as to prevent their again becoming caught, and the warp is taken off the sticks and dyed. The other qualities of silk, the " vána " and the refuse or " kachar," are dyed just as they come from the winder. The various kinds of dyes used have already been treated of in the first volume. I will only recapitulate the principal colors used, deriving from Mr. Cope's paper a list of the costs of dyeing each. Before dyeing, the skeins of silk are boiled in a solution of sajji (impure carbonate of soda) and then in soapsuds.

To make white silk, the skeins are merely taken out. washed in several waters, and then bleached over the fumes of sulphur. The other colors which are produced best are :—

Yellow, dyed with " akalbir," the root of (*Datiscus Cannabinus*) ; also with " ásbarg," the flower of a species of *Delphinium*, which comes from Kabul.

Orange color, or golden " suneri " with " harsinghár," the flower of *Nyctanthes arbor-tristis*, and some red of cochineal.

Scarlet dyed with *cochineal* which produces crimson and given its vermilion tone with " harsinghár " and its mordant, " kishta " and " bozgand," the galls of *Pistasia Tercbinthus*.*

Crimson, with cochineal alone, and "bozgand" as the mordant. Mr. Cope remarks that the cochineal is not obtained at the " pansáris " or grocers and druggists, but the silk merchants themselves supply it to the dyers. A paler shade of cochineal dyeing produces *pink*, and the paler shades varied with yellow dye will give shades of orange, salmon color, &c.

Deep purple " úda," is dyed with crimson and indigo blue.

Lilac, " náfarmáni," is dyed with the same materials in lighter proportions.

Blue can be produced from several shades almost black, to deep blue, bright blue, and pale blue or (" ábi ") all with indigo.

Black is dyed with indigo acid.

Green, of shades, very dark, bright green or " zamrúdi," pea green or " angúri " (a favorite color with natives when woven with a scarlet stripe), and pale green or " pista," &c. are all produced with shades of indigo and the various kinds of yellow dye, " ásbarg," " ekalbir," " harsinghár," &c.

Brown silk is comparatively uncommon, and is used principally in the form of thread by the persons who embroider on pashmina and want silk to match, or who weave brown and white silk check pieces in the European fashion. The colors are deep brown,(" túsha"), brown ("dar chini"), pale redish brown, ("sandali," sandal wood color) and "badámi" (almond color)

Grey or *Khákí* is also a color much used, it is produced with " kahi," (sulphate of iron) and galls (maiñ).

Madder is not used in dyeing silk. Indigo when employed is first dissolved in acide, forming what has been called " sulphindylic acid" or " murabba-rang" by the natives. I am

* Mr. Cope, at page 11, calls them 'flower buds,' identifying " bozgand " with " gul-i-pista," and seems to consider Dr. Royle wrong in calling them galls. The native name is no proof at all, seeing that the little bulbous galls look like unopened flower buds, but all the samples I have seen of " bozgand " are most certainly galls, or some similar excrescence, certainly not flower buds. (The word is also printed Vozgund instead of Bozgand.) It is doubtful whether " kusumbha " is used in silk dyeing. The wily Khatri knows too well what he is about to allow his valuable silk to be dyed with the worthless safflower, which fades in the air and light, and leaves a dingy pale yellow red, which would of course sell for nothing ; crimson is always produced with cochineal.

not aware that lac dye is used, except perhaps for purples or with blue.

Colour.	Loss in weight of the silk after the process of dyeing is complete.	Cost of dyeing.	How long the operation takes.	REMARKS.
White, ...	4 or 5 chittacks out of 16.	8 annas per seer, of raw silk delivered to dyer, ...	3 days.	
Yellow, ...	One quarter, ...	1 Rupee per seer, ..	3 days.	
Greens, ...	No further loss after the first dyeing of yellow is completed,	¼ per seer, ...	Somewhat longer.	
Crimson, Scarlet. Purples.	One quarter, ...	For ½ and ⅛ to 1 Re. per seer, the dyer gets 8 annas as his share.	6 days, and more for the colours that have two dips of colour.	The cochineal is given to the dyer; it costs from Rs. 5-8 to 6 or more a seer. For the various shades of pink, crimson, scarlet, from 1 to 4 chittacks will be used per seer of silk.

I have only to add, that the use of the Aniline dyes of Europe is now extensive. At first nly the red or "Magenta" was used, but now the fine mauves and purples are common. I confess I have not yet seen the beautiful blue, or the green ; but these will follow no doubt.

The silk is, when dyed, ready for the weaver, who is called Daryaí-báf.

The loom is exactly like that for cotton weaving, it is arranged on the ground ; the weaver sitting with his feet in a large hole previously dug out, which hole also contains the treddles and foot-boards, by means of which the threads are depressed and raised.

The treddles are the two frames which hang transversely across the threads of the warp, the threads of the one being attached to the lower threads of the warp, the other to the upper. By raising and depressing them alternately by aid of foot-boards underneath, and attached by strings, the threads of the warp are crossed and recrossed as the weft is put down. The treddles are supported over the warp by strings from the roof of the room. There is also a frame called the batten or lay, divided by a number of fine wires, or thin slips of bamboo, through which the warp threads pass ; the object of this is to strike it against the weft as the work goes on, thus tightening and compacting the whole fabric. It is also suspended from the roof by strings;—the weaver moves it, when required to strike against the weft, with his hand. The only other parts of the simple loom, are two beams called the warp and cloth beams, the cloth beam supports the warp at the end where the weaver sits, on it the cloth is wound as it is woven; the beam at the other end carries the end of the warp stretched out, and also all the superfluous lengths of the threads wound on it, which of course can be unwound, as the finished cloth is wound on to the beam at the other end.

To prepare the loom, the threads of the warp are passed by hand through the two treddles, and the batten or lay, the weaver seats himself with his feet in the hole, and with his shuttle in hand; he is ready for work, the silk being previously reeled in small reels ready to be transferred to the shuttle. The solid parts of the loom and the shuttle are made of the khair wood (*Acacia catechu*).

The number of the threads in the warp varies from 350 to 1,700. A very broad silk would be worked with 2,000. Some silk of this extra breadth was prepared for the Exhibition of 1864, by MESSRS. CHAMBA-MAL AND DEVI SAHAI of Amritsar.

In the days of the Sikh Court, Mr. Cope mentions, Mahárája Sher Singh introduced a silk of 2,400 threads broad, but the day of these very fine and large silks has passed away.

Mr. Cope gives the following particulars of the weaving of a piece of 'Gulbadan' or striped silk :—

The length of the warp is reduced in weaving from 54 to 46 yards; the breadth being 1,700 threads, the weaver takes from 50 to 60 days to complete the piece, doing a yard in a day (very narrow silk can be woven at the rate of 3 yards per diem). In the completion of the piece, 3¼ seers of dyed silk are required; 12 rupees are the wages for weaving one piece such as this, of 46 yards. When taken off from the loom, it is cut into 3 lengths, and is ready for sale. The ends of the silk that project from the piece in weaving are picked off with pincers.

I will now describe briefly the kinds of silk made.

Most of the silks are very thick and close, according to this their value is fixed; they do not shine, nor have they a beautiful gloss and lustre like European silks and glacés. Such are extremely despised by natives as far as their value goes, although they cannot help admiring their beauty, and employ them for chogahs and gowns of state.

The most common perhaps of all the native silk fabrics, is the "Gulbadan" or striped silk. It is a plain fabric of any colour, striped down its length with lines of another colour;—the favourite colours are pale green with scarlet stripe; dark green, nearly black, with scarlet stripe; yellow with scarlet or crimson stripe; purple with yellow stripe; white with dark stripe; crimson with white stripe; besides these, other varieties are occasionally met with; This kind of silk is much used for the close fitting pyjámas worn by the wealthier classes of Hindoos and Sikhs.

Plain silk without a stripe is called Daryái. If it is shot with two colours, (usually red and green, but others are intermingled also) it is called 'Dhûp chân.' In the Kashmir Collection, fabrics shot with different colours are described as Par-í-táús—"peacocks' feathers," the application of which name is obvious. The native shot silk is by no means so lustrous and beautiful to the eye as European.

Silks are now often woven in a small checks of black, brown, blue, or black and white: these are principally used by European ladies, and are described as "Daryái chár-khána."

The 'lungí' or scarf described under Class V, is also manufactured in silk, sometimes of a plain color, sometimes of a fine check.

When made of silk, it is usually enriched by a beautiful border of gold or silver and variegated silk, and finished off with a silver or gold fringe. Silk lungis are not so much worn for head-dresses as the cotton lungs are, but are much admired for scarves and waist-belts or sashes.

The 'khés' is also woven in Silk, either check pattern in squares, or plain silk, with a gold border, and edged with some fancy pattern edging on either side of the gold ; beautiful thick scarlet kheses of the kind are made at Lahore, and are much sought after. The silk in these latter, is quite plain, but it is woven on the principle of a khes, and in that style of weaving called "Khés báfí" which is different from the ordinary "Daryaí báfí."

These are the principal varietíes of plain silk. Next come those which have a silken gloss, and are soft like satinette. They are woven on the "Khés báfí" principle, and exhibit the "bulbul chashm," or damask pattern, in their fabric, either in one color or two ; sometimes they are striped, with figures on the stripe, and gold threads are introduced. Such silks are principally produced at Bhawalpur, and are distinguished by the generic name "Shúja khání," probably from the name of the person who was the first to introduced them.

All figured or damasked silks are thus called, but it must be remarked, that the varieties as yet woven are not very many,—all the damask patterns being some combination of right lines or diamond shapes in small patterns. Tho native weavers are not able to produce any thing like the groups of flowers and other patterns that beautify the silks and damasks of the European looms. Shuja khání silks all have a lustre of floss silks, are soft, and not stiff like the "daryái."

Silk enters into the manufacture of various other fabrics that are not included in this Class. In all brocades or kinkháb pieces, silk is the foundation on which the gold is woven.

Fine silk, and muslin and net, "malmal" and "dúlmiyán," is also much used, but principally for brocading with gold for mandîls or turbans or kerchiefs, and dopattás or scarves, which are much worn at weddings and on ceremonial occasions.

Several fabrics are also imported from Europe, the art of making which is unknown.

Velvet or "Makhmal" is not made in India, but it used to be imported from Russia ; that trade has almost died out on account of the facilities of the English and French trade, which supply a much superior article. The Russian velvet was thin, and also often mixed with cotton.

Satin also, called 'atlas,' is imported. The English and French are the most beautiful, but are thinner and much less valued than the Russian, which is thick.

The Russian satins are both plain and flowered, as damask satins. I have seen among the articles presented by the Khokân Envoys who came to Lahore in 1864-65, several pieces of most brilliant and gaudy flowered satins, which are apparently much admired by Oriental connoisseurs, but would, if worn in Europe, excite a suspicion of madness in the wearer !

Besides woven fabrics, silk is extensively employed in embroidery, and also in kinds of manufactures which are included in the present collection in this Class. These consist of netted fabrics, such as girdles or izârbands, which are long netted sashes, ending in ornamental tassels, and are universally employed to fasten the pyjámas round the waist. Next come every variety of silk rope, cord, and-tassels,—used both in native horse trappings, and also for tying down the coverlets of beds in the native fashion; tassels, head ornaments of silk for plaiting into the hair; necklaces of silk threads to carry charms or gold coins worn round the neck; loops and buttons for chogahs and other articles of the same kind. They are all made by men called "kinâra bâfs," (that is 'edging or fringe-weavers') or "ilâka band" or "patoli".

In specifying the contents of the Silk Class, I must not forget to mention a rather clever manufacture, worked only, as far as I am aware, by one or two men who reside in the Gujranwala District, and come into Lahore to sell their goods. This is the work in coloured chenille.

The chenille or thin velvet piping, is, I believe, imported, and the art consists in arranging lengths of it as required, in circles, loops, lines and patterns (the colour and form being according to the taste and design of the workman) on some surface, either of cloth or wood, so as to form a pattern. In this way the workman will produce on a cushion beautiful groups of flowers and leaves, all made of pieces of chenille of shades sown on, the ground work being filled up uniformly with rows of black chenille.

If the work is on cloth, as for sofa cushions, the chenille is delicately sown on with silk; if on wood, as is often done with trinket boxes, glove boxes, and also on leather shoes, the chenille work is stuck on with gum or glue.

The manufacture of silk in the Punjab will be found to be very much more confined to certain localities than others.

The great place for daryai and gulbadan weaving as well as for plain khes, is Lahore. Amritsar also shares the manufacture to a considerable extent.

Multan is also celebrated for its Silks, especially for its khes and lungis of Silk with gold borders, which are of great richness and beauty. Some 'Shuja khaní' silks are also produced at Multan.

Bahawulpur is especially noted for its Shuja khání silks, and also for a peculiar fabric woven like a gulbadan or striped piece, but made of silk and cotton thread together, which is afterwards highly glazed like European chintz.

At Peshawur silk is woven to a considerable extent, and there is an export trade to Kabul and Turkistan.

In Kashmir the silk manufacture flourishes in all its branches.

There are several other localities in the Punjab noted for peculiar fabrics. The weavers of Khusháb and Bhera in the Shahpúr District make silk lungís and kheses, a few of them are also made in the neighbouring district of Jhelam. There is a silk manufacture also at Bátala in the Gurdaspúr District, in which also the most successful of the attempts to produce raw silk in Punjab, have been made.

The manufacture of netted silk and miscellaneous articles is more widely spread. They are always to be found wherever the original silk weaving goes on, but are extensively made in Nurpur, Pattiala and Nabha.

The following is a list showing the principal varieties of indigenous and imported silk fabrics known in the Punjab.

EUROPEAN SILK FABRICS.

Silk (general name.)
"Governet"—lining silk.
Makhmal, (velvet).
Atlas, (Satin).
Mushajjar, flowered satin (from Arabic *Shajr*, a 'tree,' *Mushajjar* "having trees" or branching flower pattern).
Debái Rumi. Thin crimson silk of Turkey.

INDIAN FABRICS.

Kinkháb : brocade, stiff silk with gold pattern.

Jámdáni, silk with sprigs or flowers wrought in the loom.

Lúngi Banársi : scarves of Benares, made either "yak rukhá" *i. e.* with one right side, or 'do rukhá' or both sides right sides.

Dopatta : a silk piece made for a veil or women's scarf.

Pitambar : a soft silk worn by Hindus for 'dhotis' : it is 10 yards long (*see Glossary*).

Mutka : a coarse silk, 10 yards long and 1½ broad, generally of green color, worn by Hindus for dhoti or waistcloth.

Korá :—a softer kind of mutka : generally white.
Thalla-bund : the same as 'korá' only of white silk with colored spots.
Bund—soft spotted silk for kerchief. Stiff spotted silk is called bund-múmí.
Tassan : a silk cloth worn like a 'mutka,' now out of use.
Tafta : Silk tafeta made of twisted (táfta) thread.
Mahmúdi : a silk fabric not now in use.
Jhirmil :—thin silk cloth (soft).
Rájmahali (not now in use) : thin flowered silk made in Rájmahal in Bengal.
Mushká : a cheap and coarse silk, striped green and white.
Chaklá : a fabric in broad stripes of green and black.
Ambrí : coarse silk, in green and white stripes : not now used.
Kapúr dúr or Kapúr thúria :—Silk gauze with or without a narrow satin stripe.
Bádlá : very thin gossamer like silk cloth.
Zarbáft, a similar fabric woven with gold.

Mandíl Guzráti : a close woven thin silk and gold fabric for turbans of that sort which is formed of coils of cloth tightly twisted up almost like rope.

Bulbul chashm : Silk woven in a diamond pattern.

Mashrú *i. e.* "permitted."—As noticed under Shuja kháni silks, pure silk is not lawful for wear by Mussulmans. A fabric made with a cotton warp and woof (petá) of soft silk in a striped pattern, and having a satiny lustre, is "permitted," and hence called mashrú. "Súfi"—or Bahawalpúr silk and cotton 'gulbadan,' is also lawful, and differs from mashrú, that it has no satiny lustre, and indeed looks like our glazed calico.

Panjab.

Daryái (plain silk) Gulbadan (striped silk) and Dhúpchán (shot silk) lúngi, khes, and súfi, are all described in the sequel (p. 66 &c.)

China, Thibet and Central Asia.

Chíní—large flowered china silk.

Táwár khatai: narrow, thin silk used for temple banners.

Mashrú, solchi } kinds of satin on cotton warp as above described.
" bádshahi }

Nánka—namkin silk, green with black lines, often used for chogas by Kábulis.

Makhmal Iráni: Persian velvet: also Persian satin (atlas).

Dárái Iráni: plain silk of Persia.

Kanáwez:—Shot silk—with a lustre of two colors: the best comes from Bukhára or from Yazd in Persia.

Par-i-pasha—very soft striped silk of Bukhára.

Ráwa: a plain soft silk kerchief or veil 5 yards long.

Alácha—silk cloth 5 yards long, and has a sort of wavy line pattern running in the direction of the length at either side.

Darúa: a fabric of silk and cotton (Yarkand and Kokán) in a pattern most hideous to European eyes: it consists of splashes of color as if one had run into the other.

Rumál Andijání. Andiján silk is famous in Central Asia; this species is a very soft thin silk used for kerchiefs.

GULBADAN.

The samples of this striped silk are numerous, and in great variety as to colour. There are usually two qualities observable, differing principally in their thickness.

The first set are from Amritsar.

439.—[6613]. Silk piece, value Rs. 9.

440.—[6620-4]. 4 pieces of gulbadan by MESSRS. DEVI SAHAI AND CHAMBA MAL.

These were woven expressly for the Exhibition of 1864, being of the finest quality and the greatest breadth (2,000) threads; one of the pieces is dyed with the 'Magenta' or Rosanline dye imported from England. They value from Rs. 4 to 5 per yard.

The next from LAHORE:—

441.—[6637]. Gulbadan, Lahore Central Jail; a narrow silk in drab and white lines of equal breadth, after European fashion.

442.—[6638 & 40]. Two Gulbadan pieces one blue and white stripe; the other dark brown and white, (Lahore Central Jail.)

443.—6654 to 6666]. Series of silk pieces by PAL SHAH, Merchant, of the following colors:—

Green and white,	... value Rs.	29	1	0
Rose color, ...	"	32	0	0
Scarlet, ...	"	40	10	0
Crimson, ...	"	33	0	0
Shot, green and red,...	"	30	12	0
Grimson (yellow stripes),	"	33	8	0
Grape green, ...	"	33	0	0
Do. with scarlet stripe,	"	21	1	0
White with green stripe,	"	30	8	0
Yellow with black stripe,	"	34	8	6

444.—[6670 to 6690]. a series of Lahore made Silks by MESSRS. NATHUMAL AND BHAGWANTA.

Red and green, shot silk, Value Rs. 41 4 0
Lilac, ... Rs. 30 14 6
Rose color and black stripe, „ 36 2 6
Pale lilac and scarlet line, „ 46 8 0
Black with crimson line, „ 38 4 0
Green, ... „ 13 12 0
Scarlet and black line, ... „ 48 8 6

The following are from MULTAN :—

445.—[6850]. Blue and white check gulbadan, 'gulbadan chár khání,' value Rs. 22.

446.—[6851]. White and crimson gulbadan, value Rs. 25.

447.—[6852]. Pink gulbadan, value Rs. 25.

And from DERA GHAZI KHAN.

448.—[6872-5]. Samples of gulbadan value from Rs. 1-8 to 1-12 a yard.

The collection from NABHA contains the following :—

449.—[6902 F to J]. Samples of gulbadan in red, white, scarlet, green and pink, exhibited by the RAJA OF NABBA and PATYALA.

450.—[6907]. 5 pieces of gulbadan of various colours exhibited by His Highness the Maharajah.

DARYAI AND PLAIN SILKS.

These include, check silks, shot silks, silks made on European patterns, handkerchiefs and all plain fabrics.

The AMRITSAR collection contains of:—

451.—[6630—1]. Two pieces of silk of 25 yards each, green and rose colour, value Rs. 37-8 each, by the AMRITSAR JAIL.

452.—[6616]. Piece of silk called "Dargi" * value Rs. 30, by GUJAR MAL.

453.—[6617]. Piece of silk called "Garbi," which is half silk and half cotton, value Rs. 7, by the same.

The following is from the LAHORE collection :—

454.—[6336]. Broad ribbon in European style, pink and white plaid, by the LAHORE CENTRAL JAIL.

* I believe this is only a corruption of "daryai" in the sender's list.—B. P.

455.—[6642—6653]. Series of plain (Daryái) and (dhúp chán) shot silks by PAL SHAH.

Shot, lilac and scarlet, value Rs. 32-8 the piece.

Shot, green and red, value Rs. 32 the piece.

Green shot silk, ... Value Rs. 27-11-6
Green and purple shot, „ 32-13-0
Purple shot, ... „ 38-10-0
Blue and crimson shot, „ 37- 8-0
Black and white check, „ 31-11-6
Brown and white check, „ 31-14-0
Blue and white check, „ 32-13-0
Plain scarlet silk, ... „ 34-11-0
„ gurple, ... „ 28- 3-6
„ bright green, ... „ 29-12-0
„ dark green, ... „ 26-14-6
„ amber coloured (káfúri) „ 27-12-0
„ rose colour, ... „ 33- 0-0
„ crimson, ... „ 24-14-0

456.—[6674 to 6685]. Series of plain and shot silks by NATHUMAL and BHAGWANTA.

2 samples of shot silk, value Rs. 29-8-6 and 41-12-3 the piece.

Black and white check, Value Rs. 29- 6-6
Blue and white check, „ 28- 2-6
Dark green, plain silk, „ 31- 6-6
Purple silk, ... „ 39- 6-0
Yellow silk, ... „ 31- 6-6
Scarlet silk, ... „ 49- 0-0
Dove color (fákhtáí), „ 32-13-0

457.—[6669]. A dozen crimson silk handkerchiefs, and [6669 A]. 7 white silk handkerchief by MESSRS. NATHUMAL and BHAGWATA.

458.—[6671—3]. Three dhotís or soft silk waist cloths worn by Hindus, in yellow white, and crimson.

Value Rs. 27, 14 and 28 each, respectively, by MESSRS. NATHUMAL and BHAGWATA.

Dhotis in silk of a yellow color, are imported in numbers from Benares, under the name of "Pitambar."

These are woven plain like daryáí, but are soft silk, like a European silk pocket-handkerchief.

The following are for the MULTAN JAIL.

459.—[6860]. Neck handkerchief, pink and white plaid, value Rs. 2-8.

460.—[6863 & 3]. Lady's dress, grey, striped with black.

461.—[6864]. White and black check, value Rs. 9-15.

462.—[6855]. Pink and white small check, value Rs. 18-6.

463.—[6866]. ditto larger check, value Rs. 18-12.

464.—[6867]. White and grey stripe, value Rs. 10-15.

465.—[6869]. Black and white stripe broad, value Rs. 18-12.

466.—[6868]. White and rose colored value Rs. 18-6.

And from DERA GHAZI KHAN.

467.—[6870—1]. Red and yellow handkerchiefs ("rumâl daryáí,") by ALLADITTA.

468.—[6875 & 6]. 2 specimens of "daryáí."

469.—[6877]. A silk cap, a skull cap worn by Pathans &c., under the turban.

PESHAWUR.

470.—[6890 & 1]. Silk handkerchiefs, worth Rs. 4-1 each.

471.—[6892]. "Aláícha" silk piece for pyjamas.

472.—[6902 A to E.] 'Daryáí' from Nabha, contributed by the RAJA OF NABHA. viz:—green, purple, red, pink, yellow.

473.—[6904]. 3 plain silks, Patyala, exhibited by HIS HIGHNESS THE MAHARAJAH.

474.—[6996]. Red silk muslin, Patyala.

TURBANS, LUNGIS AND KHES.

These article will be found manufactured in the greatest perfection at Multan, Shahpur, Bhera and Khusháb in the Shahpur district, and at Jhelam. A few come from Batála of Gurdaspur, they are generally woven with a gold or ornamental border. The Lungi and Khes are woven exactly as in the cotton fabric.

The Khes are sometimes plain, sometimes checked but woven on the same principle. The distinction, as before observed, consists in the fact in the khes báfi, the weft is by a skilful design woven in and out of the warp by the aid of multiplied treddles, so as to display the colour of both warp and weft, one thread upon another thread forming a pattern or damask.

The collection in this department in 1864 was rare and very beautiful, the manufactures being quite peculiar and characteristic of the cities above named.

The AMRITSAR district contributed:—

475.—[6614]. A scarlet and green check lungi, gold border, value Rs. 38, by MEAN MAHOMED SHAH.

476.—[6615]. Kamarband or waist sash, value Rs. 7, by GUJAR MAL.

477.—[6629]. Another sash, value Rs. 5.

478.—[6618]. Silk pagri, value Rs. 6, by the same.

GURDASPUR.

479.—[6334 & 5]. 2 plain Khes, of silk and cotton mixed, with gold edges, value 45 and 36, respectively, made at Batála.

JALANDHAR.

480.—[3814]. 6 turbans of silk, made at the Jalandhar Jail.

LAHORE.

481.—[6889]. White patka, or silk scarf with border in silk and gold (kalâbatûn,) value Rs. 175, by MESSRS. NATHUMAL and BHAGWANTA.

BAHAWALPÚR SILKS.

482.—[6890]. Pair of Lahore scarlet Khes, of thick twilled silk with gold border, and narrow edging in black and white, value Rs. 175, by MESSRS NATHUMAL AND BHAGWATA.

JHELAM.

483.—[6808]. Lungi or pattern of Khes, value Rs. 61, by LARINDA SHAH of Pind Dadan Khán.

484.—[6801]. A short silk Lungi by the same, value Rs. 31.

485.—[6810]. Purple Lungi, by the same, value Rs. 22.

The next collection is from SHAHPUR :—

486.—[6811—14]. Lungis in purple, white, scarlet, and with crimson border, (Lungi kinári surkh) from Khûshâb, (valuing Rs. 55, 48, 75, and 25 each.

487.—[6814-12]. Turbans in crimson, white, dove colour, white with black edges, made at the SHAHPUR JAIL.

The following are from MULTAN :—

* "Seven hundred maunds of raw silk are "brought to Multan every year by the Lo- "hanis, chiefly from Bokhara and Turkistan: "these are manufactured in one hundred and "fifty workshops. One man will finish an "ordinary khes or silk scarf in six days, "perhaps three yards long and a foot and a "half wide, taking eight days previously for "the arrangement of the weaving apparatus. "A very handsome khes is finished in sixteen "days. That of the red colour is most valu- "able: it is dyed with cochineal, which is "brought from either Bombay or Bokhara; "that from Bombay is rupee a seer, about "a shilling a pound."

488.—[6986-3]. Turbans in red, blue, black (súrmí) and shot yellow, exhibited by NAZIR KHAIR-ULLAH KHAN.

* Extracted from a personal "Narrative of a visit to Ghuznee, Kabul and Afghanistan, by G. T. Vigne, Esquire," page 21. ("Khes" is spelt in the original, kaish.")

489.—[6789]. Purple khes, gold bordered; by the same.

490.—[6833-9]. Series of Kheses in silk contributed by the MULTAN LOCAL COMMITTEE :

In purple, ...	value Rs.	70
" scarlet, ...	"	75
" crimson,...	"	32
" Yellow, ...	"	60
" crimson 'sâda' or plain khes,	"	35
Another, ...	"	50

491.—[6840-3 & 6856 & 7]. Specimens of Ikláhí or square scarf, in kháki (grey) green, black and yellow, crimson and lilac, value Rs. 28 to 30.

492.—[6844-49 & 6855]. Turbans (dastár) in crimson, scarlet, white, sky blue, grey, lilac and blue black, from Rs. 21 to 23.

493.—[6858-4]. Specimens from the MULTAN JAIL.

Sky blue turban, gold bordered,	value Rs.	12.
Check silk pagri, ...	value Rs.	4-8
Grey turban, ...	"	5-0

SHUJA KHANI SILKS.

494.—Called also Súfí, or lawful for Mahamadans to wear, instead of pure silk, which is not lawful.

They are made at Bahawalpúr; they are exactly like gulbadán (or sometimes súsi) pieces, striped on colored ground; but the fabric is of silk and cotton mixed, the warp being cotton: it is rather stiff and hard, and is glazed with a mucilaginous emulsion of quince seeds.

BAHAWALPUR LUNGIS.

These are soft silks made for scarves or wrappers, having a satin lustre and a pattern produced by the loom; and gold thread is often interwoven ("zar báft").

495.—[6705]. Lungí in pink soft silk and gold.

496.—[6706]. Blue and gold lungi in striped pattern.

497.—[6707]. Check in crimson, black and gold.

498.—[6708]. Khes, showing a different color on either side, called 'dorukhá,' the 'two-faced.'

499.—[6719]. Dove coloured satinette, is unicolorous, but a pattern is damasked in the fabric.

500.—[6735]. Fancy satinette; from the GOVERNMENT TOSHAKHANA.

501.—[6736]. Pink and grey "sari" or wrapper, (GOVERNMENT TOSHAKHANA.)

IMPORTED SILKS.

SUCH AS ARE NOT MADE IN THE PUNJAB.

The principal of these are European, French, English, and Russian.

A few, as the Dakhan silks, Mashru, are fetched from Hindustan, Ahmadabad, Guzrat. &c.

Dopattas, or fancy scarves, are brought from Benares, together with the yellow silk "pitambar," and white spotted black silk called "Bund."

There are also the silks imported from Kabul and Bukhara by the North-Western merchants.

The samples exhibited were from LAHORE:-

[6692]. Blue plush velvet (has the pile flattened down sideways). English.

[6693 and 4]. Samples of rich green, and purple velvet. English.

[6695]. Figured, striped and shot silk (Lyons).

[6696]. Striped fancy satin, brilliantly shot in scarlet and green (Lyons).

[6697]. Another of the same pattern, but shot with brilliant purple instead of scarlet, (Lyons).

These were selected for exhibition from the Government Toshakhana, on account of the extreme beauty and lustre of the colouring, as well as for the clever grouping of the damask pattern introduced.

[6698]. Green satin, with yellow ornamentation (Lyons).

[6699]. Black rich silk, damasked with groups of flowers in satin, (Lyons).

[6732]. Black satin damasked with small bunches of flowers in colors.

The following were imported from CHINA:-

502.—[6726]. Brown figured silk.

503.—[6725]. Yellow figured satin.

504.—[6724]. Figured satin.

505.—[6893]. China silk cloth, imported overland, contributed by HIS HIGHNESS THE MAHARAJA OF KASHMIR.

A few from CENTRAL INDIA, contributed by BRIJ NATH, Darogah of the Lahore Central Jail.

506.—[6727]. Green silk, shot with gold. (Dakhan).

507.—[6728]. Red and gold "sári," flowered border.

508.—[6729]. Shot silk scarf.

509.—6774]. Purple, Mashrú, (a satin, worked with gold in stripes) Dakhan; contributed by the GOVERNMENT TOSHAKHANA.

From BENARES, contributed by the GOVERNMENT TOSHAKHANA,—

510.—[6871]. Khes dorukha, Kalábatúni" gold bordered khes, exhibiting purple face on one side, and yellow on the other.

511.—[6782]. Crimson and gold khes.

512.—[6783]. Gromson and yellow (Dorukha).

From KABUL AND BUKHARA, contributed from the Peshawar District.

513.—[6880]. "Kánawez banafsh," value Rs. 12 for 10 yards, from Bukhara by MUHAMMAD AZIM.

514.—[6979]. "Kánawez Par-i-táus chikini," shot silk kanawez embroidered, Bukhára—the same value.

515.—[6881]. "Gulbadan Kannidár," value Rs. 15 for 7⅓ yards, from Bukhara; contributed by KAZI AMIR JAN.

516.—[6882]. Kanáwez, (red), from Kábul, by MUHAMMAD AZIM.

517.—[6882]. 'Rawá Surkh,'—Bukhara.

518.—[6884]. "Chunni zard, guldár," "flowered yellow chunni"—Peshawar.

519.—[6905]. Two pieces of Kanáwez, a green and purple, contributed by HIS HIGHNESS THE MAHARAJA OF PATYALA.

The KASHMIR Collection exhibited some peculiar fabrics in silk.

520.—[6567]. Piece of "Bádshahi."

521.—[6568]. "Tuwár" of grey (múshi) color, with gold stripes.

MISCELLANEOUS SILK MANUFACTURES NOT BEING WOVEN.

A few of these are mere curiosities, but others are a standing manufacture, such is the Izarband, which is a long netted silk sash, ending in two tassels more or less ornamented, it is used to fasten the pyjmas round the waist.

The following are from AMRITSAR.

522.—[6619]. Silk braid and string by ALLA DITTA.

523.—[6624]. Sets of artificial flowers, roses, &c. in boxes.

524.—[6628]. Skeins of twisted sewing silk, plain and speckled.

GURDASPUR.

525.—[6632 & 33]. Two Izárbands or waist girdles, from Batála; another maker sent 13 specimems of a superior make, which were not included in the original catalogue.

From GUJRANWALLA were sent :—

526.—[6807]. A silk pillow of patchwork of various silks, made at Ramnagar.

527.—[6804]. Silk nets from Ramnagar.

The next collection is from LAHORE.

528.—[6641]. Broad grey braid, made on European pattern, contributed by B. POWELL, ESQUIRE.

529.—[6787—41]. Netted silk neckties, (European style), made by the prisoners in the FEMALE PENITENTIARY.

The next-series are made by AZIMULLAH, kinára báf of Lahore.

530.—[6743]. Silk tassels for a lady's cloak.

531.—[6747]. Silk cord and tassels.

532.—[6748]. Crimson "Sej band" ornamented. The Sej band is a long cord and tassel used to tie down the coverlet of a native bed to the posts of the bed; only used by people of rank and wealth.

[6749]. Is another sample, but plain.

533.—[6750 & 51]. Silk fly-fringe for horses' head. (Makherná).

The next series are by MUHAMMED BAKHSH of Lahore.

534.—[6753]. Crimson Military sash. ('Sirdawâl') value Rs. 10.

535.—[6754]. Do. in crimson and black.

536.—[6755 to 6759 &]. Izárbands in all [6765 to 6769]. varieties of colour, and with tassels variously ornamented. No. 6747 is one is in scarlet, white and green, of rather elegant appearance (from the LAHORE MUSEUM).

537.—[6762]. Three varieties of "paránda." The paránda consists of a long band or cluster of silk threads, finished off at either end with tassels, ornamented with gold thread, beads, &c. This is plaited into the long plaits or tails of hair worn by native women, and especially by girls.

[6745 and 6746]. Are two ornaments of the kind, one in black and silver, the other in crimson and gold.

538.—[6770]. Red "doria," or silken sash. They are worn round the neck to carry gold coins or charms.

539.—[6771]. "Rikâb dawâl" (in purple silk) bands holding the stirrup iron in an native gentleman's saddle, similar to the stirrup leathers of an English saddle.

540.—[6772—6]. "Bâg daur," silken cord halter for leading horses.

These are in yellow, green, and pink silk.

When a native gentlemen goes in ceremony, or in a procession, one of these is attached to his horse, and his attendants on foot run beside him holding the leading rope.

541.—[6675]. Bâg or reins of crimson silk.

The next are from MULTAN :—

542.—[6819 to 6825]. Izárbands in various colours.

543.—[6826]. Variegated sash, called "Izarband haft rang" (literally 7 colours).

544.—[6827]. Sejband "Pinjriwalla."*

545.—[6828 & 9]. Do. "Bâmchi walla."

546.—[6830]. Do. "Baôchi walla."

And from PESHAWUR :—

547.—[6885 to 89]. Series of Izarbands valuing Re 1-4 each.

From KASHMIR :—

548.—[6894]. 4 Sej bands, (silken cords and tassels) from Jammu, value Rs. 75, contributed by HIS HIGHNESS THE MAHARAJA.

549.—[6895 to 6902]. Specimens of dyed floss silk in skeins of white, turquoise blue, black, crimson, yellow, bright green (Zamrudi) light green (Angúri) and scarlet.

From NABBA.

550.—[6902H]. "Jál reshami" netted silk sash.

551.—[6902I]. Izárband.

552.—[6902K]. "Takma," buttons and loops of silk—work for chogahs.

The long pipes, both fixed and flexible, attached to hukas, are often wound over outside with variegated silk which has pleasing effect. It is quite a trade in itself. The flexible tubes are coils of zinc wire covered with Birch bark (Bhojpatr) and then with cloth, and, lastly ornamanted with silk and gold threads. The stiff tubes are made of reeds round over first with cloth, and then with silk.

* (*Vide* 'Glossary and Index' for the meaning of these.)

The forms of these pipe tubes or nechas, will be seen in an illustration to the chapter on Intoxicating Drugs, in vol. I.

Nechas with silk work were sent as follows :—

[6805] Six Pipe tubes from Ramnagar and Gujranwalla.

This Class is concluded with a mention of the chenille work (Kár-i-Makhmal) made by Káimdîn of Wazirabad in the Gujranwalla district.

553.—[6776 and 77 6790 and 6802.] Are cushions for a sofa, worked with groups of flowers and patterns, &c.

554.—[6778] Sets of tassels of colored chenille, and silver thread (such as are used by natives to ornament horses on state occasions).

555.—[6779 and 80]. Boxes ornamented with chenille work.

556.—[6791 to 803]. Specimens in chenille work as follows :—

A Ball.

A necktie.

A bracelet.

Pen-tray.

Tassels.

Boxes.

Mats.

Slippers.

NOTE.

No report on silk fabrics has been received from the Jury of the Exhibition of 1864, but their award of prizes is as follows :—

VII.—SILK MANUFACTURES.

District or Locality.	Prize taker.	Description of articles.	Medal.	Certificate.	Special prize.
Amritsar, ...	{ Devi Sahai and Chamba Mal, }	Seven finest and fast pieces of silk, Nos. 9620—9624,...	1	1	1*
Lahore, ...	Nathu and Bhagwanta,	Collection of silks, ...	...	1	...
Nabha, ...	Raja of Nabha, ...	Collection of silks of local manufacture, ...	1	1	...
Lahore, ...	Muhammad Baksh, ...	Netted and twilled silk manufactures, Nos. 6751—6775, ...	...	1	...
Wazirabad, ...	Kaim Dín, ...	Chenille work, ...	...	1	...
Shahpur, ...	Superintendent Jail, ...	Silks, ...	...	1	...
Multan, ...	Ditto Ditto, ...	Do., ...	1	1	...
Ditto, ...	Manfacturers of the town of Multan. ...	Do., ...	...	1	...

* Lady Montgomery's prize of Rs. 50.

CLASS VIII.
FIBROUS MANUFACTURES.

This Class is of course intended to include only such miscellaneous fibres as are used in manufacture, and other than cotton, silk, or wool.

The Class has been sub-divided into three Divisions, according to the different kinds of articles made.

The first Division will include loom woven fabrics, which are however very few in number: Flaxen and Linen fabrics which would occupy so large a portion of this Class in an European Exhibition, are almost entirely wanting here. In a few jails, a stout canvas has been made from flax, but that is all. As to the native flax, it has never been utilized, except to produce a coarse sting. No other fibre is woven in the province except 'san' (*Crotolaria juncea*), and that only into a sack-cloth or matting called "tât."

The second Division contains the various kinds of paper. The original and ordinary kind of native paper would be the only one in the class, were it not for the more recent experiments in paper making in the various jails, and the varieties introduced by the attempt to utilize various fibres, as tow, madár, *daphne*, straw, and others. The third Division includes ropes, mats, baskets, and all miscellaneous fibrous manufactures generally. Ropes are manufactured principally of san, or of "bánmunj," (*Saccharum munja*—grass). There is not of course generally that demand for cables of all sizes and strength that there is in a maritime country, but still the demand is considerable for agricultural and general purposes. Various fibres are pressed into service as occasion requires, and many species of grass, as well as the bark of the mulberry tree, the fibrous sorts of the Dhâk (*Butea frondosa*), and many others—are included in the class of Raw Fibres, as useful for rope manufacture.

The reader is invited to examine this Class in conjunction with the former Class, (III sub-class E.) in Volume I, as all the botanical and statistical information that could be obtained relative to the fibres themselves, is there detailed.

In the hills, the inner bark of the Dhaman (*Grewia oppositifolia*), resembling gardener's 'bast,'—is much used for ropes, as is also the bhabar, and bagar grass (*Eriophorum cannabinum*). Straw and grass are used in the higher hills for making the rude sandals worn in crossing the precipitous and rocky passes of those regions; and the rope and twig bridges, which are often the only means of crossing many mountainous torrents and rivers, bring into use many strong fibrous barks, twigs of *Fothergilla involucrata*, and the nettle tree bark (*Celtis*) and others.

The use of these fibres is universal all over the tracts of country indicated, and beyond this it is impossible to say that there is any special locality celebrated for fibrous manufactures, except in the case of a few specialites, which will be below enumerated.

Baskets and chicks are made of the invaluable bamboo cut into slips, and but a few articles of this Class are made of the thin flower stalks of the munj grass. Large chicks are also made of the stout munj, then called "*kána*," or of strips of bamboo. Course baskets are made of pilchi, the pliant branches of the smaller Tamarisk. Peshawur and other places are noted for mats and baskets of "patta", and where the date palm grows, date leaves are utilized for fans and mats. Reeds called Dub and dib are made into floor matting.

DIVISION I.

Fibrous Fabrics.

The fibrous manufactures in the form of piece goods or fabrics, are few; 'San,' for matting, and flax recently introduced in a few of the jails, are the only fibres employed. To these may be added the madár fibre, or rather floss for the seed-pods. This has been at tried; but is present more of a curiosity than a useful fibre.

[6908]. "Tât patí" from the Jail Sirsa.

This is a coarse matting made in narrow pieces from string of 'san' fibre (*Crotalaria juncea*): the sample in question costs 0-2-3 per yard. It is much used for packing purposes, and for coarse flooring. It is made at every Jail, and is common all over the country. Particularly good samples were from Hushyarpur, [6927] by Mr. Christie, and from Lahore, also [6935 A.] [6967 & 8] from Gujrat.

557.—[6933]. Canvas made from Flax grown at Syalkot.

558.—[ ]. Several scarves and handkerchiefs of fine linen made at Belfast from flax grown at Syalkot by the Indian Flax Company.

Canvas was also sent from Lahore Jail and from Multan, of two qualities, valuing $5\frac{1}{2}$ anas and 0-4-8 per yard, respectively; also from Agra Jail (7041) and Gugaira (7008).

559.—[7019]. Table napkin made from madár floss, Dera Ismail Khan.

The Shahpúr Jail gained a medal in the International Exhibition of 1862 for its manufacture of madár.

In the Punjab Exhibition, besides the above, some towels were shown made of madár and cotton mixed, also a rug made of madár (coloured).

This fibre which is short, smooth, glossy, and looks like short lengths of pale yellowish white floss silk, is produced from the ripe seed-pods of the madár or *Ak* (*Calotropis Hamiltonii*). Dr. Forbes Watson reported on it thus:—It is deficient in strength and difficult to spin on account of the smoothness of the individual fibres. Attempts in England to work it by means of machinery have hitherto practically failed.

* * * * * * * *

Some of the fibre has been sent to Messrs. Thresher and Glenny, who have for a long time been devoting attention to the subject. These gentlemen are at length enabled to report their ability to turn it to account, if obtainable here in a good clean condition at 35£ a ton ($3\frac{3}{4}$d. a lb.). Dr. Walker (of the Agra Jail) reported that it might be collected at about Re. 1-8 per maund, or about $1\frac{3}{4}$d. a lb. From experiments made at Dera Ismail Khan, however, it appears that the collection of the floss has not been accomplished at the desired rates.

The fibre requires bleaching, and answers best when mixed with cotton.

It has been tried with the cloth made by the warp of cotton, and the weft of pure madár or the warp half cotton and half madar, and weft three parts madar to one cotton. Also it has been tried with cotton in various proportions, uniform for all the threads of the fabric.

The fibre only requires cleaning and separation from seeds and dirt by aid of the usual bow. No charka is required when made into threads. Before weaving, the thread requires steeping for four and five days in water, sometimes a little Methi seed (*Trigonella*) and gum is added.*

* Journal of the Agri-Horticultural-Society of Bengal, Volume VII, page 25.

It is important not to confuse the fibre of the seed-pod, which I have called floss, with the fine strong fibre which is obtained from the stem of the plant.

To produce the latter fibre, sticks of the madár are cut about 12 or 18 inches long; the outer bark is then carefully peeled off, and the fibre is drawn from the inner part next the stem. Several threads are then placed together and twisted up by hand. No water is used at all. Madár fibre is used on the Indus for fishing nets.

The fibre is very strong, and is also suitable for weaving, as it amalgamates with silk. It is valued by the Agri-Horticultural Society of Bengal at 30£ to 40£ a ton.*

Besides giving these two fibrous products, madár is useful medicinally. Its wood makes charcoal, (especially the large species, *(A. Gigantea)* common in the lower provinces; and its juice yields a substitute for gutta-percha.

* Journal VIII, page 74.

DIVISION II.

PAPER.

Leaving aside the subject of imported papers, and those manufactured at Serampore, the papers used in the Punjab may be divided into three classes.

1.—Native paper, which is made in many places, but especially at Sealkote.

2.—Native paper made in jails. These are often made of various fibres, and made experimentally. In this class I include Daphne paper, &c.

3.—Kashmir paper.

Ordinary native paper is made of various sized sheets, and of different qualities, which are known by different names; the material from which it is made is almost always the same, the old "tât patti"—which is bleached, washed, and reduced to pulp. The only other material commonly used is old paper; but European paper, as also that printed or written on with English ink is useless, the former from the difficulty of reduction to pulp, the latter from difficulty of bleaching and removing ink stains. * Native paper-making as practised without assistance from Europeans, is worse than it was; no improvement has been made in machinery, and the makers will not adopt new fibrous substances. The process of making paper is simple, but is such that even with the utmost care, fine and thin paper can never be produced by it. Even at Gujrat, where the best jail made paper is produced, the paper is only excellent as native paper.

At first the fibrous material, chiefly old gunny cloth, or tât, is cut up by hand into little pieces with a rude iron chopper; the dust is then shaken out of it; it is next moistened; mixed with a certain quantity of "sajji," and is submitted to the "jhandar" or pounder. The pounder consists of a heavy beam of wood, working on a pivot, so as to form the long arm of an unequal lever; the end of the arm is fitted with a cylindrical block of wood, on which is fixed a small iron tooth or central hammer, which strikes upon a stone placed below: this lower end of the lever strikes down into a pukka trough, which is partly filled with the fibre to be pounded. A workman stands with one foot on the shorter end of the beam or "jhandar," and by pressing it down, forces the loaded end up, which in its turn falls by its own weight, crushing the fibre that is beneath it. A man crouches down in one corner of the trough, and keeps throwing the fibrous material on to the stone under the beam each time as it descends with a heavy thump. Of course the quantity of fibre submitted to the blow each time is very small, but by gradually throwing one piece after piece, the whole gets pounded. The material is then taken out, washed in a stream of water, made into square cakes with more sajji, and left exposed to sun and air for some time, after this it is again pounded, and again washed. When the whole is in a rude pulp and tolerably clean, it is mixed with water in a masonry trough, stirred up continually by men with bamboo sticks, and when the whole pulp is of a proper consistency, the paper-maker sits down with his strainer frame, and dipping it in with a peculiar knack, catches a fine layer of pulp on the strainer, which, when the water has drained off, forms a sheet of paper; these sheets are placed one over the other as they are made. When a sufficient number has been collected, the mass is taken away to a dry wall previously prepared with a smooth coating of plaster. The workman then takes a thin broad

* The difficulty has recently been overcome in the Lahore Central Jail. The paper produced is good, but by no means cheap.

and stiff brush, like an English house brush, only thinner, and detaching sheet by sheet, spreads each flat against the wall, to which it adheres by its own moisture; the workman gently smooths it over with the brush. When dry, the paper readily peels off, and is then ready to be polished. This is effected by smearing each sheet all over with a kind of starch prepared from wheat, and when this is dry a gloss is imparted to the paper by rubbing over and over each sheet with a round smooth flint stone over a concave surface of smooth wood.

The frame or strainer on which the pulp forming the sheet is collected, is a wooden frame covered with a strainer of fine grass stems. It is obvious that by this means a very thin or fine paper cannot be made; to make fine paper, requires a strainer of inconceivably fine metallic wires.

This process is followed with but slight variations wherever paper is made, the difference in quality of paper results from the fineness and good pounding of the fibre, the quantity and clearness of the water available for washing the fibre,* and the skill of the workman in straining it.

I now proceed to enumerate the known kinds of paper, beginning with the ordinary paper manufactured at Sealkot. The manufacture at other places of the common sorts need no special remark.

560.—[10105]. Sealkot paper made by Alfá, Sealkot.

[10113]. A sample of the paper imported into Lahore, and shewn by HAR BHAGWAN.

The following account of paper making has been received from Sealkot :—

" Nothing can be ascertained as to when the manufactories for paper started, and who was the originator. The origin of the manufacture is however supposed to have been about 600 years ago, in Imperial times, when Sealkot was a city of great importance. The common story runs, that a man whose name has not been handed down to the present time, used to have the pulp beaten by the people, but lifting the pulp from the water was done in secret, in a walled enclosure, and each sheet was valued by him at the then current Rupee. One day his son-in-law was rather curious to know the art, and through a hole in the wall of the enclosure peeped and found out the way it was done; after this it became quite common. The chief places for paper manufacture in the Sealkot District are Rangpúr, Hírapúra and Nákapúr, suburbs of the city of Sealkot. From excavations and ruins it seems that the site where these villages are were the old manufactories for paper. The mountain stream, the Aik, flows by these villages, and the manufacturers attribute the excellency of their paper to some quality in the water of the Aik. The paper of first quality manufactured in this district is called Jahángírí—is named after the great Mogul Emperor. It seems he came to Sealkot and ordered a superior kind of paper to be made, the quality made was what is now produced. It is the most expensive, and lighter in weight than other descriptions of native paper. It is chiefly used in manuscripts of the *Kuran;* the *Pothís* of the Hindus; and for Sanads. The rest are, for common use, of different qualities. One half of the total

* This is a very important point. The excellence of the Kashmir paper is no doubt largely owing to the abundance and clearness of running water available for manufacturers. At Sealkot also the manufacturers employ the water of the Aik, a hill torrent, which runs freely at certain seasons. Jail Officers wishing to improve in paper making, will do well to turn their attention to the means of increasing the facilities of washing the fibre.

quantity of paper manufactured is sent to Amritsar, and the other half taken by the Kakezais, who are *Bopáris*, as far as Peshawur: very little finds its way lower down than Amritsar.

The paper makers are a mixed community of Awáns, Tarkáns, and Lohárs. Each factory or Kárkhána is a separate firm. In the time of the Emperors the yearly proceeds used, it is said to amount to 8 lacs. The paper was in popular use at Delhi; during the Sikh rule the business declined to 20 factories, and a sale of Rs. 25,000. Under British rule, the manufactories have again increased: there are 82 factories in all, giving employment to nearly 1,000 men, and yielding an income of ¾ths of a lac yearly.

In 1855, the statistics* of the paper manufactories of Sealkot and neighbouring villages were as follows:—

Village.	Factories.	No. of Jhandars or pounders.	Men employed.			Quantity and value of paper made per annum.	
			Proprietors.	Laborers.	Total.	Number of Reams.	Value at Rs. 3-8 average.
Rangpúra, ...	44	105	200	225	425	8,925	Rs. 31,237
Rajpúra, ...	30	100	185	205	390	8,500	22,650
Hírapúra, ...	8	21	45	61	106	1,685	6,247
Total, ...	82	226	430	491	921	19,110	Rs. 60,134

561.—[10116]. Quality of paper called Jahângírí, (a quality supposed to have been ordered only by the Emperor). It is of extra large size. HAR BHAGWAN OF LAHORE.

JAIL MADE PAPERS.

562.—[10,028]. Country paper from Delhi Jail, at 4 anas a quire.

563.—[10,036]. From Sirsa, and [10,037]. The same made from old paper.

564.—[10,041]. From Ambálla Jail.
[10,060]. From Kotla.
[10,448]. From Dharmsala.
[10071] From Kangra.
[10192—10204] From Jhang, of all colors.
[10210]. Muzaffargarh.
[10240]. Dera Ghazi Khan.
[10258]. Peshawur.
[10271]. Malerkotla, and Agra.

All these are manufactured in the manner above described, either of old tát or of old paper (raddí).

565.—[10,135]. Paper made from Madár fibre, Sirsa jail, value, Rs. 3-4-0 a Gadi or ream. In both white, red, green and yellow colors.

The process of making the paper is thus described by the Assistant Commissioner in charge of the Sirsa Jail:—

This paper is made from the fibrous stalks of the Madar plant. The stalks are picked during the winter months after the plant has flowered. They are then dried; the fibre separated by hand, and thick ropes made. It is from old and worn out ropes that the paper is manufactured. The old rope, which is much used in this District and adjoining Bikanir territory, is cut into small pieces, well pounded, and

*Extract for Prinsep's Settlement Report, page 25.

soaked for 3 days with sajji and chunam—lime (slaked). This material after being well washed, forms a pulp from which the paper is manufactured. Rope made from this fibre is undoubtedly stronger than flax rope, and at the same time possesses the fineness of silk. The finest cord and twine can also be manufactured.

The paper in the Exhibition was of the fibre of the stem, but it is equally possible to make it out of the silky floss of the pods. This requires bleaching, but is by nature so short and fine a fibre, that the labor of pulping it is inconsiderable. I have not yet seen a piece of this paper from the Punjab.

566.—[10,056]. Daphne paper by Mr. G. Jephson, Simla.

567.—[10057]. Daphne paper for Sangaum, Kanawar, by Captain G. Houchen.

568.—[10,063]. Daphne paper from Kangra (Dharmsala) Jail.

Several species of Daphne and Desmodium, yield an inner bark, which furnishes a strong and supple paper. The species commonly used are *Daphne papyracea* and *oleoides*—'Jiku', *Sutlej valley*; 'Katilál', *Kàghàn*; 'Laghunai' (Pashtú); 'Nigi' *Kullu*; 'Sanarkat' *Kashmir*; and *Desmodium tiliæfolium*, 'Kálímurt,' *Sutlej valley*; 'Chamkát' *Hazara*; 'Bre or Kathí,' *Kullu and Kangra*.

The latter is more easily prepared than the former. It is used in the jails of Dharmsala and Rawalpindi. The Daphne is more confined in its range of growth than Desmodium, and is also of a smaller size and more difficult to work.

The following account of the growth of Desmodium and Daphne, and the method of preparing the lower bark for paper making, is extracted for a paper communicated by Dr. Cleghorn, to the Agri-Horticultural Society.

Daphne oleoides.—This appears to be one of the characteristic plants of the valleys of the outer Himalayas, occurring at an elevation of 4,000 to 8,000 feet, the basin of all the Punjab rivers from the Tonse to the Nainsukh.

Local names.—These vary in the different provinces: "Jeku" in Bussahir; "Nigi" in Kullu "Kutilál" in Hazara and Khagan; and "*Sanarkat*" in Kashmir. The yellow berries are considered purgative by the natives, in this respect the plant coincides with its congeners, and finds a place in the Materia Medica (see Honigberger's Thirty years in the East" p. 268.), but the use of the fibre is not known.

Process of preparing fibre.—The inner layer of bark is separated from the pliant branches without any skilled process or other treatment, than the careful removal of the outer bark or epidermis, with any knots or asperities attached to it. The manipulation requires patience, but may be easily done by women or boys;—a fair price for the labour would probably be about 2 Rs. per maund.

The inner bark is the best part, and the properties which render it valuable are toughness and good color. The way in which I prepared the fibre was this: twelve small boys went to the hill side returning to my tent with freshly stripped bark; they sat down and cleared off the epidermis with their own blunt knives; the fibre was then placed in the sun and when thoroughly dry it was tied up in small bundles The boys received one anna each in the evening and returned next morning in great numbers. In this way 12 boys in two days cleared 40 pounds of dry fibre under my supervision, but with practice a larger quantity might be expected.

The main points are, to see that the fibre is *cleared of woody integument and epidermis*, and that it is *received* and *kept dry*.

Experience gained.—Several facts have been ascertained which may be mentioned. (1) The plant does not suffer from free cutting of the branches, throwing out vigorous shoots in a few months. (2) The bark of one year old shoot separates more easily than that of old branches. (3) The operation becomes more difficult as the weather becomes colder. (4) Plunging the branches into hot water for ½ hour facilitates the stripping process. The bark should then be steeped for several days in running water and bleached in the sun. I have not *tried the boiling in a lye of ashes* but this operation would *probably apply equally well to the bark of Daphne oleoides, as to that of Broussonetia papyrifera, which is thus treated in China and Japan.*

The cleaning might be done more cheaply by machinery than by hand—the bark should be placed in hot water and then dried in the sun. It should afterwards be passed under rollers—(as in a common mangle) when the remaining portion of epidermics will fall off.

Trial at Dharmsalla.—Two bundles of the fibre were sent for experiment to the Jail at Dharmsalla, and specimens of paper manufactured from it are submitted to the meeting. Major Mercer states that too much time was employed in bleaching, but being satisfied as to the excellence of the material, he is in treaty for a supply of 200 maunds from Chumba.

Desmodium tiliæfolium.—I have to notice another plant which attains a *larger* size than the *Daphne*, occupies a *wider* range (in the same valley), and grows much lower, so that the fibre will be available at a less cost in the plains.

Native Names.—There are *Shuk-sing, i. e.*, Paper tree on the Rotang Pass;—*Kanti*, at Dalhousie,—*Kulanchi* at Murree,—and *Chamkát* in Khagan.

My attention, was drawn to this plant more recently. The bark has also been used as a paper material in the Dhurmsalla Jail, and also in that of Rawulpindee. The fibre is coarser, but more suited for the native process, and it certainly can be procured at a cheaper rate than that of the Daphne from the ease with which the layers of bark are separated.

When it is remembered that the quantity of paper manufactured in our Jails depends very much on the quantity of tat (*i. e.* old ropes and gunny bags) procurable that the supply of this material is uncertain, and that usual cost is about the same, viz., 2 Rs per maund, I trust these remarks may not be considered as wholly useless. It remains to be seen, if the preparation of these fibres can be conducted on a large scale how far they would be remunerative if so conducted."

When made into paper, the Daphne or Desmodium fibre is usually treated in the same manner as the ordinary tât fibre; paper made of it usually turns out the same colour as ordinary native paper; but it as such tenacity, that the paper can be made very thin, and yet of surprising strength and durability.

In 1863 I experimented on the fibre at the Sealkot Jail. I found that it would not answer if it was merely submitted to the ordinary pounding process under the "jhandar." The paper turned out was indeed of great strength, but was full of flaws and bits of black looking fibre. Very fair paper was made by mixing tat-pati &c., or old paper with it. To make really good paper, the fibre requires boiling with alkaline lye: this I observe is always done in Nepal. The paper made at the Dharmsalla and Rawalpindi Jails is more remarkable for its strength, than for its excellence in their respects: the other varieties of the paper are especially suited for lining or packing tea boxes.

In Nepal, the manufacture of paper from Daphne is celebrated. It would be foreign to my purpose to give a detailed account of the process; but the reader can obtain information for himself by consulting Volume V of the *Transactions of the Agri-Horticultural Society of India*, at pp. 220—231.

The Nepalese process consists of first boiling the slips of inner bark (which they commonly take fresh from the tree) in a strong alkaline solution obtained by passing water through the ashes of oak wood. After the boiling has gone on about half an hour, the bark will be quite soft, and have nearly absorbed all the liquid. Next the mass is placed in a shallow stone mortar, and continually beaten with a mallet or pestle till reduced to a pulp.

The pulp is then mixed with a little pure water. To make paper, a wooden frame, the size of the sheets required to be made, is taken (the frame being covered with very porous cloth, or fine grass or wire meshes as usual,) upon the pulp the frame or sieve is placed, and both are floated in a cistern of water. A quantity of the pulp is put in the sieve, which is then shaken about, the fine pulp passing through on to the paper frame, and the workman, by skilfully agitating the latter, causes the pulp to spread all it over, after which he withdraws it in the usual manner, and the sheet of paper is made: the sieve retains all the lumpy or coarse particles of the pulpy matter.

Some samples of Daphne fibre have been sent to Europe, and fine letter paper, admirably suited for "foreign post," has been made therefrom. I have seen a specimen of this light paper, which could only be torn with the greatest difficulty. The Daphne paper is said to resist the ravages of insects, and specially of the *Lapisma*, or fish insect, so destructive to paper. The Nepalese frequently prepare the paper by coating it with a surface of yellow arsenic *(hartál)* afterwards glazing it with rice starch; but it seems that the paper is almost as durable unprepared. In one of the papers in the transactions of the Agri Horticultural Society before quoted, Dr. Campbell, mentions that he had seen a work in fresh and perfect preservation, 150 years old, and adds that the natives say the paper lasts unchanged for 300 to 400 years. The arsenicated paper just now described is admired for manuscripts from its gloss and yellow colour. Dr. Campbell mentions that the paper has been successfully used for making ceilings of rooms: the paper can be made of any size up to thirty feet long by twelve broad.

569.—[10139]. Paper from old rags, RAWALPINDI JAIL.

Paper made from this material is the normal kind at home, but in the Punjab it is rare, and only made in jails: ordinary native manufacturers never use cotton rags. Although cotton forms the universal clothing of all classes, yet rags are not abundant as they are in Europe. This is partly owing to their not being in demand, partly that the very poor people continue to utilize, in some way or other, cloth which would in Europe be consigned to the paper-maker. Practically, I believe there would be considerable difficulty in collecting a few tons of rags even in a large city.

570.—[10148]. Paper made from date tree leaves (*Phœnix sylvestris*) RAWALPINDI JAIL.

The paper is of a green colour, and is seldom made: it is very tough. The leaves of the palm are used for mats and baskets, but would no doubt yield a paper material if well boiled with alkali and pounded.

571.—[10149]. Paper made from Bhúsá, RAWALPINDI JAIL.

This paper is made of chopped straw or bhúsá; it is not a good paper, though it might be used for packing purposes: it is also interesting as showing how even a brittle, stiff, siliceous substance can be made into paper. In Europe great advance has been made in the manufacture of straw paper by subjecting the material to the chemical action of substances which destroy and remove the siliceous coating of the straw leaving only the fibre; but the paper hitherto made in the jails has not had the benefit of such treatment. If the bhúsá is mixed with a proportion of old tát, or other soft paper material, the quality of the paper is much impreved.

572.—[10152]. Paper made from flax fibre, refuse or tow, GUJRAT JAIL.

In a vernacular account of the manufacture of this paper, which I have before me, it is stated that the flax is in the form of taut before it is cut up and made into paper. I do not know the reason of this, nor was I previously aware that flax was ever made into "taut"; the common country tát which is used for common paper is made of san. The Rawalpindi specimen, which is valued at 6 annas a quire, is apparently made from the fibre.

The refuse, or tow, of flax, is an excellent paper material. At Sealkot, the Indian Flax Company produced a large quantity, but the Commissariat Department bought it up at so high a price for packing and other purposes, that the jail manufactory could not afford to buy it! In the Gujrat Jail the process of making the papers is thus described—the frequent repetition of the pounding process under the "jhandar" at every stage is not usual.

The material after being cut up, is put under the "jhandar," after this it is washed, and after being mixed with a proportion of sajji (crude soda) and lime, it is continuously pounded for three days. The fibre being then moulded into great cakes or flat lumps called "thoba," is exposed to the air and sun for thirty days; after this it is again pounded during two days under the jhandar, after which the fibre is washed and again pounded for another day. This washing and pounding is next repeated for another day; the fibre is once come collected into cakes called "chaklis," and exposed to the sun for 10 days more. When thoroughly dry it is pounded during 8 days in a dry state, then moistened and pounded again, after which it is washed, and then undergoes a final pounding for 2 days; after which the pulp can be prepared in the masonry tank, and the paper made in the usual way. I should observe that the fine thick even quality of this paper, and its good colour, is the result of the frequent washing and pounding to which the fibre is subjected: none of the common qualities of paper get half so much labor expended on them.

In order to produce on the above principle, one "gadi" or ream, and 5 "dastas" or quires of paper, a period of two months is requisite, and the labor of 98 prisoners.*

* Pounding paper for	22 days	@ 3 men per day		=66
Washing &c.,	6 days	@ 3 men		=18
Sizing	1	4 men		= 4
Polishing paper	...	...	...	= 6
Making paper	...	...	...	= 4
			Total	98

The profits yield 1 anna per diem per man.

The materials used are—

A maund of old flax, taut, worth Rs. 3.

Sajji 1 maund	... =	Rs. 1-9.
Chuna (lime) 5 seers	... =	1 anna.
Soap, Wood, Oil &c.,	...	8 annas.
	Total	Rs. 5-2.

The price of the paper per dasta is 12 annas, so the total value produced is Rs. 11-4, and the profit Rs. 6-2.

573.—[10160]. Paper made from Chichrá root (*Butea frondosa*)—GUJRAT JAIL.

This paper is made of the following materials:—

Root of chichra, 30 seers,	... =	6 annas.
Old taut and paper 10 seers,	... =	12 annas.
Sajji one maund,	.. =	Re.1-9
Chuna (lime) 5 seers,	... =	0-1
Miscellaneous,	... =	0-8
	Total	Rs. 3-4

The root is first pounded and cut up, and then submitted to the jhandar for two days, after which it is washed, then sajji and lime is mixed in, and two days more pounding given; then it is dried in the sun for four days; afterwards, the earth and sand is washed out, and the pounding repeated but in a dry state; then it is soaked for 3 days and pounded again and then washed and again pounded for three days. The fibre is now made into flat cakes called (chakli,) and dried in the sun. It is again pounded first in a dry state, and then after being wetted once more it is washed and pounded. At this stage the rough pulp is mixed with old taut and old paper, (10 seers) and the whole pounded together for two days, and then washed. After this the pulp is ready for the tank.

The cost of paper of this kind, is as above stated, Rs. 3-4 and it takes 4 months to make two reams, worth Rs. 5, so there is a profit of Re. 1-12 for the prisoner's labor. 98 men are employed as before: 3 pie is the profit per man.

The paper does not sell well, nor is it strong, but breaks when folded.

574.—[10156]. Paper from plantain fibre, with a specimen of the plantain leaf fibre employed—GUJRAT JAIL.

This paper is made of—

Plantain stems,	20 seers,	Rs.	0	4	0
Old taut and paper,	20 „	„	1	8	0
Sajji,	... 80 „	„	1	2	9
Lime,	... 4 „	„	0	1	0
Miscellaneous,	... „	„	0	6	3
	Total,		3	6	0

The plantain is cut up and pounded much as before, with a slight difference as to the time required for pounding, as the fibre is more easily reduced to pulp. The cost is Rs. 3-6, and the result 2 reams, worth Rs. 5, and it takes only 1¼ month to make. So the profits are Re. 1-10, and only 68 men are employed;* the profit of labor of prisoners is 4 pie per man. The paper is not yet in use and was made for an experiment.

575.—[510150]. Blotting paper—RAWULPINDI JAIL.

This paper, as also that from Gujrat (10161), is very well made, and almost equal to European blotting paper. It is however rather thicker, and not so soft and bibulous. It consists of rather a fine class of native paper, left unsized, but smoothed and dyed pink with kussumba (safflower). The Gujrat price is 5 annas a quire.

576.—[10109]. Paper made from the fibre of maize, and of the *Sorghum saccharatum* or Chinese sugar-cane. MR. B. POWELL.

The leaves and sheaths of the plant yield a fibre from which paper can be made, and is used very largely in Austria. The sample exhibited was made only experimentally. I do not know where it was made, probably at one of the Jails. *See Vol. I, page* 516.

577.—[11010]. Kashmírí paper. LAHORE.

This beautiful paper, the best of all native manufactures, can be purchased everywhere. It is in great demand for making manuscript copies of all the more valued authors; it is also used for complimentary letters and polite correspondence amongst natives generally. It is distinguished by its fine gloss and polish, its evenness and freedom for flaws, also by its white wax-like color and appearance.

578.—[ ] Several qualities of paper from Kashmir, HIS HIGHNESS THE MAHARAJA.

1. "Dah Mushti."
2. "Reshami."
3. "Sadar jû."

Some of these such as Dah Mushti, refer to the size of the sheets—viz., so many hand broad, (dah) ten (musht) hand,—paper ten hands broad.

579.—[10111]. Series of gold ornamented papers. LAHORE.

These papers are for complimentary letters or "Kharítas." They usually have a gold and colored ornamental border, and are prepared by hand labour on Kashmírí paper.

The varieties are—

---

* Pounding at the Jhandar 13 days @ 3 men

per diem, ...	=	39
Washing at 5 days @ 3 men, ...	=	15
Sizing, ...	=	4
Polishing, ...	=	6
Paper making, ...	=	4
Total, ...		68

"Zar fishán," (sprinkled with gold all over).

"Tikli dar," having spots or flowered sprigs in gold paint arranged over the paper.

A letter written on this paper is placed in a large envelope of brocade with gold embroidery, or of cloth of gold, the strings of which are then closed and sealed with a hugh solid mass of sealing wax bearing the seal of the Raja or dignitary sending the letter. The letter is sometimes still further enclosed in a bag of white net, which is called "Dul miyán." Several of these were exhibited from Lahore by PANDIT MANPHUL.

580.—[1039]. Coloured papers. RAWAL PINDI JAIL.

These papers were also exhibited from several other Jails They consisted of the ordinary native paper colored pink with safflower; yellow with turmeric; blue with indigo, and various other mixed colors. All the summons of the District Criminal Courts are printed on yellow paper, and warrants on lilac, so these papers are in some demand. Colored papers are much used by natives for making fancy lanterns used at festivals, and at this they are very expert. The lanterns are made up of bits of talc, colored paper, &c, the frame work being of slips of bamboo, or rarely wire.

DIVISION III.

Fibrous Manufactures, other than Fabrics.

In this department not much novelty, and very little elegance is displayed ; but there are many articles which are extensively useful and extensively traded in, which come under this Division. The materials which principally come into use for these manufactures are—

1. Straw.
2. "Dib," the Bulrush, (*Typha elephantina*).
3. The leaves of the Palm, (*Phœnix sylvestris*).
4. Leaves of the Dwarf Palm (*Chamærops Ritchiana*).
5. Slips of Bamboo, (*B. arundinacea* and *A. utilis*).
6. The sheaths of the flower-stalk, and also the flower-stalk itself, of *Saccharum munja*.

Besides these, the materials for making string rope &c., both in the hills and plains, are very varied ; every tree or plant that has a fibre, or is known to the people of the places where it abounds, can be occasionally pressed into service.

581. [ ] Matting of the Rush—*Typha elephantina*. "Chatai"—Lahore.

This is the best and most durable kind of matting made in the *plains*, and is seen in all houses. When dry, the flag or reed, is flat, tough, and pliable ; the mat is made something on the principle of a "durree." A long pole, the breadth of the intended mat, is perforated with a series of holes about an inch apart, through these holes a number of parallel lines of string made of 'munj' are passed, forming what would be the *web* of an ordinary fabric. This *web* being stretched out to its full length, is attached to a pole or bamboo at one end ; and the other end of the strings are gathered in twos or threes and fastened off on a row of pegs. The workmen now sit down on the web, and commence at one end with the rushes, twining them in and out, and over and under the munj strings forming the web, as in cloth weaving. The beam with the holes can of course be moved further back as the work progresses, and the web is by this means kept firm and taut. The rushes are moistened and well beaten with a wooden mallet, which makes them flat as well as pliable for the weaving process. The *sides* of the mat are finished off as the process goes on, by collecting the long ends into little bunches, and then turning one under the other, which forms a long sort of plait at the edges of the mat ; the *ends* of the mat are secured by being sewn up with long stitches of double munj string. If the mat is well made, it has a firm, elastic, and striated surface, of a light brown color. I have seen them so well made as almost to supersede the use of a carpet. They are generally used under a durree or carpet on account of the floors which are usually of pucka or lime plaster. The price of such matting is about Rs. 12 per 100 square yards.

582. [ ] Matting of the Palm leaf.

This species is almost as much used as the former for a floor cloth ; but the fibrous flat leaves are also split and made up into hand-fans, fly-flaps, and baskets. The long palm leaf is cut down, and side leaflets are torn off the central mid-rib or stalk ; each leaflet thus forms a piece of smooth, flat, and very tough fibre, of a pale drab-green color, and can be utilized as it is, or may be split up into fine pieces, according to the work required of it.

Fly-flaps are frequently made of bunches of the leaves split up into fine shreds, and secured on a wooden handle; for this purpose also some kinds of grasses are used.

The mats of date leaves are not made like the 'dib' mat, on a foundation of string, but are solely formed of an interlacement of long narrow leaves, and finished off at the end, with the aid of string, being stitched round the sides—munj string is not used for this purpose, but "san" (*Crotolaria*).

The fans and baskets are made on a similar principle, only the work and the slips used are finer, and greater care is taken in finishing off and cutting the projecting ends, which are carefully turned in.

These date palm leaf mats, &c., are only made in districts where the trees grow. In the southern parts of the province, as far as the Derajat, the tree abounds, and there we have these manufactures in the greatest excellence.

583. [ ] Matting of the *Chamærops Ritchiana*, from PESHAWUR, KOHAT, &c., "*Patta.*"

These mats are made from the *Chamærops*, which is indigenous in the Salt Range and beyond, in Hazara, Peshawar, Bunnoo and Waziristan. The leaf is more fan shaped than the date palm, and is familiar to all who has seen the *Palmetto* leaf; but it has no stem to speak of. The flower rises from a tall thick stalk covered by a number of overlapping, scaly spathes, on this the flower-head rises covered with branches. The flowers when they burst forth are like those of other palms, small colourless fleshy bells, growing in clusters on the ends of the little branches of the flower stalk. The fruit is a round, hard stone or berry, which hangs at the end of the branches of this stalk, and is used to make rosaries. The local name (in Pushtu) of the plant is "mazáré" and in Sindh "Pfís"

From Peshawur I have received the following account:—

"Smooth matting is made from the smaller and more slender strips of the "patta," and where a particularly fine kind is not obtainable, the object is gained by splitting up the larger patta into slips of the required breadth. Matting is made both at Peshawur and Kohat, but usually of a coarse kind The finest and most expensive is that obtained from the Doába, and made by Mohmands and Otmánkhails in the hills; those of Pindyálí are locally famed for their expertness in this work. The prices vary according to quality, the smoother sorts being somewhat expensive.

Baskets are made of the finer matting, and they sell at from 4 to 20 per rupee. A piece of smooth matting, usually about 4 or 5 feet long by 2 or 2½ feet broad, sells for a rupee if of the very best; and the coarser kinds vary in prices, some even selling as cheaply as 8, 12, and even 20 pieces per rupee.

The mats are very neatly made, are compact, glossy, and of a pale yellowish or drab color; they are manufactured on the same principle as the date mats, but can be readily distinguished by their superior texture and smoothness. Fans and small mats from Peshawur are largely imported into Lahore, and other places where the Patta is not found.

584. [ ] **Baskets and other vessels of Patta—BUNNOO.**

They are made of the same material as the last, but exhibit a peculiarly neat and solid texture unlike the interlacing of the mats. They look as if constructed of a series of smooth rings closing compactly one over the other. They are made doubtless upon a foundation of

* Royle's Fibrous Plants, p. 925.

circular ribs, woven over with very fine slips of patta. Some of the articles were in the form of flat dishes; others of baskets; and some were made round mouthed like "lotas" and gharas.

585. [ ] Chicks—Lahore and Gujrat.

These are of two kinds: one a fine close meshed sort, suitable for windows, and the other of stouter material and more open, suitable for enclosing verandahs. The former are made of thin strips of bamboo, which are strung together upon longitudinal strings, each strip of bamboo bring left at a little distance from the other: the whole is painted green, and bound round the edge with cloth. Hung before doors they keep out flies, &c. and yet admit light and air.

In the Lahore museum are two Chinese chicks made of some kind of small grass stalks. These are of exquisite fineness, and far superior to the best chicks made here. The best and finest bamboo chicks I have seen were made in the Gujrat jail.

The large chicks for screening verandahs are either of stout parallel slips of bamboo strung on longitudinal strings; or else made of the long glossy flower-stalks of the munj, *Saccharum munja*, which are strung parallel to each other in the same way. If the stalks are not long enough for the whole breadth of the screen, the ends of two are spliced, and the necessary string passed through thus—

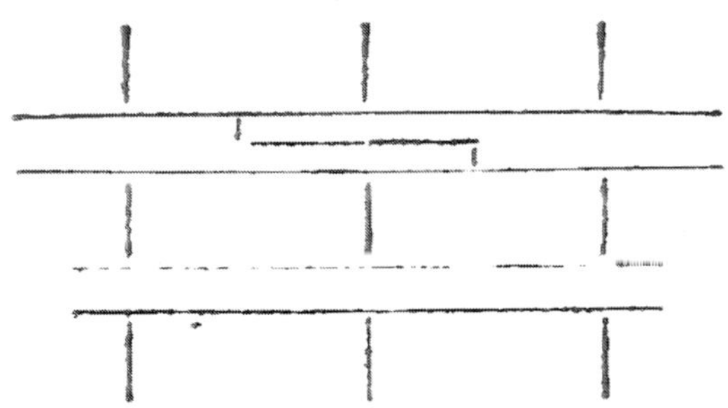

586. [ ] Múnj ropes, twine, &c., Lahore, Gugaira, (and *passim*).

This grass, *Saccharum munja*, may be seen growing everywhere in tall masses or tufts of narrow green leaves, from the centre of which, at the end of the rainy season, the tall flower-stalks with their graceful feathery flowers rise. It springs up readily where it can get a little moisture, by road sides or river sides, and indeed anywhere. In some places it covers whole tracts, and the sale of it is very productive. The leaves themselves (contrary to the opinion of one author) are quite useless for all purposes except thatching, for they are rough, and cut the hand if rudely grasped.

The useful part is the flower stalk (called *káná*): the long hanging sheaths and spathe covering this are carefully removed, and these when shredded up fine, form the material called "Bán-múnj," for string making. The glossy flower stalk, as high up as it remains of a uniform thickness, is cut to make chicks as before described, while the tapering top of the stalk is cut off for another purpose, *viz.*: to form "sirki." These smooth thin stalk ends are placed side by side forming even sheets of stalks, and then are all (at the thicker ends) kept together by being bound along with grass edging, which keeps the whole piece firm together; the other ends taper off to their natural points. These mats or pieces of roofing can now be utilized: they are often set up pent house like, tied to a bamboo, to shelter a cart and keep the contents dry; or they are laid flat over the roof beams of a room, piece overlapping piece; on the top of this lie the other materials of a flat roof, tiles, earth &c., This way of roofing is of course strange to English ideas, but is too familiar to an Indian to need description.

The thin part of the culm is in some places called "tili". Inside the culm is a pith called "khil" or "khul," which is eaten in the Muzaffargarh district. The tops of the grass as it comes into flower are given to cattle to increase the milk.

There are several grasses which, in general appearance, somewhat resemble the *S. munja*, and are sometimes mistaken for it; but *S. munja* is far the largest in size. The three species are—

Saccharum sara.
Saccharum spontaneum.
Saccharum munja.

The first reed yields káná, but not of a good quality, for this purpose the culm requires to be smoked, and dried up, which turns it brown.

The *S. spontaneum* is the *cásá* of Sanskrit writers, and is known by its beautiful wavy feathery flowers of silky whiteness.

The Gugaira district had quite a large collection of articles ingeniously worked from the tili, or fine upper stalk of the munj.

These were often worked over in places with patterns of colored worsted, and adorned with shells (cowries) sewn on to the borders. There was as a fan, or "Panka;" a sieve call "Cháj," used for winnowing grain; several baskets called "Phachhi," or "Khawa;" the latter used for holding cotton. Of the munj fibre there was a large net called "Tangar," used to hold *bhúsa* or chopped straw when transported from one place to another. Another article is called "Chînka," and appears to be a kind of string or net in which to carry plates or crockery. The porter's knot replaced here by a thick ring of rope for the head, is exhibited under the name of "Indavi." Some mats of munj, used for sitting on, and also for spreading out grain to dry &c. are shown under the names "Khirí" and "Pírí."

The string of munj is easily made: the thin slips are first of all wetted, one end made firm to a sort of weight or bobbin, and the fibre is twisted with the fingers, the bobbin at the end spinning with it and keeping it straight; as the string is thus twisted, it is wound on to the stick or reel which the operator holds in his hand. When the damp fibre dries it retains the twist, and evinces no desire to open out. Rope is made in the same way, only of several strands of string and then twisted together till it forms the required gauge. In the Rukhs* where the munj abounds, it is cut and purchased in a peculiar manner. Four persons join together on purpose to buy up all the munj cut in a certain place, the four men get a lot of coolies armed with short sickles or datris, and go out to cut the munj stalks. Each joint-purchaser's share of the whole quantity cut is represented by so many "dàtris" or 'sickles.' Supposing forty men are employed, all the day's cutting will be put up into 40 bundles, and the owner who has 10 sickles, will take only ten, and the man who has 20, will take his 20 bundles, and so on, paying the coolies accordingly.

The common ropes used for agricultural purposes are made in the rudest way. A long bundle of the fibre is made fast to a tree, and the fibres rudely twisted on till a long

* Tracts of waste land covered with trees, 'scrub' or firewood.

loose rope is attained. A man then fastens a stick to the other end, holds out the rope at full length, and twists the stick round and round till the whole fibre is duly twisted up; he then secures each end of the rope, and the operation is finished. Other ropes are exhibited made of san—*(Crotolaria juncea)*, and prepared with the aid of a rude machine described under Class XXIX *s. v.* 'Implements of the rope-twister or Rassi-bat.'

Sunkokra, Patsan, (*Hibiscus cannabinus.*)

This is made into a good rope, as its fibre is of great length, it is less strong than 'san.' The Lahore Central Jail sent a door mat made of tufts of this fibre; and some dyed to shew that the fibre will take a color. Nearly all the Jails make a profit by manufacturing coarse netted bags of 'san' string; these are in common use at all treasuries to hold rupees, 1,000 in each.

587. *Cotton ropes.*—These are principally made for punkah ropes, &c, being an even and finished rope, which is twisted of two or more colors for the sake of appearance.

588. *Rope of the Palm spathe.*—MUZAFFARGARH. This is almost peculiar to the southern districts. The central branch of the palm *Phœnix sylvestris*, comes forth enveloped in a shroud consisting of an interlacement of fibre, this, when separated, is converted into ropes. The *reticulum* is called "Kabal."

589. *Rope of the Palm leaf.*—This is called Patta-ka-rassi.

590. *Rope from the bark of the* Behul. HUSHYARPUR. KANGRA, &c.—*Grewia oppositifolia.* This is common on the lower hills, as san rope in the plains. The bark from which it is made, is the inmost bark of the tree. It is not unlike the Russian bass of gardeners, which is derived from the Lime or Linden-tree (*Tilia.*)

Several species of rope prepared as curiosities, or to exhibit the fibre, have been mentioned in Volume 1, Chapter IV, Sub-class E. to which the reader is referred for particulars.

590.—[6936-6950]. Straw Hats made at the Central Jail, LAHORE.

This is a new branch of manufacture introduced by Dr. Gray. Very creditable hats, in great variety, were sent to the Exhibition. We had white straw, and black, also mixed, and fancy chip, and straw plaited up with velvet; also straw dish mats and other articles, the work of the prisoners. The black straw is obtained by dyeing.

The fibrous samples in the Exhibition were examined by the Jurors, one of whom undertook the class of paper, and the other the remaining fibrous fabrics: their reports are here printed. The former jury alone furnished a detailed report, the latter jury supplied the list of prizes awarded.

VIII.—FIBROUS MANUFACTURES.

District or Locality.	*Prize taker.*	*Description of Article.*	*Medal.*
Madhopore, ...	...	Tát or Canvas, ...	...
Kangra, ...	L. E. Committee,	Tát bags, ...	...
Gujrat, ...	...	Do., ...	...
Multan, ...	Multan Jail, ...	Canvas, ...	...
Lahore, ...	Central Jail, ...	Flax Canvas, ...	...
Gugaira, ...	...	Ditto ...	1
Lahore, ...	Jail, ...	Door mat, ...	...
Lahore, ...	Jail, ...	Door mat of munj rope,	...
Dehra Dhún, ...	Jail, ...	Aloe fibre, and fabrics, ...	1
Lahore, ...	Jail, ...	Hemp and other ropes,	...
Kangra, ...	L. E. Committee, ...	Fine twine, ...	...
Bunnoo, ...	Dy. Commissioner,	Mats and fans, ...	...
Peshawur, ...	L. E. Committee,	Fans, ...	...
Lahore, ...	Híra Nand, ...	Ditto ...	...
Gujranwalla, ...	L. E. Committee, ...	Ditto, ...	...
D. G. Khan, ...	Mohandí, ...	Ditto, ...	...
Peshawur, ...	L. E. Committee, ...	Floor matting of Patta,	...
Lahore, ...	Central Jail, ...	Straw hats, ...	...

REPORT ON MISCELLANEOUS MANUFACTURES.

PAPER.

Jury :—

Mr. A. M. Dallas.
Mr. B. Powell.
Lalla Kunhya Lall.
Major T. W. Mercer.
Major J. E. Cracroft.
General VanCortlandt.
Mr. T. H. Thornton.
Mr. C. P. Elliot.

Mr. W. P. Woodward, *Reporter*.

The paper made in this country by the natives is of one kind only, * but of several qualities—all are however thicker, heavier, and coarser, than the commonest description of English paper.

It is impossible now to determine exactly when or by whom paper making was first introduced into India. Native historians are silent on the subject, as they are on most interesting and material questions; but it would not be far from the truth to fix the date some time between the 10th and 11th centuries A. D, or contemporaneous with the invasion of Hindustan by the Moslems. That it was not brought here before that, the following facts would appear to put beyond doubt.

It is well known that the art of making paper from cotton was flourishing in China so early as the 2nd century of the Christian era. A commercial intercourse existed then, and for some time previously, between China and India, and India and Europe, *viâ* Egypt. But paper of cotton was not known in Europe till about the † 9th century, when it was introduced into the southern countries by the Arabs, who, it is recorded, found a large manufactory of this paper at Samarkand, when they conquered Búkhárá. It was by the same route that the silk worm, though at an earlier date, was introduced into Europe from China. If then, it be supposed that paper making was known in Hindustan before the rise of the Moslem power, it is unaccountable why it was not carried into Europe at a very much earlier period, seeing the intimate intercourse that existed between the countries.

The above idea is also favored by the fact that all the private manufacturers to be met with now are Mahommedans,—a Hindú paper-maker being unknown. Caste objections would also have been an invincible difficulty to the Hindús initiating an experiment of this kind.

It is believed that previous to the introduction of paper, the leaves and bark of trees, the palm and plantain—and especially the "bhojpatr" and "talpatr,"—were used for writing on. Perhaps also Papyrus was brought from Egypt, for it used to be made into a kind of paper in small sheets, formed by the thin fibrous membranes of the plant being stripped off and pressed together. The use of vellum (calf-skin), or parchment, (sheep skin), as used in Europe, may be seen in the case of Mohammedan M.S.S. in the Delhi Mosque.

Whether introduced from China, or by the Moslems on, or subsequent to, the invasion of Máhmúd of Ghazní in the 10th century, it appears certain that such as was the process of

* Made only from inferior kinds of flax and hemp, called tat.

† See Hallam's Middle Ages, and Taylor's Modern Europe, and Roberston's Disquisition on India.

manufacture at the time it was introduced, so it continues to this day. There is of course every allowance to be made in respect of the non-improvement of the apparatus, on the score of an absence of the inventive talent in the matter of machinery, and the cheapness of labor not making this a necessity; but what is remarkable, is the non-improvement of the description of paper, and the non-utilization of the variety of raw materials which abound in the country, as it has been thought that there is not a country on the surface of the globe which is more adapted, from the nature and variety of its indigenous, as well as cultivated plants, to supply an almost infinite quantity of raw material for the manufacture of textile fabrics, of great diversity and commercial value, and from the refuse of which alone we have the means of manufacturing paper. Besides, there are innumerable fibres which, from their coarseness and shortness of staple, are unsuited for weaving purposes but still are eminently useful for the purpose of paper making.

The process of manufacture is as follow :—

The material having been procured, the manufacturer proceeds to reduce it to a state of pulp. Ten maunds of the tát is cut up into small fragments by means of a common axe, after which it is thrown into a vat made of bricks, generally four feet deep, seven in length, and six in breadth. In the bottom of this vat at one side of its lesser diameter, is imbedded a large block of stone, procured from the beds of rivers; these vary in size, but are for the most part two feet broad by four feet long, and one and a half to two feet in depth. A portion of water, sufficient to wet the whole mass, is then added, and it is now subjected to the process of pounding.

This is effected by means of the following apparatus, viz :—

A beam made of bábúl wood, ten feet in length, and nine inches in breadth and thickness, into one end of which is fixed an up-right round piece of wood or pestle, four feet in length and nine inches in diameter, and bound at the lower end with iron; on the under surface of this pestle, two teeth, or rather beaters, are inserted, made of iron, and placed parallel to each other; these measure five by three and a half inches. Four feet from the pestle end of the beam is driven a round piece of wood right through; this is supported on two notched up-rights driven firmly into the ground, and forms the fulcrum on which the lever moves.

The power is applied five feet from the fulcrum, and the space through which the end of the lever traverses is eighteen inches.

It is worked by six men, three on each side. The lever is depressed by the men simultaneously applying one foot on the beam, and the force is delivered at the pestle, and by their suddenly taking their feet off, and in this way the work proceeds. Two men sit in the bottom of the vat, and feed in the cut tát &c., in small qualities between the beaters and the block formerly mentioned. This pounding operation is carried on for three days successively.

The stuff is then washed and dried, and exposed to the sun for three or four days. It is now returned to the vat, and has added to it 100 pounds of "sajji," a very impure sub-carbonate of soda, and 50 pounds of slaked lime, moistening with water at the same time, and mixing all well together.

It is now beaten for eight days more, washed, and dried in the sun as at first; then sajji and lime added in the same quantities, beaten for eight days, dried, and exposed as before; then

50 pounds of sajji is added and 25 pounds of lime; again beaten till fine enough, which is generally three or four days; then washed, and put into the paper making vats. Washing the pulp is performed as follow :—It is put into earthen vessels or nânds, at a river side if possible, and trodden with the feet, adding from time to time fresh water; then thrown into a sheet tied at the ends round the waists of two men; they take this into the middle of the stream, and allow the running water to pass through the sheet (not over it), shaking at the same time the pulp to and fro; this constitutes the process of cleansing. The pulp is now considered ready to be made into paper; this is accomplished in the following manner, premising that four vats are considered the proper complement to one beating machine. The vats are four feet square, and also four feet in depth; they are filled with clean water, and a quantity of the pulp is placed on a space at the right hand of the spot on which the paper maker squats; he breaks this pulp up with his hands, and with an earthen cup adds water from the vat, with which he washes portion of the pulp into it, this operation goes on until all the pulp is got into the vat. He then with a long bamboo diligently stirs it about in the water, giving a striking motion every now and then to break up any larger portions; after this has been continued for about an hour, the pulp is allowed to settle down in the vat; the heavier particles of course reach the bottom first, and leave all the finest of the pulp uppermost. When this is effected, the paper maker then puts two bamboos in a longitudinal direction from the front of the vat across the top. He then takes a barred frame of wood, upon which he puts a screen or chick made of fine grass, fixing two pieces of wood at the sides to regulate the breadth of the paper, its length being determined by the length of the chick : the usual size is twenty two inches long by nineteen broad. He takes hold of this frame in both hands, and after passing it frequently across the water, to bring up some of the pulp, he dips it vertically into the vat, and then brings it into a horizontal position on a level with the water. He moves the frame gently to and fro so as to spread the pulp equally; raises it, and again dips it into the pulp, repeating the same process as at first; he then raises it, and puts a bamboo horizontally across the two longitudinal ones formerly mentioned, and rests one end of the frame on this, in an oblique direction, the other edge being placed on the side of the vat; the superabundant water thus is allowed to escape, and after removing the two small pieces of wood from the screen, he turns down the top of it a little, so as to facilitate the separation of the sheet, and puts it down flat on the space at his side from where the pulp was washed into the vat In this way he goes on laying one sheet on the top of the other without any intermediate cloth or substance of any kind, until he has got ten quires made, or a " Gadi," consisting of 240 sheets; this generally takes him the whole day to accomplish.

This heap is pressed by means of a board about two thirds the breadth of the paper and twice its length, two men adding their weight to this. The board is first placed at one side, and the moisture as far as possible expressed, and then it is removed to the other side of the upper surface. It is now allowed to remain all night, and in the morning the process is repeated.

This is all that is thought sufficient before the paper is dried. Drying is accomplished thus :—each sheet is separated, and spread by a brush upon a wall which has been made smooth for the purpose. In fine weather this is done in the open air, and then the process is a very easy matter, but in wet weather, or during the rainy season, it is difficult to get space enough to put the paper upon as soon as made in a large manufactory, owing to the time it takes to dry.

When dry, the surface which was in contact with the wall is tolerably smooth, the other is still rough ; this roughness is rubbed down where most conspicuous, by pieces of burnt bricks. The paper now is ready for sizing. This operation, like all the rest, is sufficiently primitive. The sheets are arranged smoothly in heaps ; a size made of wheaten starch is applied with a kind of mop made of rolls of coarse flannel or blanket, dipped into the starch, and passed over the paper ; it is afterwards hung up on lines to dry.

The paper has still to go through another operation before it is fit for use. This consists in polishing it, which is effected as follows.

A curved piece of wood, about three feet long and nine inches broad, is fixed firmly on the ground, having its concaved surface uppermost (this is generally made of mango wood). The workman leans down on his knees, and takes a cloth slightly moistened with oil. He lays a sheet of paper on the wood and passes the oily cloth very gently over its surface ; he then with both hands commences polishing it with a piece of common agate or bloodstone, made convex, and generally about two or three inches long. This stone is imbedded firmly in an elliptical piece of clay, about six inches long, so as to allow a firm hold being taken of it with both hands. The workman passes this rapidly up and down the paper with considerable force until a polish appears on the surface ; having turned the sheet, he repeats the same process. The paper is now folded, sorted, cut, and made up into quires and gadis, two of which make an English ream. The quantity of paper that one man can polish, if expert, in one day, is five quires or 120 sheets.

What a contrast is the result of the present process in England, where successive improvements have brought the art to such a state of perfection, that a continuous stream of fluid pulp is now passed round the cylinders with unerring precision, and not only made into paper, but actually dried, pressed smooth, and every separate sheet cut round the edges, in the brief space of five minutes !

In the Serampore manufactury alone, it is believed, has machinery been employed. In 1825, Mr. Marshman of Serampore imported one of the famed self acting cylindrical machines of Messrs. Donkin & Co., the celebrated paper-machine makers. But how this has worked, and what have been the practical results, the outside public do not appear to have been at any time informed. The official public are however familiar with what is called Serampore paper, made from cotton, which is served out to public offices, and is used in matters of an ephemeral nature. It answers very well for print'ng official reports and text books, and for any purpose not requiring any rough or frequent handling, as it is far from durable.

Very excellent paper is made at Kashmir. It is particularly smooth and white, and by far the best specimen of the collection exhibited. It is held in high estimation all over the country, especially at native Courts, and is used only for first quality writings and correspondence with native Princes and Chiefs. Nothing is known of the process by which the paper is made in Kashmir, owing to the extreme jealousy with which any communication between the manufacturers and natives of the plains is guarded. A Kashmiri paper maker is never met with out of the territory, as they can leave it only at their peril, or when bound to silence under the severest penalties. But there is no reason to suppose that the process is anything different from what it is all over India, the superiority in the texture being unquestionably due to the natural abundance of water and to the use of mills moved by streams, such as existed at Fabriano in the Picenum, and at Colle in Tuscany, the vat-made paper of which places was pronounced "superb" by the Jury of the English Exhibition of 1851.

Paper making has long been one of the chief manufactures in Government Jails, as affording one very appropriate description of "hard-labor," and ensuring a maximum of profit from a minimum of capital. The paper heretofore made has been of the coarsest kind, the native process and materials being used. But of late years increased attention has been paid to the subject, and not only has the old description of paper been improved in quality, but new materials have been laid under contribution, as the marginal* list indicates, with more or less successful results.

* Flax fibre .... Gujrat.
Dhák root .... do.
Plantain leaf .... do.
Rags (old)............Gujrat and Rawal Pindi.
Ganni (old) .... Do. and Jhelam.
Date leaves .... Rawal Pindi.
Bhúsá .... do.
Daphne... .....Kangra, Simla, Kanawar, Lahore.
Dhâman bark............Kangra.
Tát (old)............ Do. and Jhelam.
Mâdár............Sirsa.
Hemp ropes .... do.
Raddí or waste paper .... do.

The great draw-backs which exist, and will continue to exist until the subject is practically taken up by European enterprize, is the want of machinery to cut and beat the pulp fine enough, and of a continuous and regular flow of water to wash it clean enough.

The specimens from the Gujerat Jail attracted special notice, and there is no doubt that great attention has been paid to the subject in this district. In the Rawul Pindee Jhilam and Sirsa Jails also, great improvement has been made.

A large and flourishing native manufactury exists in the district of Sealkote, where paper known by that name is made of an excellent quality. The jury are surprised to find none of it in the exhibited specimens, nor from Delhi and Ludhianah, where there are private manufactories of no mean pretensions.

The following is a list of the prizes :—

I.—Kashmir paper, ...	*1st*, Special prize, value Rs. 50.	By Mr. C. Gordon, Editor Lahore Chronicle.
II.—Gujrat Series of papers from Dhak root or Ch'ichira, Ganni, Plantain leaf and Flax fibre, and Blotting paper, ...	*2nd*, do. value Rs. 32.	By Lieutenant Nisbet, Assistant Commissioner.
III.—Jhilam—For excellence of manufactures cleanness and freedom from blemishes, ...	3 shares, value Rs 30.	By Exhibition Prize Committee.
IV.—Gujrat—Paper from old rags, ...	2 shares value Rs. 20.	By do.
V.—Sirsa—For application of Mâdar fibre to paper making, ...	Certificate.	
VI.—Rawal Pindi—For skill in dyeing paper,	Certificate.	

W. P. Woodward,
Reporter.

CLASS IX.

ARTICLES OF EMBROIDERY.

Two branches of art are involved in the manufacture of goods of this class. For in the first place, the gold and silver has to be prepared in the form of tinsel, spangles, ribbon, thread, &c. &c., before the embroiderers can use it, and next there is the art of embroidering itself.

The manufacture of the gold thread, &c., will be considered afterwards, under the head of Works in the Precious Metals.

The bulk of gold embroidery is done with kalábátún, or the common gold thread—a body of silk over wound with a thin flattened wire of gold or silver, as the case may be. Gold is wound on orange colored or red silk; silver on white. The former is called *kalábátún surkh*; the other *kalábátún safed.*

There are two principal kinds of gold embroidery; one of a solid and rich kind called "*kár-chob*;" the other an ordinary and cheap kind of work, being merely a gold thread described as "tilá kár" or "kár-chikan."

Gold and silver embroidery of the kind called "kár-chob" is principally employed for large and handsome articles, such as cushions of State, elephant trappings, saddle cloths, masnads, or carpets spread out before the seats of princes.

The second kind of embroidery is principally employed in articles of dress, in ornamented caps, and in edgings to garments. Chogahs, or long coats, richly embroidered with gold, are worn on State occasions.

At Delhi, a variety of other articles of dress are made up, figured with gold and with embroidered borders,—ladies' scarves, "dopattas," shawls, and various other articles, especially of native female attire. Such glittering raiments figure greatly at marriages and other ceremonials.

A number of very elegant articles are prepared on a foundation of net or fine muslin, the material being merely worked over with sprigs of flowers here and there. Such fabrics are called "bútidár," and are finished off with a bordering, in which not only embroidery takes its place, but fringes, spangles, and pieces of tinsel polished and sewn on to produce the effect of jewels, are introduced. Such articles are very brilliant, but are rather *outré*, and gaudy to European taste.

The embroidery of a heavy and rich character is worked upon velvet or cloth, for the purposes of jhúls, or saddle cloths, masnads, &c. and which is termed "Kárchob," is so called because the velvet or other material to be worked on is, in the first instance, stretched smooth and tight on a wooden frame,—(chob). The frame consists of two stout side pieces, the ends of which are perforated; into the holes are inserted the pieces that form the remaining bars of the frame, these are moveable, and held in their places by wooden pegs, and by placing the pegs in one or other of a series of small holes in the bars the frame can be enlarged and contracted at pleasure. To the edges of the cloth on which the embroidery is to be done four flaps of stout cloth are next sewn, and the flaps are tightly lashed by string to the bars of the frame, and stretched till the whole is tight. The pattern is in the first place lightly printed or stamped on the material with a wooden carved block, as in calico printing, or else is drawn out with the hand by a brush charged with yellow paint made of hartál or orpiment* and the

* I subsequently learned that this is done in the way described at the top of page 99 *sqq*.

workmen commence by working over the pattern in long stitches of yellow silk or thread, to give it body and make it stand out in relief; over this the gold thread is laid down and fixed in its place by sewing it down with a fine needle charged with either orange or white silk, according as the work is in gold or silver.

Where a continuous surface of gold is required, the gold thread is laid on in consecutive rows, generally in a herring bone pattern; and the foundation or cloth being already worked, as above described, with a substratum of yellow thread or silk, it is soft and impressible, and thus the result is that the pattern appears quilted on. Variety is obtained by quilting some parts in higher relief than the rest; and also by changing the direction of the threads. The texture will be easily seen as well as the method of quilting, by closely inspecting the annexed illustration, which represents a chárjáma or saddle cover made at Lahore.

The bulk of the work being in the ordinary gold thread, the rest is varied by the occasional introduction of pieces worked over with flattened and waved wires or ribbons called "mukesh,"* of bright gold, overlaying one another like the scales on a fish: a suprisingly rich and gorgeous appearance is thus obtained. A most splendid elephant cover was exhibited of this work: the foundation being velvet. the whole of the immense surface was richly quilted over with gold and silver, and finished off with a fringe of twisted gold wire two feet in length; but the beauty of these works is familiar to every one who has seen a native durbar.

The value of the embroidery is entirely dependent on the quality of the gold thread employed. If the silk thread is richly and well covered with gold the weight is greater, and the work presents a richer appearance; if the silk thread is only lightly and sparsely covered with gold, and shewing silk between, the work looks poor. Consequently, when a man commences a work, he always asks what sort of kalábatún he is to use; how many rupees per tolah it is to cost?

The art of embroidery in this style does not now flourish. Formerly, in the days of native rule and brilliant courts. all sorts of embroideries were in constant demand. Now, in British territories, these things are less in demand. and the manufacture would die out all together, except for the courts of the native princes that remain, and the demands of a few of the wealthier inhabitants. A few men are found in the large cities who can work well: they never make anything except to order, and require an advance to enable them to buy materials.

In Lahore and Amritsar there are only a few shops where this work is carried on, and even in Delhi, I am informed, there are only about 10 or 12 establishments giving employing to about 150 individuals, who are not confined to any particular caste. They begin as children to learn. At first, when a ***shagird*** or apprentice goes to an employer, he presents his master with a dish of sweetmeats, and is then installed and set to work first in thread only; when he has advanced sufficiently, he pays the master a fee of 20 rupees, and then is allowed to work in silk or gold thread, till he is perfect in the art.

Such embroidery as comes into use for ornamental caps, chogahs, and other articles of male and female attire, still flourishes, indeed is rather spreading since a number of articles for European wear are now made for export at Dehli.

This kind of embroidery is much less troublesome then the work called kárchob, for it is all done in one operation with the needle charged with gold thread. somtimes plain, sometimes in chain stitch. The kárchob is occasionally employed in embroidering caps, and chogahs.

* The art of making this wire which appears thus— is described further on in the book.

In Kashmir, the embroideries are especially beautiful, both in design and execution.

The Kashmiri embroidery reaches its climax in the hand-worked or 'amlikár' shawls: these have already been to some extent described.

They also work floor cloths, and table covers and other articles, with great success, sometimes introducing figures of men and animals into their work.

At Ludhiana also, a considerable quantity of work in colored silk embroidery is done, but principally for sale to Europeans. Slippers, caps, that are worked on cotton or cloth, or merino, grounds, in colored silk, both in patterns of arabesque device, or in leaves and flowers.

One of the commonest kinds of embroidery is that done on pashmína cloth, usually in silk of the same color. This is principally used in making chogahs, and also articles of European dress.

It is best done in Kashmir, whence some very magnificent specimens are occasionally seen; but it is also done with considerable success both at Amritsar and Ludhiana.

This is in fact a kind of braiding done with silk thread, and in a peculiar stitch. It looks rich and handsome, as the work, owing to the thickness of the silk, stands in slight relief on the ground material.

As to pattern, though considerable variety is exhibited, and great intricacy in combination, yet the basis of the design is usually the same. One of the most commonly introduced form is that pear shaped figure, so often seen in shawls, which is called "saro," or cypress tree, from a fanciful idea of the form of a cypress,—the slender top bent over by the wind—and is a form something like this—

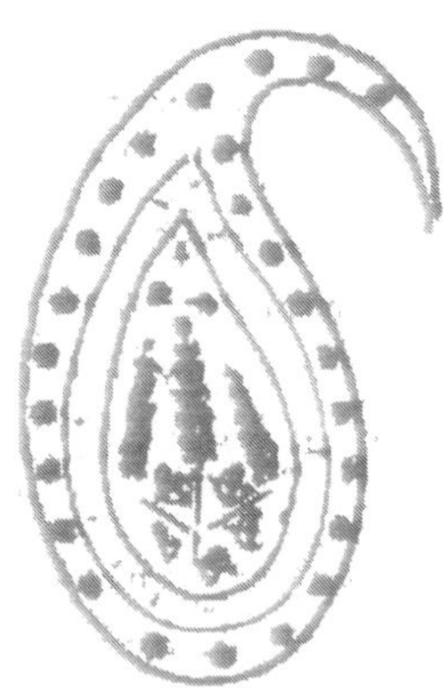

This form, more or less elongated, is a ground work of many designs, the spaces being filled up with sprigs of flowers and leaves; and long curved lines "dauri;" the borderings and edgings are quite conventional and have various names, according to the idea of form which has suggested the pattern—one of the names are described in Moorcroft's account of shawl weaving quoted previously.

I am informed, in Delhi, that the people have no settled rules as to pattern, but describe the various forms, as "saro," and a long pattern having a stem and flowerets branch off, "bel"—sprigs "buti," &c., &c. There is not much originality in design, and most works are now executed from copies already made; though a clever workman will vary them. Most patterns are merely different arrangements of the irrepressible "saro," "bel," and so forth.

BLACK NET SHAWL.

The pattern is usually drawn on paper, pricked out with a pin: this paper being stitched over the cloth to be embroidered, color—generally yellow orpiment—is put on over the lines of pin holes, and small specks of color penetrate the holes, and mark very slightly the cloth beneath. The embroiderer then works over the marks. In other cases the pattern is lightly stamped on the cloth by means of a wooden block charged with color, just as in colico printing.

Delhi Embroidery.

592.—[7045]. Scarf embroidered with gold, value Rs. 70.

593.—[7046]. A chádar, or scarf, with gold (chádar kalábatúní) value Rs. 60.

594.—[7047]. A square shawl (rúmál) embroidered, value Rs. 25.

595.—[7048]. A mantilla (peshwár) embroidered, value Rs. 60.

596.—[7051]. A scarf, "dopatta," embroidered, value Rs. 135.

597.—[7000]. A small scarf, "patka," embroidered on pashmina.

598.—[7055]. Dáman alkhálik.

599.—[7057]. Madákhil.

600.—[7059]. Angí and kúrtí, (boddices,) embroidered.

601.—[7061]. Embroidered cap with fur, "topí samúri."

602.—[7062]. Cap, "topa chabba dár."

603.—[7065]. 'Partla' or sword-belt embroidered in gold.

604.—[7071]. Battúa "in gold thread. These are the peculiar loops and buttons for fastening the choga.

Scarf embroidered in floss silk on net.

Do. Do. in floss silk on merino.

Muslin piece embroidered with sprigs and flowers in gold:—"Jàmdàni."

Ludhiana Embroidery.

605.—[7088]. Caps embroidered in colored silk by Ahsan Shah, upon cotton cloth &c.

606.—[7096]. Mat or flower vase stand, embroidered by Azíz.

607.—[7095]. Embroidered fan.

608.—[7100]. Embroidered purses and tobacco pouches.

609.—[ ]. Slippers, embroidered on cloth and merino.

Amritsar.

610.—[7152]. Gold embroidered shawl, (shál zar-doz).

611.—[7153]. "Zínposh," saddle cover, embroidered.

612.—[7155]. Masnad, on velvet, with rich gold embroidery (kárchob.). A carpet or cover used for covering the throne or dais on which grandees sit on State occasions.

613.—[7156]. Chogas embroidered all over in gold, (Messrs. Devi Sahai and Chamba Mal.)

614.—[7170]. Rampúr scarves embroidered in silk, "kár-i-sozan."

615.—[7176]. Embroidered neckties, waistcoats &c., pashmina ground, embroidered with silk of the same color, Lahore.

616.—[7202]. Embroidered velvet masnad (kar-chob) exhibited by Raja Harbans Singh.

617.—[7203]. Zín-posh, saddle cover, (karçhob).

618.—[7204]. "Jhúl," or horse housing, embroidered on scarlet cloth, by Azim ullah.

(The embroidery is gold and silver relieved with silver spangles (sitára), and ornaments of the green beetle-wing).

619.—[7206]. Green velvet choga embroidered all over with gold thread, "zar-doz," Government Toshakhana. This was made in Kashmir.

620.—[7207]. Masnad of pashmina, spotted with gold.

621.—[7218]. Purple silk "angarka," or frock embroidered in gold thread ("zar-doz")

Some of the coarser kind of embroidery in cotton and silk was also exhibited Such work is used principally in ornamenting the chadar, dopatta, or scarves usually worn; the commonest and coarsest kind are made of dull-red cloth dyed with madder, embroidered with silk generally in rude flowers in sprigs of green and yellow.

Such are the following:—

622.—[7247]. Cotton "bâgh" embroidered, value Rs. 1-5-0, by THAKUR DAS, LAHORE.

623.—[7268]. "Phúlkárí" (*lit.* 'flower work') scarf, value Rs. 11 as. only.

624.—[7250]. Skirt or "Lenga" embroidered.

This kind of embroidery is especially noticeable among the articles of clothing from Bunnoo and the Derajat, and from these localities it is very well executed. The work is done with thick threads of floss silk, and is worked by women on the bodies of their dresses. also on the "chola" or stomacher: some of the devices are very quaint.

KASHMIR.

625.—[7371]. Square shawl embroidered with the needle, "amlikár."

626.—[7374]. A table cover worked in figures of men and animals, (chikan-kár taswír-dár).

627.—[7376]. Square shawl embroidered with gold thread (rumál zerí-kár).

628.—[7379]. Khes or scarf of pashmina embroidered with gold thread (zarí kar).

629.—[7382]. Embroidered cap.

FARIDKOT.

630.—[7390]. Two "lungis" or scarves embroidered with gold or silk.

JHIND.

631.—[7391]. A saddle embroidered all over with silk.

632.—[7392]. A saddle embroidered with gold thread.

NABHA.

633.—[7395]. "Anga chikní" or embroidered frock.

634.—[7396]. "Chautahi zaríñdar," or embroidered red coverlet.

PATYALA.

635.—[7413]. Specimen of embroidery in gold thread.

636.—[7415]. A "chop" or woman's scarf embroided in silk, (kar-i-chikan).

MALERKOTLA.

637.—[7423]. A piece of muslin worked with silk.

638.—[7224]. Muslin and spotted with gold and silver.

Sozni, bed cover—Kashmir.

This is a favorite kind of work. It consists of a double surface of cotton cloth slightly padded and quilted down, not in squares, but in curved patterns of flowers &c. The quilting work is done with pale blue or pale pink silk, and the raised parts of the work sometimes appear to be tinted by having a colored cloth below the outer surface, the color of which partly shows through the white.

This work is best done in *Kashmir*, but also at Lahore, Amritsar, and elsewhere.

The following are specimens of embroidered leather:—

Most large cities have workmen who embroider shoes and sword-belts. At Kasúr, in the Lahore district. there is an embroiderer who has carried off more than one prize at Local Exhibitions for his embroidery in plain gold thread, or in gold thread and colored silk worked on leather, and for his embroidered saddlery.

[7064]. Sword belts by RAMI MAL of Delhi. Specimens also from Amritsar, Hushyarpúr, Ludhiana &c., &c.

[8712]. Saddle trappings, of gold and velvet by MUSTAKIM of KASUR (LAHORE DISTRICT.)

[8073]. Letter bag elegantly embroidered in gold and silver thread.

[8174]. A gold embroidered belt, and leather powder flask (belonged to the late Raja Teja Sing)

(For an account of Horse, Camel and Elephant Trappings, see Class XI—LEATHER).

CLASS X.

ARTICLES OF CLOTHING—AS SUCH—INCLUDING ETHNOGRAPHICAL SPECIMENS GENERALLY.

This class is designed to embrace those specimens which are always to be met with in museums, having been brought by travellers, or sent in by collectors who have intuitively almost, taken them up as indicative of the religion, manners, dress, food, habits, and capabilities of the people they have visited.

To some extent the whole volume furnishes an ethnographical sketch, inasmuch as the various manufactures are all more or less special: the fabrics, the vessels, the pottery, the jewellery, the fine arts, all exhibit some peculiarities, but there are nevertheless a few articles which might be called ethnographic specimens, as specially illustrating the habits of the people. A large portion of these specimens exist in forms of clothing and costume more or less remarkable, and hence the prominence given in the heading to "Articles of Clothing." The Punjab territories are made up of tracts of country so wonderfully different in climate, physical appearance, and geographical position, that it is not surprising to find the utmost difference between the various races inhabiting the province and its environs.

In the hill country we have all the varieties of Indian and Thibetan races; the districts of Kangra, Simla, Ladák, Lahul, Spiti, Kanáwar, Kashmír, Kaghán, and Kabul, all furnish us with differences of dress, appearance, manners, customs, and implements of trade, art, or religion. In the plains we have all the distinctions of Kashmíris, Biluchis, Pathans, Hindus, and Mohamedans, Hindustanis and Central Indians. Among the Hindus again we have different castes, and all sorts of people who belong to no caste at all: Gipsies, Chúras, Chángars, and the like. All these exhibit, more or less, differences, and especially in their dress.

I have expressly avoided all mention of such physical peculiarities, as Ethnologists lay most stress on, viz: conformation of the skull, height, carriage, strength of form, and so forth; such matters could not form a portion of a work like this; indeed if they could be legitimately included, I have neither space to give to the delineation nor knowledge to complete it. For a similar reason, peculiarities of language are not here noticed, save incidentally in giving the local vernacular names of the articles described.

All that can be attempted under my present heading is to describe those articles of dress, and other objects of manufacture and art, which are ethnographically interesting.

With this preface I may now proceed to an enumeration of the collection. The first series are dresses of castes &c., inhabiting the plains.

We have first two classes of them: those who are agriculturists, and those who live in cities.

The former will be found principally to include the following classes, *viz.* Sikh Jats, Mussulmán Jats; Raiens, Dogars, Gujars, Brahmans, Rajputs; but in some places there are some considerable aggregations of castes called Lubánas, excellent agriculturists, who, in the Lahore district are much collected together along the banks of the Ravi, and they have a dialect so peculiar as to be with difficulty understood by ordinary people. Kambo is another rather prevalent Hindu caste in some places, so is the Arora. In the Frontier districts we have different races altogether: Wazíris, Bilúchis, Afrídis, Pathans, &c. These will appropriately form a class by themselves.

In the districts just below the hills, and in the lower hills, Rajputs predominate.

Besides these regular classes, all over the country other classes are to be found, the enumeration of which is not within the scope of this work; but, as far as dress is concerned, the several classes of persons who have more or less distinctive dress and occupations, as Fakirs, Nais (Barbers—who also arrange betrothals), Mirásis, wandering bards; also the very low castes, Bhangis, Chúras, and others, are to be met with everywhere: but they generally are very poor: they wear very little clothing at all, and nothing at least that deserves the name of a distinctive costume.

In the cities, we have besides the native gentry, Hindu and Mohamedan, Khatris, and shop-keepers of all classes, banyas and various Hindustani traders, Sikhs, Mussulman Kashmiris, Munshis, to say nothing of all those individual traders and occasional visitors who represent castes and tribes having no local domicile. The dresses of such will be described.

Costumes of Lahore, Amritsar, and other similar districts.—In the cities, Mussulmans of the higher rank generally wear an angarka, or coat with a skirt, the body fitting tight: over this a choga; in cool weather this may be made of figured muslin or else of silk, very gay colors being often selected; in colder weather embroidered pashmina, or European merino, or other warm material is made use of. White stockings are worn, and shoes of fine leather, more or less embroidered with gold; white or colored turbans are worn according to custom. The ordinary class of respectable Munshis will wear a similar dress, but without the gay colors, generally a plain white dress; if any part is colored it is a scarf &c., of the printed muslin which in Europe is only used for female dress.

When trowsers are worn they are usually narrow and long (Gharáradár wa tang). But some classes of Musulmans wear loose trowsers, and Hindu merchants, shop-keepers and others wear a waist-cloth or dhoti of white cloth, sometimes with a red printed edge; this is worn so as to fall in folds on each leg, and fastened up in the middle and tied round the waist.

Females wear loose trowsers, a sort of shirt or kurta of fine cloth, and a large 'dopatta' or scarf, which is gracefully folded over the head and covers the whole body almost.

Kashmiris are abundant: those who trade, and are called Sádhu, wear dresses like other merchants; their females wear a long shirt or kurta, trowsers of súsí, blue striped with white, a small cap on the head, and a veil called 'burka.'* Their shoes are of red or green leather, of a somewhat peculiar shape, and called 'kaush;' other Kashmiris who work as shawl weavers &c. generally shave their heads and wear a small quilted skull cap and loose trowsers, often wear no clothes on the body at all, except perhaps a dirty chaddar or wrapper; they are nearly always very dirty.

Julás and weavers and many other working people wear instead of trowsers, a 'tahband' or sheet worn round the waist like a skirt and tied up in a knot in front of the waist.

Of Hindu castes: among the Munshis, Kashmírí Pandits are common; they wear white angarkas and chogas and turbans like other Munshis, and black leather shoes. The wealthier classes wear a white angarka, and sometimes for a wrapper a silken scarf with gold

* The *burka* is not a veil but a bag, like a bottle cover on a larger scale. It consists of a cylindrical bag for the head, having holes cut out, and covered with net work to see and breathe through: while attached to the head bag a pleated skirt covers the whole figure downwards: the woman so encased looks like a mummy, and is of course invisible to eyes profane. The whole dress is made of coarse white cloth.

border, or a shawl, and these also wear ornaments round the neck, and gold karas or bracelets.* The Hindu shroffs or money changers (saráf), the cloth seller (bazáz) &c., wear 'dhotis' or large sheets tied up into loose trowsers, close folded pagris of white, or often pink cloth. *Nauriyas*, a class of traders from Bikanír and thereabout, wear a very long turban of red cloth and a white dhoti, which is worn like other Hindu dhotis, but is confined by a silver chain girdle furnished with a clasp; the ends of the chain are visible and hang down for ornament; such a chain is called "tarágí." The Hindu castes of Káyaths called 'Bharpúnja' (literally grain roaster); also engage in mercantile and clerks' business, sometimes they wear a cap, and sometimes a turban.

The Sikh gentlemen wear trowsers tight fitting round the calf of the legs; they wear also a kurta or shirt with a scarf round the waist, and some adopt a choga, others wear a khes or scarf: they often wear a double turban, as presently described.

Sikh ladies wear a kurta, of silk or fine muslin; trowsers, which are tight and made of striped silk or gulbadan; sometimes a skirt or lengá is worn over this and the usual scarf or dopatta of fine muslin, which covers the head as well as the body.

Sikh villagers generally wear very little clothing. They will wear a coarse pagri, and a khes or chaddar for a scarf;—and often wear short drawers coming down to the knee, or else a sort of 'tahband' or waist-cloth. The women wear a skirt or lengá, a chádar, generally of red coarse cloth embroidered with rudely executed sprigs of flowers in green and yellow silk,—some also wear a "choli" or sort of stomacher, which generally leaves the arms bare and also exposes part of the body down to the waist.

Among the Sikhs, the class called Nihangs or Akálís should be noticed: very few are now to be seen, but they dress entirely in dark blue; having a high peaked turban, which carries three steel flat rings—the war quoit of ancient Hinduism—and also certain short knife-like pieces of steel stuck into the body of the turban. They wear a large iron flattened ring round the neck and iron rings on the arms.

The villagers usually at work wear nothing but a coarse 'patka' or turban, and just such a waist-cloth or "sáfa," as serves for a covering. † If coming into town they put on a chādar, or wrapper. They wear shoes of stout coarse leather called "dhauri." The women wear a lenga, or skirt, sometimes coarsely embroidered, and pajámas or loose trowsers generally of súsí (already described). Some classes of Mussulmans, Malis and Raeíns, wear dark blue cloth instead of white, and a waist cloth tied in front like a tight skirt.

The better class of villagers and the headmen or lumberdars wear white turbans and a white shirt, also a khes, also probably a well woven lungi for a waistcloth, or a white cloth of better texture than usual.

I will only add to this note a word or two concerning turbans.

Hindus, especially banyas and shop-keepers, wear a "pagrí," which is a turban closely bound in regular folds on the head, and the proper binding of it is an art in itself.

Others who do not wear the pagrí choose a loose full turban wound on without any particular care, and called "dastár."

* I shall describe the jewellery of the country in its proper place. A kara is a thick ring which not a complete circle, but the two ends are brought together and bent open to put on.

† Called by Hindus "langoti."

Sikhs sometimes wear the pagri, sometimes the "dastár," but Sikh gentlemen often wear a double turban. A small close fitting turban (colored) called "sáfa" comes down over the forehead, and a loose dastár, generally white, or of a different color to the sáfa, is so disposed as to shew a little bit of the latter underneath and just over the forehead; the effect, when the colors are well assorted is pleasing.

Mohamedans wear a dastár usually, or else a large and loosely folded turban of shawl or scarf material; this is called "amáma" or "shamla;" the large turbans formed by endless coils of muslin tightly twisted into a rope are called by the same name.

I now proceed to give extracts which describe the dress and habits of the people in special districts.

The Ambala District.—The dress of the men consists of a turban, twisted round a skull cap; a dhoti, or cloth fastened round the waist, and drawn up between the legs; shoes; and in the cold weather, a sheet or counterpane stuffed with cotton. Only a few of the better dressed men wear the chapkan (jacket,) or mírzai (coat.) so common in the provinces. The fact is that only a few of the zemindars have hitherto been sufficiently well off to afford these luxuries. Those who can afford it wear a thin cotton jacket, in the hot weather and rains, and one of dyed cotton stuffed or padded, in the cold weather.

The Sirsa District.—The principal castes in the district wear dress as follows:—

Sikh Jats wear a turban (dastár), a kurta, a short coat or jacket, a short cloth worn round the loins called "kach," and over all a "khes" or "chádar" as a wrapper.

The women of this class wear on their heads the "orna," a sheet sometimes embroidered on the edges with silk; a "kurti" or chemise; and paijamas of which the lower part fits close round the leg, but being very long is gathered into folds or wrinkles; this article of clothing is called "suttan" or "paijama churidár;" a skirt is superadded called "lenga;" the richer classes have this of silk, or "mungasbári" (mixed cotton and silk).

Another caste is called "Bajra." They wear a sáfa or short turban. (The dastár is a very long cloth, wound round the head; some classes wear a dastár of one colour, and wind the shorter turban or sáfa of another colour inside, only leaving a little piece of the color exposed). In this district the "sáfa" is called "potaba." The body is covered by a "kamri," or short coat reaching to the waist (kamr), which is the same as an "angarka" only half the length; it opens down the middle and fastens by strings below the breast; below this is a "dhoti" wound round the loins, and hanging loose about the legs. A "chádar" is worn over all, or a shawl of wool (lohi) in cold weather. The women wear an "orna" as before, and an "angya," a small stomacher covering the upper part of the person only. A skirt or "lenga" completes the dress.

The next caste is the "Bishnavi." The men wear clothes like the Bajra Jats,—the women wear a head veil or sheet always of wool,—either in the form of "orna" or "lohi,"—a woollen stomacher or "angya," and the skirt with its tying string (called dhaila) is also of wool.

Brahmans, Aruras, Bakâls, &c., wear a dastár on the head, on the body an "anga" before described, and around the loins a "dhoti"—and as a wrapper,—a "khes," "dohar" (double sheet), "dotahi," "chadar" or blanket "lohi" according to the season. The women wear the same dress as the rest; they call the "lenga," "gagra." In the Punjab proper there is a difference; the "gagra" is a cheaper or common kind of "lenga."

The Mussulmans, Lohanas &c, wear on the head a pagri (dastár) and some a salári—(a cloth, which is white striped with black lines.) Some of then wear on the body an anga, others nothing.—round the waist they wear a "taimat" or taiwand (answering to the "dhoti" of the Hindus) and over all a "lunghi" or a chádar.

Women wear the usual head sheet or veil, "orna"—on the body the angya or kurta, and either the 'paijamas" or "lenga," or in cold weather both.

*The Shahpúr District**.—The every-day dress of the male portion of the Mahomedan population living north of the Jhelam river consists of four garments—a "mujla," a "kurta," a "chádar," and a "turban," or "pag" as it is here called. The first is a piece of cloth about three yards long and a yard and a half wide, which is tied tightly round the waist, and allowed to hang in loose folds over the lower part of the body. The "kurta" is a full-cut tunic, with large open sleeves reaching a little below the waist. The "chádar" is made of three breadths of cloth, in length about as many yards, and is worn something in the manner of a plaid. Of the turban nothing further need be said, than that its size depends much on the social position of the wearer, and increases with his importance. South of the Jhelam the "kurta" is discarded, in the Bâr it is never seen, indeed the man who would wear such a garment there must be possessed of more than ordinary moral courage to endure the jokes that would certainly be made at his expense. The material of which this simple clothing is made, is the ordinary coarse country cloth, except that along the rivers, especially the Chenab, colored lungis are often used as "mujlas." The "Kaliars," the chief camel owners of the Shahpúr Tehseel, are also much given to wearing "lungis." The Hindus to a great extent follow the fashions of the Mahomedans among whom they live, in regard to the use of the "kurta," but their mode of tying the turban is somewhat different, and the "dhoti" replaces the "mujla," the difference between garments being in the manner of putting them on.

The Mahomedan women also wear the "mujla," (tying it somewhat differently to the men), and this is usually a colored "lungi." Their other garments are two, the "choli," and the "chádar." The former has short sleeves, and fits closely round the breasts, leaving the remainder of the body bare, except where a small lappet hangs down and hides the stomach. The "chádar" is a piece of cloth about three yards long and one and a half wide, worn as a veil over the head and upper part of the body, from which it falls in graceful folds nearly to the feet behind. The "choli" is generally made of strips of many colored silk, the "chádar" of a coarse but thin description of country cloth called "dhotar," sometimes dyed, but more often plain. To this the "Thal" is an exception, where veils of many colors, the patterns formed by spots disposed in a variety of ways on a dark ground, are the rule. In the hills, colored garments are scarcely ever seen. The Hindu women of the Khatri class wear full trowsers called "suttan," made of a striped material called "susi," the ground of which is usually blue. Over the head is a thrown a "chádar" of coarse cloth, prettily

* From Major Davies' Settlement Report.

embroidered in many colored silks, called "phulkári," and round the upper part of the body is worn a loose "kurta" of silk or muslin. The women of the "Arora" class are clothed like the Khatranis, except that in place of the trowsers, they wear a skirt called a "gagra," and sometimes the "mujla." It may be added, that it is the invariable rule, even among Máhomedans, that a girl shall wear a "kurta," and plait the two front tresses of her hair, until she is married.

For the costumes of hill districts, and those about the foot of the mountains the following series will serve as descriptions.

In Hushyarpúr, the Jats, Raíñs, Musulman Rajputs, and Hindu Rajputs, Gujars, Brahmans, abound. The Gujars and the Hindu Rajputs and Brahmans are mostly in the hills, and the Gujars are here described as peacable and quiet, unlike other districts where they are the reverse,—being great thieves of cattle.

The costumes of the plain-dwellers do not differ from the foregoing descriptions. For the rest the following extract will supply information. It is taken from Barnes' Report.

Clothing. Men.

Kangra District.—" 291. The ordinary clothing of the poorer classes are, for the men, a 'topi' or skull cap, for a turban is seldom or never worn, a 'kurti' or frock reaching to the waist, or a 'cholu' which is a similar garment only extending somewhat lower, and 'kach' or breeches, for long trowsers are not " in vogue. In addition to these three articles, the peasant usually carries with him his " 'pattu' or blanket, which in hot weather he twists as a turban to defend his head from the " rays of the sun, or in winter wraps round his body, as a highlander flings his plaid.

" The frock and breeches are usually made of cotton woven by the village weaver or " julaha, and cut and sewn into shape by the village 'sui' or tailor. The pattu is of home " texture, generally in alternate squares of white and black wool, the only variety being in the " size of the squares. In the rains people travel about bare-foot, as the wet weather spoils the " shoes, but in all other seasons they usually possess a pair of slippers or 'júta.'

" The higher classes of course wear whatever they please. Their clothes are usually made " of English fabrics, and formed into shapes to suit the fashion or pleasure of the wearer. " The only peculiarity is that the 'kurti' is commonly retained by all, and in the head- " dress they all shew great coxcombry and taste.

" Two or more turbans of different colours are artistically mixed together, and bound " round the head so as to display the colours to advantage, and to fall in heavy yet graceful " folds over the right ear. The usual mixture is a red ground with a white exterior turban, " and the effect is always becoming. Like all other fashions, it is sometimes ludicrously " exaggerated, and I have seen as many as seven turbans of different hues, not very judiciously " chosen, wrapped round the head of a hill dandy. The hill people are also very fond of " wearing colored vests and scarfs. They also adopt the effeminate habit of wearing ear-rings " of gold, graced sometimes with pearls, and those who can afford it will display gold or silver " bracelets, and necklaces of beads alternately with gold.

Women—their dress.

" The female dress is also very picturesque. On ordinary occasions they wear the 'gagra' or petticoat, the 'choli' which covers the breasts, " and the 'suthan' or long trowsers, with a 'dopatta' or mantle " to form the head dress. In the winter they adopt a gown, called 'doru' which covers the " whole body, fitting close under the neck. For ordinary wear, these garments are all made of " simple colors and are both modest and becoming. But on gala days, though the habili- " ments are the same, the texture and colors are strikingly altered. The petticoat is adorned " with printed silver or gold patterns, which set off the extremities, or the whole garment is " made of streaked colors tastefully associated. The 'dopatta' or mantle instead of being a " simple white is transformed into a pink or yellow scarf. The 'choli' is made of equally " gay material, and the person is ornamented with various articles of jewellery. The nose ring " or 'bálu' is the most common ornament. Every woman who is not unmarried, nor a " widow, displays this piece of finery. It is a sign of married life, and shews that the wearer " still rejoices in the society of her husband. The lower classes are restricted to silver, other- " wise the 'bálu' is always made of gold, in circumference limited only by the taste of the " possessor.

" There is a great variety of female jewellery, which it is not necessary to detail. The " Girth women are very foud of a profusion of necklaces; some are constructed of coloured glass " or pieces of poreclain (kach) and beads, the vegetable produce of the forest. This dress is " the costume adopted by Hindus. The Mahomedan women do not evince such taste or " coquetry. They never wear the gagra or petticoat, and very seldom the doru or gown. " They restrict themselves to loose trowsers and a mantle. The gown of the lower classes is " made usually of coarse chintz. There is another dress, confined, however, to the higher ranks, " the paswaj, which is a cotton gown of very light texture almost approaching to muslin, and " made of various gay colors".

Lahul.—The Lahul people wear a dress of which the principal material is woollen cloth, and which resembles the dress above described.

The men wear a coat (chola), trowsers called "sutni," a waist-cloth "gáchi," and shoes made of a thick leather sole oblong in shape save that it is extended at one corner to make room for the great toe, the upper part of the shoe is a net work of string: such a shoe is called "púla." In the very wild parts shoes or rather sandals made of "bagar" grass (*Eriophorum sp:*) and also of plaited straw are used, especially for crossing over rocky paths and snowy places. The upper covering of all is a thick "chádar" or wrapper of woollen cloth, fastened over the shoulder by the aid of a kind of brass brooch called búmni.

The scarf that the Lahul women wear is called "pecha."

Kulu.—The Kulu men wear a dress not unlike the Lahulis, the topa, or cap, the gachí or girdle a frock called chola, and also "khuntí," and other articles the same.

The Kulu women's head cap is called "dháthú, " and they also wear a long tail of black woollen thread plaited into their own hair like the " paranda" of the plains and called "jathi."

The shawl or wrapper is called "dhúmkar," and the women wear long leggings, which being made far too long for the leg are worn gathered in folds round the leg, and this is for the sake of warmth in the winter; such leggings are called "paunche."

As ornaments women also wear enormous anklets, like huge fetters, of zinc and lead, rudely carved with patterns &c.: these are called "gunkare" and another variety 'kangnu.' The weight is considerable.

Ladakh Custome.—The following account is extracted nearly verbatim from *Cunningham's Ladakh, p.* 303. " The men of Ladakh wear a cloak of woollen, thick and warm. * * " The cloak is called *la-pa-sha,* it is made like an ordinary choga or dressing gown, either " white or 'khudrang,' the natural dirty grey of the wool. It is never washed and never " taken off till it falls off.

" Round their legs from knee to ankle they have coarse woollen leggings (called *rKang-* " *Phying*) of felt, fitting tightly or else wrapped close round the leg and secured by a garter " (called *rKang-gDub*) which is wound spirally round the leg from the ankle upwards. The " garter is generally black (a woollen tape) but sometimes red. On their heads they wear " either quilted skull caps, as filthy as their cloaks, or caps of sheepskin with the wool inside " and with a large flap behind which covers the back of the neck as well as the ears.

" Those in better circumstances have fur caps of the same shape. Their boots are of felt with soles of sheep or goat skin, which are turned up all round and sewn to the felt.

" The upper part of the felt boot is open to the front, and is allowed to fall over something " in the manner of the boots worn in England in Charles II's time. The " Lamas " wear red " boots, and the others mostly have theirs ornamented with small bits of colored cloth in the " front.

" The Ladakhi women wear a black woollen jacket with a large striped petticoat of many " colors (and stamped with a pattern on the stripes) generally green, blue, red and yellow, " reaching below the mid-leg. Over all they wear a sheepskin with the wool inside, secured " or rather skewered in front by a large iron or brass needle.

" The poorer classes have the outside of the skin plain, but those in better circumstances " cover it with coarse woollen baize, either red, blue, green or yellow, and with a broad border " always of a different color. The upper classes cover this sheepskin cloak either with brocade " or with silk. Their heads are always bare, the hair being arranged in a border of narrow " plaits which hang round the head like a long fringe.

" From the forehead over the crown of the head they all wear a long narrow band of " (red) cloth studded with coarse many-flawed turquoises, which hangs down behind as low as " the waist, and is usually finished off with a tassel of wool or a bunch of cowries.* The ears " are covered by semi-circular woollen lappets, fastened to the hair and edged with brown or " black fur, generally of the otter skin, called *kundaz.* * * * * They are made coarse " or fine according to circumstances; for the Ladakhi women seem to pride themselves upon " the style and material of their lappets, just as much as European ladies do upon the fashion " of their bonnets.

* This is the " perak," to be described presently.

Costumes of Spiti.

It is now time to describe the dress of the remote province of Spiti. Excellent illustrations of this will be found in photographs (which are better than pages of letter-press) in Mr. Egerton's volume on his tour in Spiti.

The dress of the men consists first of a pair of boots, of which the foot is of leather and the legs of woollen cloth of different colors, first a bit of yellow or red, and then a bit of black, secured under the knee by a garter. These are called "hlam." The upper garment is a loose coat of thick home-made blanket, with long skirts, belted round the waist with a coarse scarf.

They all wear ear-rings and necklaces of turquoises, coral and amber beads : every one has an iron pipe stuck in his belt ; a tobacco pouch with its flint and steel hanging to it ; and a little wooden bowl in the breast of his coat used as a drinking vessel. On their heads they generally wear a little round cap, but some wear a kind of Scotch cap, the loose top of which hangs down over the neck. Youths, except those in high position, ordinarily go bareheaded. The women also go bareheaded. The unmarried ones have one or two turquoise beads in their hair, but the married ones a most stupendous ornament called a "perák." * The dress of the women is a long gown like that of the men, and a pair of long loose trowsers tucked into the boots, which are worn like men's. They have no pipe or flint, for to their honor be it said the Spiti women do not smoke. When working in the fields (for all the farm work except ploughing is performed by women) they remove the perák (which is heavy) from their heads and let it hang down from the two ends, one of which is fastened to the shoulder, the other to the belt.

Captain Hay mentions that the large cloth boots being much larger than are requisite for the size of the leg, the vacuum is filled up with bhúsa, *i. e.*, chopped straw, or else with wool.

The women wear their hair in a number of plaits. The men also have their's done up into one long plait. Women are not secluded. The Lama has a variety of head-dresses, but in the Chinese fashion. The food of the people consists of wheat, barley and pease; they eat yak's flesh and make soup of it also. Animals are killed by strangulation to avoid shedding their blood. Tea is much drunk but prepared with butter and salt. †

The collection illustrating the Kangra, Kulu, Lahul, and Spiti dress, consisted of the following :—

639.—A perák or women's head ornament from Spiti.

This consists of a long leather strap or cloth strap ending in a double tassel, which hangs down from the back of the head ; in front there is a gold, silver or brass fan-shaped ornament, which comes down to the forehead ; on each side of the face two long ornamented tassels hang down, and behind hangs the tail of the perák, the strap before alluded to, which is covered with large turquoises pierced, and sewn on ; they are not fine stones,

* Egerton's Spiti, page 25. † Captain Hay's Report.

but large coarse pale blue pebbles full of flaws, and not worth above 5 rupees an oz. : they are brought from China. Mr. P. Egerton mentions he had great difficulty in obtaining the specimen (an inferior one) which went to the Exhibition of 1864, and even for that he had to pay Rs. 80 or £8. Only married women wear these perāks, but every married woman must have one ; consequently, as the turquoises are obtained with difficulty, fathers have sometimes long to wait before their daughters can be married.

640.—Hill woman's dress flowered with silver and gold (Kangra and Kulu.)

This is a scarlet skirt made of imported cloth and covered gaudily over with sprigs and flowers in gold and silver. It is made by first stamping the desired pattern on the cloth by means of wooden blocks charged with a gummy mixture, over this common gold and silver leaf is put, which adheres where the gum is, thus forming a pattern in gold or silver on the cloth ground. Such gaudy dresses are worn on festival occasions.

641.—Woollen girdle, Kulu.

This is nothing more than a long rope or rather piece of felt piping which is wound round and round the waist for a girdle : it is not twisted up like a rope, but is a smooth piece of " piping," the wool holding together owing to its felting property.

642.—Woollen jacket, Kulu.

643.—Woollen gaiters or leggings, Kulu.

644.—Cap, Kulu. This is a thick ring of felt, which encircles the head, the middle of the ring being covered with cloth. Otherwise describing it, it may be said to be a small cap of coarse black cloth, the edge of which is developed into a thick roll or ring.

645.—Coat and Trowsers, (Kangra.) The coat of the whitish blanket seen commonly in all the hills from Hazara to Simla. The trowsers are of a thin soft toad-colored leather of great pliancy and softness, and are, I believe, peculiar to Kangra : I have not seen them worn elsewhere.

646.—Shoes of Bagar grass.

These are a rude kind of sandals made up of *Eriophorum cannabinum* : they are bound on to the feet for walking or rather clambering over jagged rocky paths, and narrow ridges where the bare foot would be cut, and where the ordinary shoe could not be worn.

647.—Shoes of hemp called " Sheli." The best are made at Plách, and are often seen on the road between Kulu and Simla. The sole is either of felt or of hemp made up in to a thick mat and shaped 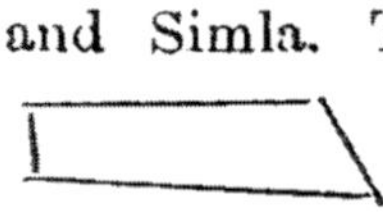 ; the foot is sustained by a rim of closely woven net-work of woollen thread.

648.—Shoes made of wheat straw, Kulu (vide *infra*).

649.—Dress from Lahul—Revd. H. A. Jæsche, and Tara Chand—consisting of a man's coat and trowsers (all of wool) a woman's dress, and socks, and shawl, and cap, and

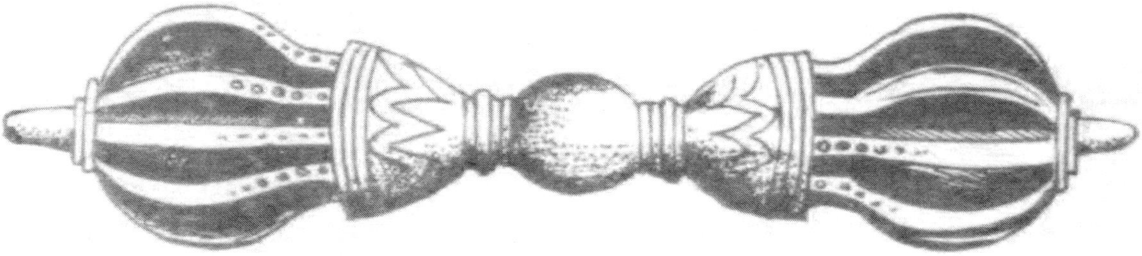

"Dorjé" or sceptre
(nearly full size)

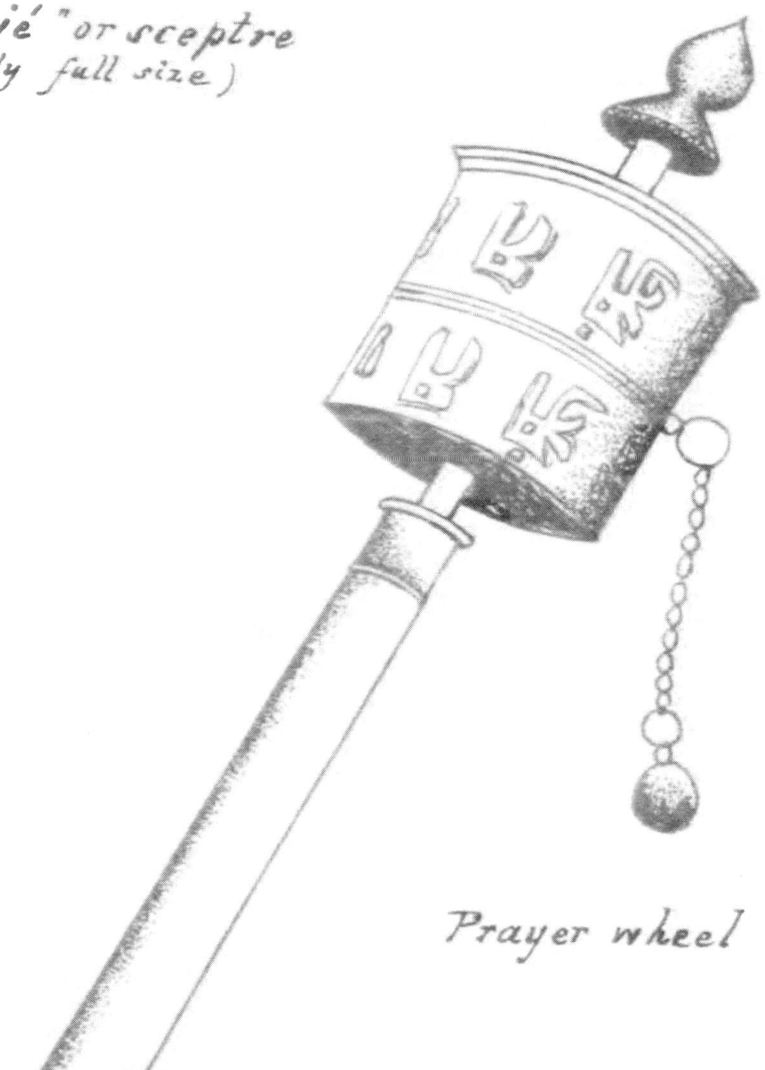

Prayer wheel

to face page 111 No 650

a girdle,—also some straw shoes. In Thibetan the woollen cloth is called "rNambu"—*pronounced* Nambu.

The warp is of Changthán wool, used on account of the length of hair, the short Lahul wool is used for the shuttle thread. A coat costs Rs. 3-0-0, the trowsers Rs. 1-4-0, the girdle 6 annas, and cap 8 annas. The trowsers are of immense length, but this is remedied by wrapping or rather gathering them in folds round the leg up to the knee, for the sake of warmth.

The straw shoes are made by soaking the straw in water, after which it is beaten with a mallet and twisted into the requisite form. Everybody makes his own shoes. Coolies on a long journey usually carry as many pairs with them as they expect to spend days on the march.

650.—Lama's dress, girdle and shoes.—Lahul, Revd. H. A. Jæsche.

This appears to be a mere woollen gown and girdle of the common Orders: the superior Lamas and Abbots wear yellow robes on state occasions, and other satin robes on which are Chinese figures: their head-dresses are gigantic pieces of carved wood work. They are illustrated in Mr. Egerton's Journal.

I have since seen a very curious dress of a Lama of the Dengpa sect: it consists of a jacket of dull red woollen cloth (dyed with madder) called stod-tse (*pronounced* tötse); trowsers, a cloak called blagos (*pronounced* lagö) a "meditation band," which is a broad strip of red cloth, which is strained tightly across the shoulders and helps to sustain the devotee in the peculiar stooping posture he adopts when engaged in meditation. This belt is called 'sgom-thag.' "

This dress was accompanied by three instruments: one, the prayer wheel, called "mannaphanna"; it consists of a copper cylinder which turns on an axis of iron wire fixed into a wooden handle. Sometimes the cylinder is made of silver, or ornamented with silver letters embossed on it; the cylinder contains a central core of cloth, &c., round which is wound the strap or tape on which prayers are inscribed; the cylinder is made to rotate by jerking it with the hand, and as to the upper part a short piece of chain with a weight at the end is attached, when once set going it is easily kept in motion: the prayer is supposed to be said when the cylinder turns. Prayer wheels of this kind are often set up near villages on the side of a hill stream and so turned by water-power. Another sacred emblem is a dorji or sceptre, a small implement made of a bell metal called "khro" (*pronounced* tho). Its shape will be seen in the annexed plate.

A third implement is a blunt dagger, the blade of iron, the handle shaped something like the dorji and of the same metal; it is used not for fighting purposes, but for incantations and charms, &c.

651.—Woollen cap—Revd. H. A. Jæsche. This is a felt hat something like our English wide-a-wake: it is made either white or black of thick coarse felt, very easily turned into any shape, the rim can be worn up or down &c.: these are made by Chinese workmen at

Yarkand. Those sent to the Exhibition had first received a binding round the edge with velvet. A cap costs Rs. 2, but if made of pashm or shawl wool Rs. 4.

It was interesting to find in the Exhibition among the curious products of the wild regions of Lahul, a set of worsted stockings made by Lahuli girls under the superintendence of the ladies of the Kyelang Mission.

Chamba Costumes.

The people of the Chauráh district wear the usual greyish white woollen cloth, a girdle of dark brown woollen or felt rope; their head-dress is a tall woollen peaked cap of the same color and material as their dress;—the cap has a deep rim which is turned upwards, and the rim being cut through in front ends in two projecting points into the top of the cap. The people frequently have a string or garland of dried yellow and purple flowers strung on alternately with pieces of white talc: this has some religious import.

The men here, as all over the hills, have rude silver ornaments and great beads of amber, sometimes also coral and turquoises of a coarse kind. Samples were sent of a cloak or choga, a tall cap and waistband and girdle; these came from Barmaor.

The women of the "Chauráh" district of the Chamba Hills, wear a small cap of cotton cloth, with a triangular peak or tail hanging down behind, a woollen coat, and narrow trowsers gathered into folds on the leg.

In the Pangí district the men wear a short thick grey woollen coat reaching to the knees, secured by a heavy girdle, either of woollen rope or of a blanket, wrapped round the waist. The legs are usually bare, except in the case of the richer agriculturists who wear woollen trowsers. Straw shoes called "púla," are universally worn. On the head is a woollen skull cap: small necklaces of amber, coral, &c., are worn. The women wear a large blanket as a skirt, a broad girdle of woollen cloth, and the body is covered by a blanket worn round the breast and with the ends thrown over the shoulders like a plaid and secured with brass pins. On their head they wear a high woollen cap, the crown of which is broader than the base and hangs over. Their ornaments are large ear-rings, neklaces of coral, &c. Every woman also wears a large round brass plate suspended by an iron chain, and hanging over the breast, a brass bell, and generally a bunch of brass pomegranates, which are hollow and jingle together: zinc bracelets or 'karas' are also worn.

The Buddhist villagers of Pangí are rather better dressed—at least the wealthier classes. The men wear woollen caps, small ear-rings, and a woollen coat. The women wear a cotton jacket with tight sleeves, woollen trowsers, a blanket for a scarf. They also wear the bell and the plate, together with an immense profusion of long and short necklaces of cowries, beads, amber and coral chains. On the head a small cap lying in folds on the top of the head. A silver fan-shaped ornament hanging over the forehead, and chain and fringes descending on either side of the face. Anklets of bunches of brass pomegranates are also worn: the 'pula,' or straw shoes complete the costume.

The furthest province of Chamba consists of Chota Lahul: the Lahuli costume has already been described.

Costume of the Hill Tribes of Simla.

Men wear a long woollen coat, and rather baggy trowsers, tight at the ankles; a long rope or piece of cotton cloth serves as a girdle; the cap is usually of black woollen felt, having the thick edge or ring, such as before described, and which is also worn in Kulu and figured in a photograph at page 8 of Mr. P. Egerton's Spiti Journal before quoted. Their shoes are of woollen felt with leather soles.

Women wear a dress consisting of a body and petticoat stitched together, or made in one. They do not wear trowsers as a rule—unlike the other hill people. The hair is plaited and make into long tails with black wool, the ends being finished off with red wool, and a gaudy colored kerchief is thrown over the head.

The people in the lower Hill States appear excessively fond of dresses covered with silver flowers, &c.: all cotton cloth is imported from the plains.

The Simla collection contained several pairs of shoes, and also snow shoes; men and women's caps, and several excellent blankets. The people here dye their wool with madder, &c., and occasionally vary their fabrics with lines or edgings of red. I have not noticed, however, the check or plaid so common in Kulu.

Costumes of the Frontier.

Leaving the Himalaya we now proceed to the costumes of the frontier. Any one who wishes to gain a good idea of the people themselves and their customs, I would refer to Pollock's account of Dera Ghazi Khan; to the Dera Ismail Khan Settlement Report; to the late Major James' charmingly graphic Report of Peshawur; and to Dr. Bellew's Yusufzai Report; besides the works of Burnes and Elphinstone on Kabul, and to Vigne and to Jacquemont's Travels.

652.—Dera Ghazi Khan. Of the clothing worn in the Derajat I have obtained the following particulars:—

There are two principal classes, Hindus and Bilúchis. Hindu men wear loose paijamas called "sharai," and sometimes dhotis—generally white, but occasionally colored. "Angarka" is a long coat reaching down to the knees. "Pairáhan" is an under-shirt worn under the angarka; a wrapper or chádar is worn above the angarka, when requisite.

Dastárs or turbans are not manufactured in the Derajat. A 'thán' or piece of muslin is divided into three pieces down its whole length and forms three turbans; sometimes red or pink turbans are worn. A cotton cap is worn under the pagri.

Mussulmans wear paijamas reaching to the ankle; instead of these a sheet called locally "dedha," or "táwad" or "taiband," it is worn either dark blue or white. A pairáhan or kurti is worn as an under-shirt, and also a chádar for a wrapper, or else the chádar is replaced by a "patka" or scarf, sometimes embroidered on both sides.

The Bilúchis wear loose paijamas with many folds, and the kurta as before, and the chádar or patka.

Hindu women wear a pleated skirt called "gagra," a bodice or stomacher called "chhola," embroidered, and a scarf called "pochan."

Mussulman women wear either a "gagra" or trowsers, and a chola or stomacher "sínaband," sometimes both, and a "pochan."

The Bilúch women wear a "kakka" or long bodice in lieu of the chola and scarf.

653.—Hazara Costume.

The dress of the residents of the plain country differs little from that of the inhabitants of the Punjab generally. A loose white kurta and flowing paijamas, the latter sometimes loose and open at the ankle, and sometimes drawn like a Turkish trowser, constitutes the dress of the majority, to which the higher class add a lungi as a girdle and another as a turban. The Khans wear the latter embroidered with gold. In the hill country, near the border, the garments, both tunic and trowsers, are often dyed of a deep blue, with a small skull cap for a head covering.

The prevalence of the dark blue dress and the blue turban, often with a bright crimson border, will strike the traveller in Hazara. On passing through the district from Abbottabad, the people struck me as looking much better dressed than is usual in the plains; there were none of those dirty looking, half naked men, whose costume is made up of nondescript pieces of cotton very dirty and ragged.

654.—Wazírí Costume, Banu District, and Banuchi Costume.

The following particulars were kindly obtained for me by Mahomad Hayát Khán, Extra Assistant Commissioner at Banu.

The Wazírís are the hill people in the territories adjoining the Banu and Marwat plains; the Banuchis are the inhabitants of the Banu plains.

The people eat wheat, maize, barley, and bread made of them, and mutton—meat is much used, also porridge of roughly pounded maize.

The clothing of the men is as follows:—A turban, dastár, is locally called "dastúr." It varies in length from one yard to six, and is of coarse cloth; it is usually of a dark blue color, and in the branch clan of Tewár Khel, red, and in some other clans white: some of the Maliks wear turbans of still larger size.

The next article of dress to be described is the chádar, which in Wazírí dialect is called "patkí," it is usually white and of coarse texture: some few Maliks wear a blue "lungí." The body clothing or shirt—kamíz—is of three descriptions: the first is made of coarse sheep's wool, either of its natural color or white: it is a large loose article called "angarka," and on the breast of this shirt the Waziri women work embroidered patterns in silk or cotton. Such a shirt is called locally "shári," and its price varies from one rupee to three, this is very commonly used.

Maliks and rich people wear "angarkas," made of white cotton cloth, without seams, and which are locally called "halka."

Other clothes are made to fit the body (*i. e.* are made with seams "chín," and not left loose like the rest)—these are called "etkoi."

Paijamas or trowsers, called in Pashtú "pardek" or "partok," are worn loose and large, and of white cloth; and in the Masúd clan, the poor people and laborers wear them made of white wool.

The women's clothing is thus described:—

They generally wear on the head a "sipatta" of dark blue color, and made of coarse cotton cloth—they locally call this "takrai." Old women do not wear blue cloth, but one dyed grey with earth; and young women (as they call them in Pashtú Niyázmana Shanzai) do not wear a "sipatta," but another scarf called "jamai," which is white and embroidered with sprigs of colored flowers; for this a scarf called "langái" is sometimes substituted. It is a striped cloth, in black and white, and with a silk border.

The "kurta zenana," or body garment, called in Waziri dialect "khat," is of two kinds: one "jalána khat" and the other "giridana khat." The first sort is worn by unmarried women, and is loose and seamless, and of red colored "chet" or print; the second kind is worn by married women. It is made of dark red or dark blue coarse cloth, and is often embroidered with silk down the front: the Waziri women work this themselves. Just below the breast the skirt commences in a great many pleats, and reaches down to the feet. When these women go out on a journey or to work in the fields, &c., they tie the end of this skirt up on to their backs.

The women's trowsers are called "partek" or "pardek": those for unmarried women are white, and for married women are made of "susi." There are several kinds of "susi," called "vegamai," "zadr khesh," "sísar khesh," which are used for making paijamas; their fashion is this, that they fit tight to the leg as far as the knee, and above are loose. Children's dress does not differ from the former and is called by the same name; difference only being made of course in size. Young children do not wear the paijamas, they only wear a kurta (jacket) and kamíz or shirt. They wear on their feet sandals, called "jablimizri" and "kalbal chirmi," and exceptionally shoes.

The food of the Banuchis consists chiefly of barley and Indian corn. They rarely use wheaten flour, and the females are never allowed this luxury. A singular feature in the Banuchi costume is that the men never wear woollen clothes out of doors. In the coldest weather they generally appear in linen (cotton) garments, and this not from poverty, nor from any prejudice of caste or religion. The only cause they can assign is custom, and its origin is not to be traced, (Correspondence on Settlement of Dera Ismail Khan, Sec. 25.)

The Banu people wear dark blue clothes and lungis with a red border. I notice the following account of them from Masson's travels (1826—1838)* which may be interesting to the modern visitor of Bannu.

" On the same plain as Marwat, the Bannu people have besides a difference in their " costume, a smaller stature than the inhabitants of the former place. The Marwati is " generally clad in coarse white linen (cotton), in much the same manner as the Pathans on " the banks of the Indus. The people of Bannu wear dark clothing, and are fond of lungis " with ornamental borders. Both in dress and appearance they assimilate with the moun- " tain tribes. They are very brave, and remarkable for entertaining an *esprit du pays*. " They are eloquent in eulogiums upon their country, and the exclamation 'My own dear " Bannu!' is frequently uttered by them.' "

655.—PESHAWUR COSTUMES.

The dress of an Afghan—male or female—has been correctly described by the Honorable Mountstuart Elphinstone, at page 313, Vol. I., of his "Caubul." it may be mentioned here in addition, that the lungi or scarf, of various degrees of cost and excellence, is common to all, from the Chief or Khan who struts about consequentially, displaying the gold embroidered border of his finer scarf, to the humble ploughman, who must be contented with one made of the coarsest material, with a border and edging of a different colored thread merely. These scarfs are of various colors; but the most common are blue, whether of the finer or coarser textures.

Amongst the agricultural population, a scarf of the darkest blue, with a deep border of crimson and yellow silk gaudily, but not inelegantly, intermixed, is much in fashion and sure to be worn at fairs and festivals. The best of these are made at Hangú in Kohát. The prices of scarves vary from Rs. 4 to 100, or more even, according to the costliness of the embroidered border. The lungi is often twisted into a head-dress, the border, whether colored or embroidered, being conspicuously displayed. It is also sometimes used as a waist-band, and occasionally to cover the whole body like the plaid of the Scotch highlander. The usual mode of wearing the turban amongst Afghans is graceful and becoming. Amongst the young men much stress is laid upon the proper twisting up and adjustment of this adornment to the head. The most approved are generally worn around a small Persian skull cap, the tip of which peers from amidst the compressed folds of the patka. The trowsers or " paijamas" are invariably loose: amongst agriculturists, of a blueish grey color streaked with crimson. The better classes wear white, or silken trowsers of various colors.

The dress of the hill tribes is an inferior imitation of that of the peasants in the valley. Some tribes have a distinguishing peculiarity, as for instance the Swatis and Bonairis, who recognize each other at once by certain stripes peculiar to the trowsers worn in each country, somewhat analagous to the distinguishing stripes of tartan amongst the Scotch highlanders. Amongst the Afridis who trade most with Peshawur and Kohat, as

* Vol. I., 97.

the Adamkhail and others, drab or "khákí" seems to have become a favorite color, mainly, it is presumed, on account of the concealment it affords to the masses of filth which these wild men cherish around their persons.

The Peshawar collection contains a number of interesting specimens.

656.—[7645]. Kazlbáshí hat, called "pupákh." A tall black curly lamb-skin hat made of "post barrá sya" (skin of black lamb of Karákal.)

657.—[7647]. Choga or long over-coat of gram-colored pattu, (choga pattu nakhúdí).

658.—[7648]. Choga of camels' hair? Choga kurk.

659.—[7649]. Choga from Kashgár.

660.—[7650]. Khosa Kandahári. A stout cloak with sleeves of solid white felt.

661.—[7651]. A woman's head dress, chauni or parándá. A long silk band ending in gold tassels, used for plaiting in with the hair.

662.—[6532]. Small cap of Kandahar, also one from Peshawur. These are small skull caps quilted, of cotton or silk, and embroidered—similar caps were sent from Kabul. The caps are in various styles, called "Jamrodi," "Lálpúra," "Peshawarí": the cap itself is called "kullah."

663.—[7667]. Shoes for men and women from Peshawur, Kabul &c. These are often of green leather or "kimukht," and embroidered with gold or colored silk.

Postín, a wool lined cloak—"dálah khafak."—Badákshan.

Khaftán of samúr or Russian fur.

Postín kirsák, from Bukhara.

Khaftán of sanjáb or sable—Russian.

664.—[7678]. Belts containing powder horn, steel and flints, &c. These are very curiously embroidered on leather with silk, and contain a retort shaped leather horn, with a mouth-piece like an European powder flask, for powder; a number of tubes fixed side by side and cut off slantwise at the mouth to hold shot or bullets; a pouch or an apparatus for flint and steel and tinder, and places for knives, &c.

665.—[6769]. Clothes worn by dancing girls. Principally a robe with a tight body and sleeves, and a skirt rather short and having an immense number of pleats or gathers; and over all a large ornamentally bordered scarf, which the dancer moves about and folds gracefully in different postures as she moves: an immense nose-ring, rings, thumb-rings, ankle-rings, complete the ornamentation.

666.—Paijamas worn by Afrídí women.

667.—Coat and trowsers worn by Yuzufzaí men.

668.—Shoes made of "patta" or palm leaves, called "chapli." The collection also contained some leather shoes called "justah," and another kind called "kufshi."

669.—[7686]. Caps made of straw.

The ordinary dress of the Yuzufzaís consists of a loose kurti or "kamiz," and wide trowsers called "partog," with a "patka" or turban to wind round the head. All are of coarse cotton cloth of home manufacture, and are frequently worn without a change till in tatters. The dress of their Chiefs and well-to-do men is of the same kind, but of better material, and of English manufacture. The of dress the women only differs from that of the men in the substitution of the "orna" or chequered sheet for the turban. The sheet is of the same material and pattern for the whole tribe. *

NOTE ON THE DRESS OF FAKIRS IN THE PUNJAB.

Some of these of course wear no clothing at all but a thin bit of cloth for the waist, and wander squalid and filthy with matted and rank hair for place to place, staff in hand, and with the beggar's bowl often made of a large kind of cocoanut shell.

A class of Musulman fakírs, called Bánawá, wear a sort of white high cap, worked over with blue thread, and on the body an "alfa" or white shirt, having no sleeves, and embroidered over with blue thread : this is generally very ragged.

Baba Nának's fakírs often wear a similar dress ; some of them wear an ordinary turban, except that several lengths of hair rope are bound round it.

Rasúl Shahi fakírs cover their faces with the white ashes of wood ; wear a tall cloth cap on their heads, their bodies naked, a waist cloth (tahband) and plain shoes. These fakírs use spirits and eat meat with broth and rice.

Sanyásis and *Udásís* are wandering beggars, who are partly naked, and wear what clothes they do wear stained with ochre, and have a bowl in their hands, either of a cocoanut shell or of turned wood.

Bairágis are stationery fakirs, and wear large marks and streaks (*tíka*) on their foreheads.

"Jangam" fakírs wear on either side of the pagrís, and in front also, three brazen concave plates indented at the edges to represent the sun.

Saráwi or Pûj fakírs are the Gurus of the Bhábra caste ; they always wear a bit of cloth over the mouth to avoid killing any little insects in the air with their breath, also they carry a stick headed with a sort of brush to clean away insects from being trodden upon : they wear no shoes.

* Bellew's Yusufzai, page 215.

APPENDIX TO CLASS X.

NOTE ON A FEW OF THE MOST REMARKABLE DRESSES IN THE LAHORE CENTRAL MUSEUM.

Central Asia.—(A Láma of the higher order)—A flowing tunic of dark blue satin, with very long sleeves like a modern barrister's gown, the sleeves having broad stripes of green and scarlet silk. An apron of blue satin hangs in front, on which is worked the head of a huge dragon, his gaping mouth and fierce eyes being very prominent ; over the shoulders hangs a sort of cape hanging down in a point before and behind. It is in fact a square bit of brown satin edged with yellow, with a hole in the middle for the head.

A Láma of an inferior order has a dress of common red woollen cloth dyed with madder or kuámi root ; it is a long gown reaching to the feet, secured by a girdle of woollen cloth ; a scarf of woollen cloth is worn : his head-dress of red cloth, being an immense head-dress like a very large Scotch bonnet, projecting in front. On gala days a Láma wears a peaked red cloth cap edged with fur (foxes skin), and has the boots of cloth already described. The implements of a Láma are also held in the hand—the dorjí or thunderbolt, and sacred knife. The most curious article of the Láma's dress is his pocket handkerchief, a piece of thick woollen cloth about 1¼ feet long and 8 inches broad, dark colored, but striped across with white, blue, red and green. In his girdle he carries an iron pen case containing a pen, viz., a slip of bamboo.

A Báltí man is plainly dressed in a grey or dirty white woollen suit, a tunic with belt, and pyjamas all of the same material ; shoes like list slippers, all made of wool : he has a black skull cap.

A Báltí woman's dress is not represented, except by a cap of red woollen cloth hanging down in a long peak or tail behind.

There are two Ladákhi men's dresses : one sent from the Kangra district has pyjamas and tunic of whitish woollen cloth with a woollen shawl ; a leather bag to hold food, a rude tobacco pipe, a pouch for flint and steel, and a knife or dagger in a wooden sheath completed the Ladákhi's requirements. His cap is of brown wool somewhat rolled up by way of a brim : the top of the cap is red. A plume or bit of artificial flower is stuck in the cap, made of bits of talc and dried flowers tied on to a slip of bamboo. His feet are bare, or he wears grass shoes. The other dress, a Ladákhi shepherd's, sent by Dr. Cayley, has a long coat with red facings, no pyjamas, but bits of felt bound round the leg by goat hair laces; boots of grey cloth with leather soles, ornamented by a triangular bit of purple cloth over each instep. The girdle is a black woollen fringed one : his dagger, pipe, &c. he carries like the other. Two caps were sent, both like long bags, which, placed on the head, hang down on one side like a night cap ; one is of soft black cloth, the other of brown cloth with a pattern rudely embroidered on the front.

The Ladákhi woman's dress sent from Kangra district has a coarse and thick coat of dark brown wool, and pyjamas of the same ; her feet are protected only by grass shoes : a girdle of woollen cloth completes her attire, and she wears on her head the perák.

The Ladákhi woman's dress sent by Dr. Cayley appears to be a winter dress : the gown, a body and skirt, is made up of strips of cloth alternately dark red, dark blue, black and dingy yellow, and printed with a pattern. She wears a woollen girdle, from which depends a "chatelaine" of strips of leather with tassels of cowrie shells, also a very long string with an immense bunch of goats' hair tassels reaching down to the ground—sometimes this last is suspended from the head; for a cloak she has a square shawl of thick sheep skin, the fur worn inwards. The outside is covered with red and green cloth. The head dress consists of two large lappets of black fur over each ear, and kept in its place by the hair being bound round and round in plaits: she wears the perák, and, in front, jingling ornaments over the forehead. Woollen boots, the tops the same material as the dress, completed the costume.

The Spiti dress has already been described, but I will describe the dresses in the Museum. The woman has loose red trowsers of woollen cloth ; clumsily made boots of leather, the tops being of wool. Her tunic is black and short, confind by a red girdle, all the red being a dull madder tint; over her shoulders a small woollen kerchief ornamented at either end with a fringe and a border of large white spots: on her arms are bracelets made of circles of white conch shell. An immense necklace of white beads also cut out of shell is round her neck, and a smaller necklace of large lumps of crude amber and turquois with coral beads between ; on her head she has a perák.

The Spiti man has boots like the woman's, no pyjamas, but a long woollen coat reaching to his ankles ; his cap is a little skull cap of red, with a black border.

A woman of Yárkand's dress was sent by Dr. Cayley. It consists of white cotton pyjamas fastening at the side, while the man's fasten in front ; a tunic or vest of the stiff Yárkand silk of curious pattern—crimson with white blotches—edged round the neck and at the opening with a band of green silk ribbon, two or three bars of which green are also sewn on to the body of the tunic over the left breast only ; as a girdle she wears a white kerchief embroidered with silk, and over all a choga of Russian print ; her boots are like small Wellingtons, the tops of pale leather with a black border, the lower leather of darker color, ornamented by a strip of green leather over each instep, and a crest of green floss silk down each foot; under the boots large felt socks are worn : a small skull cap of black cotton, prettily embroidered with silk, covers the head in summer, and a thicker cap, lined with fur, in winter.

The Chamba State sent some articles of dress from Barmaur. The dress consists of a thick grey woollen coat called chúí (choga), with a long twisted dark brown girdle of goats' hair—the hair generally felted together into a solid rope or piping ; gray cloth trowsers are worn, or, when the snow is on the ground, the legs are wrapped in strips of woollen cloth. The cap is of grey wool, peaked with a flap to cover the back and sides of the head, but generally worn turned up against the peak: the flaps *turned down* are worn in mourning for a relative. A kalgí or tuft of pheasant's feathers is sometimes struck in the cap, as in Kulu; also a 'bid' or bunch of flowers, made of pieces of talc tied to bits of stick, or dried red and yellow flowers, forming a primitive idea of artificial flowers.

CLASS XI.

LEATHER MANUFACTURES.

Three classes of leather are to be met with in the Punjab : one the country leather, bulls,' calves,' buffalos' hide, goat skins, and occasionally camels' hide, with some few others of local manufacture. The other includes leathers from Kabul and Peshawur. The third consists of European imported leathers.

In the 1st class there is little to notice in a manufacturing point of view. The greater part of the leather produced is thick and hard, but of strength inferior to European. The process of tanning is uniformly rude and troublesome, though the results are occasionally satisfactory as regards softness of the hide. The slow process by which the skins are allowed to soak for days together, only to receive another soaking when the first is done, is the best calculated to produce a pliant and supple leather, and is quite suited to the slow, patient, and sedentary habits of Oriental workmen.

Bullocks' hides yield the strong leather used for shoes and general use ; buffalo hide, the thickest of all, where great strength is required ; goat skins furnish thin leather, and camel hide is rarely and locally used—Delhi being the only district which sent a specimen to the Exhibition of 1864.

The process of tanning consists in soaking the skins in lime water for some days to loosen the hair and surface of the skin, the hide is then scraped, and, after washing, is sewn up in the form of a sack, the interior being filled with the bark of the kikar (*Acacia arabica*); water is frequently proved over it, the skin bag is then reversed in position, and the watering repeated. The length or duration of each stage in the process varies according to the nature and thickness of the skin to be tanned.

The finishing process consists in taking the skin when still just damp and spreading it on the ground, it is then rubbed over with a wooden block or mallet furnished with a handle, and called "hathelí :" it is rubbed on both sides.

The finer skins are polished by a bit of horn or of agate, let into a lump of clay or wood for a handle. Among the best varieties of leather made in the plains are the soft wash-leather and hides of the Kangra and Hushyarpúr Districts, and the red skins of Núrpúr. The former are of very soft texture, generally a greenish buff color, so soft that the thinner skins are made into gloves and constantly worn as breeches by the Kangra hill-men. The same art applied to skins produces a pleasing result to the fancier, inasmuch as all about Kangra leopard skins and other ornamental furs can be obtained, the leather being beautifully and completely preserved, but with all the fur uninjured.

I have obtained from the Kangra district the following account of the manufacture:—

First the skin is wetted and then steaped in a 'matka' or earthen pan full of lime and water, the mixture to be sufficient in quantity to cover the skin completely. Every day the earthen pan, which is kept carefully closed over, is opened and the skin turned and shaken in the lime-water; if the skin is thin, 20 days of this treatment suffice; if thick, one month. After this the skin is washed in clean water, and then the skin is well rubbed with the dried and powdered leaves of the Dhao tree (*Conacarpus latifolia*) for two hours successively. After the rubbing is over, the leaves and skin are put together in a vessel and water added. Next day the skin is tied on to a stick and wrung out (as a dhobi does clothes). Again it is steeped in a fresh solution of leaves, and this process of steeping and wringing out is repeated for four days consecutively: fresh leaves are to be used each time. The skin is then sewn up with múnj string into a hollow sack and filled with "dhao" leaves, and hung up like a "massak"; on being taken down it is reversed and hung up again by the other end; this ensures both ends very well impregnated—the hanging process occupies two days. After this the skin is opened out and dried, and then rubbed with oil, and eventually washed. When dry it is scraped with a sort of iron scraper called 'rambí,'* after this it is again rubbed with oil. After 3 or 4 days it is washed in cold water and dried. After that it is rubbed with a mixture of curds and water, and again washed. The leather thus prepared is then soft. The skin principally used is that of the Sâbur or Sámbar deer; but other skins can be used—goat's, buffalo's, deer's, &c.: the color is a sort of toad color. The leather is made into gloves, gaiters, and also trowsers, worn by the hill men about Kangra, &c. Besides the art of making this soft leather, the people are very skilful in dressing animals' skins with the hair on. The same process appears to be followed as that above described, but the hair is carefully preserved, and the scraping rubbing, &c., done on the inner side. Skins of tigers, bears, leopards, cheetas, &c., are thus prepared.

Two men in a year can prepare 18 scores of skins. The process cannot be carried on during three months of the rainy season.

Much of this preparation of skins is done in the village of Bulwán, iláka Jíjun of the Hushyarpur District.

The Núrpúr leather manufacture has been thus described in a letter from the Nurpúr Tahsildar :—

"The leather prepared is of two kinds, thick and thin: the thickest of all is the buffalo hide, and next in thickness the hide of cows and bulls. The thin kinds are made of the hides of goats, sheep (dumba), rams (menda), Kakrel (deer skin); and besides these horses' asses' and and camels' skins are utilized. The thick kinds are made of two colors, black and red, and the thin kinds in black, red, yellow, and green: the red or crimson is the commonest. The method of preparing the small skins is as follows:—The skins are taken off and rubbed with two chittaks of salt, and put in the sun; in one day they dry, after that they are washed, and afterwards rubbed with wood ashes, and the hair, which is thus loosened, scraped off with a piece of wood. Again the skins are put into water and rubbed with pieces of rough potsherd, which completely removes the hair, &c.: again the skins are washed. When 40 skins have got thus far, they are together put into a great earthen cauldron or 'nánd,' together with barley meal 6 seers, and salt 2½ seers, and water

* Ramba is the short spade or trowel used by gardeners: rambi is a small one.

is poured on. For four days the skins are left to soak, after that 2 seers of 'ban-kath' (coarse catechu extracted from the *Acacia catechu*) are added. The soaking is continued for four or five days longer, after which the skins are taken out and scraped with an iron 'khurpa' or scraper : this completes the final cleansing from hairs, &c. After this the skins are again soaked in a nand with 7 seers of barley meal and 3 seers of salt in fresh water, for 3 or 4 days. By this time the skins are clean and almost colorless.

In order to make red skins, 4 seers of 'lac' are boiled in water with two chittaks of 'sajji' (coarse soda), and two chittacks of the bark of the Lodar tree (*Symplocos paniculata*), the skins are then dyed in the mixture, and after that 20 seers of the bark of the Amaltás (*Cathartocarpus fistula*) are ground fine, and then being infused with water, the skins are thrown in and allowed to lie for 3 or 4 days. On being removed, the color is fixed by rubbing the skins with 4 seers of salt ground to powder.

The cost of preparing 40 red skins is as follows :—

	Rs.	*A.*	*P.*
Skins, ...	10	0	0
12 seers salt, ...	1	4	0
13 seers barley meat, ...	0	5	0
2 chittaks sajji, ...	0	0	3
Lodar Bark and Catechu, ...	0	0	3
20 seers Amaltás, ...	1	0	0
TOTAL Rs., ...	12	9	6"

Before concluding the account of the best leather prepared in the plains, I should not forget to mention that, at Gujrat, one or two men have the art of preparing goat and sheep skins into fine soft leather, which, in texture and general appearance, is hardly, if at all, inferior to European. The men will not divulge the method of preparation for fear of spoiling their trade. The leather is principally used for covering the very comfortable easy chairs known as the Gujrat or "Capperina" chair, which was the design given them by a former Deputy Commissioner named Capper. It is highly probable that the process is a more or less satisfactory imitation of the European process of softening, dyeing, and polishing leather; the skins in all probability owe their softness to that patient and long continued process of washing and soaking above described: the dyeing, finishing, and polishing being the special art. The colors are generally dark green, and claret color or maroon. The former is produced either with the aid of indigo and some yellow, or with an extracted dye stuff obtained by infusing pieces of brightly dyed English cloth—a practice much resorted to in obtaining a dye from cloth—the red is produced with lac. After the dye has been applied, the dry skin is carefully polished with a bit of horn or cornelian fixed into a handle of clay. I can, however, obtain no further particulars of the work. Any native factor with the curiosity to look into an

English manual of manufactures, and copy the process described, would, after a few experiments, and possible failures, eventually equal or surpass the Gujrat work.

Of the second class ; the leather that comes from Peshawur, and is also imported from Kabul, is the best in quality, and most pretentious in variety and color.

Thus we have besides the usual plain brown, red, and black country leathers, a black leather with mottled surface like imitation morocco ; a mottled green, and also turquoise blue leather, much used in making shoes worn by certain sects of Mussulmans, and largely exported to Kashmir, where it is used for shoes. It is also made use of in embroidering or ornamenting saddlery, belts, and the hunting and warlike accoutrements common to all the border tribes.

This leather is made in Kabul ; not I believe in British territory. There is also a sort of bronzed leather imported from Kabul, called "kimsan." A note on the Kabul and Peshawur leathers was sent me by Lalla Piyarí Lal, Extra Assistant Commissioner at Peshawur.

Bulghár leather (the fragrant hide noted in No. 646, page 157, Volume I,) comes from Russia, and is not made in India. The manufacturing process is not known.

I have been informed, however, that the skins which sell from Rs. 15-0-0 to Rs. 25-0-0 each, are said to be horses' hides, are of a brown color, and marked with the small diamond check often seen on "Russia leather." It is said that the delightful scent is due to long and careful tanning with birch bark : the tanning is certainly unequalled.

My native correspondent had however different views as to the cause of the fragrance.

"The people believe that there are great pits in Russian territory in which the tanners collect bullocks' and other hides after first cleansing them. About the date of the appearance of the star 'suhail' (Canopus) by the disposition of Providence such a breeze sets in as by its contact causes the leather to become altogether fragrant." On the completion of the process the owners remove the leather from the pits sending it in all directions for sale.

As the scent is derived from soaking in the pits (ghár) the leather is called "bal *ghár*."

Both European gentlemen, and the rich classes in Afghanistan, spread these skins to sleep on in the hot weather. No insect will touch them.

About 100 skins are annually imported into Peshawur.

Another kind of leather is called "Chamra Irák." It is considered a valuable kind, and is made in Persia (or those provinces included in the somewhat indefinite term Irán, which, I believe, is hardly confined to Persia proper). The hide is bullock's hide : a second quality is made in Kabul. As it is much used in the manufacture and ornamentation of horse

LEATHER WARE.

trappings it has got the name of "irák."* Leather of this kind is sold of red and roan (badámi, color of the almond) color; about 50 skins are imported into Peshawar and are sold by *weight* at Rs. 2-8 a seer. "Kimukht" is another kind of leather. It is made of asses' skin, and of two colors, black and pale green or turquois color; in texture it is rough with speckles (*dánadár*): as many as 300 skins are annually made in Peshawar, of which about 100 skins are reserved for export down country. I have seen numerous specimens of Kashmiri shoes made of this leather, and also horse trappings ornamented with it in Deraját, I therefore suppose that it is made in Kábul also, and is among the north-western imports. The green shoes are worn by Mussulmans of the Shía sect, but Súnnis would object to wear them (See note to No. 719, *post.*)

The last class of leather now commonly met with, is imported from Europe. In every large town shoemakers and saddlers are to be found who work with European leather; and book-binders also buy calf, imitation morocco, and other leathers. A good deal of harness and shoemaker's work, which really is of Cawnpore work or made of better sorts of native leather, but in European fashion, is palmed off as European work.

Delhi.

Specimens illustrating this class are as follows :—

670.—[5523]. Bullocks' hide.—Skin of kid.—Camels' hide.—Buffalo hide.

Sheep skins and goat skins are called "nari" as a general term.

The leather of the first kind is used in shoemaking (see note on Shoes).

The raw hide is soaked one day in brine, and for one month in lime-water, after which the hair easily comes off with scraping. The hide is then steeped six days in an infusion of kíkar bark (*Acacia arabica*) or ámla (*Phyllanthus emblica*). It is then rubbed with alum.

Sirsa.

671.—Leather húka.—This is a leather vase for holding the water of a húka, it is ornamented with stripes of green kimukht leather and studded with little nails of silver.

[8222]. Is one with brass mountings.

[8223]. Of plain leather.

Very pretty húkas are made in Chúnián of the Lahore district, the leather being stiffened with bands and studs of bright engraved brass. The Hissar district also sent similar specimens; also the Mukatsar pergunna of Ferozpore district [8275].

* Irák is the name applied to a tract of country between Persia and Arabia, including the ancient Chaldea and Media. The adjective "iráki" is applied to the breed of horses produced in these countries.

672.—[8225]. Chágul—a leather water vessel. This very gracefully shaped vessel is figured in the annexed plate ; it is carried on journeys, and as for miles in this part of this country you may go without seeing a village or a well, such provision is necessary.

673.—[8215]. Bridles—Rohtak.

SIMLA.

674.—[8255-6-7 &c.] Ornamental leather work exhibited by the Rajas of Kyunthal, Biláspur &c.

These articles consist of glove boxes and other fancy boxes, cigar cases, &c., made out of stout black leather lined with red leather ; the surface is sometimes variegated with patterns of red, green, and gilt leather, but the distinguishing feature is that the whole is embroidered over in a white pattern with narrow slips of the quill of the peacock. The work is done, not at Simla, but in villages in the Kangra district and elsewhere, the work being mostly taken for sale to Simla. The men can work to order, initials and even crests on the leather. The work is remarkably cheap—a cigar case costs from 14 annas to 1 rupee.

KANGRA.

675.—Specimens of the soft greenish yellow Sábar leather before described.

[8242—5 &c.] Pantaloons, value Rs. 5, or Rs. 10 per pair.

[8244]. Socks, value Re. 1.

[8245]. Gloves.

[8246]. Purse.

[8247]. Gaiters.

676.—[8249] Red dyed skins from Núrpúr.

These skins are called Lákhí or lac-dyed skins. Specimens of book-binding in black and red leather of this kind were sent. The process of manufacture has already been described.

HUSHYARPUR.

677.—[8263 &c.] Kakrel skins of various qualities, from Re. 1-2 to Rs. 2-4-0 each.

These are prepared at Gurshankar and Húshyarpúr.

678.—[8254]. Waist-belt worked with gold thread (petí) by Jíwan of Anandpúr.

679.—[8255]. Black embroidered sword belt (gátra).

Formerly there was an extensive manufacture of this article in the Hushyárpúr district : now it has fallen into disuse.

680.—[8208]. Leather breeches made at Garshankar—of similar fabric to that described in the Kangra District.

Lahore.

681.—[8276]. Shield of "genda" or rhinoceros hide, said to have belonged to Guru Gobind Singh. These glossy black shields were once in general use ; many of the Multání and Frontier Chiefs still carry them.

Gujranwala.

682.—[5635 &c.] Series of hides—buffalo, bullock, goat, and sheep.

683.—[8300]. Shoes used by thieves (khosa) to muffle the feet of cattle so as to prevent their being tracked.

Shahpur.

684.—[8313]. A leather huka vase.

685.—[8314]. Horse trappings, value Rs. 2.

Gujrat.

686.—[8302]. Skins of polished leather by Umra of Gujrat. I have already alluded to this special manufacture.

Montgomery—(Gugaira).

687.—[8338-9]. Leathers from Sayadwalla.

688.—[8334]. Red leather from Harrapa. This is made like the red leather of Núrpúr.

689.—Leather rope.

690.—Ornamental huka vases.

691.—[8334]. An inflated hide used as a float for crossing rivers on, called "sandhrí" or sarnáí ; in the Peshawur list it is called "shináz." The word sarnáí is applied to an inflated bag, also to a bag-pipe ; "shinaz" is derived from the Persian "Shína" or shaná swimming. Properly speaking the sarnáí is a small float made of a goat skin ; while the large skins used in the hills are called "dreñ," or "daráin." They are in use on most of the rivers in the hills, and below, for crossing : the large skin is thrown into the river, the swimmer throws himself on it on his face and paddles along with surprising rapidity. Europeans and others often cross rivers seated on a four-legged bed or charpoy which is placed crosswise over two skins places together, other men on single skins with paddles accompany the machine and conduct it on its journey. In the proper season, when violent floods are over, a most pleasant journey can be made in a few hours on one of these charpoy floats : the Ravi and Satlej are constantly navigated in this way.

The following particulars concerning the preparation of the skins was obligingly furnishd me by Mr. G. C. Paul, in the employ of Messrs. Brassey, Wythes, Henfrey, and Co.

" The skin is only taken off a bullock that dies a natural death, because, if the throat were cut to kill it, the cut would interfere with getting the skin off whole ; for the skin of the head, too, is taken off.

The skinning commences by slitting open the skin from the inside of the right hind leg, a little below the knee joint, to the root of the tail. The ankle and hoof of each of the three remaining legs is cut off and thrown away, and then the whole skin taken off from the slit in the right hind leg. Turning the skin inside out, the openings of the ears, eyes, nose, mouth, and horns, and any other openings about the body, are then sewn up in such a manner as to make them perfectly airtight.

After arranging the above mentioned openings, turn the skin right side out and gently scrape off the hair from the skin, and then firmly tie the ends of the two forelegs and left hindleg. Through the large opening in the right hind leg fill the skin with either pounded bark of the "kíkar" tree, or with dried leaves of the 'als' (a tree which bears a long fruit, about 2 feet in length and 2½ inches or 3 inches in circumference, the inside of which is black and sweet) and hanging the skin head down on a tree, pour as much water into it as the bark or leaves will absorb, and for three days water must be continually added as fast as it oozes through the pores of the skin. On the fourth day the skin is emptied and allowed to dry. The slit of the right hind leg is then closed by gathering the skin in folds into a neat knot, brought as near as possible into the part where the tail was; through this knot make an opening sufficient to let in a piece of wood about ¼ inch thick, and 1 inch broad, then, placing a stick of this size in this opening, tie the knot firmly and make it airtight. The length of the above mentioned piece of wood must be 7 inches over what is necessary for fitting into the entire thickness of the knot, and these 7 inches project out in the same line as the three legs. This done, the end of the left hind leg is no longer permanently closed, but a cord is attached to close the end when through it the skin has been inflated. The "dreñ" is now ready for use. Sometimes the word "masak" is substituted for "dreñ," but it is a mistake, the word "masak" can only be applied to the skin bags used by "bhístis" or water-carriers, to whom the word "máshkí" is also applied. Throughout the Punjab "dreñ" is the expression, except when "khalra" is used; but this may be applied to any kind or form of skin or leather—"khal" means skin.

The man using a "dreñ," uses a paddle, of which the handle is about 18 inches long, and the blade about $8'' \times 5'' \times \frac{1}{2}''$; the thickness of the handle corresponds with that of the blade. The paddles are made of "deodar" wood, that they may float: if the man drops his by chance he can pick it up.

Before using a "dreñ" about two quarts of the oil, extracted from the very oily parts of a piece of "deodar" are poured into it, and by thoroughly inflating the skin every two or three hours during one day, the oil is forced through every pore of the skin, thereby rendering it, to a great extent, proof against damage from wet. Great care and every precaution should be taken to guard the skin from the sun. When using it on the river it must be kept wet by splashing water over it occasionally; when carrying it by land it is carried inflated (for which purpose a cord about ⅛th of an inch in diameter is tied loose roun, about the breast of the skin) with a wet cloth thrown loose over it, and when not in use the air is expelled, and the skin folded up into *three* folds, but must never be allowed to become very dry from want of the oil, or the creases formed by folding will split when the skin is again inflated. Also, always before inflating the skin or opening the folds, immerse the folded skin in water till it softens, in order to avoid all chance of the skin splitting; and, when not in use, the skin must be kept safe from the attacks of rats.

When by accident an opening is formed in the "dreñ," the knot to which the stick is attached is opened, the skin turned inside out through that leg, and a piece of leather sewn on so as to again make it air tight.

As regards the management of the "dreñ," when using it on the water it is placed legs upwards, and the head of the skin to the right of the man. He throws himself on so as to allow as much of his breast to go beyond as will be balanced by his legs, and to keep the skin from being carried away from under him, he presses it with the left arm from the elbow upwards, and the right leg from the knee upwards. The skin is then propelled by working the legs from right to left against the water, and a wooden paddle used in the right arm. The "dreñ" can only be forced in the direction of the right arm of the man, but to avoid a breaking wave an experienced man can back his "dreñ" a little.

The use of the stick which projects in place of the right hind leg is to allow of one man on a "dreñ" placing himself face to face with another, when each man holds with his left hand the stick of the other hide, and by this means they help one another to a great extent, especially when crossing a rough river with loads. In this way the two men will cross 5 pucka maunds safely."

With a few exceptions the "sarnai" or goat skin is prepared in the same manner as the "dreñ." These exceptions are :—

1. The head is cut off leaving as much of the neck as possible, and when the skin has been taken off (in exactly the same manner as that of the "dreñ,") the end of the neck is tied firm.

2. Instead of the "deodar" oil, the oil of the "til" seed is put into the "sarnai," and only one quart, or less, if it be a small skin.

3. The stick is not attached to the knot of the right hind leg, nor is it used at all in the "sarnai."

Besides these, the only difference is in the management of the "sarnai," it is placed legs upwards, and the man rests himself on it so as to get the neck between his thighs and the two fore legs also pressed between the thighs. His head and shoulders thus project beyond the hind legs of the skin; then he passes his left arm round the outside of the left hind leg and holds the knot of the right hind leg in that hand, by which means he can keep the skin stationary and pressed to his chest. He works his legs and right arm exactly the same way as in swimming.

On a large " sarnai " a man can take a load of about 30 pucka seers, and two men on " sarnais " can cross a third man by each holding the end of a stick, and the third man holding it in the middle, his body hanging in the water.

692.—Kuppa and Kuppi.

[8335]. Specimens also sent from SIRSA, ROHTAK &c., &c.

The kuppa is a huge vessel made of a leathering material, which is, in some cases, I believe, made of hide—camel hide and others—but more often, especially in the smaller sizes, of a glutinous skin, made by boiling the intestinal integrument of horses, cows, &c., into a gluey mass. A large clay block of the size and shape of the intended vessel is taken, and the softened material plastered all over it, well beaten together, and left to dry. After this is finished the interior clay is broken up and picked out.

The Rohtak collection exhibited some small vessels of this material, in the most fantastic shapes, some like jugs, others flattened and perforated apparently with large holes, which of course can open only longitudinally in the thin flat body of the vase. The jars are sometimes ornamented with patterns cut out in white parchment and struck on. The smaller vessels (kuppí) are used for holding oil, &c., and the large ones (kuppa) for holding oil, molasses, &c., in store : some of them are so large as easily to realize the familiar oil jars in the story of Ali Baba and the forty thieves.

They are mended easily when worn into holes by plastering on fresh integument.

Kuppas are sold according to size—a kuppa to contain one maund so much, or six maunds so much.

693.—A water bag called kúní.

694.—Scale dishes (tarázú) made of camel hide.

This sort of scale is very common in many districts for weighing grain, &c.

695.—[8341]. Native horse trappings. I describe these in a separate note on Native Saddlery, &c.

696.—[8142]. " Khopa "—Hollow leather caps put over the eyes of cattle when employed in turning wells, oil mills, &c.

697.—[8343]. " Khosa "—Mufflers for feet of cattle (before described).

BANNU.

698.—[8359]. Camel's head gear—Marwat.

An apparatus of leather adorned with strips of green and red leather, tassels, and white cowrie shells strung together. Camel trappings in the Deraját and Bannu are often exceedingly ornamental ; woollen rope and tassels, and bridles of cowrie shells being the prevailing fashion. A large necklace is added covered with cowries or little bells, and a large tassel dangling in front.

PESHAWUR.

699.—[8162]. "Khal sabz," green leather.

Some account of this has been given already, but the secret of making the color is not disclosed. I believe it is produced with acetate of copper.

700.—[8766]. Black leather, value Re. 1 a skin.

701.—[8363.] Fine leather (chamra irák, above described) called "Mesha Badámi," value Rs. 2.

702.—[8365.] A "Shughla," or leather bag for carrying flour, rice &c., on a journey.

703.—Shákh, or horn or leather powder flask shaped like a horn.

These were used all over the Punjab, and by the Sikhs, sometimes made of leather highly embroidered with silk and colored leather, as in the Deraját specimens, sometimes made of metal; the powder is extracted by a small hole with stopper in the flat covering of the broad end of the horn.

704.—"Kamr Khísa," soldier's or hunter's belt, having attached to it a small leather flask with long neck for shot, a knife or series of knives, flint and steel, and slow match for the matchlock, and a series of short bamboo tubes sewn together side by side and covered with leather to hold bullets. These are everywhere worn in the Deraját, and by the frontier tribes; the Deraját ones are of soft rough leather, but prettily embroidered with colored silk. The various implements including the powder flask hang from the belt by straps after the fashion of a lady's "chatelaine."

705.—Water vessel of leather for a journey, value Rs. 2 called Mathara or Chágul.

HAZARA.

706.—[5681]. Hide from Palki. DEPUTY COMMISSIONER HAZARA.

Skins are soaked first for 15 days in water and lime, then cleaned and the hair removed, the skin is then sown up, leaving one aparture, and filled with particles of oak or cheer bark or "bán," (*Rhus cotinus*) or leaves, and on these water is constantly poured until the skin is thoroughly saturated. The price is about 1 rupee per hide.

NOTE ON NATIVE SADDLERY AND TRAPPINGS.

Native saddlery is generally much more ornamented than European.

The saddle (zín or káthí) is made of wood covered with leather or cloth, or velvet, and padded : it is very high both behind and in front, so that it is almost impossible to fall off. Under the saddle a namda or felt is placed to protect the horse's back from rubbing. Poorer people use a fold of blankets &c. ; middle class people the felt; and nobles and rich people a chárjáma or saddle-cloth of velvet richly embroidered and padded with felt. Sometimes the saddle is ornamented by a number of huge silk tassels which hang down on either side of the horse, both in front of the saddle and behind, being attached thereto by leather straps: these are only worn on gala days. A saddle so ornamented is called "laryanwáli kathí," or in the Deraját and Multán, where the ornament is oftener used, "dhákáwali." The girths are made of "newár."

The stirrups are made of leather covered with red cotton cloth, or silk, or brocade; a crupper is commonly used, and called "dhumchí." The horse has on the head a "sirdawál," or púzí (head stall); the "zerband mah nukta," nose band and martingale, and round the neck a "hainkal" or necklace of great glass beads, or shells, or gold coins, or coral. A hainkal taken in 'lute' at Lucknow, was found to be made of beautiful amethysts, set in gold.

The bit is called "lagám" of whatever pattern it may be. Native bits are nearly always very severe ones, furnished with rings, spiked or barbed bars, &c. The reins are called "bág."

A riding or sowárí camel is furnished with a double saddle for two riders, called "káthí," and is ornamented with a neckband called hainkal, which usually has a large colored worsted tassel hanging down in front. On grand occasions silver ornaments are worn.

A camel of burden has a pack called "pálán," made of rough "tát" or matting stuffed with straw, &c., in lieu of the saddle.

An elephant is fitted with a gadela or felt pad, over which a "jhúl" or richly embroidered housing is thrown. It is the jhúl that looks so brilliant on State occasions on the elephants of the nobility. Immense sums are spent on embroidering in gold on velvet, these huge saddle cloths.

The haudá is either an open one flat, like a shallow box or tray, or is made like a chair, or has a dome or canopy—the latter is called 'haudá amárí.' Haudás are often covered with plates of silver chased and brought into patterns.

SADDLERY.

NOTE ON SHOES WORN IN THE PUNJAB.

I reserved this subject for a separate note, with an illustrative plate, as it is a sufficiently curious one. Nothing so well indicates the strange diversity of tribes in the Punjab territories, as the curious variety of shoes worn. Thus we have shoes suited for the snows and mountain paths of the Himalaya ; broad strong shoes for the frontier warlike tribes strangely sewn with leather thongs and bright with silk embroidery; we have the green slippers with high iron shod heels worn by Mussulmans at Peshawur ; delicate little gold worked shoes for the ladies of the Jach Doab ; gorgeous brocade shoes from the Delhi bazars ; classical Greek buskins from Bannu ; descending at last to the imported patent leather boot, now esteemed by the smarter class of office baboos.

HILL SHOES.

707.—[7456]. Hill shoes from Jubal.

708.—[7458]. Do. from Basáhir.

709.—[7570]. Do. made of Bagar grass (*Eriophorum Sp.*) Kulu.

710.—[7511]. Do. wheat straw—Kulu.

711.—[7532]. Pair of snow shoes (Spiti) called in the local list " feelum momani."

712.—[7532]. Wooden shoes for walking on snow—Spiti, called "kair" or "ker."

The design of nearly all these shoes is alike. The straw ones are represented in the annexed plate. The grass shoes are made up of wisps of the dry grass plaited together, the principle in all cases being to make a thick hard sole, with or without a covering over the toe, and with straps to secure them like sandals. Every traveller takes two or three pairs with him, and as soon as one is worn out he takes a new pair ; it is almost impossible to slip on either rock or snow with them. Grass shoes are called 'phulharru' in Kashmir, and 'patáwa' towards the plains. " Púla" is also a common term in Kulu and Chamba.

A more pretentious kind of shoe is that to be met with all about Mandi, Plách, and Rampur : near Plách the people told me they were called "shelli." The sole consists of a bit of mat woven up of strong hemp string and rudely shaped to the foot, it is kept in its place not by straps or string, but by a close edging of woollen net work sown up over the toe. Some shoes of this kind have felt, and some leather soles. They are very comfortable for an European to walk in if he has soft leather socks to wear under them. Shoes of this kind have already been described.

DERAJAT.

713.—[8350 &c.] Shoes from Rájanpúr, Dera Gházi Khan, &c.

These are made of stout rough leather, sewn with leather thongs or thick cotton thread, and ornamented with cloth and with silk embroidery.

Figure 2 represents a pair of men's shoes with thick soles called "chuni rámi" from Bakmála. A pair a little less thick are called " Bakhmála zenáni kábuli " in the Museum. A curious pair of shoes of a very squat form, were sent from the Mazári hills by Imam Bakhsh Khan. The shoe is of coarse reddish colored leather, sewn with leather thongs, but elaborately embroidered all over with silk. The structure of the shoe is curious—see figure 3. The toe piece is sown on last, the sides and heel being formed of one curved leather.

714. Sandals.—Specimens are included in the lists of Dera Ghazi Khan, and Dera Ismail Khan, and Hazara, under the name of " chapli." They are much worn in the hills skirting the Deraját and Biluchistan : the specimens came from Bozdár hills, Harand, &c., &c.

Some of the specimens are of grass or *patta* (palm leaf), but the prevailing chapli is a leather sandal, made of folds of leather, and secured to the foot by the aid of straps. One pair from the Derajat hills, now in the Museum, I have drawn (fig. 4,) and it is worth describing. The sole is made of two or three folds of hide, sewn all over fantastically with thick white string, shewing the stitches on both sides ; towards the heel the sole is slit up on either side, and thongs of leather thus detached, forms the support of the main brace which holds the sandal over the instep ; this brace or strap is covered with little bits of lead sewn on like beads : two other broad straps, rudely embroidered with silk and gold thread, go over the foot, being held together by a longitudinal strap also covered with lead beads.

Shahpur.

715.—" Kheri "—Leather sandals much worn in the Salt Range.

Bannu.

716.—" Chapli "—Leather sandals.

717.—Leather boots, like ancient Greek buskins, worn by the Khans and better class ; they lace up the front with a leather thong passing through little iron rings sewn to either edges of the opening in front; the boot extends a little above the ankle and is of flexible brown leather, and has the rudest attempt at ornament in the shape of two bars of silk work on the instep. The pair in the Museum were given by Major Urmston from the Marwat iláka, Bannu.

Shoes of the Plains.

Common shoes of bullocks' hide of various qualities are made everywhere; the commonest kind are worn by poor people ; for the middle class a little ornament is introduced—an edging of red leather, and so forth. The wealthier classes wear shoes of fine leather embroidered or stitched with gold. Some tracts of country are specially celebrated for shoes—the Chaj or Jach Doab, the Doába (Hushyarpur), and Delhi.

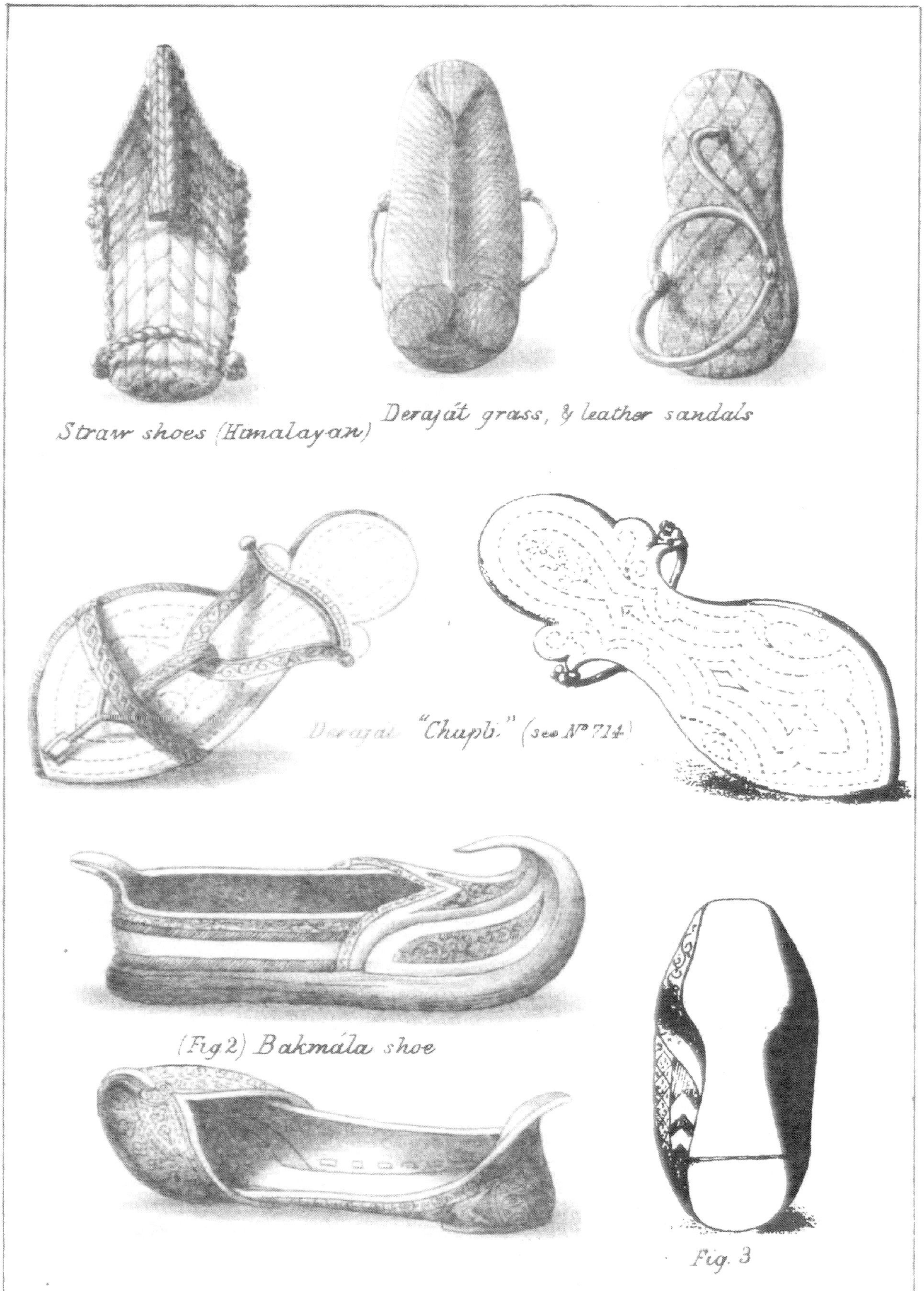

S. Sedgfield Lith:

All about Pindi and Jhelam shoes may be had quite different from common country shoes; the ladies' slippers are uniformly finely made, neatly lined with leather or red velvet worked with gold, and finished with a rosette of purple or red floss silk on the toe.

The men's shoes are much neater and smaller than common country shoes, of smooth brown leather, uncolored, and edged with a neat stitching of gold thread. A sketch of these shoes accompanies.

In the Hushyarpur district, country shoes of bullock's hide for general wear are largely made; they are always stitched with thick cotton thread unwaxed, the consequence is they are easily cut, but the leather is much softer and loosely sewn than in a European boot, consequently there is not so much strain on the sewing.

Shoes are always made with the pointed toe, a little tag of leather bending over, plain sides and heels slightly rising.

Delhi is the great place for shoes, principally for ornamental shoes; gold and tinsel being the material worked on leather or on cloth over leather. Five pairs of shoes were sent to the Exhibition in 1864, under the names of, "júta sulma wa sitárá"—"júta kalábatuní—júta ghetta or nagphani, of sulma and sitará,"—" kafshí of sulma work."

The pair of Delhi slippers called "ghetta" (figure 5) in the plate, are strange in appearance, very gaudy with gold thread and red leather, the lining being red, with an open work ornamentation of silvered leather; the toes curled up, and the whole shoe so broad that it is difficult to understand how it can be worn. The broad curled toe resembles the head of the cobra snake when erected, hence the shoe is fancifully called nagphani—the snake's head shoe.

Delhi shoes are exported chiefly down country to the value it is said of 4 lacs of rupees yearly: there are some 100 shoe manufacturers in Delhi. The Hindi word ghetta is simply used to signify a shoe with no back leather to support the heel—it is practically the same as the Persian ' kafshi.

PESHAWUR.

718.—[7687]. Shoes called *instáb*, made of leather covered with embroidered cloth, lined throughout with stamped leather.

719.—Slippers called kafshi—" Kafshi" are slippers without sides or back, the sole towards the heel being narrow, and excessively raised by a small high heel shod with iron. The specimen sent is figured in the annexed plate. The shoe is of green leather, the sole of double brown hide; the inside is prettily variegated with a spray of green leather flowers stitched down on a ground of gilt leather. The price is Rs. 2-8 0 a pair.*

* I also alluded to the circumstance that these green shoes are only worn by the Shías: green is the color of the Imam Husain, whom the Shías venerate, and red is the color of the Imam Hussan esteemed by the Sunnis. I heard an old Mussulman relate that once the Almighty sent to the Prophet two garments, one green, the other red; he offered the choice to Hussan and Husain, who chose the red and green respectively. A saint, whose name escapes me, forthwith predicted that he who had the green robe should be poisoned, and he of the red should be killed with the sword, which duly came to pass.

720.—Lama's boots.—Dr. Cayley.

These come out of place here, but I must not leave them altogether. They are worn in Thibet by Lamas: they are of Chinese manufacture. He upper part is of thin Russian broad cloth, embroidered in shades of blue with Chinese silk; the sole, which is the most curious part, is of immense thickness, and consists of a series of folds of cotton cloth closely packed and sewn together. This curious boot is figured in the plate.

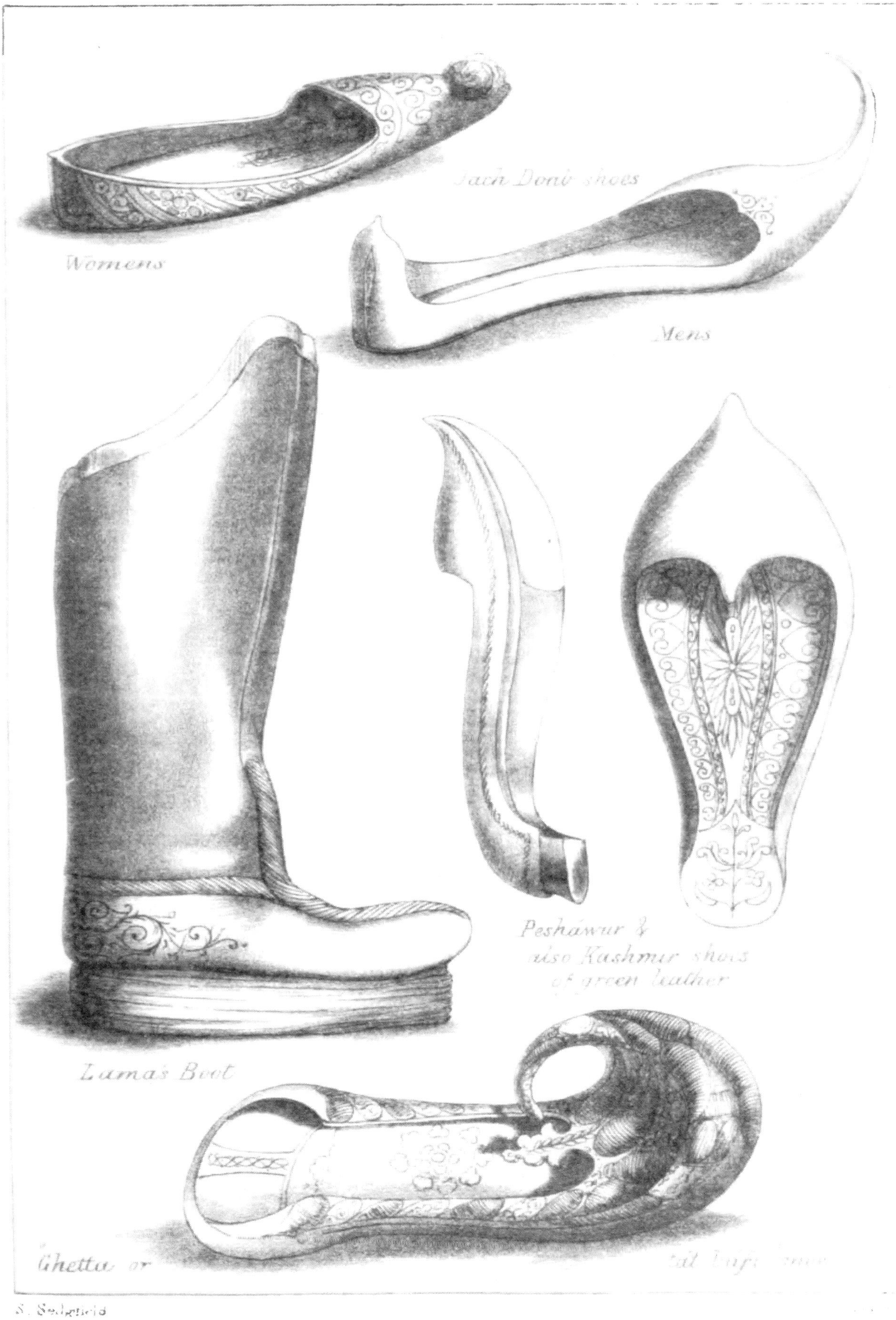
Womens
Jach Doni shoes
Mens
Lama's Boot
Peshawur &
also Kashmir shoes
of green leather
Ghetta or

S. Sedgfield

GROUP OF BRASS WARE.

CLASS XII.

METALLIC MANUFACTURES.

DIVISION I.

WORKS IN NON-PRECIOUS METALS.

SUB-CLASS A.—BRASS, COPPER AND COMPOUND METALS.

The collection is not very interesting, consisting of ordinary works in brass, copper, mixed metal—zinc and pewter.

KARNAL.

721.—[7734]. Betel nut cutters, 'Sarota.'

These are of brass with iron blades, they are like a pair of sugar nippers, two brass handles and short blades; the upper blade has a brass edging from which projects small ornaments, one in the shape of a peacock; the brass handles are rudely ornamented by being set with bits of tinsel and glass to look like stones.

The sarota is used to slice up the betel nut preparatory to mixing it with the lime and spice and wrapping it in the pán leaf.

722.—[7735]. A Surmadán.

A small vase for holding powdered antimony. To the stopper is attached a brass bodkin or blunt spike, with the aid of which the powder is drawn out and applied under the eyelid and lashes. These little toilet articles are made of brass, silver, wood, and ivory in various shapes.

723.—A brass box.

This manufacture appears peculiar to Karnál. It offers the neatest and best specimen of native work in metal that I have seen. The box is of metal covered with red velvet, and over the velvet again is an open work case of brass with solid edges and corners. A very pretty one was sent to me fitted with blue velvet, and the brass open-work silvered. The boxes are oblong, true and straight, and well made. A box sells for about Rs. 13.

AMRITSAR.

724.—[7802]. A brass huka vase, ornamented.

725.—[7803]. A large brazen vessel to hold water.

726.—[7806]. An open work brass bird cage.

(The illustration shows the design.)

At Amritsar a good deal of work is done in the way of manufacturing vessels from copper, sheet brass, and the mixed metal or bell-metal called "phúl" and "kánsí". Specimens of cups and platters of the latter metals beautifully chased and engraved in various patterns, may be had. Two good specimens are in the Lahore Museum collection.

Lahore.

727.—Series of brass vessels of household use.

Under this head I note, once for all, that large class of goods which really forms the staple of the work in metals of the Punjab. The number of fancy articles is few; but in every large town great quantities of metal vessels, drinking cups, cooking pots, lamps, &c.,—in short, all articles of household use, are made for local consumption and export. Amritsar, Ambala, Ludhiana, Jálandhar, all export brass vessels; they go up into the hills and across the frontier into Kábul and Kashmír and to every part of the Panjab.

Metal vessels in a native household supply the joint place of porcelain, glass, and silver plate in a European family. Hindus use brass vessels and Musalmans generally copper vessels, except in the case of small drinking cups, &c. There is hardly any one so poor but he has not some brass pots, if no more than the "lotá" in which he boils his porridge, drinks his water, and holds water to wash in. The wealthier a man is the better off is his house as regards his vessels. In the 'rasoi khána,' or kitchen of a big house, the array of brass vessels, cooking pots and water holders, all scoured bright with earth every day or oftener, is quite formidable. The native gentry use silver drinking cups and some other articles of silver, but the staple article is brass or copper. I believe, however, that glass and crockery are coming more and more into use, even among those who do not ape foreign manners at all. The lamps employed in a great house where European candles and lamps have not found their way, are huge brass candelabra with a broad dish below and a number of branches for little lamps filled with oil and having a wick in the spout of the oil holder. The dull light, quantity of smoke, and dreadful smell these "chár-dívás" (lamps with four wicks) emit, would be intolerable to the European idea. Such a lamp is figured in the plate annexed. Brass vessels are sold by weight, so much being allowed extra for workmanship. They are nearly always made of imported sheet brass and copper. Some mixed metal including brass are made by natives, but in small pieces, and useful only in making smaller articles. The process of making these vessels is described further on.

The common vessels are as follows :—

Lotá.—A small brass pot, round, contracted towards the mouth, and having just above the neck a short lip all round.

Kaul or Katora.—A rather flat drinking cup, supposed to resemble in shape a lotus flower (Kaul, Kanval.)

Abkhora.—A drinking pot more or less like a lota or shaped like a vase, sometimes made with a handle, cover and spout. Those with spouts are called 'Abkhora tútídár.'

Gilás.—A straight drinking cup shaped like a tumbler ; with or without a cover. The name is a corruption of our word "glass" in the colloquial sense of a drinking glass.

Baltoa.—A large vessel for holding water—a brass bucket, with or without rings at the side. Hindus use a baltoa to boil a large supply of food for distribution at a feast.

Dol, or Dolchí.—A round vessel to hold or draw water with, sometimes made of iron ; Hindus use it.

Ganga Ságar.—A large brass ewer with spout for holding water.

Degchá.—A large cooking pot, broad mouthed and round, with a lip; used by all classes.

Degchí.—A smaller size of the same shape.

Garwá—A vessel for drawing water and holding it for drinking purposes; used by Hindus. *Garwí* is a smaller size.

Tháli.—A flat plate.

Parát.—A flat brass tray with a rim.

Tabalbáz.—A brass bowl used to hold curds &c. at feasts; the name is derived from the kettle-drum used for hunting to frighten the game, it being of the same shape.

Silfchí or Chilamchí.—A basin for washing the hands in.

Aftába.—A brass ewer from which water is poured.

Patíli.—A small cooking pot with a cover used by Musulmáns.

Tumbiya.—A drinking cup shaped 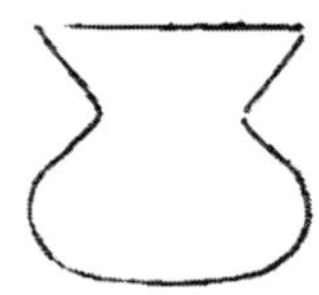

Chakla.—A stone slab (or wooden—when used by Hindus) to grind spices and prepare pastry on

Belna.—The rolling pin used with chakla.

Pauní—A cullender or straining ladle; skimmer.

Chalní.—A sieve.

Kharchá, Kharchí.—Ladles.

Síkh.—A spit for roasting meat on.

Hawang-dasta (vulgarly hamám-dasta). A brass pestle and mortar. A wooden one of the same shape is called "Chattú."

Phahauri.—A sort of shovel to rake out ashes from the oven.

Sahánsi or Sandási.—A pair of tongs with broad curved hooks at the end, to grasp a cooking pot round the neck and remove it from the fire.

Karáh and Karáhí.—A flat iron baking plate.

Kafgír. A ladle for taking the scum off cooking pots.

Tawah or Loh.—A thick iron plate.

Rafída.—An iron plate on a long handle by which a baker reaches a cake when formed into the oven.

728.—Suráhi, of zinc—LAHORE BAZAAR. Water goglets of zinc can be had for camp and travelling use; not liable to break.

729.—Water goglets and cups of pewter ornamented with brass—DELHI.

A few miscellaneous articles from Lahul, Kulú, &c., are more interesting.

730.—Inkstand. "Nakdu" from Spiti. This is a mere steel or polished iron tube, with a cap or sliding lid, having a small receptacle for ink. The Thibetan writing is performed with a small flattened and pointed bit of bambú.

In several of the Hill States very pretty inkstands are in use. I saw one at Kumharsen, near Simla: the ink pot was of brass with a prettily closed lid, and the receptacle for pens attached to one side at right angles; two small chains were fastened to it; the whole was beautifully though roughly carved. Such pen cases are always worn, stuck in the girdle.

731.—Tobacco pipes, 'Kangu padam,' SPITI AND LAHUL.

Every Láhúli is seen with one in his girdle: it is a long iron or brass tube slightly fluted for ornament, curved slightly at one end, the curve being terminated by a small bowl, all in one piece with the stem.

732.—"Dungsmo—" a tea pot, SPITI.

A most remarkable article: it is a broad wooden cylinder about 18 inches high and 5 inches diameter, bound at intervals with rings of brass and edged with the same; some of the rings are set with bad turquoises; the cylinder is fitted with a central stick or piston, the lower end charged with a disc of wood fitting to the cylinder. The tea in use is hard brick tea, or tea cemented with gum of some kind and a little blood. The portion of tea to be used is put into the cylinder with a portion of a salt called "phulli," (See Vol. I, page 97) and ghí or rather butter (for ghí is not used in Láhúl), and the whole pounded and churned with hot water; the result is a thick soup, which is much relished. It has this advantage that there is no waste of tea leaves!

When prepared duly, the tea may be transferred into a rather elegant shaped copper jug with a handle and spout; the sides of the jug are prettily ornamented, and tinned in a pattern.

The skill of the people of Thibet in metal ornamentation is not to be despised, it is rude indeed, but often shows a great idea of ornamental design. I have seen flat copper boxes to contain amulets and charms (furnished with little rings to tie them round the waist or hang them about the neck) very prettily worked over in a sort of filigree brasswork. In Dr. Leitner's collection there was a bell with the handle and sides beautifully ornamented in relief. I believe that this art has come from China; the best specimens of bells (used in worship) "dorjés" or sceptres, coming from the Chinese territory, where the work is beautiful, and have been imitated, and so a certain facility of ornamenting metal has become common.

733.—A Kashmíri tea vase.

This is in the Lahore Museum: it is an elegantly shaped jug with handle and spout covered all over with a pattern of little sprigs and leaflets raised above the surface,—a pattern familiar to all who have seen or purchased the pretty silver 'surahis,' or goglets of Kashmír. The material is copper tinned. Whether the tea is infused in this or is first worked up in some other vessel I do not know, but I believe it is simply boiled with water in a cooking pot or degchí. Green tea is always used, and that imported overland from China is sold as high as 7 and 8 rupees a seer. All Kashmíris and Kábulis are great tea drinkers. (See Chap. "Tea" in Vol. I.)

734.—Iron vessels from Mandi territory, consisting of 'Launda'—an iron pot for cooking. "Dharmchi," an iron ladle for carrying fire or for use as a ladle. "Karáhi," an iron shallow cauldron used by confectioners for boiling milk, syrup, &c., &c., (used everywhere). "Sijrí" a small iron stove for carrying fire.

I will now describe the two kinds of factories in which vessels are made: that of the "bhartya," and that of the "tatyár."

The workman who makes small solid, and large hollow, vessels by casting, whether in brass, copper, zinc, or other metal, is called Bhartya.

For all small kinds of articles he has a pair of iron shallow boxes called "halka." They are made horse-shoe shaped, and one fits exactly over the other; at the centre of the curved side each box has a hollow lip, being in fact half a tube; when the two are put together there is a hollow receptacle with a tube in the upper part though which metal can be poured. The two boxes are held together with small clamps at the side. To use these halkas: they are separated and each filled to the edge with a composition of oil, wax, resin and clay, well kneaded together; on this bed the mould is formed: it is generally done by taking an article already finished and which it is desired to reproduce, and pressing it into the clay so that one half is in the clay and one half out: the other 'halka' is then put over, and this takes the impress of the other half. The article is taken out and there is of course a complete hollow mould; the halkas being now clamped together a spike is passed down the tube at the top to put it in communication with the mould and metal is poured in. This form of mould is used for small and solid articles. The halka varies in size from 6 inches × 4 and 1 inch deep, to four times that size. For large vessels, *viz.* cauldrons, deghchas &c., the following process is adopted. A solid block mould is made on the ground of the shape of the inside of the hollow vessel required. It is made of clay. Over this is spread a layer of lál mitti or clay found with a red tinge, mixed with múnj fibre chopped fine (to make it bind); over this again a layer of red clay and cow-dung, and over this a layer of red clay mixed with múnj; again, and lastly, a coating of red clay mixed with finely chopped blanket. This being complete, wax is taken and beaten into thin plates, as thick however as the brass vessel to be made is intended to be, and the mould is covered all over with wax plates. Over the wax four layers of clay and material as before are smeared. The rationale of the process is now evident: a wooden fire is lighted about the mould, the clay layers harden, and the wax layer melts in the midst, part of it running out by a little hole left at the botton, part being absorbed by the clay; a hollow space is thus left, which is a hollow mould fit to receive the melted metal. A close earthen crucible is now prepared with melted brass, usually three parts copper to one of zinc; a hole is made in the top of the mould and the small hole below carefully closed, and the molten metal run in. When cold the mould is broken up, and the vessel taken off, it is finished by being mounted on a turner's wheel and turned with steel tools till it is even and fit for use.

The other workman called "Tatyár" makes the lighter sort of vessels of copper and sheet brass, while the Bhartya casts the heavier and more solid vessels. The Tatyár's implements are—

Ahran.—Large square anvil without points.

Sandán.—An anvil with two points, smaller than áhran.

Chauras mekh.—A "sandán" with both points cut off, leaving only the square centre.

Kubbi Mekh.—An anvil which has the head hooked thus :—

Tundi Mekh.—The one-armed anvil, an anvil with one point only. The word 'tunda' is applied to a man with one arm.

Sanni.—Pincers.

Hathaura.—Hammer.

Parkár.—Compasses.

Chaurasa.—A hammer, shaped like an adze.

Udála and událi.—The same, only the blade of the hammer is narrower and broader, the section giving an oblong instead of a square.

Chaurasi.—A small chaurasa, for fine work.

Domuhí.—A hammer, with a striking surface at either end of the head.

Kharwa.—An iron form on which small vessels are fixed while being hammered into shape. *Kharwánt* is a wooden frame which holds the kharwa in position (sometimes called "dosángí.")

Níl.—A round iron rod to clean tubes, spouts &c, with files.

They use either sheet brass and copper imported, or else they make an ingot of mixed metal in a crucible and then hammer it—these vessels are cold-wrought.

Addendum on Metallic Leaf and Foil.

In Patiála, Nábhá, Lahore, Amritsar and most large places, gold and silver leaf is made, the metal being beaten out under sheets of jilli or gold-beater's skin: of this hereafter. Tin foil is made, and sheets of bright brass foil or orsdew, in pieces about 8 inches broad and 2 feet long—and called "bindlí." This is used for decoration purposes on gala days.

SUB CLASS B.

HARDWARE.

If the Sub-Class A was uninteresting, this is still more so. Hardly anything is to be noted. The iron employed is either Native or European, and an account of imported iron will be found at page 7 of Vol. I.

Nails of soft flexible iron are made, and screws—the latter more rarely. Baking plates for cooking the universal bread or chapáti are made of hammered iron, and large shallow bowls or open cauldrons, made of sheet iron bolted in pieces, called "karáhi" are used both by saltpetre makers, dyers. sweetmeat makers, and in all sorts of manufactures where any substance has to be boiled in large quantity in an open vessel. Iron stoves and chafing dishes are in use but require no special notice.

Looking over the catalogue of the Exhibition of 1864, I do not find a single specimen under this class worthy of record.

SUB CLASS C.

CUTLERY.

There is more variety under this class, and in some cases a fair superiority of workmanship.

The common articles of daily use, knives, scissors, tweezers, horse bits, stirrup irons, and such like, when of native manufacture and pattern are generally rough; but the practice of making articles with something approaching to European finish and in European style, has taken root in the Sealkot district and at Wazírábád and other places in the Gujranwalla district, as also in Gujrat.

Still more recently Mr. Spence, a gentleman employed in the Medical Store at Sealkot, has taught certain workmen at Sealkot with the aid of European steel not only to make scissors, penknives and table cutlery equal to European, but to prepare and finish in the highest style delicate surgical instruments. I had the satisfaction of sending to Paris in 1867 sets of instruments for operation in cataract and other eye diseases, sets of dental forceps, amputating knives, scalpels and lancets, that must have been respectable even in the city, *par excellence*, of such manufactures.

In Delhi the cutlers are very clever in imitating surgical instruments, knives fish-hooks, and other European instruments: but they have not been *taught* like the Sealkot men, and it is said that their instruments when once blunted will not readily take an edge and polish again, but remain harsh and rough. The workmen use principally old sword blades, European and Persian, for steel instruments; but for small instruments, requiring toughness and strength, they seek for an old steel ramrod and work it up. The Delhi cutlers are all congregated in one part of the city.

The facility for learning such work is traceable to a cause. In former days, there was a demand for weapons of all kinds; swords, daggers, battle-axes and spear heads were made, and the corresponding defensive weapons—shields, chain armour and plate armour. Very early in the history of India the blades of Irán or Persia were famous, steel was imported from the south-west, and also from Central India, and workmen soon acquired skill in making it up. The best workmen also learned to use other kinds of iron, to weld and temper, to produce water-mark in steel, to color it blue, and in short to do all that the best sword makers of Europe can do. Nor has the art died out: where the demand survives, in Kashmir and in Peshawar, and just beyond our frontier, men of considerable skill work at these handicrafts. I have seen a Kashmíri blade of welded bars of several varieties of iron, a small quantity of silver being hammered in to produce a beautiful wavy "water mark." But in other parts of the country, and especially in the settled provinces of the Punjab, no sooner had the stormy days of the later Sikh rule passed away, than the demand for such wares ceased or was greatly diminished. The men who wrought the arms turned their attention to works of peace, and settling in the districts of Gujranwalla, Sealkot and Gujrat, took to making guns, hunting knives, table knives, clasp knives and other articles, having imitated European articles given them for the purpose.

The class of workmen whose special branch was the ornamentation of arms and armour in inlaid gold and steel chasing, have mostly settled down into the class of 'Koftgars' whom I shall describe presently. But inlaid arms, chain armour and swords are still to be had,—mostly being specimens preserved from past years. It is needless to add that the operation of the Arms Act has done much to diminish the number of weapons; but a few of the best makers who still remember the Sikh days or have learned from the armourers of those times, hold licences and are able to ply their trade. I should here mention the steel employed is either imported steel or steel made by heating iron bars in contact with charcoal till it has imbibed the necessary quantity of carbon, steel being a carburet of iron. Steel I am told used to be imported in flat plates or discs, probably made in this shape for facility of carbonizing, from Central India. I am not aware whether any of the iron ores of India are spathose or producing in fusion a crystalline carbonized iron like the German *Spiegeleisen*.

The specimens illustrating this class, are as follows :—

Ambala.

735.—[7743]. Office penknifes (handles made of betel nut.)

This is a favorite fancy work. Pen-holders, rulers and knife handles are made of betel nut cut to shape, and the various pieces cemented together and held by an iron shaft down the centre. The appearance of the mottled brass and white nut, which hardens and takes a slight polish, is sufficiently pleasing. Price of the knives 1 rupee each.

Ludhiana.

736.—[7748]. A sword.

This is of rather soft native iron polished by Gúrmúk. Gúrmúk appears to be the best cutler at Ludhiana.

737.—[7762]. "Mochana," tweezers. Every native barber has a pair.

738.—[7764]. Native penknife.

The usual penknife is a small pointed blade fixed in a rather long handle. The common clasp knife (when a European pattern has not been imitated) is a very rude affair, and is more like a razor. Of all native cutlery it is observed, that in the cheaper and smaller articles, the surface of the iron rarely has a smooth or lustrous appearance but exhibits the scratchy surface left by rough filing or grindstone work.

739.—[7765]. Penknife. English pattern.

740.—[7766]. Scissors.

It is difficult for an European to hold native scissors: they are often made so that one blade serves as a knife, and the finger holes are made one smaller than the other, so that when closed one falls under the other: such scissors are held with the little and middle fingers, not with the thumb and first or middle finger. 'Darzis' (tailors) nearly always use scissors made in European fashion.

Simla.

741.—[7778]. Razors, "Ushtara."

Very rude, though sharp. The process of shaving with them would be eminently unpleasant. They fold between two side-pieces very like an European razor, only they are smaller and shorter.

742.—[7780]. Knife. Náligarh (Simla Hills). Rude knives with wooden handles, used indiscriminately for all purposes, are carried in the belt in a leather sheath by every man in the hill districts.

SEALKOT.

743.—[7826]. Office Eraser.

744.—[7827]. Penknife, 3 blades; another with 4 blades.

745.—[7829]. Scissors, large; and a pair of small scissors.

746.—[7831]. Hunting knife.

747.—[7833]. Bread knife.

748.—[7834]. Tobacco cutter.

These and many other articles, some of best native iron and others of imported English steel, are made by Sealkot workmen under tuition of Mr. W. Spence of the Medical Store Sealkot, (see "Surgical Instruments.")

749.—[7835]. A sword, worth Rs. 120, by Karmdín of Kotli Loháran. This is a blade well made of plates of different kinds of iron welded together and tempered.

The collection included a Persian knife, daggers, a battle-axe, and a hatchet made at the same place, all well finished and polished. The following account of the Sealkot cutlery manufacture has been received.

Forging.—They forge *cast* steel at red heat (my correspondent uses throughout, the phrase, "cherry red heat"), and shear* steel at a low white heat. The work is then cold hammered.

Filing.—The forged article is put into shape and has the scales and blurred surface removed with files, leaving the edge rather thick (the process described is of making knives, swords, &c.)

Hardening.—This is effected by heating the article to a "cherry" red in a fire of charcoal and old leather, and then plunging it into cold water with a layer of oil floating in the surface, sometimes it is plunged into pure oil: this depends on the nature and quality of the steel and the purpose for which it is intended. Percussive tools are mostly hardened in sweet oil.

Tempering.—I quote the account sent me, *verbatim.*

"This is done either in the common way, or by placing the articles to be tempered "in a vessel containing oil, along with some alloy, the melting point of which answers to "the temper required. Springs, if small, or if equal in thickness, are blazed off in the "usual way; but if otherwise, they are roasted in flaming oil, in order to render unequal "thicknesses alike in temper. The alloy consists of lead, tin and bismuth, melted "together in various proportions to suit the different tempers required in cutlery."

---

* Steel is of three kinds—"common," "shear," and "cast." Shear steel is tough and elastic. "Tools, says Dr. Ure, "which require great tenacity without great hardness are made of it, such as table knives, plane-irons, &c. 'Cast' steel is made by melting steel in covered crucibles with bottle glass, and casting in iron moulds, the ingots are hammered into rods; the steel takes a good polish; and scissors, penknives and razors, are made of it."

The finishing processes are—(1) grinding, (2) glazing, (3) polishing. For an account of the European method see " Ure's Dictionary of Arts, under Cutlery."

At Sealkot these processes are done with the aid of wooden wheels, some of which are faced with thick buff leather, others with lead. The grinding is done on stone wheels ; glazing on the wooden wheels with emery of various degree of fineness, according to which also, the size of the wheel varies. These wheels are known as " buff wheels," " wood glaze wheels," and " lap wheels." They are turned by an endless band and a fly wheel.*

The emery used is known according to fineness, as " con-emery," " washed-flour emery," and " double washed flour emery." The corundum, or " karund pathar " ground to powder is sometimes substituted. These are used with the wood and hard wheels.

Polishing is done on the leather wheel, the surface being covered with per-oxide of iron, a yellow oxide called " crocus of iron."

All this the reader will observe is a simplified copy of the European process.

Common and cheap native cutlery is, after forging and rough filing, ground on a grindstone, which is turned either by a boy, who keeps pulling a twisted leather band round the projecting end of one axle, or by a bow and leather such as the native carpenters substitute for a centre bit. Polishing is not done at all : but for the better class of work a little corundum powder or European emery is used on a wheel with a leather edge. The " Sikli-gars," men whose trade is to clean and brighten arms and iron work, remove rust and stains with a set of smooth hand-iron scrapers or small chisels, which they laboriously rub and scrape up and down, and they finish with rubbing, with iron rust mixed with a little acid, and with powdered corundum and oil, with the aid of leather or rags. Brass they polish with soft earth and rotten-stone and oil. (See also under the head of " Trade Implements," *v.* Sikligar).

GUJRANWALLA.

This district has settlements of cutlers at Wazirábád and Nizámábád, who imitate European cutlery: these men make self-acting tobacco cutters, neatly finished with blue steel catches, engraved brass plates, &c., all at a cost of Rs. 5 (!)

The commonest manufacture is a large sort of pocket knife with implements, as button hooks, corkscrews attached, or campainger's sets, consists of folding knife fork and spoon ; but the cutlery as a rule is not nearly so well done as that at Sealkot, and the use of iron of the class called ' aspát ' is commoner than of steel, also the final processes of glazing and polishing are badly done or not done at all. These men seem to excel in making guns, and mechanical works like the self-propelling tobacco-cutter.

The following specimens will give an idea of the work turned out :—

750.—Razors. By Umr Baksh of Rámnagar.

751.—[8020]. Crochet needles, by Mubárak of Nízámabad.

752.—[8026]. Knife and Fork, value Rs. 3.

NOTE.—The native names of the wheels will be found further on, and in the glossary. I had not ascertained them when I wrote the above.

753.—[8035]. Letter Clip in blue steel, (by the same makers.)

754.—[7988]. Pocket knife, Wazírabád.

755.—Tobacco cutter.—The action of the knife or cutter propels the cake to be cut.

756.—[7991]. A pair of Pistols—value Rs. 16, by Husain.

757.—[7993]. A double-barrelled gun,—value Rs. 45, by Fazldín.

758.—[7794]. A Carbine—value Rs. 80—by the same.

759.—[7795]. A single-barrelled gun,—value Rs. 25.

760.—[8000]. Horse's bit,—snaffle, &c.

761.—[8001]. Spurs and Military Chain Straps &c., Nízámabád.

Jhelam.

762.—[8059]. Iron horse bits.—Jhelam seems to produce the best cutlery of this description.

There are two specimens : one is called " nari," which is I suppose a sort of snaffle, an European snaffle is called " kajai " The other is the " dhána," which means 'curb.' The cost is only 6 annas each. Made at Rhotás.

763.—Stirrup irons. They are made occasionally on the European model. These are almost circular, narrowing up to the point of suspension.

The commonest stirrup iron has a flat broad plate at the bottom for the foot to rest on.

Shahpur.

764.—[8806 &c.]. Carving knife, bread knife, table knives and forks, large [Rs. 18 a dozen, small 15 a dozen] ; also penknives.

These articles constitute almost a specialty of Shahpur, and are made with handles of bone, or of a pretty translucent green stone, which is *plasma*, or with the mottled and variegated marble or limestone found in the Salt Range and elsewhere.

The green stone handles deserve a more special notice. The plasma is a green silica brought from beyond Kabul. The native name is " Sang Yesham," which is the term applied to jade or nephrite. Jade differs however from plasma. The constituents are as follows :—

Jade.		Plasma.	
Silica, ...	50·5	Silica, ...	96·75
Magnesia, ...	31·0	Alumina, ...	0·25
Alumina, ...	10·0	Iron, ...	0·5
Iron, ...	5·5		
Chrome, ...	0·05		
Water, ...	2·75		

Plasma has been found among the ruins at Rome. It is infusible, while jade melts before the blowpipe into a white enamel. The best jade comes from Persia and Chinese Tartary: it occurs in granite and gneiss. Plasma occurs in beds associated with chalcedony. Plasma, it will be observed, contains *no magnesia* and a much larger proportion of silica than jade.

The following account of cutlery, kindly communicated by Major Davies, then Deputy Commissioner of the district, I transcribe *verbatim*:—" Information received from Shuruf-din, Lohár of Bhera. The iron is obtained from Bombay. The process of manufacture of cutlery is as follows:—A seer of iron say, is heated and hammered continuously for about a day. Borax (sohága) about a chittack in quantity, is put on this iron when hot, and it is then fit for manufacturing into the required shapes.

" These shapes are roughly obtained by means of hammers and moulds, then filed and again heated; they are cooled in water with an eighth part of oil floating over the top, which hardens the surface of the iron.

" The polishing process is now begun, and is performed by means of the "sán" and the 'matsán,' of which descriptions must be given.

" The 'sán' is formed by heating a kind of fine sand obtained from the Salt Range in a vessel and then mixing 'lákh' with it, until the whole is formed into a sort of dough, after which it is well kneaded and then forced into a mould, which, when it is cold, turns it out in a round shape with the appearance of a very thin grinding stone.

" The 'matsán' is made in the same way: a stone containing much silica called 'kurand' being, when pounded, substituted for the sand. The kurand is said to come from Hindustan."

The article—a knife say—to be polished, is first moved backwards and forwards on the sán, turned rapidly, with a very little fine common sand applied.

The article is then applied to the matsán in the same manner; the matsán however is first prepared by the application of oil and a piece of 'kurand,' after which charcoal is rubbed on it and it is well dried with a cloth. This preparation takes place three times during the polishing, which from first to last takes about two hours. Large articles, such as talwárs &c., are not polished in this elaborate manner, but oil and pounded 'kurand' are merely rubbed on with a piece of wood.

The pale green plasma called 'sang-i-yesham is cut by means of an iron saw, and water mixed with red sand and pounded 'kurand.' It is polished by application to the sán wetted with water only, then by being kept wet with water and rubbed with a piece of 'watí' (a smooth fragment of stoneware, crockery, or potsherd) and lastly by rubbing very finely pounded burnt sang-i-yesham on it. This last process must be done very thoroughly.

The other stones used for handles come from the Salt Range and the hills near Attok. Each is polished by being rubbed with 'watí' and its own burnt powder as above; when the stone is very hard, oil is used in the process instead of water.

Montgomery (Gugaira.)

Some of the coarsest class of native cutler's work was sent from this district, including the usual knife, scissors, tweezers, razors, and a pair of " camel shears " from Shírgarh in this district,—and costing 4 anas.

Peshawar.

The cutlery works of this district, as might be expected, are principally of a warlike nature. The workmen have the advantage of the iron from Bajaur, which is excellent in texture and easily convertible into steel, (*see* Vol. I, pp. 8 and 9).

The Settlement Report has the following brief notice of the sword factories.

" Sword blades of a coarser quality are manufactured at Peshawar, but those in " greatest request, other than Persian and Damascus blades, are those [called] " 'Tírai, " " made in the Makzai hills of Tírah at what is known as the Mírzakhání factory. The " temper of these swords is highly appreciated, and some, purchased perhaps at a small " price, are valued nearly as much as Irání (Persian) blades."

The specimens exhibited as cutlery can hardly be separated from those coming under the class of " Arms." I beg to refer the reader to that class for the strange variety of swords, knives and daggers this district produces.

Lahore.

The works of cutlery here are principally arms ; ordinary rough knives, scissors, tweezers &c. &c., are made in this district as well as in every other. I may here mention that a few cutlers, like those of Nizámábád, seem to have settled at Kasúr, and that a few articles, superior as compared with ordinary native cutlery, were sent to the Exhibition of 1864 from that sub-division of the Lahore district.

The specimens are as follows :—

765.—[7855].—A sword, 'Talwár,' with waved edge.

766.—[7856].—Steel sword made by Amán Ali of the Mochi Gate Lahore, value Rs. 12 (an inferior quality).

767.—[7857].—A sword of steel finished with water-mark, by the same, value Rs. 30.

768.—[7858].—A sword with a device engraved on the blade, Rs. 20.

769.—Small curved daggers, made at Lahore.

770.—A dagger made of embossed steel by Amán Ali.

Kashmir.

771.—[8175].— A steel mirror. Before the importation of European glasses, and before the process of silvering Aleppo and European glass for mirrors was known at Delhi, small round mirrors of polished steel were in use, and still are to be had. This is one : its value is Rs. 7-8.

In bringing this class to a close, I most enumerate the tools used by the blacksmith in metal works.

The details of the blacksmith's work are familiar, and there is nothing special in the native method. Charcoal is used in the forges.

The tools emplyed are :—

(1).—" Ahran."—(anvil). (2) Wadhán (Sledge hammer) for hammering large works, used with both hands.

(3).—Hathaura (hammer.)

(6).—Hathauri, small hammer.

(7).—" Sannya," pincers of five kinds and sizes.

(8).—" Chaini," cold chisel for cutting iron.

(9.)—" Sumbhá," to make holes in hot iron.

(10).—"Dedhí," an iron-piece with a hole in it placed under the iron to be drilled with the Sumbha.

11.—" Chaurasi reti," square file, for filing with either side or face.

12.—" Nímgird reti," half circular file.

13.—" Tirsál reti," triangular do.

14.—" Reti," common file.

15.—" Katíra," pair of shears or pincers with sharp edges for cutting metal.

16.—" Golrá reti," round file.

17.—" Parkár," compasses.

18.—" Hathkali," hand-vice—" bânk" is a big vice for bench use.

19.—" Mús," screw mould in which screws are made—the female screw.

20.—" Jandri," plate bored for wire-drawing.

21.—" Tappa," a shaping block.

22.—" Kundi," hook for stirring iron in the forge.

23.—" Khalwa," bellows, or two skins to form bellows.

24.—" Bilol," mouth-piece of the bellows.

25.—" Khal," single skin used for a pair of hand bellows.

26.—" Kauncha," forge tongs.

27.—" Sandán," small anvil with points at either end.

28.—" Bánk," a vice (copied from the European implement).

29.—" Nímgira."

30.—" Tappa golf," a round block for shaping round plates in.

31.—" Bhattí," forge.

32.—" Muddhi," wooden block let into the ground on which the anvils are fixed.

....

The Jury Report on the Collection of 1864, may be printed as a suitable conclusion to this class :—

CUTLERY AND HARD-WARE.

JURY :—

Colonel Sim.	G. Burnell, Esquire,
H. Gunn, Esquire.	Dr. Elton.
Nawab Allee Reza Khan.	B. Powell, Esquire.
Nawab Abdool Mujid Khan.	T. D. Forsyth, Esquire, *Reporter*.

The articles exhibited in this class comprise a wide range of utility, and being such as are intended for the daily wants of life, rather than for ornament, it is necessary to look carefully to the workmanship, design and ultimate use of the articles displayed.

In this department novelty of design is not likely to be met with, for, as a general rule, the implements of trade, and the articles coming generally under the head of hard-ware, are produced in greater perfection by Western nations than by Orientals.

Thus it is found that, whilst most of the articles manufactured after native models are comparatively rude and uncouth, those made according to English patterns have some pretensions to neatness of finish and utility.

The exception to this is to be found in the swords and large knives, exhibited from Peshawar and the frontier. The manner in which match-locks are made, and native gun-barrels are twisted, is curious; but this is not a trade which is likely to be fostered under the British Government.

The articles exhibited may be divided into two heads :—

1st.—Culinary or household.

2nd.—Sporting or warlike.

Under the first heading there are knives and forks, penknives, scissors, erasers, from Umballa, Loodiana, Sealkote, Lahore, Goojranwalla, Goojrat, Shahpore, and Jheend.

Scales and weights from Umballa and Loodiana.

Padlocks from Rohtuck, Simla, Umritsur, Lahore, Goojranwalla, Rawul Pindee, Googaira, Dera Ghazee Khan, Bunnoo ; a door-lock of excellent construction after an English pattern made at Umritsur.

A large collection of brass and copper cooking pots, cups, goglets, hookah bottoms, and other native utensils.

Under the head of sporting and warlike—there are swords, daggers and long knives, from Umritsur, Sealkote, Lahore, and the frontier districts, and some presented by the Chiefs of the Cis-Sutlej States ; a sword from Loodiana, a 'kúkri' from Simla, sporting knives from Sealkote, Goojranwalla, and Dera Ismael Khan.

Guns after English patterns were sent from Goojranwalla and Cashmere, and a specimen of a twisted gun-barrel has been supplied from Kohat by Mr. R. E. Egerton, whose interesting account of the manner in which these barrels are twisted is appended.*

Native matchlocks and pistols are sent from Peshawur.

---

* See Class 'Arms.'

Horse bits and stirrups from Hissar, Rohtuck, Lahore, Goojranwalla, Jhelum; horse shoes from Her Majesty's 89th Regimental Workshops.

Knives and Forks, &c.—Most of the penknives and scissors are of exceedingly poor and rude construction.

The way in which some of the purely native made cutlery is got up is clever, as far as appearance goes, but it will not bear close inspection.

The external imitation of English cutlery is excellent, but does not stand the test of use, there being scarcely a blade which would bear ordinary trial. The natives in some instances have evidently procured English steel, but not understanding how to work it, have destroyed the temper in making up the blades.

The exceptions are—

[7826 to 7833.]—Knives, eraser, 2 penknives, 2 pairs scissors, sporting knife, and bread knife. These are by far the best articles of cutlery exhibited, and are really good specimens. The blades are made of English steel apparently, but it is understood that they have been worked up by native artificers under English superintendence. They are neatly finished with ivory and horn handles.

Good specimens of penknives are exhibited by Goojranwalla workmen.

[7997-98-99].— by Amir.

[8002.] A knife; [8003.] Carvers } by Ameroodddeen.

[8005.] Very good specimen.

[8006. 8007.] } Knives by Shahabooddeen.

[8012.] Knife by Gholam.

[8024. to 8030.] } Knives, forks, erasers and penknife. } by Nubbee Bux.

[8031.] to [8035.] } the same by Mobarik.

The scissors exhibited by these manufacturers are very poor indeed.

[8063. to 8067.] } Shurufdeen, of Shahpoor, exhibits good looking carving and dinner knives and forks, with imitation jade handles. But they are worthless for use, not being made of good steel.

[7749.]—*Scales and Weights.*

[7750. 7751.] } Scales and set of weights, letter scales, by Goormookh of Loodiana. These are after the English pattern, and are remarkably well made.

The ordinary native padlocks are supplied in abundance, and are not worth notice.

[7739] A lock on Chubb's principle is sent from the Rohtuck Jail, but it is quite a misnomer to use Chubb's name in connection with the lock exhibited, for it is of the most ordinary and rude nature, the principle of the lock being that which would be turned by a large watch key. Externally the lock has an imposing appearance.

A curious puzzle lock from Bokhara is exhibited by Misr Meg Raj, Lahore, No. 7874.

[7872.] Is a very bad specimen of a common English padlock.

[8009.] Letter padlock (brass) by Golam.

[8041. Do. Do. brass. } Local Exhibition Committee,
8042.] Ivory Do. ... }

are very good specimens of padlocks, for which the workers deserve honorable mention.

[8005.] A cleverly contrived native padlock, on an English pattern.

Door Lock.—Sirdar Bhugwan Sing exhibits an excellent specimen of a door lock, No. 7808, made after an English pattern. It would be very desirable to encourage the manufacture of such articles, as they would be much sought after if produced at a moderate price, as doubtless they could be.

Sporting aud Warlike.—There is a very small show of guns, and none have been sent from Kangra, where formerly very fair specimens used to be seen; the best Mundee iron being procurable in the neighbourhood, and clever workmen being found in a colony at or near Teera Sujanpoor.

[7994.] Gun, double-barrel, price Rs. 45.

[7995.] Carbine, breech-loading, price Rs. 80.

[7996.] Gun, single-barrel, price Rs. 25.

[8004.] Gun, double-barrel, price Rs. 60.

are exhibited by Shahabooddeen, who deserves special notice for the workmanship and finish of his weapons. The manner in which the breech-loading carbine has been bored is highly creditable. The locks of No. 8004 are very superior.

The guns from Cashmere are well wrought, and the finish is excellent.

A hunting knife, no number, sent from Nizamabad, is well made, and appears to be of good steel.

[8000.] An English bit made by Shahabooddeen, Nizamabad, deserves notice.

[8203.] Quoits } Specimens from Soldiers' Workshops are highly creditable,
[8204.] Horse shoes } and deserve special notice.
[8207.] Wad cutter }

Prizes, &c.

The Jury do not consider any articles in this class of sufficient excellence to deserve a medal, but they would, as much as possible, encourage this branch of manufacture by the grant of money prizes and recommendatory certificates.

They would award to Shahabooddeen of Goojranwalla for his guns, three shares of prize money.

To Mr. Spence, Sealkote, Sir Robert Montgomery's special prize might be given for general superiority of finish and excellence of material.

To Goojranwalla, 5 shares of prize money might be sent for distribution to the different workmen employed by the Local Committee; and to the following exhibitors, who ought also to have certificates:—

Shahabooddeen.	Gholam.
Amerooddeen.	Mobarik.
Shurufdeen.	Nubbee Buksh.

Two shares to Sirdar Bhugwan Singh for the superior sample of a door lock.

Three shares to Goormookh, Loodiana, for his brass scales and weights.

Two shares to Sergeant Ord, Her Majesty's 89th Foot.

One share to Sergeant Bates, Her Majesty's 93rd Highlanders, for superior specimens of hard-ware.

Honorable mention should be made of the guns from Cashmere, and of the air gun from Puttiala; a certificate should be given to Local Exhibition Committee Kangra for delivery to the maker of an ivory and steel letter clip of superior make and finish.

For Mr. Burnell's prize for sudder bázár block, or rough-filed iron-work, there was no competition.

T. D. FORSYTH
Reporter.

29th March 1864.

DIVISION II.

WORKS IN THE PRECIOUS METALS.

SUB-CLASS A.—WORKS IN GOLD OR SILVER WIRE; AND B—FABRICS WOVEN WITH GOLD AND SILVER WIRE AND THREAD.

The demand for fabrics of this class is immense. Every wealthy man has his shoes embroidered with gold, for which spangles (sitára), and thin tinsel (sulma) are required. Gold ribbon (ghota, kinára &c.) is largely used in trimming dresses, both male and female : gold thread (kalábátun) is used in embroidery ; and for the heavy rich embroidery, already described as kár-chob, tinsel wire of sizes (called mukesh) is required. Silk cloth with patterns woven in gold wire,* is called kimkháb, is used for dresses of the wealthy, for cushions and state coverlets and cushions (masnad), and for the envelopes in which royal and princely correspondence is enclosed (called kharíta). Native ladies demand muslins figured with tinsel, and public dancers wear the gaudier and more showy kinds of tinsel ornaments. Small skull caps covered with gold work and tinsel are much worn on gala days, especially by children. Delhi is the great place in the Punjab for shoes embroidered with gold, or with spangles and tinsel wire worked on to them. Such shoes are said to be made with "sulma wa sitára," and the neater and quieter article is worked with gold thread, which is less sparkling and showy, is said to be "kalábatúní."

Dehli also is the manufactory for caps showily embroidered with tinsel and spangles : sheet tinsel being often sewn on to imitate jewels. All kinds of embroidered muslins, gold edged turbans, and fancy articles of tinsel ware, are to be obtained at Dehli.

At most of the large cities, embroidered shoes are made, and at Lahore and Amritsar the kar-chób is done, the manufacturers being the relics of the once flourishing class who supplied the Sikh Court and nobles with embroidered velvet coverlets, cushions, floor cloths, saddle cloths, &c. The demand has now fallen off, and the embroiderers obliged to take to other classes of embroidery more in demand by the general public. Kimkháb (corruptly kincob) is not made in the Punjab : it is possible that in some places a stray workman from other parts may be found, but that is all ; all our kimkháb is brought from Benares or from Ahmadabad in the Bombay Presidency. The qualities of kimkháb are very various in inferior sorts: the last yard or so is fairly well woven, the gold flower standing out bright and glistening from the silken-surface, the "thán" or piece is so folded for sale that the good parts form the few outer folds ; on going towards the inner lengths the gold flowering gradually becomes thinner and poorer. The unwary purchaser who only looks at the outer folds is thus often sadly cheated.

I do not think there is any great demand for kimkháb now ; the fashion of wearing European silks and satins for chogas and robes is so prevalent that kimkháb seems to be driven out.

The Maharaja of Kashmir has however imported kimkháb makers into his territory, and in 1868 presented to the Lahore Museum a piece of very elegant material, gold flowers

* I must adopt throughout this class some general word to indicate the narrow tinsel ribbon which is formed by flattening a gilt wire of various thickness according to the work it is required for. I call it tinsel accordingly. A gold thread means (kalábátun or) gold tinsel upon silk.

on a white ground, and so neatly worked as to bear inspection on both sides; the work is equal to Benares, but hardly to the *best* " Dakhaní " work.

To illustrate this class I must describe the process of making:—

Silver and gold tinsel wire, plain and fancy—sulma, tila, mukesh, gokru, &c.

Gold and silver thread—kalábatún.

Tinsel spangles—sitára.

The foundation of all work in this class is the " kandla " or silver ingot.

At Lahore the kandla is particularly pure: it is never allowed to be alloyed with more than a fixed quantity of copper. The whole ingot weighs 63 rupees or tolas standard, and 68 rupees Nánakshahi (Sikh rupees) This size has descended from long custom. The Municipality tax the " kandla-kash " or kandla making community, at so much per cent on the value: a contractor farms the tax, it being put up to auction, and he collects the per-centage due on each kandla. If the number of kandlas made that year is very large, the total of his per-centage will exceed the price paid for the farm and he gains, otherwise not. The present contractor tells me that about 1500 kandlas are made in the year, but that the number varies.

The kandla consists of a round bar of silver, slightly tapering at each end and covered with gold all over. To make it, the first thing is to get a long narrow silver ingot about 8 or 9 inches long and 1 inch thick, called " raini ;" this is made by melting silver in a small kuthâli or open crucible with sohága (borax) as a flux, which leaves the silver perfectly pure: it is then mixed with the proper quantity of copper alloy and poured into an iron mould having a handle and called " reza." The reza is simply a thick narrow bar of iron with a trough in the middle, long enough to admit the required quantity of metal.

So soon as the " raini " or ingot is cold it is taken to the Municipality office to be tested. This is done to prevent the deterioration of the Lahore manufacture and consequent depression of the trade: if it were not, the kandla could be easily adulterated, and also those bankers who give over silver to be worked up would be defrauded. For this reason also all the kandla-kashes work together in the old mint buildings " Tankshál " of Lahore; this facilitates supervision. All the kandla-kashes are in one partnership, about 15 or 20 of them, and their earnings are thrown into a common stock and divided out: if a member is sick and unable to work he gets his share all the same; it is only when a person renders himself obnoxious or becomes lazy that they refuse to give him a share, and then the matter often ends in a law-suit. This arrangement is a matter of ancient custom. Recently a workman from Hindustan made his appearance, but has been obliged to go and sit in the Tankshál, being looked on with much disfavor by the others as an interloper.

The testing operation is performed as follows:—

Each kandla has in it 64 rupees Nánakshahi (Sikh coinage) weight of pure silver; five kandlas are taken and a small portion cut off each. Of the fragments, one rupee weight (according to a standard rupee kept for the purpose) is taken, and mixed with a proportion of lead and melted in a crucible. The pure silver when taken out (the lead and copper being separated from it in the melting), ought, if of proper quality, to weigh exactly against another standard rupee made 32 rice grains weight less than the first, *i. e.*, every true kandla contains 32 rice grains = four rattis * of alloy to the tola: if more

* 8 rice grains equal one ratti, the red seed of *Abrus precatorius.*

than 32 rice grains weight is lost, the kandla is immediately destroyed as spurious; if it is correct, the kandla is stamped with a die bearing the letter "L. 32." L for 'Lahore,' '32' to signify that in the testing 32 rice grains weight of alloy exists in the tola.

The oblong ingot when stamped is called "raini." It is then made into a kandla by hammering and filing (when the shape is that of a candle, round and somewhat tapering at the ends,) and by covering it with gold. The gilt bar thus ready is also called kandla. The raini by being filed into the kandla ("kandla kilái huí") loses 1 tolah in weight. For making a kandla the rate is Rs. 2-8 to Rs. 3, including 1 tolah of silver which comes off the raini or ingot in the process of making it into the kandla.

The gilding process is done by means of gold in thin narrow plates, and quite pure ("sona patra"), which, by the aid of fire and hammering, are plated on to the surface; the doing this part of the work well is the kandla-kash's art: he makes no secret of it now, and will teach any one who wishes to learn.

The quantity of gold put on is more or less according to the color and quality of the tinsel ultimately required: if but little gold is put on, the tinsel will be of a pale yellowish color, if plenty, it will be of rich gold-red. The tensile capacity of the gold is wonderful, for however fine the bar may be drawn out, the gold surface always remains; the fine wire used for making thread must be produced by drawing out the kandla to thousands of times its original length, and yet the gold surface, and also the color of the gold never changes: if the kandla is thinly gilt and pale in color, so is the wire, and if the kandla is dark red, so is the tinsel.

The kandla has now to be drawn out by the "tárkash." His apparatus is simple, but powerful. A small oblong trough about 3 feet long or 4, and 2 feet broad, is dug in the ground and bricked round. Across this a stout roller of wood is laid, supported at its two axle ends in wooden sockets at either side of the trough. Through the roller pass stout wooden arms, or spokes, one sloping one way, the other the other, like the letter X.

The roller is called "jandar." A stout chain, called "sangal," terminating at one end in a ring, and at the other with a pair of pincers or a crab, is now fixed to it by simply passing the ring over one spoke and turning the roller half round; the chain is thus secured with a good purchase, is now extended towards the opposite end of the trough; here, just to where the chain reaches, are fixed two very stout posts deeply driven into the ground, and having the upper end projecting about a foot above the ground and cut with a slit of say four inches broad down the centre, these are called "kila."

A stout steel plate is now produced having a series of holes in it, just so large that the kandla cannot pass through any one in its present state, though the tapering end (made tapering for this reason) can. The kandla is well rubbed with wax and the end forced though the "jandri" hole: this is then placed point inmost against the two posts of the "kila," and held there by a man's foot. The projecting point of the kandla is firmly caught and held by the pincers, and then by turning the roller, exactly on the principle of a rack, the kandla is stretched out and gradually dragged through the hole; in length it is now about trebled or quadrupled. This process is repeated with finer holes until the wire is drawn as fine as ordinary small wire, and then it is made up into coils of so many tolahs weight. In this state it is called "veri." The tárkash's work is now over. The annexed plate shews the three machines described.

Fig. 1.

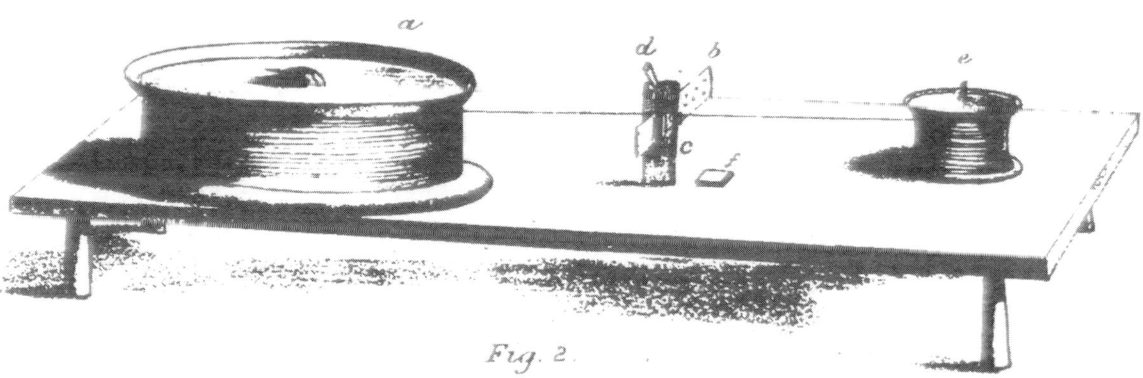

Fig. 2.

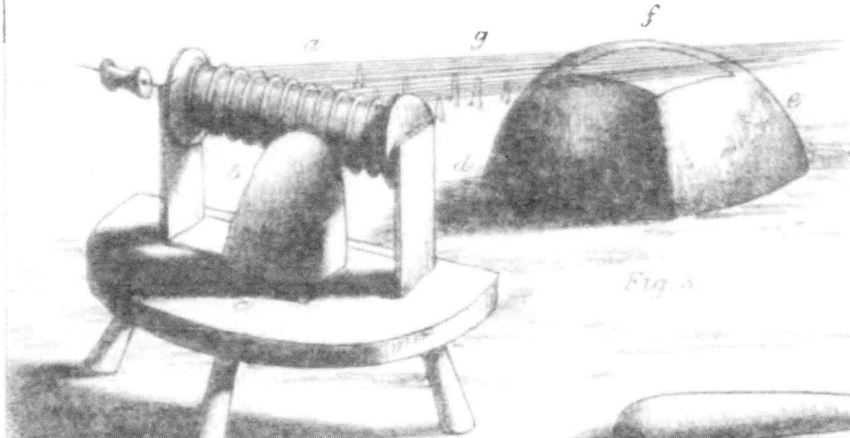

Fig. 3.

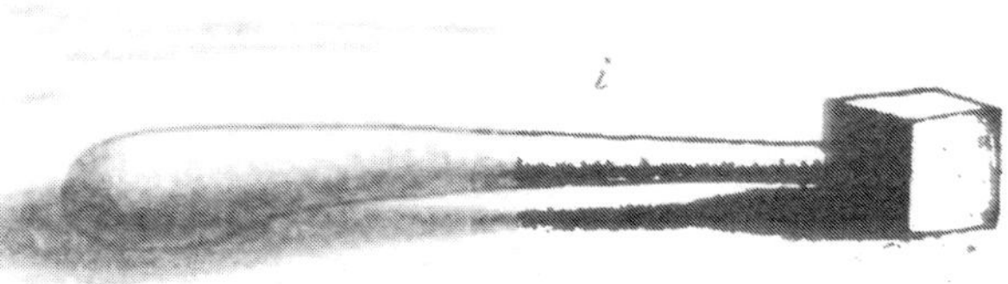

Fig 4

The veri passes to the "kataya" or fine wire drawer, who has to draw it out still finer, but his apparatus does not require to produce such a powerful tension as the tár-kash's. He has merely a low board supported on four short legs: this is called 'patra.' On it is fixed an upright iron spike ("kil") on which a small wooden wheel—broad edged and rimmed (to prevent the wire wound on it slipping off)—revolves. This is called "charkhi." The wire has to be softened before it is drawn, this is done by putting it on a copper drum or charkhi, and then after heating, transferring it to the wooden one.

The coarse wire to be fined is wound on this: one end of the wire is passed through a pierced steel plate—the hole being gauged to the fineness of the wire required. The steel plate called "jandri," is held in its place between two little iron uprights suitably placed, called "mareli," by help of a little wooden wedge made of "pilchi" or other soft wood and called "tor"—the point of the wire passing through the jandri hole is pulled by the hand gently till a sufficient length comes out to fasten the end to a larger and much heavier wooden wheel (charkh) revolving horizontally at the other end of the patra. The workman sitting before the patra then turns the heavy wheel by a dexterous application of his hand to the flat top of the wheel or drum, which has a little dent in it to catch his finger: sometimes the drum has a little hole in it, and is propelled by a small tool like an awl whose point goes into the hole: this is called "bailoni." The drum is heavy enough to exert a force sufficient to draw the flexible wire though the hole and keep winding it off till all is finished. In order to commence work, the end of the coarse wire has to be ground down, so as to make it pass through the hole, after which the man catches the end in his fingers and exerts force enough to compel the wire through the hole, thus drawing it out till he gets a bit long enough to attach to the wheel, after which the weight of the revolving wheel continues the drawing. The patra is furnished with two little round bits of rough glazed china or pottery, (bits of an old cup or saucer rounded and beveled) called "pewáñ," the end of the wire is sharpened by rubbing it between them.

I must say now something of the jandri. It is a small tongue or plate of hard steel pierced with a series of holes, called "bára." Each bára or hole is made with difficulty as it requires the successive use of 32 small steel punches called "katár." One is first applied and given one blow with the hammer, then another, and then another: the result is a beautifully smooth even hole. Each hole, as originally made, is of the same size: but as the wire requires to be drawn finer for some work and coarser for others, the workman has accordingly to adjust the hole in the jandri, which he does by hammering it up close with a little steel hammer, having one end pointed, (and called "chándá") and then re-opening it of the required size by passing a steel spike or needle called "silái," through it—gauged to the size of wire required. Another sort of spike is also used, called "chaurasa" (the silai is round, the chaurasi has four facets terminating in a sharp point.) The finest gauge draws the wire so thin as to be almost invisible: the art of sharpening the end of the wire so as to get it through the fine hole and have a handle to commence pulling from, requires no little delicacy and skill. It is needless to say that the hole is always smaller than the wire, otherwise the wire would only pass through without becoming longer and thinner.

All these operations being done, the owner of the veri or coarse wire, requires an equal weight of fine wire to be delivered. The tárkashes and katayas are more numerous than the kandla-kashes.

The fine wire is generically called "tand," *i. e.* 'pulled material.'

Four gauges of wire (tand) are made :—

1. The coarsest, tárí ka tand, for making spangles (tári or sitára).
2. Mukesh ki tand (for mukesh, used in embroidery.)
3. Kinárí ki tand, for making kinárí and gota or gold edging.
4. Wattan ki tand, or tila ki tand. the finest of all, for making "tila," the thin kind of tinsel used for making gold thread, and for sulma, and for weaving chunibádla, and the thinnest and lightest gold wire fabrics.

The fine wire now goes to the "dabkái" who flattens it out into 'tila,' 'mukesh,' 'gokru-mukesh,' 'mukesh batí-hui,' for ribbon and lace making, according to order and according to the fineness of the wire.

The dabkai's apparatus is simple: a stout block of hard wood is driven into the ground, leaving only the rounded head projecting; this forms a solid anvil into the centre of which a piece of steel is let, curved slightly on the surface, as being a segment of the dome shape; this is finely polished and always kept perfectly free of all dust and scratches; the operator sits before this, hammer in hand, and hammers the wire flat on the steel, with the aid of a rather heavy but small steel hammer one end being beautifully polished and slightly concave to fit the surface of the anvil. The end of the handle is thickened by a good covering of wax, which gives a firm grasp. The wooden anvil is called "kunda," and the steel plate let in to it "nihaí," the hammer "hathaura".

But the means of applying the wire has to be described :—

A long reel is taken, being 15 compartments (called "girdhának"), it revolves on an iron pin between two uprights, and at one end of the axle pin, which projects, a wooden reel is fixed. The wire owner who hands over the "tand" to be flattened, gives it over by weight, *wound on to the* compartments of the reel, leaving one blank. The object is to have an exactly equal quantity of wire on each compartment, and this is adjusted by removing any surplus and winding it on to the reel at the end of the axle pin. The compartment reel and its stand and uprights is now placed on a little three-footed stool called "tirwai" (corruption of tirpai) opposite the workman and some little distance in front of his anvil, and it is kept from revolving on its axis until wanted by laying a flap of leather against it, and on the leather a heavy square iron weight called "dár". The wheel is let go a little and 14 strands of wire drawn out to a sufficient length.

Just at the end of the steel nihai on the anvil, between the anvil and the girdhának frame, two tiny little bits of leather, the edges sliced like the teeth of the comb, stand up: they are kept there by strings: the strands are taken and passed over the combs of leather seven strands between the slits of each: they are thus gathered into an even skein, which is slowly pulled over the steel with one hand and simultaneously hammered flat with the other. In order to keep the wires separate between the girdhának and the leather combs, small weights, called "dhellar," consisting of a string with a courie shell at either end, are hung over the strands: this keeps them taut and prevents the fine spider lines from becoming entangled.

GROUPS OF KASHMÍR SILVER VASES.

The wire when flattened is thrown into an earthen pan as it comes off in pieces, this being the best way of keeping it clean. It is then gathered and tied up in skeins, called "lucha," and weighed: it is sold by weight also.

According as the gold has been applied, thick or thin to the kandla, so is the color of the wire rich or pale. For silver wire, the kandla is of course left ungilt.

The fancy kinds of tinsel are made in the following ways: twisted mukesh, (bati-hui) is made by taking the fine wire 'tand' and winding it by means of an ordinary 'charkh or spinning wheel, on to a long narrow steel spike, so as to form a narrow ringlet: this is opened out till the wire is waved only, and then flattened; the mukesh when thus waved, is much used by karchobs for a gold ground work, being sewn on edge over edge.

Sulma is made of very fine wire wound on to a steel needle (silái) so as to form a thin close curl like the tendrils of a creeping plant, only very much finer and closer, and comes off in pieces a few inches long. This is the prettiest form of gold tinsel. The pieces of sulma look like pieces of fine chain, or, if I may be allowed the comparison, like gold vermicelli. Two kinds were sent me from Delhi: 'sulma kora,' which is rather looser in texture and made of plain drawn wire; and 'sulma dabka hua,' made of fine wire slighly flattened and having a closer wound appearance: the difference is hardly appreciable to an uneducated eye.

The winding is done by fixing the needle on to the common charkha, and attaching a reel of gold wire: one end of the wire is made fast to a bit of string fixed at the end of the silái, and it is then wound off close and fine, row against row, on the silai, and when finished the little curl, now called "silma" or "sulma," is slipped off: it is used in embroidery of caps and shoes, principally.

Spangles (tára or sitára) are made of the thickest wire, (though still very fine) which is first wound off on to a wire shaft just as the sulma, only coarser. The long curl of wire is called "phogli." The silái is turned up at one end to prevent it slipping off.

The "dabkaya" now sits down opposite his steel anvil, and spreads all round him a clean cloth, and sets up a sort of wall or low tent of cloth round him to prevent losing his spangles, which fly about; he takes the phogli in one hand and with the other cuts the coil of wire up the side with a pair of scissors having fine points, but one blade much shorter than the other; the point of the short blade goes in under the wire coil and the other presses on it, the result is that when the silai is shaken and turned up, little coils of wire, shaped thus (C) fall off; as each drops on the steel anvil a single blow with the hammer flattens it out into a spangle thus ⊖ and the work is done; the spangles lie all about the cloth, and are afterwards carefully collected.

The materials are now ready for use: the tila or plain thin flattened wire goes to the kalábatún sáz—(in Panjabí tilá-bat) or gold thread maker, and to the kináre báf or weaver of gold lace, edging, &c. The mukesh, and the sulma and sitára, go to the embroiderer and shoe ornamenter. 'Gokru mukesh' (which is mukesh puckered up, or crimped with a pair of iron tongs), also sulma and spangles, go to the embroiderer of caps.

False tila and mukesh are made of brass gilt, and come mostly from Delhi.

Kalábatún is made by twisting the fine gold tila or flattened wire on to fine red silk, if it is gold (surkh), on white silk if it is silver (safed); it is simply done by fixing two threads of material to a small iron spindle, just the same shape as an ordinary spindle; this is kept perpendicular by the thread passing under a little hook at the end. The spindle is set spinning by a twist of the finger and thumb: the finished thread is wound off on to reels.

The kinára-báf makes gold lace (military) and ribbons of all kinds. Lace is made on a warp of firm and thick yellow silk, with 'tand,' or wire not yet made into thread: the end of the web is tied round a small stick and secured by a string to a nail in the wall, the other end of the web is fixed to a roller, it is crossed by 2 or 4 small treddles (gulla) to lift the upper and lower threads of the warp: these are suspended from the ceiling by strings, and a "kangi," to close up the woof, is hung on the warp just like a miniature loom. The woof thread in lace making is gold: it is applied, not with a shuttle, but on a plain spindle shaped stick called "kainthá."

Gold ribbon is made with a tiny loom like the above: in making it the web is of gold wire flattened (tila) and a single strand of silk at each side for the edge, to give strength to the whole; the woof is very fine red silk or white, according to color of the metal: silk is always used, even to make ribbon of imitation tinsel.

The narrowest ribbon is called "dhának" (No. 786 &c.): it is made of 5 to 7 strands of gold in the web; it is used in making "dori." "Gotá" is a broader plain ribbon with 20 strands. "Pattah" is a ribbon still broader—as wide as the finger. "Kinárí" is wider still. "Anchal" is the widest of all.

Gold fringe is also made by the kinára-báf: the fringe is twisted by hand and the tags kept together by the band along the edge woven in a loom.

The variety of articles, in the nature of materials for gold embroidery, may be illustrated by the following lists:—

Pattiala.

772.—"Laus sunehrí guldár"—Military gold lace epaulettes. These are after the European fashion. The origin of the word *laus* for epaulettes I do not know: perhaps it is a corruption of "lace," but the word "lais," which is evidently our word "lace," is used for gold lace also.

773.—[7398]. Gold and Silver lace.

Native gold lace is only used by European tailors for the bands of Military caps; it is too heavy or expensive, being of gold wire (társurkh), much more heavily gilt than the European, and therefore more expensive. "Lais" is admired by natives for waist-belts, sword-belts &c., (peti, partla, gátra &c.,) and worn in native cavalry regiments &c., &c.

774.—[7399]. Do. of silver gilt.

775.—[7400]. Sulma of gold and silver.

776.—[7402]. Gokru-i-mukesh. This has been described above, it is merely tinsel crimped or puckered up. The term 'gokrú is applied to the prickly seed vessel of the burr (*Tribulus*), thence the word has passed into other meanings. A round spinous ornament for the ear is called gokrú; the spiked three-pronged irons, which, being thrown down, are so curved that one prong must project and so harass the advance of cavalry, are called gokru. Just in the same way the Delhi jewellery in gold, pointed all over with little points, is called bábul work, from its resemblance to the round balls of yellow stamina which form the flower of the bábul or acacia.

777.—Sitára safed and surkh are the round spangles before described.

778.--Gota, surkh and safed. Gota is a bordering of gold made in a loom as above described. Júta, (or false) gota, is very cheap—the tinsel being merely brass and water-gilt.

779.—[7402]. Dhanak (safed and surkh).

780.—[7408]. Zanjírah (gold).

781—[ ]. Silver wire gilt.

782.—[7412]. Mukesh (described above).

DELHI.

783.—[3437.]—Gota, gold ribbon called 'Hor' in local list.

The same from Ludhiana, Ambala &c. &c.

LAHORE.

784.—[8684].– Mukesh,—and gold thread made from it (kalabatun), reeled gold wire, and reeled red floss silk used for making kalabatun. The little wooden reel is called "pechak." The same with silver wire and white silk for silver threads (hence the use of the names 'safed' and 'surkh' for silver and gold thread).

785.—" Kaitún mothradár," a kind of edging of green and scarlet silk and gold.

786.—[8689].—Kaitún mothradár, gold lace edging: this is woven with gold thread in the web and woof; not like gota, which is made of tinsel.

787.—[8694].—Kaitún "safed," silver braid by MUHAMAD BAKSH. This is a narrow braid, such as ladies use in embroidery or braiding work.

788.—" Dori sabz wa siya," green, black and gold edging or braid: a narrow braid made by plaiting gold or silver dhanak (*q. v.*) with silk.

789.—[8700].—Anchal safeda.

790.—[7801].—Kinári, edging. Anchal and Kinári are ribbons of silver and gold, either plain or woven in a pattern. The manufacture has been described above. The plain ribbon of the broader sorts has often a pattern pressed on the material so as to stand out in relief, by printing with a hard iron block or die after gentle heating.

791.—[8703]. Gold "Sarpech."

This is a strip of thin gold woven ribbon, a foot broad, worn round the turban by the bridegroom on the day of his marriage; when so attired he is called "Nau-Shah," the new king. The sarpech was formerly only worn by Kings and Emperors and such nobles as they chose to allow the distinction of wearing it. The bridegroom who wears it is king for the occasion.

792.—[8705]. Chúni bádlí, a scarf of fine muslin woven with gold, worn at weddings: it is very light, hence called "bádlí," and glitters prettily enough.

793.—[8706]. "Son-sehra," an ornament consisting of a piece of very deep fringe (a foot deep) made of thin strips of gold tinsel; it is tied round the forehead of the bridegroom at his wedding and allowed to hang over the face.

794.—[8707].—Kalghi, a cockade or aigrette of gold tinsel and feathers, worn in a child's pagri on gala days &c.

795.—Tinsel ornaments for the ears. These are rosettes not unlike a guelder rose, stalks and flowerets being imitated in tinsel, and worn stuck into the ear by dancing girls. They are called "Karnphúl."

PESHAWAR.

796.—[9095].—Gold thread (Russian) worth Rs. 1-1-0 a tola.

797.—[9096].—Gold thread made at Peshawar, Rs. 1-4 a tola.

Russia gold thread is sold in Peshawar, both real and imitation, ("jùta kalábatún.")

NABHA.

798.—[9163.] "Sanjáf," a border of brocade (silk is often substituted) and sewn inside the lining of a garment at the edge.

799.—[9166.] Patha or fíta, a narrow edging.

800.—[9176]. "Zari," gold and silver, the same as "chuni bádla."

801.—[9183]. Gokru, gold and silver.

The collection also included sitára, sulma, mukesh, dhanak and gota.

FABRICS WOVEN WITH GOLD.

The following are the specimens.

802.—[7396]. Kimkháb, woven at NABHA. This was, I suppose, woven by a workman employed by the Chief of this State.

803.—[7422 &c.]. Specimens of muslin woven with spots of gold and silver, MALER KOTLA.

DELHI.

804.—[8441 &c.] Series of fancy gold woven fabrics by Lála Rami Mal. The names, toí, chín &c. mean thin fabrics of net or gauze embroidered.

"Toi ganda," Rs 2-8 a yard.
"Toi bíjdár," (spotted or speckled with small spots or seed—bíj) @ Rs. 2-4.
"Toi Saburja"—@ Rs. 1-2.
"Toi phúldar" (flowered) @ Rs. 1-7.
"Chán phúldar."
"Chuneria," @ Rs. 1-1 a yard.

LAHORE.

805.—[8711]. Muslin, printed in gold, (chúni malmal cháp tilaí) by Anand Ram.

This is simply gold leaf applied to muslin, by printing the pattern first in some glutinous size, and then applying the gold leaf.

SUB-CLASS C.

VESSELS AND ARTICLES OF GOLD OR SILVER FOR USE AND ORNAMENT.

I do not here include personal ornaments; putting them by preference under the head of "Jewellery." The class does not exhibit any very interesting articles.

For design and variety in the form of articles we look in vain; but in this class of work, as in many others, great delicacy and ingenuity is discovered in chasing, ornamenting, and engraving patterns on the various articles.

Most of the silver and goldsmith's work is rude, and always exhibits a want of finish, and a carelessness of accuracy which is distressing: circles are always out, the lines of a casket never true or straight, a vessel is often slightly lop-sided, or the work shows marks of the file and the burnisher.

The silver vessels in use in rich men's houses are the ugliest things imaginable; all that is wanted is to have pure silver, dull, white. and heavy. Polishing silver, and the contrast of bright and frosted silver is unknown and hardly appreciated.

But under this sub-class, some of the inlaid work of Sealkot and Gujrat, and the flower-chased vases of Kashmir, redeem the series from being utterly uninteresting, and, fortunately, form and design are here both excellent. In the case of 'Koftgari,' or inlaid work, besides arms and armour, caskets vases and ornaments are made, but on European and other good designs, wherein the indigenous taste for delicate tracery comes out in full force in the inlaying work. The Kashmir work again is almost confined to the production of the water goglet or "surahi," copied from the clay original, whose elegant shape I have before remaked to be probably fortuitous. A few other articles are made, such as little cups with covers, and trays of a very pretty pattern—four cornered—the corners being like a Muhamadan arch.

The following articles in silver will illustrate the class. I have not repeated the names of the household vessels, drinking cups and so forth; almost any of the vessels mentioned under No. 727, *ante*, except the very large ones may be found in wealthy houses, made of silver instead of brass.

LUDHIANA.

806.—[84611]. Salt-cellars (silver) by Gurmukh of Malondh.

807.—Silver water-goglet and cups.

808.—A pair of silver slippers (fancy article, for ornament).

809.—Silver "dibba" or round box for keeping trinkets, &c.

810.—Silver snuff-box.

The snuff-boxes in use are either made of silver, or else of a bêl fruit dried and mounted with metal, or even of glass; but all are on the principle of a hollow egg with a very small opening, and stopped with a little stopper: 'to take a pinch' out of such a box would be difficult.

Snuff is principally taken by Kábulis, Peshawris and by Biluchí people, rarely if ever by the Panjábis, and never by Sikhs.

Simla States.

811.—Silver box from Kanaití.

812.—Silver pen box and inkstand. Júbal. This is prettily chased.

Each of the small Hill States having his own Chief, Rája, Rána or Thákur, a silver-smith for the Court is required, and a workman with sufficiently rude art is generally forthcoming.

Amritsar.

813.— Gilt box. This is of silver gilt ; a casket ornamented with flowers, done in sort of repoussé work.

There are one or two workmen at Lahore and Amritsar who make very handsome patterns chiselled out in relief on very hard wood or brass ; and then hammer a thin silver plate over it till the silver takes the impression of the pattern in relief. Such workmen can make pretty caskets, or designs for book covers, in any style.

814.—[8522]. Silver Surmádan or antimony holder. A small vase or bottle for holding antimony, applied as a cosmetic to the eyes. Such vases, having a narrow neck and a silver bodkin with which to apply the powder, are made in great variety of shape and style of ornamentation.

815. An " Atar-dán." A casket for holding little pots of attar or otto of roses, jessamine, &c. Some of them are very elegant. There was one sent by the Nawab of Patondhi to the Paris Exhibition in 1867. It is probably Delhli work. In shape it is oblong, with the sides gracefully curved like the body of a guitar and the corners rounded. It is mounted on claw feet, and has a raised lid ; the work is partly plain and partly silver open-work, the latter portion being gilt. The whole is set with turquoises, and the lid surmounted by a small peacock in enamel.

Lahore.

816.—" Guláb pásh." A vase with a long narrow neck and a perforated mouth piece, for sprinkling rose water.

817.—[8658]. "Abkhora tútídar." A silver drinking vessel, with a spout, cover, and handle.

818.—' Kulfi.' A small silver vessel with cover, used for preparing ices in.

819.—A scent bottle—" Atar-dán."

820.—A silver huka vase, with stem, bowl, and every thing complete. Such a silver huka would be used by a nobleman or Raja : it is an extremely handsome affair.

821.—A perforated silver ball.

Whether this is meant for a toy, or to be used as a " salki," to infuse tea in a cup or other vessel, instead of using a teapot, I do not know.

822.—[8678]. " Keta nukri," silver marbles for children's toys.

823.—A Chauri or fly-flap, with silver handle.

The servants in attendance in every great man's house has one or more, standing behind the chair and waving the chauri gently to keep off the flies. They are either made of peacocks feathers (for state ceremonies) or of the tail of the yak (see Vol., I, *s. v.*).

Kapurthalla.

824 —Dates imitated in silver.

825.—Series of vessels of glass covered with filigree silver.

There is a Kapurthalla workman and one at Amritsar. The stems of the glass and the rim are covered with silver gilt and flowered (not filigree work) and the bowl with a covering of silver net, made of fine wire. Drinking cups and vases are made in this way.

Kashmir.

The Kashmir work made, both in silver and gold, at Srinagar, is the best work under this class. but wants finish and neatness. The work is uniform in design consisting of a pattern of small sprigs of leaves all over the vessel in relief: it is done with a hammer and tiny steel chisels and punches. Sometimes the work is made with the ground silver and the sprigs gilt: this is called "Gangá-jamní" work.

To give some idea of the prices, I enumerate the following :—

The prices are rather high, as might be expected at an Exhibition.

Silver cup, partly gilt,	... ...	Rs. 20—13
Large surahi, Do.,	... ...	" 70
Silver dish,	... ...	" 47
Cheroot case,	... ...	" 22
Salt cellar,	... ...	" 6 —11
Silver surahis,	... ...	" 50 and 65

The purchaser in Srinagar can hardly be cheated, except in quality of work, as all these goods are sold by actul weight in silver, with a fixed rate for workmanship added.

Inlaid Ware.

The inlaying is mostly on steel or iron, in gold, and occasionally silver, and sometimes both; when gold and silver are employed in unison, the work is called "Ganga-jamní."

The inlaid work of steel and gold is called "Koft-gari," the people who do it are "koft-gars."

I have already explained that originally arms and armour were the only things in demand, but now, in times of peace—Othello's occupation gone—the workmen have nearly all settled in the Gujrat and Sealkot districts, and make inlaid work on caskets, vases, pistols, combs, brooches, bracelets and so forth. In Sealkot the workmen have been greatly improved by the teaching of Mr. Spence, before alluded to. This gentleman has induced the Sealkot workman to apply that care in finishing, in which native work is usually so deficient. The rough undersides of the inlaid work and the joints, which were formerly left bare or rudely marked with silver in a check pattern, are now finished by the aid of electro-gilding.

Koft-gari is done by first drawing out the pattern on the steel surface with a hard steel needle or silái. This leaves a line sufficiently deep to catch the very fine wire laid on. The wire is of pure gold, drawn through a steel jandrí, just as described under the head of "Gold wire drawing," only that the wire is gold. and not silver gilt. The wire is then hammered into the iron according to the pattern and lines already drawn, the whole is then heated and again hammered, and the surface is polished with a white, porous stone; where the soft gold is required to be spread, the rubbing and hammering are repeated with greater force. The gold used is pure and very soft.

Recently Mr. Spence has introduced inlaying on bronze. and some pretty specimens were sent to Paris in 1867. The gold for this must be of the richest and darkest color, or it does not show out.

For a particular account of the implements used in koft work, see note to No. 833 (Multan) *post*.

SIMLA.

826.—[8490]. Axe inlaid with gold—Kyunthal.

HUSHYARPUR.

827.—Specimens of inlaid work, in silver on iron—a pen stand, a buckle, and a knife. This work is rather rude, and has little to recommend it—made at Una and Hushyárpur.

AMRITSAR.

828.—Koft-gari arms, contributed by Sirdar Bhagwán Singh of Amritsar, consisting of the long native gun, daggers, swords, helmet and armour. There are still some workmen, relics of the Sikh days, both at Lahore and Amritsar, who can, to order, work up swords &c., in gold inlaying, and do it beautifully, if allowed expenses for a liberal supply of gold wire. Imám Baksh, Mehtáb Singh, Amánulla, and a few others, are the Lahore workmen.

LAHORE.

829.—[8749]. Hunting sword, the blade inlaid with devices of tigers, dogs &c. &c., value Rs. 35.

830.—Inlaid shield, value Rs. 125.

831.—Inlaid pistol, on blue steel.

832.—Huka vase and pipe, inlaid.

These samples are sufficient to show the style of work done.

SEALKOT.

Koftgari was exhibited from Gujrat and Sealkot, and some from Nizámábád and Wazîrábád, and Múltan.

The Sealkot work is now the best, owing to late improvements.

There is no interest in a long list of articles. I may say that the men will work from full size drawings and copy any vase, or card tray, &c. Ladies' trinkets, caskets, pen-cases, inkstands, letter-weights, are all to be had. A very complete model of an Armstrong gun, with the screw and smaller parts in electro-gilt, was sent to Paris in 1867 and priced £45.

I subjoin the following list to give an idea of the price: this is taken from the Paris list of 1867, and the rates are decidedly high.

Caskets of all patterns,	... ... from Rs.	20 to 180
Card trays and dishes,	... ... „	20 to 35

Model of Armstrong gun, finished to scale, and complete in every respect, ...	Rs.	450
Paper weights, various, ...	„	8 to 20
Letter clips, ...	„	5 to 10
Penknife, 2 bladed, ...	„	6
Octagonal cigar stand, which, by turning a knob on the centre, reverses the sides of the case, displaying cigars in racks, ...	„	200
Bracelets, ...	„	6 to 10 each.

Can be had with Persian inscriptions wrought in gold: these are much admired.

Brooches, various, ...	Rs.	5 to 10
Solitaires, buckles, &c.	„	10 to 25
Scent vases, ...	„	70
If inlaid on brass with fine gold they cost more.		
Shield inlaid with gold, ... according to richness of work.	„	140 and upwards,
Inlaid gun, ...	„	150 to 500
Paper knife, ...	„	5, 8, 12
Table bell, ...	„	20
Set of scales and weights	„	75
Centre piece, ...	„	250

Writing sets, consisting of pen tray, inkstand, candlestick and portfolio can be had.

833.—Koft work from Multán. My correspondent writes:—

" The invention of this art dates from the time of the great physician Luqmán,* who first introduced it into India. It was not known in Multan some two hundred years back, when it was first introduced and practised by one Muhamad Murád, a resident of Multan. The art is not carried on to any great extent here, nor are the articles of this description of manufacture generally exported to any foreign country: in the time of the former rulers the manufacture of such articles was confined to the requirements of the city. I believe it was not the intention of the artizans solely to derive their means of livelihood from this profession. They had occasionally, but not often, to go to Sind or Bháwalpur to execute this sort of workmanship. "

The following are the names of implements used in the manufacture.

Hammer or Hathaura made of steel.

Mohárí or rubber of agate or cornelian (ghori).

Sohán or file made of iron.

Chimta or pincers made of iron.

Kalam-faulad, or carving pen made of steel.

Pathraini made of 'rukh.' a sort of iron.

Kath or goldsmith's scissors.

Parkár or compass made of rukh. a sort of iron.

Charna or splitter, do. do.

Ráwatí or file made of common, do. do.

Silaí or pencil made of 'Tava' iron.

* This is, probably, nonsense. B. P.

Jandri or an instrument for drawing wire, made of rukh iron.

Zambúr or pincers made of rukh iron.

The gold wire used, if of superior description, is that which is drawn to a length of 12 yards from a single másha of gold: but as the task is delicate and difficult, it requires a person of good sight and strength.

The inferior description of wire is only drawn to a length of one yard from a másha of gold, but as the work is not superfine, it can be done by a person possessing ordinary strength and eye sight. The process of wire drawing by passing it through the jandri has already been described.

The rate of wages for workmanship is entirely dependent on the quality and description of work done. If an artist was to manufacture a gold worked hand axe, like the one sent to the Exhibition of 1864, which was the best that could be made here, the wages would be 12 rupees for every tola weight of gold thus wrought. But if the work done were of an inferior quality, it could be executed for five rupees per tolah.

The following are the terms and phrases used by artisans of the above profession.

Khingrí.--A kind of clinker or porous scoriæ from potters' kilns—it is used in cleaning and smoothing the surface of the article on which the inlaid work is to be done.

Pechak or Reel.—Made of wood or paper, is used for coiling the gold wire.

Tânchí.—Is the process of carving the pattern on the surface with a steel pen or style.

The method of working is as follows:—Suppose a hand axe is to be inlaid The blade of the axe is first made smooth with a ráwati or file, after which it is polished with the khingri or pumice stone, on this being done a rough wooden handle is inserted in the hollow part of the hatchet; the outer end of the handle is pressed inside the arm, and the hatchet is placed on a stool one and half feet high, and then the process of carving is done with the steel pen, according to the design which the workman is furnished with.

The hatchet is then heated for a few minutes in a fire of charcoal, quite free from smoke, until the steel changes its natural color into azure blue. The gold wire is then also heated so as to make it soft, and is coiled on a reel.

Again the hatchet is placed on the stool in the manner above described; the artist takes the wire and presses it into the lines with the iron pencil, pathraini, following the outline design engraved with the style. When one flower or the whole work is completed, it becomes necessary to cut the wire, which is done with "kath" or gold smith's scissors. Should the wire, after being first fixed, become loose in any part of the hatchet, it is again heated in the coals, and the wire is beaten with a small hammer which refixes it. The hatchet is then rubbed with mohári or stone rubber, so as to draw out its brilliancy and lustre.

After the above process is completed, the hatchet is well rubbed with sour lime-juice, but as this changes the color from azure to white, it becomes necessary again to put it on a clear fire, so that it may resume its former color of azure, together with its brightness and lustre.

Gilt.—If an article is to be plain gilt all over, it is first smoothened with the ráwati or file, and afterwards cleaned with khingri or pumice stone ; it is then drawn over with chequers with the carving style, and sprinkled with lime-juice, after which it is heated ; gold or silver leaves (as the case may be) are then applied with pincers, and lightly hammered, and are rubbed with the mohári or stone rubbers, which causes the gold to adhere to the surface roughened by the chequered lines—and then the soft gold spreads out under the rubber, and covers the whole surface.

The rate of wages is as follows :—

Gilding,	per tola of weight,		3	Rupees.
Silvering,	do.,	do.,	12	Annas.

SUB-CLASS D.

SPECIMENS OF PLATING IN GOLD AND SILVER.

This class is a very small one. The art of electro-plating in the European method has become known to a few persons; and, in Lahore, it is easy to get silver dishes, spoons and forks, replated, with very fair success.

The specimens in 1864 were but few, and only from Amritsar.

[7810].—Iron hinges gilt (one by Sirdár Bhagwán Singh himself).

[7810—1.]—Coffee pot and milk jug, plated.

A large silver bird intended for a centre piece, very rude and ugly; plated.

What is called water gilding is also done, in imitation of the European process. The original native process of gilding, applied by them to large works, as gilding temple domes, elephant howdahs, &c., is now described.

In plating such articles, they use the process called "thanda mulamma." In small articles they use water-gilt. If the article be of copper, it is to be well scraped, cleaned and polished, and then heated in the fire to remove all oil or dirt that may have been left on the surface by polishing. After this it is dipped in an acid solution of the 'kishta,' or dried unripe apricots. After this it is rubbed with the powder of half burned bricks, or some other earth. The surface is then rubbed with mercury, which adheres by combining with the metal. The article is next placed in clean water for some hours, and again washed in the kishta solution, and dried with a clean cloth. Gold leaf is now applied to the surface, to which it adheres, being adjusted by the workman blowing it with his mouth or touching it with a cloth. The gold then, by reason of the effect of the mercury coating, appears all white. The article being subjected to heat, the mercury sublimes, and the dull yellow metallic tint returns; more gold leaf is now applied, and is all rubbed and ground into the surface by means of agate rubbers called "mohári." These are merely convenient shaped points of jade and agate fixed into iron or wooden handles. The quantity of mercury used is always double in weight that of the gold: the plating is of course done more lightly or more heavily as the work requires. This is the process employed in plating the domes of temples, &c., they are of copper gilt, plated in separate pieces, which are afterwards joined.

If it is desired to plate with silver, the surface of the copper is scratched with chequered lines and beated, when the metal turns black they put on silver leaf and rub it in with the mohári while still hot, and after that the remainder of the silver intended to be consumed is put on: the final polishing is done with agate or jade.

Where gold and silver leaf is required to be applied to an iron surface, as in the case of armour, knives, or ornamental work, the surface is scratched over with chequered lines, this process is called ('khizán'), and washed with hot solution of kishta; and then dried it is heated to what the workmen called "shitáb" (corruption of siya táb, 'black heat') *i. e.*, the greatest heat it will reach without becoming red hot. In this state leaves of gold or silver, as required, are layed on, and rubbed in with a "mohári."

In plating on brass, if gold is to be used, the process is as with copper; if silver, the process is that for iron.

I do not describe the water-gilt process—it is done by means of a solution of gold in nitro-muriatic acid: it is only known in the Punjab since the days of the British rule. The process is therefore only a copy of the European art.

NOTE ON THE PROCESS OF GOLD-BEATING—"DAFTRI KUT."

These people consider themselves possessed of a great art, inasmuch as the possession of gold-beater's skin (jillí) is necessary, and the art of making it is supposed to be difficult. I was informed that an elaborate composition of 23 'masálas' was necessary.

These are given for mere curiosity. It is obvious that two-thirds of the substances are quite useless, and added only for show and to involve the process in seeming mystery.

Gold-beater's skin is prepared from the scarf skin of the sheep—that thin skin which lies immediately below the wool, and can be removed separately.

Persons of the "Katík" caste take 100 skins with the wool on, and soak them for eight days in a mixture consisting of 3 seers of wheat flour, 1½ seer of rock salt, and one seer of the milky juice of the madár plant (*Calotropis*), the whole being diluted with water to suffice for soaking 100 skins.

When the soaking is completed, the hair is scraped off with an iron scraping rod—'rambhi.' The skins are then spread on stones and the scarf skins removed entire: this seems to require practice and delicate manipulation. The upper skins so removed are thoroughly washed with 1 seer of dahi or curds and water, and after that twice with clean water. They are now dried in the sun.

Next a mixture is made of the following drugs, in proportions of 32 to 34 máshas each.

Cloves.
Jalauntri (mace).
Kangumandí (a round root, probably of *Crocus Sativus*).
Nakhún. They look like broad dirty brown wrinkled nails, as if from the foot of some animal.
Dates.
Cocoa-nut kernel (garí).
Akarkarha (*Spilanthes oleracea*).
Jaiphal (nutmeg).
Dálchíní (cinnamon).
Zafrán (saffron).
Sandal sarkh, } Sandal wood.
Do. safed, }
Iláchí—cardamoms, both small and great.

These spices are boiled over a slow fire in 4 seers of water till the liquor is reduced to 2 seers in bulk.

Then another set of 23 drugs &c., is taken, in quantities varying from 4 to 8 tolahs.

Ratanjot (Onosma, used as alkanet root).
Chalchalíra (a tree lichen *Parmelia*).
Buddhi-budha, (a common tree lichen, black underneath and white above.)
Málkangni (*Celastrus*).
Birmi (yew wood).
Indarjau (seed of *H. antidysenterica)*.
Kahi kahela (*Myrica sapida*).
Taj—aromatic bark.
Bahman, safed and surkh—(*Centaurea*).
Phul dháwí (flower of *Conocarpus*).
Belgiri—(*Ægle marmelos* fruit).
Bálchir—(*Nard root*).
Kapúr kachri (aromatic root of *Hedychium*).
Pán roots.
Tej bal—aromatic leaves.
Red "ratti," (*Abrus precatorius* seeds).
Isabghol, (*Plantago* seeds).
Tamál patr (aromatic leaves).
Pipla múl (fruit of *Plantago amplexicaulis*).
Mothrán (root of *Cyperus longus*).
Camphor, which is to be ground up with saffron.
Ghee, 8 tolahs.

The above substances, which are mostly astringent and aromatic, are to be well mixed in one maund of water, and the camphor and ghee added last; the whole is to be boiled down to 20 seers. This done, the clear liquor is strained off through a basket lined with "dhák" leaves, into an earthen "kunál" or naund, and the "phog" or dregs on the strainer, thrown away. The first prepared liquor is now mixed with the second, thus making 22 seers an all, which is again gently and slowly evaporated down to 15 seers. It is strained through cloth, and then the camphor and ghee of the last list, are added, after which it is again warmed and the 100 skins will soaked in it.

The object of the liquid appears to be to affect the fine skins by a sort of tanning with the astringents, to preserve it from decay by the aromatics, and to soften it by the oil and other demulcent substances employed. The skins are now spread on separate clean stones to dry, after which each skin is cut up into leaves of a convenient size; 100 hides thus yield 1200 'jilli' leaves. They do not all turn out of equal thickness, so the "daftri kut" selects the thicker ones for silver beating, and the finer for gold. The skins are separately rubbed with plaster of Paris made by burning and grinding 'ropar' stone, also called 'makol'. 300 of these skins after being separately dusted with a clean cloth are collected into a book and tied up in a leather case, which is subjected to hard beating on a stone with the gold beater's pestle: this goes on for 2 days, after which each skin is again rubbed with a clean cloth. Gold intended to be beaten is made in thin strips of plate called "díwáli." The slips are enclosed between layers of skin, till a sort of book or pile is formed—120 plates go between the 300 skins—they are tied up in the leather case, and beaten with an iron hammer on an anvil of stone; the blows are delivered first round one edge of the parcel, then it is turned half round and the other edge gets beaten, and so on. Four times the packet has to be opened and the position of the gold bits shifted to prevent the skins being cut. After that the gold is too thin to be moved again. A "daftar" of gold leaves is ready in 3 or 4 days, and requires a lakh and a half of blows with the hammer.

....

CLASS XIII.

JEWELLERY.

This class is almost impossible of separation from Class X. A large number of the articles in it are curious from an ethnographic point of view, and are neither beautiful in design, nor costly in material.

It is hardly necessary to say that jewellery is as much worn by men as women, but the kinds of jewellery worn by each are distinct in form and name.

It is very curious to remark what an immense number of names for different kinds of ornaments the people recognize. In European languages we call every kind of ornament for the arm a bracelet; we hardly adopt any distinctive terms for varieties of necklaces: but a Punjabi has at least half a dozen names for different patterns of these articles.

The country people, and indeed the poor and middle classes, wear mostly silver ornaments; those better off have the same in gold. It is only the very wealthy who wear richly jewelled ornaments.

Silver ornaments are almost the sole form of wealth among the villagers. If a man has a few rupees to save he makes a great 'hass' or necklace, and gives it to his wife to keep; or he makes a lot of karas (armlets) and so the money is converted.

The gold and silver ornament makers are by far the most numerous; they are called technically "sádákár"—a "plain metal" worker. The people who can cut, polish, and set gems, are few and far between.

As we leave the plains and go further into the hills, the number of silver ornaments decreases and the men also wear much less jewellery, having mostly perhaps but one necklace and a few charms or amulets. The women have large necklaces of beads, and of rough bits of amber, red coral, and turquois pebbles. Besides these, strings of imported glass beads. and sometimes of large beads cut out of the white conch shell are worn: the latter are imported from beyond Yarkand and Kashmir. Silver engraved charms and armlets are much worn; in Ladákh and Láhul they often wear small copper boxes, the surface ornamented perhaps with brass and turquoises, and containing scraps of writing, prayers, incantations, and the like: these boxes are generally worn and hung or tried round the waist. The women in the Simla States wear immense "pázebs" or anklets of zinc, which close round the ankle, being bent together till they meet; they are often six inches broad, and are rudely engraved with devices: thick zinc bracelets are also worn on the wrist.

In the hills all the women seem partial to ear-rings, which resemble bunches of flowers; in Kulú they are generally of silver. An immense number of little balls hanging by short chains to a ring, is a common pattern. One in the Museum is in the form of a pyramid suspended by the point, and the base fringed all round like a tassel.

I here seen more ornaments in silver worn by the Kulu women than in other Hill districts. They also have many species of silver enamelled work, brought from Kangra: particularly graceful is the Kulu silver head gear.

The subject of jewellery will be best treated in the following order :—

1. Description of hill ornaments Western Himalaya, Chamba, Pangí, Lahul, Spití, Ladákh, and Kulu.
2. Ornaments used in the plains generally, and in Shahpur, Gugáira (Montgomery), Rohtak.
3. Imitation of European jewellery and Delhi work.

The people in Hazára and Kághán, in the Western Himalaya, wear ornaments in silver and zinc, and some few of gold.

The names given are those current in Hazára, and the names in brackets are the ordinary vernacular equivalents.*

"Pairkará" (chúra). Silver rings worn on the ankles by women—they are flat worked metal; the elaborate anklets with fringes, little bells, &c. are here, as elsewhere, called "pázeb."

Flat rings called gúthyán are worn on the toes. Finger rings, commonly known as "múndri" are here called "chap;" and the big thumb ring (ársí) is called "angúthrá."

Small bracelets worn on the wrist are called "wangan," whether of zinc, glass or silver; these are the "churis" of the plains. An amulet fixed on the upper arm with a silk tie is called "bhawata." For necklaces, a "dulra," consisting of metal beads on a silk thread; "hansam" (haslí) a silver ring or collar (worn also by children); chamkali (champakalli) (literally the "necklace of champa buds") an elaborate ornament with pendants; "hamayal" (har) another necklace with pendant ornaments, complete the list. In Mansera, a necklace consisting of a broad chain work is called "pajútra."

In the ears. plain rings—"chala" (dandi, báli.) are worn by women also. "Chitkan" (zaujír) ear-rings of chain work, hanging about the ears; also "lúrke," colored glass ear-rings. A "jedu" is an ear-ring consisting of a metal cup or bell hung by a silk thread to the ear. "Paizwán" (bulákh) is a plain nose ring worn by women; and "chárgul" (four-flowers) a nose stud worn by married women (called *laung* in common vernacular).

"Tawíz"—Amulets. are worn on the arms, on the forehead, and round the neck. by both sexes. "Dáditak" a silver ornament worn by women hanging over the forehead.

A plain small cup-shaped metal shield, called "Máin," is worn on the head on great occasions.

Pangi, Lahul, Chamba, &c.

The women wear a sort of flat folded cloth cap, from this depends over the fore-head, a silver moon-like ornament with pendants, and a border with a fringe of silver is worn over the temples following the angle of the hair.

Round the neck a profusion of necklaces are worn, some fitting close, the next set a little longer, and the largest hanging down to the waist.

The close ones are made of large shell beads or silver beads; several more are of small glass beads, coral, amber. &c. A number of brass beads are also worn, and necklaces terminating in small hollow brass pomegranates, which, having a metal pea inside, clink and

* For this list I am indebted to Mr. A. L. Home, Assistant Conservator of Forest (Jhelam Division.)

jingle like small bells. Each woman wears suspended by three chains of iron, a round concave plate of brass, which hangs down from the right shoulder; on the other side a brass bell is worn.

The ear-rings are either large round rings of silver, or chains terminating in great studs. The stud is stuck into the ear, and the chain hooked into the hair above. Some of them wear round the ankles bunches of jingling brass pomegranates.

Bracelets are not worn in any profusion, and then only the thick " karas " of zinc or silver.

Spiti and Ladakh.

The Spiti men wear round ear-rings, and one or more long necklaces of amber and turquois beads round the neck. They do not appear to wear any armlets or bracelets.

Every man has an iron pipe stuck in his belt, his tobacco pouch, and a flint and steel. Unmarried girls wear in their hair one or two beads of turquois;* ear-rings and necklaces of beads of amber and coral. Bracelets are usually made of beads cut out of shell, or circles made by sawing off a round section of a conch shell : these are imported.

The married women fix to the front part of the perák (already described in Class 10), a large moon-like silver ornament which hangs over the top of the head, the fringe of it drooping on to the forehead ; on each side of this, a broad flat plait of silver chain-work hangs down on either side of the face, and terminates in a silver tassel. Every woman has at her waist a tassel of leather ornamented with cowry shells.†

Ladákh.—The women wear, as in Spiti and Láhul, a profusion of long necklaces of coral and amber and turquois beads rudely strung together with conch shell beads and European glass beads ; also great amulets of brass studded with turquoises or silver. As in Láhul, the Ladákh women wear round the neck, suspended over the breast, a round brass plate, sometimes replaced by a huge bit of conch shell. Their bracelets are of silver or shell as above described.

The women likewise carry a brass spoon, a convex brass mirror, and a case of small needles attached to their girdles ; to these may be added a small metal or wooden cup, a single or double flageolet, a metal spoon and plate, all of which are stuffed into the slackened breast of the dress next the skin, along with a ball of wool, a coil of rope, and a few unleavened wheaten or barley cakes.‡

The men wear necklaces, but I think not bracelets. The necklaces serve principally to carry amulets; these consist sometimes of small tubular boxes containing written prayers or charms, sometimes of flat boxes ornamented rather prettily, and sometimes of flat engraved plates of silver.

Both men and women have a pouch edged with steel for flint and tinder purposes : the leather part of the pouch is prettily ornamented with brass or silver.

---

* Egerton's Tour in Spiti, p. 25.

† See the Photograph at page 30 of Mr. Egerton's book on Spiti.

‡ Cunningham's Ladak, p. 305.

Simla States.

The Kanáwar people, and also those toward Simla States, wear huge zinc rings or tubes round the ankles; silver or zinc bracelets, round silver ear-rings, and have also a large open brass brooch, of which the characteristic form is—

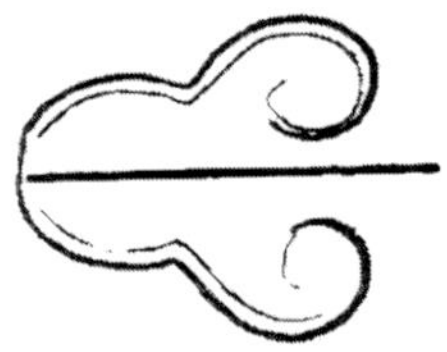

This brooch serves to fasten the upper shawl, or waist girdle: the plate at page 304 in Cunningham's Ladákh shews it to advantage. Necklaces of glass beads, and coral and amber, are here in fashion also.

Kulu.—The profusion of large bead, amber, and coral necklaces disappears among the Kulu people; they wear mostly silver, not a little of it is prettily enamelled: this latter work is done at Kangra and at Jagat Sukh.

A Kulu woman wears round her neck chains of small coral or glass beads, and chains of silver beads cut into facets, and having small enamelled pendants hanging therefrom. They wear a nose ring of gold or silver with a pendant spoon-shaped ornament hanging from the ring.

They wear also round ear-rings with bunches of silver bobbins and chains attached; also bracelets like those in the plains. Some of the richer women wear a head ornament, which is fixed over the forehead under the plaits of hair and woollen thread, which form a coronal. The ornament consists of two broad plaits of silver wire work, which, separating from the central point of suspension, are worn like braids of hair on either side of the face, and terminate in silver tassels: they resemble those worn in Spiti, but are smaller.

Ornaments worn in the Plains.

Derajat.

The ornaments worn in the *Derajat* are described as follows, from a set sent to me by Jamál Khán, chief of the Lughárí tribe.

The necklaces are—

Hassi, a 'torquea' of stiff solid metal. The plate shews one.

Chamkalli, a necklet consisting of a string of twisted silk, on the edge of which a number of long narrow and pointed gold beads, like the pointed buds (kalli) of the jessamine (chamba) are fixed. The effect is of a collar or fringe of gold rays or spikes.

An amulet of silver on a black silk chain (see plate).

Kath-mála, a necklace consisting of 4 rows of gold beads about the size of small peas; they are tied round the neck with a silk chain ending in tassels.

The handsomest neck ornament is a thick twisted silk chain from which hang, by a number of silver rings (which fit tightly over the silk), 3 "takhtas" or flat amulets, one large one in the centre and a smaller one on each side; attached to the lower edge of the amulets is a fringe of little silver bells. This ornament is called 'patrí.'

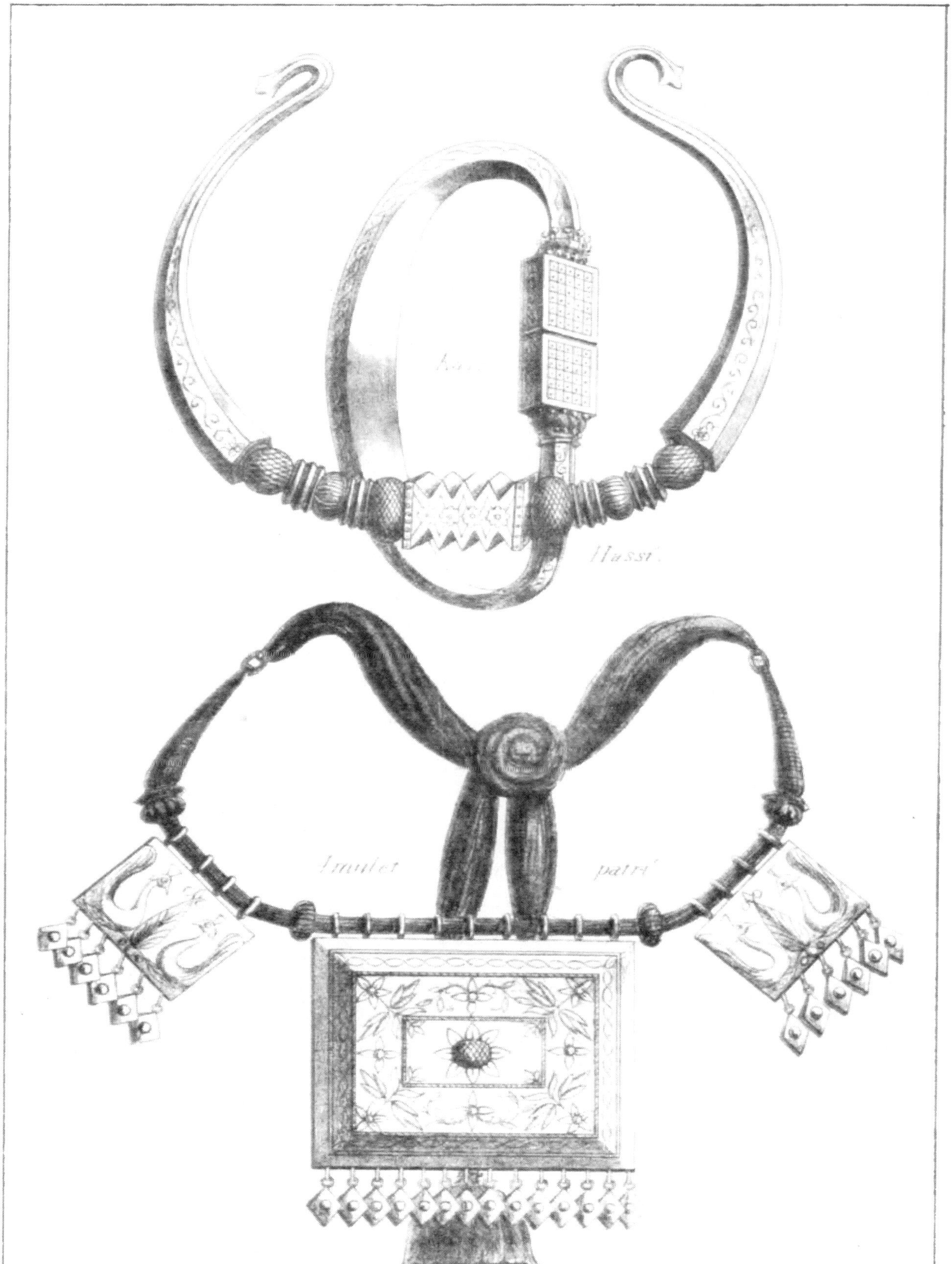

S. Sedgfield. Lith. Calcutta

Derajat ornaments p. 118

For the arms there are the usual bázuband,—a flexible band of gold tied round the upper arm by silken ends and tassels. A pair of "dastí" or "pouchis" being just like bázuband in style, only worn on the wrists, and consisting of a number of long gold beads strung on silk and ending in large colored silk tassels.

"Kangan."—Small bracelets on the arms, which open with a hinge and are fixed together by a rude sort of stud and pin—these are the "karas" of other parts.

On the feet there are "karí," a huge pair of hollow rings, which are bent round the ankle, and the two ends where they meet, end in square pieces as the plate shows.

"Tora."—Apparently the same as "jhánjar" of the plains, are hollow rings of silver, which open by a hinge and are fixed by a stud, worn round the ankle. The peculiarity is that inside the hollow, small bits of metal are placed so as to rattle when the wearer moves. These rings are sometimes worn on the arms towards Sind and Shikárpur.

"Pontha" are a pair of ornaments for the ankles, worn by children; they are stiff silk thread circlets, to which are fixed all round, small hollow pomegranates in silver with metal inside, that they may tinkle like bells.

Ear-rings of the common sort are worn as elsewhere. The usual bálí with its pendent tassel (patra) is drawn in the plate. The nath or nose ring is also worn.

Shahpur.

From Shahpur we having an account in the interesting report by Major Davies. The original report is accompanied by a sheet of well-executed drawings.

The neck ornaments consist of the following:—

Hár.—A broad collar, being a net-work of silver chain, worn both by Hindus and Musulmáns.

Hasli.—A silver solid *torquea* or stiff ring of silver, tapering at either end, is put on by opening and bending, and closing up again when in position: the front is adorned with pendants.

Táviz.—A thick necklace of crimson silk threads clasped at intervals by silver rings, from which hang silver flower-shaped pendants: in the centre a large oval silver amulet depends.

The bracelets are—

Chúris, thin silver rings, opened by bending.

Tád.—A broad silver ring worn on the upper arm.

Bahúta or "bázuband" a flexible armlet, composed of silk strings and silver plates, tied round the upper arm, the tying strings terminating in silver tassels.

Gokru, a thick silver bracelet, so called from having its edge nicked with points like the burr fruit: it is worn by Hindu women.

Chankangan.—A band of silver with small chains and pendants all round, worn above a set of the chúris by Hindu women.

Bahín.—A sort of silver tube wrought in a checked pattern, clasped round the arm, and is about 4 inches long.

The thick armlet called "kara" is worn by both sexes.

Finger rings are called *challa*, and one having three prominences like acorns is called "tridodya"—it is worn by Hindu women on the first finger. The ársí is worn here, as elsewhere, on the thumb. Ear-rings are in some variety under the name of "bálá" or "bálí."

The bálá is thicker, like a small "hasli." The bálí is a large thin circular ring of silver wire ornamented at one side by broad silver studs. The bálí or válí, worn by Mussulman women, is a silver ring terminated at either point of junction by a silver stud, on it hangs a bunch of small silver chains terminated by little silver balls.

On the toes broad thin rings are worn called "challi"; on the ankle a flexible coil of chain work with small pendants is worn: it is called "pázeb." A rather graceful silver pendant or châtelaine, called kharítí, is worn at the girdle by unmarried women.

The most characteristic ornament is worn on the top of the head by women of the Arúra caste, it is called "choti-phúl," and consists of a small round shield or silver plate worked and chased in circles.

Montgomery.

The Montgomery district collection in 1864 contained the following list :—

Chandan hár.—A silver necklace for women.

Haslí. A thick ring like the 'torquea' of Roman and British antiquity, worn round the neck; it tapers at either end, and the thin ends meet when it is bent into shape.

Kanthí. A necklace.

Champakalli, do.

Dúlra, do.

Hamáil galo, do.

Tavetarí, a gold charm or amulet.

Sáorah, a necklace (gold.)

Lar, a necklace of several threads (silver.)

Dughdugí, a necklace.

Bálí-patar, ear-rings worn by men and women.

Murki, do. (gold) do. do.

Dhedó, do. (silver or gold, either.)

Baháduriya, do. (women's.)

The following are all kinds of finger rings :—

Chala, angúthí, gokrú, birmgand.

The bracelets appear to be much the same as the Punjabi ones generally, viz. bawatta, paunchi, bázuband, kara, &c.

General List of Jewels.

A list of all the jewellery worn in the Punjab generally, and excluding local peculiarities, shews the following copious vocabulary :—

I.—HEAD ORNAMENTS.

Men's.

1. Sarpech—Jigháñ, the jewelled aigrette worn in front of the turban.
2. Kút biládar.—An oval pendant worn over the forehead (fig. 1).
3. Kalgi.—Plume in jewelled setting.
4. Turah-i-marwaríd.—Tassels of pearls worn on the turban.
5. Múkat or Mutakh.—A head dress worn by Hindus at weddings &c.

Women's.

7. Sisphúl, chaunk, or choti phúl.—A round boss worn on the hair over the forehead, it is cut or indented so as to resemble a gold flower like a chrysanthemum.
8. Phúl.—A boss like No. 7, only smooth, hemispherical, and set with jewels; it is worn on the top of the head—one or two are worn at pleasure.
9. Maulí.—A long chain made of rows of pearls separated by jewelled studs, about 8 inches long hanging from the head on one side.
10. Sir máng. A chain and pendant worn on the head by Hindus.
12. Boda.—An ornament of silk and silver plaited into the hair of children.

II.—ORNAMENTS WORN ON THE FOREHEAD.

(*By women only*).

13. Dámni, or dáúni.—A fringe hanging over the forehead on either side of the face (fig. 2). Some of these are richly jewelled.
14. Do. Kutbí, } Varieties of No. 13.
15. Do. Sosaní, }
16. Tíka or kashka.—Small ornament on the forehead (pendant).
17. Chánd bíná.—A moon-shaped pendant.
18. Táwít.—Small amulets worn on the head.
19. Jhúmar.—A tassel-shaped ornament or pendant (fig 24). Mostly worn towards Delhi, not in Punjab.
20. Guchhí marwaríd. A cluster of pearls.
22. Bindlí.—Small tinsel forehead ornament.
22. Barwata.—Tinsel stars worn over the eye-brows, (not to be confounded with *Bhawata* an armlet)

III.—EAR-ORNAMENTS.

Men's.

23. Bálá.—Very large thin rings worn by Khatris, Sikhs and Dogras. They have a pearl or so strung on the gold wire of which they are made.
24. Murkí.—Smaller ear-rings of the same shape.
26. Zanjírí.—A chain worn with the bala to keep it up.
27. Dúr (gold)—A small ear-ring with three gold studs one on side—(fig. 3).
28. Birbali.—A broad ear-ring with 3 studs (fig. 4).
29. Durichah.—A ear-ring with pendant tassel (fig. 5).

Women's.

30. Bálí or goshwára.—A set of rings worn all round the edge of the ear.
    Bálí bahádurí, (see fig. 18)—it has a large pointed stud in the centre.
31. Karnphúl, dhedu, and jhúmká. All forms of tassel-like ornaments, made with silver chains and little balls, fringe of silver chain work, &c., &c. A handsome pair of Karnphúl is figured in the last plate of the series.
32. Pípal-watta, or pipal pata, like a murki, but has a drop or pendant to it ending in a fringe of little gold "pípal" leaves.
33. Kantalá.—A similar ornament, has a stud besides the pendant, (see fig. 6.)
34. Bálá khúngri-dár.—A heavy fringed ear-ring (fig. 7).
    Bálá katoriwalla sádá (see fig. 18).
35. Khalíl.—Small ear-ring, (fig. 8).

Women's.

36. Jalíl.—Just the same, only that the central stud is jewelled.
37. Phumní.—Silk and tinsel tassels.
38. Machh Machlian.—A small gold figure of a fish worn as an ear-ring.
39. Tid,—patang.—A crescent-shaped jewelled pendant; along the lower edge of the crescent hang a row of gold pipal leaves.
40. Tandaura, dedí.—A huge star-shaped jewelled stud.
41. Mor phunwár.—A pendant of jewels being a rude imitation of the figure of a peacock.

IV.—Nose Ornaments.

Women's.

42. Nath —A large nose ring, one side of the ring being ornamented with a belt of jewels or a few pearls, and gold spangle ornaments &c. hung on to it.
43. Bulák.—A small pendant (fig. 10) either worn hung to the cartilage of the nose, or else strung on to a 'nath.'
44. Latkan.—A sort of ornament of pendants put on to the thin gold ring called a nath, and hanging from it.
45. Morní.—A small pendant for the above, shaped like the spread out tail of a peacock.
46. Laung.—A small 'stud' let into the flesh of the nostril on one side, generally of gold, with a pearl or turquois on it.
47. Phúli.—A small ring with a single emerald, or other stone of an oval shape, as a pendant.
48. Bohr —A jingling pendant of gold pipal leaves—(see fig. 11).
49. Machhlián be-sir.—(Headless fishes).
50. Rekháñ, made of gold and worn on the *teeth*;—a stud of gold or silver fixed into the front teeth.

V.—Necklaces and Neck Ornaments.

Men's.

51. Málá.—A necklace of large beads hanging down long and loose.
52. Kanth-kanthí, (worn by women also) (fig. 1.) This fits rather close to the neck—the pendant may be omitted.
53. Nám.—An amulet, round or star-shaped, suspended from a twist of colored silk thread fastened round the neck by tying at the back (see "júgní" below).

Táwíz.—A square amulet, jewelled, or otherwise.

54. Takhtí.—A flat square plate engraved with figures, &c.
55. Hainkal.—A chain of twisted silk, from which depend, by little golden loops, various coins, amulets, &c., all round.
56. Zanjírí.—A set of chains.
57. Chandarmáh.—A large gold flat medal suspended by a single ring on a silk chain or cord.

Women's.

58. Chandanhár.—A collar or necklace of a great number of chains (fig 22).
59. Málá.—Hár.—A plain necklace of pearls or gold beads &c. hanging down long.
60. Champakali.—A necklace like a collar with pendants, &c. described under 'Derajat' ornaments. The pendants or rays are either plain metal or set with stones.
61. Júgni.—A single jewelled pendant, hanging from a necklace of silk—like the "Nám," only more elongated in shape.
62. Mohrán.—A gold mohur or coin hung by a silk necklace.
63. Haul dil.—A sort of amulet of jade; not square as a táwiz always is, but cut in curves round the edge.
64. Saukan mohrá. A small gold medal or large coin worn like No. 57.
65. Hassí, or hass, like a *torquea.* A ring or collar of silver, thick in the middle, and thin at either end.

Women's.

66. Guluband. A jewelled collar (fig. 13.)
67. Mohnmálá. A long necklace made of large gold beads, with an interval of gold twisted thread between each bead.
68. Atrdán.– A square jewelled (or plain gold) pendant, attached to a silk chain, at the back is a small box like our vinaigrette to contain 'atr' or perfume.
69. Kandí.—A chain of silk carrying amulet cases (fig. 14.)
70. Silwatta.—An amulet case shaped like a small gold pillow or bolster, with two rings attached to suspend it.

VI —Arm Ornaments.

71. Bázuband.—A broad belt-like ornament, generally mounted on silk and tied on the upper arm.
72. Nau ratn, is the same, the ornament consisting of a band of nine gems set side by side, and tied by silk ties.
73. Távíz. An amulet worn on the upper arm.
74. Anant—("the endless.") A large thin but solid ring of gold or silver, used chiefly by Hindus.
75. Bhawatta.—A square gold ornament, worn on the upper arm (fig. 23.)

VII—Bracelets.

Men's.

76. Ponchi, worn on the wrist. A series of strings of shells or small gold elongated beads.
77. Kangan or kará or gokru. A bracelet of stiff metal, worn bent round the arm; when the edges are serrated it is called gokru.

Women's.

78. Ponchian kútbi.*
79. Chuadandí (rats' teeth.)
80. Iláchídána. (grain of cardamoms.)
81. Kangan or kará zanána (as before.)
82. Bánká, thick gold bracelets. Hindus wear them (fig. 15.)
83. Gokrú (as before.)
84. Gajra. A flexible bracelet made of square gold studs mounted on a silk band.
85. Chúri of sorts, as ch: kantakhárat, ch: chauras, ch: kangani-dár. They are generally made of a flat ribbon of gold or silver, bent round, (fig 16.)
86. Báín, or long silver *sleeve* or tube worn on both arms, like a lot of churís fastened together.
87. Band—An armlet, broad and heavy (see fig. 19.)
88. Jhankangan. Small hollow '*karas*' with grains introduced into the hollow to rattle.

VIII.—Finger Rings.

89. Angushtri.—A ring set with stones called also "mundri" (Hindi) or angúthí.
90. Challa. Large challas are worn on the toe also. The challa is a quite plain hoop or whole "hoop" ring (with or without stones) being gold or silver, but the same all round.
91. Angushtána, angúthá. A big ring with a broad face, worn on the great toe.
92. Khari panjángla (a set of finger rings of ordinary shape).
93. Shahálmí or kharí, a ring of long oval shape (fig. 20).
94. Birhamgand, a broad ring figured at No. 21.

* There are several sorts of Ponchis called Kútbi: chúadandi (the beads like rats' teeth); iláchídána, like cardamom grains &c.

IX.—Anklets &c.

95.—Pahzeb.—Various ankle ornaments made with chains and pendants of silver, which clink together when the wearer walks.

96.—Chánjar.—A large hollow ring, which rattles when the wearer walks.

97.—Karíán-pair or khalkhal. Like karas, worn on the ankles.

98.—Khúngrú.—A ring or ankle of long ornamental beads of silver, worn on the feet.

99.—Zanjírí —A set of chains with a broad clasp—called also tora.

The enormous variety of names cannot fail to strike any one: every little change in the pattern or size of an ornament seems to secure it a different name. The general form of each kind of jewel is always maintained, but of course the details of ornamentation vary immensely. Very fine jewellery is but little made in the Punjab; most of the necklaces and turban ornaments made for the nobility are got at Jaipúr &c. The design for them is drawn out by the head jeweller himself, and he gives the drawing to workmen. All the finer specimens of jewelled ornaments are beautifully enamelled on the back, (unless the stones are clear set).

The fine enamelling is done at Jaipúr and Benares, &c. Only inferior enamelling (compared to Jaipúr work) is done in the Punjab.

The gold and silver work, as far as the plain form of the article required, or as far as it can receive the required pattern by merely hammering on to a die or into a cold mould, is done by the *sunár* or goldsmith, (also called zargar or sunyár.)

If the ornament has then to be ornamented with bossed patterns, &c. it goes to the 'chatera,' embosser and chaser.

If jewels are to be set, the enamelling at the back is done by a 'mínákár,' and then the stone is set into the places prepared by the goldsmith, &c. by the 'murassiakár' or 'kundansáz,' whose sole work consists in putting some lac into the receptacle or hollow in the gold prepared to receive the stone, putting in a tinsel or foil prepared by the "bindlígar," and then pressing in the stone, putting on a gold rim to keep it in place.

It will be proper to describe the tools used by each workman in his separate processes.

The first operator is the goldsmith or sunâr.

He makes up gold ornaments as far as their mere form is concerned; he neither finishes nor sets them with stones, nor does he ornament his work, except when he can do so with a die-mould.

He has a small anvil or square block of iron slightly convex on the surface, on which he works the metal. This is held firm in a block of wood. It is called "ahran." His tools are:—

"Hathaura"—hammers of sizes.

"Nál"—a blow pipe.

"Sannu"—forceps, plain pointed.

"Rezá"—a mould.

"Katíra"—a pair of pincers with blades for cutting metal.

"Sanni"—a long pair of pincers with the claws turned down.

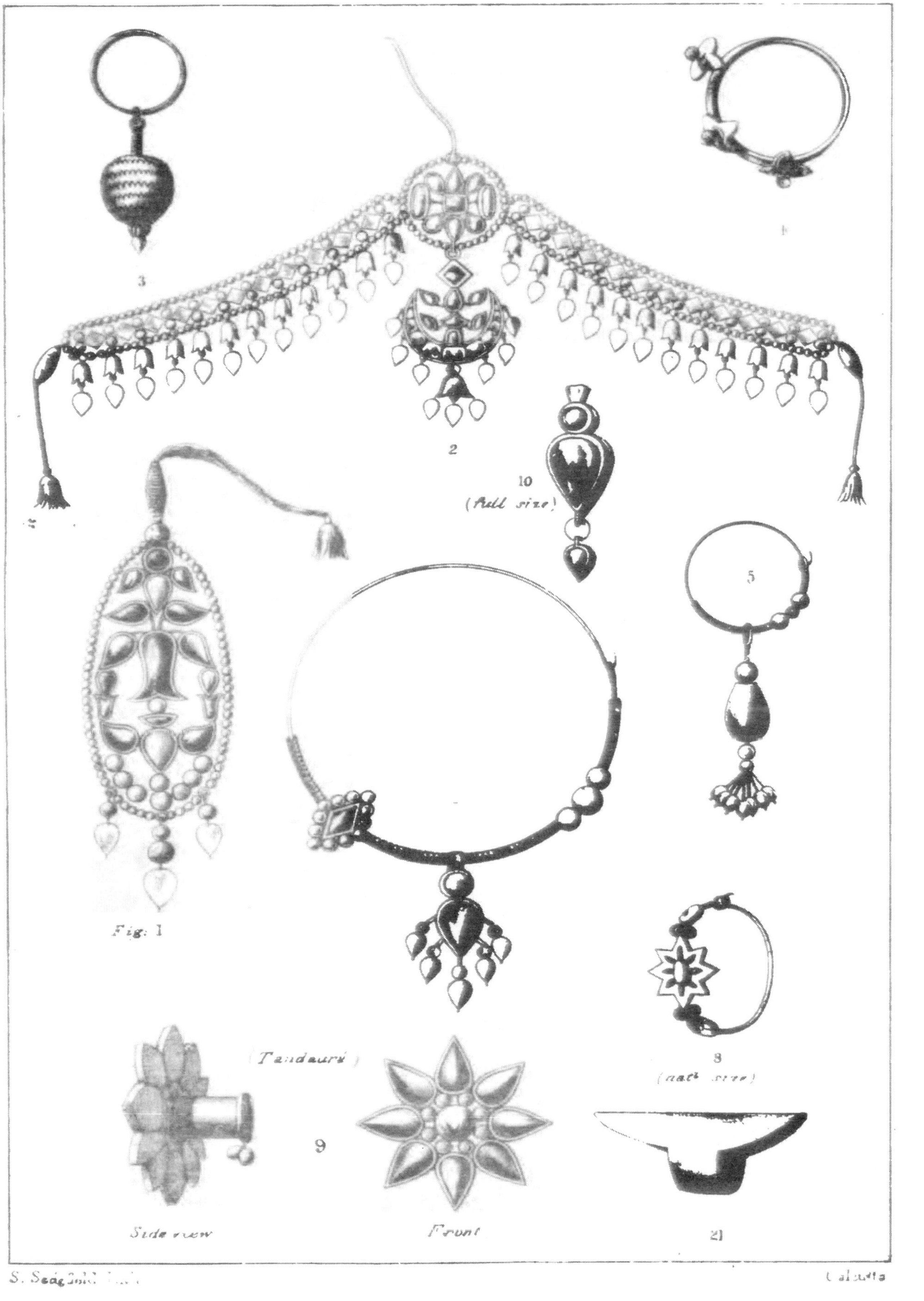

S. Sedgfield Lith.   Calcutta

S. Sedgfield Lith. Calcutta

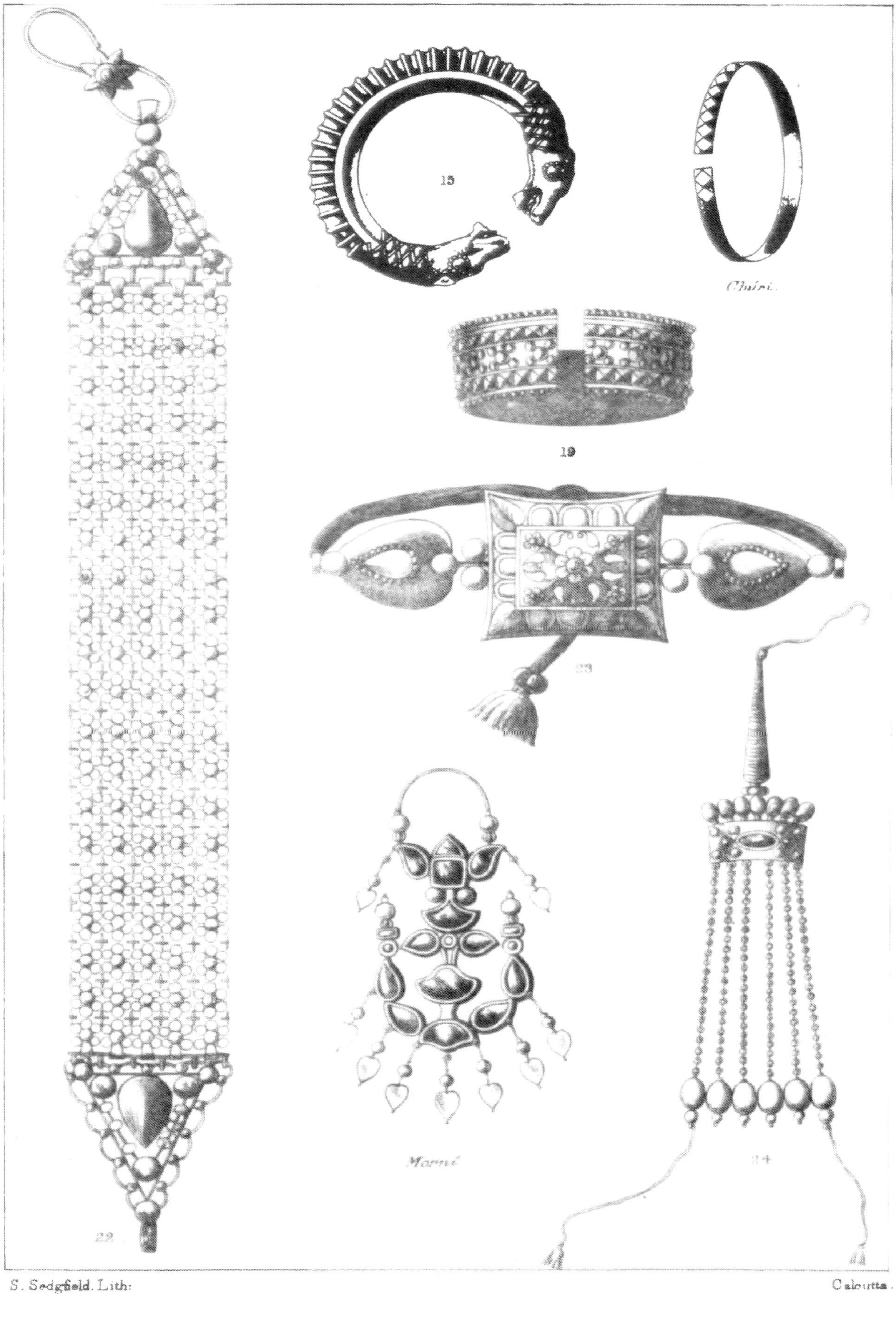

S. Sedgfield. Lith: Calcutta.

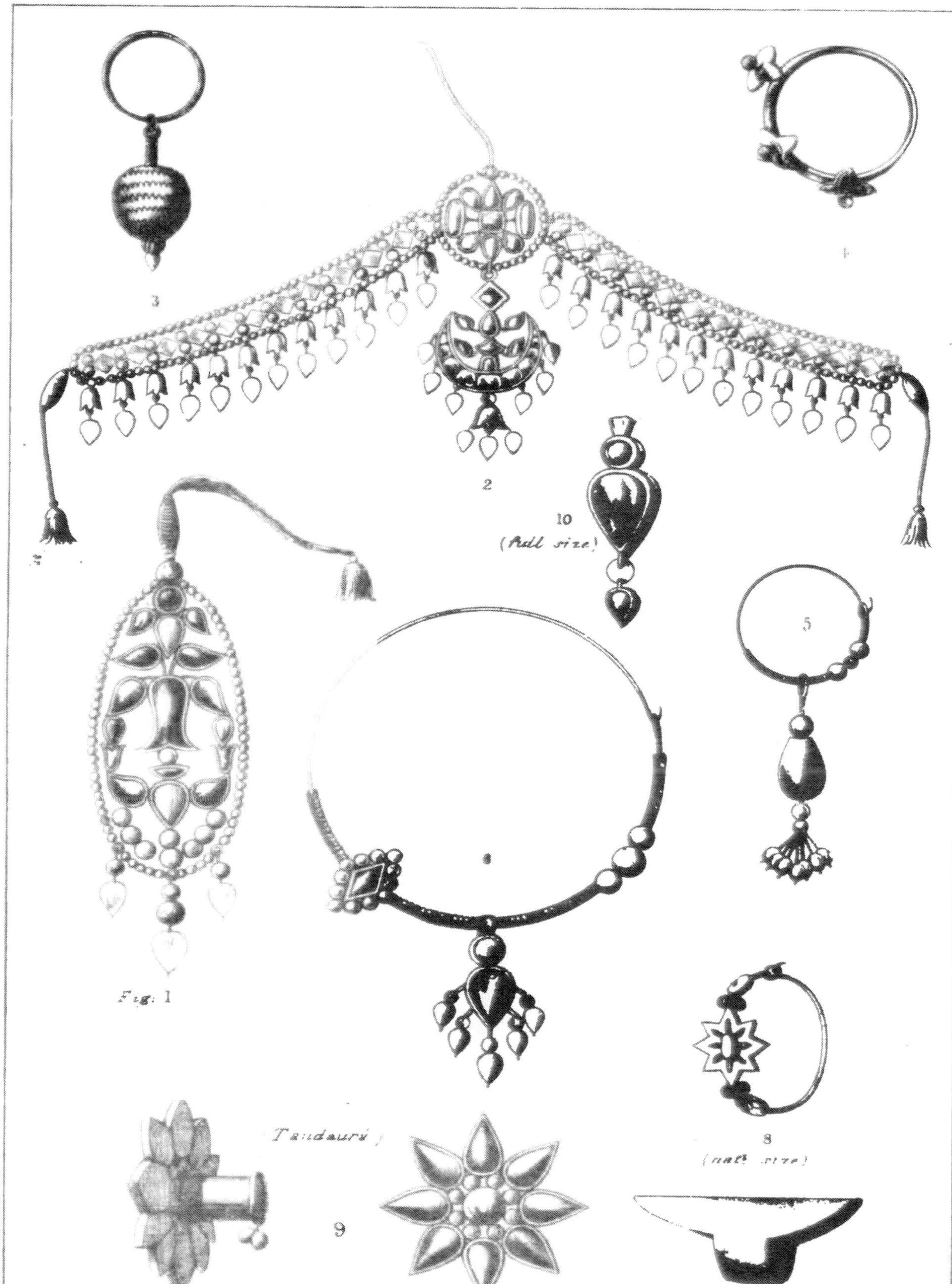

S. Sedgfield lith.

Calcutta

S. Sedgfield Lith. Calcutta

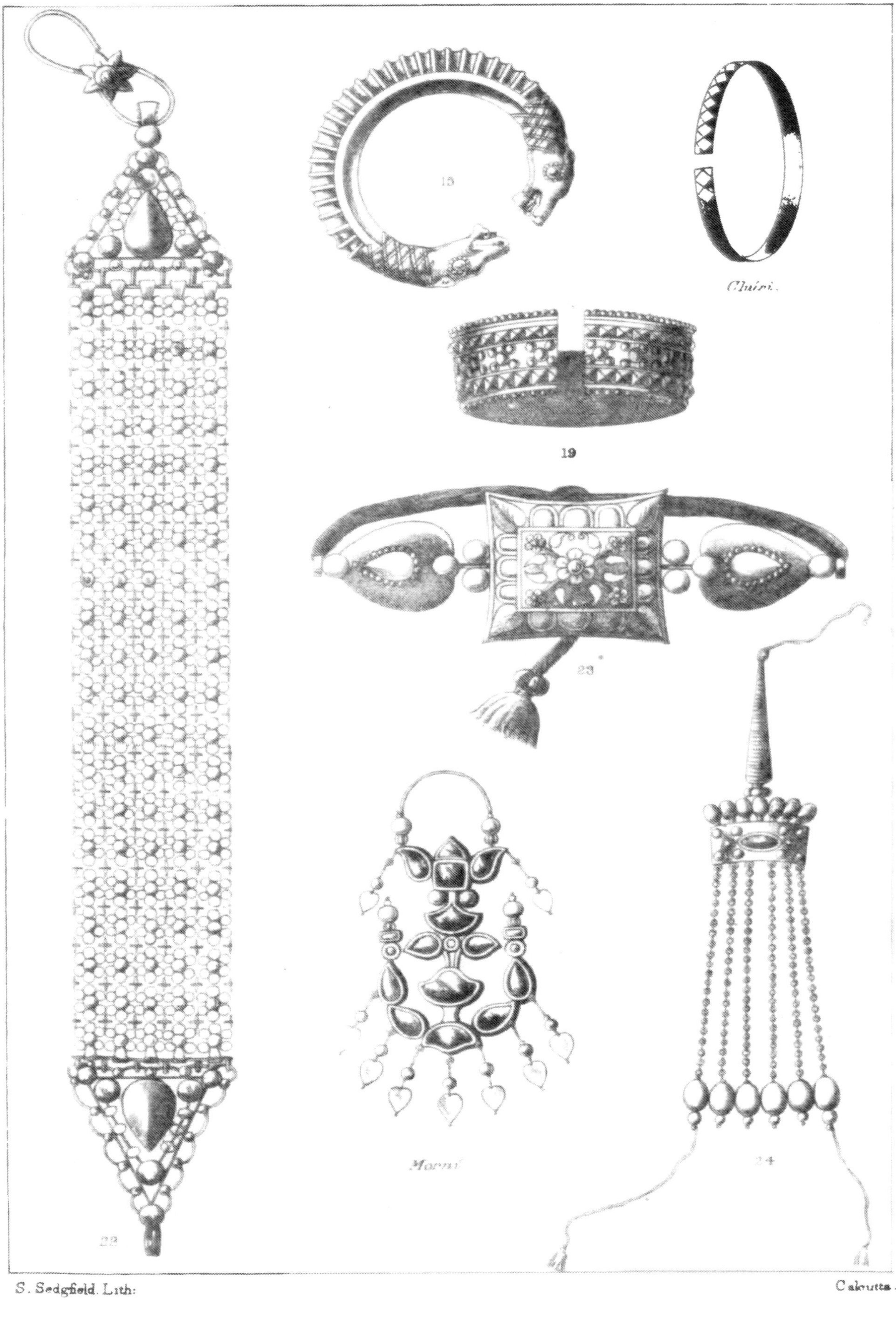

S. Sedgfield. Lith: Calcutta.

No. 14 "Khanch"

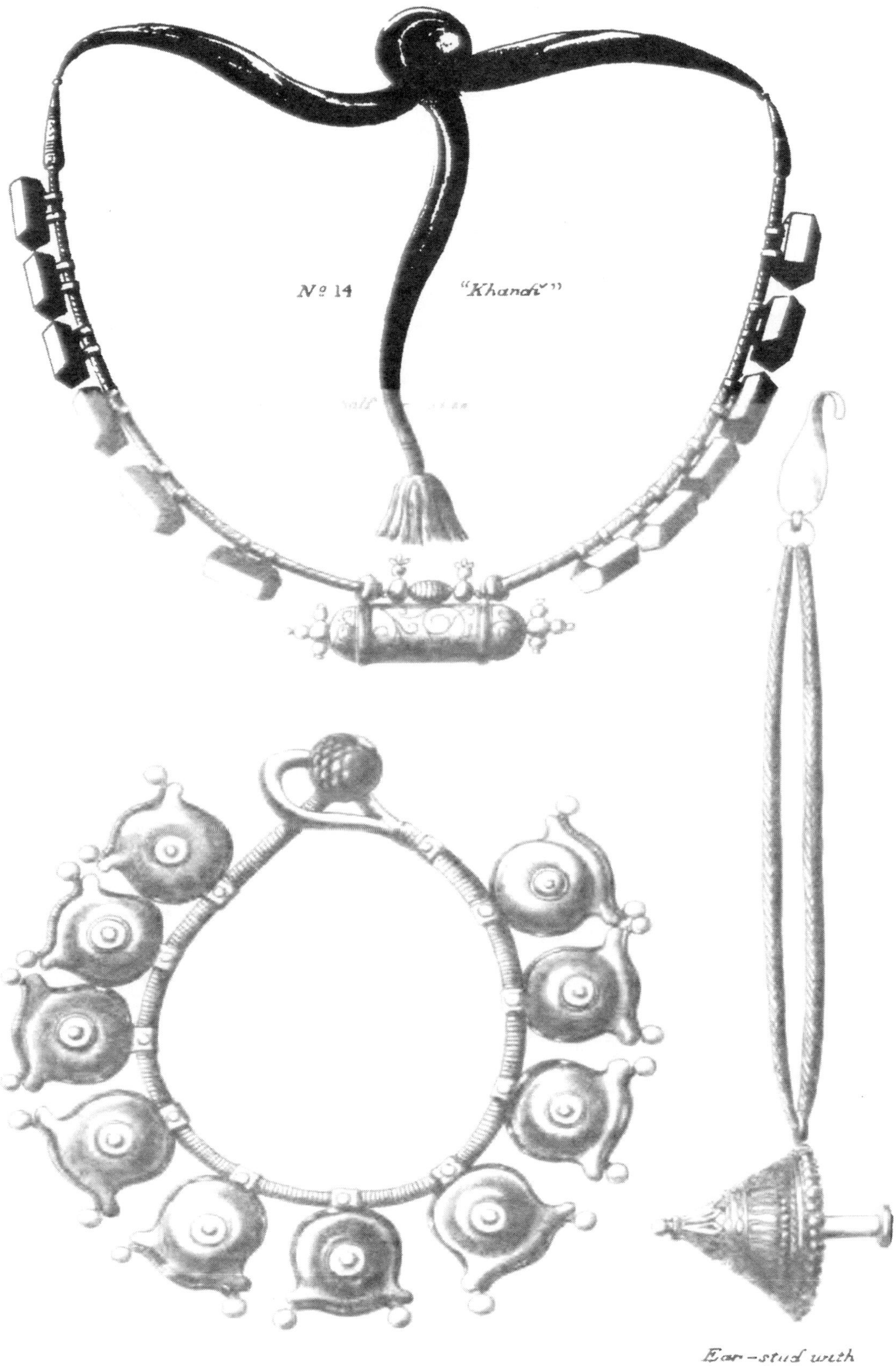

Póntha or Gungrú worn on the ankle.
nearly full size

Ear-stud with
Suspender
(Kútí)

S. Sedgfield. Lith:

Kangan
Bázuband.
Jhumká.
Dastyára or Kara.
Champakalli.

" Jandri "—a steel plate for wire drawing.

" Zambúr "—heavy pincers, straight blades.

" Chaurasi "—a small square headed hammer.

" Tappa "—dies, to produce patterns.

A bit of silver or gold is placed over the mould or die and struck (while cold) with the hammer; silver bracelets (chúrís) are given their pattern in this way. The 'tappas' are made of kânsí or bell-metal, which is hard. The tappa only impresses a small part of the metal at once: it exhibits perhaps ½ an inch of pattern.

The roughly formed metal now goes to the chatéra or embosser and chaser. He uses a broken pot to hold fire called " taur " (it is just the curved portion of the bottom of a 'ghara'); a crucible, kuthâli; a small anvil with a point at either end, called 'ekwâí;' and the ornamenting is done with a great variety of steel tools to be described presently in detail, but whose general characteristic is that they are all like large steel nails with a head to receive the blow of the hammer, and the points variously rounded, flattened, slant-edged, straight-edged &c., and there are also differences in the size and thickness of the tools. They are like stone-mason's chisels and pitchers on a small scale, as far as appearance goes.

Those with the point flat and edged, are called " chírná," and these are in four sizes. The same still broader and flatter is called " chaini." When the edge is slightly curved like a gouge or scoop the tool is 'kanerna'; when the point is flat and the edge blunt, the 'chírna' becomes a 'lúrtá'; and when the tool is thick and large and has its point squared off, showing a neat smooth sectional square, it is called " thalna." 'Ekwásá thalná' is similar, but the point slants off so as to exhibit a sectional rhomboid. Each one of these tools is made in four or more sizes.

I should add that these 'thalnas' are specially used to polish and burnish the ground work of metal or field, from which the embossed flower &c., stands out.

Another tool of this sort has a smooth round point with a small hole drilled in the centre of the cone; when this is struck on a piece of metal and the blow repeated, while the tool is moved along, a series of small points are raised on the metal which has something like the effect of our " engine-turning." This tool is called 'gul-sam.'

The same tools with smooth blunt points, and *without* the hole drilled, are called 'golra,' and are as usual made in four sizes. The same form, but where the point is slightly more conical and point like, receives the name of 'súmbhá.'

With these tools all sorts of ornamental work and flowers are produced. The men do both chasing and embossing, and also repoussé work. When chasing &c., on a hollow ornament, the workman fills it up with resin to get a firm basis to work on.

There is a verb, 'chitarna' to paint, adorn, emboss, from which the word 'chatera' is derived.

I must here add that it frequently happens that small filings and bits of gold are dropped on to the earthen flour of the workshop; this repeated over a number of years renders the soil valuable, and when a goldsmith leaves his shop, the people called nyárias or gold-washers, buy the right to dig up the earth, which they wash by means of a 'kátrá' or wooden tray and collect the gold grains.

If the ornament has been made of gold, and is to be set with jewels, it will have to go to the 'murassia-kár' or kundan sâz. If it is intended to be highly finished, *i. e.*, to be jewelled in front and enamelled on the back, of course it goes to the enameller or 'míná-kár' first, but I will leave the enameller for the present. The "murassia-kár's" tools are :—

A tirpai or workstool; chimta or forceps; and a number of polishers, besides siláis or steel probes.

Let us suppose he wishes to set a stone in a ring: the ring has been made by the sunâr, who has left a hollow place for the stone.

The jeweller will place a little lac in the hollow, and on that will press down a "dánk" or bit of foil, provided by the "bindligar," of whom presently.

He rubs the "dánk" into the requisite curve, and presses it with a small tool consisting of a wooden handle brass bound, and carrying an agate point to polish with. Where the point is large and rounded the tool is called "ghota"; where a very hard bit of agate is set so as to make a very small point, suitable for preparing the place of setting a very small gem, it is called "khilauri": another size of agate polisher is called "rokhá." The foil being in place and the stone placed on it, sometimes the edge of the cup in which it rests is worked up all round so as a over-lap the stone; this is the European way, only the natives rarely do it neatly. The esteemed method however is to put a "kundan" on: that is, to press with a probe or silái thin gold foil all round the edge of the gem till a rim is formed, and then the foil by continual pressure consolidates and is burnished. The process reminds me more of a dentist stopping a tooth with gold than anything else. The size and quality of the rim put on, as to thickness and purity of metal, can be varied to suit the means of the purchaser. They sometimes set jewels "clear," but more usually with a foil behind, and sometimes they color the back of the stone to deepen it, but they never color the foil itself. The art of fixing gems by little claws is only done by those who have learned the way of making European jewellery.

Jewellery in the European fashion is now largely made in Delhi, at which place almost any kind of work can be executed to order. In most of the large cities some kind of work can be executed in the European fashion. I have seen rings very well made at Lahore and at Kangra, and even watch chains of simple pattern. The 'chateras' can imitate the European method of chasing admirably.

The most original work of Delhi jewellery is that know by Europeans as bábul work. The native workmen call it "khárdár," literally work of thorns (khár) or points. Gold ornaments (generally spherical, or in such form that a number of circular convex pieces can enter into the pattern) are covered all over with a number of minute golden points,* and then this surface, like a tiny hedge-hog's back, in gold, is 'frosted.' Indeed, no comparison describes the work so well as the term bábul work, which indicates its resemblance to the flower of the *Acacia Arabica* (bábul or kikar) familiar to every Indian reader; but for the sake of others I may describe it as a little ball of yellow filaments. The ornamentation of gold by raising on the surface a number of little points was probably suggested by the slight of the flower, or perhaps originally by the seed vessel of the burr

* It is often said that pure gold is necessary to make the points with, but while the gold used must always be less fusible than the 'tánk' or gold-solder, it need not be quite pure, and I have seen some of very poor metal indeed.

(gokru) : indeed a coarser work of this sort, and made for native wear, is called ' gokru.' The work was first brought to notice about 30 years ago, and his since been increasing in demand, and has improved in quality up to a certain point, though purchasers must now be on their guard against bad gold, gilt over and frosted so as to deceive the eye. As I said before, the ornaments made are always spherical or at any rate convex ; thus we have ball-shaped ear-rings, boss-shaped studs ; solitaires, brooch settings composed of a row of little bosses &c.

Thy are all hollow and are sometimes filled up with lac; each point is separately made and fixed on the surface. They are not " repoussé " work, as one might at first suppose, though the convex metal base is so.

Through the kindness of MAJOR MACMAHON of Delhi, I have obtained further particulars about this manufacture, to imitate which all efforts in England have, I understand, failed.

In the first place, as before said, the ' points ' and the convex base are of different qualities, the latter is generally of inferior gold, while the points are made of gold at Rs. 17 or 18 a tola. One of the manufacturers, however, says in his answer, that the alloyed gold is preferred, and he gives Rs. 14 a tolah as the value of the gold used. The workmen get from Rs. 2-8 to Rs. 3 per tolah as the price of their labor, and are allowed from 12 annas as to Re. 1 per tolah of gold advanced to them, as " chij " or wastage.

The goldsmiths are usually Hindus, and have their residences in the tahsil Rasauli, at the following villages :—

Kewáli. Rádna. Rohat. Mangal Kalán. Morthal. Kakrohi.
Bilri Kalán. Mohána.

The work is of some antiquity, as various castes wore ornaments of this sort before its suitability for the European market came to notice. The Ját men wear as an earring a ' gokru,' but generally women do not wear them ; Chumár women however wear them without objection.

It is now time to examine the process of manufacture.

As before intimated, the little points are all separately made and afterwards soldered on to a convex surface in regular rows.

In order to make the points, a ' tappa,' which is a flat circular block or ingot of "kánsi," (the hardest sort of bronze or compound metal,) is requisite. Two and a half tolahs of the metal are melted in a small ' kutháli ' or crucible over a charcoal fire, with the aid of the brass blow pipe. When melted, 4 mashas of ' sohága ' (borax) and one of black sajji (impure soda) are stirred in, and the whole poured out into a circular mould (kálbút) about the size of a military metal, and deep rough to hold the 2½ tolahs of metal. When the metal is set, but still hot, it is hammered out flat, but not thin, on an anvil, and in the flat surface 5 or 6 small holes, the size of grains of poppy-seed, are hammered in with a punch, taking care that the holes do not entirely perforate the plate. Next, the gold has to be prepared for use on this mould or block.

Four and a half máshas of gold are made into wire, and then drawn fine through the hole of a wire drawer's plate or " jandri " till it is as fine as possible : * it is wound on a metal rod or reel, and thrown into the fire till red hot ; when taken out it is soft and flexible, and is cut with scissors into shreds of short length, which are set to

* The whole art of gold wire drawing has been described a few pages back.

soak in a little dish of oil. This done, the workman takes up shred by shred with the forceps, places it over the little hole in the 'tappa' before described, and with a tiny hammer, no heavier than 2 tolahs, gives a dexterous blow, which drives the gold into the hole. Turning the 'tappa' upside down, the workman taps the back lightly and the grains of gold having no disposition to stick owing to the oil, readily fall out and appear like so many seeds or tiny pyramids with flat base and conical apex.

The points being ready, the convex base or matrix on to which they are to be fixed has to be made; it is generally of inferior gold. This is made by hammering out a flat thin plate of gold and then knocking it into a mould (in the manner of repoussé work) which leaves a smooth convex surface. On this the gold points have to be arranged in regular rows. This operation is one of great delicacy, for if the rows of points are not perfectly regular and parallel, the appearance will be spoiled.

In order to make the points stick in their places before the final soldering, they are immersed in a sticky compound, made by boiling half a tola of the 'dál' or split pulse of the sort called másh, with one chitak of water and six ratis of 'sohága' (borax) till quite soft; the grains of gold so prepared, are taken one by one with the forceps and placed in position.

The solder is prepared thus:—Take one másha of gold and one rati of copper, and melt together; hammerit out till as thin as a sheet of paper, cut the foil into shreds as fine as hair, and across into minute pieces; having mixed these shreds with some of the dál mixture before described, the prepared ornament is anointed all over with it, and the whole put into the fire, and urged with a blow-pipe with great accuracy. The solder melts, while the points do not at so low a temperature; and this is the reason why the ornament must be made of gold superior to the solder. The melting solder is so spread by the heat of the fire and the dexterous use of the blow-pipe, as to settle down evenly on the surface, leaving the points exposed, and they are thus firmly coagulated and fixed together. Should the solder be too thick at any part, it would of course cover the points and spoil the appearance, and the melting has again to be resorted to till the required even deposit of the solder is attained. All this requires great niceness of handling, and much experience also; for if the fire is too hot or applied too long, the points would melt as well as the solder, and the work be irretrievably spoilt. The ornament is returned in its present state to the jeweller who employed the workman, but it is still dirty and unpleasing in appearance, and has to be cleaned by lighty heating with borax, and then receives the clear yellow frosty appearance by being plunged, when clean and perfectly hot, into a strong acid solution of 'kishta,' or unripe dried apricot brought from Kabul.

Ear-rings and other ornaments are often made perfectly spherical. This is done by making two hemispherical bases in the mould as before described, they are bound together by iron wire, and then with ordinary jeweller's solder joined into one globe or ball: the iron wire can now be removed. The points are afterwards put on in the manner already detailed.

This class will be now brought to a close by an extract from the Report of the Jury in 1864; and this will be followed, by way of an appendix, by notes on the art of enamelling, and of the trades of the pearl-borer, the seal engraver, and the lapidary (hakák) who engraves stones for signet rings.

....

EXTRACT FROM REPORT ON WORKS IN PRECIOUS METALS AND JEWELLERY.

Jury :—

Mr. F. Cooper.
Mr. Lepel Griffin.
Dittu Mull, and
Mr. E. L. Brandreth, *Reporter*.

* * * * * * * *

Delhi was, and perhaps is still, the principal place in India for the manufacture of all kinds of jewellery; but since the extinction of the King and Court after the mutiny, the trade in jewellery is not what it was, and the best artizans are emigrating to the native states.

* * * * * * * *

Delhi has contributed a great variety of silver brooches, several beautiful turquois ornaments, gold rings, jewels set in gold for necklaces, bracelets &c. &c., enamelled bracelets, bàbul ornaments, gold work fans, &c. Kurnal, Rhotuk, and Umbala, sent a few gold and silver ornaments; Loodianah a silver jug and cup, pair of silver shoes, and some silver and gold personal ornaments; Simla several silver and other ornaments; Kangra some enamelled and other ornaments; Amritsar a large collection of ornaments of different kinds: bracelets, ear-rings &c. &c. also gold inlaid daggers and sword handles. Lahore had a very large collection of ornamental work of various kinds: silver scent bottles, jewelled sword handles, mínákári work, jade cups, enamelled armlets and bracelets, diamond head ornaments, diamond bracelets, ear-rings, and various other ornaments for the person. Mooltan sent some enamelled silver goblets, and gold worked knives. Googaira (Montgomery) had a very large, and a most complete collection of every kind of the ordinary silver ornaments worn by the great mass of native women. Dera Ghazee Khan, Bunnoo, Peshawur, Kupoorthulla and Chumba, exhibited a few gold and silver ornaments. Cashmere exhibited some very beautiful gold and silver cups and surahis and other silver ornaments.

A few of the most interesting articles exhibited in this class may be mentioned. Among personal ornaments, a superb diamond, emerald, and pearl necklace, very beautifully set, and richly enamelled at the back, exhibited by Behárí Lál of Delhi.* A magnificent diamond and emerald turban ornament with emerald pendants, richly set, exhibited by Lalla Hurjus Rae of Lahore. Among the Kashmir contributions, a richly embossed golden chalice, and the silver and gold richly embossed flagons, deserve special notice. Some glass bottles and cups, ornamented with silver net work and gold border, exhibited by Ralyá Rám, appear of a novel character.

Of the koftgarí work, the shield exhibited by Emamdeen and Shurfdeen appears the most striking; there were also some beautifully and richly inlaid caskets and inkstands.

The following is a list of the prizes awarded.

		Rs.
1.	A magnificent necklace, exhibited by Behárí Lál, ...	50
2.	A magnificent turban ornament, No. 8822 exhibited by Lalla Hurjus Rae,	25
3.	Rich diamond crescent necklace, clear set in silver, emerald and ruby pendants, exhibited by Hazáree Mull (?)	25

* This is shown in the plate, the last of the jewel series.—B. P.

		Rs.
4.	Bracelets, studs, and brooch, set in turquoises with enamelled backs, by Hazáree Mull (?)	25
5.	Ruby bracelet with enamelled sides, No. 8411, by Jowahir Lal, is well finished, unique, and tasteful, ...	10
6.	Pair of diamond armlets set on green colored chequered ground, flowered setting, No. 8482, by Jowahir Lal, ...	10
7.	Necklace of emeralds and pearls, very graceful, by Beharee Lal, ...	10
8.	Bábul work solitaries and brooches by Hazáree Mull, ...	10
9.	Enamelled bracelet set with diamonds, dove colored ground, chequered pattern, No. 8836, by Harjus Rae, ...	25
10.	Blue Bhawulpore enamelled silver personal ornaments, consisting of anklets, armlets, necklace, &c. No. 8778, exhibited by Lahore Museum,	25
11.	A large and curious collection of silver rustic ornaments, No. 8972, and following numbers, by Local Committee Googaira (Montgomery),	25
12.	Cashmere gold cups, No. 9118 and 9129, exhibited by the Maharajah, ...	50
13.	Glass bottle with silver net work by Ralyá Rám, ...	10
14.	Koftgari work, especially shield and dagger No. 8929, exhibited by Imamdeen and Shurfdeen, ...	50
15.	Koftgari inkstand, richly inlaid, No. 8572, by Imamdeen, ...	25
16.	Koftgari box and other contributions, No. 8652, by Gholam Aindeen, ...	10
17.	Koftgari richly inlaid casket, No. 8584, by Futtahdeen and Kurmdeen,	10
18.	A richly embroidered gold waistbelt, with diamond and emerald buckle, Delhi, ...	25

NOTE ON THE ART OF ENAMELLING.

Enamelling (minákárí) is done in the south Punjab, (Multán and Baháwulpúr), and also at Kangra. It is also rarely done by individual workmen elsewhere. There is a man at Lahore who knows the work, but who states that he can only make a sort of black enamel, and that he has to get the green, red, and blue, in pieces from Multan.

In Multan it is said that the first maker was one Naulú, who worked 400 years ago, and that since then the art so increased in excellence, that Multan enamelled ware was highly esteemed and exported to other districts.

The term " míná " means, in Persian, a glass vase or blue glass ; also applied to the sky "the azure deep" &c., and hence to the blue vitreous enamel, which is the commonest sort.

The enamel is usually seen in flat, vitreous cakes : there is opaque white, yellow, pink and red, green and blue. All these are vitreous in substance, the melting glass being prepared with various metallic salts or compounds, as oxide of cobalt, iron, manganese &c., and thus colored.

A rude kind of black enamel is made without any glassy substance, as will be described here after.

The article to be enamelled is never made of pure gold or silver, but is one-half alloy, to stand the heating and the treatment ; generally the metal used for the work is therefore said to be " nímá chándí " &c.

The silver vessel to be enamelled is first heated and made quite clean with the 'kishta' solution before alluded to. The pattern to be engraved is marked out with a probe or siláí, and the pattern is then finished off like " chatera's " work, with such tools as he uses : in Multan these implements are called " toghra " and " handi." The pattern is produced in relief, so that the lower parts being filled up with colored enamel, the silver leaf or whatever it is, may show out on a colored field. A small quantity of the enamel is now finely powdered with a tool called bilohá (Multan), and the powder is mixed with a little borax into a paste with water. The paste is put on to the engraved silver, so as to fill up the dents and hollows cut by the engraver, and leave a clear pattern on the enamel ground ; the tool used for applying the colored paste is in Multan called ' súrjan.'

To burn in the enamel is the next work. A bit of clean talc is put at the bottom of the furnace and on it the article enamelled ; over this again a small iron cage or dome (to keep off the ashes of the furnace) and the whole is surrounded with lumps of charcoal, well burned and well washed, so as to yield no ashes, and is set on fire.

If on taking the vessel out it is found that the enamel has not spread evenly, or has coagulated or run over the edge, &c., the excess has to be ground down with a file and tool called barbá, consisting of an iron bar coated with a mixture of lac and corundum or emery powder. When the enamel is level and even, it has to be heated again, and it probably requires a further filing down, which is done with sand and water and a bit of soap-nut. It is now finally heated, and after washing in the kishta solution, the work is finished.

The black enamel that the Lahore workman makes is not vitreous, and merely shows a dull black ground, on which the silver flower pattern appears more like the "bidrí" work of Central India.

The black enamel called by the Kabulis (whence the art came) 'sawáth,' is made by melting two parts of silver, one part of lead, and four parts of sulphur together, but this is done in a closed crucible and with exposure to a fierce heat; when sufficiently melted the material is poured into a mould (reza). The black substance which results is finely powdered, and being mixed with borax into a paste, is applied in the manner described.

The enamelling on the back of jewellery is called "pharfúra," and is done at Jaipúr, not in the Punjab.

The Mooltan enamelling is principally of cups and plates &c; that of Bahawalpur of large necklaces, bracelets, and other ornaments for the person. In Kangra, smaller works, amulets, belt clasps, and even articles of European form, are enamelled.

Enamelling is understood at Delhi also.

The best enamelling comes for Jaipúr; no one will tell the art by which the colors are produced, but I have gathered the following :—

Dead white enamel is made by a "calcine," made by reducing lead in a crucible over a slow furnace, by tossing in a few bits of tin the lead gradually runs into a white powder: this is the basis of all of the opaque colors, when mixed with (kanch) glass powder and borax. Yellow is produced either with oxide of lead or iron filings reduced by calcining repeatedly with a little salt. Blue is produced with 'reta' (see Class XIX *post*), with or without white enamel, according as a deep or pale blue is required.

The Bahawulpur and Multan enamellers produce an opaque red or salmon color, obtained with white enamel and some litharge or lead, reduced further than the yellow oxide, and approaching the 'minium' or red. Pink and purple are produced with 'anjaní,' (oxide of manganese) and the white enamel.

The Jaipúr enamellers have a beautiful transparent red, which I cannot find out, but expect it is made by boiling acetate of copper with sugar, and obtaining a peroxide of copper, which, if skilfully applied at a moderate heat, gives this color (see Ure's Dictionary of Arts, *s. v.*—"Enamel"). Green is produced with calcined oxidized copper and 'kánch'; opaque green by mixing the said copper color with yellow enamel. I have of course no information as to the exact quantities used: a great mystery is made of all this.

THE PEARL BORER.

Pearl borer's tool.

The pearl borer, "moti-winh" (from winhna to bore), fixes the pearl into a little hole in a block of very soft wood, generally *sembal*, &c. The boring is done with the usual mechanical contrivance: a pointed tool set revolving by a bow and string passed round, and moved to and fro with a sawing movement. So here the borer is a light pointed tool with a long handle. To make a loose handle for this, the workman selects the end of a cocoanut shell, the extreme end bit of which makes a mushroom-shaped piece, this he holds his hand upon, while the end of his boring tool revolves in the hollow. The bow used is of course very small and light.

HAKKAK—RING STONE POLISHER OR LAPIDARY.

His tools are,—a grindstone, which revolves on a wooden axis between two uprights; the uprights and stand are called 'adda.' The wheel or grindstone called 'sán,' is a disc made of corundum powder and lac melted together: it is kept revolving by a bow and leather string, like a turner's wheel. The sán is made of two sorts: one to grind coarse, the other fine. 'Mitta sán,' is one to grind finer, this is made with sand instead of corundum.

A third wheel is called 'chilása' and is smaller, and serves to polish the stone with the aid of a paste called "bari," made of pounded burnt crystal or flint.

I may add in this place, that no one in the Punjab knows how to cut diamonds; they say only one or two people at Jaipúr and at Benares do: they have not the diamond powder necessary, and they say it costs two or three thousand rupees to set up a wheel. Other stones they can polish, because the powdered corundum or emery they have, will suffice. The lapidary's wheel is a heavy 'lap' or disc mounted on the end of a wooden spindle, the spindle is supported between two uprights, and worked with a bow; the wheel is often weighted with lead to increase its rotatory power: the edge is charged with a mixture of lac and emery. The stone to be polished is stuck with lac on the end of a wooden holder, this is pressed with the right hand against the wheel, and the left works the bow: the facets are produced by the eye only, and are often not very regular.

SEAL ENGRAVER.

The seal is used by all classes, not so much as a seal, but as a signet, especially when the wearer cannot write his name (which is unfortunately very often the case).

The 'mohr-kand' or engraver's stand, consists of a solid heavy pyramidal box, on the top of which is a long wooden ledge carrying three uprights; one at either end is fixed, but the third can be slid along and fixed with a screw, so as to hold the graving tool, which is mounted between the end and middle, in a horizontal position, with the graving end projecting.

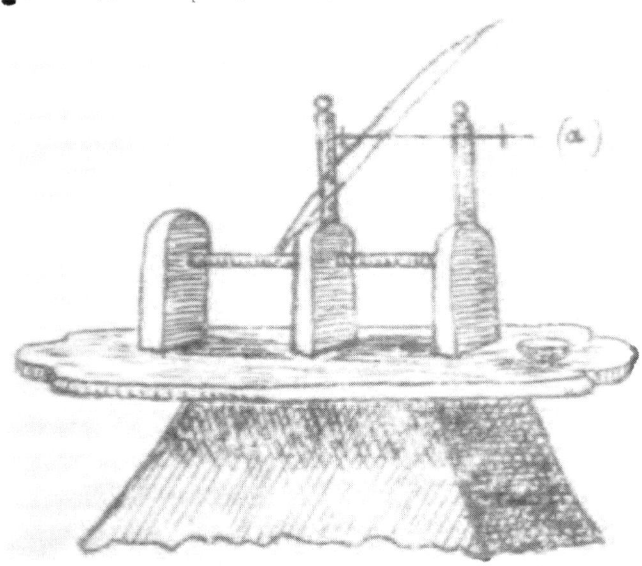

Engraver's "Adda."

The tool itself is set revolving by the usual process of the bow. The point being adroitly pressed against the seal stone, and touched with oil and corundum, kept in a cup below, a dot or line, or other mark, is engraved: the stone is stuck with lac on to a wooden handle for convenience of holding. The graving tool or 'barma' consists of a light turned wooden shaft carrying a steel spike, at the very point of which a small copper head, like a pin's head, is fixed. This little head touched with oil and corundum does the work. If a fine *line* has to be engraved, the headed barma is removed and one placed inthe proper position, which carries a little disc of copper at the end; the disc is perhaps ¼ of an inch in diameter, and the edge can be filed exceedingly thin.

It is this thin edge, when pressed revolving against the seal stone, that cuts a fine line The whole process, however, requires the workman to be exceedingly adroit in adjusting and turning about his stone so as not to get the lines too thick or too deep, to get the curves smooth, &c. Very nice seal-cutting is done with letters of amazing smallness and fineness at Delhi, but perhaps the Kashmiris are the best of all at this trade.

BINDLIGAR—MAKER OF TINSEL ORNAMENTS.

Bindli means a small spangle. In Kangra they are worn stuck on to the face and forehead with gum.

The bindligár makes the 'foil' to place beneath stones set in jewellery, and also the small gold pendants like tiny hollow spoons : they form a fringe to náths (nose-rings) and other ornaments, and are called "jhamkan."

his tools are—

Ahran.—A small anvil.

Chamra charmi.—Parchment.

Mikráz.—Scissors of sizes.

Chumti.—Forceps of sizes.

Sanní.—Small pincers.

Fire holder ; agate polisher (mohárí) ; a smooth stone ; and a three-legged stand or low work table.

They have thin sheets of gold or silver called 'sitta,' and cut out the form of the 'bindli' with scissors ; these they color yellow or red. They give them a concave form by pressing on the leather with an agate tool called "gotá."

NOTE ON THE KOH-I-NUR DIAMOND.

I have a series of papers communicated to me by the late Diwán Hukm Chand Peshawria, which were prepared by the late Fakir Núr-ud-dín. In the form in which they reached me they do not present any connected narrative, I have therefore extracted the information they contain, and having added other matter, have arranged a note on the history of this celebrated diamond, going as far back as it can be traced. I have also been able to consult Tavernier's Voyage des Indes, now a rather rare book. There are also some good, but not perfectly accurate, notices of this diamond in the *Encyclopædia Brittanica*, and the Catalogue of the Great Exhibition of 1851. The Encyclopœdia has reproduced Tavernier's drawing of the diamond.

The legend of the origin of this diamond is, that it was found in the mines of the south of India, and was worn by one of the heroes of the Mahábharat, Karna, King of Ánga; this would place it about 5,000 years ago, or 3,001, B. C.*

Nothing more of it is heard till it appears as the property of Vikramaditya,† (Bikramajít of modern Indian vernaculars) the famous Raja of the great Central Indian kingdom of Ujain; it descended from him to the Málwa Rajas, who kept it till overthrown by the Muhamadan power. The Muhamadan power was first felt in the Dekkan towards the close of the thirteenth century; Alá-ud-dín Khiljí, nephew of Firoz, the first sovereign of the 2nd Ghori dynasty, several times invaded the Dekkan, and his General, Kafúr, as early as 1310, brought back from the Dekkan a treasure consisting of several *chests* of jewels, pearls &c.‡

Alá-ud-dín died in 1316.§ I take it that this Alá-ud-dín is the one intended, and not the other prince of the same name, once the slave of a brahman astrologer, and who afterwards became the founder of the Brahmani dynasty in the Dekkan (he died in 1357). For if it is this latter, it is difficult to understand how the diamond found its way to the Delhi treasury, seeing that the weak and disorganized monarchies that characterized the close of the 2nd Ghori dynasty were never able to cope with, or to overthrow, the Dekkan power. There was also another Alá-ud-dín in 1446. Assuming then that the diamond was with Alá-ud-dín Khilji, it must have remained there in possession of his successors, the last of whom was Sultán-Ibrahím, son of Sikandar, son of Bahlol Lodi. The possession of the diamond by Alá-ud-dín and his successors is stated as a fact by Sultán Bábar in his memoirs, who fixes the date of Alá-ud-dín's acquisition of the diamond as 1306 A. D.

It was at this time that Bábar, a descendant of the great Taimúr-leng, after several invasions,‖ at length, in 1526 (A. D.) attacked Sultan Ibrahím, and entered Delhi: Ibrahím was defeated and slain. One of the native historians says that, on reaching Delhi, Bábar shewed great kindness to the family of the late emperor, assigning a

* Catalogue of the Great Exhibition of 1851, Vol. II., p. 695.

† According to the Memoirs of Bábar, the diamond was actually in possession of Raja Bikramajít of Gwalir at the time when Humáyun (Babar's son) took it. The said Bikramajít was holding Agra on behalf of Sultan Ibrahím against Babar's force. Perhaps this gave rise to the idea that the great Bikramajít had it.

‡ See Mill's History of India, Vol. II., p. 203.

§ Mill, who *always* garbles Indian names, calls him 'Alla,' which is no name at all. He also calls the brahmin Gangú—Kongoh!

‖ He invaded India five times between 911 and 932 Hijra.

pension of 7 lacs of rupees to the mother. She, in gratitude for this, presented Bábar with the diamond, or as the Khulásat-ul-tavárikh, calls it, a 'piece of diamond,' saying it weighed '8 miskáls.'

The weight, of which I shall speak presently, is quoted from Bábar himself, who does not say that it was actually 8 miskáls, but was about, or probably (ghálibàn) 8 miskáls.

In Wilson's Glossary of Indian Terms, the miskál is equal to 63½ grains troy, which would make the diamond weigh 508 grains or (taking 4 grains = 1 carat) 127 carats.

The native historians fix the weight differently. Ferishta makes 8 miskáls equal to 224 ratis; and the translator of Bábar's memoirs, to 320 ratis: but the weight of the rati also differs.* The miskál also is sometimes estimated at 72 grains: this would make the diamond 576 grains, equal 144 carats.

This story of the diamond being given by Ibrahím's mother is not countenanced by Bábar himself, who (p. 308 of the translation) relates as follows:—

'The family of Bikramajít and the head of his clan, were at the moment in Agra, '[Bikramajít, not the earlier celebrity of that name, but the Raja of Gwalior, was at Agra 'holding the city for Sultan Ibrahím]. Upon Humayún's† arrival they attempted to escape, 'but were stopped by the parties stationed to watch their movements, and were brought in 'prisoners. Humayún would not permit them to be plundered, and of their own free will 'they presented to him a peshkash, consisting of a quantity of jewels and precious stones, 'amongst which was one famous diamond, which had been acquired by Sultan Alá-ud-dín. 'It is so valuable that a judge of diamonds valued it as half the daily expenses ‡ of the 'whole world; it is about 8 miskáls in weight. On my arrival Humayún presented it as 'a peshkash to me, and I gave it him back as a present.'

Jean Baptiste Tavernier, who visited India about the middle of the 17th century, gives a different account of the origin of the Koh-i-nur, and if his story is true, that of Bábar's cannot be; nor is it possible that there should have been two diamonds of such extraordinary size at Delhi at the same time; for Tavernier, who was allowed to handle and weigh all the jewels, would surely have noticed the fact. It is of course possible that the diamond which Bábar had and gave to Humayún, was not the one which descended to Shah Jahán and Aurangzeb. The writer in the Official Catalogue of the Great Exhibition of 1851 concludes that Tavernier's account is not true. There is nothing in the method of cutting the Koh-i-nur (as it was seen in 1851) which would lead me to suppose, necessarily, that it is the work of an European, nor can there be any objection to the greater antiquity of the diamond on the ground of the art of diamond cutting being unknown. It was not known in Europe before the end of the 15th century (or 1486 A. D.), but it may have been, and probably was, known long before that in India.

Tavernier does not seem to have been aware of the existence of Bábar's account, and does not relate any special enquiry as to the origin of the diamond he saw. His

---

* Some give it as 1·953 of a grain, others 2¼ grains. Natives say that one rati equals 8 average sized grains of clean husked rice.

† Bábar's son, who was sent on the expedition.

‡ I suspect we should read 'income' instead of 'expense.' The copyist wrote خرج instead of خراج the 'alif' was omitted.

drawing and description do not certainly correspond exactly to the shape and facets of the Koh-i-nur as it was in 1851, and there is no reason to suppose that it had been touched between the date of the Mogul reign and its possession by the Sikh power. On the other hand, if the diamond really had its origin in only the preceding reign, there must have been persons at the Court who were well aware of the truth. There is, however, a great improbability in one particular about the story, and that is, that the rough diamond weighed 900 ratis, equal to about 787 carats ! The diamond Tavernier saw and weighed was only 280 carats, so that there must have been 500 carats lost in cutting, which is hardly possible.

Tavernier's story is as follows :—

After mentioning that on 1st November 1665 he was shown the jewels in Aurangzeb's treasury, he says,* 'the first jewel put into any hand was the great diamond, which is a 'round rose diamond, very convex on one side (fort haute d'un côté) ; on the under side 'there is a small nick with a little flaw in it.† It is of fine water, and it weighs 319½ 'ratis, equal to 280 carats (of 4 grains) : the rati equal to 7-8ths of a carat. When 'Mirgimala, (*sic.*) who betrayed his master the King of Golconda, presented the stone to 'Shahjahán, it was uncut, and then weighed 900 ratis, equal to 787½ carats, and had several 'flaws. Had this stone been in Europe it would have been differently treated, some good 'pieces (pendants) would have been taken off it, and the stone itself left much larger ; as it 'is, it has been quite polished away. It was Le Sieur Hortensio Borgis, a Venetian, who 'cut it, and who was poorly recompensed for his pains. They reproached him with having 'spoiled the stone, saying that he could have left it much larger. Instead of paying him for 'his work, they made him pay 6,000 rupees, and would have taken more if he had anything 'more for them to take. If Hortensio knew his work better, he could have taken some good 'pieces off without doing wrong to the King, and without having had so much work to 'polish it, but he was not a very skilful diamond cutter.'

Whether this account of the origin be accepted or Bábar's, there can be no doubt that this diamond came from the Golconda mines. Tavernier expressly says that it came from a mine which he calls Gáni‡ (or Coulour, in Persian) which is seven marches east from Golconda. This is the Gáni Partiála visited by Dr. Voysey in 1823 ; and the early history of the stone in Bábar's memoirs points to the Dekkan as its origin. Now these mines of Golconda were known to yield larger diamonds than any of the others of Raolconda and Visápúr.

It is commonly said that this diamond used to adorn the 'peacock throne.' This, however, was certainly not the case in Aurangzeb's time. Tavernier (p. 241) gives a minute description of this splendidly jewelled couch, but the great diamond is not described as being in it. One large diamond is described, but that weighed 80 or 90 carats only, and does not correspond in size to the Koh-i-nur.

In Chapter XXII there is a further description and a plate of this large diamond : it is represented as cut in uniform facets, and there is an irregularity in the shape at one side, he says :—

* Voyage des Indes (Paris, 1676, vol., II., p. 249.)

† See foot note to page 198 *post*.

‡ The word gání or kair, means mine.

"Ce diamant appartient au Grand Mogol lequel me fit l'honneur de me le faire
" montrer avec tous ses autres joyaux. On voit la forme où il est demeuré etant taillé, et
" m'ayant esté permis de le peser, j'ay trouvé qu'il pese 319½ ratis qui font 279 $\frac{9}{16}$ de
" nos carats. Estant brut it pesoit comme j'ay dit ailleurs 907 ratis qui font 793 $\frac{5}{16}$ de
" nos carats. Cette pierre est de la méme forme comme si l'on avoit coupé un euf par le
" milieu." *

Tavernier also mentions that the rati used in weighing diamonds at Goloonda and Visápúr, is ⅛ less than the European carat of 4 grains.

The writer of the Note in the 1851 Catalogue, before quoted, questions Tavernier's measurement of the weight, as, if a rati is equal as he says to 7-8ths of a carat, it should equal about 3½ grains, which no rati ever does; the maximum being 2 $\frac{5}{16}$ and the average received weight 1·9 grains. If weighed by the higher scale it gives 700 grains or 175 carats, which is very near the actual weight of the Koh-i-núr, *viz.* 186 carats.

The diamond remained in the hands of the Mogul sovereigns down to King Roshan Aktar Muhamad Shah (who ascended the throne in 1720) at the time when Nádir Shah invaded the Empire of Hindustán. Nádir Shah, after the battle of Karnál entered Delhi in March 1739 A. D. He seized the entire treasury of Delhi, including the peacock throne and the great diamond, which he called Koh-i-núr or "mountain of light": this is the origin of the name by which the diamond has since been known. There is no reason to suppose any truth in the story which represents Nádir Shah as changing turbans with Muhamad Shah, and taking the diamond along with the turban. Nádir Shah took the Koh-i-núr with him, but nine years after his return to Persia he was murdered by his nephew Ali Kuli Khan. Soon, however, the country fell into a state of anarchy, and Ahmad Shah Duráni, who had been a yasáwal or chief porter in Nádir Shah's service, became King at Kandahar and Kabul, A. H. 1161. The Kingdom of Persia, however, did not immediately pass into the possession of the Duráni. Karím Khán Zind reigned seven years after Nádir Shah, and possessed the diamond; his brothers Jáfir Khan and Lutf Ali Khan succeeded, and had the diamond also. Lutf Ali was eventually defeated by Aghá Muhamad Khan Kájár, and fled for his life. During his flight he fell in with 90 Seistáni troopers, to whom he shewed the diamond, which was then worn as a bázuband or armlet for the upper arm; the diamond he offered to them as the price of his safety. With characteristic treachery the Seistánís took the diamond, deserted Lutf Ali after hamstringing his only horse, and made their way with the precious jewel to Kandahar. In this city they attempted to sell it, but Ahmad Shah Duráni having heard of this, sent for the men and seized the diamond. Ahmad Shah died A. H. 1184, and was succeeded by his son Taimúr Shah, who, after a reign of 23 years, was succeeded by his son Zamán Shah. Zamán Shah was defeated and deposed by his brother Mahmúd Shah.

Zamán Shah when defeated at Ghazni, fled towards the Khaibar, and took refuge in the fort Ashik (*sic* in Nurdín's papers). In the walls of the fort Zamán Shah hid the Koh-i-núr along with some other valuables. Shah Shujá, a younger brother of Zamán Shah, did not allow his brother Mahmúd to reap the fruits of his victory, but, having gained over a considerable body of troops, established himself on the throne. To him Zamán Shah

* This is very like the real stone, which is quit flat below and is nearly oval, except a slice cut off one side; viewed endwise, and from the end opposite the gash or slice, it is quite like Tavernier's plate.

revealed the hiding place of the Koh-i-núr, and it was dug out and given over to Shah Shujá. Shah Shujá was however unable to hold the throne against Mahmúd Shah, but was defeated and forced to take refuge at Rawalpindi, carrying the precious diamond with him.

While there, the Governor of Kashmir sent to assure him of fidelity, and invited him to Kashmir. Shah Shujá believing him, moved to Hassan Abdál, and thence to Attock. Meanwhile, Mahmúd Shah, Shah Shujá's successful rival, sent though his Wazir, Fatih Khan, overtures for the friendship of Maharaja Ranjit Singh.

The Kashmir Governor (Ata Muhamad Khán) no sooner heard of this, than he sent renewed solicitations to Shah Shujá to come to Kashmir. Shah Shujá did so, but first despatched his wife Wafá Begam to Lahore, carrying the diamond with her. Shah Shujá, as is well known, immediately on reaching Kashmir, was treacherously seized and imprisoned.

Wafá Begam was well received by the Maharaja, and suitably lodged and entertained at Lahore. So soon as the news of the Shah's fate reached her, she sent to the Maharaja, begging his assistance in procuring his liberation, and offering the Koh-i-núr as a reward for the service.

Meanwhile Wazír Fatih Khán (Mahmúd Shah's Wazir) had made still further interest with the Maharaja, and induced him to aid in the Wazir's design of invading Kashmir. Ranjit Singh advanced as far as the Rohtás fort (Jhelam), and instructed a number of his Chiefs and Rajas to assist Wazir Fatih Khan in his expedition against Kashmir, but secretly ordered them to secure, at all hazards, the liberation of Shah Shujá.

The Maharaja returned to Lahore and immediately acquainted the Begam with the measures taken for the Shah's release, demanding the promised diamond as his reward ; the Begam prudently, however, declined giving it up till she saw her husband with her own eyes. Maharaja Ranjit Singh was obliged to be contented, and made arrangements for conveying the news of the success of the Kashmir expedition so soon as the event would occur.

The Kashmir expedition succeeded, Ata Muhamad Khan, the Governor, in great distress released Shah Shujá, and placed him on the throne of Kashmir. Wazir Khan and the Sikh army were, however, completely successful.

It is needless for my present purpose to detail the intrigues which followed the success ; how Ata Muhamad Khan made overtures to the Sikh conquerors, and how Fatih Khan was afraid, in consequence. Shah Shujá, afraid to trust either Ata Muhamad or Fatih Khan, adhered to the Sikh Díwan Mohukm Chand, who, according to his instructions, set out from Lahore, taking Shah Shujá with him.

On reaching the capital the Sikh Chiefs left Shah Shujá at Shahdara, and reported the events of the expedition to the Maharaja. Next morning Shah Shujá, accompanied by Prince Kharak Singh, entered Lahore with royal pomp, and was lodged in the "Mubárik haweli."

The Maharaja now made several efforts to get possession of the diamond: on one occasion it is even said that one of the Maharaja's Sirdars kicked the Shah. In Nur-u-din's papers, some extracts from Sohan Lál's history of the Maharaja are given, from which I gather the following particulars ;—

Bhaya Rám Singh and others were sent to solicit the delivery of the diamond. They pressed him exceedingly, but he made pretences to avoid giving it up. He was therefore put under a strict guard, and "every day served to add to the severity of his confinement." Shah Shujá sent a deputation to the Maharaja saying, that the diamond was mortgaged for 6 crores of rupees due at Kabul, but the Maharaja was not satisfied. At last it was agreed that the Mahajara should pay three lacs of rupees in cash, and grant a jagír of the annual value of 50,000 rupees. On receipt of the Maharaja's promise, Shah Shujá said he would deliver the diamond within fifty days.

"On the 29th Jamádi-ul-awal, (1st June A. D. 1813,) Fakir Azíz-ud-din, Bhai "Gurbaksh Singh, and Jamadár Khushál Singh, went to Shah Shujá and demanded the "diamond. The Shah replied that Maharaja Ranjit Singh should come for it himself. "The Maharaja on hearing this, cheerfully mounted his horse, and accompanied by troops "on the right and left, and taking with him a sum of 1,000 rupees in cash, went to Shah "Shujá's haweli. The Shah received him with respect and bended the knee to him. "The Maharaja then sat down * * * * The Shah produced the diamond "and gave it to the Maharaja, who signed an agreement to secure the Shah from further "molestation." Presents were then exchanged, and the Maharaja returned to the Fort.

In Nur-ud-din's papers a number of statements are given of various persons who were questioned as to whether the three lacs agreed to be paid were ever granted. It seems quite clear that, although from time to time sums of money were presented to the Shah, the agreement alluded to was never fulfilled.

As to the weight of this diamond, I already stated that the Khulasát-ul-tawárikh, speaking of the diamond in Bábar's time's says, the weight was 8 miskáls=144 carats. When obtained by Ranjit Singh, "wise examiners" of the time gave its weight as 42 mashas = 336 ratis = 735 grains = 183⅗ carats, which is close to its exact weight.

The diamond was set in gold, and worn as a bázuband or armlet, and is still remembered at Lahore by the name of the bázuband diamond. It was in the state in which it was exhibited in 1851, 186 carats in weight and worth £270, 768: it has since been re-cut.

No one in this country had an adequate idea of the value of this stone. It is commonly said that Ranjit Singh on being asked the value said it was "ikbál,' or the power which could conquer the state which possessed it; but what the Maharaja really said, more humorously, was, that the price was 'shoes'—*i. e.*, he who could give his enemy a beating (shoe beating is the oriental sign of defeat) and take it from him. The meaning is, however, the same.

Fakir Nur-ud-din writes as follows, about what he heard Wafá Begam say on this subject :—

A few months after the diamond in question came into the possession of the Maharaja, "I was called back from Jálandhur to Lahore, and deputed by the Maharaja to Wafá "Begam, to find out what opinion she had of its value. By order of this Highness I "visited Wafá Begam, and begged her to inform me what she had heard or knew to be its "value. Wafá Begam, in reply, said that its value could not be described in one way, but "in several ways. According to what she had heard from her ancestors, its value is equal "to a heap of precious stones and gold mohrs filling a space marked by five stones, each

" thrown on four sides and upwards by a strong young man. Some have said this even to be an inadequate value; others have said that its value is equal to half of the daily income of the whole world. And the real price by which it has passed from one hand to another, is presentation of a weak to a powerful party, which price brought it in the possession of Saduzai family, and at last into the hands of the Maharaja.

The subsequent history of the diamond is too well known to need repetition. It was ceded to the British in 1849, taken by the Marquis of Dalhousie, Governor General, to Bombay in 1850, and entrusted to Lieutenant Colonel Mackeson, C. B., and Captain Ramsay, who sailed with it to Europe, reaching Portsmouth on 30th June 1850. They handed it over to the Board of Directors East India Company, and, on the 3rd July 1850, it was delivered to Her Majesty. It has since been re-cut in a completely round form, losing considerably in weight, but gaining vastly in beauty and brilliancy. It can be worn either in a bracelet or in a necklace; there are two pendants mounted with it.

CLASS XIV.

ARTICLES OF VERTU.

All that can be done in this class is to give a list of the more remarkable specimens that have come to notice.

LAHORE.

Powder-horn, made of polished shells of some large species of *Turbo;* the mouth being closed with copper gilt covering.

There was one from Amritsar in the 1864 Exhibition [No. 10100].

[8772].—Horse trappings of gold repoussé work on velvet, (value Rs. 2,900) belonging to Raja Harbans Singh of Lahore.

[8774].—Necklace of gold and coral for horses, (value Rs. 370). Another of large white glass beads. Another of jade beads. Another made of gold coins (ashrafies) strung on silk cord. Another of large beads of cut rock crystal.

[8778].—Small cups of rock crystal. These are brought from Yarkand, &c., and are much admired in the houses of the wealthy.

[8780].—A cup of green serpentine. This is called " zahr mohra," because, if poison is poured into it, the stone is supposed to crack, and so " reveal the poison."

[8781].—A jade cup, inlaid with precious stones.

[ ].—A large onyx stone cut into the shape of a frog (Kabul) in the Lahore Museum.

[8784].—Various sword handles of jade, amulets and charms of the same, inlaid and set with stones.

[8800].—A fly-flap, yak's tail, in gold and jewelled handle (Raja Harbans Sing, Lahore).

[8803].—Series of agate knife handles. This stone is brought from Cambay.

[ ].—A jade cup. These jade articles are all brought from Yarkand, and are not made in the Punjab.

[8809].—Ornament for the point of a scabbard, set with rubies. Another of jade.

[8810].—Figure of a tiger carved in agate.

[8811].—Beads of clouded amber.

[8813].—Vases of dark green jade (loot from China).

[10123].—A hooka vase of carved marble.

[ ].—A marble book-stand—two plates of carved marble, crossed like the letter X; the Koran is rested on this in a mosque at prayer time (it is called " rihl ").

AMRITSAR.

[10087].—A crystal bowl, value Rs. 150.

[10090].—An onyx cup, value Rs. 100 (or agate, " sang ghauri ").

Also a series of pen holders, little dishes and salt-cellars, of agate and serpentine (zahr mohra).

PATYALA.

[10264, &c.].—A boat carved out of white Jaipúr marble. A pen-case ditto, ditto.

TABLE MADE OF VARIOUS PUNJAB WOODS.

CLASS XV.

MANUFACTURES IN WOOD, USEFUL AND ORNAMENTAL.

Division I.—Furniture.

„ II.—Carved and Inlaid Work.

Furniture is so little used by natives, that this class is a small and uninteresting one. A rich man's house is often well furnished with carpets, hangings, low cushioned divans, and " masnads," but ornamental furniture is unknown save to those few who have adopted the European style. Tables, often inlaid, or with legs covered with silver plate, and arm chairs, are alone in use, and low wooden stools for sitting on.

The number of natives who are skilled in wood carving is however considerable. The form of articles produced by them is rarely good and never beautiful; it is only in surface design that they seem to excel.

All the furniture that was really good in the Exhibition of 1864, was made by carpenters who had taken patterns from European articles, and brought their own skill in design and carved tracery to bear on the work.

The following articles may be mentioned as shewing the more curious articles of furniture :—

[9571].—An arm chair, entirely made of white marble; the back and sides being perforated and carved. A similar one was sent from Lahore (Sirdar Bhagwan Sing, exhibitor,) Amrítsar.

[9578]—An arm chair entirely covered with plates of ivory and mother-o'pearl (nímrú), Nawab Jahangir Khan, Lahore.

[9581].—Tún wood table inlaid with ivory.

[9581].—A watch case ornamented with gilt brass. This is a copy of the 'Louis Quatorze' style.

[9707].—A chair painted and gilt, " kárí-kalamdání (See Lacquered Ware), Kashmir.

[9708].—A round table in painted wood. The design of this being of the shawl pattern, was really beautiful, and the coloring chaste and subdued. The cost of such a table is 81 Rupees.

The following specimens are all of European fashion :—

[9570].—Round table, the top inlaid with 50 different kinds of Punjab wood, the stem and base representing reeds on a lake, with swans supporting the table, carved in white wood, and with water lilies. The plate shews this elegant piece of work, executed by native carpenters under directions of Mr. J. Gordon, c. e.

[9568].—A drawing-room chair, elaborately carved (Sirdár Bhagwán Singh). This shews how delicately natives can carve; the material is tálí or shísham wood.

SIMLA.

[9554 &c.,].—Book cases, chiffoniers, small tables, arm chairs, couches, &c.

Simla is celebrated for its carved ware. Several carpenters may be seen in the bazar at work. The patterns are supplied them, and the imitation is excellent. The woods most used are walnut, and a beautiful zebra wood known as "kakkar" (*Pistacia*). The work is cheap enough : a pair of teapoys cost Rs. 20 ; a book-stand for the table Rs. 3 ; a flower-stand Rs. 20 ; a couch (the wood work) Rs. 25.

JALANDHAR.

[9565].—A side-board or chiffonier carved in shísham wood. This elaborate carving is figured in the annexed plate.

OTHER DISTRICTS.

In Shahpúr, a remote and rather wild district, Major Davies, the Deputy Commissioner, got some native carpenters to make excellent furniture. At Lahore, in the Railway Workshops, with the aid of good tools and effective superintendence, almost any article of joiner's work, plain and fancy, can be produced. The Raja of Kapúrthála sent to the Exhibition a table with a marble top, and a carved arm chair, very well finished and polished. The last item is not often well done ; as a rule native workmen are contented to varnish with copal instead of actually polishing.

I should not close this class without alluding to the "Gujrat Chair." This is an instance of how an article of manufacture can be introduced and localized within narrow limits and then rendered permanent. Some years ago a Deputy Commissioner of Gujrat, named Capper, interested himself in manufactures. Mrs. Capper gave some carpenters a pattern of a folding easy chair. It was at once imitated in tún wood, and has a loose hanging cushion of leather. I have already alluded to the leather.* These chairs are made only at Gujrat, and have obtained a Punjab celebrity : they are called by the natives Gujrat or "Capperína' Chairs."

* See page 123.

CARVED FURNITURE.

DIVISION II.

CARVED AND INLAID WORK.

It is hardly worth while to make a separate class of the carved and inlaid work. I have already described under the last head the skill many natives possess in the art of carving; but for want of suitable objects, almost the only articles on which the art is exercised are pen-cases, boxes, cups, and legs of the universally used charpoy or flat bedstead.

The following specimens may be mentioned:—

Delhi.

[9192].—Carved sandal wood box, the sides bound with silver, and set with oval "Delhi miniatures" (of which hereafter). These sell, according to size and number of paintings, from Rs. 250 to Rs. 25 each.

Ambala.

[9207].—Carved spoons and forks, for salad &c.

This work seems to have been learnt from Sahāranpúr, not far off, where beautiful carved work of the soft white wood of the *Wrightea* is executed.

There are a variety of similar carvings from Ludhiana.

Hushyarpur.

[9279 &c.].—Boxes of dark shísham wood, inlaid with a flower pattern in ivory.

Amritsar.

[9339].—Walking sticks of olive wood, and of the "Rāuns" (*Cotoneaster*) carved. A favorite sort of carving is on a short stick, carried, I believe, by Bairágí fakirs, and consisting in inscriptions carved in relief in Gurmúkhí, Hindí, and Persian characters.

[9349].—A carved vase for a húka, of wood.

Gujranwala.

A model in carved wood of an elaborately carved verandah of arches and pillars, in an ancient báradari. This piece of work may be seen in the Lahore Central Museum. It is a faithful representation of a very elegant and interesting specimen of domestic architectural wood carving.

Jhelam.

I may note from this district neatly turned and polished cups of shísham wood, and a similar series from Shahpúr.

The Jury Reports on "Furniture" and "Wood Carving," prepared for the Exhibition Committee of 1864, may conveniently be printed as an Appendix to this Class.

JURY REPORT ON FURNITURE AND WOOD CARVING.

Furniture, in the common acceptation of the word, is unknown to Orientals. The articles requisite to the inside of a house differ in little beyond the material of which they are made, in the halls of an Indian prince and the hut of a peasant. Each must have his charpoy, but one will have it of silver, while the other will have it of wood. As in their ordinary dress and food, so in their domestic comforts, all classes are more or less equal. Tables are as superfluous to them as knives and forks; chairs are used on occasions of ceremony rather than for comfortable repose, and are chiefly looked upon as a species of social thermometer by which a man's position may be at once determined. Only persons of quality sit on chairs at a visit; dependents and inferiorshave to sit on the ground. The idea of household comfort is but faint in the native mind, but it is increasing with their advance in civilization. In no country is comfort so well understood as in England. Continental habits in this respect have decidedly an oriental tendency. Uncarpeted floors, uncurtained windows, uncovered tables, and uncomfortable bed rooms, are the characteristics of ordinary French and German houses. On special occasions they make a display which English houses seldom pretend to; but seen in the garb of every day life, the solid qualities of an English home come out to the best advantage. The difference is not in any one thing, but in the whole tone of the furniture and fittings. This love of solid comfort, as opposed to cold display, is gaining ground rapidly among our fellow-subjects in the east, as if by sympathy. In the Presidency towns rich natives display their wealth rather in an extravagant indulgence in European luxuries, than in the barbaric pageants of former days. One of the most magnificent chandeliers ever made is now under preparation for the Nizam of Hyderabad; and nearer the locale of the Exhibition may be see a suite of rooms in an Indian palace that make the spectator forget he is in the East.

The result of all this is that in calling for an exhibition of furniture, even in the Punjab, it is needless to look for articles invented by natives and intended for purely native use. The designs will be European, and the articles will be such as Europeans are likely to approve of. That this has been the case, the contents of the Furniture Court in this Exhibition will show. The specimens exhibited are few in number, and with one or two exceptions, commonplace both in design and execution. In this, as in so many other departments, it is evident that much more could have been done had more time been allowed, and had the objects of the Exhibition been better understood. As it is, there is sufficient in the articles exhibited to show what *can* be done in the province. Woods of all kinds exist in abundance; skill can be commanded to almost any extent. It needs only a steady demand to bring out the real capabilities of manufacturers in this respect.

A circumstance that operates strongly against the manufacture of good and valuable furniture is the migratory character of the European population, from whom encouragement for the manufacture is chiefly to be looked for at present. A family seldom lives in one station for more than two or three years at the most; hence economy and durability are the points kept in view in furnishing a house, rather than elegance and costliness. It will be long before this depressing influence will cease to operate, but there are symptoms of its decline discernible even now. The style of furniture of a mofussil house is very different now from what it was ten or twenty years ago. On the other hand, there are circumstances which will always tell strongly in favor of an indigenous manufacture of furniture. One of these is, the serious expense of getting any other; another is the unsuitability of finely polished or veneered European furniture for such a climate as this: it cannot last any time. The defects are in the material as often as in the style of work. The desiderata in furniture for Anglo-Indians are that the wood be suited to the climate, that it be left as much as possible in its natural state without the unpleasant adjuncts of sticky varnish, cracking veneer, or jagged brass binding; that it be portable and light, so as not to incommode a traveller; that it be elegant in shape, and calculated for coolness both is appearance and practice, and that it be moderately cheap. These qualities are rarely found together in Indian furniture. One of the objects of the Exhibition is to ascertain what improvement can be made in this respect and how. There is perhaps scarcely a house in the Punjab that contains a complete set of furniture, that is, a series of articles all of the same wood and in the same style. Houses are furnished piece-meal, one article being the production of one man, another of another, living in far distant ages: most of the articles have a history of their own full of interest if they could but unfold it. These anomalies are the result of stern necessity, and not of choice. A few years may see them vanish.

To the European eye there is nothing in the Furniture Court equal to the chiffonier made in the 89th Regimental Workshop, for finish and solidity; the joining is excellent, the polish and the exact fit of the shelves and doors are all that can be desired. Native made furniture always seems unfinished; the artificer seems to tire of his work as it approaches completion. The superiority of the work of European soldiers over that of natives is very noticeable. The inlaid table from Amritsar, however, shows that under European superintendence native workmen can attain a high degree of success.

The districts contributing furniture are Loodiana, Simla, Jullundhur, Amritsar, Lahore, Goojrat, Shahpore, Mooltan, Gugaira, Kuppurthula, and Kashmir. The following Regiments also sent contributions:—Her Majesty's 89th, Her Majesty's 93rd Highlanders, Her Majesty's 101st Regiment, and the 2nd Battalion Rifle Brigade.

The following articles were specially noticed:—

[9570].—A round drawing room table, the top inlaid with 64 different Punjab woods; and with an elegantly carved and ornamented pedestal. Both in design and workmanship it leaves nothing to be desired, while it derives additional value from its exhibiting at a glance the resources of the province in woods suitable for furniture.

[9764].—A chiffonier exhibited by Sergeant Ord, 89th Foot, made in the Regimental Workshop. It has been already noticed above.

[9679].—A carved side board from Shahpúr. The carving is rather coarse, but it is effective, particularly at a little distance.

[9680].—A round table from Shahpúr, not very ornamental, but serviceable and solid.

[9554—64].—Ten pieces of furniture from Simla. They are all in the same style, or nearly so. They are chiefly of 'kakkar' wood. The carving is clear and effective, and the shape of all the articles good. They form a very elegant set, and are creditable to the manufacturer.

[9675].—An iron easy chair from the Gujrat jail. It consists of a piece of fine durri stretched on a light iron frame. It moves easily and is well balanced.

[9578].—An arm chair made of ivory and mother o'pearl, exhibited by Nawab Jahangeer Khan. The shape is not elegant, but the construction is curious. The blending of the two materials gives it a very silvery appearance.

[9579].—An arm chair carved in marble, exhibited by M. Ter Arratoon. A beautiful piece of work, in thorough oriental style.

[9768—71].—A wire chair, a stool, flower stands, &c., from the Regimental Workshop of the 101st Regiment. These are the only specimens of this elegant and useful kind of work in the Exhibition, and are very creditable to the makers. The flower stands would ornament a verandah, and the wire seats would prove very convenient in a garden. This species of work might be largely developed in the Punjab, and would prove most suitable.

[9779].—An ice box—Rifle Brigade. This is very well constructed in zinc and wood.

[9784].—Easy chair, 3rd Battalion Rifle Brigade, very solid and comfortable; wood well cut and polished, well stuffed and mounted on castors.

Wood carving.

The specimens in this department are very few in number, and are not generally of high merit. This cannot be for want of good woods to carve in, as these are known to exist in abundance. The native idea appears to be to have their small ornaments and figures cut in ivory or stone, or moulded in precious metal. They like a little rough carving in wood over a doorway or on a balustrade, but they do not seem to care so much for that minute artistic carving which pleases the European eye. An exception must be made in favor of the hill districts, where wood carving is practiced to a considerable extent, as well as stone sculpture. This taste is, in them, much more advanced than their social and intellectual condition in other respects would lead us to suppose.

After all, fancy carving in wood is not an art that is ever likely to meet with much encouragement, except, in as far as it can be made subservient to utility in connection with furniture or architecture.

In this, as in all other arts practised by the natives of India, it is surprising what creditable results they arrive at with the use of the coarsest and simplest of implements. The idea of subdivision of labor, even in turning out small articles in large quantities, would never enter into a native's mind. He would commence, carry on, and finish, each one himself, not leaving a single one of the various processes to be performed by another. The hill carving, in particular, is executed with the rudest of tools, and must occupy the patient artist many a weary day. The remuneration would be incommenserate with the labor expended, in any country but this.

Some of the best carving in the exhibition was the work of other provinces. The style of carving displayed in the massive black furniture of Bombay, and its occasional imitations in the Punjab, is characteristic of a different department of the art altogether, and one which is calculated to play a much more important part in the manufactures of the country, and the social comforts of its inhabitants, whether native or alien. It must be admitted, however, that the chief excellence of the Bombay specimens, sent to the Punjab Exhibition by way of comparison, is in their color and boldness of design. As far as workmanship is concerned we do not see what is to prevent the artificers of Simla from equalling their brethren in Bombay. The chief want about the specimens of Punjab carved furniture, is a want of finish. The last touches are left undone, and the result is an appearance of incompleteness, which is fatal.

" *Districts.*—The districts which contributed specimens of wood carving, are Delhi Kurnal, Umballa, Loodiana, Jullundhur, Kangra, Hooshyarpore, Amritsar, Lahore, Gujranwala, Simla, and Shahpore. This list includes some of the districts under Class XV, because wood carving can scarcely be separated from furniture where the articles are of an ornamental character. It includes also districts which contributed specimens of simple wood turning, not sufficiently ornate to be styled carving, and yet not capable of being classed under lacquered turnery.

" *Kinds.*—The kinds of articles exhibited are sandal wood boxes, boxes of other kinds of wood, some of them on the Bombay pattern, charpoy legs, walking sticks with fancy heads, ornamental spoons and forks, spices and fruits in wood, paper knives, paper weights, combs, card cases, cups, carved furniture, and a few miscellaneous things.

" *Articles noticed.*—A carved chair—No. 9568 of Class XV—exhibited by Sirdar Bhagwán Sing, made by Karm Sing of Amritsar. This is one of the most striking objects on entering the Furniture Court. It is evidently not intended for use, and certainly not calculated to ensure comfort, but for elegance of form and excellence of execution, the Jury consider it a most creditable specimen of Punjab workmanship. All the lines are in flowing curves ; the feet consist of the claws or paws of some animal, probably unknown to naturalists, proceeding out of the mouths of many teethed dragons: rather a grotesque combination, but pardonable for its very extravagance. The sides and back are adorned with similar fancies. White bone, or ivory studs are interspersed with the carving, and the whole is surmounted with the Royal Arms, evidently showing that the chair is of recent production. We believe it was specially made for the Exhibition. The carving in some places may be considered rude, and only saved from condemnation by a liberal coating of varnish ; but the same delicate work is not expected in an article of this kind that we look for in a jewel casket or an imitation of fruit and leaves.

" [9570].—A drawing-room table ; the top inlaid with 64 different Punjab woods, exhibited by Mr. J. Gordon, Executive Engineer of Amritsar. This table is mentioned here on account of the beautiful carving on the pedestal. The base consists of a mimic pond formed of mirrors, on which rest a few water-lilies carved in white wood, and two swans of similar wood, stretching their necks up the pedestal, which is surrounded by carved rushes rising out of the pond below. The whole effect is excellent. As an artistic work, there is nothing in any department of the Exhibition to excel it.

" [9192—98].—Delhi Boxes, exhibited by Ismail Khan. These were noticed in the Fine Art section on account of the ivory paintings on them, but the carving is deserving of notice here.

[9206].—Spoons and forks exhibited by the Local Exhibition Committee of Umballa. These are very cleanly carved in good wood, and are remarkable for their delicate finish.

[9211].—Cardamoms of wood—Umballa.

[No.].—Similar ones from Lahore and Amritsar. These imitations are most deceptive in their semblance of nature.

[9554—64].—Ten pieces of carved furniture from Simla, exhibited by Lieutenant Colonel Lawrence, particularly two flower-stands, which are beautifully carved, with double serpentine stem, and leaves round the top.

[No.]—A "chowri" made of sandal wood, also one of ivory—Puttiala. The patience with which each separate hair or fibre of the fly-flap has been separately cut is astonishing."

FURNITURE FROM SIMLA AND GUJRAT.

DIVISION III.

TURNED AND LACQUERED WARE.

There are two prominent kinds of work which deserve separate mention : one is the 'Kár-i-kharát' or turned and lacquered ware, known to Europeans by the name of Pák-patan work ; the other, the turned work of Dera Ismaíl Khán.

The kharát work consists of turned wood boxes, cups and toys, the outer face of which is prettily colored with a coating of mottled lacquer.

The best work in the Punjab is done in the Montgomery district (*late* Gugaira) at a place called Pákpatan; but the art is by no means confined to this place. I have specimens from Delhi, Amritsar, Lahore, (both the city and the sub-divisions of Sharakpúr and Kasúr,) Shahpúr and the Derajat. Of the Derajat work I shall give a separate notice

The lacquered work has a fine polish and generally a marbled or mottled appearance, often in two or three colors, and the article finished with a flowered border, which latter is done by a species of handiwork different from the rest, and certainly affording a good instance of the delicacy of native handling.

In describing the work of Pákpatan, I may be excused for introducing the account given of this remarkable town in the Settlement Report :—

" The census gives Pákpatan five thousand (5,000) inhabitants, a number which the appearance of the town would cause a stranger at first sight to believe to be under estimated. The conspicuous situation of this town, on an elevated mound which overlooks the plain for many miles, creates, at first sight, a very favorable impression, which a nearer acquaintance however soon dispels. The streets are narrow and steep, the houses are badly constructed, and the place is especially noted for its sanctity and filth. The latter requires no further remark here, but, from its peculiar construction, this town is not likely to be improved by any sanitary measures, unless at a vast expense. Its sanctity is renowned throughout the Mahomedan part of Asia. It contains the tomb of the celebrated saint and martyr, Bábá Furreed, who converted a great part of the southern Punjab to Mahomedanism, and whose miracles entitle him to a most distinguished place among the " pírs " of that religion. The fair held near his shrine, which is still kept in good repair by his descendants, attracts annually between fifty and sixty thousand pilgrims. The miraculous wooden chapatti, dates, &c., which the worthy saint is related to have tied to his stomach when he felt hungry, and which composed his sole nourishment for thirty years, are still preserved for the reverence and worship of the faithful. The most remarkable part of the proceedings at this fair is however the passage through the " Gate of Paradise," a narrow opening in a wall, about five feet by two and a half, through which the pilgrims force their passage during the afternoon and night of the fifth of the Mohurrum. Every devotee who contrives to get through the gate at the prescribed time is assured of a free entrance into paradise hereafter. The crowd is therefore immense, and the pressure so great that two or three layers of men packed closely over each other generally attempt the passage at the same time, and serious accidents, notwithstanding every precaution taken by the Police, are not unfrequent."

The process of making the lacquered were may now be described:—

The turner's apparatus is very simple: he has first a strong wooden frame made fast to the ground and furnished with two uprights, between which the block of wood on which he is to operate revolves. One upright is fixed, and furnished on the inner side with an iron spike which forms one point of suspension; the other upright is capable of adjustment at a quarter or less distance, according to the size of the work—it slides along the under bar of the frame, and is fixed by a peg in one of a series of holes in the bar. When adjusted to the required distance, a piece of hard wood, generally shisham or box, is supported by the iron spike in the fixed upright, and a rather long iron pin run through a hole in the second, and thus the block is freely suspended on points between the two uprights. The iron pin is prolonged beyond the support, and is turned by a bow. The bow is fitted with a leather cord, which, being once twisted round the projecting end of the pin, is worked backward and forwards saw-like, thus communicating a rotatory motion. The turner sits on the ground, gains a fine purchase by putting his foot against the frame work, and moulds the article with chisels. The machine is kept going by a small apprentice, who saws away with the bow, and is supposed to learn the art meanwhile.

So soon as the article has attained the required shape, it is ready to be lacquered.

The coloring matter consists of thick short sticks (battí), of a composition of lac, resin, coloring matter, and, it is said, with a certain admixture of sulphur and bees wax.

Mineral colors are mostly used. The yellow is made with orpiment; green with arsenite of copper; red with red lead or vermillion; blue with imitation "lájward" (see Volume I, *sub voce*) or Prussian blue ('wilaiti níl'). But a pretty transparent crimson is produced with the red of the lac insect; and black with lamp black. When about to apply the sticks of lacquer color, the wooden article duly smoothed and clean, is set on the turner's frame and made to rotate. If the color to be produced is an uniform surface of lac color, the lac-stick is pressed rather hard against the wood and the color comes off, as the heat produced by the friction is sufficient to soften the lac and detach a portion. When enough color has been applied, the article looks dull and streaky, but a piece of bamboo is taken and a fine edge put on it with a chisel; this is skilfully rubbed over the surface of the article till the color has evenly spread, and by skilful manipulation a polish begins to show on the surface, which is enhanced by a gentler application of bamboo edges, and finally completed with oil and a rag. To produce the mottled appearance so much admired, the sticks of color are selected of a rather harder composition, and less easily softened by heat. The article to be colored is set revolving, and the workman, holding the color stick against it very lightly, allows a point here and a point there of color to attach itself; the wood soon appears to be sprinkled over with colored dust.

The workman takes another color, and repeats the process, moving the stick up and down along the revolving block, when by his skilful manupulation the second color adheres at points which the first color has left blank; sometimes a third color is touched in in the same manner. When enough color is on the surface, the different points of colors are rubbed together and combined into a mottled or marbled appearance by rubbing, as before described, with a bamboo edge, and finishing with a rag and oil. The prettiest mottle is that of crimson and black, crimson and white, and blue and black. Around the rim of a box or lip of a cup, a border is often put on, with a flower pattern on it, which is done in a different way.

GROUP OF LACQUERED WARE.

KASHMÍR TABLE.

The article is again set spinning on the frame, and color applied where the desired border is to come, in a uniform band, and well rubbed in and smoothed with the bamboo; a coating of red is always given first, over the red, a coating of green is applied till the red disappears, and over the green, black.

The flower pattern is produced by hand with a small sharp chisel; so delicately does the workman adjust the force and depth of his cut, that he will, for the flower, let us say, make it appear red by cutting away the black and green coats and exposing the red layer, for the leaves he will scratch down to the green one, and for a white line he will cut down to the wood. A mistake seems never to be made in this work: a slip of the tool would of course spoil the whole.

The turned work from the Deráját (Dera Ismail Khan), differs from that of Pakpatán. The variety of articles made is much less: the favorite article is a round box with a domed lid. The mottled surface is not given; but three coats of color, red, green and black are applied as just described, and the pattern entirely produced by the chisel. The lines produced are often silvered with an amalgam of mercury and tin-foil, and the appearance is very pleasing. The boxes are further ornamented by carved ivory knobs, &c.

It will not be interesting to give a list of specimens. At Pákpatan all kinds of cigar boxes, glove boxes, vases and trays, croquet mallets and balls, children's toys, &c., are made, and a list of them would be useless.

I conclude the class with a descriptive list of the turner's tools:—

(1). 'Nán.'—A large, heavy, narrow bladed chisel, for the first operation of rough clearing the wood.

(2).—'Nihán.'—A broad chisel, rather heavy, with long wooden handle, for neat cutting, also called Máthná.

(3).—They rest their tools on an iron bar 'addi', placed close below the revolving block of wood, and press the edge of the tool against the wood, moving it from side to side.

(4).—'Burákí.'—A pointed chisel to cut out screw, grooves, &c.

(5).—Chírná.—A heavy iron bar, terminating in a flat blade at either end, only the point of which is sharpened edgewise. Grooves can be cut, and a cylinder separated into pieces by this.

(6).—'Rachí,' and 'Roda'—A bar worked into a blade at either end.

The 'rachi,' blade being shape as *(a)*

and 'Roda,' thus *(b)*

(a)

(b)

(7).—'Sathra' 'Sathrí.'—Narrow edged chisels of sizes.

(8).—'Bánkiya'—for cleaning out the inside of vessels intended to be turned hollow. It is like a hooked bar, the edge of the hook being flat and sharp

(9).—'Tesha'—Adze.

(10).—Rangáta—the polishing stick.

(11).—Varma of sizes—This is the universal tool for boring holes.

He has also saws and files, which need no description.

CLASS XVI.

IVORY CARVING.

The places where ivory carving is done are numerous, but the only respectable work comes from Delhi and Amritsar. I exclude Patyála, because I understand that a workman there, who far excelled every one else in the Punjab, is dead, and I am not informed that the manufacture is sufficiently established to find him a worthy successor. A few articles are made in Ambala, Ludhiana, and Lahore.

The best work, even of the Patyála artist, is far inferior to Chinese work.

The ivory with which these carving are executed is obtained from the tusks of *wild* elephants. The natives say that the tusks of domesticated elephants yields only a brittle and inferior ivory, liable to crack on exposure to air. I quote the remark, but am unable to produce the result of any practical test applied to judge of its correctness. But my informant further asserts, that the cause of the brittleness of the tusk of the domesticated animal is the salt that is given him with his food.

The tusks of tame elephants are, however, far from valueless, and I am told the Native Princes—Gwalior, Jaipúr, &c.,—dispose of ivory obtained in this way. The Maharajah of Patyála is said to have store houses of ivory, which he does not sell, but makes into ivory bracelets, (churís) and distributes them on the occasion of weddings. The ivory sold at Delhi varies is price from Rs. 3 to 12 per seer. The Tarai in Oude, to the south-west of Náipál, called by natives "Khajli ban," appears to yield a large supply of ivory. The inhabitants collect the tusks of dead elephants and dispose of them. My informant mentions a place called "Ganj bélerí," in Bareilly, as a local market.

The manufacture is dependant on the skill and patience of the workman; the carving is wholly done by the aid of the rudest files, chisels, knives, and steel styles. The workman often holds the bit of ivory firmly between his toes as he sits on the ground, and carves it with his hand.

The Delhi specimens are various boxes, crochet needles with tiny figures carved on the handles; minute toys representing men and animals are among the best.

A workman, Panah of Ludiana, seems to produce a variety of work for the Ludhiana city.

One of the commonest form of work in ivory, is the manufacture of colored ivory bracelets, slender rings, worn by women on the arm in dozens. The bracelet maker is called 'Churgar,' and his tools are the following:—

1.—'Rachi'—A pointed chisel.—(*a*)

2.—'Chírna'—A pointed ditto, but with fine point.—(*b*)

These blades are generally ground at either end of the same iron: there is no wooden handle.

(*a*)

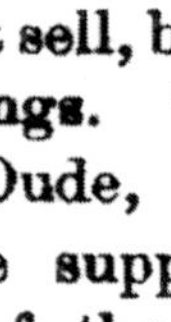

(*b*)

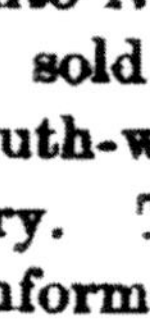

3.—'Roda'—A thick flat iron ground to a flat edge shaped thus

(*c*)

4.—'Kharát'—The usual turner's frame. The workman mounts a bit of ivory on the turner's frame, and works it till it is in a smooth cylinder, then he divides the hollow cylinder into the number of circles required for bracelets by a pointed tool which cuts into the ivory and separates the circles while revolving—this tool is called 'singhári' and is shaped thus:

The cutting points being at either end.

In order to color the rings, they are mounted on a wooden cylinder called 'kálbút,' which is set turning by the lathe wheel. The rings are colored with lac to a deep crimson, and polished with a 'rangáta' or polishing stick of date tree wood (khajúr).

The following extract from the Jury Report on Ivory to the Exhibition Committee of 1864, notices the best specimens of work exhibited. They should great delicacy of style, and patience in handling. Few people would like to sit down to cut a fly-flap out of a bar of ivory, each hair having to be produced by a separate cut of the fine saw!

"The articles included in this Class are more ornamental in their character, than useful. The actual number of articles exhibited in this department is great, as may be seen from the Catalogue, when the series extends from No. 9192 to 9549, but they do not make a great show, or occupy a large space, being for the most part of small size.

"The East has long been famed for its ivory manufactures. From the very earliest times of which we have any record, India has not only had a sufficiency of ivory for its own requirements, but a large surplus for exportation. It is not improbable that cargoes of ivory from the west of India, with the gold of Ophir, were carried in ships of Tarshish to decorate the palace and temple of Solomon. From the presence of this valuable material in such abundance, and the luxurious tastes of the Princes and nobles who successively surrounded themselves with all that skill could produce and wealth command, it is natural that India should produce the most cunning workers in ivory. This has been to a certain extent the case, but the skill attained in the art has been chiefly confined to certain localities, such as the neighbourhood of Moorshedabad in Bengal, and has not been co-extensive with the distribution of the material. Ivory carving, as distinguished from mere turning, is, from its very nature, an art that will always be most extensively practised in Oriental countries, where the people have plenty of leisure, require very little for their support, and have unlimited patience. The agency of machinery can never be largely introduced into such an occupation, and there is therefore little fear of Western competition. The monopoly of the manufacture will long lie between India and China. If the demand for ivory ornaments has declined in India itself, which probably it has done with the decline of Eastern power, it has largely increased in the most opulent countries in Europe. There is therefore every reason to encourage the art among the manufactures of this country, and to direct it into such lines as will ensure success. The tendency of Orientals is to keep for ever to the same beaten track. Originality of design will only be the result of pressure from without. Skill in manipulation exists, it has only to be utilized by the suggestion of new fields of labor. Our ideas of ivory work, as well as of almost all the beautiful arts practised by the natives of this country, are formed from the travelling pedlars who bring round their wares for sale. We have little information regarding the process of the manufacture, the numbers of artificers engaged in it, or where they are to be found. We know that from father to son for many generations such arts as ivory carving are handed down, but it is with the utmost difficulty that we can find a carver when we want one. This difficulty must have been noticed in almost every department of the Exhibition. The only way to remove it, is to encourage something like a commercial spirit among manufacturers, to teach them the value of their trades, and to point out gradually the best means of making themselves and their manufactures, known throughout the country and abroad. Many an Indian art is languishing for want of some stimulus of this kind.

" A glance at the collection of ivory articles in the Exhibition shows that the contributors have not sent their best specimens.* If the Punjab can produce nothing better than what this collection contains, the art is at a low ebb ; but there is reason to believe that the manufacturers have not done themselves justice, and that when the objects of an Exhibition of this kind are more generally understood, and encouragement is held out, a much better display will be made.

" Among a collection of ivory articles of all kinds, may be noticed an elegant and delicately cut bouquet-holder. It catches the eye at once by its superiority to the rest of the things, but it is somewhat disappointing to find it marked " China," though apparently exhibited by an Amritsar gentleman. There is nothing either in the quality of the ivory, or the skill of the manufacturers, to prevent the natives of India equalling those of China in this department, but the Exhibition contains no proof of their present ability to do so.

" The districts from which ivory manufactures have been received for exhibition are Sirsa, Umballa, Loodiana, Simla, Jullundhur, Kangra, Hooshyarpur, Amritsar, Lahore, Goojranwala, Shahpore (?) Dera Ghazee Khan, and Patyala. Those which contribute most largely, are Lahore, Amritsar, Loodiana and Patyala. The kinds of articles exhibited are numerous, but may be included under the general heading of boxes, paper knives, chessmen, figures of men and animals, muffineers, combs, bracelets, rings, walking sticks, and dagger handles, and a few miscellaneous articles incapable of classification.

" The most noteworthy articles are the following :—

A camel with two riders, from Loodianah, No. 922, exhibitor Panah. It is neatly cut, and in good proportion. There is no great ornamentation about it but it is a fair specimen of work.

[9383].—A camel similar to the above, Lahore, exhibited by Khuda Baksh.

A collection of ornamental combs and paper knives from Amritsar, included under No. 7812, exhibited by Devi Sahai and Chamba Mall.

[9384].—An elephant, Khuda Baksh, Lahore.

[9523].—A native bullock carriage.

* I am inclined rather to doubt this. I do not think that better work, as a class, could have been produced. Individual workmen could, when urged and encouraged, do better work, but ivory carving as a trade is at a low ebb in the Punjab—B. P.

GROUP OF IVORY CARVING.

[9524].—A boat with rowers, contributed by the Maharajah of Patyála. These and the following are the best specimens of Punjab ivory carving in the Exhibition.

Two daggers with ivory handles and scabbards. These are very handsome, and exhibit an application of the art not very common.

Chauris from Patyála, with carved handles—and thin strips of ivory forming the brush.

[9356].—A small pen box, carved, with a minute pad-lock cut in ivory—Khuda Baksh, Lahore."

CLASS XVII.

PAPIER MACHE AND PAINTED WARE.

This is a class which is constituted solely for the benefit of Kashmir: the work known as kár-i-kalamdáni is quite peculiar to that country.

The work is by no means always of papier maché, indeed it is the method of glazing and ornamenting the surface, rather than the nature of the material that is to be looked to.

The work goes by the name of kár-i-kalamdání, or "pen case work," because usually applied to the ornamentation of pen cases, and small boxes; but since an European demand has arisen, tea-caddies glove-boxes, paper cases, and vases, have been made at Srinagar to order, and even articles of furniture ornamented by this art. It is also called 'kár-i-munakash' or 'painted-ware.'

The work is done on articles either of smooth wood, or papier maché prepared by pulping coarse native paper, and moulding the softened material to the required shape. The article is covered with a coating of white paint, on the surface of which a delicate pattern in colors, chiefly crimson, green, and blue, is drawn with a fine brush; flowers, and the curved designs seen upon shawls, are most commonly produced. A very pretty pattern is also done by painting with gold paint a spreading series of minute branches and leaves on a white ground,—a border of brighter coloring is added: sometimes figures of men and animals are introduced. When the painting is done, the surface is varnished over with a varnish made by boiling the clearest copal (sundras) in pure turpentine. I do not think boiling in oil, (which is the ordinary carriage varnish) would yield a clear enough varnish. The varnish has to be perfectly transparent, or it would spoil the appearance of the painting. I am not sure that mastic varnish is not used: *(Mustagi Rúmí)* mastic is abundantly brought from Kabul. Referring to the material "papier maché," the only other specimens I saw in the Exhibition of 1864, were some cups and bowls rudely silvered with mercury and tin-foil, sent from the Sitpúr parganah of the Muzaffargarh District.

The following extract from the Jury Report of 1864, will be read with interest:—

"Papier maché is, as the name expresses, "mashed paper". It is surprising to see the beautiful forms into which this material can be wrought. The art of working it in its more ornamental phases has only become general in Europe within the last 20 or 30 years, but it has probably been known from a very early period. There are various* modes of preparing the pulp, but the general principle is to reduce strips of coarse paper by boiling or soaking to a kind of paste, which is then stiffened with gum or some other glutinous substance. In this form it can be worked or moulded into any shape, and when the required outline is attained, the surface is hardened and glazed with lac, or some similar substance, and sometimes lamp black, and colored according to the intended design. Sometimes another process is adopted: sheets of coarse paper, saturated with flour and gum, are laid upon each other on a metal mould to the required thickness,

* This does not refer to the native manufacture.—B. P.

GROUPS OF KASHMÍR PAPIER MACHÉ WARE.

this is dried in a hot room, the surface is glazed with lac and lamp black, and the ornamentation is proceeded with. A surface of this kind is impervious to moisture, and even to heat. The chief difference between the two processes is, that in one the paper is reduced to a paste, and in the other it is fastened together in layers: sometimes the two are combined. The black varnish so common in Europe does not seem to be used in India. In Europe, the introduction of mother o'pearl imparts great brilliancy to the work. This does not appear to be done in India, or at least it is not to be seen in the specimens exhibited; nor is it usual to blacken the material, which process gives such a suitable ground for ornamentation in European work. The art in India is chiefly applied to small articles, such as pen cases, salvers, cigar cases, and the like. The successful artificer in this department is more dependent on the excellence of his outer coloring and varnish, than on the quality of the paper pulp. Color and design come greatly into play, but the specimens in the present Exhibition show very little variety; nor does the work last long, for by keeping the varnish darkens, and the colors lose all their brilliancy, as may be seen in the specimens of old Kashmir work exhibited from the Lahore District. The work is peculiar to Kashmir.

"There would be a great demand at home for fancy articles of this description, not that they can equal European papier maché, but merely on account of their being Indian, and indeed quite different in appearance and style of ornament from European papier-maché. The fact that the native demand for them is properly understood, seems to be fully proved by the number of "kalamdáns" exhibited; they are always likely to sell. Other articles also are made, which are equally suitable for European and native use, such as trays, salvers, caskets, chess-boards, ornamental cups, and the like.

"The following articles here noted by the Jury:—

[9708].—A lacquered table contributed by the Maharajah of Kashmir. It exceeds two feet in diameter. The whole surface is colored richly in flower work which predominates. The varnish used is very transparent, and gives a fine smooth surface. The effect is very pleasing, but unfortunately the top has become warped, which seriously detracts from its beauty, and will probably never be remedied. This defect is probably caused by the thinness of the wood. Had the top been made of a thicker piece, the table would have formed an elegant drawing-room ornament.

"[9707].—A lacquered chair from Kashmir. In the same style as the table, but much inferior.

[9726–9727].—Cups and saucers, Kashmir. These are very highly wrought. They seem to be in the Chinese style, and have a very soft appearance. The coloring is excellent."

CLASS XVIII.

PORCELAIN AND POTTERY.

DIVISION I.—GLAZED POTTERY.

It does not appear that the natives of the Punjab ever practised *generally* the art of glazing pottery for domestic use. A few samples here and there indicate the existence of the art in a rude form, and the greatest progress has been made in the manufactories attached to the larger jails, where special efforts have been made to improve the color and the nature of the glaze. But the art of glazing and using encaustic colors has existed from an early date, and has, strange to say, in the form in which was practised with success, almost entirely perished. The form I allude to, is that of the glazed encaustic tiles, or glazed flower work composed of inlaid pieces of encaustic work, used to ornament mosques, tombs, and public building.

The Wazír Khán Masjid in the City of Lahore, built A. H., 1044, in the reign of Shah Jahán, is covered all over with encaustic work. The Shálimár gardens * have various buildings similarly ornamented : these latter have the patterns inlaid like mosaic work, each piece being separately colored and glazed, and afterwards fitted together with cement.

The whole vicinity of Lahore abounds with ruins ornamented with glazed work; so in the Districts of Multan and Muzaffargarh are numerous tombs, some of them of great age, ornamented with glazed tiles. The Shams Tabrez, in the Multan Fort, is a notable example.

This art is not actually lost. The Exhibition of 1864 contained specimens of the modern glazed tiles executed at Multan, and there was one specimen of a rather elaborate pattern executed by a workman resident at Jalandhar.

A workman at Sealkot also furnished large tiles glazed of a deep blue color for the churches in that Station.† Glazed pottery is made at a few places: I have seen it at Multan and in the Peshawur Bazaar. In the Rawalpindí, Sealkot and Lahore Jails, glazed pottery is made, and in the latter jail especially ; the work, though not equal to European, is remarkable good. The art was introduced by a native.

A small pamphlet has been published at the Central Jail, Lahore, from which I derive some particulars as to the method of producing glazed colors. The pamphlet should be procured by any one who wishes to carry the processes into practice, for, in spite of the author's lame style, and faulty phraseology—a combination of high Persian words with very ordinary Urdu phrases—it contains a good deal of useful matter. Two substances are of cardinal importance in the process: one is kánch, a vitreous glaze ; the other is a calcine or oxide of lead. As regards kánch, the specimen sent one is a pale clear bluish glass, like English bottle glass in lumps. There is *Angrezi kánchí* and native or "*desí.*" The former is made of "*sang-i-safed*" and pure alkali ; the *desí*

* Made in the time of Shah Jahán.

† See the note on this subject in the Jury Report appended.

kind is made either out of reh or alkali earth with sand, *i. e.*, a natural efflorescent alkali and fine siliceous sand; or with ground stone and potash, or with stone, borax and sand.

To make kánch on the English plan: take "sang-i-safed," (a quartzose rock obtained in the form of rolled pebbles from the bed of streams near the hills) 25 parts, pure soda six parts; purified borax (*sohága telia*) three parts; salamoniac, (*nausádar*) one part. Each ingredient is finely powdered and sifted, and mixed with a little water, and made up into white balls of the size of an orange. These are burnt in a furnace, till they become red hot; they are allowed to cool, and again ground up and sifted. The material is again put into the furnace till it melts; when thoroughly melted, one-fourth seer of fine, clean, picked saltpetre (*shora kalmí*) is stirred in. A foam appears on the surface, which is removed with a skimmer, and set aside for use. It is the "kách-lún" of the druggist.

A glass making material is however to be obtained ready ground in powder from England, and requires only burning and melting as above. The native kánch is less clear and transparent, and has a dirty green tinge. In making kánch a small quantity of oxide of manganese may be added (*anjani*); but too great fire must not be applied, for, if the manganese gets too highly oxidized, it will color the mass pink or lilac; at a low degree of oxidization it parts with a portion of its oxygen, which facilitates the destruction of carbonaceous impurities, and also destroys the green color, by imparting more oxygen to the iron, which causes the color. The *desi* kánch is made by grinding the ingredients already named, sifting, burning, and treating as just described. The proportions are as follows:—

(1).—Sang-i-safed or 'sang-i-surkh nagori', a siliceous grit, used for mill stones, and sajji, *equal parts*.

(2).—Sang-i-safed, 4 *parts*; sohága, *three parts*.

(3).—Siliceous sand, and sajji *equal parts*.

Two maunds of dry wood will fire a furnace to produce 10 seer of kanch; Kikar or Karir (*Capparis*) wood is preferred, cut into small pieces.

The next important articles are the calcines, or oxides of lead. There are "sikka safed," the basis of white and of most of the blues, greens and greys; "Sikka zard" the basis of yellows &c.; "Sikka sharbati," a pale reddish oxide (litharge); and "sikka lál," a red oxide. Sikka safed is made by putting two parts of lead and reducing by tin. The furnace used is a closed one, and consists of an hemispherical open crucible, resting on a base or pedestal of clay, and surrounded by fire, with a conical covering of some dried bricks; holes are made to enable the workman to introduce his iron skimmer and stirrers.

The lead being melted in the crucible, one part of tin is gradually added in little bits; vapour rises, and a white powder forms on the surface, which is raked on one side and lifted out into a vessel placed for the purpose: the melting material is constantly stirred. This goes on till the whole is reduced. Care must be taken that no particles of uncalcined metal remained: this preparation will be spoken of hereafter as sikka safed. Six seers of lead and three seers of tin can be reduced in hot weather in one day in winter in two days. The furnace to produce this quantity requires two maunds of

Jhand wood (*Prosopis,*) dry and in large billets ; the fire must be steady, neither very fierce nor very slack. " Sikka zard " is made by exactly the same process of reducing one seer of lead with only one-fourth part of tin or one half the quantity used in the last. " Sikka sharbattí " is made by reducing one seer of lead with four chittaks of zinc instead of tin. This is, I presume, a yellow oxide or litharge of lead, which is partly oxidized above the yellow stage, and approaching the minium or red oxide stage. Sikka lál is the metal oxidized till red, and made by calcining one seer of lead with four chittaks of zinc. The above materials form the basis of all the glazes. The color and the glaze is applied together.

White glaze is made with—

One part " sikka safed,"
One part kánch,

well ground and sifted and mixed, put into the kánch furnace and stirred with a ladle. When melted, borax, in proportion of two chittaks to the seer is added. While this is being done the fire must be slack. If the mixture gets a little blackish, add a small quantity of saltpetre. When all is ready, the material is taken out and thrown into cold water, this splits it into fragments, which are collected for use in the manner to be presently described.

A white glaze used at Multan gives a better and more opaque white than the above.

Take sang-i-safed two parts, kánch one part, and grind together; a little borax improves it. It is mixed with máwá, the gluten of wheat in solution, and applied to the vessel; over it again a coating of finely ground glass powder is spread. This glaze is not so often used, as it is liable to crack and come off.

This white glaze, if mixed with certain other ingredients, will give the tints shown in the following table. The glaze is mixed with the required coloring matter, and both are ground together to an impalpable powder ready for application to the vessel.

I should add that the " reta " or zaffre, spoken of in the table and elsewhere, is a powder consisting of the black oxide (ore of cobalt) which has been roasted in a furnace and powdered, mixed with a little powdered flint and siliceous sand. The cobalt ore is found in Central and Southern India, and has been known for hundreds of years past. The calcining of the ore drives off the sulphur, arsenic, &c., which it contains, and completes the oxidization of the cobalt, which is important : I expect some of the zaffre is imported from Europe. It sells in the bazaar at 4 rupees per seer. In the pamphlet I am referring to, it is said to come from " Kiráua Jhanjhána."

Color.	Weight of the white glaze used.	Material to be mixed in order to produce the required color.	Weight.	REMARKS.
1. Firozá—turquois blue,	1 seer,	"Chhil támba," thin flakes of oxidized or calcined metallic copper, ...	1 chittak.	
2. Kásní—pink or lilac,	Ditto,	Anjani—oxide of manganese,	1 do.	These are merely shades of the same tints.
3. Sosni—violet, ...	Ditto,	Do., do., mixed with reta or zaffre, ...	1½ do.	
4. Udá—purple or puce,	Ditto,	Anjani, ...	2 do.	
5. Khakí—ash grey, ...	Ditto,	Reta—Anjani, ...	1½ do.	
6. Níla—deep blue, ...	Ditto,	Zaffre or Reta, ...	4 do.	Ditto Ditto.
7. Asmáni—sky blue,...	Ditto,	Ditto, ...	1½ do.	
8. Halka-ábí—very pale blue, ...	Ditto,	Ditto, ...	1 do.	
9. Fírozí-ábí—pale Prussian blue tone, ...	Ditto,	Chhil támba as above, ...	1-24th of a seer.	This is a pale shade of No. 1.

Another method of preparing the dark blue glaze for use by itself. The ingredients are—

Flint powdered, ...	4 parts.
Borax, ...	24 do.
Lál Sikka, ...	12 do.
Sang-i-safed, ...	7 do.
Sajji, ...	5 do.
Zinc, ...	5 do.
Zaffre, ...	5 do.

All these are burnt together in the kánch furnace as before. Whenever they have a white ground, they are able to produce patterns, flowers &c., on it, in blue and other colors. For turquois blue calcined copper is used ; for purple, manganese ; zaffre for blue : the blue zaffre and "chhil támba" require to be burnt before use. "Lohá chun" (iron filings), when prepared as hereafter described, gives a yellow. The colors are applied with a paint brush, after being very finely ground up with gum and water. To produce green flowers, they mix "Kahi lál" (bi-chromate of potash) one tolah, with a little "sikka safed," and dissolving them in a seer of clear water, filtered through unglazed paper, the powder that is collected in the filter is used and gives a green mark. Orange color patterns are done with surma (black antimony); and blue with sulphate of copper (tútyá.)

* This is said to be "the English method ;" and various other colors are given at pages 38—39 of the pamphlet, which I have not quoted.

Just as the white glaze is made to be the basis of a set of colors, in a similar manner a yellow glaze is formed, of which the "sikka zard" is the basis, and this forms the foundation of a series of tints.

The yellow glaze is made of :— "Sikka zard" 1 seer.

"Sang safed" or mill-stone, or burnt and powdered flint, 4 chittacks.

These are fused in the furnace, and when melted, some borax (1 chittak to the seer) is added.

The tints produced are :—

Color.	Proportion of yellow glaze.	Material added.	Weight.
Zamrúdí, deep green, ...	1 seer, ...	Calcined copper, chhil tamba,	3 chittacks.
Sabz—full green, ...	1 Do., ...	Ditto, ...	1 ditto.
Pistákí—bright green, ...	1 Do., ...	Ditto, ...	1¼ ditto.
Dhání—pale green (color of shoots of young rice, dhán,)	1 Do., ...	Ditto, ...	$\frac{1}{128}$ ditto.

Another green is produced by burning one seer of copper filings with 'nimak shor' (sulphate of soda). The dull red or 'sharbatí' color is made in Rawal Pindí by mixing one seer of sharbatí sikka, one seer of sang-i-safed, or powdered burnt flint, and melting them together as before with "sohága." In Lahore and elsewhere a similar effect is produced by simply applying a transparent glaze of two chittaks of borax and half a seer of kánch, which shows through it the natural red of the pottery.

The dark copper color producing a burnished metallic lustre is made as follows :—

"Lohá chun," or fine iron filings, are calcined in a crucible in a fire made of "upla," (cow dung cakes) which give a slow smouldering fire. They are calcined with a little salt, and when cold are ground fine in a pestle; the burning and pounding is repeated four times, when the iron is completely reduced.

To one seer of borax, 4 chittaks of the prepared iron are added, and the whole is stirred up with the gluten used in applying the color, and is put on to the vessel prepared to receive it.

"Lákhi," the glossy deep brown generally seen on jugs and teapots, is made by a similar mixture, but substituting 1-16th of a seer of a manganese (anjani) for the iron.

"Kakrezi" a blackish green or olive color, is produced by—

Kánch, ...	½ seer.
Prepared iron (as above), ...	1 chittack.
Calcined copper (Chhil támba), ...	1 chittack.

The color having been prepared and reduced to a fine powder, it has to be applied with a brush to the surface of the unbaked pottery. The vessels to receive it must therefore be carefully smoothed over, and cleaned with a bit of wet rag. Inasmuch as the

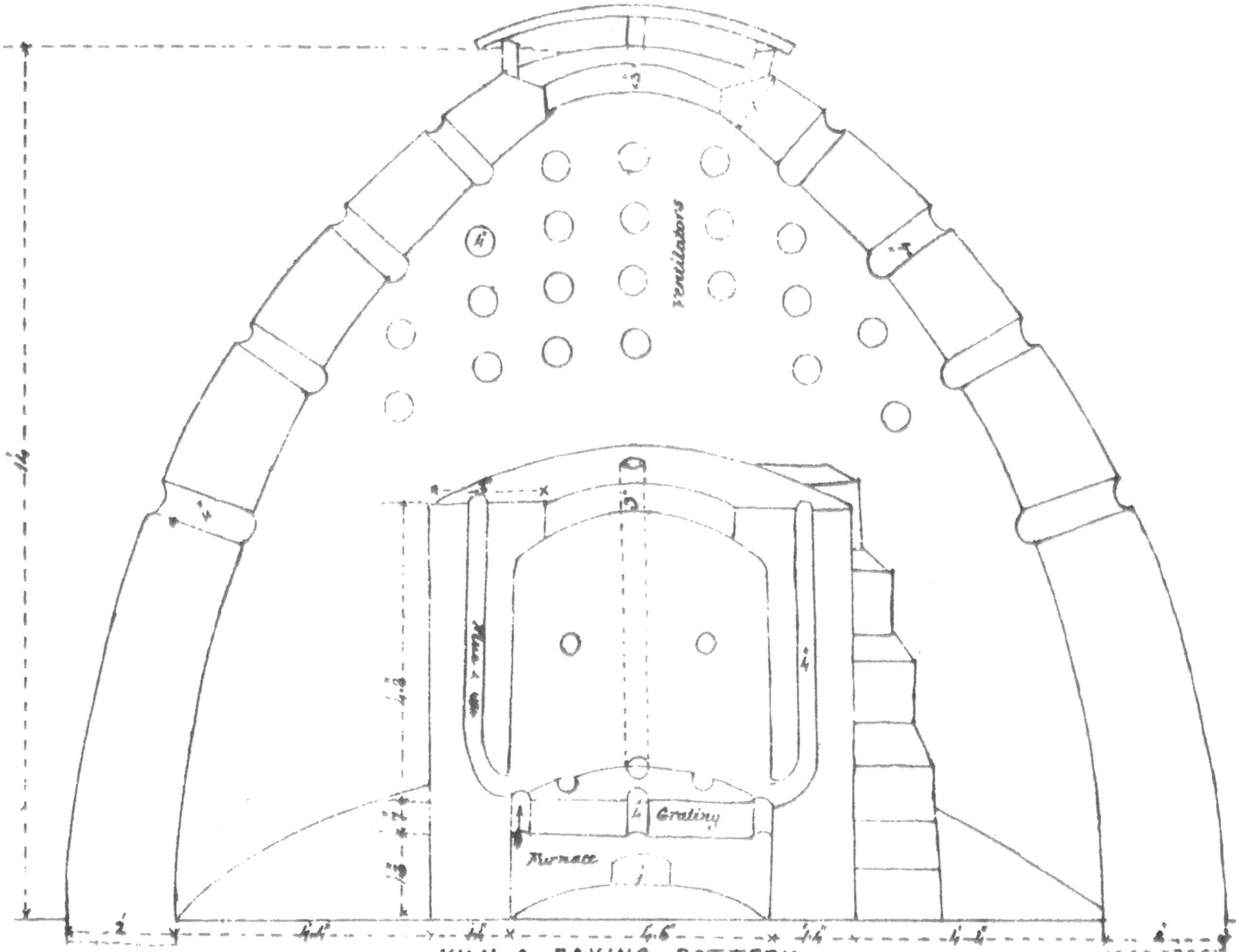

KILN for BAKING POTTERY:

Scale 1 inch = 3 Feet

pottery clay is red when burnt, there is fear of the more delicate colors being injured; accordingly they first prepare the surface of the vessel, after cleaning and smoothing it as just described, with an 'astar' or coating painted on, of kharya-mitti, a soft soapy-feeling whitish clay, brought *viâ* Multan from the Derajat and elsewhere.

The kharya-mitti is prepared as follows :—One seer of it is finely ground for two 'pahars' with two tolas of the 'bhimbri' gum. (*Acacia modesta*), and 'chál' * gum (*Conocarpus*) two tolas ; this is worked up with half a seer of water, then four seers more water are added. The whole mixture is strained through a cloth; the residue is ground up again with more gum till all passes through. The whole being left to stand, a fine precipitate is deposited, the clear liquor is drawn off. Two chitaks of borax, and two of finely powdered glass are mixed in, and the preparation is ready to be applied. With this mixture also they tip the points of the supports which hold the vessels in the baking furnance.

The vessel being so coated, the color glaze to be applied is mixed with one seer of "máwá," a liquid glutinous substance made with 'nisháta,' the gluten obtained by washing wheat flower and collecting the subsidence.

The 'nishásta' is ground with the color and a little water, for $\frac{1}{8}$ of an hour, then again with more water till the required consistence of a paint is obtained, and the mixture can be applied to the vessels. The vessels being carefully dried are placed in the furnace. The furnace is shewn in the plate. It consists of an outer bee-hived shaped dome or covering, perforated with ventilators; and an inner hollow cylinder, underneath which is a furnace fitted with four flues, one passing up each side of the cylinder. The bottom of the cylinder is grated, and on the grating, which has a circular area of size according to the structure of the kiln, the vessels are placed. Each is separately supported on small stands (sipái), being tripods of burnt clay, having three points on which the vessel rests; these are tipped with the 'astar,' because otherwise they would stick to the glazed surface when it melted, and require to be detached by force, leaving little holes on the surface of the vessels. The 'sipáis,' require to be made fresh for each changing of the kiln.

The kiln is fired with "ber" (*Zizyphus*) or "kikar" wood, cut in small pieces; these give very little smoke, which of course is a desideratum. Five maunds of wood supply a furnace of the size given in the plate. After five hours of heating, the fire begins to take effect; after seven the color swells; after nine, it melts and begins to spread, after ten it is transparent and smooth; the fire is then stopped and raked out, and water poured on.

Every ventilator and hole must now be carefully closed, for draughts of wind or dust would ruin the bake. On the third or fourth day, according to season, the the kiln will be cold, and the vessels may be taken out.

The great difficulty with native pottery is the extreme coarseness of the pottery clay, which gives a red color, and its liability to crack in the furnace, thus throwing away the glazer's trouble. The clay cannot be worked up very thin.

The jail potter recognizes the usual three kinds of clay: whitish, red—(or rather clay having a cast of red,) and black (having a grey tinge,—it is not a *black*). He says that

* Also called káthi gond.

no good clay can be got at Lahore; even that from the village Kot Khoja sai (black) is not good; he gets good clay from Gujranwalla and Hushyarpúr.

The following articles are included in the list of glazed pottery in 1864.

[9826].—Enamelled tiles, prepared under directions of E. GARSTIN Esq., of Amritsar.

[9833].—Glazed bricks for flooring (cost 8 annas each) by KUTBA of Sealkot.

[9835 A].—Cups and saucers, bowls and cream pans, by the same.

The following were from the LAHORE JAIL.

[9837—9850].—Breakfast service, turquois blue; Jars—pale lavender color; vases in green glazed pottery;—Soup tureen and dishes—10 pieces.

Jugs in various patterns, embossed with designs; &c. Plates glazed in burnished copper color; brown teapot; candle-sticks; basin and ewer; cheese cover and dish; two large glazed earthen vases suitable for a garden.

[9854].—Two vessels, one glazed, one unglazed, experimentally made from Kaolin obtained at Dalhousie.

Disintegrated granite rock may be seen in various parts of the Himalayas, and some of it would probably be found to yield a fairly tenacious Kaolin. The difference lies in the pureness of the color. It frequently happens that a slight yellow tinge is acquired in baking; this is ascribed to the presence of oxide of iron, but may be due to some fault in the furnace. During 1869, a bag of an apparently fine and white Kaolin was sent for trial from the Agror Valley (Hazára), but proved a failure: it had no tenacity, and was merely a disintegrated quartz rock.

[9855.]—Two pieces of pottery in black clay, which have been glazed with the lac colors described under the process of wood-turning and lacquered ware. A specimen of the same on glass was also sent, the lacquer seems to stand well on the pottery, but on glass shows a tendency to crack and peel off.—(The specimens were from Kasúr in the Lahore District).

[9867].—Specimens of variegated encaustic tiling (modern)—Jálandhar, exhibited by PANDIT MANPHUL.

[9877—9890].—Various glazed vases, basins, articles for table and domestic use, mostly plain, green and brown—RAWALPINDI JAIL.

[9897—9903].—Glazed articles for household and table use, JHELAM JAIL, and Pind Dádan Khan, (by MEGHA SINGH and GANESHA SINGH of Pind Dádan Khan).

[9909].—Various glazed bricks, ancient, and modern; glazed pottery in blue and white pattern and in plain colors, MULTAN,—(from the Jail and City manufacturers.)

[9948]. Encaustic tiles from ancient tombs.—Muzaffargarh.

[9958 &c.,]. The same from Dera Ghazi Khan.

[9966]. Glazed cups and basins, white, with a pattern in blue, and other plain colors (Peshawur Bazar).

[9970 &c.,]. Porcelain cups and teapots—imported Russian manufacture.

[ ]. Specimens of glazed pottery from the Jálandhar Jail.

In a memo. on the Delhi District by Mr. Thornton, there is the following notice of indigenous glazed pottery:—

"A rude kind of pottery, with a red and yellow glaze, is manufactured, but used chiefly in making toys and 'chillams' (the bowl of the 'huka'). The glaze is produced by an application of oxide of lead and borax. There is also a rude kind of porcelain, known as "Hindustani chíní", not unlike old Majolica. It is manufactured from *burbura* (a powder formed of disintegrated felspathic rock), and covered with a glaze produced from powdered glass (kánch) and a quartz powder. A blue color is produced by adding the powder known as rang níla* and brought from Jaipur; green is obtained from copper; and yellow as above described. This porcelain is not much used, except to make the small round ink-pots (dawát) for holding native ink, which are exported in considerable numbers."

* This is sold in the Bazar in the form of a blackish sand, and is an oxide of cobalt, the zaffre above described.

DIVISION II.

UNGLAZED POTTERY.

The only distinctive kinds of unglazed pottery in the Punjab are—

(1).—Ordinary clay pottery, either red or black when baked, made in all districts, in some better than others.

(2).—The fine pottery work of Rohtak.

(3).—The pale yellow and grey clay ware of the Deráját; the texture is gritty and very porous, hence the 'surahis' or water-coolers, are very excellent.

Under the first head however there is a considerable variety. In some districts there are skilful potters, who make bowls of pottery clay almost as thin as stout paper; they being porous, if filled with water, soon render it extremely cool owing to the rapid and easy evaporation. Such bowls are made in the Gujranwalla District. In Lahore I have seen thin pottery vases made double,—one vase within the other, and the outer layer perforated to show a pattern.

In some places the pottery is ornamented with an amalgam of mercury in patterns. Kangra sent some thin earthen vases, first silvered, and then covered with a coating of transparent lac coloring over the silver.

All pottery of every kind is done with the same rude apparatus. The kumhár or potter has a heavy wheel, made of clay mixed with bits of cotton, wool, or other material to bind it. A wooden axis projects from the centre of the under side, and works on a pivot of wood let into the ground; the workman sits with the wheel in front of him. In order to communicate a rapid motion to the potter's wheel, a small nick is made on the upper surface, in which the workman impinges a stick, and with a series of jerks urges it in spinning. The wheel remains only tolerably level while at its full speed, and soons begins to have an irregular eccentric motion, this renders it very difficult to mould any vessel perfectly true with such a wheel. The wheel is called "chak," and the turning stick "danda." The wooden block on which the axle turns is called "chopat." In the Upper Punjab a larger and steadier kind of wheel is made by a disc mounted on a wooden spindle. On the lower limb of the spindle a second disc, but made of wood, is fixed. A hole is now dug, across which two perforated bars are firmly fixed. The spindle or axis is held by them, so that the upper disc revolves just above the surface of the hole, and the lower one serves as a tread-wheel. The workman sitting on the edge of the hole, with his feet inside, turns the wheel by pushing the lower wooden disc with his foot. This produces a steady motion; this wheel is preferred for all large sized vessels. More information will be found in the Jury's Report which is printed further on.

Whichever wheel is used, a lump of kneaded clay is placed on the centre, and the workman moulds it in the usual way, constantly dipping his right hand in water, a bowl of which he keeps at his side. When the vessel is formed, he detaches the base of it from the wheel by dexterously sliding a tight stretched string across; this cuts the clay. If it is desired to make a very large vessel, such as a gharra, the workman uses a sort of short wooden mallet called "tathwá," to aid his right hand with which the moulding is done; in his left hand he holds another round mallet called 'karíru,' which he uses inside the vessel as it forms up. Natives do not take any very great pains in preparing the clay. They select material from a place which is known to yield it, and bring it in on donkeys, &c., in bags. When dry, they pound it well, and sift out all the coarse particles, putting the fine powder aside. The coarse pieces are thrown into water to soak, and when they are dissolved, the liquid clay is mixed with the fine powder already obtained, and the whole is trodden and kneaded with the feet.

In some jails, a masonry tank is built, and the clay well agitated with a large quantity of water ; the coarse particles at once fall to the bottom owing to their weight, but the water above is thick like pea-soup, this is poured off, and after a while settles, leaving a very fine mud deposited, and clear water above ; the clear water being cautiously drained off, a fair tenacious pottery clay results. The coarse particles in the first tank are worked up with water till they dissolve and form a similar liquid.

The potter's clay found in the alluvial plains of the Punjab is of four kinds : white, grey, red and black ; or rather is recognized under these names, by each kind having a whitish, reddish, or grey cast color. The first is not common ; the Derajat and Multan Districts alone have pottery made from it, and under this is included the Dalhousie Kaolin, *safed matti.* A sort of pipe clay is abundant however in the Salt Range, and at Aurangpúr near Delhi (see vol. I). The red and grey clays are the common ones ; they turn red on burning. Really black clay is not commonly found, but is so occasionally ; black clay, when of good color, makes very neat vessels, when burnt it is still black, but is aided in color by mixing in lamp black.

The specimens of unglazed pottery may now be described, with such notes to each specimen as may appear necessary.

ROHTAK.

[9787 &c.,].—A series of vessels executed in well burnt pottery, the surface ornamented with engraved devices and patterns. The articles are of a well tempered material, and of a pale reddish brown *(badámi)* color ; the pottery is finished with a shiny pearl-like substance, probably talc ground to an impalpable powder. This is the best pottery (unglazed) I have seen from any district. The collection consisted of fancy-shaped water-vessels, plates, cups, pipe bowls, covered pots &c.

LUDHIANA.

[9813].—Series of vases, jugs, &c., in baked clay. The vessels consisting of rather indifferent copies of classical and quasi-classical vases, are made of ordinary burnt clay with devices moulded in relief, and are colored with an unburnt smooth coating of dead white or pale pink paint (but see Jury Report *post.*)

KANGRA.

[9819].—Two small vases of thin unglazed pottery ; the surface has been silvered over with an amalgam of tin-foil and mercury. In one instance the silver was covered over with transparent purple lac varnish, giving a purple metallic lustre ; on the other was partly painted with green, shewing green and white (silver) pattern, and varnished over with lac varnish.

Hushyarpur.

[9822 &c.,]—A large "degcha" or water cauldron, of very well burnt pottery, would hold several gallons. Another specimen, showing successful burning of very large vessels in this district, is a huge oval jar, about five feet high and two feet in diameter, used for storing grain.

Amritsar.

[9832].—Besides other ordinary pottery, some of them well baked, there was a large terra-cotta garden vase, made under the directions of J. Gordon, Esquire, C. E.

Lahore.

A number of toys in pottery were in the collection ; and also an excellent series from Hushyarpur. They are made by pressing thin clay into hollow moulds, half the figure being formed in one, and half in the other mould, the two halves are afterwards joined, the figures are burned, and eventually colored by hand. Figures of men, birds, animals &c., are thus produced.

[9869].—A set of vases of burnt clay, painted with a white ground, and then with flowers on the white field, the whole being thickly varnished over with copal varnish. This is a very poor and perishable substitute for glazed pottery.

Gujranwalla.

From this district I have received some well burnt drinking cups and basins in perfectly black clay, very thin and porous ; also some brown clay basins as thin as paper almost, by Hayát, potter, of Gujranwalla.

Jhelam.

[9982].—Some very well polished and burned water goglets, of a bright even red color (Tahsil Chakowal.)

Rawalpindi.

There are some classical looking water goglets of rough gritty porous clay, spherical and much flattened, narrow mouth, and two handles on either side : the form is rather classical.

Shahpur.

The plain pottery of this district (Khusháb Tahsil) is well finished and good.

Montgomery.

A great variety of pottery was also sent from the Montgomery district, Tehsils of Hujra, Kamália, and Pák-Patan (No. 9920—9947).

Dera Ismail Khan.

We have here the specimens of white gritty porous pottery already alluded to. The material seems suitable in color and texture for producing large terra-cotta articles for garden use.

DERA GHAZI KHAN.

[9955].—Vessels similar to those last described of pale porous clay.

The pottery of Kálábágh (Bunnoo district) of a similar kind also deserves notice.

HAZARA.

[9974 &c.].—There are some black clay basins ornamented all over with an amalgam of tin and mercury, which, unlike those of Kasúr and Ludhiana district, have the silver pattern burnt in. The vessels are accordingly useful, as the silvering does not wash off. A large " surahi " of smooth red clay was similarly ornamented.

KOHAT.

[9975].—Here again we have pottery of pale yellow or white porous clay, like that described under Dera Ismail Khan. The vessels sent were a water jug of classical shape, a butter dish, and some other articles.

KASHMIR.

Specimens of the " Kangrè, " a sort of chaumière were sent. They are earthen pots contained in a peculiar sort of basket work, with a handle at the back, and are carried under the clothes for warmth in winter.

JURY REPORT ON PORCELAIN AND POTTERY.

The following is printed from the papers of the Exhibition of 1864 :—

Jury.

1. Dr. A. M. Dallas.
2. Mr. Baden Powell.
3. Mr. O. DeCortanze.
4. Lalla Kunhya Lall.
5. Major T. W. Mercer.
6. Major J. E. Cracroft.
7. General VanCortlandt.
8. Mr. T. H. Thornton.
9. Mr. C. P. Elliott.
10. Mr. W. P. Woodward, *Reporter.*

* * * * * * The process of manufacture in India is simply as follows :—

The clay having been procured, is mixed with water, and after one or two days standing thus, is well kneaded for four or five days more. A lump of the clay is then taken and turned on the wheel, until, under the dexterous handling of the potter, after going through a variety of forms, the requisite shape is attained. The vessels are then gently removed, being dissevered from the wheel by a string passed along while on the turn. They are first dried in the sun, and then baked, being closely piled together in a sort of kiln, the smaller articles being enclosed in large vessels kept for the purpose. Some few articles are cast in moulds.

The Indian potter's wheel is a rude and clumsy looking thing, but is not in all places of the same make and shape. In the lower provinces it is a large circular stone, resembling the upper mill-stone, turning on an iron or wooden pivot securely fixed in the ground. It is turned with a stick, and as long as the impetus lasts the potter works the clay in the centre, and then again uses the stick to quicken the motion. In some places the wheel is not unlike that of a common cart, but is fixed and turned in the same way.

In the upper parts of the Punjab, however, the construction is different. A hole is dug in the ground three feet or more deep, and the same in diameter. In this is fixed vertically, by two horizontal supports, an axle of wood, carrying at the lower end a wooden disc, and in the middle the working disc or table. The potter then sits on the edge of this hole with his feet inside, and turns the lower disc with his feet, and works the clay on the upper. This wheel has none of the defects of those first described, as it ensures a regular motion, without any delay or trouble in turning or throwing.

In the Punjab, and it may be said in India, there is no indigenous manufacture so common as pottery, almost every village having its potter. In some places they excel, as at Agra and Aligarh. At Rohtak, Gujranwala and Jalandhar, it is made remarkably thin, so as to be distinguished by the name of paper pottery ; but generally the out-turn is a rude rough description of pottery, though of great variety of form. It is made nearly altogether from the clayey deposits of marshes, tanks and canals, called "chikni" and "káli matti," with a slight admixture in some cases of river sand, but of no stony ingredient. This is pronounced to be the great defect which renders the pottery liable to suffer if subjected to the heat necessary for the commonest glazing.

The generality of articles made are water jars, drinking and cooking vessels, and other such vessels of great variety used by the poorer classes, though the first are in general requisition by rich and poor Europeans and Natives, and would not be improved by glazing. In some articles a rude sort of glazing is attempted, as in toys and chillams.*

In all the imperial cities of India, and as regards the Punjab, especially in Lahore and Delhi, may be seen on the walls of the public buildings and mosques, specimens of tiles. This art has been thought to be dying out, and among the specimens of glazed tiles exhibited, the Jury were struck with one set, which they at first supposed to be antique, but it has been since ascertained, very much to their surprise and satisfaction, that these were made expressly for the Exhibition by one Sharfdin of Jallandar; very good specimens of glazed tiles have also been contributed from Multán.

This art is known under the name of "kási." According to local tradition, it was introduced from China through Persia, by the Moguls, through the influence of Taimúr Lang's Chinese wife, and it is remarkable that the commencement of the practice of ornamenting the walls of mosques with colored porcelain, appears to be synchronous with the Mogul conquest of Persia; on the other hand, the art of glazing bricks, &c., was known to the ancient Semitic races,—*e. g.*, the Chaldeans and Arabians, and was introduced by the latter into Europe, and it is noteworthy that the word "kási," is not a Hindi or a Tartar word, but an Arabic word, akin to the Hebrew "kás" (a cup or glass.)

It has been remarked as somewhat surprising and unaccountable, that having advanced so far in the manufacture of porcelain, as to be able to cover their buildings with a coating of enamelling of the most brilliant colors and tasteful designs, the artizans seem to have come to a stand still, and never to have applied the art for purposes of domestic utility. The truth appears to be that they received no encouragement, there was no demand for such articles, and there is none still; among the natives themselves, as the higher classes universally use gold, brass, silver or copper dishes, there is no taste for ornamental crockery. Among the Hindús, a religious prejudice prevents them from using an earthen vessel twice, so that to break a *China* dish every time after using one, the cost being about four times greater than common pottery, would not answer in a pecuniary point of view. As regards the Mahomedans, they were ever moving about in camps, in the train of the Emperors, and to them, costly vessels of porcelain would be a nuisance.

Attempts have lately been made in some of the larger Punjab jails to manufacture glazed pottery, and as the Catalogue will show, all kinds of articles of English design have been attempted. By far the greatest attention has been paid, and success attained, in the Lahore Central Jail, but the energetic officer under those intelligent superintendence the experiments were conducted and have advanced so far, will be the first to acknowledge that the results, though encouraging, have not been thoroughly satisfactory.

Some specimens of ornamental plain pottery, urns and vases, from Loodiana, attracted attention. The designs, being uncommon and even elegant, bespeak an intelligent workman. It appears that about 25 years ago Colonel Claude Wade, for sometime on political duty at Loodiana, and known there as "Bakshi Wade Sahib," gave the manufacturer of these specimens, Jassa, some patterns of English pottery, which he has followed very successfully. He uses no glaze, but a paint made of chalk and gum.

* A description of the Delhi glazed pottery is omitted, as it has already been noted in the text.

The following is a list of the prizes :—

I.	Lahore Central Jail, ...	For best specimens of glazed pottery, ...	1st special prize—value Rs. 50, ...	Sir R. Montgomery.
II.	Ludhiana—Utum, ...	For elegancy of design and superiority of finish of specimens of plain pottery, ...	6 shares, value Rs. 60, ...	Exhibition Prize Committee.
III.	Jalandar—Sharfdin, ...	Glazed ornamental tiles,	2nd Special Prize, value Rs. 25, ...	Major Medley.
IV.	Multan, ...	Ornamental do.,		
V.	Lahore Central Jail, ...	Four large glazed garden vases, ...	3rd Special Prize, value Rs. 25., ...	Mr. J. Gordon.
VI.	Rawalpindi Jail,... ...	For good attempts at glazing, ...	3 shares, value Rs. 30, ...	Exhibition Prize Committee.
VII.	Rohtak, ...	For skill in mixing the materials,...	Ditto	Ditto.
VIII.	Multan Jail, ...	For attempts at glazing,	2nd Ditto 20, ...	Ditto.
IX.	Gugaira (Montgomery) Jail,	Ditto ditto	1st Ditto 10, ...	Ditto.
X.	Gujranwala, ...	For paper pottery, ...	Certificate.	
XI.	Kasúr, ...	For application of kharadi work to ornamenting pottery, ...	Certificate.	

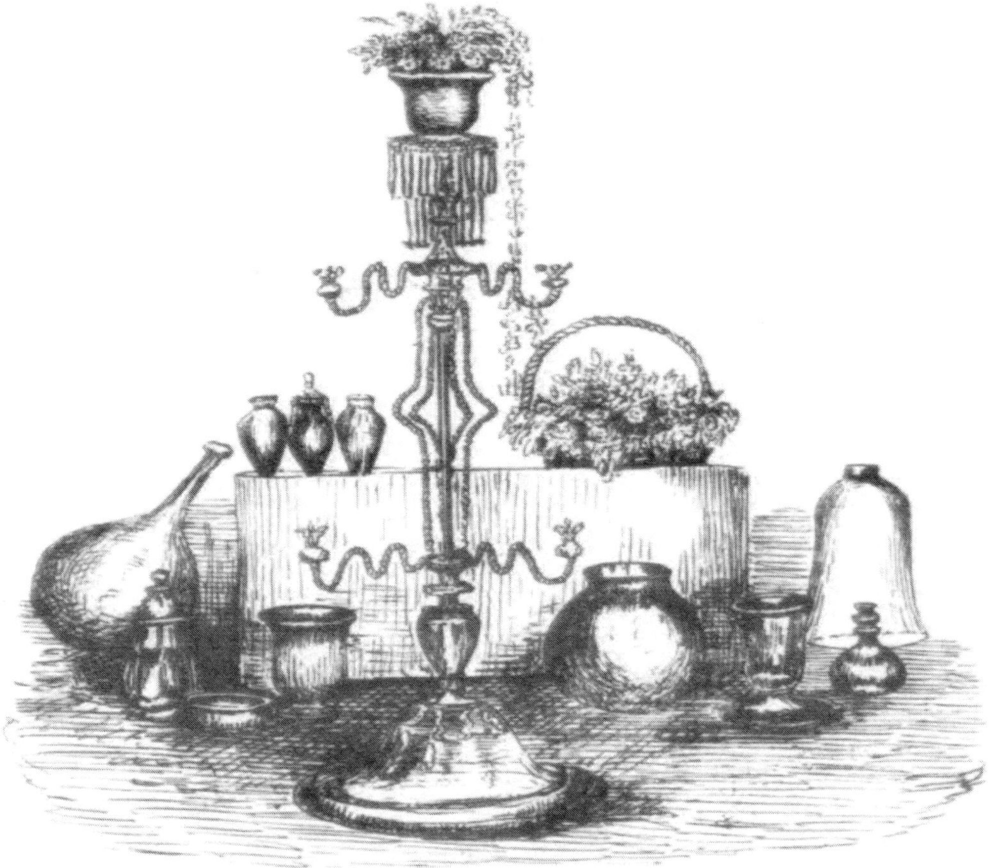

GROUP OF GLASSWARE.

CERAMIC VASES.—LUDHIÁNÁ.

CLASS XIX.

GLASS MANUFACTURE.

This manufacture is still in its earliest infancy in the Punjab. There is neither good material forthcoming wherewith to make pure glass, nor suitable furnaces to melt and to anneal it.

Two kinds of glass are made: white glass, and coarse blue or green glass, generally full of flaws and air-bubbles. White glass is made either of fused glass imported from Europe in the lump,* or of melted fragments of European vessels. The pieces are melted in a crucible and blown into the required shape.

Only small articles are produced. There is a tolerably good workman at Patyála and one at Lahore; both these can make small candle-shades, small vases, glass globes, and bottles. Lamp chimneys are so much in demand that they are often made, but these articles, in common with all native glass, from want of proper annealing, are very brittle and stand heat badly. To save the lamp chimneys, it is the custom to boil them in a pot-full of hay and water before putting them on a lamp.

At Lahore the workman was intelligent, and I succeeded in teaching him to draw glass rods, and thus to make flower stands of the pattern well known as "Exhibition vases." He also produced some twisted or spiral glass rods, which, fitted on to a dish of tin or glass, made a pretty flower-holder, the twisted handle appearing above the leaves and flowers which conceal the less sightly part of the stand or dish.

The coarse kind of glass is made by re-melting lumps of a crude greenish glass slag called "kánch."

This is made by collecting the sandy soil in certain places where it has a natural admixture of carbonate of soda efflorescing from the soil, and melting the mass over a fire. The "Reh" or 'Kalr' soil described in Vol. I, has generally a predominance of sulphate of soda, but in some places it is carbonate, and not sulphate, and the soil, if sandy, can be easily melted into glass. In some parts of Oudh the reh soil is full of carbonate, and it is melted into coarse glass, from which glass bracelets or bangles (churis) are made.

In places where the natural soil is not to be had, glass is made by melting quartzose pebbles (sang-i-safed) ground to powder with khár (potash) in equal parts. I believe this latter is the commonest way of making glass in the Punjab.

The only specimens of glass worthy of mention, came from—

Lahore, Hushyarpúr, Patyála, and Karnál.

The specimens are enumerated to show the sort of article produced, and a note of any peculiarities is added.

Lahore.

834.—[9999].—Flower baskets, with crystal glass handles (see annexed plate.)

835.—[10000].—A glass ornamental centre-piece for flowers (see annexed plate.)

* See extract from Jury Report after the Patyála specimens.

836.—[10001].—Table vase in the pattern of three small *amphoræ* joined together, and standing on three points.

837.—[10002].—A small chandelier, with glass drops; samples of glass rods, gum-pots, bottles, lamp glasses &c., were also sent, all these made by a man named Azím Beg and his pupils. I visited this man's workshop, a dingy little hovel, furnished with two or three dome-shaped furnaces covered in and made of clay.

The glass is melted in a crucible in one, and when melted a portion of the glass is withdrawn on the tip of an iron blow pipe and blown out. If the glass is to have a wide mouth it is opened out with a pair of iron compasses which are passed round inside while the glass is soft, and till an even circular rim is obtained. When bottles have to be made, the glass is blown, and while still soft, shut into a mould to keep it to the right shape. I believe the old man knows how to cast fused glass in a mould, provided the article is small enough; but he did not show me this. When the glass vessel is ready, it is put into another furnace, which consists of a hole in the ground with a flattened dome built over it, having a hole in the centre. The articles to be annealed are placed on the flat dome near the aperture, through which the heat escapes, the whole is covered over with a second dome of clay furnished with a door.

Sometimes the furnace is made in the ground, with a small passage down to the flue, and the surface of the ground above then forms the resting place of the vessel, the fire being underneath: there is an earthern covering built up outside. The furnaces are very small,—not above two feet in diameter. The Lahore workman had made some retorts and other vessels, including a good sized alembic of bluish semi-transparent and very vesicular glass.

HUSHYARPUR.

838.—[9993].—A glass jar (price Rupee 1.)

Small drinking cups, (3 annas each,) by KARIM BAKSH of DASUA.

These are of a deep blue color, but full of air-bubbles.

Some similar glass vessels were sent from Núrpur in the Kangra district, unaccompanied by any description. The following account has been received from Hushyarpúr.

Karim Baksh, "Churgar" (the glass maker or maker of glass "churis") says that the manufacturers select a sort of stone which is known by its readily pulverizing and yielding a white powder. (This is I suppose a quartzose or siliceous pebble.) This is powdered fine and mixed with fine flour in equal parts. Small lumps being made of the paste, they are dried on a fire, and baked in a forge, when a white powder or 'gach' results. If it is to produce white glass it is mixed with a solution of saltpetre and again burned; if they wish to make blue glass, they mix with two seers of gach, two tolahs of prepared or dead copper (*mará huá*) which are burnt together. The more copper, the deeper the blue. In order to prepare the copper, two tolahs of metal beaten out thin are taken, and spread over with a mixture of six mashas of salt, mixed with the 'gul' or refuse of the huka bowl, and then the whole mass is burned in a forge all day. The copper comes out black and powder like. This is collected in an iron ladle and once more heated, after which it is ground fine and mixed with the 'gach'.

The 'gach' melts under heat into glass, which is converted into vessels with a blow-pipe. A green color can be given by adding to the gach, tin and lead prepared (*mará huá*). Black anjani (manganese oxide), which can be had at Núrpúr in Kangra, being added to the gach, a purple color (*úda*) is obtained; paler or deeper according to the quantity added. Tin and lead prepared and mixed with the gach together with a small proportion of anjani, give a yellow color (*basanti.*)

There is nothing remarkable in the method of blowing glass. They separate the vessels from the blower's tube by a touch of cold water, and mould the vessels while soft with an iron tool to adjust the size of the mouth and lip of the vessels.

The processes which now remain to be described, are first, the manufacture of silvered glass of Karnál and Pánipat; second, the manufacture of glass churis, ornaments which are worn by the dozen as bracelets on either arm, chiefly by the lower orders; and thirdly, the manufacture of looking glasses, practised only, as far as I am aware, at Delhi.

The Karnál District collection consisted of—

839.—[9988].—Large pear shaped vessels of thin and course blown glass, used in subliming salammoniac:—From Kaithal. See Vol. I p. 89.

840.—[9989].—Glass globes silvered inside. These are intend to be hung up for ornament; they are not unlike the silvered globes sold in Europe, but are not so well made, and the orifice being very large, has to be clumsily filled up with bits of glass and a fringe of gilt tinsel.

A string of large beads, silvered inside, was exhibited from Pánipat.

The following account of glass making, and glass silvering, has been kindly furnished me by Major Parsons, Deputy Commissioner of Karnál.

" A mixture of powdered and sifted " sang-i-surkh," (red sandstone, obtainable at Agra) and sajji in equal parts, with a seer of saltpetre to each maund of the mixture, is baked in a brick tank or oven, until the material becomes white. It is then subjected to further heat in a closed furnace, in which the mixture is kept at a high temperature for two days and nights until completely melted. A seer of the mixture is then removed at a time on the end of an iron blow-pipe (*dhanyári*) and blown out gradually into a globe. When the globe is complete, a wet cloth is passed round the neck, after which the globe can be separated from the pipe by a slight blow from the edge of the fire-tongs;—the concussion causes the neck to snap through at the wetted part, and the globe which is resting on the ground, becomes detached. An iron rod smeared at the end with lac is then applied to the bottom of the globe outside, thus:

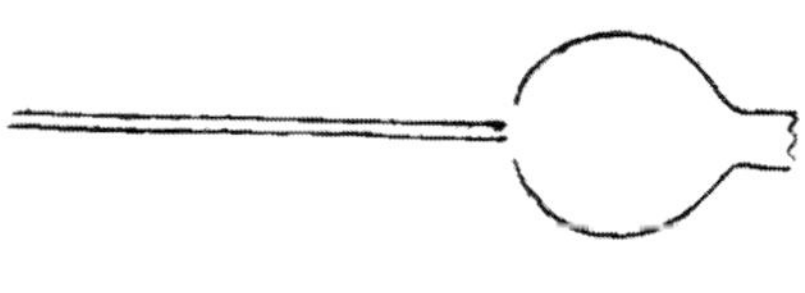

to which rod the globe adheres; the globe is then held in the mouth of the furnace and again heated for a few seconds, after which it is taken out. While held at the end of the rod, neck upwards, a spoonful of the silvering mixture (afterwards described) is poured in through the neck, the globe is turned round and round while the mixture spreads all over the inner surface, adhering as it spreads. The rod is now removed by a slight wrench (this however invariably stars the bottom of the globes).

" *Silvering mixture ;*—A seer of pure tin (kalai) and a maund of lead, are melted together, and 4 tolas of quicksilver are added to the mixture. An amalgam is thus formed.

" The glass globes, are generally made about the size of ordinary gharas : they are then broken up and sold in pieces, to be subsequently cut into different shapes for spangling women's dresses, or ornamenting the walls of ceilings of rooms * &c. A few globes are occasionally kept intact for disposal, but there is no trade in them.

" The manufacturer is not able to dispense with the breaking of the necks of the globes. I got him to make some glass bottles for the Dispensaries, but as the necks were all broken off, and he was unable to make lips to them, the bottles were not of much use.

" The art has been practised for four or five hundred years ; especially the manufacture of silvered glass used for ornamenting the walls of palaces, for trinkets as " ársis " and necklaces, and for making studs of pieces of looking glass which are put on to women's scarves in parts of the country ; such a dress has already been described."

The remaining specimens of fairly well made glass consisted of the following :—

PATYALA.

841.—[10015].—Candle-shades.

842.—[10016].—Two ink-stands.

843.—[10017].—Two glass plates.

844.—[10018].—Two glass bottles.

The Jury Report on glass gives the following note of Patyála glass.

" Good specimens are exhibited of glass articles made at Patyála and Lahore ; the former being the clearest and best. This is, however, owing to the material. The manufacturer of the Patyála articles is in the employ of the Maharaja, and he has two assistants. The raw material is imported from England in the shape of bricks or blocks weighing about 4 lbs. each ; it costs at Patyála Rs. 40 per maund. He also uses bits of broken white bottles, which are melted down and blown through an iron tube. The articles exhibited are little inferior to similar articles of European manufacture. He acknowledges having learnt the art about 30 years ago from a gentleman at Cawnpore, whose name he forgets.

" The Lahore manufacturer uses only broken English glass, and the result is very fair. The designs of the articles exhibited were furnished by a member of the Jury. "

Before closing this Class, a note must be made of the churis or glass bangles of colored glass. Some were sent from Gúrgaon, Karnal, Rohtak, (Jhajjar), Hushyarpur, Jhelam and Maler Kotla. Some of them were. I expect, made of the natural alkaline earth, particularly those of Gúrgaon, Karnál, and Maler Kotla.

These glass bracelets are worn, a good many on each arm, by children and the poorer class of women, who cannot afford silver or gold ornaments.

* Most of my readers will have seen the " Shísh mahals " in the Lahore Fort and at Delhi, and elsewhere, the ceilings are covered with bits of looking glass fixed in stucco.

The art of making glass bracelets or churis is as follows :—The workman is called churi-gar. His tools are :—

Kundi, of sizes—Iron hooked rods with wooden handes.

Tirkala—A long iron wire pointed, mounted in a reed handle.

Málá—A long narrow iron spoon, shaped like a spear-head.

Síñkh ; A long pointed iron rod.

Sarhindi—An iron rod with a cone of clay on one end, so that circles of different sizes can be obtained by using the point of the cone for small circles and pushing it farther in to produce a wider aperture.

Kharchi—A small ladle.

Nali—Blower's tube.

Silái—Iron spikes of sizes.

Tongs and furnace.

A wooden cylinder—' muttha '—to keep the bracelets on.

They have three furnaces : one called " haus," in which they prepare the ' kach ' or glass ; one, in which the melted material is kept for use by the maker of glass articles ; and thirdly, a small furnace in which they make the míná or enamel glass coloring for ornamenting the bracelets.

The furnace is fed with ' karír ' (*Capparis*) wood, as it gives a fiercer fire.

Glass is made by melting ' lál-pathar,' a red sandstone with sajji. They make the material into balls (pinní), and burn it all night with a slow fire. Next day they heat it more fiercely, and then it fuses into ' kach.' The glass is then removed with the aid of the kundis or hooks.

To make bracelets, some kach is placed in an earthen pot and melted, the progress being tested with an iron rod. The workman then takes a " síñkh, " and lifting a portion of the glass, makes a thick ring on the rod ; he loosens this when cool, and hanging it on the pointed end of the rod, puts it into the furnace, spinning it round and round on the rod till the ring opens out and forms a bracelet, he then withdraws it, and slips it over the conical mould or ' sarhindi, ' so as to adjust it to the size required ; when cool, it is finished.

The coloring is done afterwards, with lac applied to the glass while warm, so that the color sticks, or else ornaments are made by melting small points of colored glass rods (míná) and applying them.

LOOKING-GLASS MAKING.

Last of all, I have to make a note of the " 'ainasáz," or looking glass-maker's trade. The art is almost entirely confined to Delhi, where also the glasses are set in a variety of ornamental wood and ivory frames, and the backs finished up with a sheet of plain glass, painted in rather gaudy patterns on the inside to give the effect of enamel. In a note on the Delhi District already quoted, Mr. Thornton says :—

" This is a thriving manufacture. The glass is brought in an unpolished state from Damascus and Halb (Aleppo), *via* Calcutta." I should say that the glass is of two kinds: first, that intended for looking glasses, which is always extremely thick. A native or Delhi mirror is at once recognized by its nearly always having the edge of the glass bevelled off or cut down towards the frame, showing how thick the glass is. Some are however made flat and plain like English glasses. The second kind of glass is the clear white glass, generally oval in shape, used for covering the Delhi ivory miniature paintings. These glasses require to be well smoothed off at the edges and to exhibit a beautifully clear and polished surface. Mr. Thornton continues, " the glass is polished first with 'burbura' (a powder of disintegrated felspathic rock) and afterwards upon a hone made of the wood of the semal (Cotton tree—*Bombax*) sprinkled with powdered flint or emery.
* * * There are about thirteen manufactories, and about 200 artizans employed."

The looking glass maker " 'aina-sáz " is the workman who silvers the glass.

His tools and materials are the following :—

1. Diamond pencil (cutter).
2. A flat perfectly smooth stone slab " sil," generally of the red sandstone of Jaipur &c.
3. Pincers, files, compasses, saws, scissors.
4. Corundum or emery powder.
5. " Potli khákistar."—A small bag or dabber filled with wood ashes.
6. Mercury, tin-foil, and glue.

He first spreads tin-foil evenly on the stone slab, and pours over it the quicksilver, which he gently spreads by the aid of his bag or dabber (No. 5); the mercury adheres to the foil, and the surplus is allowed to run off. The sheet of glass is now let down delicately and exactly over the silvered surface; the silvering adheres of itself to the glass. The plate being removed, is left for a time in a slanting position, so that an excess of mercury which still remains, may completely drain off. This done, the glass is ready to be framed.

CLASS XX.

ORNAMENTAL OR FANCY MANUFACTURES.

There is not much to be entered in this Class, but my account of Punjab manufactures would not be complete without an enumeration of a few of the fancy articles which Punjab workmen make. The enumeration is quite heterogeneous like the Class itself.

845.—[10042].—A small round box, made of transparent horn, by Kanyha Lál of Kotla, (Ludhiana district).

846.—[10043].—A parrot imitated in paper, price Rs. 1-8, by Bhawáni of Ludhiana.

847.—[10045].—Paper flowers by Teka of Ludhiana.

Natives are very good at making paper flowers: the green leaves accompanying them are often made of talc stained green.

848.—[10100]—A narrow necked bottle, in the interior of which letters in Persian and English are painted in black—AMRITSAR.

Several of these articles were exhibited. In some cases; the letters were cut out in black paper and stuck on after the fashion of the now somewhat bygone art of "Potichomanie," others were painted with a brush.

849.—[10103].—Wax flowers—Amritsár (exhibited by Sirdar BHAGWAN SING).

850.—[ ].—A toy, consisting of a round looking glass to represent a pond, with a number of small paper ducks thereon, having their heads suspended so as to move at the least shake.—LAHORE.

851.—[ ].—A peep show. A small square box with a lens to look through, displaying a small gilded temple, trees, and flower beds, multiplied by reflection in small mirrors placed at the sides. (LAHORE.)

852.—[ ].—A small cannon of silver, mounted on a marble slab. This is furnished with a sun dial. Over the touch hole of the cannon two upright pieces support a burning glass, with a slide to incline it to a proper angle, and to the dial. The angle being such that the focus of rays converges on the touch hole at midday—the gun is supposed to fire of itself at noon—(I doubt this article being of native manufacture.) Exhibited by NAWAB JAHANGIR KHAN of LAHORE.

853.—[10170].—Boxes made of straw—Chakkowal, JEHLAM.

854.—[10269].—A boat carved in marble, also ducks of white marble, made hollow, so as to float (PATYALA.)

855.—[ ].—A "Jack in the box". A narrow wooden box, on drawing the lid of which, a cobra snake, made of horn, starts out.

856.—[ ].—Boat made of pith. This is an article made as a toy, of narrow strips of pith joined together.

857.—[ ].—A glass bottle with a narrow neck, which contains a wooden charpoy, a ball, and other articles. The wonder is how these articles were introduced.

858,—[ ].—Ornament made by shaving up a piece of soft white fig wood (*Ficus glomerata*), these shavings curl up, and so a sort of Catherine wheel ornament is produced.

Paper lace.—This is most ingenious. It is all done with hand cutting and fine scissors. The patterns are beautiful. It is executed by Karím Baksh, Gulám Husain, and Kallu, of Shahábád in the Ambála district.

859.—[ ].—Siphon toy in pottery. Being a large cup, with a female figure in the centre, holding a child on her head. The cup is filled with water, but so soon as the water reaches the brim, the whole runs out through an aperture underneath the figure. This is effected by some syphon arrangement, but I have failed to discover it. The toy is supposed to represent the mother of Krishna, who crossed the Jamna with the child on her head: fear for the child's safety being excited by the depth of the flood, she was gratified by finding the water suddenly recede so soon as it touched the child's body.

860.—[ ].—Lac bracelets, ornamented with beads, Delhi.

I must add to this class an account of making lac bracelets or churis, which are worn like the ivory and glass churis already described. They are made in many places, especially Delhi, and the process in the Punjab exactly resembles that described in a report on one of the Central Indian Districts, which I have unfortunately mislaid, but which I have used for the purpose of quoting the recipe for making the gold solution that gives the gold lustre to these pretty but fragile toys.

Refined or purified lac, is mixed with the fine powder of burnt bricks, and the two are heated together in an iron pan and stirred till perfectly combined. The lac is drawn out into sticks of the thickness of the intended bracelet, and this is done by rolling the sticks on a flat board while still hot. Pieces of the requisite length are cut off, and each piece is bent round and joined, and placed on a wooden cylinder to cool, and to be further ornamented. The glazing with gold solution and silvering is generally done before the sticks are cut up.

To silver the sticks, tin leaf or foil is mixed with half its weight of dry glue, and these are pounded and ground together for a long time, till in about six hour's time they amalgamate. The mass is then thrown into very hot water, when it crumbles into little pieces. They then stir this up and pour off the water, repeating the operation till all dirt and impurity in the water disappears. When the solution is quite pure, they boil it up and let it stand, carefully covered, for the night.

Next day the silver solution is found deposited. This is spread with a brush on the lac, and burnished by rubbing over with strings of glass beads. If it is desired to produce the effect of gold, the silvered lac is painted over with a transparent yellow varnish prepared as follows:—

Gum myrrh (bol) is boiled in sweet oil in proportion of 40 to 48. The liquid is strained through a cloth; the sediment thrown away and the oil set aside. An earthen pot is now smeared with clay on the underside, and its mouth is closed up with an earthen cover, the edges of which are luted over with clay, so as to render it air tight. This is heated red-hot over a fire. When quite red, the mouth is opened, and little bits of sundras (copal) are thrown in. The same weight of sundras as of bol is used; the mass is stirred and the mouth again closed. The stirring and heating are repeated till the copal is thoroughly reduced. The myrrh and oil solution is now added to it, and the whole heated and stirred, after this the mixture is strained through a cloth and is ready for use. The lac bracelets are often further ornamented by having little glass beads and bits of tin foil stuck along the edge.

CLASS XXI.

PRIME MOVERS &c.

This Class is unrepresented.

CLASS XXII.

DIVISION I.

MACHINES FOR RAISING WATER.

The only machines which are used for raising water are, the Persian wheel, used in most wells in the Bari Doab, and but little used in those parts of the Punjab bordering on Hindustan; the "chalár", or small wheel on a similar principle, used for raising water from tanks, ponds, and low level canals; the "Lao-charas" or rope and bucket, used in the Ambala District and elsewhere; and the rude long armed lever and pot called "Dhanklí,"* used in Hushyarpur and elsewhere.

I have given a drawing of the Persian wheel, and described all the above named machines in Vol. I, at page 206 *et seq*, where the subject of irrigation is treated of. But under this Class I can appropriately inform the reader of the different parts of which these machines are made; nor will it fail to strike the student of languages how minute the people are in their nomenclature. Every peg and bit of iron or other material used in making up these implements has its appropriate and distinctive name.† It will be observed also that the name varies according to the District. This change of agricultural nomenclature has already been noticed when we spoke of the various soils in Volume I.

The parts of the 'Lao-charas' are those given by MR. WYNYARD.

'Láo'—the hempen rope.

'Bhawan'—the wheel over which the rope passes, (made of 'kikar' or 'shisham' wood and iron.)

"Kohar"—the groove on the edge of the wheel for the rope to run in.

'Mán dal'—an iron hoop which keeps the mouth of the water bag open.

---

* This has been in the first Volume, incorrectly written "Dhenkli."

† The same remarkable variety of names will be observed in the jewellery list, and above all in the names for the kinds and varieties of cattle in use among the Gujars or Bar tribes, whose principal occupation is cattle grasing. Not only is every shade and combination of color distinguished by an appropriate name, but the turn of a horn, the shape of a tail or ear, is sufficient to give rise to a distinct epithet.

'Charas' or 'charsa'—the leather water bag.

'Kilì'—the pin which unites the lás and the yoke.

Partala—a leathern apron, worn behind by the driver of the bullocks—this prevents his getting cut by the tight strained rope.

The parts of the Dhankli are merely :—The long lever of 'sál' or 'shisham' wood called "dhanklí." The earthen pot, wide mouthed and large, in which the water is raised is called 'karwála'; and the rope which is attached to it is 'berah.'

I will now give a table showing the parts of the Persian wheel, both in the Panjabi and in the Cis-Sutlej dialects.

The reader is referred to the sketch of the Persian wheel at Vol. I, p. 208.

Parts of the well gear.	Panjabi Name.	Cis-Sutlej Name.
1. The horizontal lantern wheel, ...	Dhól, ...	Chakal.
2. Its shaft or axle-tree, ...	Trikala, ...	Bhalohal.
3. The upper rim of the lantern, also the lower, ..	Ganyá.	
4. The bars between the rims, into the interstices of which the teeth of the vertical wheel work, ...	Khubba.	
5. The small wooden pegs which secure the ends of the "Khubba" projecting through the surface of the upper "Ganyá," ...	Dhatúrí.	
6. The beam resting between two pillars which form the socket into which the upper point of the axle of the Dhol works, ...	Kárjan, ...	Gangan.†
7. The crooked stick which passes through the beam and holds the axle of the Dhol. ...	Makra, (?) ...	Makra.
8. The vertical wheel, the teeth of which work in the lantern wheel, ...	Chuhakli, ...	Chaklí.
9. The teeth of it, ...	Búrya.	
10. Its axle or shaft carrying at one end the chuhakli, and at the other the well wheel (bair,) ...	Lath, ...	Lath.
11. The cross beam or main spoke of the chuhakli,	Dhakar.	
12. Two lighter spokes crossing it at right angles,	Bázú.	
13. The catch which prevents the vertical turning backwards, ...	Kutta, ...	Addá or Kutta.

* In Cis-Sutlej it either rests on walls or pillars, or on a forked pole "tak" at one end, or an upright or "Dho'i" at the other.

Parts of the well gear.	Punjabi Name.	Cis-Sutlej Name.
14. The beam fixed across the centre of the well's mouth, which supports the shaft or "lath" of the skeleton wheel on which the ropes and water pots are fixed, ...	Jallan, ...	Jhálu.
15. A hole in the Jallan to serve as a socket for the end of the axle "lath," ...	Tálwa.	
16. The wheel at the end of the Jallan, ...	Bá'ír, ...	Bá'ír.
17. The rope frame which hangs over the bair and dips into the well, ...	Málá, ...	Mál.
18. The water pots fixed on the málá at intervals,	Tind, ...	Tíndar.
19. Sticks which project from the side of the well and touching the 'Ba'ir' wheel, keep the mal or rope work in its place. The two act as forestay and backstay, ...	Sútlar, ...	Jal thaman on the one; side Súttar, on the other.
20. Cross bars, like the rounds of a ladder between the two ropes of the málá, ...	Arerián, ...	Gíri.
21. A wooden splash board or guard, fixed at the inner side of the well to prevent dirt being kicked down by the bullocks in passing, ...	Baríla.	
The water being raised in the pots, pours into a series of troughs over the well's mouth.		
22. The first which is fixed under the wheel and parallel to it, ...	Párchá, ...	Párchá.
23. The second at right angles to it, ...	Bári.	
The third leading from the "Bárí" to the field or reservoir &c. ...	Níshár, ...	Násár.
24. The pole with seat for the driver at the end, formed by two forked branches, and with a webbed seat of string, ...	Gádí, ...	Gádhar.

(N. B.—See also the class "Agricultural Implements.")

DIVISION II.

Is not represented by any indigenous exmaples.

DIVISION III.

The common forms of carriage are three :—

(1). The country cart is called "gárí," or "gadah,"* and with the epithet "do-baldí," char-baldí," according as it is drawn by two or more bullocks. Less than two are never employed. The term hackery,† so often used by Europeans, is not known in the Punjab.

(2). The "Ekka" or "Yakka" (*i. e.*, the one horse) and

(3). The "Bailí," a sort of large "Ekka" drawn by two bullocks.

The "Rath" is a large four-wheeled vehicle, with a domed and ornamented pavilion of cloth and tinsel over it; though seen towards Delhi, is not used in the Punjab.

A country cart, though very clumsy, is very well adapted to the style of travelling; great speed is not required, and the roads traversed being "kacha," that is, made without metal, are soon worn into deep and irregular ruts, which would tell sorely on a cart of neater manufacture, and with much stiff iron work and joinings. The native cart, from its style of build, and the few joints it has (and those always of wood) gives and yields, creaks and groans along, but never breaks down ; even a wheel giving way is a rare occurrence.

A cart with two bullocks will carry 20 maunds of 80 lbs, and do 15 miles in a day. A three bullock carries 30 maunds, and a four bullock gárí 40 to 45. More than this is not ordinarily wanted in a cart.

The wood work of a cart is made of Kikar (*Acacia*), Ber (*Zizyphus*) or tút (Mulberry) or Shisham (*Dalbergia Sissu*). The Coniferous woods are neither strong nor elastic enough to stand the wear and tear.

The cart is framed upon the principle conveyed by the conjunction of the lines in fig. 1 of the plate.

The bottom of the cart is formed by two stout shafts called (ûd) inclined to one another, as in the lines *a. a. a.* These are kept in place by cross bars *b. b. b. b. b. b.* called "tíkání". The ends of the shafts (ûd) meeting into one, form the pole on either side of which the bullocks are yoked; at the point where they meet a wooden but or cap is fixed, called "sunni," to which the yoke beam, "jhúla" is transversely tied. To form the platform at the bottom of the cart, short planks are filled in between the bars (tikání—*b* &c.) The wheels are supported by iron axle-pins, between the axle "tura" under the shafts *a a*, and the outer beams *d. d.* called "painjni." These beams are supported by two cross beams fastened under the platform of the cart (*c. c. c.*) and called "tír."

* Called chakrá in Rohtak and neighbouring districts.

† What this word is I cannot discover. It is neither Arabic, Persian, Hindi nor Bengali, and had it been one of the Southern or Western dialects, PROFESSOR WILSON would have noted the fact. In Wilson's Glossary a derivation from a Portuguese word "accuretai" (to carry) is suggested. The nearest Hindi word is "hakarna" to drive cattle.

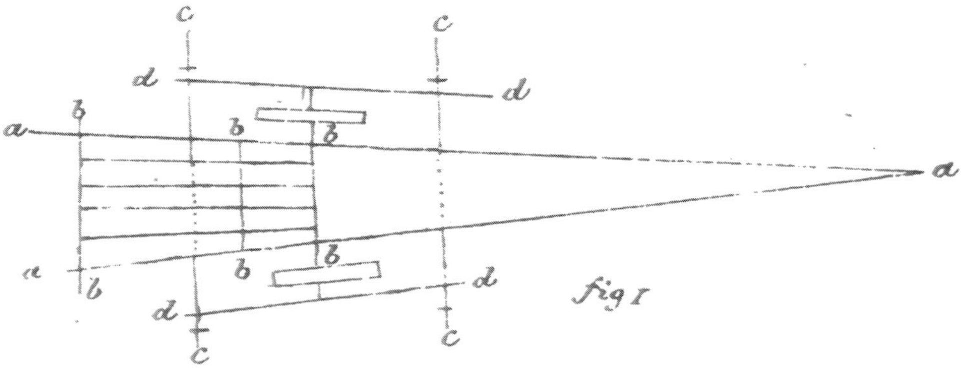

fig I

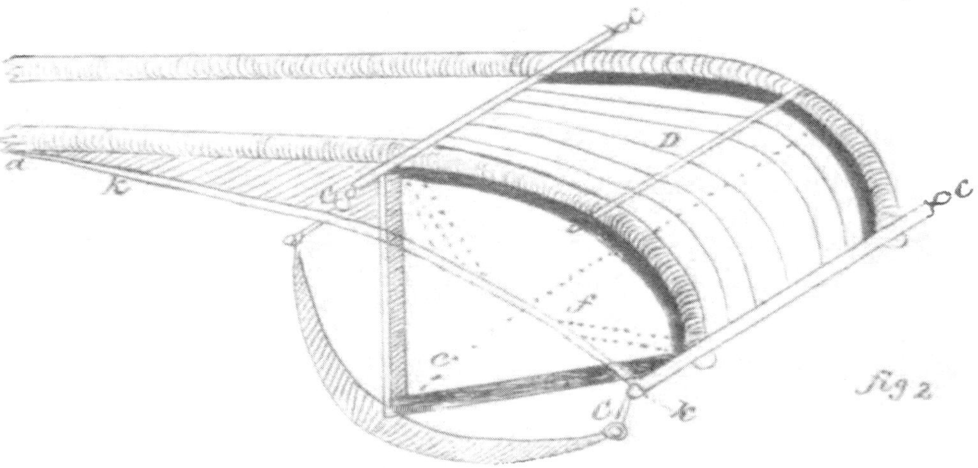

fig 2

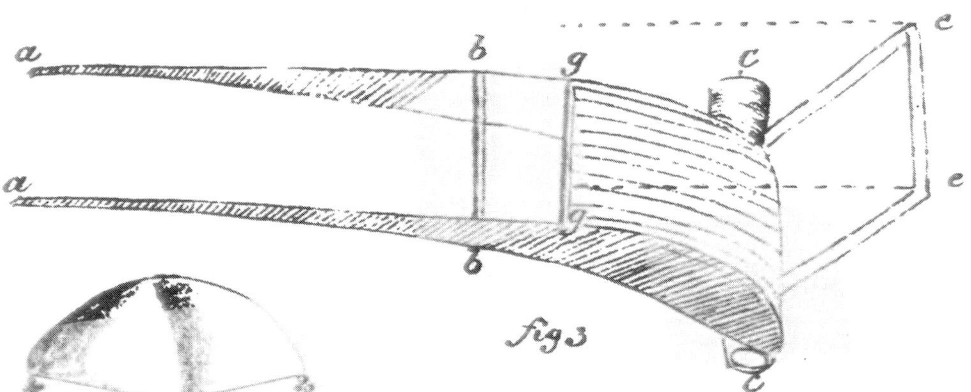

fig 3

fig 4

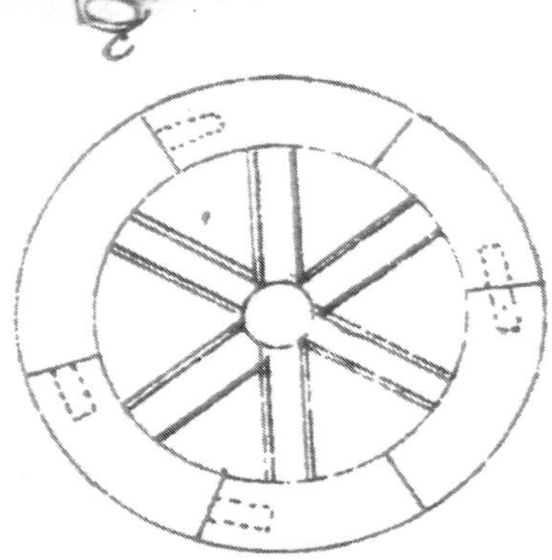

fig 5

Goods placed on the platform are prevented from falling off by a high railing on either side, called "munni" or "khalúah" (Cis-Sutlej), the poles of which are stuck out into the shafts *a. a. a. a.*, and which can be filled in either with net work, matting, or simple railing bars, according to the nature of the goods to be carried.

The wheels of a cart are made with a very heavy felly, in separate pieces, and no tire (fig. 5). The spokes are six in number, each consisting of two parallel bars, as in the cut. The pieces of the felly are deeply mortised one into the other as indicated by the dotted lines: no nails or bolts are used, except that occasionally an iron plate is nailed over the joint. The wheels are consequently very tough, but yielding, and are well adapted to the deep-rutted country roads.

In the Cis-Sutlej, Mr. Wynyard gives the following names for parts of the cart. The body without the wheels is "rerá;" the axle "awan;" a ring of iron round the axle "ánda;" a second and smaller ring "ándi." The other names are as before given.

The "bahli" is a carriage for conveyance of people, and is drawn by two bullocks; it is comparatively light in actual drawing weight, though clumsy in appearance, being constructed principally of bamboos covered with leather. The frame work, or basis on which the whole depends, is illustrated by fig. 2.

Two bamboos, *a. a.*, curved at the lower end, are inclined so as to enclose a broad space at the one end and come to a point at the other, these are called "phar." They are crossed at the commencement of the curve down and at the extreme end by cross bars *C. C.*, and *c. c.*; called, the front one, "tikání," the hinder one "ánk." The space between is filled up with five bamboos called "májá" and little cross bits "dandia" (not shown in the figure); and the whole is strengthened by the iron side bits between *C.* and *c*, and by a cross bar of iron called "talwattí." A small curved bamboo, indicated by the dotted line *K. K.*, joins the bottom of the curve with the shaft, and various wooden cross bits, indicated by the dotted bars *f. f.*, support it, and a cross bar underneath, parallel to *D.* (called mairâb) holds the whole firm. This entire frame work is covered with leather.

The wheels are supported by two bars (called tulawaí) which meet at the point *G.* At this point the axle pin of the wheel is inserted, and the other end rests in the curved beam *H. H.* (painjní), which besides receiving support from the under beam "mairâb," is firmly tied at either end by ropes to the knobs of the cross bars *C. C.*, *c c.*

The whole frame work and wheels in this state is called "tángá," and is used to carry large loads of grass, cotton, &c. If it is used for carriage, then a flat frame or platform, with the bottom of webbing like a bedstead, and carrying four uprights, forming a canopy, is put on (fig. 4).

The whole canopy is fixed on over the sloping frame in the last figure, so that the pole *a. a.*, (saongí ki talwatti) rests on the pole *C. C.*, in the former figure, and the front of the platform on the pole *C. C.*, to which it is firmly tied down with ropes. The whole of the seat and canopy is collectively called "pírí" or "saongí." The webbed seat is stretched over a wooden frame, of which the two side bars are called "jeru" and the fore and aft ones "báí." Pieces of wood let in at the corners for strength and to hold the uprights, are called "dhíwat"; the four uprights are called "dandá;" and the cane work roof and the cloth covering called "chatri;" the ornamented bars behind, (see fig.) nine in number, are called "táriya." The bullocks are yoked just as in a "gárí."

The " Ekka" or " Yakka" being drawn by one horse, it is not possible to adopt the arrangement whereby the bamboos forming the frame work are brought together so as to form the pole of the vehicle, otherwise the principle of the construction is the same (see fig. 3.)

A. A., are the shafts, made of an upper and lower bamboo, with cross sticks; *b. b.* is the dandya on which the driver puts his feet, *g. g.* is another bar, and from this the space is filled in by seven bamboos, and the frame work covered with leather. The lower cross bar of the frame carries two wooden blocks (addí) which support the axle tree " dhura." It is in the method of supporting the wheels that the " yakka" differs from the " bahli." In the former there is a regular axle-tree, which the support of the wheels in the "bahli" has been explained to be without such a piece. The seat and canopy, " píri" and " chatri" are fixed on to the frame from *g. g.* to *e. e.* just as in the case of the " bahli." The shafts are furnished each with a stick attached by a ring near *A* and called " supai," by which the carriage can be propped up, otherwise the balance when the horse is out would be to throw it down on the shaft ends. The wheels of an " ekka" are made like those of the cart, only lighter, and the pieces of the felly are not mortised together, but joined by small iron plates on either side secured with bolts.

In connection with this Division, I think a suitable opportunity occurs to print the report of the Jury at the Exhibition of 1864, which describes the carriages in that collection. Though of European fashion, and nearly all made under European supervision, the actual work is native. There is one native carpentering firm, Bhujjan Lal and Co. of Jullundur, which builds European carriages; and at every large station native workmen are to be found who can paint, repair and restore carriages. A great deal of the success attained in such work is due to the knowledge of iron work and painting acquired in the workshops attached to the Punjab and Delhi Railway at Lahore.

JURY REPORT ON CARRIAGES.

Jury :—

Mr. G. Stone.	Captain Mercer.
Lieutenant Colonel Wintle.	Mr. L. Saunders.
Mr. H. Gunn.	Captain Black.
Sirdar Bhagwan Singh.	Mohamed Shah.
Lieutenant Colonel A. Taylor.	R. Bocquet, Esquire (Locomotive Superintendent, Punjab and Delhi Railway) *Reporter*.

Class 23* of the Catalogue forms a prominent feature in the Exhibition building, and is deserving of more notice than the public has bestowed upon it. When we consider the great skill, technical and mechanical, requisite in all the followers of the trade, and its necessity as affording the means of inter-communication and comfort to the public, we cannot but uphold all endeavours of enterprising people in the Punjab to acquire that vitality, which would tend to invest them with the same importance as the richest among the rising merchants of the country. Although the trade is in its infancy in the Punjab, and its followers perhaps necessarily despised, we feel assured that the period is not far distant when carriages, as complete and comfortable as those procurable in Calcutta, will be manufactured here at far more reasonable prices, possessing the advantages of being constructed of well seasoned timber and properly welded iron work. It would indeed prove a boon to the public generally if any competent parties would devote their capital and time to so laudable a pursuit, for laudable it undoubtedly would be, if the intense and continuous application necessary to combine and adapt the manifold intricacies of carriages, which leaves but little leisure for any other pursuit, be taken into consideration. Those people who have been put to the trouble, anxiety, and expense, of obtaining conveyances from Calcutta, will readily concur in the above.

The catalogue mentions upwards of 40 articles belonging to this Class. A large number of these are roughly constructed, representations of the different country vehicles used by the natives; there is nothing novel in the design or excellent in the workmanship.

The first full size carriage, we notice, if taken in the order in which they stand in the Exhibition annexe, is a species of Victoria Park Phaeton, with a hood and coach-box. The outlines of this carriage are, on the whole, good, and the interior is neatly fitted, and presents a very cosy appearance. It is strong and serviceable, but has evidently been constructed by some one who shares in the popular, but delusive idea, that weight is strength. Next come three very light, elegant, and strongly built, open carriages. One a Stanhope Phaeton or Waggonette; the second a Droshky on four wheels, and lastly, a Mail Drag by Mr. Chapman of Umritsur. These small carriages are strikingly bold in their outline, and with their double-spoked wheels, finely tempered springs, and masterly style of under-framing, contrast strongly with the heavy looking wheels, short springs, and to say the least, cumbersome under-framing of the other four-wheeled conveyances on show.

* (Class XXII, Division III, of this Book.)

Of the Waggonette, we have to observe that it has a very tasty outline, and looks very light and smart, with room enough to carry six persons with comfort. The height of the back and front wheels are well proportioned, the springs lengthy, and the deep black colored side panels show well against the chocolate colored wheels, picked out with vermillion and black.

Of the Droshky, we have to notice that the design is original. The curves are easy, and flowing well into one another. The wheels are light and high, the springs lengthy, the fittings are drab morocco with green trimmings. This carriage is painted a neat bottle-green, picked out with bright green. This trap is got up with great taste, and presents a very favorable specimen of the conveyance adapted for one horse or a pair of ponies. The splinter bar can be removed in such a manner as to form a perfect one horse vehicle. The Mail Drag by Mr. Chapman of Umritsur stands close by. It is unpretending, very neat, and forms a vehicular link between the four-wheeled Dog-Cart, and the Mail Phaeton so much in fashion at the present time. It is very well mounted on a neat iron framing, has elastic springs, and tapering wheels. The tastily shaped body tooks well ; the side panels are of sheet copper over toon wood. The iron work is blackened, the body, springs, and wheels are painted bottle-green picked out with bright green. The cushions, etc., are of drab morocco leather, which tends to give this trap a similarity of decoration to most others seen in this part of India. We are of opinion that on this account the appearance suffers from this sameness of hues, but these are the favorite colors for this style of conveyance. The trimmings are of rich drab silk ; and handsome circular lamps set off the whole so well, that the Jury has justly awarded to this unique specimen of coach-building by an amateur, the prize medal.

Bhujjun Lall of Jullunder has on show two specimens of his work : a four-wheeled Dog-Cart with canvass top, and a two-wheeled Dog-Cart without. Of the four-wheeled Dog-Cart we have to remark, that as a native production it deserves great praise, but it is wholly unadapted for one horse, or even for anything but good roads ; not only on account of its appearance of weight, but also on account of its short springs and the absence of springs in the cushion. The canvass top is an admirable contrivance, and it is a pity that some sort of arrangement of this kind has not been adopted in the case of the open conveyances above noticed. The Dog-Cart on two wheels and spider springs presents a method of disconnecting the shafts from the body, the object of which however is not obvious. It is consequently, rather of doubtful advantage, as it entails much extra weight and complicated iron work. The finish and general workmanship however has gained a certificate of honorable mention from the Jury. There is one other two-wheeled dog cart on show, which is in the opinion of the Jury much better adopted to the uses to which this class of conveyance is usually put, than anything that has yet appeared in this part of the country. The driving seat is something like that of the Mail Coach of England, and of very easy access. The wheels are of convenient height, and the shafts very elastic, obviating totally that disagreeable oscillation known as "knee motion." The price of this cart, 350 Rs., commanded a ready purchaser. Bhujjun Lall's cart at Rs. 500, is, as has been observed, a peculiar specimen of its kind, entailing expensive iron work, hence the difference in price. This last specimen was constructed in Lahore.

A pair of Buggy wheels, by Mr. Burnell, deserve to be noticed. They are varnished 'Shísham,' with very stout tires. They are heavy in themselves, but are strong enough for the heaviest two wheeled conveyance. The idea seems to be to show, how strongly and of what good materials they have been constructed. They have won the prize which has been offered for the best pair of wheels, and as there are no others on show, it has been thought fit to award it to the mistree who made them, and whose name appears upon the boss of each wheel. Two "dandies," one by Mr. Watson, the other by Captain Dyas, well deserve the prizes awarded them. They are a very considerable improvement on the wretched contrivances that are everywhere to be met with on a cruise through the hills.

Prizes awarded by Exhibition Committee.

The Mail Drag by Mr. Chapman of Umritsur,	Medal.	
Dandy* by Captain Dyas, ...	20	Rs.
" by Mr. Watson, ...	20	"
Ekka by Bhugwan Singh, (Model)	20	"
Carts by Bhujjun Lall, ...	Certificate of honorable mention.	
Phaeton by Francis, ...	Ditto.	

Special Prizes.

Model of a Waggon suitable for conveyance of troops to be awarded by the Inland Transit Company	100	Rs.
One pair of wheels to be awarded by Mr. Burnell, ...	50	"

* Light sort of chair or hammock, strung on a pole, for carrying a lady or gentleman in the hills.

DIVISION IV.

RAILWAY PLANT.

There is nothing in this Class of indigenous Punjab work; but I may take this opportunity of mentioning a model of a first class carriage, made to scale by native carpenters, who had learnt in the Workshops, which was Exhibited in 1864, and is now in the Lahore Central Museum. It is finished in every respect as a real carriage, even to the door-locks, hand-rails, windows, roof lamps, springs, grease boxes, buffers, &c. &c., every thing being workable. It was made *without* aid or supervision. At the same time I may notice a full sized carriage intended for use on the Punjab Line, also made by native workmen.

The following description is taken from the Jury Report (Lieutenant Colonel G. Sim, Reporter.)

"The Jury examined also a beautifully executed model of a 1st Class Carriage, such as is now in use on the Punjab Railway, but which is not included in the Catalogue, as it was stated to them it had not been registered or sent when the latter was compiled.

"The model was made by five Native workmen belonging to the Railway Workshops, but made in the city, without any aid whatever from Europeans. It is on the scale of 1¾ inch to the foot, complete in every detail of iron, wood, brass, and external and internal arrangements. It is a marvel of correctness, even to the glass windows and venetians, which can be pulled up or let down, to the buffers, and buffer springs, wheels, axles, grease-boxes, steps, door handles, guard's locks, doors, hinges, bolts; and also to the rails, chairs and sleepers on which it rests and runs. The Jury consider it a remarkable specimen of the skill and minute carefulness in execution, to which, under the teaching and example of Europeans, the Native artisans in the Punjab have attained since the railway was first commenced. It proves also how useful in all the handicraft requirements of a railway the Native workmen are found to be; a result that the officers of the railway have often cordially acknowledged in their official reports.

"*No.* 10,458—*A first Class Carriages made for the Punjab Railway.*—This carriage was of course built in the railway shops, and will be used on the line. The work was done by the native workmen under the usual European supervision of the Carriage Building Department. It is of the Saloon pattern, with seats at the ends and sides, but open in centre. The cane work of the seats is of an improved and more regular pattern than ordinarily given, the seats not being cushioned. The windows are of much larger openings than usual, as the carriage is intended to be used if required by Sirdars and Native gentlemen with their suites, and the ventilation has been more carefully studied. The joiner's work is very accurately done; the wood carving to the window and sash frames being of tasteful design, and the relief being more deeply undercut, showing, on the part of the native workmen, a great improvement over the ordinary style of the country, which is flatter."

GROUPS OF BOATS

(Models)

PLEASURE BOAT.

KOHALA FERRY.

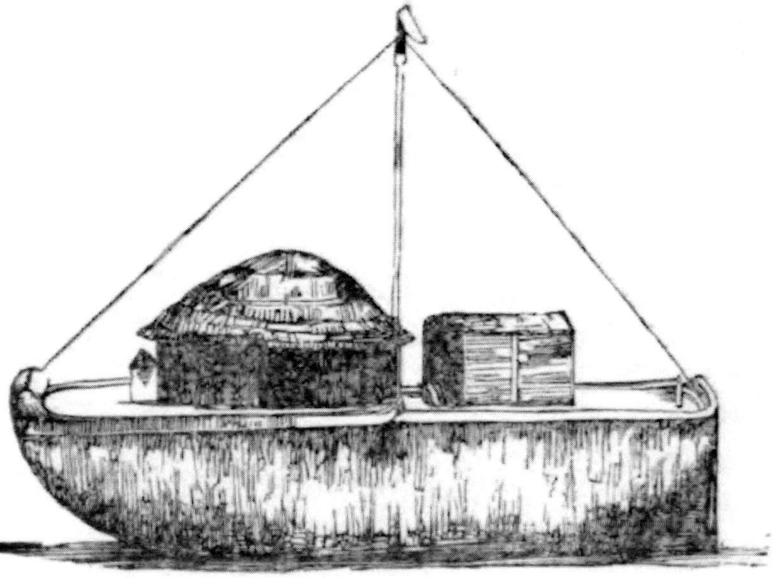

ZARAK.

"PARINDA" OR HUNTING BOAT.

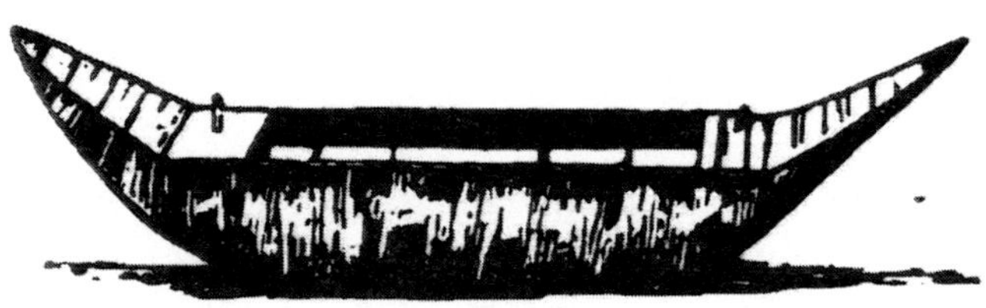

DONDI.

MODELS OF BOATS.

DIVISION V.

BOATS.

In the province of five rivers this Division may be expected to be well represented. The boats, however, are very clumsy in construction, and have remained unaltered for ages.

The following kinds are mostly in use :—

1. "Berí"—This is the large traffic boat on the Ravi, Chenáb, and Jhelam, and also on the Indus. It carries from 500 maunds or less, up to 1,000 maunds.

The "Berí" is always of the same shape, except at Attok, where it is of a narrower and more tapering shape. Thus the "Berí" of the Ravi, &c., is shaped like the model in the *lower* group of boats in the annexed plate, viz., the small boat immediately in front of the one with the mast; the Rawalpindi (Attok) "Berí" is figured in the *upper* group, being the little model to the extreme left.

In the Rawalpindi District however the form seems to have undergone a change, for the catalogue of the 1864 Exhibition contained two models, "Beri namúna sábik" (former shape) and "Beri namúna hál" (present shape). The boat just described is the former pattern; the "namúna hál" is a square stemmed and square sterned boat, like those on the other rivers.

A rather larger outline will better illustrate its general shape.

The flat bottom or hull is constructed on a skeleton of longitudinal beams with transverse ribs ; the sides are not, however, ribbed up to the top, but are constructed of stout deodar planks, which, as shown in the cut, are scarf-jointed together, and afterwards further secured by small iron clamps. The sides and the bottom are held together by still larger iron clamps. The scarf-joints, are not secured by nails, but by pegs of bamboo, driven slantwise through the edges of either timber and then smoothed off on the surface.

I may give a more particular account of the "Berí" described from one on the Ravi. These large boats perform the journey down to Sakkar, and when they do so, avail themselves of a sail. The mast, "kúa," merely rests on its end in a hollow socket in the mast beam (adda), which crosses the boat from side to side and flush with the edge, about two-third of the length from the stern. The mast carries a large square or rather oblong sail, called "sidh" or "sirh," wider than the boat. The sail is made of coarse cloth called "khaddar." The mast is supported by two stays "geru," which are fixed to the sides of the boat, close to the (adda) and are immoveable. Two other stays (chotíye) support the mast lengthwise to the boat, and are fixed at stem and stern. There are also two moveable stays, on loosening which the mast can be let down, called (táliye). The mast carries its pulleys

(yárí) with pully wheels (ráwat,) on which move a rope "usran" fixed between the "táliye" or fore-stays. This rope is the support for the cross yard "ár" which carries the sail. A similar lower beam or boom extends the sail below. The sail can be reefed by aid of string tags called "bandar." The sail carries two other ropes, one at each end of the yard "vera," and two others attached to either end of the boom "hanj" these aid in shifting the sail. There are other ropes, but I do not pretend to give them all. The above are the principal. The boat is built of deodar, or when built towards Sindh, my Lahore informant said, of woods which he called 'sál, 'dúpla', 'árni' and 'pona.' At the end of the boat in the figure will be seen a set of arches, these lead into the "khanji" or places for the boatmen to sleep.

The 'Beri' then represents the heavy traffic boat of the principal rivers, but is used on the Chenáb and Jhelam for a ferry boat also. On these latter rivers, however, a flat boat pointed at bow, and square and very low at stern, is now often used for a ferry, because being placed stern on to shore, the carriages, &c., which are to pass the river can be so easily rolled down an incline made on the bank—and the gradual slope of the stern end forms as it were a continuation of the incline, so that there is little difficulty in getting even a heavy "Dâk" carriage on board.

"Zárak"—on the Sutlej, the heavy traffic boat is called by this name, and it has also a square stem and stern, and is broad and heavy, and much higher in build than a "Beri." The plate shows in the lower group a "zárak" with its mast up, and with a thatched hut erected on the deck for accommodation during the long voyages which these boats make with grain, &c., for the Kurrachee market.

"Kishtí" or chapú. This word is sometimes incorrectly applied to all sorts of vessels, but it properly applies to those flat 'tray-like' punt boats, with their bow sharply pointed and inclined upwards as shewn in the plate.

They are built without curves of any kind. The bottom is perfectly broad and flat, and made of planks nailed to transverse ribs, the bottom is broader to the stern end: the sides are low, and consist merely of straight boards fixed at an angle to the bottom. The planks are usually of chíl or deodar wood; the sides and transverses of kikar (*Acacia arabica*) of Dalbergia (*Sissú*) or

Mulberry (túť.) The clamps are also of túť. The pointed prow is joined by a sort of dovetail to the bottom and is secured by curved clamps of hard wood at the edges.

The term kishtí or navak is also applied to the flat boats mostly of European or quasi-European pattern, used in constructing the bridges of boats which span our large rivers as soon as the monsoon floods subside.

The native boat (kishti) may be constantly seen as a ferry boat on the Sutlej, and as an ordinary traffic as well as ferry boat on the Bias. The Bias not being a trading river (it runs into the Sutlej at Haríkí, too high up to be a trade route) the 'beri' does not appear to be in use.

The smaller boats are known by the names of 'dondá' or 'dondí' (according to size) and chapú (?)

The "Dondí" or "dúndí" is much used at Jhelam as a ferry boat: it is much smaller and lighter than the "beri", and has its stem and stern both pointed, the stem having a longer point and raised higher than the stern: it is not unlike the small boat in the upper group. Similar small boats were in the Dera Ghazi Khan collection for use on the Indus.

A ferry boat used at Kohála on the Jhelam is shaped almost like a filbert nut, very much bowed and curved, the prow pointed, but the hull curving upwards towards the prow, and the stern square cut.

In Kashmir, as elsewhere, besides the ordinary boats, a number of fantastically shaped pleasure boats are in use: the upper figure in each of these groups shows specimens of such.

In Kashmir the population is so aquatic, and its city so like an Eastern Venice, as far as its water traffic is concerned, that a special notice must be devoted to Kashmir boats. A large and heavy boat like the Punjab "beri" will be found much in use, while on the lakes and rivers around Srinagar the higher classes adopt as a pleasure boat a long narrow boat fitted with an awning, and called "parinda," the "flyer," from the speed at which it can be urged by its many oars: such a boat is figured in the upper group. A variety of this boat of smaller size, for hunting and fishing purposes, is called "parund" or "shikarí"; and a broad boat or punt in the collection of 1864 was marked "Dúngá." The large heavy boats so often the dwelling place of whole families in Kashmir, are thus described by Lieutenant Louther :—*

"The vessels are curious contrivances, the farthest from architectural improvement I ever beheld. The larger craft are not bad models of "Noah's Ark," equally solid, and equally capacious, built entirely of fir (deodar) timber; the breadth of beam enormous, and the length so unmanageable, that it often takes a *whole* day to turn round into a canal after discharging the freight. Those employed as "lodging houses" are even more unwieldy, and often contain a strange medley of society. They are thatched nearly to the water's edge, and any holes which time and the poultry may have perpetrated in the roof, are patched from time to time with party-colored rags, or with any remarkable rubbish which may be at hand. Four or five families, (including always many squalling brats,) tenant these crowded berths; their goats, fowls, ducks, and dogs always accompanying them, and assisting in the general uproar and impurity. Every cabin has its fire-place, and every fire-place its attendant volumes of nauseous smoke, the produce of wet sticks

* Journal A. H. S., Volume VIII.

or still more unfit materials. From sunrise till sunset, this crowded community furnish a fearful picture of debased humanity, too idle or too helpless to work, or what is more probable, quite shut out from the *opportunity* of working (except occasionally gratis on the tyrant's account). Subsisting on wild fruits and weeds, with goat's milk, (their poultry, and its eggs being kept for the white visitors, whose money paid for the same will perhaps benefit some watchful soldier),—their persons barely clad with rags, and unapproachable as bad-living, dirt and vermin, can render them,—their angry jabbering in constant warfare with each other, altogether form a hideous Babel of human misery in the centre of Nature's most lavish gifts, and which reveals the gross system of misrule under which the people are struggling."

In concluding this Division, I shall extract a detailed account of the boats used on the Indus, which will be found in Volume XVII of the Bombay Selections, called "Sindh,"—Part II.

"The boats upon the Indus are of simple construction, and their figure perhaps the best that could be given considering the kind of navigation in which they are employed. They are easily constructed, not very expensive, and for stowage of cargo no form could be better devised. Their proportions, though not elegant, are pleasing, and tacking or under sail their appearance is pretty. The employment of the Indus craft is confined to harvesting the crops, serving the ferries, and keeping large towns in fuel ; for these purposes the supply is ample.

"Between the sea and Attok two kinds of vessels are in use : the Zohruk on the upper, and the Doondee upon the lower Indus. In boats belonging to the latter classes a slight difference in the build gives rise to a further classification, and of this description of vessel, the mohana (boatman) enumerates more than one variety ; but before particularizing each, a description of the Doondee is necessary. Her good and bad qualities are shared alike by them all, and the following notice of this boat is therefore applicable to every vessel upon the river.

"*Form and Method of construction.*—The hull or body of the boat is formed by the junction of three detached pieces, namely, two sides and bottom—at variance with our ideas of naval architecture; the three parts are first separately completed and then brought together as a cabinet-maker does the sides of a box. The junction is thus effected :—When each of the three parts that are to form the whole is complete in itself, the sides are carried to the bottom of the boat, and at once secured by crooked pieces of timber to the flat future bottom of the Doondee. To bring the bow and stern up to the corresponding parts of the sides is more difficult, and to effect this many days are necessary. Where the bow and stern are to rise, the planks are lubricated with a certain composition, which gives them a tendency to curve upwards, and this is further increased by the application of force. The extremes thus risen, a trackle is stretched between them, and by a constant application of the heating mixture, and a daily pull upon purchase, the ends rise to the required angle and are secured to the sides, while an advantageous curve is imparted by this process to the planks in the boat's bottom. The bow of the Doondee is a broad inclined plane, making an angle of about 20° with the surface of the water. The stern is of the same figure, but subtends double the angle.

"To the slight curve in her bottom planks, she is indebted for the following advantages in descending a river. Should she strike upon a sand bank, the boat turns like a top, and presents no stationary point for the stream to act against.

"The Jumptee is the State barge of the Sind Amírs, and is used by them and their principal officers on all occasions whether of business or of pleasure. Perhaps the appearance of this boat, as she approaches the capital, is more characteristic of the Indus and of Sind, than aught else to be seen in the country. On this day her Meerbar puts on clean clothes and the national cap received from the Amírs in a recent river excursion : the bright hues of the cap formed of the gaudiest colored chintz, vie with those of a Kilmarnock bonnet or a Paisley tartan. The crew are dressed becoming the occasion, and as they bend to the rope the breeze distends their ample robes, and a further character of stateliness is imparted to the Jumptee. Large red flags wave over her stern, and from the raking mast streams a long party-colored pennant that anon skims the water as the breeze lulls and freshens. In the bow of the boat is a small crimson pavillion, in which royalty reclines, and in the other extreme of the vessel is a roomy cabin of elaborately carved work for its numerous attendants. The steersman on an elevated platform stands out in bold relief, and while he guides the boat, encourages the rowers. The Jumptee's crew are a noisy set, but for aged men, wonderfully good humored; they are divided into two gangs or watches, and are as partial to a cup of good bhang as sailors are to grog!

"These boats are decked, and of considerable tonnage. One which I saw at Hyderabad measured 120 feet over all, with a beam of eighteen and a half feet; her draft of water was two feet six inches, she pulled six oars and a crew of thirty men. They are built of Malabar teak, chiefly at the ports of Mughribee and Karachee.

"The Zohruk.—What the Doondee is in Sind, the Zohruk is on the Upper Indus, namely, the common cargo boat of the country. The planks of this vessel are held together by clamps instead of nails, and the junction is often neatly enough executed. This class of boats is not so strong as the Doondee, but they sail faster and draw less water. They are more roomy than the Doondee, and though less adapted for the conveyance of goods, are much superior for transporting troops.

"The Dugga.—This is the clumsiest, and, at the same time, the strongest built boat upon the Indus. She is confined to that rocky and dangerous part of its course lying between Kalabagh and Attok. The form of the boat differs but slightly from that of the Doondee: the Dugga has neither mast nor sail. Her name is the Sindian word for a cow, and the awkward, sluggish motion of this boat, shows that it has not been misapplied. If the Dugga drops down the river to Mittun, there she must remain, and be sold for whatever sum she will bring, for to drag her up against the stream of Kalabagh would cost more money in the hire of men than the boat is worth.

"Boat building materials—Suggestions.—The Upper Indus is principally supplied from the banks of the Chenab, where the Talee tree, the Sissoo of Hindustan, is seen with a trunk measuring twelve feet in circumference: three such trees furnish plank enough to build a large sized Zohruk.

"The Attok boats are built of good fir, brought down the Kabool river, and from the forest, of the lower Himalaya.

"Iron work—The Lower Indus is supplied from Bombay, and the Upper portion of the river from the mines of Bunnoo and Bajour."

CLASS XXIII.

INSTRUMENTS FOR WEIGHING AND MEASURING.

Under this Division there were only two specimens in the Exhibition of 1864.

One a large clock, made entirely by a native, but with materials and tools obtained from Paris; and another, a small clock which worked a musical box, and had a sort of mock waterspout, which played when the clock worked. It consisted of a spiral of glass, which turning rapidly caught the light against the edges, and produced the effect of flowing water. The works of this clock were not of native make: they were put together by a native workman in the service of the Maharaja of Patyala. They are alluded to in the report on philosophical instruments, which will be found a few pages on.

The second division of this Class is unrepresented. Natives are however well able to copy, and that with fair accuracy, European scales, letter weights, &c. &c.

CLASS XXIV.

MATHEMATICAL AND PHILOSOPHICAL INSTRUMENTS.

The Exhibition of 1864 contained not a few specimens of modern instruments made under European supervision. Mr. Spence of Sealkot produced an Electro-Magnetic battery. The workshops of Rurkí (North-Western Provinces,) and Madhopúr, produced levelling and surveying instruments. The somewhat elaborate machinary of Colonel Dyas' rain-guage, as improved by Mr. J. L. Watson, is successfully turned out at the Madhopúr foundry. There can be no doubt that almost any amount of success may be obtained in this direction : the fine materials however have to be imported, and constant supervision exercised.

A report appeared in 1841, on the construction of philosophical instruments in India, by Captain J. Campbell, Assistant Surveyor General. From this paper I make the following extract :—

" Sir John Herschell in his " Discourse upon Natural Philosophy," has thought it necessary, for fear the fact should be doubted, ' to assure the reader that balances have ' been constructed capable of rendering visibly sensible a quantity of matter to even the ' millionth part of the whole ' ; yet this which by the passage is evidently considered a great effort of mechanical skill, I have been able to effect by the hands of an Indian workman, totally untaught, except by myself ; and with regard to its outward appearance, no one who has yet seen it but has remarked—' How beautifully it is worked ' or that ' no one would for an instant believe that it was made in India.'

" It might be remarked in contravention of my propositions, that I endeavour to assert the possibility of rivalling in India the productions of the genius of Ramsden and Troughton, and that the idea is absurd ; but however such it is my intention to assert.

" From their unimpassioned character, their slow and quiet habits, their delicate appreciation of touch, and their untiring application, it is probable that a clever native, if once taught properly the art of dividing the circumference of a circle, might very probably surpass the best effect of the most celebrated workmen of London.

" It is supposed by many, that modern discoveries in optics have improved refracting telescopes by the lenses being better made ; but such is not the fact. The lenses of the present day are not in the least better than those which Galileo and Huygens were able to make ; and it is probable there is hardly a Chinese workman who does not possess a great deal more skill in polishing a lense, than the best optician in London. I once bought in London a Chinese toy, an imitation of a compound microscope, from which I took lenses so beautifully polished, as to be admired by one of the first opticians in London, and I have little doubt that a clever workman in India could fashion lenses with which a refracting telescope could be put together quite as good as the best which Tully or Dollond ever made.

" The above may appear a startling assertion, but no optician will deny the possibility of its being correct ; for the fact is, that workmen are totally unable to give a particular required figure to a lens, and lenses of required focal distance for forming the achromatic object are selected from among numerous failures (whence the high price). Modern science has only improved these instruments by teaching the proper theoretical principles upon which to compound their various parts."

Further detail cannot however be permitted to this subject, my plan confining a descriptive account to those articles which are of purely native manufacture.

Almost all the instruments that were exhibited, were astrolabes, dials, and other instruments used either in the fancied computations of astrology, or in those real calculations of ancient astronomy in which it is well known the Hindus attained considerable excellence. His Highness the Maharaja of Kapurthala exhibited two fine astrolabes, one a small hand one, the other represented in the plate. Each is furnished with a number of variously engraved discs or plates, which are used in turn according to the purpose of the observation.

The method of taking the time by this instrument is described in the report. Other observations can be made.

The following list of astronomical instruments was compiled for me by Pandit Rádha Kishn, late astrologer to the Court of Ranjit Singh, and by Pandit Durga Pershád.

1. Digyantram—A brass disc with a moveable index, used for finding the exact time of the sun's crossing the meridian, and for fixing the quarters of the heavens.
2. Trikon shankú yantram—Consisting of a wooden tringle with a cross bar, like the letter A ; the cross bar is graduated, and a string and a ball depending from the apex shows how much out of the perpendicular it is, and what the angle of the ground is.
3. Sambhúmí yantram—An ordinary spirit level.
4. Ghati yantram—A water clock. A copper bowl perforated with a little hole, which, placed in a vessel of water, gradually fills and sinks : exactly one hour is consumed in filling. This article is in common use, and by it all police guards, &c., keep the time, striking their gong as each hour comes round.
5. The hour glass of sand is also used, called ' bálú ka ghati yantram.'
6. Shankú yantram—Graduated scales used in measuring.
7. Pratod yantram—A long graduated beam for finding out the time by the aid of the shadow.
8. Chakra yantram—A graduated disc, and needle, for determining the zenith distance, and the altitude of the sun.

   The " chap yantram " is a half disc, also used in determining the zenith distance.
9. Túrí yantram—The quadrant.
10. Samay prabodhak yantram—A dial graduated so as to show the sub-divisions of time.
11. Dhruv bhraman yantram—A square plate, having circles inscribed on it and an index rod, by means of this the time is ascertained at night, by the polar star (*Dhruv* polar star—*bhraman*—going, wandering.)
12. Rátri pradíp yantram—Another instrument for telling the time at night (*ratri*—night *pradip*—lamp.)
13. Dakshinodak bhiti yantram—(*Lit.*—" from south-northerly separation ")—A square plate with graduated quadrant of a circle, an index, and plumb line, used in ascertaining azimuth distances.

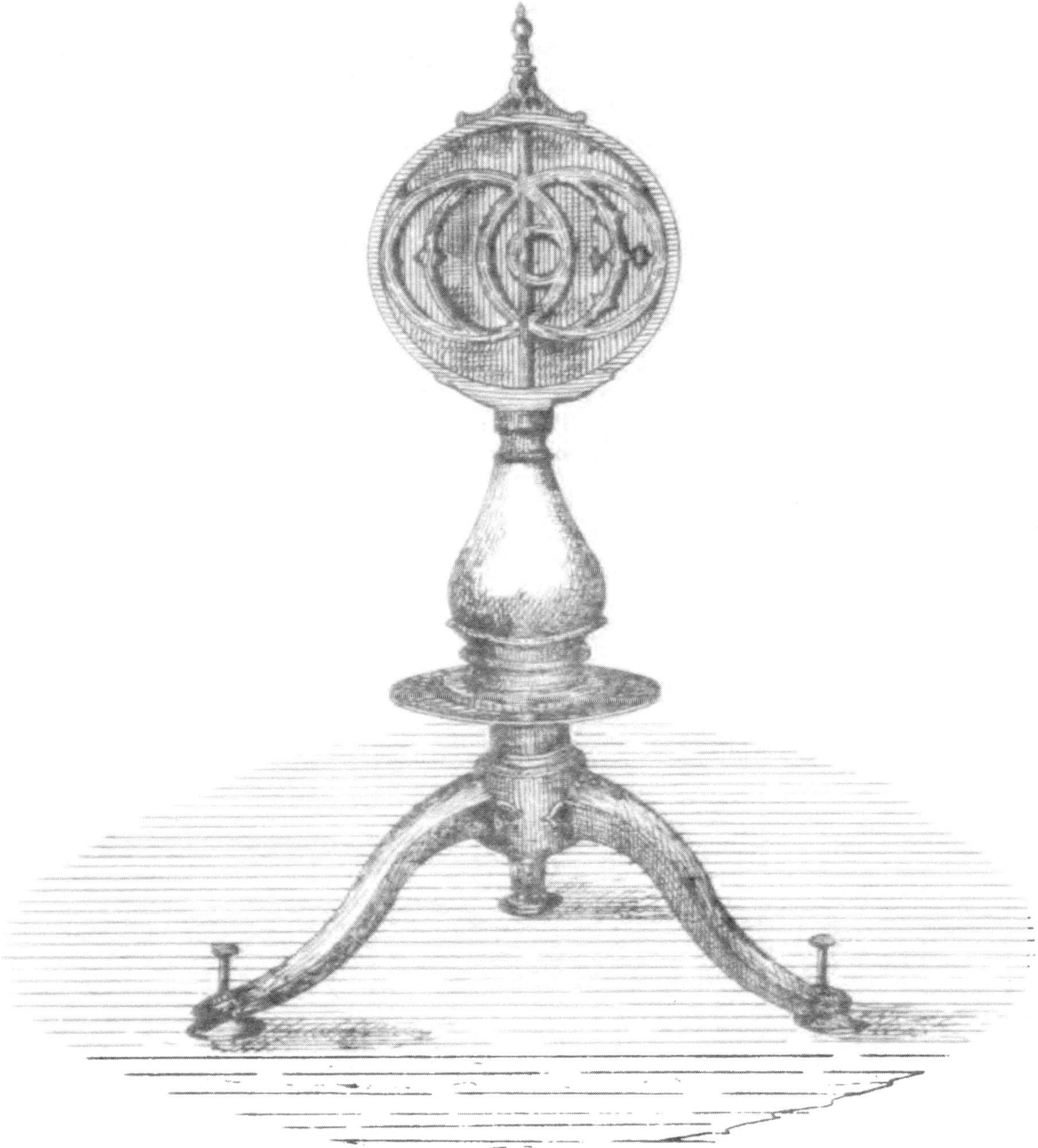

ASTROLABE.

14. Sextant.
15. Octant.
16. Rám yantram—used to show the declination.
17. Yámyottara yantra—A dial with tube for shewing zenith distance and the meridian shadow of a *Gnomon*, when the sun is in the equinoctial line—(*yámí*—south *uttara*-north.
18. Falk yantra—A graduated oblong plate, with inscribed circle and bar to give the shadow—for measurement of hours, angular distances, &c.
19. Yashti yantra (or ishtí) a dial for computing time.
20. Digansh yantram—In geodesy, to ascertain the bearings of a given object.
21. Nárí balay yantram—Shows the time according the Indian division of " Nári"—the hour of 24 minutes.
22. Samrat yantram—The form of the instrument is a semicircle, superscribed on the hypothenuse of a right angled triangle; the circle is graduated and intersected at its extreme ends by another arc. The brass plate on which the whole is engraved carries an observing tube. The instrument is used in measuring zenith distance and declination.
23. Jaya prakásh yantra.
24. Yanti ráj—The usturláb of the Yunání or Arabian astronomy.
25. Budhi yantra—A large gnomon, the shadow of which is observed when the sun is in the equinoctial.
26. Jar kalíya yantram—To show altitude and ascensional difference.
27. Gol yantra—To show the motion of the planets, according to the Hindi divisions of the sphere.
28. Kránti yantra—declination instrument.
29. Játul halka yantrí—For finding longitude, &c.
30. Bhugol yantra—Globe.
31. Swayambahu yantra—A revolving disc, set turning by a stream of water, which flows by a siphon tube out of a vessel properly placed and dropped on to the cogs or teeth of the disc. A revolution is maintained at a certain rate, and by this means the time is ascertained after the machine having been once started at a known hour.
32. Vakra darsaná bhangí—A vessel showing the reverse revolution of planets.

The Jury Report of 1864 is as follows :—

JURORS.—Colonel Maclagan, R. E.
Major MacLeod Innes, R. E., V. C.
Kanhya Lall, Executive Engineer.
A. Neil (Meteorological Superintendent) *Reporter.*

The articles to be reported on were in the Exhibition, contained in Section C. Those most worthy of notice are now described.

[10676—7].—Two Hydrometers, made of brass, exhibited by Goormook of Loodiana, of ordinary form, and very rudely finished.

[10683].—Brass tubular beam-compass, exhibited by J. D. Smithe, Esquire, of Madhopúr, and constructed in the Baree Doab Canal Workshops. Their fitting up was rough and unfinished, but the instrument itself is tolerably well made. The jury awarded an Honorary Certificate.

[10684].—Electro-Magnetic Battery, of ordinary construction, but well finished, exhibited by Mr. W. Spence, Sealkote.

[10685].—Clock, scientifically and elaborately finished (original cost Rs. 4,000), exhibited by Rajah Hurbuns Singh of Lahore.

This clock is made to strike the hours and half hours, and shews the diurnal position of the sun in the ecliptic throughout the year, and the lunar rotation throughout the month. It was constructed under the immediate management of Bhugut Ram Sohai, in the time of Runjeet Singh. The finishing is in most of its parts exceedingly good, and very elaborate. The Jury awarded a medal.

[10686—692].—Astrolabes, exhibited by the Rajah of Kapurthalla. These instruments are now almost obsolete, and there seems nothing in the construction of either of those exhibited worthy of being noted. A short description of one of them will suffice. In Hindi, the instrument is called Yantra Raj, in Arabic, Ustarláb. On the back of the dial there is a moveable copper tube attached to a flat narrow plate, each end of which is pointed. Here the margin is divided into 360°, and these again into fourths by a vertical and transverse line, which intersect each other at the centre of the dial. In the front or anterior side of the dial, the margin is divided into 60 gharies—2½ of these being equal to one English hour. Each ghari is divided into 6 equal parts. Within the anterior margin, which is raised, there is a moveable circle of brass attached to the centre of the dial by a pin. On the edge of this the twelve signs of the zodiac are marked, each compartment being divided into 15°.

How to use the Instrument.—Raise the tube to such a position that the rays of the sun may pass through it. Mark the position of the tube with reference to the degrees on the margin, counting from the transverse line. Ascertain from the calendar in what sign of the zodiac the sun is together with the degree. Bring the sign and degree to bear on the inner circle on the anterior side, and on the transverse line then mark the degree opposite the projection of the inner circle. The degree marked on the posterior side of the dial should be traced on the flat plate on the anterior side. Bring the sign and degree of the upper circle upon the plate, and mark again the degree opposite the projection of the circle. The *gharies* contained between the two marks made opposite the projection will be the time of the day.

[10693—5].—Gold and Silver mounted Magnetic Compasses, exhibited by the Maharajah of Kashmir. Creditably constructed.

The object of these is to furnish the Musulmán with the means of knowing which way to turn towards the Kibla (Mecca) at prayer time.

The Jury awarded an Honorary Certificate.

[10698.]—A clock, said to be made by a workman in the service of the Maharajah of Patyala. There is a musical apparatus attached to it, but nobody can make out the tunes. An ornamental water-spout is also attached, in which a short twisted glass rod is the water ; the light catches the edges of the spiral, and as this is kept in motion produces a glancing like the glimmer of falling water. Workmanship very creditable.

[10699.]—A model of the Electric Telegraph apparatus, also made by a workman in the service of the Maharajah of Patyala, neatly finished.

The Jury award an Honorary Certificate.

[10702—7].—A set of Surveying Instruments, made in the Rurki Workshops, and consisting of an Everest Level (20 inches), levelling staves, telescopic staves, case of Spirit Bulbs; ground agates for compass needles, and small pocket compass. Exhibited by Major Allen. They are all beautifully constructed, the Everest Level especially so.

The Jury awarded an Honorary Certificate.

CLASS XXV.

SURGICAL INSTRUMENTS.

Native Surgery is unfortunately in an extremely backward state. The operations known are very few and very rude. The implements are mostly so coarsely made, that it is wonderful how any result whatever can be effected with them. Fortunately, however, the natives of the Punjab are extremely willing to profit by European art and science in surgery, much more than they are in the case of European medicines. They still cling desperately to the exploded fallacies of the old Greek school with its dry and moist, hot and cold, remedies.

There are no books on surgery worth reading. The art of surgery was looked on with contempt, and was consigned to barbers and such like craftsmen. A respectable physician hardly dared to attempt the practice of surgery, or he was nicknamed 'barber.' Hakím Muhamad Ishák, a physician of some note, who came to Lahore in the reign of Alámgir (Aurangzeb), and entered the service of Nawáb Amánat Khán, Subadár of Lahore, turned his attention to surgery, but was much derided in consequence. He had learnt something about surgery from an Italian in the Nawáb's service, named Antún (Antonio). Muhamed Ishák wrote a treatise on surgery, called "Tashkara Ishákiya".* Although it is one of the best extant, it contains very little that is useful. Of several diseases, the cure of which is perfectly easy, he makes no mention, and declares some of them irremediable. Thus of stricture of the urethra he says—"The cure of this disease is known to God only." They had only a rude idea of lithotomy, and nearly always killed their patients, although the native surgeons, who have learnt the operation in the European method, are, from their impassive and steady manipulation, particularly successful in it. The native operation for stone consisted in passing the finger into the rectum, and feeling for the stone till by pressure it protruded so as to make the exterior of the perineum bulge, the operator then, with a lancet or razor, cut a gash over the protrusion, taking his chance of what membranes or tisses he cut through, and pulled out the stone. It is needless to add, that in many cases the laceration and injury of delicate structures was such that the patient did not survive.

It was hardly possible to have a limb amputated, although the frequency of battles in those days rendered it compulsory to make some attempt. I was quite unable to find any native surgeon who knew anything of amputation. Many told me that they could extract a bullet with a sort of hook and forceps, and that when a limb was shattered by shot they would remove the splinters of bone, and trim the ragged edges of the wound, and heal it. Whenever amputation was attempted, the flesh being cut, or the bone sawn through, (they generally however availed themselves of the fracture of the bone, by pulling out the splinters as before said,) and then hemorrhage was prevented by dipping the limb into melted rosin or hot ghee! This agreeable method of dispensing with ligature of arteries and suture, in one process, was occasionally practiced in the case of criminals in the Sikh days, who had a finger or a limb amputated as a punishment. Nature seems

* A good manuscript copy of this has been obligingly lent to me by Fakir Syad Jamál-ud-dín, of Lahore, among whose ancestors, the physician was numbered (he was the Fakir's father's mother's great-grandfather). I take this opportunity of acknowledging the frequent assistance I have received from this gentleman in preparing the various sections of this volume.

to have gifted these people, as a compensation for their lack of knowledge, with a proportionately powerful *vis medicatrix*, as regards suffusion from veins, &c. It is uniformly noticed how much fewer veins a native patient needs to have tied than an European.

Dr. Farquhar told me that after the battle of Chiliánwála he was about to render assistance to a Sikh soldier who had been wounded in the leg by a cannon shot; amputation was necessary. The man loudly protested, thinking he was to be killed, but when he was pacified as regards his safety, he was again horrified by seeing, as he thought, no means of staying the bleeding, and cried out for the 'hot ghee' wherein to dip the stump. He was quite astonished at the use of a tourniquet and ligatures for the arteries. The use of the hot ghee always incapacitated a man for work for several weeks, and even months afterwards, always producing a painful sore, with sloughing, and not unfrequently mortification. No native surgeon will at the present day attempt amputation.

The different surgical operations are performed by the following classes of people:—

(1.) 'Shikasta-band'.—These men reduce dislocations, and attend to fractures. They have no apparatus of any sort. They reduce dislocations by the application of force, and apply stout bandages. They are, however, tolerably skilful at reducing simple dislocations, and frequently effect considerable relief to the patient by their system of rubbing, pulling, and manipulating the muscles in cases of straining. The people who perform these operations are often 'Kamángars' or bow makers, and also wrestlers.

(2.) Banjáras or oculists.—The most remarkable operation is that for cataract, in which, in spite of their rude apparatus, they are very fairly successful. As far as I am aware, their operation is always for depression. For instruments they have a very small lancet, which consists of a short handle, wound round with silk, and exhibiting the triangular point of a blade thus 

This is used for incising the cornea.

They have also a probe of steel, but more often the probe ('súá') is replaced by one of the long fine white thorns of the Acacia. The younger trees have very long and finely pointed thorns, which have a beautiful white siliceous coating, and certainly offer a smoother and finer point than any steel work made by an ordinary workman. The thorn is extremely tough. They have also two hooked instruments ("kundi"), one rather thick, made of copper, the other of steel, and much more slender and finely pointed, and also a blunt probe.

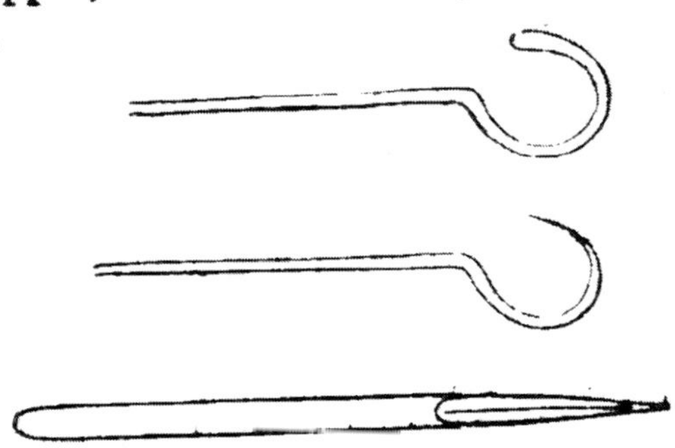

The probe or thorn is used in operations where they simply puncture the cornea and *depress* the cataract. In other cases they make an incision with the lancet (in lieu of the Beer's knife of modern surgery), and then introduce the copper hook to open a passage for the depressing instrument: the smaller hook being used in depressing the film if it cannot be removed by the probe alone. A small razor (ushtra) is among the instruments of these practitioners. The Banjáras occasionally brand the temples, with a view to strengthen the sight and prevent blindness.

(3.) Jaráh.—This term is, perhaps, a more generic word for 'surgeon,' than indicative of a special class. All operations, however, such as bleeding with lancets, lancing of tumours, swellings, treatment of hemorrhoids, extraction of teeth, is done by the jaráh. His instruments will now be described. In the Lahore Museum there is a case of mother-of-pearl and steel containing a series of implements inserted through holes in a plate which stops the mouth; this looks more like a lady's work case for scissors, crochet hooks, &c., than a surgeon's box, but in it the tools are better made. There is an attempt at polishing, and the various knives, &c., are made to screw into handles.

The usual instruments are as follow:—

"Sanní".—A rude pair of iron square pointed pincers, one handle of which is hooked at the end. This frightful apparatus is for drawing teeth.

"Naherná".—A thin iron blade, with a sharp slanting edge or point, used for lancing the gums previous to extracting a tooth. Some rather broader bladed "nahernas" are used for paring nails, and chiropodic operations.

"Patri"—A hone for sharpening instruments.

"Chamúta" is a leather strop for the same purpose.

"Mochana"—Tweezers.

"Ushtra"—Small razors, used either for shaving any part to be operated on, or else for making a deeper incision or gash than the lancets (nashtar) will make.

"Toká"—A small hook, the point of which is flattened at the sides and sharpened. The stem being flexible, it is placed in position, and being drawn back, is let go and strikes smartly on the place, which is punctured by the sharp edge. It is used for opening veins in the forehead.

"Míkráz"—Pointed scissors.

"Nashtar" (fasd-ki)—Lancets for bleeding.

Needles and thread; Bandages, &c.

"Zambúr and Zambúri"—Forceps of sizes.

"Dastúr"—A sort of syringe used in administering an enema.

"Suá and Silái"—Probes.

"Pichkárí suzák"—A syringe for injecting remedies in urinary complaints.

For bleeding and cupping they have the following:—

The use either a horn, or an earthen cup called 'rummí', or a hollow vessel called "tumbiya" or 'kuppí'. When they apply the horn after cutting the vein, they apply the mouth to the point of the horn and draw in the breath, thus exhausting the air and causing the blood to flow and fill the vacuum; or else they prick the skin over with a lancet

and then apply the earthen pot which is heated, so that the air on cooling may contract and a vacuum be formed, to fill which the blood will exude.

In some cases they merely wish to excite a tumour or boil, and they heat the "tumbiya" or kuppi and tie it tight over the place, which causes it to rise and swell, or to suppurate.

When bleeding by venesection is being done, the surgeon gives the patient a short round stick or "latti", which he is expected to keep twirling with his hand, thus keeping up circulation by the motion.

The case alluded to, contained a small saw (ári), and a "pech", an iron wire terminating in a spiral like a small cork-screw, used for worming out foreign matter from the ear or from a wound. In the Montgomery collection a looking glass was added to these articles, and the whole enclosed in a leather case called "rachyání".

(4.) Gagras—These people are solely occupied in the application of leeches ('jok').

(5.) 'Madári'.—These people cure the bites of snakes and animals, not by surgical or medical means, but by spells, incantations, and charms. These are invariably resorted to by the people in cases of snake bite!

"Kán maflyás".—Ear surgeons. These men occupy themselves with the treatment of ear-ache, and with removing obstructions in the passages. The use of a syringe is unknown. Their favorite remedy for ear-ache is the introduction of a little sweet oil.

They use a pair of forceps, "chimta,"—a broad pointed probe used for digging out foreign matter, and called, "silai aríz nok-wali,"—a blunt probe, "gol-nok-wali,"—and a probe for inserting cotton wool for cleaning the passage—"silai-pamba wali".

The paring of nails, removal of corns, and other work of the chiropodist, is done by the barber, "hajám" or "nai."

I must here mention one of the few operations in which the surgeons of the country are eminently successful. One, that of the cataract has been described, the other that I allude to, is the work of the Kangra "Khangars" in restoring the nose. Jealous husbands bite or cut off the point of the nose of their wives in spite, and cutting off the nose seems also to have been used as a punishment in former days. The annexed plate, copied from a native drawing, will show the process. The patient is laid down, and the surgeon, with a lancet, or rather with a small razor (ushtra) cuts a triangular bit of skin from the forehead,* which he turns down, and then dexterously and lightly twists just at the junction of the nose with the brow, so as to bring the right side of the skin in front; he lays this down over the nose, and having by dexterous manipulation and working drawn down the remainder of the original cartilage so as to form a basis, he disposes the new skin over the whole, and fixes it by strips of plaster and bandages. The gradual treatment of the healing surface, and the patients lying by, flapping away the flies, are quaintly, but accurately, portrayed in the plate. The only implements the "Khangars" use are a razor or lancet, a needle for sewing, and one or two tools for smoothing down the skin.

* The skin is taken from the forehead, and never I believe from the cheek.

These are all the classes of people which make any pretence to be surgeons. The practice of obstetric art in any form is unknown; midwives or dáis attend, if necessary, but are unable to render any assistance beyond what their hands can afford. It is needless to remark that they are utterly ignorant. In the list of drugs of the first volume will be seen various remedies given to women before and after child-birth. It is to be remarked, however, that especially among the lower orders of the agricultural population, cases of difficult parturition or birth appear to be comparatively rare. Should such a case occur, the life of the child or the mother, or both, is invariably sacrificed through ignorance of any proper treatment.

Under this chapter, I may mention that veterinary surgery is no better understood than that applied to the human frame. The Bétár or Salotri has a few lancets for bleeding and some bandages: branding with a hot iron is a favorite remedy for most diseases in cattle. The pious Hindu will not touch the sacred animal himself, letting it die rather, he performs the operation however, *vicariously* by a Mussulmán, and it is all right!

I may take this opportunity of including a notice of the Bhátra or ear-borer. Every native woman considers it necessary to have the ears bored, and some times not only one hole but many are made, to admit of all the mass of bális, bálas, murkis, &c., &c. that are fashionable to wear. *

The Bhátras tools are as follows:—

Murki—a stout zinc wire bent round so as to form a nearly complete circle, the two points are sharpened. One of these points is forced though the lobe of the year, and the ring drawn though and left there till the wound, which is a severe one, heals. When the murki has done its work, a "bunda," or second zinc ring, thicker than the murki, is inserted to enlarge the hole. The bunda has also a small weight hanging from it, so as to pull down the ear and ensure the hole being made. I am told that the operations necessary to gratify the hideous vanity of wearing clusters of ear-rings are so painful, that women sit in the house for days crying with pain, and the wounds do not heal for three months sometimes.

I append the Jury Report in the collection of 1864, which shows also how far European instruments are imitated by native workman (see also the class "CUTLERY.")

REPORT OF THE JURY ON SURGICAL INSTRUMENTS.

Jurors:—

Dr. Farquhar.	Dr. Thom.
Dr. Penny.	S. A. Surgeon Raheem Khan,
Dr. Dallas.	Dr. J. B. Scriven, Reporter.

The Districts exhibiting articles are, Kangra, Hooshyarpore, Sealkote, Lahore, Shahpur and Goojranwala. Besides these, articles are included in the catalogue from Amritsur and Patyala, but have not come to hand.

* The sight of these rings ought to cure European ladies at least of the barbarous practice of boring holes in their flesh to stick ornaments in!

The collections reported on are eleven in number, *viz*:—

1st.—A rudely constructed razor and lancet sent up by the Local Exhibition Committee at Kangra.

2nd.—A set of three ivory handled vaccine lancets, exhibited by Dr. Aitchison of Hooshyarpore.

3rd.—A similar set of lancets with horn handles, also exhibited by Dr. Aitchison of Hooshyarpore.

4th.—A case of Lithotomy instruments. These are of the kind commonly provided for hospitals in India. They are not of the newest or best pattern, but their finish is good, in fact equal to that of the instruments usually supplied to Medical Depôts from England. They are highly creditable to native artificers, and the jury think they are deserving of a prize of Rs. 20. The exhibitor is Mr. Spence of Sealkote.

5th.—A case of midwifery instruments. The finish of these is also creditable. The silver catheter is particularly well made, but the pattern of the forceps is not good. The jury consider this case deserving of a prize of Rs. 10. The exhibitor is Mr. Spence of Sealkote.

6th.—A case of instruments for extracting teeth. The key and gum lancet in this case seem to be very good. The forceps and elevator are made after a pattern not much used in the present day, and certainly not to be recommended, nevertheless the finish of all is excellent, and the jury recommend a prize of Rs. 10. The exhibitor is Mr. Spence of Sealkote.

7th.—An abscess lancet; and

8th.—A bleeding lancet, both by Mr. Spence. These two instruments are well polished, sharp, and apparently of good quality.

9th.—A case of razors and other instruments used by the Native barber surgeons: these belong to the Lahore Museum.

10th.—A lancet and probes used by native Surgeons in the operation for depression of cataract, exhibited by Dr. Henderson of Shahpore.

11th.—Two rudely made bleeding lancets and a gum lancet, from the district of Goojranwalla: the name of the exhibitor is not given.

The prizes above recommended are as follows:—

No.	Article.	District.	Exhibitor.	Prize.
10713	Lithotomy case.	Sealkote.	Mr. W. Spence.	Rs. 20.
10714	Midwifery case.	"	Do.	Rs. 10.
10715	Dental Instruments.	"	Do.	Rs. 10.

CLASS XXVI.

MUSICAL INSTRUMENTS.

The musicians of the Punjab, whether Hindu or Mussalman, use the Hindu system exclusively. The Arabic system of music is not known.

It would be impossible for me to give under this Class any account of the musical *system*. I have only to describe the musical instruments in use as one of the branches of mechanical manufacture.

I may however add a few words in preface to a descriptive list of musical instruments, and explain as much of the system of notation, tuning and melody, as will render what follows intelligible.

The musicians who accompany regular nâch players,* are always Mussulmans of the caste of Mír or Mirási (barbers and astrologers &c.) and are called " Dôm "; this term is not however considered complimentary, and would be a positive insult if addressed to any one else. The Dôms use only a " sarangi " a sort of fiddle, a pair of little bells or small cymbals, and a drum ; but at more elaborate nautches, in the houses of the wealthy, I have seen other instruments introduced. Some classes of Hindus perform as nautch dancers, and accompany them with music, such persons are called Rásdhári. Professional players on the tambúra (a sort of guitar) are called " Kaláñwat " ; those on the bín, are ' Bín-baz." Amateur musicians are called " atai, " whatever instrument they prefer.

I should note that music is strictly forbidden to Mussulmans, excepting only a drum called " daf, " at marriages or ceremonies, and then apparently only for the purpose of publicity or proclamation of the event. It is needless to say that this prohibition is little attended to ; and as early as the reign of Kai Kubád (1285 A. D.) one Amir Khisro, in spite of the prohibition, introduced the guitar known as the " tambúra, " which accompanies the voice ; and this has ever since been a very popular instrument. Amateur musicians are rare, and professional ones are looked on with a sort of contempt, like surgeons.

The Hindu system of music does not appear to be very different from our own, at least as regards the division of the scale or gamut. The octave, with seven full tones, (the eighth being a repetition of the first) is recognized, and called ' saptag.' Instead of the letters of the alphabet C. D. E. &c., or the notation do, re, mi, the notes are named—

Do—Kharj.
Re—Rikab.
Mi—Gandhár.
Fa—Madham.
Sol—Pancham (' the fifth ') or dominant.
La—Dewat.
Si—Nikádh.
Do—Kharj—again, &c.

* This word is now almost naturalized as " nautch."

Sub-division of tones ('sur') are recognized, and a half tone is called " múrchhan." The quarter tone is recognized, and both half and quarter tones are easily produced, even on the fretted instruments, by putting the string to one side of the fret, which of course tightens it slightly, and raises the tone. In a " saptag " there are 21 'múrchhans' or sub-divisions, as will be seen by dividing the scale into fractions of tones as, C. C.♯, C.♯♯, C ♯♯♯ D. &c.

The term 'ras' is used apparently as our 'base'; " dirg " as tenor; and " palutt " as treble.

I should remark that the instruments are tuned to a convenient pitch to the voice, or to about half a tone lower than our full concert pitch. To tune an instrument is 'sur karna.'

I will now proceed to a description of the instruments in use.

DIVISION I.

STRINGED INSTRUMENTS.

The most favorite of these appear to be the varieties of guitar.

When these have more than one string, it will be invariably found that only one string is designed to be fingered; the others, remaining as open strings, and form the common chord of C. major, which is played as an unvarying drone or accompaniment with the thumb, and while the " chantarelle " or melody string is struck with the finger, which is generally armed with a skeleton thimble made of iron or steel wire, and called " mízráb." Those instruments which have frets (sundri) have them moveable, as it is the invariable practise to set the frets according to the rág or melody to be performed, and there are certain set tunes appropriate to the different hours of day or evening.

861.—[ ].—Tambúra—This guitar has only four strings, and no frets. It is a very favorite instrument, and accompanies the voice. The tambúra is called " chherwala," *viz.*, " the accompanier," as it is shaken (chherna) or twanged to the voice. The strings consist of " madham " or first string, which gives the melody; and three others form the base or drone, tuned to the octave and fifth. The tambura is a large guitar, with a large hollow body made of a gourd, faced with wood, and with a long stem or handle. It carries four strings, one of brass and three of iron wire: the strings are much thicker than those of the " sitár " (which follows). One string gives the melody, and the others the base or drone, but usually the instrument being used to accompany the voice, the changes of tone in the first string are few.

862.—[ ] " Sitár "—There are several kinds, all of the varieties of guitar, to which word the name has a clear affinity. In form these instruments are not inelegant. The body is gourd shaped, and exceedingly bulging; in fact consisting of the half or section of a large gourd, with a flat face, the shoulder sloping off into the long wooden handle: the manufacture will be described presently. The instruments are often prettily and elaborately inlaid with ivory or else painted in gold and colors and varnished. The varieties of " Sitár " to be now described are the " Madham Sitár, " the " Chárgah Sitár," and the " Tarbdár Sitár." The favorite form of " Sitár " is called " Madham". This is the instrument introduced at Dehli by Amír Khisro in the reign of Kai Kubád, as already intimated.

The Madham Sitár has the handle long and hollow, or deeply concave, but faced with a thin piece of " tûn " wood. The frets are of brass, and grooved in the middle, so as to retain the cat-gut belt which holds the fret to the handle, but admits of it being moved up and down to the position proper for the " rág " or music to be performed, as already explained.

The frets are 16 in number, that is, prepared to produce on the first string, two octaves; in compass, a large instrument is sometimes made with twenty-one frets or three octaves.

The Sitár has commonly five strings, but sometimes six. The first string, called madham, is of thin steel wire, obtained from Delhi or Barelí; the others are two of brass, and the third of steel wire.

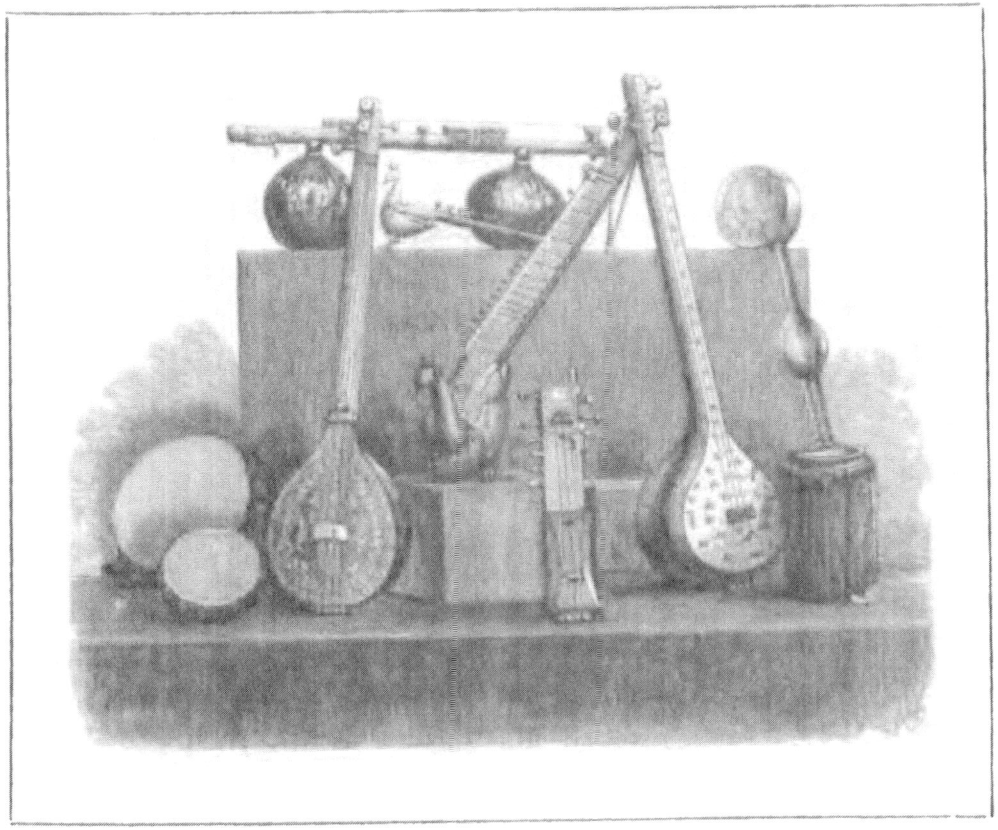

GROUP OF MUSICAL INSTRUMENTS.

The three last are the drone or accompanying, and always open, strings, being tuned to the key note, fifth or 'panchma,' and the lower octave of the key note; if there are six strings, the key note is doubled in unison; if seven, the third is given as well as the fifth, thus giving the whole chord.

863.—" Chárgah Sitár," is like the Madham, has four strings, and no frets, but permanent marks on the handle indicating the position of the fingering.

864.—" Tarbdár Sitár," or Sympathetic Sitár, has the handle slightly concave, and under the frets and under the playing wires a set of very thin steel wires are extended, tuned to the ascending notes of the gamut. The pegs which hold these strings are at the sides of the handle, those holding the playing strings at the head. The "tarb" are purely sympathetic strings, vibrating and producing a shrill twang in unison, and by sympathy with the corresponding note struck on the upper strings. The admirers of the Sympathetic Piano-forte of modern times will perhaps be surprised to note so very ancient a recognition of the principle. The 'tarb' strings appear to me to be tuned rather flat of the true tones, which produces a greater twang, and there is always one tone below the key note. Thus, suppose the first strings of the drone strings is tuned to C, then the lowest of the "tarb" strings will be tuned to the B below and so on, upwards.

865.—"*Bin.*"—The next instrument of this class is a 'bín.' It consists of a long hollow bar or key board, flat above, and concave below; on this the wires rest, and it is supported at either end by a large gourd. The form will be more readily understood from the plate.

The "bín" is the best sounding of all the stringed instruments played by aid of the fingers and the "mizráb" or wire guard.

It has six strings, and moveable frets; the first string alone, which is played with the frets, is called "báj." The other six strings are strung at some distance off the "báj," so as to leave room for the play of the finger The second and third are of steel wire, the fourth of brass, the fifth of steel, and the sixth of steel also, but with fine brass wire coiled upon it. This string is called "larz."

They are tuned thus—

2nd.—Kharj	C.	unison.
3rd.—Kharj	C.	
4th.—Pancham	G	above.
5th.—Madham	G.	octave below.
6th.—Lars	C.	octave below the second string.

The bín has also the sympathetic strings called "tarb," whose screws are on the side of the handle. They are nine in number,—that is, eight notes of the gamut and one below; thus the second string of the upper set being tuned to 'middle C. "Kharj"—the lowest note of the tarb will be B natural, the second C natural, corresponding to the second string above, and so on up the scale.

The bín is frequently made of a very large size with proportionately stout wires, and can then produce a loud sound: it is used more for instrumental music than accompanying the voice. It is not to be confused with a sort of *pipe* also called 'bín.'

866.—*Rabáb.*—Is an instrument much used in Lucknow and in Hindustán, but not in the Punjab. It has six strings, and a long handle about three feet long. The strings are attached to screws in the broad head of the handle, and arranged in a peculiar manner, which will be understood from the figure in the annexed plate.

I have now only to add a few instruments, which are hardly fit to be called instruments at all, being rude and unmusical sounding guitars, fitted with only one or two strings, and capable only of affording a sort of accompaniment to the voice. Such are generally used by fakirs and wandering singers.

867.—" *King.*"—A rude instrument, deriving its name from the twanging shrill noise it makes. It consists of a single wire stretched over two small bridges resting at either end of a stick or bamboo, which passes through a small half gourd at either end, like our basket stick: the face of the gourd is left open (fig. 1.)

This instrument is used by Brahman beggars when singing for alms, &c.

868.—" *Yak tára.*"—This is a rude instrument with one string, for accompanying the voice, and used by fakirs sometimes: also accompanied with the "kartal" or "bones." It consists of a long bamboo handle. with a small circular body made of half a gourd, and with parchment strained over the front, on this is a small bridge over which the brass wire passes. The wire is secured to the end of the bamboo projecting slightly through and beyond the body. A large wooden peg or screw at the end of the handle enables the player to adjust the tone of the string.

869.—" *Chártára.*"—Played with a wooden stick or plectrum, ('jawa' or jaba), which is a thin piece of wood shaped as (fig. 4.) The chártára is shown in (fig. 2.) It has four strings, three of steel and one of brass wire. An instrument I saw of this name at Delhi, had only two strings, and was played with a bow like the 'Kamánch' (fig. 3.)

870.—" *Saród,*" also called Rabáb, from Bunnoo. This instrument is mostly used by Kábulis and in Khorásáu, and so is found in our frontier districts One specimen in the collection of 1864 was described as "rabáb." The instrument, which is rather elegantly shaped, is figured in the plate. The great depth of the body, as shewn in the side view. is remarkable. The body and a part of the handle, (as far as the fret marks) are hollow, and made of 'tûn' or 'shísham' wood.

The handle and body as far as the central bend or waist, are faced with wood, and the rest of the body with parchment. There are six catgut strings which are played on with the 'jawa' like the last described instrument. These strings pass over a small wooden bridge on the parchment, and are secured to a piece of leather, which is fixed to the bottom of the instrument, and has the end split into tags. to each one of which a string end is fastened off. There are also five sympathetic brass wires. (*tarb*) which pass into the hollow body of the handle through small holes made for the purpose, and are wound on screws the handles of which project at the side.

The Rabáb called "Rabáb Banársi"—Benares rabáb—is an instrument with a bow.

The next series consists of three stringed instruments, which are played with the finger, or with small sticks or hammers. These instruments no doubt suggested originally the design of the Virginal, Clavichord and Harpsichord. which have been improved into the modern Piano-forte: they correspond with the Dulcimer and Psaltery of ancient writers.

Of these instruments, only one exists in the Museum of Lahore, as in use in the Panjab, the others are obsolete.

871.—"*Kánún.*"—This is the psaltery or sort of harp. It consists of a frame shaped as in figure 6. The strings, which are steel, are twenty-three in number, to include three whole octaves: they are fixed by moveable screws at the upper end. It differs from our harp in principle of construction, inasmuch as the strings which are fixed to the sounding board, are thence carried, not diagonally upwards to the curved upper beam, but horizontally to a beam opposite the sounding board. There are 28 strings.

872.—"*Kantúra.*"—This instrument consists of a hollow and flat sounding board, made of tûn wood, and of an oblong shape, supported partly on a hollow square box, and partly by two tressel legs or rests. The specimen I describe from was about 20 inches long and 8 broad. In the upper part (the end opposite the box) the screws for holding the wires are fixed upright and perpendicular to the face of the sounding board; the strings, twenty-two in number (3 octaves) are of steel wire, and of equal length, the requisite adjustment as to length being attained by the wires passing over or rather through some ivory pegs arranged diagonally across the board.

The instrument is played with the finger and 'mizrab.' It is tuned from one note below the key note, and then regularly up the scale by full tones.

We now come to the stringed instruments, which are played with a bow (gaz or kumání). There are several varieties: the most pretensious is the—

873.—"*Táús.*"—A long handled instrument, of which the body is in the form of a peacock, whence the name. The upper part of the body is covered with strained parchment, and the lower part highly colored, gilt and varnished to resemble a peacock. This curious instrument is figured in the plate annexed. The handle, which is very long, is hollow, but faced with a thin slip of tûn wood. It carries sixteen moveable brass frets. Along the left side of the keyboard or handle, a small bar of wood is attached, which carries sixteen pegs, which hold sixteen sympathetic steel strings "tarb," which are arranged slightly diagonally, so as to come down to the bridge of the instrument, which supports the four main strings on the upper edge, and the sixteen "tarb" strings through sixteen small holes in the centre of it. The four strings are arranged as usual: one alone at the right side, which is changed by fingering to produce the melody; the other three tuned to the key note, fifth and octave form the bass or drone accompaniment: the four strings are made, the first three of steel, the fourth of brass wire. All are of equal length and attached to four large pegs, two in front and two at the side of the extreme end of the handle, but as the second string produces a shriller tone than could be got by having the full length and tightening the screw, it is shortened by a small ivory peg through which it passes, just below the fifth fret. The instrument, which I have heard played with considerable skill, is played with a bow fitted with a number of black horse hairs, and stiffened with rosin (biroza); the hairs of the bow are not arranged flat as in an European violin bow, but in a bunch, with a piece of wood at one end, which can be adjusted to tighten the hairs. When once set right they are tied down with string, there being no screw arrangement as in the European bow.

874.—“ *Sárangi.*”—Is the common fiddle used by all the nautch players. It has a thick short handle, almost as broad as the body, and is like it, hollow. The body is also hollow, and faced with parchment; it is chamfered or pared away at the sides towards the middle. The strings are of catgut, four in number, and attached to screws with large knobs fixed in the handle, two in front and two at the sides. There are also eleven or thirteen brass wire ‘ tarb ’ or sympathetic strings, which are fixed to screws or pegs arranged in two rows: these pass through the body of the handle and project at the side. The end of the wires are introduced through small holes in the surface. The sound of this instrument is very harsh and disagreeable. The first strings and the second, in order to shorten the length, rest on a small bridge near the tightening screw, called “ sír ” or “ pilak ;” the third rests on a tag of tightly wound silk, possibly to deaden the sound: this tag, which can be pulled under the string at pleasure, is called “ batti.” The curious shape of the head and handle will be seen in the plate.

Another instrument was described to me as in use in Pattiala, as the Chång, (fig. 7). I have some misgivings that this is either the same as Saranda, or only a variety. I have not been able to procure a specimen, but am told that it is at once recognized by the body being in the shape of a kite (patang.) The body is made of wood, and the upper part is hollow and open, the lower part is covered with parchment and carries the bridge. There are five strings attached to screws placed thus:  in the handle, and also eleven sympathetic strings, which are attached at the side. The instrument is played with the “ gazi ” or bow.

875.—“ *Tid* ” or “ *Tad.*”—This is a much ruder instrument than any of the foregoing. Its body is of roughly cut deodar wood, shaped as in fig. 8, the upper part being hollow, the lower covered with parchment; it has four strings, three of steel wire, and the fourth of thick twisted copper wire, and is played with a rude bow. This instrument is only to be found in villages, and is said to be much used in Márwár.

876.—“ *Dotára.*”—An instrument called dotára, but having however four strings, is not unlike in shape to the Chártara, but has a short thick handle like a sárangi.

877.—“ *Chikára*—is the fakir fiddle. It is represented in fig. 9. The three strings are made of bunches of black horse hair, and there are five sympathetic strings. The handle is covered with wood and is hollow, the lower part of the body is covered with parchment.

878.—“ *Kamánchi*”—is a sort of large fiddle, twice the size of a “ sarangi, ” and used mostly by Kashmiris (fig. 3.)

Before passing on to the wind instruments, I should mention that the manufacture of stringed instruments is a specialty of one class of workmen ‘ Khátamband ’; they never make drums or pipes of any sort.

Their tools are like those of ordinary carpenters, but capable of doing smaller and finer work. They have the “ tesha ” or adze; some saws, a “ chosá,” or long thin rasp, a “ tikora ” or three cornered file, a “ miyán-tarásh,” or gouge or scoop to make the hollow handles of instruments with; a “ nímgira ” or half round file; a “ kanassi ” or two edged file with a fine or “ smooth ” cut; a “ sathri ” or “ chaurasi ” (small chisel); “ sanni,” forceps; “ parkar ” or compasses, and a “ barma,” to bore holes. The wood used is invariably “ tûn,” which is tolerably hard, does not split, has no resin or oil, polishes well,

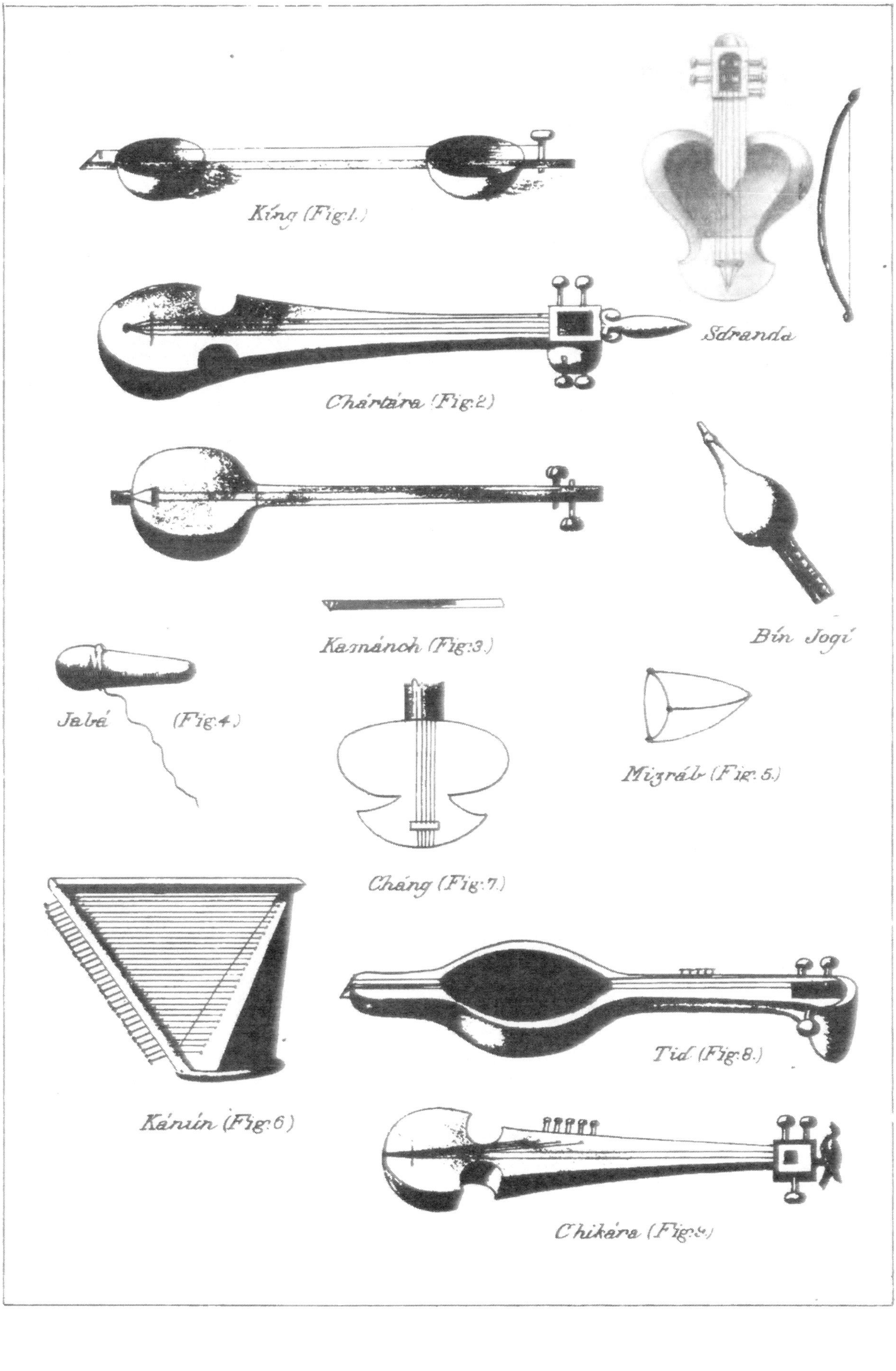
Kíng (Fig:1.)
Sáranda
Chártára (Fig:2)
Bín Jogí
Kamánch (Fig:3.)
Jabá (Fig:4.)
Mizráb (Fig. 5.)
Cháng (Fig:7.)
Tíd (Fig:8.)
Kánún (Fig:6)
Chikára (Fig:9)

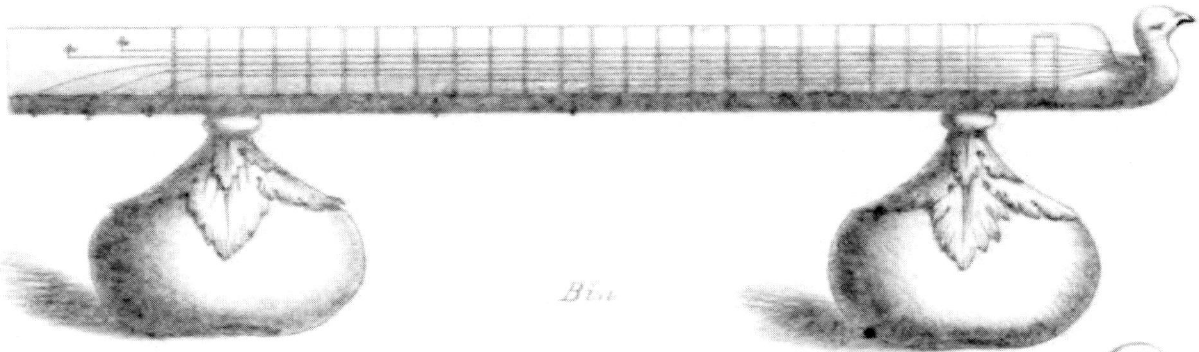

Bín

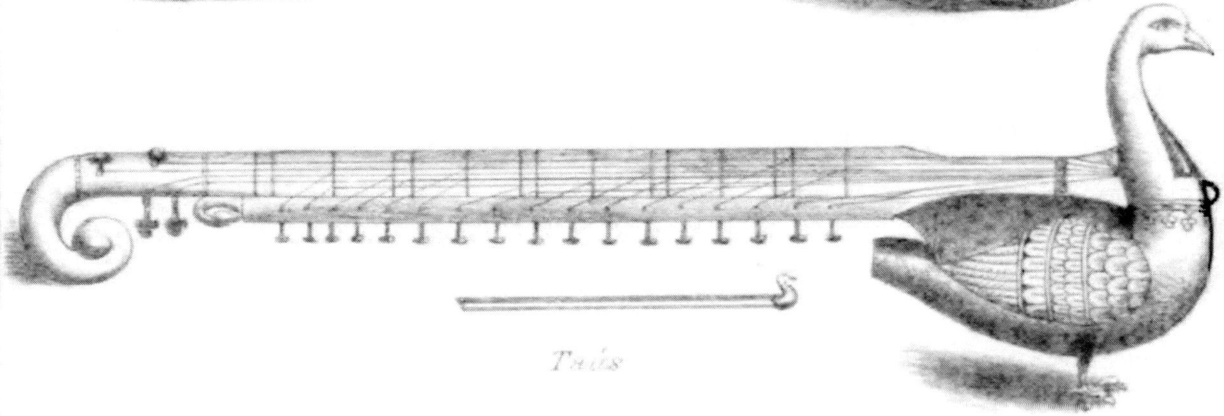

Taús

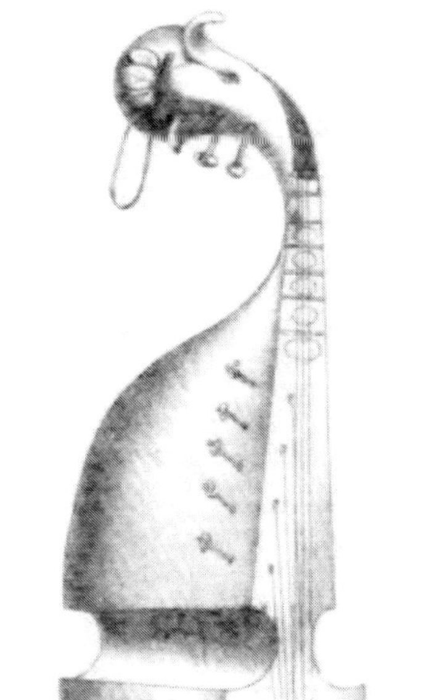

Sarod or Rabáb

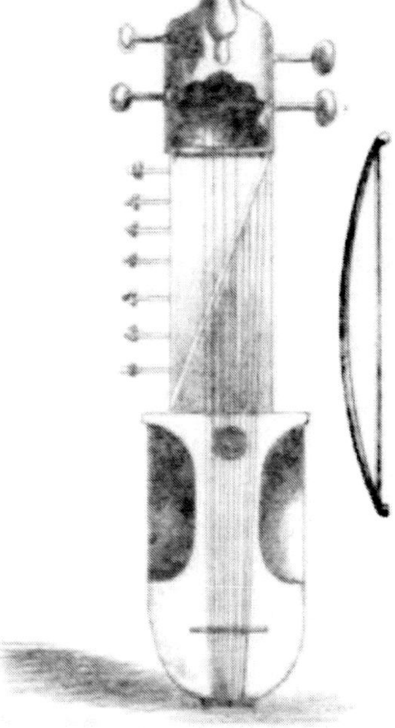

Sárangi

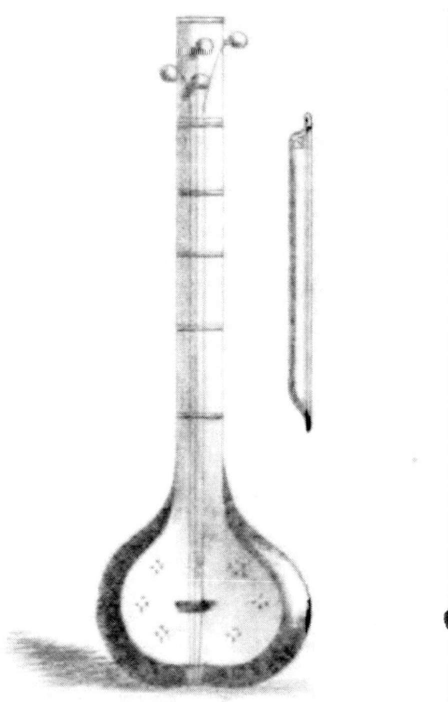

Rabáb Banársi

and is not liable to insects or to decay. The dry shell of the great gourd *(Cucurbita maxima)* and *Lagenaria* (the bottle gourd) are in request for the bodies of all sorts of sitárs, bíns &c.; ivory is required for inlaying and for the bridges (ghori or surdhárí) of the instruments.

DIVISION II.

WIND INSTRUMENTS.

These are not so numerous as the stringed instruments, nor are they commonly used, except perhaps the bánsri or flute, and a sort of flageolet; snake charmers carry the "bín," and trumpets are used in heathen worship.

The following is a list;—

879.—"*Bansrí*"—A flute or fife with four holes, made of bamboo.

880.—"*Nai*" is a straight pipe somewhat similar.

881.—"*Alghoza*"—A sort of flageolet also made of bamboo, has seven holes, is slightly funnel-shaped, and played either singly or with two in the mouth at once.

882.—"*Surná*"—vulgarly called "túti"—A wooden tube with a trumpet shaped end. In fact a sort of clarionet.

883.—"*Nafrí*"—A flageolet played by Kashmirís, very like the last named.

884.—"*Bín.*"—This instrument consists of a double flageolet, fitted to a hollow and narrow necked gourd. It is figured in the annexed plate. It is principally played by snake charmers.

885.—"*Sharnao.*"—From the Bunnoo hills, and also to be met with in other hill places of the west Punjab. Is a regular bag-pipe, or set of pipes fitted with an inflated goat's skin.

886.—"*Mardang*"—is a sort of postman's horn.

887.—"*Turí*"—is a very long, and loud sounding straight brass trumpet, used at marriages, religious festivals, &c. When curved it is called "karná." Horns (narsingha), and conch shells (shank) are also used on such occasions.

DIVISION III.

MISCELLANEOUS.

The following are miscellaneous :—

888.—" *Jaltarang,*"—consists of a series of thin porcelain cups of sizes, partly filled with water, according to the note required, and so tuned to two or three octaves, note by note. They are played with small bamboo sticks, like our harmonicon, &c.

889.—" *Talli* "—a small bell worn round the neck.

890.—" *Jora or Kainsi* "—two small bells, struck one in the other.

891.—" *Santúr* "—a steel triangle, similar to that used in bands with us.

892.—" *Chaina*"—Large cymbals.

893.—" *Jhánj* "—Also a kind of cymbal.

894.—" *Mejra* "—A name for cymbals appearing in the Gugaira (Montgomery) collection.

895.—" *Kartál* "—two pieces of hard dark wood, generally shisham, played just as the " bones" are by Negro singers.

896.—" *Múnchang or muchang* " is the Jew's harp. This toy appears to be of great antiquity in India, and is of exactly the same form and construction as those used by children in Europe. I am told that at Kalka (Ambala District) at a certain season of the year these toys are made and sold by hundreds.

DIVISION IV.

DRUMS.

Drums are so universally admired, and form such a necessary accompaniment of every entertainment, procession, or ceremony, that it is not surprising to find a great variety of every possible size and shape.

897.—" *Tambúr* "—is an English Military drum.*

898.—" *Dhol* "—Is a very large barrel-shaped drum, held horizontally, both ends being fitted with leather or parchment, and struck with slightly curved sticks.

899.—" *Dholki* " or *Dholak*—is the same shape, but somewhat smaller.

900.—" *Pakáwaj* "—A large drum of barrel-shape, but *much* more elongated, and consequently having the parchment end much smaller in diameter. It is used in processions.

901.—" *Nakára* "—Is a kettle drum.

902.—" *Dhaussa* "—A military kettle drum carried on horse back.

903.—" *Naubat* "— A very large kettle drum carried on camel back.

* Not to be confused with tambúra, the sort of guitar before described.

904.—*Tabla.*—The pair of small drums played on to accompany the "sarangi" at a nautch. The body is made of turned and lacquered wood; the bases being rather broader than the upper end, they stand upright, and have parchment at the upper end only, which can be adjusted and tightened by long leather thongs. The tabla are always in pairs, tuned differently: the one with a high note is marked with a large black spot on the parchment, and is called "agaura;" the other or lower toned drum is called "pichaura" or "dháma"—played with the hand.

905.—"*Tásha*" is a sort of tambourine. Its body in fact consists of a sort of basin of pottery ware, covered with goat skin and played with sticks. A hole is made through the basin at the back. The instrument is worn suspended from the neck by the performer by strings, and used in processions, weddings, &c.

906.—"*Daira or Darya*" is a large tambourine without bells.

907.—"*Khanjri*" is a smaller tambourine with bells, set in the rim, just as in the European tambourine.

A native book of musical instruments I have seen, contains a small but rather deep made tambourine, with bells called "dafli."

908.—"*Mandil*" is a small barrel-shaped drum, of turned wood. hung by a string sound the neck, and played on at both end's with the hand. This is used by itinerant showmen &c.

909.—"*Daf*"—is a sort of tambourine, used only by bhangis, and chúras (sweeper caste). A circular wooden frame, the front covered with parchment and the back by a network of catgut (or rather goat-gut) leaving, however, a round hole in the centre.

910.—"*Daurú*"—A small drum, used by Kahárs (hill carriers) and also by itinerant showmen: it is shaped like a 'dumb-bell,' is of turned wood, and has a parchment face at either end; two small strings are attached, each armed with a pellet covered with cloth. The little instrument is grasped in the middle by one hand, and then being twisted about, the pellets hit the parchment and produce the sound.

The Kahárs, when sitting round to sing, will frequently use an earthern 'ghara' for a drum, or will support a metal plate on an inverted 'ghara,' and lay a bracelet or bangle on the plate, and strike it as a drum; the bracelet causes a jingling sound, as well as the drumming noise.

911.—*Tumbanári.*—A drum used by Kashmiris. It consists of an earthen pot, narrow at the bottom and wide at the mouth, shaped in fact like a flower pot; the mouth is closed with parchment or skin, and the instrument is held under the left arm and drummed on with the right hand.

CLASS XXVII.

SMALL MACHINES FOR VARIOUS PURPOSES.

This Class cannot be expected in the present state of advance to which this country has attained, to be very numerously represented, or to exhibit any very great skill. I shall have little else to offer by readers, than a list of the best of such articles as were exhibited in 1864, and have been elsewhere met with.

The first kind consist of locks.

912.—Ordinary native padlocks.

Every man fastens his house door, and even his boxes, by means of a chain and staple with one of these padlocks.

The padlocks are of two kinds, one of which is considered insecure, and the other other more difficult to open.

The upper one (fig 1), in the annexed plate, is closed simply by a catch which is pressed forward by a spiral spring, so as to fix the end of the handle which projects downwards for the purpose.

The key is a mere screw; it is inserted at the mouth of a short tube, which carries at one end the iron catch, and is surrounded by the spiral spring. It is wound in till the thick part touches the outer shell of the padlock, when the leverage causes the internal spiral to be contracted, by which means the catch is withdrawn and the handle let loose. A thief could of course effect the same thing by inserting almost any old screw key of the same size. A single blow would also remove the end of the case, and then the catch could be pushed back with ease. A glance at the sections shewn in the sketch will explain this.

The second kind of lock, though still ruder in appearance, and having the awkward bar or iron (shewn at fig 2) for its key, is yet stronger and resists the burglars of this country better. In this lock there is a strong iron bolt thrown across (fig 3, *a*) and is held there by the upper bolt (*b*), being furnished with a stiff spring in either side (*c. c.*) This cannot slip through the hole at the end of the case (*d*) without being first compressed by the fork of the key. A thief, unless he happens to have a key of the right size to catch the springs (which may vary considerably), has to break the whole lock. At best however this is a very rude and by no means secure padlock. Some remarks about native locks will be found in the Jury Report on Cultery and Hardware at page 152, *et seq.* They should have more properly been inserted here, but it was found impossible to break up the report.

Among the most noteworthy of these locks, is that sent from Basahir (No. 7779), and used in other parts of the hill districts also. In principle it is not unlike the second figure in the plate, as it consists of a bolt thrown across the aperture in the lower part: the key is however different, it has to be inserted vertically through a slit in the upper part, which is made with a flat top, and then being inserted, has to be pushed sideways till it catches the spring inside, and allows the bolt to be pushed back. The key is shaped as at fig. 3.

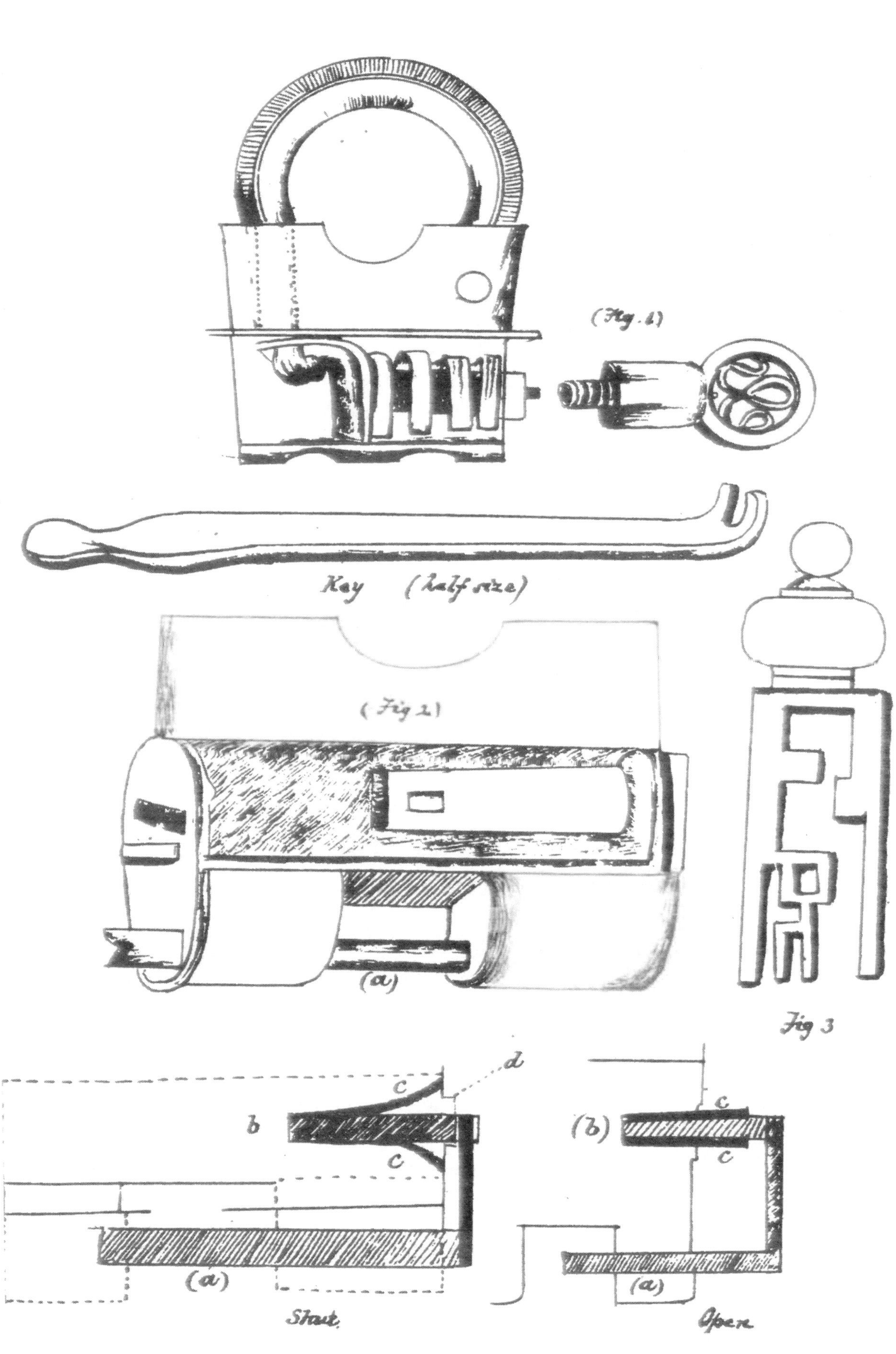
(Fig. 1)
Key (half size)
(Fig 2)
(a)
Fig 3
d
c
b
c
(a)
Shut
(b)
c
c
(a)
Open

Omitting locks imitated from European models, the ones worth extracting from the Catalogue of 1864 are—

913.—[No. 7870].—Monster lock of polished iron (valued at 40 Rs.) made by Ilahí Baksh of Lahore. This is on the principle of figure 2, and opens with a lever bar.

914.—[No. 7873].—Puzzle padlock.—This is in shape like a horse: it is from a maker in the distant province of Bukhára. It is certainly difficult to open. The key is fixed in it, but has to be properly applied, so as to enable the bolt to be withdrawn. In shape it is made to resemble a horse. I had no opportunity of discovering the secret. The great difficulty is to find out how to insert the key, which carries a small moveable bar at one end. If the key is once inserted the puzzle is overcome, as a push throws back the bolt.

915.—[No. 7890].—Was a padlock, made in the form of a tiger, and gilt. It was made by Pír Baksh of Lahore, who valued it at 20 Rupees.

A series of neatly made scales and weights for postage purposes was sent from Ludhiana.

CLASS XXVIII.

ORDNANCE, AND ARMS EXHIBITED AS SUCH.

In former days, as already intimated, the art of making swords and guns, as well as of defensive armour, was successfully practised in the Punjab. It is at present only to be found in the workshops of a few artificers, relicts of the Sikh days, and of apprentices who had learnt from them. In Kashmir, however, both swords and firearms are well made, and the sword blades of Peshawur are famous. The cutlers of Sealkot, Nizámábad, and Wazírábád (Gujránwala district), and of Gujrat, are still able to make such weapons, but not of a very good description of metal.

DIVISION I.

ORDNANCE.

It may be as well to make some mention of the art of cannon founding as practised in this country.

The casting of cannons in brass was understood, and a few well finished specimens may be seen in the Lahore Fort Armoury, and one good specimen (Mohamadan work) in the Lahore Museum.

Outside the latter building stands the once celebrated gun called " Zamzama," or " Bhangiwalla töp."

It was cast in the time of Ahmad Shah Dúrání, and was evidently considered a wonderful work, even after making allowance for the Oriental metaphors of the inscription.

The gun is 14 feet 4½ inches in length, exclusive of the cascabel, and the aperture of the bore is 9½ inches.

The following is a transcript of the descriptive account placed in the Central Museum.

The great gun called " Zamzama, " or the " Bhangíanwalí töp, " was cast A. D. 1761, by Shah Walí Khan, Wazír of Ahmad Shah Dúrání.

After the departure of Ahmad Shah, the gun was left in the possession of the Sikh Sirdars of the Bhangí *misl* (whence its name " Bhangiánwalí töp.") It came to be regarded as a talisman of supremacy among the Sikhs. Eventually, Ranjít Singh possessed himself of it, and it was used by him at the siege of Multan, in A. D. 1818. From that date it used to stand at the Delhi gate of Lahore, until removed in 1860.

The gun now stands near the Central Museum, facing the Sadr Bazaar, in which position it was placed on the occasion of the Duke of Edinburgh's visit to Lahore, in February 1870.

The inscription on the gun is translated as follows :—

" By order of the Emperor [Ahmad Shah] Dúr-i-dúrán,
Shah Walí Khán, the Wazír, made this gun, named
Zamzama, the taker of strongholds,
The work of Shah Nazr.

1

" In the reign of the Emperor, possessing dignity like the Feridún,
Dispenser of Justice, robed in equity,

2

[In the reign of] his present Majesty, Ahmad Shah Dúr-i-Dúrán,
A Prince occupying a throne mighty as Jamshíd's,

3

There was issued unto the Chief Wazír,
From the threshold of His Highness,

4

An order to have cast, with every possible skill,
A gun, terrible as a dragon, and huge as a mountain :

5

[Yea, the order was given] to his heaven-enthroned Majesty's devoted servant,
Shah Walí Khán, Wazír.

6

So, in order to effect this great achievement,
The master-workman called up his endeavours ;

7

Till, with consummate toil, was cast
This wondrous gun—Zamzama,—

8

A destroyer even of the strongholds of heaven—
Under the auspices of his Majesty.

9

I enquired of Reason for the date of this gun ;
Reason angrily replied—

10

" If thou wilt give thy life in payment
I will repeat to thee the date."

11

I did so, and he replied ;—' *What a gun is this !*'
' *The form of a fire raining dragon.*' "

The last lines give the chronogram of the date of the gun, 1174 A. H., or 1761 A. D.

The letters in the words have a numerical value, according to the "Abjad" system.

This gun is mounted on a large carriage (takht). The Sikhs used shísham wood for the carriages, but always preferred Kikar (*Acacia arabica)* for the wheels, on account of its toughness. They thought this of so much importance, that for the supply to the arsenals in Kashmir, the Sikhs attempted to form a plantation of the Kíkar in the uncongenial climate of Srinagar, where a few of the trees may still be seen. Besides guns cast in brass, long narrow iron guns may be seen at Lahore, and also a few of wider bore, made of bars of iron secured by iron rings or bands.

Iron small bore cannons, mounted on the wooden saddles of camels were in use, and called Zambúrak.

The principle of making guns in bars with rings, was considered as the early and rude idea, and was abandoned when the art of casting was invented.

The cascabel of a cannon is called " dumeli" or " badeli"; the trunnions " hathúa."

The frame of the carriage on which the gun rests is " parh"; " makkí " is the sight mark on the muzzle; and "dídbán" the sight at the other end. The touchhole is called " piála".

Guláb Singh invented a very small gun (of iron) mounted on a small carriage for hill warfare, it was drawn by a man or by a goat.

The " Obchí " or howitzer, was only introduced after the contact of the British power with the Sikhs, and was used to discharge shells (gola-sél) made of zinc, because they did not know how to cast hollow iron shells.

The Obchí is said to be kothídar, or having a chamber at the end of the bore, which the cannon has not.

The shell is made in a mould having a solid centre and a layer of wax over it; over the wax other layers of clays are smeared. The wax is melted (as described at page 141) and thus a hollow is left, which is filled by the melted metal.

An other way is to take an iron " reza, " or hollow iron mould, which separates into two halves ; each is filled with a mixture of sand and oil, and a wooden ball of the required size first impressed into one half and then into the other : a hollow sphere is thus formed when the halves are closed together, but in the middle, an earthen ball (bacha mittí ka) is fixed to an iron pin, projecting from the bottom of the mould. The " bacha " is made of the same size as the interior hollow of the shell is to be. Metal is then poured in.

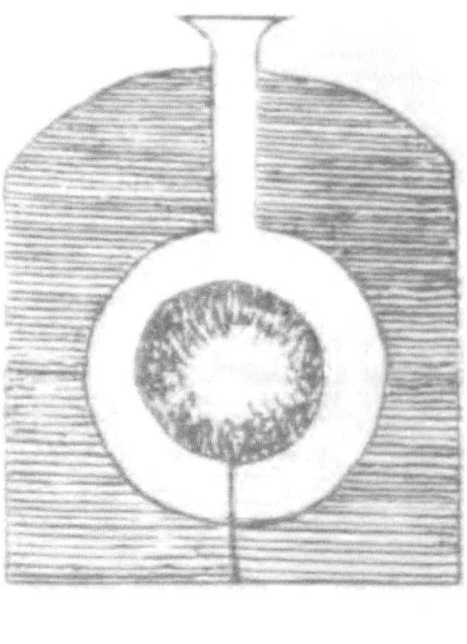

The mouth of the shell is fitted with a tube of box wood, through which passes a falíta (or fatíla) or slow match, made of cotton thread soaked with a paste of powder and spirits.

The "obchí" was made for shells of 10 seers, 15 seers, or 20 to 25 seers.

The next kind of gun to be described is the "Hôth"—always constructed of the length of nine times the diameter of the aperture; either shell or shot could be fired, and could be sent much further than by the obchí. This gun was also made without a chamber (kothí.)

The large mortar was called "Ghubára ;" the length of the piece being half as much again as the diameter of the mouth : it was made of gun metal, never of iron.

Large shells were made with a series of thin iron bars, called "kapánch" inside. This was done by simply taking an earthen bacha, or ball, to keep the centre clear, over this the iron bars were arranged all round, fixed with wire at the bottom and round the neck. Each kapanch was shaped thus  Over this frame wax was spread, and then earth. The wax being melted out, as before described, and metal poured in. When the shell case was thus complete, the earthen bacha was broken up, and picked out in pieces, leaving the collection of "kapanchs" inside, which remained attached by the neck to the shell by the contact of the melted metal. The explosion of the shell caused the plates to separate, and a dangerous discharge of these sharp pieces of blade-like metal was the consequence.

Several guns called "jazail" have been used in forts. They are merely very large long muskets, so big that a man could not use them.

These particulars were given me by Nidhán Singh, an old man who used to cast guns in the Sikh times. He tells me he has cast 700 pieces in his day, and originally learnt through his father from a Kábulí.

DIVISION II.

FIREARMS FOR WARFARE OR SPORTING PURPOSES.

These will be best illustrated by enumerating, with the addition of descriptive notes, where necessary, the collections sent to the Exhibition of 1864.

Amritsar.

916.—[10364].—A pistol (the English term is used in Pánjábí—pistôl.)

917.—[10365].—A blunderbuss, called "karábín" in the vernacular catalogue. It is a short and somewhat wide mouthed piece, but the short and trumpet shape barrelled weapon generally known as the blunderbuss, is not called karábín, but "sher bachá."

Lahore.

918.—[8731]—Matchlocks inlaid with gold.

These matchlocks are of the form which will be seen in the plate representing 'a group of arms.' There is one near the right edge of the pillar. It is fired by a "falíta" or slow match, and called "bandúk tora dár." This latter word is said to be derived from the "taur" or "tor," the Elephant creeper, the fibrous stalks of which, when dry, were used for slow matches. The air roots of the "pipal" (*Ficus religiosa*) and of the "bar" (*Ficus Indica*) are similarly used.

"Bandúk pathar kalah."—A long barrelled piece, firing with flint and pan.

"Bharmár lahori."—A kind of weapon that has both flint and a slow match, in case either should fail to go off. It was invented in Ranjít Singh's time by a Hindústaní called Mirza Bharmar, whence the name.

"Rafl."—This is merely a corruption of the English term rifle, and is made on the European model.

"Bandúk masála-dar"—"Masála-dar" means a weapon that is fired by a cap containing the explosive composition or "masála."

"Karábín."—A short barrelled gun, with the muzzle slightly trumpet-shaped.

"Sher bachá"—A short barrelled and very trumpet-shaped weapon, not larger however, than a large old-fashioned horse pistol.

"Bandúk rakh-dár" has a rifle bore.

PATIALA.

919.—[8107].—An air gun. (This is imitated from the European model.)

SIMLA.

920.—[10301].—A native matchlock—Sirmur State.

DERA ISMAIL KHAN.

921.—[10409].—A Pathan matchlock.

DERA GHAZI KHAN.

922.—[10413—34].—A matchlock from the Khurásán, exhibited by the LUND CHIEF.

923.—[10414—312].—Another from the Bozdár hills.

924.—[10416—314].—Another from Rájanpúr.

925.—[10417—315].—Another sent by the GURCHAIN CHIEF.

926.—[10418—316].—Another from Rájhan by IMAM BAKSH KHAN.

Shooting belts, called "Kamr-khísa," accompany most of these guns. They are furnished with a series of parallel tubes bound together, for holding bullets, a shot flask, a powder horn or "shákh," flint and steel, and a knife.

PESHAWUR.

927.—[226].—'Tofung Sindí'—value Rs. 500, from Sind, exhibited by MUHAMMAD ALI KHAN.

928.—[ ].—'Bandúk mah sipaia'—The long heavy matchlock used by the hill tribes: it is always known by having two prongs or metal supports to steady the barrel,

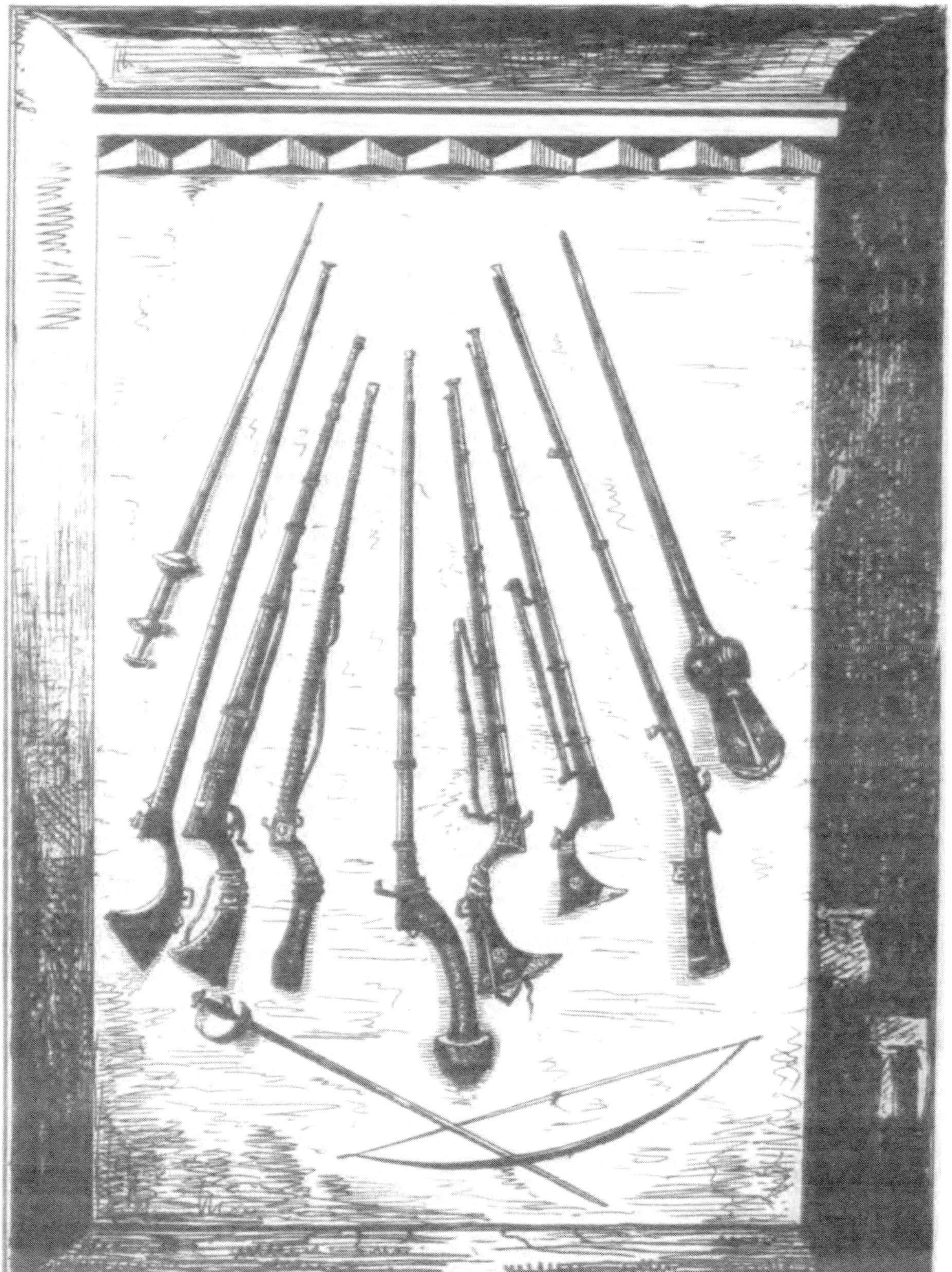

GROUP OF ARMS.

the weapon being too long and heavy to ensure an accurate shot without such support. Though these guns take a great time to load and adjust, yet, in the hands of Afrídís and others, when they *do* go off, they prove very deadly weapons.

It is now time to describe the method of making guns and boring the barrels.

The stock of a native gun is an unimportant part, and is generally narrow in form as will be best seen from the plate, showing a group of arms on the wall of the Exhibition of 1864.

The matchlock farthest to the left, and next a huge double-handed sword, is the usual form of a native gun: the one represented is "tora-dár," *i. e.*, fired by a slow match: the stock is of shísham wood. The two guns next to this having curiously carved stocks, so broad at the but end, are from Baháwalpur. The stocks are made of stained shísham, and have some silver and ivory inlaid ornaments. One of the long guns from the Deraját has a sort of knob or pad at the end to protect the user from the effects of the recoil. Such a piece is shewn in the centre of the group in the plate.

The locks of guns need no remark. There is first the simple matchlock, which consists merely of a trigger, with a small bar, which allows the piece of hooked metal which holds the 'falíta' or match, to drop and come in contact with the pan; there is also the common flint and steel lock, in no way differing from old fashioned pieces of European manufacture. Such locks as are now made with nipple and cap, are copies of the simple European model.

Gun barrels are made in three ways:—

First the common way, which is inferior; but guns for the rank and file in the Sikh army were thus made. The gun so made is called "patta-ka-bandúk." It consists simply in bending a flat broad bar of iron round a mandrel (láthi) into a tube, and hammering together the edges till they are thoroughly united. One good point about these guns was, that if they burst, which they often did, they did not do much harm.

The second way is to take a series of strands (gaz) of iron: each strand is originally square, and then called kandla, but has to be first twisted, so as to form a spirals sixteen of these strands are then longitudinally arranged round a shaft or "láthí" of iron, and tied in their place with iron wire. "Chikní mittí" a sort of fire clay, is next smeared over, and then the barrel is heated, a few inches at a time, and hammered together. The spiral twist of the strands leaves a peculiar water-mark in the iron, hence the barrel made in this second way are called "jauhar-dár."

The third way differs from this, in that no "láthí" is used, and the barrel is made of a spiral band of iron, over which strands are again wound the reverse way. This sort of gun is said to be "chúrídar."

This species of gun is said to be best made in Baháwálpur, and next to that at Kohat. Gun barrels are mostly made with "Guleri" or with "Bajaur" iron.

I shall only add, that in these " watered" guns, the outer surface is either round, or filed into eight facets, whence called " pahldar."

The following account of the Kohat manufacture has been kindly communicated to me by Mr. Robert Egerton, C. S., who saw the process.

" This is the piece of forging from Kohat, which I saw the gunsmiths there do before me in about an hour.

" They take a flat bar of Bajaur iron, straighten the edges, and reduce the bar to a uniform thickness by hammering and heating: they then hammer the bar to a point, and work it with a hammer under several heatings to a coil. No rod down the centre is used. The coil is hammered tight by hitting it on the ends, and is welded by covering it with a yellow clay (common at Kohat) and heating it. The clay has a reducing effect, and the surface of the iron becomes very fusible under its influence, so that when heated, the joints of the coil are easily welded with very light hammers and light blows. When the first coil is welded, another coil of finer iron, or of mixed metal, used to give a fine grain, is hammered on, the twist of the coil being reversed so as to break joint with the first coil. The upper coil is welded in the same way as the lower, and the whole mass becomes united.

" The barrel of a long gun is made by the process above described, more strips of iron being welded to the end of the first piece of the coil.

The points about the forging worthy of note appear to me to be—

1*st.*—The quality of the iron, which is remarkably fine and free from scale in working.

2*nd.*—The curious effect of the yellow clay. I think the clay should be analysed: its effect on the iron is surprising.

3*rd.*—The forging being completed without a mandril or any contrivance of preventing the sides of the barrel from collapsing under the blows of the hammer at welding heat."

I may here mention that the broad strip of flattened iron which is made into the inner tube or coil, is called " patta ". The thin rod which is used in the outer coil is in its first stage merely a thin square rod, and is called kandla ; before its application to the barrel it is twisted into a spiral stick (in the state called " kandla bata hua ") and it is this spiral, that when the rod is coiled on the barrel, leaves the water mark.

Gun boring is done as follows :—A gun, smooth-bored, is called sádá (*i. e.* plain) and rifle-bored is said to be " rakh-dár."

Every gun barrel, whatever kind of bore it is designed to have, is first cleaned with a number of iron tools called " silai," shaped like the " burkú," which is the next applied.

This is a round iron bar about ¼ inch in diameter, furnished with a handle thus :

At the end the bar is squared for about three inches of its length, and the square end is generally made of harder iron than the shaft; this end has also two plates of hard iron (aspát) welded in on either side, so as to give two sharp edges. This tool is touched with oil and forced into the rough barrel, and twisted about till the barrel is smooth inside.

The next tool is a "sáfi," shaped like a burkú, but the squared end is not only three inches, but a foot and a half or more in length, and is armed with welded plates on two of the sides as before, but the plates are not of aspát merely, but of the hardest and finest steel (fauládॱ)

After this, a tool called "nizák" is used.

The nizák consists of an iron rod about 4 feet long, with a short wooden handle. At the end of a rod are attached by a point, two half circular files, which hang down like the limbs of a flail: the flat sides being together and the file surfaces facing outwards. When put together they form one cylindrical file, which fits the mouth of the gun barrel, and is made to do so accurately by the introduction of one or more slips of leather between the two files.

This is worked up and down the barrel by hand, till the final smoothness and polish are given.

For the smooth bore, the process concludes with the use of the "nizák."

To produce the rifle bore, the above processes are followed, and when the nizák has been applied, the rifle bore tool, "rakh-bur," is applied. This consists of a long shaft of iron, at one end is an iron head shaped thus:

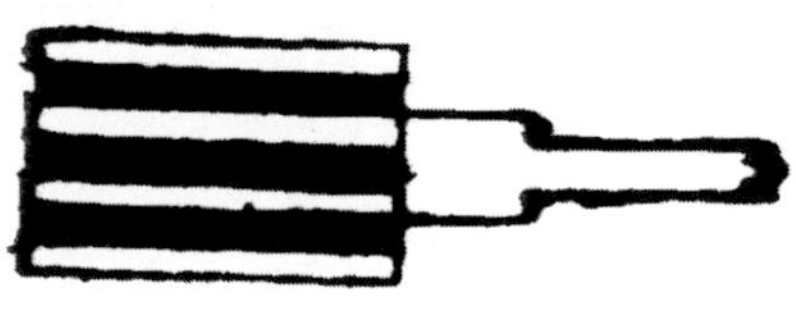

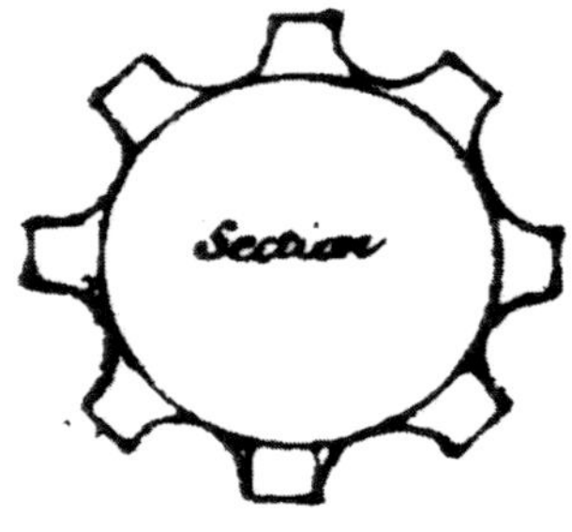

The head is thus milled, in order that it may be fixed firmly to the apparatus presently to be described, which gives the peculiar spiral motion required. At the other end is the head with which the groove is made. It consists merely of the end of the shaft, split down the middle, so as to be capable of being widened by the insertion of a "patri" or little wedge-plate of iron, and furnished on either side with a little bit of file about $1\frac{1}{2}$ inch long, and made of the hardest steel.

When the end of this is first forced into the barrel, the files make only a slight mark; but as by the working of the files (by the motion presently described) the grooves get deeper, it is necessary to widen the filing end. This is done by knocking the 'patri' farther and farther into the slit, till the greatest distention is produced that can be required. But this file head cannot be merely forced into the barrel and worked straight up and down the groove, but has to be regularly cut in a spiral, hence it is necessary to communicate to the "rakh-bur" an uniform spiral motion, coupled with considerable power.

This is effected by the following piece of simple machinery. First, a long and solid plinth or bench of brickwork and clay (*a. a.*) is built: it is about 7 feet long, 2½ feet high, and 2 feet broad, the surface is not perfectly horizontal, and has one end slightly higher than the other. On the surface of this slope a stout plank is fixed, the end of which projects some distance beyond the plinth. On to this two stout parallel bars (*c. c.*) are fixed; secured at one end by a cross brace (*f*), in which there is a hole, and a central pole or shaft of hard heavy sâl wood (*e*) passes through it. The other end of the pole or shaft is held by a moveable cross bit, (f^2) which slides up and down in appropriate grooves in the side bars; the projecting end of the central shaft is furnished with a knob and two stout arms (*d*), which the workman lays hold of to push the shaft forward and draw it back. The milled head iron shaft carrying the files as before described, (*h*) is now firmly fixed into the end of the wooden shaft, and the barrel to be bored is fixed with iron staples down to the end of the projecting plank, so that the end of the iron rod enters the mouth of the barrel(*g*). The arrangement will be easily understood by a glance at the diagram.

As at present described, however, the motion of the central pole or shaft would be straight up and down, whereas it is required to have a spiral motion. The hard wood pole is, therefore, deeply grooved by two spiral incisions, and the upper cross brace f^1, is perforated, not merely by a round hole, but by a round hole armed with two teeth, which, catching in the groves, cause the shaft, although simply propelled by the arm, to assume a spiral motion.

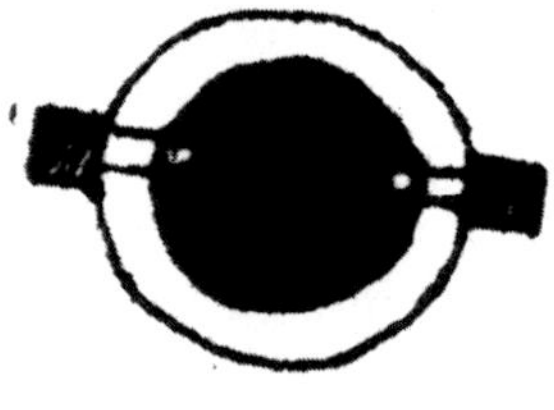

The barrels are bored usually with four grooves or more, two only are made at a time, and the position of the barrel then changed to receive two more.

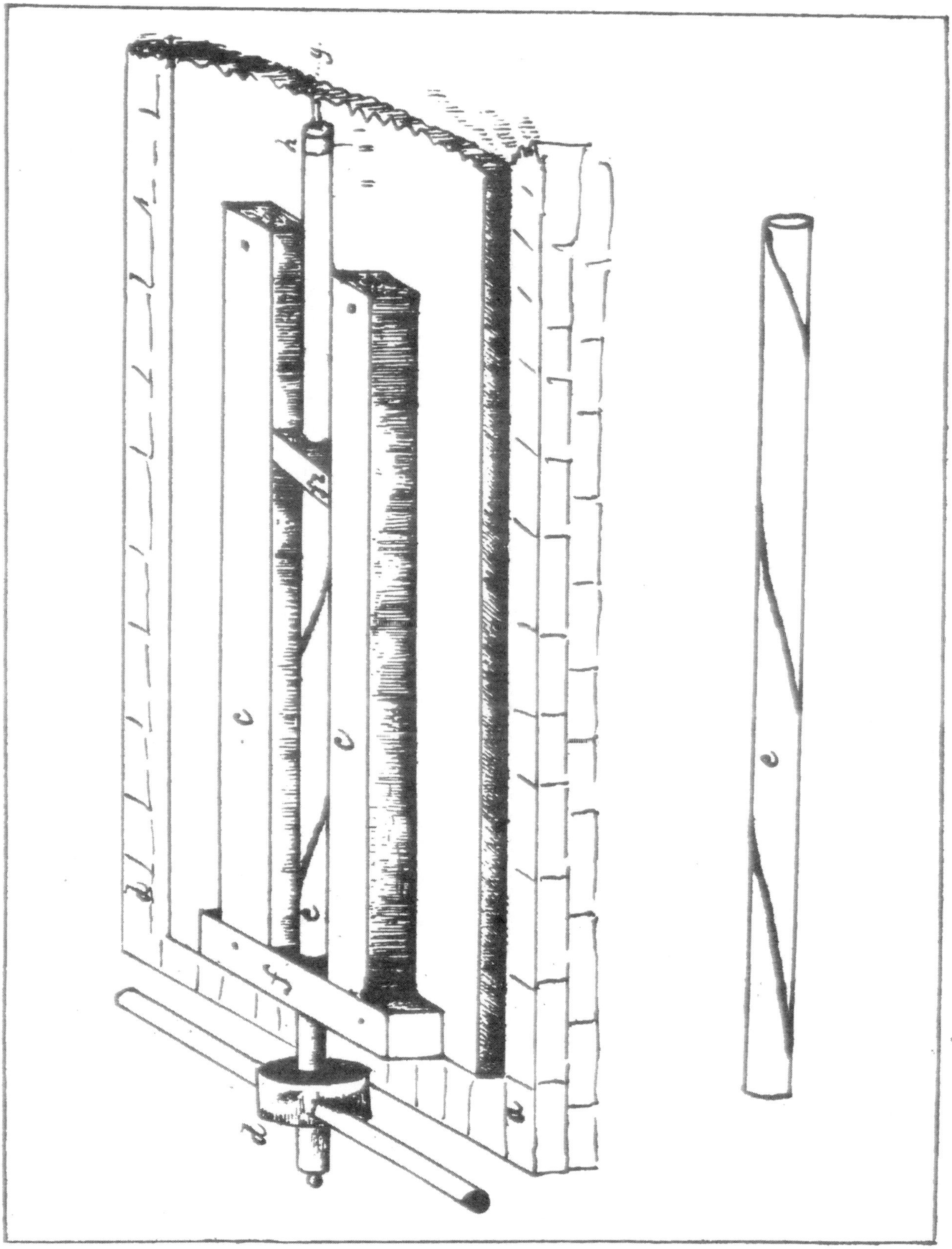

to illustrate rifle boring

(p. 2[illegible])

DIVISION III.

SWORDS AND DAGGERS.

Nearly all good blades are imported, and we hear constantly of 'Iráni' as a term implying excellence in a sword blade, meaning that it comes from Persia (or from Syria even.)

Sword blades of tolerable quality may perhaps be made by a few remaining workmen in some parts of the Punjab; but not many. The Kashmir State has an armoury, in which good blades are still made, or might be made. But the best blades are made beyond Peshawur. The late COLONEL JAMES's Settlement Report contains the following brief notice :—

" Sword blades of a coarser quality are manufactured at Peshawur, but those in " greatest request, other than Persia and Damascus blades, are the Teerahí, made in the " Oruckzye (Urakzai) hills of Teera, at what is known as the Mírzá Khání factory. The " temper of these swords is highly appreciated, and some, purchased perhaps at a small " price, are valued nearly as much as Iráni blades ".

In form the swords do not vary much. The varieties most known in the Punjab are the 'talwár' and 'kirch'; shamsher, the Persian word, is the equivalent of the Hindí talwár.

The talwár has a slight curve in the blade; the handle has either a side guard or not. The straight cross handle shaped in the sketch is generally seen in Persían and Khurásán and Kábul swords.

The basket guard like our Infantry sword, or like the Highland sword, is called " Shabakka ".

The "*kirch*" is a straight sword. The European Infantry sword would be called by this name. The Sikh Artillery men had heavy straight swords with iron or brass guards and hilts.

The "khanjar" is a dagger with a curved blade, like the bichúa, afterwards described, only bigger.

Sword sheaths, "miyáñ," are made of thin slips of 'sembal' wood, covered with velvet, leather, or kimkháb.

The daggers known in the Punjab are the "katár," the 'pesh kabz,' and the "bichúá." The long Afghan knife is known as "chhura," and in the Peshawur lists a dagger or knife called "babúdí" appears.

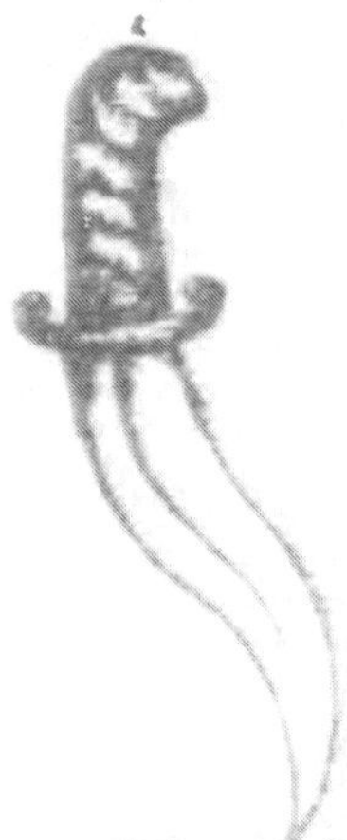

Bichúa

Peshkabz

Katár

'Katár' is the name of a triangular and heavy bladed dagger, whose chief peculiarity is in the handle, which consists of two side bars to protect the hand, and one cross bar by which it is grasped at right angles to the direction of the blade.

The "peshkabz" has a blade quite straight at the back, and sloping at the edge to a fine point; the handle is usually of shírmahi, the white bone of a large *Cetacean*, spoken of by Richardson as the "seer-fish," a sort of Tunny.* The sheath, (either of leather or velvet) is worn so as cover a part of the handle.

The "bichúá" is a dagger with a waved blade, and has the handle either of iron gilt and shaped like the sketch, or else has a handle with a side guard also like a sword.

The handles of daggers are often of ivory, of "márpech" or jade, of agate, or of rock crystal.

The blades of all these are often prettily inlaid with gold, and then are described as 'koft,' or 'kár-i-tilá.' The handle of the katár, which is always of steel, is generally inlaid with gold. One of the prettiest daggers of the 'bichúá' kind I have seen, was one *found*, (not made) at Lahore, which had a hollow slit cut down both sides of the blade, the slit being filled up by a row of small pearls let in.

Swords are inlaid with gold, usually just below the hilt, for a workman will not spoil the appearance of the water of a fine blade by working it over; but common sword blades are frequently inlaid all over, and especially hunting swords, called "talwár shikárgáh," which are worked all over with figures of tigers, dogs, antelopes, &c.

---

* No *fish* of any species has a bone of such a size: the bone is probably of a Cetacean called, I believe, the "black-fish," and common on the Western coast.

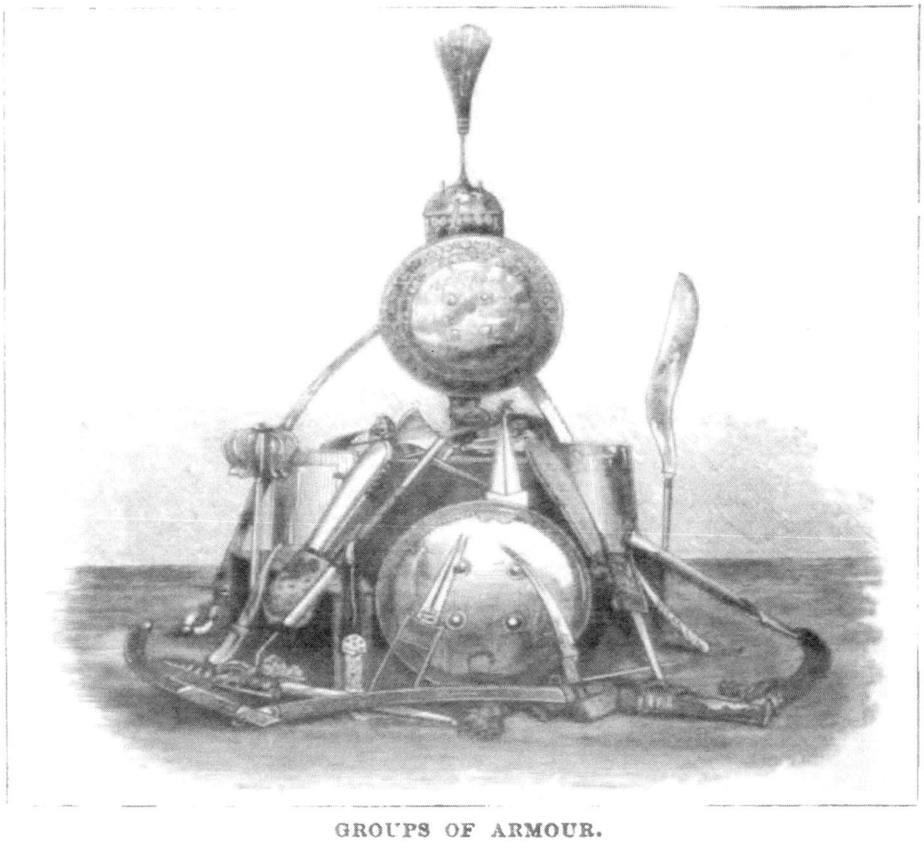

GROUPS OF ARMOUR.

Generally, it may be observed for the benefit of those who have a taste for collecting specimens of inlaid armour, the best are those old pieces preserved from the Sikh days, or which have travelled from Kabul or elsewhere. The few remaining workmen (who hold licenses for the purpose, and tell you that they are "license-dár" *) are ready to furbish up and inlay with gold, such weapons, on the conditions of an advance wherewith to purchase the necessary gold wire and other material, and a good long time to do the work in. The latter condition is indispensable, for the work is, in its nature, one of great delicacy, and requires the deliberate and patient work of an oriental hand, and the workmen knowing that they have a monopoly, indulge their fancy as to the amount of labor they choose to undergo in the day.

This is said mostly of the few old armourers who remain at Lahore and Amritsar, reminiscences of the Sikh times: they have each a few apprentices, who will no doubt pursue the trade after them as long as European travellers visit India and demand such wares. These to my mind do better work than the more modern schools of Sealkot and Gujrat, which seem to excel rather in producing caskets and fancy ornamental work, than in the much admired armour and weapon inlaying.

I need not extract from the collection of 1864 a long list of weapons to illustrate the above remarks: there were endless repetitions of the same forms of daggers, each perhaps having its own special merits in design, but offering no tangible feature to discriminate it in a printed list. There were swords of the kinds above described, some new,—some old,—some exhibited for the sake of the blade,—some for the inlaying,—some for the hilt and handle, others for the scabbard gay with jewels and velvet; but the Peshawur list will give an idea of the real varieties of swords made.

I should not, however, omit to mention that Sirdar Bhagwán Singh of Amritsar exhibited two or three swords of an unusual character. One was a huge blade, figured in the plate representing a group of arms, and carrying not only a solid basket hilt of steel, but an arm guard of steel also; there was also a sword of the cut and thrust order, intended to be used double-handed, figured on the upper and extreme left hand of the group, this is called "hata"; it belongs to Hindustan, and is used in show fighting: when very long it is called "saif." Another sword in Sirdar Bhagwán Singh's collection is in the lower part of the group. Still another, but not a Punjab specimen, was a huge kind of broad sword with a round point, used in show-fighting, and called 'katah.'

The Peshawur list contained the following :—

[202].—"Shamsher Misrí."—Supposed to be an Egyptian blade, valued at Rs. 200.

[203] —"Shamsher Iráni—chinár Jauhar".—An Iráni or Persian blade, with the jauhar or water mark, like the chinár (or grain of plane wood).

[204].—Shamsher dozabánáh. A two 'tongued' or two-edged sword.

[213].—Talwár Tírahí, exhibited by GHULAM JAN, and made in the Tíra District already alluded to.

[214].—Shamsher Shah-Husainí Iráni—A sword of the Shah Husain fashion (the blade is ribbed longitudinally) from Persia.

* Under the Arms Act.

[216].—Shamsher chinár jauhar Khurásáni—from Khurasán as its name implies.

Then we have knives and daggers. The name of one of these I do not find in any of our dictionaries.

[193].—" Babúdí tilákár," value Rs. 45, by Píra of Peshawur.—A gold inlaid knife or dagger.

[ ].—Chhurá jauhardár, is an Afghan knife, worth Rs. 120.

Chhurá Tíráhi is from Tíra, as before noted.

[223].—' Kárd khurd.'—Two small knives, one rather larger than the other. These are not used in fighting. " Kárd " is the Persian equivalent to " chhurí."

DIVISION IV.

MISCELLANEOUS.

There is not much of any interest remaining. The defensive armour perhaps is an exception, as it often exhibits skill in taste and workmanship.

In former days finely made chain armour was worn, called " zira : " it was either worn with or without lining. I have seen one suit entirely cased in velvet. There is a short coat, " kurta zira," and leggings, " paijama zira," a helmet called " kulla zira," generally consisted of a globular shaped steel cap, surmounted by a plume, and protected all round, except over the face, by a curtain of chain work.

Over the chain armour the " cháraina " was often worn, consisting of four pieces or curved plates, one for the front of the breast, one behind, and one smaller one for each side, attached by straps ; armlets of steel accompanied these. Steel helmets called ' khod ' were worn, and were furnished with a sliding bar, which could be slipped down so as to protect the bridge of the nose.

The whole " cháraina," when worn by the Sikh nobility, was beautifully inlaid with gold.

Shields were in former days universally used, and are so still by all the Biloch, Pathán, and Afghán tribes.

In former days they were either of steel inlaid with gold, or of rhinoceros hide (genda) or buffalo hide (the commoner ones), generally studded with four gilt bosses, or one larger boss in the centre ; they are always circular, and about 18 to 20 inches in diameter, but the size varies.

Among miscellaneous weapons, the battle axe or " tabar," a broad edged axe, was occasionally used ; and the armoury at Lahore contains one (beautifully wrought with steel carved work) said to have belonged to Guru Gobind Singh.

A large iron mace is also in the collection, consisting of a stout short rod, headed with a crown-shaped series of stout steel ribs, projecting or radiating on all sides from the central shaft.

The "chakra," or war quoit, has never been used in recent times, but the 'Nihangs,' or Sikh fanatics, always carried, as part of their strange dress and accoutrements, a large quoit, which consists of a large thin circle of steel, the outer edge being sharp.

Bows and arrows, as weapons of defence and offence, are now so out of date, that I could with difficulty find at Lahore or Amritsar a single workman who knew how to make them. They are still carried by the Hill Chiefs of Rajput descent; and a bow is presented as a "nazar," or offering of respect, to a paramount chief or power.

Some of the bows are shaped like ours, *viz.*, a single curve or arc; but those in the hills are mostly made with a double curve, like what we now see in pictures and sculptures as "Cupid's" bow.

The bow consists of a central piece, often of horn or bone, and to this two other flexible pieces are joined and firmly bound; these are made of mulberry wood, first inserted into the centre block or hand-piece, and then bound with strips of catgut or thin hide; they are tipped very skilfully with horn: the whole bow is then painted, ornamented with flower patterns in gold and colors, and varnished. The bow string is of crimson silk tipped with catgut loops to attach it to the bow.

The arrows are straight shafts of the munj grass stem (kána), and tipped with solid points of steel; the feather apparently of some kind of grey goose,—called "'ukáb."

The bows are made by a "kamángar," whose trade is distinct from that of the arrow maker, or "tír-gar. I found one of the latter at Lahore, who gave me the following account of his tools.

His implements are :—

"Kálib"—an iron tube or mould through which the kana or shaft of the arrow, made of kana grass, is passed, to straighten it and pare off knots, &c.: it is heated if required.

"Tirpai"—work stool.

"Barma"—to bore holes.

Arrow head or "phal," which is made for him by an ironmonger.

The arrow shaft is headed with wood, neatly bound on, so as to bear the incision of a nick to catch the bow string: the nick is called "bágar;" the feather is made by attaching the feather stripped off the quill with glue to the shaft—four feathers are applied to each arrow.

CLASS XXIX.

IMPLEMENTS USED IN TRADES AND OCCUPATIONS.

DIVISION I.

IN MANUAL TRADES.

This Division is, I fear, a very miscellaneous one, nor have I any explanation to offer of the arrangement, or even of the contents of the pages devoted to it.

Wherever it was possible, in describing special manufactures, I have included a description of the tools or machinery employed in the production, and hence there would be no object in repeating them here.

In some few cases, however, I had either omitted the details, which it afterwards occurred to me might be useful, or I had not obtained the requisite information; for it is literally impossible to understand from a native description, unaided by any diagrams, the tools and appliances used in the various handicrafts. It is necessary to go to the workshop and see both the form and use of each kind for oneself.

But there are not a few trades and occupations which could not be separately described except through the medium of a class like this, and on such grounds, I trust, the disorderly appearance of this chapter will meet with indulgence.

It opens with some details of tools used in trades already described. Thus, we have the tools of the weaver, the silk fringe-maker, and the silk dyer, also the workman who crimps and pleats cloth, a fashion once extensively in vogue.

Then follow the implements of the following trades, which, as before suggested, are merely residuary, and purposely exclusive of all such trades and occupations as have been otherwise noticed in the preceding pages.

Carpenter,	"Mistrí, or tarkhán."
Metal cleaner and armourer,	"Siklígar."
Coiner,	"Tangsáliya."
Needle maker,	"Sozangar."
Tinman,	"Tíngar."
Pipe stem maker,	"Nechában d."
Kite maker,	"Patangsáz."
Firework maker,	"Atishbáz."
Mat weaver,	"Boryábáf."
Rope maker,	"Rassi-bat."
Gilt leather maker,	"Pannigar."
Book-binder,	"Jildsáz."
Cobbler and Saddler,	"Mochi and Siráj."
Paper maker,	
Stone cutter,	"Sangtarásh."
Mill-stone rougher,	"Chakeráh."

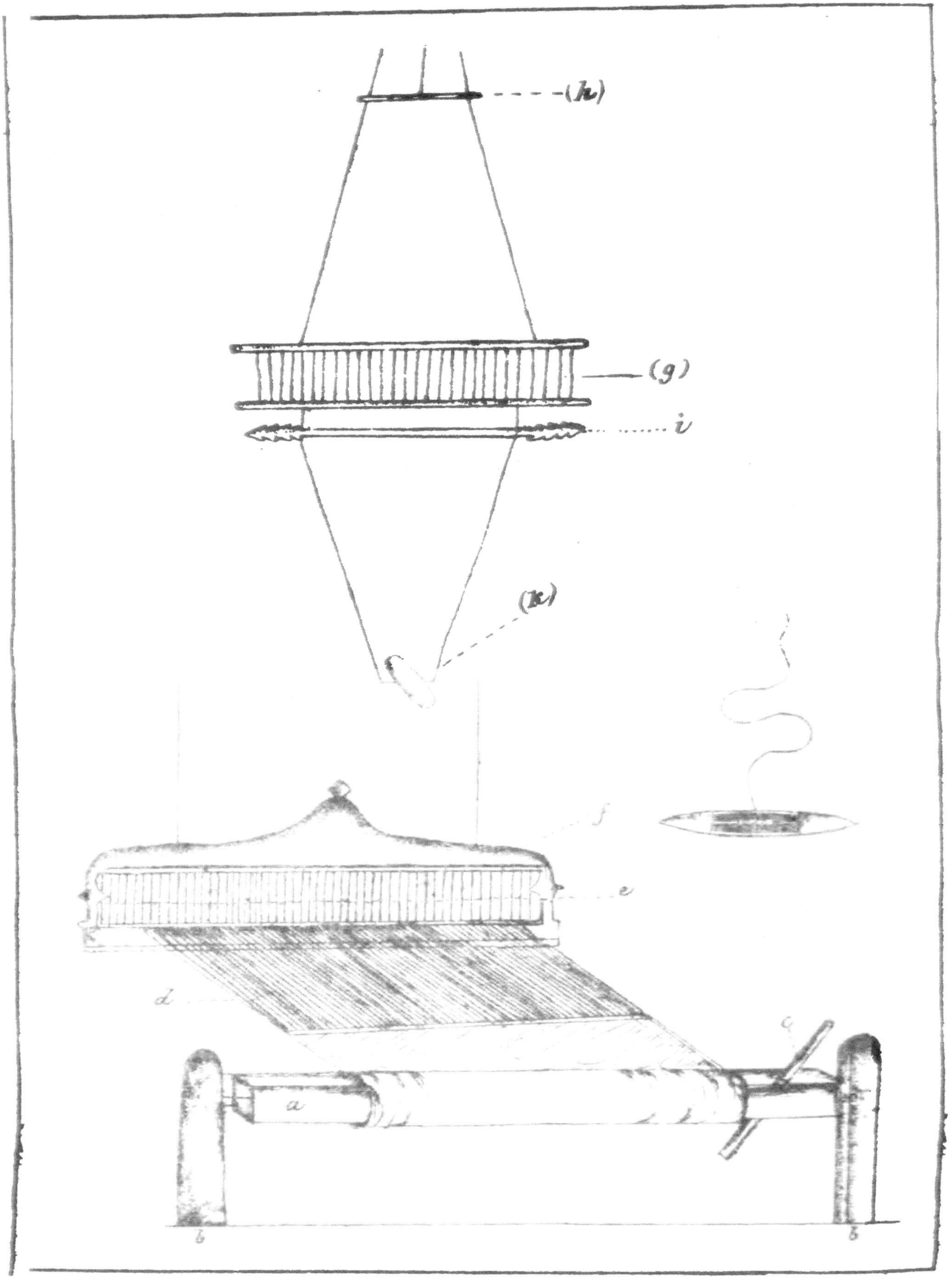
(h)
(g)
i
(k)
f
e
d
c
a
b
b

There are a few connected with the supply of articles of food, such as :—

Dosálí.—The man who makes up cups, &c., of leaves, in which confectionery and other edibles are sold.

Halwai.—The sweetmeat maker.

Panírgar.—The cheese maker.

Pápargar.—A man who grinds pulse, and also makes a sort of thin cake or biscuit called pápar.

Bharpúnjá.—A grain parcher.

And lastly some miscellaneous trades :—

The tobacconist (Tamáku farosh.)

Soap-boiler (Sábungar.)

Ink seller (Siyahi farosh.)

Wrestler (Pahlwán.)

Tight-rope dancer (Bázígar.)

" *JULA'*."—Weaver.

The parts of the loom can be understood by reference to the diagram annexed. Beginning with the front we have—

(*a.*) The " Tur," or beam on which the cloth is wound as fast as woven. It is supported between—

(*b.*) " Mekh," two upright posts, and the *tur* beam is turned by means of—

(*c.*) " Girdhának, " a straight stick passing through a hole in the " tur."

(*d.*) Táni is the web. The method of preparing it has already been described. I should mention that the web is kept extended at the point where the finished fabric commences by a stick underneath. The stick is furnished with an iron point at either end, which is stuck into the edge of the cloth : this is called " panak. "

In order to keep the upper and under threads of the web separate, moveable sticks are inserted at intervals. When it is desired to push them forward as the work progresses, the weaver beats the web with a stick called " channi," and the jarring thus produced shakes the sticks forward.

The other end of the web, or that farthest from the " tur," is held by a rope, " láns," fixed to a short peg in the wall.

The weaver seats himself on the ground in front of the tur, his feet being in a hole dug underneath. In front of him hangs the " shána " (*e.*) or comb, which consists of a number of fine slips of bamboo, and keeps all the threads distinct.

The " hathá " (*f.*) is a rather heavy wooden frame, which fits over the " shána," and is suspended from the roof; it moves backwards and forwards, and as soon as the shuttle has passed between the threads of the web, the workman pulls the hathá forward and strikes the thread home, thus compacting and closing up the weaving as it progresses.

Behind the shána and hathá hang (*g.*) the heddles called " rach "— two in a plain loom, four in a " khes báfi " loom—by means of which the threads of the web are alternately brought over and under each other.

This is shown separately in the diagram to avoid confusion. The heddle consists simply of a pair of light bits of kána or reed, with a series of threads, which have to be passed on to the warp before the loom is set up. They are suspended from a stick called "kalá" (*h.*) and ultimately to the roof of the building. The heddles are weighted and kept in place by sticks under the warp, having notched ends and called "painsar" (*i.*). The treddle underneath, by which the rach is raised, is called "karáon" (*k*).

The shuttle is called nāl, and is made of Khair wood (*Acacia catechu*). It is shaped like a small boat, having a spool of thread inside, which can be removed when the thread is expended, and replaced by another full one.

The thread when woven is first wound on to a skeleton drum, called "dhera," supported in a square and light wooden frame called "uri"; from this the thread is woven off on to the spools or shuttle spikes by means of the "charkha" already described (see page 1 *et seq* of this volume.)

Silk weaving is described at page 61; and shawl weaving, which has a special kind of loom, at page 38, and there is an illustration taken from a photograph of a loom which was at work in the Exhibition of 1864.

UTU-KASH—ONE WHO PLEATS AND PINKS CLOTH.

(1.) Matt—large earthen vessel with a narrow mouth and broader base, which, being inverted, serves as a table or stand to work on.

(2.) Angítí—small furnace.

(3.) Dhátrí—a curved iron like a small sickle.

(4.) Charcoal.

(5.) Fan.

This art is not so much followed as formerly. Gentlemen would have the whole coat pleated over in a chequered pattern, or even in arabesque or flowered pattern. This was much in fashion in the Sikh army. The pleating could be done on any material, silk muslin or satin. It is rarely seen now.

ILA'KABAND or PATHOLI.—FANCY SILK AND FRINGE MAKER.

His tools are —

An "adda"—upright stick stuck on a flat stand, serving to fasten the ends of thread in plaiting, fringe making, &c., 'silai,' or steel spikes, scissors, and needles.

He makes fringe, fancy buttons, borders, plaited strings for necklaces, izárbands or netted silk girdles, tassels, and the like.

He makes also gold ribbon of the kind called kaitún, and fringe, on a tiny kind of loom which has no frame work, and moreover is worked sideways. The ordinary loom has its web at right angles to the workman's body—this is parallel to it. The threads are changed not by heddles, but by small leather adjuncts called "kathila," which are simply turned by the hand to invert the web threads.

Fringe is made partly in this manner; the tags of the fringe being made by hand and the edging which holds them in place on the loom.

"*PATRANG*"—Silk Dyer.

His tools are —

'Karah'—iron flat caldron.

'Deg'—caldron.

'Kunál'—earthen 'naund' to hold alum solution ; another to hold sajjí solution.

'Danda kasanwala'—stout sticks used in applying force to wring out the wet 'lachha' or skeins of silk.

'Danda chalaiwála,'—for the same purpose.

'Dandí jóriwáli'—a small sized stick.

'Chattú,'—large wooden mortar with its "molá," or pestle.

'Hangi'—large horse hair sieve.

'Sil-batta'—stone and pestle for grinding up dye stuffs.

Ropes and bamboos.

'Píri,' a stand or frame to support a deg or a strainer, over the receptacle below.

The dyeing processes have been elsewhere described.

"*MISTRI*" *or* "*TARKHA'N*"—Carpenter.

His tools are as follows :—

'Tesha,' (or basola) adze. Carpenters are very clever in using this tool, and with it they will do a number of operations for which other and special tools are provided. In the hills a small adze is used, called "bela." This is smaller and lighter than the regular adze, and moreover the edge is curved.

The specimen I am describing from, came from the Pangi province of the Chamba State, on the Upper Chenab river. The coarse, but nevertheless effective and well designed carving on old houses, 'nāgs' and temples in the hills, is almost always done with a tool of this kind.*

'Kuhárí or kulhára'—is the ordinary work axe.

'A'rá," 'árí"—saws, small and large.

'Parnáí'—a small and narrow bladed saw.

'Martol,' or "hathaurá", "hathaurí"—hammers.

'Ghan,' a large sledge hammer, mostly used by wheel-rights.

'Barma kumáncha'—is the revolving awl, worked by a bow with a leathern string, which supplies the place of our gimblet, and also of our centre bit. The awl is made of various breadths : a point of any size can be fitted into the handle at pleasure. The leather string (called "tandí,") of the bow is twisted round the moveable wooden reel in the centre of the handle, and by a saw like action the tool is kept revolving.

Chisels are used as follows :—

"Sathrá"—a large chisel.

"Sathrí"—a small do.

"Chaurasí"—a sort of chisel which has a narrow stem spreading out into a broad edge.

* A drawing of a bit of this carving will be found further on (Class —*Architectural Contrivances.*)

"Chauras bírá"—a very narrow chisel, shaped 

"Gird, or "gol bírá"—a small chisel with a round edge. 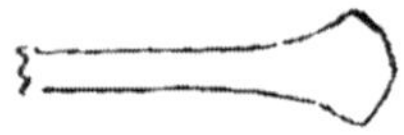

"Chapú-bírá"—a small gouge or curved chisel for cutting grooves.

"Miyángi"—another, only smaller.

"Nok"—a chisel like the chauras bírá, only again filed off till the edge is reduced to a sharp point.

The planes are —

"Randá"—common plane.

"Dráz"—a narrow plane for squaring and straightening edges.

"Golah"— a small plane with the blade semi-circular, so as to make a rounded moulding at the edge of a plank, &c.

"Cheri-randá"—a plane for bevelling edges, &c.

"Gilmi-randá"—a plane for cutting out a groove.

Carpenter's *files* are —

"Kanní-retí"—a two bladed file for sharpening and setting saws.

"Chossa"—a coarse rasp.

"Retí"—files of sorts. Ním-gird, ("*half round*" file) &c.

And he also requries —

"Gunyá"—the carpenter's square or gnomon.

"Parkár"—compasses of iron.

"Khatkash"—a tool to mark lines on planks: being an iron spike in a wooden handle.

"Nímgáz"—a foot and a half rule.

The sawyer, called 'parnáí-kash,' or "árí-kash," uses only one implement that need be alluded to, *viz.*, his adda or triangular prop, whereby he supports, in a tilted position, the log he intends to saw up. It consists simply of a triangular arrangement of bars, the third bar being moveable, so as to adjust the opening to the size of the log.

SAIKALGAR or *SIKLIGAR* (corruptly) CLEANER OF ARMS AND METAL WORK.

His implements are—

"Sán"—a grinding and polishing wheel; and "diwál charmi," a leather rope, which is passed over the end of the axle of the sán, and is alternately pulled by either of two men seated at opposite sides: this causes the sán to revolve. It is larger and heavier than the wheel used by the 'hakkák' (*q. v.*) and so cannot be turned by the bow and string. Two uprights, or "kel," support the sán.

"Kurund"—corundum or emery.

"Randá"—flat edged scrapers, made like the blade of a plane and used for scraping iron. They are made of various sizes.

"Maskala"—an iron polisher shaped like a crescent; held by one point, or by both if a flat surface has to be polished.

Horn polisher—piece of horn let into a flat handle.

"Patri"—a stone slab for a hone.

"Kaf"—a mixture of oil and corundum or emery, which is rubbed on the article to be cleaned, after which it is scraped with a randá.

"Gaddi," a pad of woollen cloth, on which the article is polished. It gets in time a coating of oil and corundum because of the rubbing that comes off the articles polished.

"Tor áhani."—a pick to clean out holes, tubes, &c.

TANGSA'LIYA.—Coiner.

His implements are—

'Bhatti'—forge.

'Kalwang'—bellows.

Pincers, anvil, hammers, as in other trades.

'Reza'—a narrow ingot mould.

'Kutháli'—a crucible.

'Chimta'—tongs.

'Wadhán'—a sledge hammer.

'Tappa'—die with which coin is struck. A bit of rounded and weighed silver is placed between two dies, and both sides struck at once with a sledge hammer.

This represents the old fashion of mint work.

SOZAN GAR.—Needlemaker.

This man makes large needles of iron wire, still used by cobblers and for coarse work, as they sell at four annas or five annas a thousand: the thinner they are the more they cost.

"Iron wire is taken, and a prescribed length cut off with a pair of heavy nippers called "kainth;" a blow with a hammer on a flat anvil, on one end of the wire, flattens it to receive the eye. The needle is then dressed to make it straight by rolling it under a wooden pin on a slightly concave surface of a thick wooden stick. These are called "darári-danda," or "mathána-danda." The needle is sharpened with a file, and then ground on a wheel. This wheel is a vertical shaft about a foot long, shod with an iron point, which revolves in the ground, and the upper end being a point which runs into a wooden arm or transverse bar, which is supported by a wooden rest.

This wheel, called 'charkh' or "bartá," is a mass of lac and corundum melted together. It is set spinning by a bow and leather string, as is usual in all apparatus when a rotatory motion is required. After the polishing the eye is bored with a "barma," but the barma consists of a mere iron silai or spike with a hollow bit of cocoa-nut shell called "toi," which forms the handle on which the workman's hand rests, while the spike revolves with the action of the bow string (*See* illustration under "Pearl Borer" page 192.)

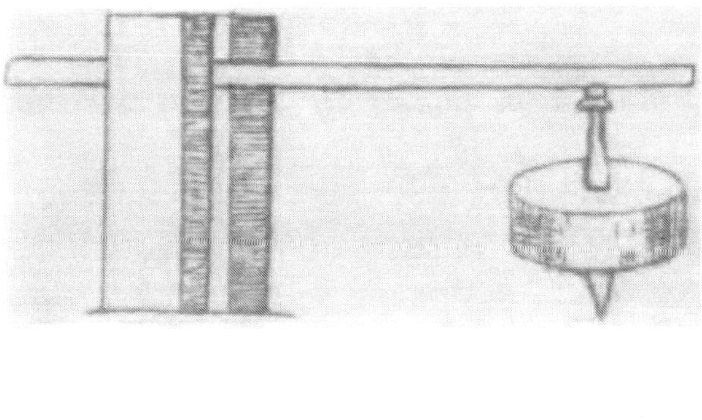

The needles are polished by being rolled upon a piece of leather with some "chân," or bran of wheat, and a little water; being rolled and rubbed together, they get smooth. About 250 are made in a day.

TIN GAR (*sic*). (TIN-MAN.)

His tools require no mention. The iron with which he heats the solder or "ránga" is called 'kábya' or 'káwya.'

NECHABAND.—PIPE STEM MAKER.

They take a small bamboo of the hollow stemmed kind (the *Arundinaria falcata* or Nírgál of the higher hills) and place it on a sort of iron neck or vice, supported on three feet, (called sipáwa,) over a charcoal fire; they are thus able to bend the tube to the angle required for the huka stem (see plate at page 288, volume I). When the bend is effected, and the stem is cool, it is sawn to size with a small saw; they tie cloth over the outside, and then insert into the end a stout curved iron wire, which is roughed all over so as to stick to the inside of the tube; this gives them a handle whereby to spin the tube round and round while they wind silk or gold thread on for ornament. The iron is called "tôr.

A long iron wire, similarly roughed with points, like the twig of a fir tree, is called nîmgaza, and is used for hollowing out and clearing the inside of the tube.

The tube of a huka which supports the chilam or bowl is made of a hollow reed (narí or nai-ábí) and the smoking tube of the small bamboo. The tube of a "pechwán" is made of a coil of zinc wire covered first with birch bark, then with cloth.

PATANG-SA'Z.—KITE-MAKER.

The passion of the people for kite-flying may be understood by the maker having a separate trade.

He requires only knife, scissors, a board, a pestle and mortar, a "dullu," a round earthen vessel to hold water and a big shell to polish the paper.

The kites are made of thin bamboo, and polished paper. The form of kite is usually that of a rude attempt at the outline of a butterfly or bird. The kite-flying that is most fashionable, is that by two opponents, each of whom endeavours to cut the other's string. For this purpose the kite-maker covers the string with a colored paste called "májha," consisting of ground glass and corundum mixed with flour paste and red lead.

ATISH BA'Z—FIREWORK MAKER.

"Mohlá"—wooden pestle, thin in the middle for the better grasp of the workman's hand, and thick and cylindrical at either end; this is used for pounding up the saltpetre &c., in the—

"Chattu"—or mortar, both being made of mango wood to prevent the possibility of striking fire. Only the rough pounding is done in this.

"Chakki"—flat circular mill or grindstone for grinding materials.

"Chaj"—a sort of basket or frame in which material is winnowed from dust and dirt, by being jerked up and down.

"Chauni"—a seive of horse hair, or of pierced parchment.

"Sáncha"—a mould or pattern tube to guide the size of the tubes in which the fireworks are formed.

"Sil batta," grindstone and slab for grinding.

"Levi," paste, and "san" for tying up &c. Nearly all the binding of rockets and tying up tubes &c., is done with strips of untwisted 'san' dipped in paste. This, when dry, is an excessively tight and firm binding.

"Khurpí," small scraper.

"Kharcha," small ladle for filling tubes with composition, &c.

"Tesha," adze.

"Hathaura," hammer or mallet.

"Barma," awl or centre bit.

Small saw.

Materials required—

Paper, bamboo, jillí (gold-beater's skin), charcoal, sulphur, saltpetre, "deg" steel filings brought from Hindustan—common iron filings are not used.

Hártál (orpiment) gives a blue color; Mansil (realgar) (written in my vernacular list manchir) gives white.

The gold-beater's skin is used to bind over certain tubes to prevent the material burning too fast, or bursting all at once.

BORYA BA'F—Mat Weaver.

His tools are—

Wooden pegs; string and rope; "hatta," a long beam perforated with holes. This last forms the 'weaver's beam,' though which the moonj strings for the web of the mat are passed and thus kept in place: the other ends of the strings, at the extremity of the intended length of the mat, are fixed to a bamboo, which is kept in its place by wooden pegs. The material used is the dry flag, *Typha angustifolia*, (dib), which is collected in bundles. When required for work, a handful of the long leaves is taken, slightly damped and made flexible with blows from a wooden mallet.

Matting made of date palm is done without any string web: broad plaits of the fibre are made and stitched together.

RASSI-BAT—Rope Twister.

They have a wooden board shaped as fig. 1 pierced with holes, called "charkh"; through these are passed sticks, usually roughly broken off boughs of a tree shaped as fig. 2 and called "sabíla"; the knot on the shoulder keeps the stick from passing through the hole altogether. To the short end of each stick a length of rope-hemp, or other material, is tied. The perforated board is now fixed firmly to two uprights, and a second and similar perforated board is put over the long ends of the sticks and is turned round and round: this causes the short ends of the sticks, with the hemp strands attached, to revolve, and thus the strands are twisted together. To secure uniformity, the strands ('lár') are passed over a wooden block called "kálbút" (fig. 3) with grooves in it; beyond this the ends of the strands are caught by a hook, which hook is fixed to the end of a bit of rope, which is made fast to a weight. (When seven strands are required, then one strand passes though a hole bored in the middle of the block). The block is at the end of the strands furthest from the turning board, and close to the weight; as the rope is formed the closing strands force the block forward, as fig. 4.

String is made by twisting on a big wooden spindle called "taowír," suspended by leather thongs.

For rope which is not sufficiently thick to require the first described apparatus, they use a mere wooden frame, carrying four revolving spools at the corners, each spool ends in a hook, to which the strands to be twisted are tied. The spools are set revolving with a band passed over them and a fly-wheel or charkha. This frame is called "takla."

PANNIGAR—Gilt Leather Maker.

His implements are, a file, a flat stone, leather, "raughan gúna," silver leaf.

They take small pieces of sheep skin, six fingers long and four broad, called "panní," and place them on the stone, where they are carefully scraped; then they place the silver leaf over the leather, and fix it there with a size made by boiling the gelatinous tendons of the goat's foot with nishásta (wheat starch). The silver being fixed, it is burnished (jilá kiya játa) with agate, and varnished with a yellow varnish consisting of copal (sundras) boiled in linseed oil and colored yellow with musabbar (bitter aloes). The finished leather is of a coarse brassy color. Panní is very cheap, a piece only costing a few pies: it is used in native saddlery and shoemaking.

JILD SAZ—Book-Binder.

The book-binder uses these tools :—

'Kap.'—A curved knife for cutting paper.

'Síl.'—A stone tablet.

'Koba.'—A mallet to beat paste-board covers, &c.

'Sui.'—Needle, and

'Rambhi, a leather cutting chisel with slanting edge; also rulers; screw press called "sikanja," scissors, &c.; chední, a tool like a rambhi, but with a straight edge, for scraping leather; 'chossa,' a rasp, to smooth the edge of paper.

MOCHI—Cobbler; and *SIRA'J*—Saddler.

They use the following tools :—

A'r—awls of sizes, being made with tapering points, but thick and heavy above, and short flat heavy handles, thus,

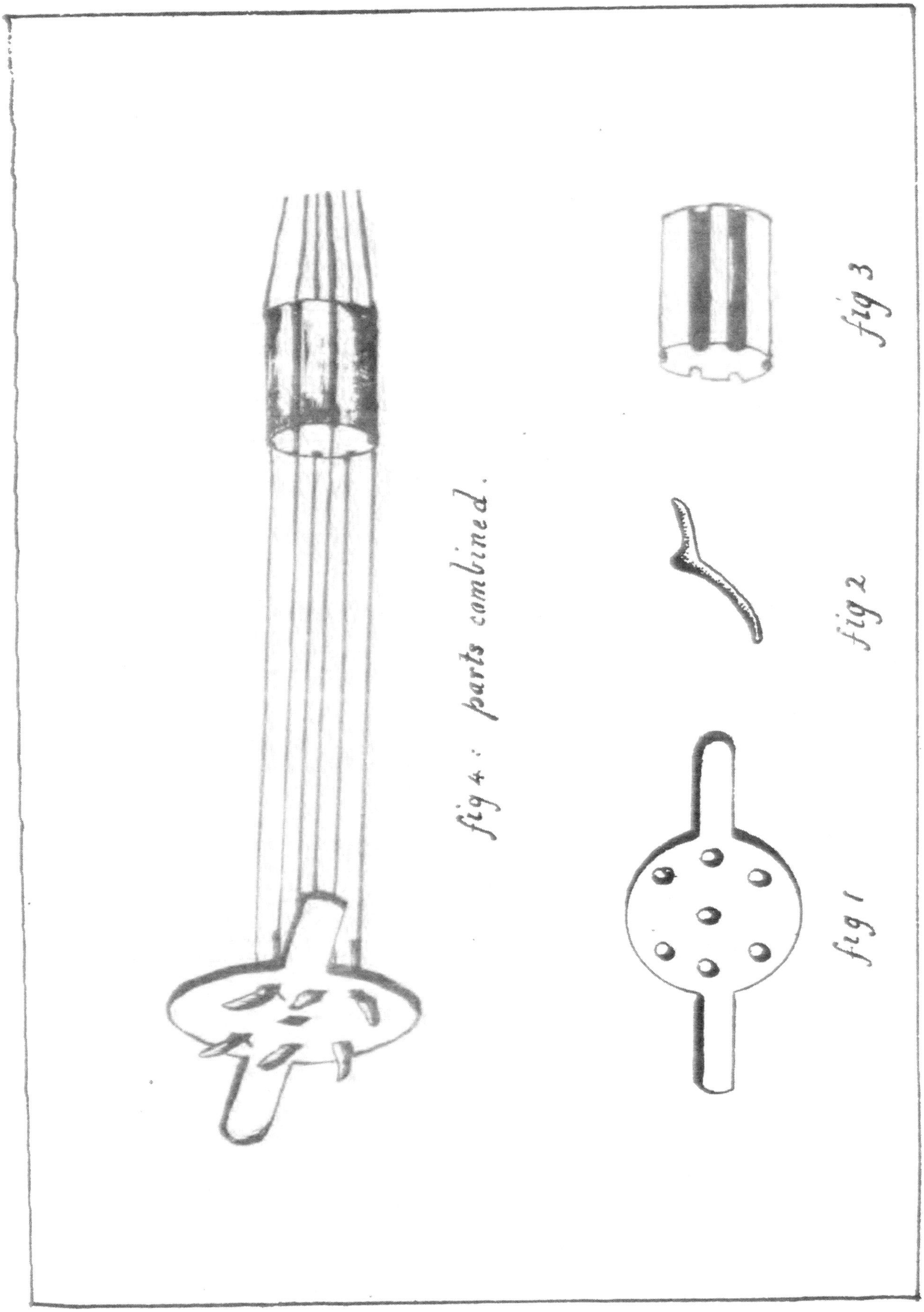

to face page 304

An awl with a little notch in the side of the point, to allow the thread being passed over it at the time of boring the hole, is called 'ár kundíwalla.'

"Chední" is a tool for paring and scraping leather thin; it is an iron blade coming to a broad slanting edge, and is fixed in a turnip-shaped handle of wood.

"Chirní" is a sharp slant-edged tool for cutting leather. The leather to be cut is placed on a flat tabular wedge of wood called 'katíra': this is made of 'karíl' wood, so as not to turn the edge of the tools.

"Koba" is the squat-formed pounder or mallet used for beating leather.

The saddler has a wooden 'tree' to make up his saddles with, called 'kátra.' The shoe-maker requires a "kalbut" or last, with "phárá" or wedge to make it fit. Both artizans use a 'pharní,' or tool for polishing leather, and a gota chobí, a wooden bar cut to an edge for a similar purpose. They have also a 'gamcha' or little lump of dough, with which they clean the tinsel or lace they put on their work.

Paper-Maker.

The implements of a paper-maker have been already partly described in the course of the description of paper making given at pages 92 and 93.

The pounding apparatus is called "jandar."

The frame which carries the fine screen on which the pulp is deposited to form the sheet is called "kháshí."

"Mír" is the screen laid over it, and formed of a series of parallel stalks of the "panní" grass, selected for their evenness and thinness. Two sticks, used to extend the 'mír' and keep it straight on the kháshí at either side, are called "such."

The brush for spreading the paper against the prepared wall to dry is called dastána.

SANGTARA'SH—Stone-cutter.

His tools are—

Hathaura,—hammer; and "gan," sledge hammer.

Tánchi (of sorts)—stone cutting chisels without handles.

"Chíní"—a chisel for dressing or squaring building stones.

"Tánki"—a thin flat chisel of hard steel for splitting slates.

Tirpái—(stool) to put the work on.

Gunyá and parkár—gnomon and compasses.

Sohán—a rasp or coarse file.

Pathri—a hone to sharpen chisels.

A copper saw.

An iron do.

A large cross-saw, worked with sand.

Sán—a polishing wheel.

Kuraud—corundum powder.

Bartá—a wooden bar covered with a mixture of lac and corundum, used for polishing.

"**Pacharkári**" is the art of joining in stone. The Pacharkár has small tánchis, hammers, a small saw, sohán, iron wire, bow with iron wire for cutting stone, a tube, which being worked with corundum powder, bores a hole and withdraws the interior cylinder; a 'barma' is also used.

In quarrying &c., the following tools are used:

"**Karandi**"—the scoop (a long wire with spoon shaped scoop at the end) for cleaning blast holes.

"**A'gal**"—crowbar.

"**Jabbal**"—jumper used for smaller blast holes, being pointed at either end and bulging in the middle.

"**Mín**"—("Dig" lower down, but both in hill districts) a lever.

CHAKI RAH—MILLSTONE ROUGHER.

The millstone rougher's whole business is to rasp or roughen the surface of the grindstones. This he does with a small pick or hammer called "chakiráh."

DOSA'LI.

A class of people who make "dhúna," (little cups) and "pattal," (plates) out of leaves, in which Hindus eat food or carry sweetmeats from the shops, &c. They fasten the leaves together with the strips of the bark or sheath "tili" gathered from the stalks of the "munj," and even work patterns on the leaves with thin strips of the same. They originally were hill people, but some few are found in Lahore, Amritsar, and elsewhere.

HALWAI—SWEETMEAT SELLER.

The halwai or sweetmeat maker uses the following vessels—

Karáh and karáhi—open iron hemispherical cauldrons.

Thál—plates of brass, or trays.

Khwáncha—large brass tray. The itinerent seller carries one of them to hold his wares when selling: he supports the tray on a sort of stool made of kána reed, called "tarauní."

Tawá—an iron plate for baking.

Dora—a cup attached to a rod, or deep ladle.

Pauni—a cullender (various sorts) some to drop 'bedána' through, (which consists of drops of thin paste passed into ghee and fried,) some to make "bundí," which is finer.

Belna and chakla—paste roller and board.

Khurpi—an edged tool for scraping the inside of kettles and pots.

Knives (churí).

Masad chobi—a round mallet used in beating the sugar used in making "halwa."

Sieves (channí).

Wooden moulds to make sugar images in, as used on festival days.

Dábí—a wooden scraper.

PANIRGAR—Cheese-maker.

His implements are—

Chiku—a shape or mould made of bamboo in which cheeses are made.

An iron pan (karáhí).

Shírdán—rennet?

Dori—an iron strainer to separate the curd.

Bojha, a stone weight to press the cheese.

Natives have only one kind of cheese. They heat the milk first, using ewe's milk, goat's, cow's or buffalo's; of these ewe's milk is mostly used,—and then stir it with rennet mixture. The curd is placed in the mould or chikú, which is first lined with cloth, and is then pressed with the addition of a little salt. These cheeses do not keep long. Kabulí cheese is imported into the Punjab. A cheese made as above is ready for use in a few hours after pressing; the cloth is changed twice during the process.

PA'PARGAR—Pulse Grinder and "Pa'par" Maker.

This man makes "pápar," that is to say, thin flat cakes made by mixing mûng or mâh (pulse) flour with salt, black pepper, spices, zíra, &c., into a paste with water, and then rolling it out with a rolling pin.

They first of all take dâl or split pulse, soak it in water, add the spices, and make it up into little balls of the weight of half a chitták each, one ball rolled out thin makes a pápar. This is a separate trade.

Pápargars only make these cakes, or else "baryán," a kind of fried savory cake, or "pití," which consists of mâh pulse ground up with water, and is sold in that state, being cooked according to taste by the purchaser. They also grind up gram in the same way, and sell it to halwáis, who make the sweetmeat called "laddú" out of it.

BHA'RPUNJA OR BHA'RPUNJA—Grain Parcher.

His implements are—

Kaunchá—shovel to take out the sand, which they first heat in the oven and afterwards use to parch grain on.

Kharchá—a ladle.

Bhattí—the oven.

Kárchí—iron plate.

Chánní—sieve, and "chaj," winnowing basket.

"Daur"—earthen vessel like a naund.

Sand.

"Muttha tílí"—a sort of whisk or brush, with which they agitate the grain along with sand in the karahí over the fire.

"Hathíkra gillí"—a hollow earthen vessel filled with kunkur to make it heavy, and then used as a pestle in crushing parched pulse so as to make it into dâl or split pulse.

TOBACCONIST.

Requires only a bit of matting or taut to spread the tobacco on, and a "múnglí" or wooden mallet to bruise it with; a "toka" or small chopper to cut it up, and a "channí" or iron sieve to sift out the coarse bits of stalk.

The powdered tobacoo is mixed with molasses and beaten with the múngli: some people add sajji to make it strong.

To make tobacco into the "khamíra," or mixture for smoking by wealthy persons various spices and perfumes are added, and apple preserve, &c.

Hindustanís chew tobacco with lime or betel nut; Punjabís do not.

SA'BUNGAR—SOAP-BOILER.

His implements are—

Kunál—earthen cauldron.

Chamcha—ladles.

Cháhbacha—small masonry tanks.

Pahauri—a wooden scraper.

Dora—a deep ladle, with a cup attached to a stick.

Channí—a sieve.

Karáhí—a cauldron, or curved iron pan, used by a soap boiler, is built into masonry, so as to form a fire-proof bottom to the tank, and then the soap lye is boiled in it.

Twelve maunds of crude soda (sajjí) and 6 maunds of whitewash (kalaí) are mixed in a masonry tank (cháhbacha) and sufficient water pound over them to cause the water to stand two fingers depth over the mixture; after being well stirred it is left to settle. The clear liquor is drawn off into a second tank placed below the first, and then into a third, in which it is mixed with 20 maunds of sweet oil: the mixture is stirred and left to stand for 15 or 20 days; after which it is put into the tank with an iron bottom and a fire place underneath (bakhárí). It is well boiled. Sweet oil is used (*viz.*, sesamum oil) not "saron" (rape seed), which yields a coarse, hard, and insoluble soap.

INK-SELLER.

Boils his lamp black with gum in a karahí, and when boiled down thick, either makes it into little balls with his fingers for sale, or smears it on a reed frame called 'pathhal,' off which it falls in scales and is collected when dry.

PAHLWA'N—WRESTLER.

He uses the following weapons:—

"Múnglí"—the callister or Indian sceptre.

"Bugdar"—short cylinders of wood, with a place cut out in the side for a handle.

" Sangtúr or Sangtola "—a much longer wooden cylinder, three or four feet long, which is held by handles cut out in the thickness of the wood, raised with both hands, and thrown backward over the head.

"Tamán"—a sort of bow, the extension of which strengthens the muscles of the arm.

The clothes they wear consist of a ' samosa,' or head cloth, worn to keep the hair confined. ' Khainch ' ornamental strips of cloth, worn on the hips and hanging down on either side ; ' langoti and jangya '—short drawers and waist-cloth.

BA'ZIGAR—Tight Rope Dancer.

His apparatus consists of a stout bamboo pole held by four stays ; up this he climbs and fixes on the top a " patrí " or small wooden stage, or foot-board, from which he exhibits feats.

He dances on a rough rope or on a slippery one ; the latter is called "nára," or rope of leather thongs. He ties a cow's horn to each ankle, so that the tip of the horn may curve outwards ; he then walks on the rope, the rope being between the sole of his foot and the curved horn, he is thus enabled to maintain a balance on the smooth surface. On a common hemp rope he dances with the aid of the balancing pole. He generally makes a show of lifting heavy beams called " sohága," and jumping over several camels placed side by side. These people mostly come from Rajauri and Punch, and are said to be Kashmíris.

The " lakribáz " is also a performer of this class : he fights with the 'gatka' or basket-hilted singlestick, also with the ' bānk,' a huge two-handed straight bladed sword ; or with the "saif" or "phatá," a kind of broad-sword ; he performs tricks also with the " maratti," a bamboo pole with a lighted torch at either end.

DIVISION II.

AGRICULTURAL IMPLEMENTS.

Under the division of agricutural implements I have included those rude machines which are used for cotton cleaning, oil pressing, sugar-cane crushing, and raising water from wells. I have also taken occasion to note some experiments which were instituted to compare the efficiency of the native cotton cleaning apparatus with improved saw and other gins. A series of rude implements will also be mentioned, and all will be described under the three divisions, which in the first volume we found convenient in agricultural matters. Thus we shall have to describe the tools and their names as used in the Punjab, (2) as used in the Cis-Sutlej districts, where the vernaculars approach more to those of Hindustan, and (3) those used in the hills.

The cotton cleaning machines have already been noticed. The separation from the seed is done by passing the cotton through two wooden rollers carried between two uprights; the ends of the rollers are formed into screws, which impinge one on the other, so that when a handle at the opposite end of the upper roller is turned, both upper and lower rollers are moved. The rollers can be adjusted closer to one another, according to the nature of the cotton. Such a machine is called " belna " or " velna." The cotton has to be carded and cleaned, which is done with a " pinjan," which has already been described as like a large strung bow, hung from the roof, and the string twanged and let fly against the cotton with the aid of a small wooden billet held in the hand; the workman is called 'nadáf. To supersede these rude processes, which, however, are cheap, and considering all things, wonderfully expeditious, various designs of saw-gins and other machines have been tried.

The following extract from the Report on the Dharwar Cotton-Gin Factory (a Government institution) will explain this subject :—

" The Supreme Government at Calcutta challenged invention by offering prizes in money of a large amount sufficient to induce the best mechanical skill of the country to enter the lists, and at the appointed trials many and varied inventions and modifications were brought forward, but the result proved that the task had baffled the skill of the competitors, and that the "time honored" churka continued to hold its sway in triumph.

" One or two points essential to success had been overlooked in all these machines, and though some of them in short trials appeared to give promise of success, and obtained prizes, still, when brought into practical use, it was found that they could not surpass the " churka " even in the single requirement of quantity of out-turn of work, and ultimately all hopes of obtaining such a machine seemed to have been abandoned.

" For some years back I have paid very considerable attention to this subject, and after careful practical study succeeded in producing a machine entirely free from the above defects ; and, on proceeding to England, I took with me working models of this machine and also supplies of seed cotton. I was thus enabled personally to lay these models before some of the first machinists of the country, and to explain where the former difficulties lay, and the exact nature of the articles now required.

"Various parties have been engaged, each introducing his own modification with regard to the application of the power &c., but the practical result is the production of machinery which, with the estimated labor of one man, gives an out-turn of upwards of 100 pounds of cotton wool per day, with the additional advantage of allowing no seed to pass through.

"At the very highest estimate, the quantity of cotton cleaned by the best native churka does not exceed 20 pounds per man per day of 12 hours. With such a great advantage in economy, not to mention expedition also, as well as the yearly increasing scarcity and cost of labour, owing to the amount taken up by railways and other public works, the benefit of such machinery, when it becomes generally known, will be appreciated, and the cleaning of native cotton by its use will in all probability become a separate occupation in itself.

"The saw-gin destroyed native cotton, and its value was lowered in the market; nevertheless, labor was scarce, and the Broach saw-gin, driven by steam, found ample employment. I saw at that place in the cleaning season of 1859, the carts laden with seed cotton crowding to the gins, and their owners striving for precedence. The exports from Broach at the time at which the above estimate of profits was taken, amounted, I believe, to about 45,000 bales per annum.

"I may here observe that, although the cultivation of native cotton is capable of extension to an enormous degree, yet the amount of manual labor available is barely sufficient to clean the quantity now produced. Any large extension without the aid of cleaning machinery therefore cannot be expected, and this remark is the more applicable, when it is considered that the chief increase in cotton cultivation must be looked for in new districts, such as those of Central India, where the population is thin and scarcely sufficient to till the land."—*Report on the Cotton Gin Factory, Dharwar, pages* 17 *to* 19.

I shall merely add a brief table shewing the result of some trials with different kinds of machinery.

It is impossible to go at greater length into the subject in a work devoted to describing the existing manufactures and machinery of the Punjab. Indeed the introduction of even as much as I have admitted can only be justified by the consideration that there has been so much interest excited by the question of cotton gins *versus* charkha or belna, that it is difficult to mention the one without some allusion to the other.

RESULTS of several trials made at Kurrachee in 1864-65 with American and English Saw and Roller Cotton-Gins upon "Indigenous Sind" (native) and "Mulleer grown Egyptian" (exotic) uncleaned cotton.

DESCRIPTION OF GIN.	Manufactures.	Price at Kurrachee.	Motor power.	Kind of seed Cotton used in experiment.	Time occupied.		Weight of seed cotton used.		RESULTS. Clean cotton.		RESULTS. Seeds.		RESULTS. Motes &c.		Clean cotton obtained per hour.		REMARKS.
					hours.	minutes	lbs	oz.	lbs.	oz.	lbs.	oz.	lbs.	oz.	lbs.	oz.	
A cotton-gin of 18 saws, can be worked by either power or hand.	Carver & Co., Massachusetts U. S.	Rs. 200.	1 man.	Mulleer-grown Egyptian.	...	5	2	...	...	8·2	1	6.7	...	1	6	3·2	Two men were employed, one relieving the other in working the gin. Is evidently better adapted for long than short-stapled varieties; does not appear liable to get out of repair and any portion of the woodwork can be repaired by a smart village carpenter. Fibre of cleaned cotton does not appear to be injured.
Do.	Do.	Do.	Do.	Sind indigenous.	...	11½	4	...	...	13·5	2	6	...	12.5	4	6	
A toothed roller-cotton gin, 12 inches wide, compact in form, and requiring to be fed with cotton seed in small quantities.	Messrs. Garnett, Cleckheaton, Yorkshire.	Rs. 125.	1 man.	Mulleer-grown Egyptian.	...	14	4	...	1	2	2	14	nil		4	13	Two men employed in working this gin, one one relieving the other; is evidently well-adapted for short-stapled varieties and does not appear to injure the fibre in any way. Seed comes out fairly stript of cotton.
Do.	Do.	Do.	Do.	Sind indigenous.	...	14	4	...	1	4	2	12	nil		4	5	
A Roller gin worked by hand, the roller of wood and not covered with leather.	Messrs. Platt Brothers and Co. Oldham.	about Rs. 80.	Do.	Mulleer-grown Egyptian.	...	6	1	...	...	4·3	...	11·6	nil		2	12	This gin cleans the cotton well the seeds coming out well stript of cotton. Fibre not injured in the slightest degree. Is slow however in its work.

Kurrachee,
17th February 1865.

A. W. HUGHES.
Inspector of Cotton of Sind.

The *oil pressing machine* has already been described. It is called "kohlu."*

The *sugar-cane mills* have already been described.† The "velna," the one like the oil mill or kohlu, used in the Cis-Sutlej districts, and the one used in Kotar, will be found in Volume I. But I should mention that the plate facing page 304 represents an improved sugar mill invented by Mr. Buchanan of Gujrat. Its peculiarity, which the plate cannot show, is that by aid of a curved iron sheet at the back, the canes pass through the upper rollers and into the lower ones again without difficulty. Mr. Buchanan furnished a memo. on this machine, which I append. The plate in Volume I, at page 304, was, I should mention, intended for this volume, but the binder appropriated it for the first, unknown to me!

"This is a model on the scale of ⅜ths the proposed size, designed to be worked by water power, by an endless band attached to a drum fixed to a water-wheel; the water-wheel being erected on the falls of the rajbahas reticulating the Goordaspoor district, or similar falls used by natives for the grain mills, as either undershot or Archimedian fly water-wheel will apply. The principle is that of the mills in general use in the West Indies, but with the addition of another pair of rollers contrived to work in opposition, the contrivance (iron plate directors) is also original. In the West Indies the mills are worked by horses or mules yoked on by levers.

"The natives bring forward as a plea for not improving their sugar-cane, that their mills are not suited or powerful enough. Their mills, although showing a fair knowledge of mechanical power hardly to be expected from them, still requires 16 men and 8 pairs of bullocks to work it for 24 hours, producing but 8 or 9 maunds of goor; this is unnecessarily expensive. Their apparatus is also rude, and it is continually liable to mishaps when working. The working of this machine will not be a quarter as expensive as the other, besides being capable of bruising stiffer cane, and giving a much greater out-turn."

Before taking leave of the sugar-mills, I propose to give an account of the parts of the "Dãl-kohlú," a sugar-mill used in Ambala, and generally in the Cis-Sutlej districts. In these it is seen the rollers (belna) are little if at all used.

The huge hollow mortar or vessel which holds the canes is made of sâl *(Shorea robusta)* or other hard wood, and is called kohlú; it has a rim of iron called "kundal."

The roller which presses the canes is called 'lat,' and is made of kíkar or shísham wood. This is kept pressing against the side of the kohlu as it rolls round and round by a beam called "mákri," and to this is attached the long lever, which is moved in a circle by a yoke of cattle, and which walking round and round cause the lât to roll like a huge pestle in a mortar. This lever is called "mának thambá," and at the end of it is the driver's seat "pât".

To work the mill, the lât is removed, canes placed all round the kohlu, and then a huge wooden cup called "dánt roda," like a lining to the kohlu, is put in: thus the canes are enclosed between two walls of wood; the lât is then fixed inside the 'dánt-roda,' and the two being thus pressed together the canes between are strongly crushed; a false wooden bottom is put into the dánt-roda and called "jár-páchar;" the expressed juice

* See Punjab Products, Volume I, page 431.

† Id. Volume I, pp. 305—6, and plates.

runs through this into the kol or hollow receptacle under the kohlu, thence it is drawn by a drain or half-pipe (patnála) into a naund or "kund," a great earthen receptacle.

It is now boiled in a "bél-karahí" and stirred with a short spoon, háthí, or a headed stick called "mūsad." The boiled juice is stored in a large pan called "chákh," being moved there into by aid of a sort of pan called "cháshní.". A long ladle used in helping this operation is called "dhora".

The Plough.—The plough used in the Punjab is a very simple affair. A somewhat long heavy beam, gradually coming to a point at one end, and rounded at the other end, supplies the place of the whole of the ploughshare and other arrangements of an English plough. This beam is called "kur;" it is shod at the point with an iron blade called phāla, which pierces the soil, and the beam behind it getting gradually broader forces the soil of the furrow aside as it advances. The furrow is not of course very deep, but in all soft sand and sailába soils this cheap plough is quite sufficient.

To continue the description: from the extreme heavy end of the 'kur,' a handle, consisting of a sloping stake and a hand-piece at the top, is erected at a slight angle, by which the ploughman guides the course of the plough; further on, a stout curved beam (sanná) is fixed into the "kur" and slopes away in an opposite direction to the handle or "jangi." This beam gets thinner towards the end, and its elongated end forms the pole on either side of which the oxen are yoked.

The plough-share is made of kíkar or ber wood. When they use the "nali" or tube for drill sowing, they tie it on to the stake called "jangi," which is fixed to the plough handle. The nali is a tube of bamboo, with the mouth rather wide and funnel shaped: it is used in sandy soil for wheat sowing, and in some soils for gram and jowár also—it deposits the grain deeper in the soil than the ordinary hand process.

The bullocks are harnessed by a yoke called panjálí, consisting of two parallel bars, one of which goes above and the other below the neck of the animal; it is fitted with four cross bars, two at either end, between which the neck of the animal is confined. The two outer bars are moveable, in order to let the yoke be put on and taken of. The upper beam of the yoke is called "júla," and the lower "phat;" the inner and fixed crow-bars are "mutyá"; the outer moveable bars or pins "arli."

On the subject of ploughs, an extract from the report on the revised Settlement of the Ferozepore district may be given.

"The plough deserves further notice. There are two descriptions of ploughs, one called the "múnná," the other the "hal." They will best be understood by the following drawing.—(See sketch facing this page.)

Of these, the múnná is considered by far the better sort of plough. It penetrates much deeper into the ground than the hal, and goes deeper and deeper at each successive ploughing, as the surface soil gets more pulverized, but it can only be dragged by strong cattle, and is used only in the rohee. The hal is the plough of the "bhet" lands.* It is a very inferior machine to the múnná; it only scratches the surface of the ground, but a heavier plough would be of no use with the small breed of cattle that are alone found in the "bhet."

* Low moist lands near the river.

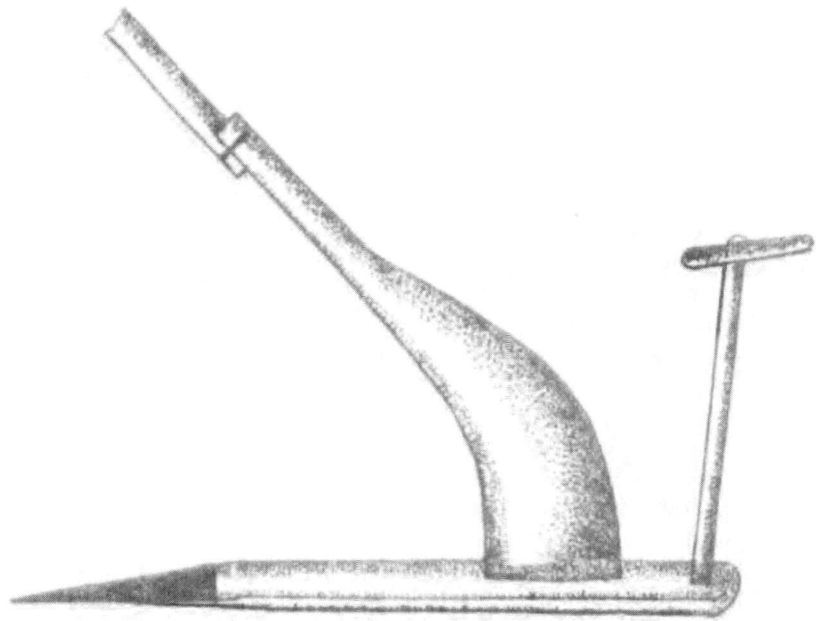

Plough in general use in the Plains

Hal (Feroze pore)

Munna.

The parts of the plough given (Amballa district) by MR. WYNYARD, are as follows : the plough used Cis-Sutlej does not materially differ from that in the Punjab proper.

Hal.—The whole plough.

Halis.—The shaft connecting the plough with the yoke (made of sál wood.)

Hal—the wooden beam that carries the ploughshare (made of kikar, shisham or khair wood.)

Pátha—the frame with iron rim (kāt) which holds on the ploughshare.

Phálí—the ploughshare of iron.

Júá—a single yoke for quiet oxen (shisham or tût wood.)

Panjálí—a double yoke, into which the necks of oxen are fastened by "gathá" or straps of leather.

Nari or Nurká, leather thong by which the yoke is attached to the shaft (halis.)

Pachwánsa—a small wedge by which the phalí or share is firmly fixed into the pâthá (made of kikar or tût (mulberry) wood.)

Paíní-sántá—bamboo handle and leather thong forming the ploughman's driving whip. The stick with a goad fixed to it at one end, and a lash at the other, is called "puráni" in Punjab.

It now remains to describe the other agricultural tools used in the plains.

Kuhárí or kulhárí—a small, somewhat heavy headed axe, used for wood cutting &c. (Kulhári—*Cis-Sutlej.*)

Dátrí—a curved sickle with a rough serrated edge (Daránti *Cis-Sutlej.*) See sketch facing next page.

Ramba—a sort of trowel with curved handle (Khúrpa *Cis-Sutlej.*)

Phaurá or Kasi—the tool shaped like a mattock, but with a broad shovel like blade, that takes the place of our spade. (Phaora, karkasi, *Cis-Sutlej.*)

Thoká— a chopper formed of a wooden handle, or back into which the blade is fixed by two points at either end (Gandása *Cis-Sutlej.*) See sketch facing next page.

Khodál (*Cis-Sutlej*) a pick for digging kankar.

Kasi or Kasolí (*Cis-Sutlej*) a shorthand hoe, used for hoeing sugar-cane fields.

Gáhan—(*Cis-Sutlej*) a sort of harrow, for scratching up the ground for rice sowing when the ground is covered with water. It is stuck full of pegs about two inches long.

Sohágá—a heavy beam, drawn by horses and oxen, to smooth over the land after sowing &c., (mera or sohága *Cis-Sutlej.*)

Karáh—a heavy beam or frame of wood, made of pieces nailed together and having an iron plate attached, used for clod crushing and levelling. (Belna or úd *Cis-Sutlej*) It is drawn by men, two men standing on it to increase the pressure.

Jandra—a large wooden rake, with a long handle and a beam and teeth of kikar. The teeth are not at right angles to the handle, but on the same plane. It is so held at an incline by one man, that it presses against the earth, and then two others, each seizing a rope that is attached just above the teeth-bar, on either side, drag it along. The jandra is used principally on preparing the kyári or small beds for irrigation, with a rim or ledge of earth round the edge to confine the water. (Jandra *Cis-Sutlej.*)

Khôpa—leather caps put over the eyes of cattle when working the wells.

The implements used in the threshing floor ('phir') are as follows. The floor itself is selected on a hard clean place, and is 'leped' over with mud, and made perfectly clean and smooth; the cut wheat, &c., being thrown down, it is trodden out by oxen, who drag after them a sort of frame called 'phalá.' This consists of four rough bars or sticks arranged as a frame, and one across the middle, the inside is wattled in with dry twigs and boughs of the cotton plant.

The action of the rough surface of this against the corn, aided by the trampling of the oxen's feet, not only frees the grain, but breaks up the straw into fragments, which forms "bhúsa." When sufficiently trodden, the whole is tossed and turned with a huge wooden pitch-fork, "tarangri" * (Jelî *Cis-Sutlej*), consisting of nine long wooden prongs, bound to a stout stem or handle with thongs of raw hide.

The rope that keeps the cattle together in the yoke in threshing floor is called "dáiras" in the Cis-Sutlej, and "jotar" in the Punjab.

In the hills the plough can only be used where there is a tolerably large area for each field; but it often happens that the fields rising in terraces one above the other are only a few feet in breadth. In such localities the plough gives way to hand hoeing and digging.

The plough, when used is just like that of the plains. Some of the tools are especially adapted for stony soil and for breaking up stones too large to move without assistance. The tools are as follows.

Kasi—a small hoe or mattock, with a rather narrow blade and handle, about two feet long.

Mend—a heavy solid bar of iron, about 3 or 4 feet long, set in a wooden handle, used for splitting and breaking stones.

Chikrí—Is made in two shapes: one is a light hand-hoe with the handle a foot long, and the blade crooked; the other (*b.*) is merely a hooked stick, shod with iron at the point; both are used for digging out weeds and thinning various kinds of crops and loosening the earth round the roots of maize, &c.

Rambhi—a hoe like the 'phaora,' the blade about four inches broad, used in rice fields only.

Besides these several of the Hill States of Simla, sent.

Daránti—the curved sickle not unlike that used in the plains.

Dhángrá or Dhángrí—a small axe. (Gandása in Kanaiti.)

Kudáli—a small hooked hoe or pick.

The 'Kudáli' of the Bhagal State is a mere bit of hard wood hooked and pointed. The point has been heated in the fire to harden it.

The reaping hooks or sickles have rather the iron part of the handles longer than those of the plains.

* A similar tool with five prongs is called Panjángula.

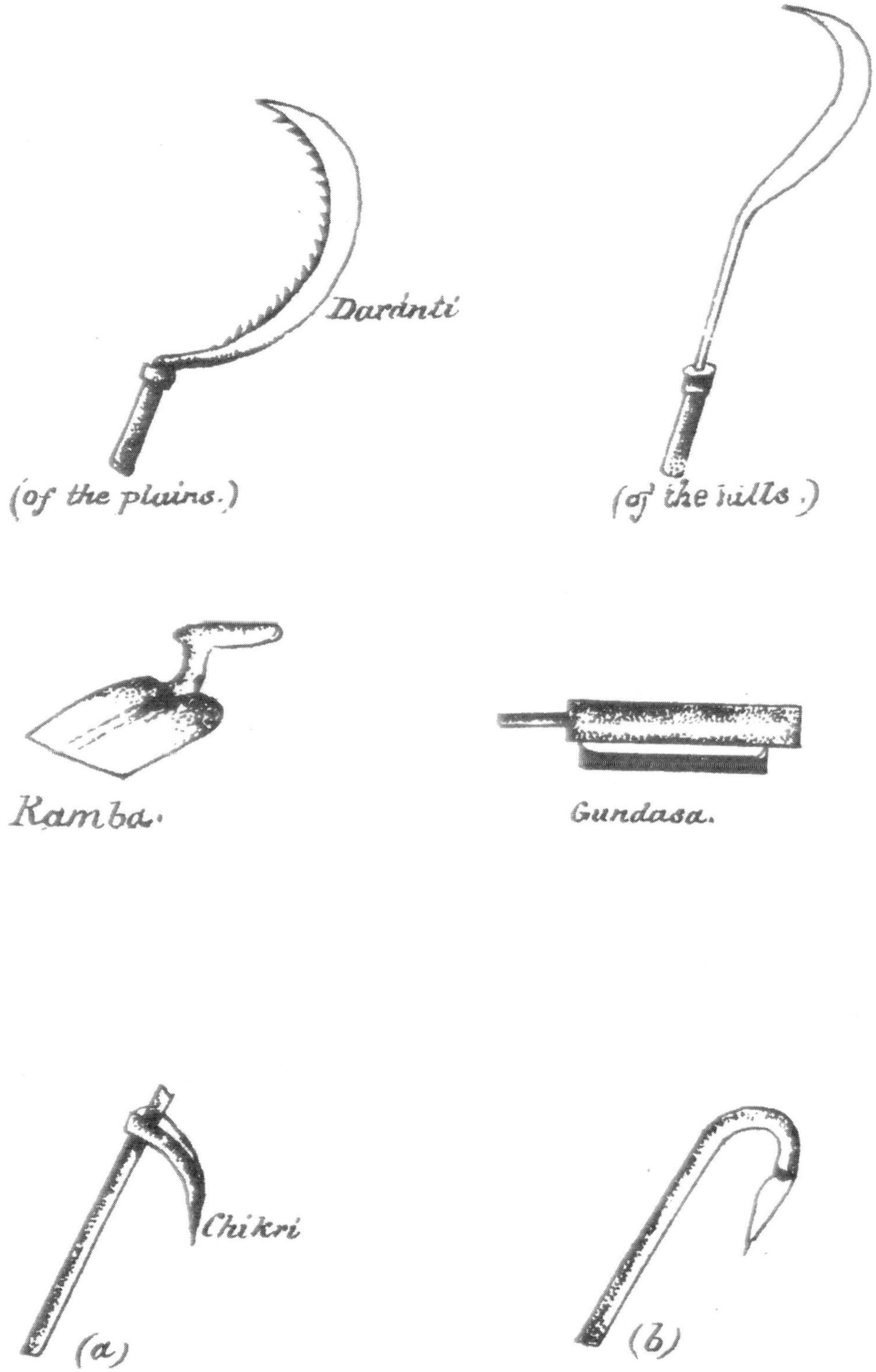
Darānti
(of the plains.)
(of the hills.)
Kamba.
Gundasa.
Chikri
(a)
(b)

In Kangra the following implements are used :—

		Rs.	As.
Hal and Lohála, ...	Plough and Ploughshare, (costs,)	1	0
Máhi, ...	A heavy horizontal block of wood dragged by oxen for smoothing surface of a field, ...	0	3
Mach, ...	Similar to the above but curved in shape and used only in muddy lands, ...	0	2½
Dandrál, ...	A harrow with eight or ten bamboo teeth dragged by oxen, used for opening the soil round the young corn, ...	0	5½
Mánjah,	Hoes for weeding,	0	8
Kodal Kodálí,		0	4
Bhukráñ or Kuthela or Bharota, ...	A wooder club used for crushing stiff clods of earth, ...	0	1
Tringul, ...	A three-pronged pitchfork, ...	0	2
Dráutí, ...	A small hook, ...	0	2
Khabar Dráutí, ...	A hook with teeth like a saw to cut long grass, ...	0	4
Kahi or Kasi, ...	A mattock, ...	1	0
Rambhá, ...	A small iron instrument for digging up grass roots and all weeds, ...	0	2
Kulhárú or Chhau, ...	Axes for cutting wood, ...	0	8
		0	4

I conclude this class by reprinting the Jury Report on Agricultural Implements in 1864. It contains also a note on an improved saw-gin.

REPORT OF THE JURY ON AGRICULTURAL AND HORTICULTURAL IMPLEMENTS.

"Under this head are found but seventy-nine articles exhibited in all—from General No. 10,590 to No. 10,669. The majority of these also, are merely rough models of the very primitive implements in use throughout the Panjab, and require no notice.

" The Section is however by no means wanting in the exhibition of articles of real and actual interest and worth. From the district of Gurdaspur, for instance, some valuable models have beem supplied, *viz:*—

No. 10,632, a sugar mill.

No. 10,633, a cotton gin.

No. 10,634, a cotton press.

" These machines were the contributions of a Mr. Buchanan, and their construction displays considerable ingenuity. A memorandum by the exhibitor explaining their mode of construction and working is attached. The Jurors regret much that these models were not made with more care, and better finish. They have no doubt that one and all of them would work well, if properly made; but the models submitted were altogether too rough to admit of their working being satisfactorily tested. It is on this account only that the Jurors do not think they are justified in awarding to Mr. Buchanan the prize of Rs. 200 offered by the Rajah of Kupurthalla for a model of a sugar mill. They however gladly award that gentleman a medal for the general collection.

" As carefully executed models none surpass the contributions of Sirdar Bhagwán Singh of Amritsar.

No. 10,619, instruments used by the gardener.
No. 10,620, ditto by the cultivator.
No. 10,630, model of an English plough.

" The Jurors consider the Sirdar to be well deserving of a medal for these donations, and this they award.

" And lastly, to Mr. McNabb, the exhibitor of a neatly contrived working model of a cotton belna of steel, the Jurors award a third medal. This little model is perfect in its construction, and attracted considerable notice, especially from the native visitors to the Exhibition, by all of whom it was thoroughly appreciated.

" The contributions of Messrs. Lepage and Co., of Calcutta, pickaxes, and kothális were also approved of not being however of Panjab manufacture, these cannot compete for the prizes offered.

" The Jurors cannot close their report on the articles submitted to their inspection under this Section without bringing prominently to notice the existence of machinery in the Hazara district for the cleaning of cotton, worked by water power. The model contributed by the Hazara Local Committee is rough, and small; but as they are of opinion that the use of water as a motive power in the working of machinery is much neglected, they notice the existence of this—to this part of the Panjab—novel method of cleaning cotton, in the hope that it may attract attention and prove useful."

MEMO. BY MR. BUCHANAN.

" The undersigned begs to state that in forming the designs for these machines, he held in view the circumstances of the country with regard to the materials to be procured for making them. Complications of the most trifling kinds had to be set aside, so as to meet the capacities of the people and the indigenous artizans; they can all, he is convinced, be made by the latter. The canal districts were also held in view as affording cheap motive power, and the designs were made accordingly.

" I.—*Cotton Press.* This model is on the scale of one-twentieth of the proposed size. It is the Surat Cotton Press principle, arranged so as to work by an endless band on a drum, to be worked either with water or animal power. The Surat press working on the capstan mode, at the base of the screw piles, is very disadvantageous and incommodious. It requires many men to work it, and the time occupied in the pressing of each bale is unnecessarily long. In this machine but twelve minutes will be required to press a bale with the drum worked by a bullock. The time will be shorter if worked by water power. The press beam can be re-elevated by lowering the endless band on the lower wheel (top of machine) by the lever appendages common and well known in all machines worked by the strap.

"At Gurdaspur, I calculated that a machine made up thus would cost Rs. 220. The screw piles, bar and cogged wheels being "sheeshum" wood, the remainder deodar. In making the cogged wheels, a little ingenuity is required: the teeth and indentations should be separate pieces dove-tailing into each other. In the teeth, the grain of the wood should be longitudinal, in the indentation pieces transverse. The reason for this is obvious, as the teeth will then bear considerable pressure (double of what will be required in this machine). If the teeth had the grain of the wood parallel to the plane of pressure, they would inevitably break off. Another advantage is gained should warpage take place in any of the pieces or they be worn away, they can be easily replaced by new ones. There are many excellent plans, I believe, in practical carpentry of making wooden cogged wheels, and the native indigenous artizans are not ignorant of some.

"II.—*Cotton Gin.* Owing to my removal from Gurdaspur, I was unable to quite complete this machine. But it is sufficiently prepared to give an idea of the principle. Both the "churka" and the Macarthy gin principle have been applied, the latter being that the staple is caught up by the rough fibres of the leather covered cylinder, revolving under a fixed blunt-edged knife, the staple being freed from the seeds by the resistance of the rack; and the seed held from following by the teeth of the rack, which is placed before the leather cylinder. This method answers fully with long stapled cotton; but with the short staple degenerate country cotton it does not act, the seeds being also small. When the indigenous cotton is improved by culture in its quality, the Macarthy principle will then answer better than the "churka:" the latter both dirties and tears the fibre. To accommodate the machine to the present native cotton, the steel knife is removed, and a polished steel cylindrical bar is substituted, so as to revolve by contact with the leather covered cylinder. The rack should also be removed. The fluted cylinder at the back is for clearing the staple from the leather one. There is a box in the machine into which the cleaned seed falls through the trellis work at the top.

"The originality in this machine is the adaption for working the cylinders by the treddle or the common foot lathe apparatus. Some substitutions have been made and the appliances simplified.

"The native churka is a very rude contrivance: a person by working all day can only gin 1¼ seers of cotton. In a medical point of view, it is much to be deprecated, as from the unnatural and awkward position the worker has to sit to it, it is very injurious and unhealthy, so that a cheap and simple machine not having these disadvantages is much to be desired.

"A gin made up thus will cost at the outside about Rs. 25. When this specimen was being made it became very popular. The carpenters whom I had employed received orders for many."

Under this head I may describe an apparatus used in the Hazára district, where small hill streams are abundant. Properly speaking the machine is made up for husking rice, but I have seen models of the same kind of machine applied to turning mill-stones, and also to turning the cotton cleaning rollers commonly used in the country.

The apparatus is called Píkú.* It consists of a small over-shot water-wheel fed by a stream of water.

Two walls or supports being built up about 7 or 8 feet apart, in the centre of each a block of wood is let in (called móndhi); these blocks have each a hole or notch in which the ends of the axle or lath rest. The "lat" is a short round wooden bar, double spindle shaped, or thus—

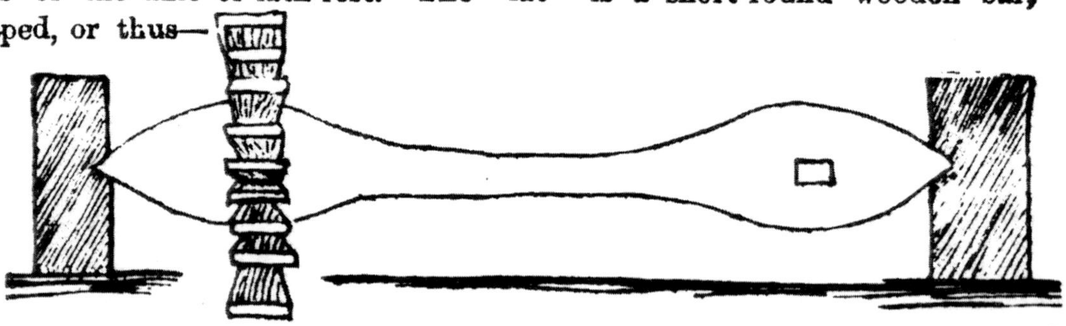

At one end, about 1½ feet from the socket, is fixed the "charakh" or wheel, consisting of from 17 to 24 radiating pieces of wood, broader at the outer edge than at the inner, which is inserted 3 inches into the body of the "lath." These radiating pieces or fans are called "kham" (= wing) and each is 15 inches long. A water-course, here called "khatta" (Punjabi 'kul') is now conducted to a convenient height above the wheel, and from thence a water trough is let down at a convenient angle to within 3 inches of the wheel; the stream of water sets the wheel in motion. The outer trough is made 8 inches wide at the upper end, gradually diminishing to 4 inches at the end over the wheel: it is 8 inches deep, and is called "parnála."

If a rice husking machine has to be made, a deep hole or excavation is made in the bank behind the axle or 'lat' (a suitable position having these features is of course selected) and in this the mortar for holding the rice is fixed; two upright posts or "mǒna"

---

* The papers from which these details are taken were furnished by Captain Wace, Settlement Officer, Hazara, and accompanied by drawings.

are erected in front of it, carrying between them a circular rod, which has a round headpiece inserted at right angles, and which, when the rod descends, hits the rice in the mortar and removes the husk The next requisite is to communicate a motion to this pounder, by making it alternately to rise and fall hammerwise; for this purpose at the end of the 'lat' opposite the wheel, and about the same distance ($1\frac{1}{2}$ feet) from the socket, a curved piece of wood, like a parrot's beak, and called "chapér," is inserted. As the axle revolves, this alternately catches the end of the rod carrying the pounder, lifts it up, and then owing to its curve slips away from under it, when the hammer falls by its own weight; and when the point of the 'chapér' comes round again it catches the rod, raises it, and lets it fall again, and so on. In 24 hours such a machine will husk six ass loads of rice, estimated at 14 maunds 25 seers standard weight, but this is at full working power.

When the water power is wanted for a mill or a cotton 'belna' the chapér is not used, but a similar wheel and the further end of the axle fitted with cogged wheels suited to give a vertical or horizontal movement as may be required.

DIVISION III.
HORTICULTURAL IMPLEMENTS.

Very few of these exist; the rougher work of preparing garden land is done with the ordinary agricultural tools, such as the plough, the 'jandra.' The only small tools the gardener uses are the following—

'Kasi' as before.

'Pháora' Do.

'Chuhá rambá,' a sort of iron fixed in a wooden handle; it is made of a bar of iron, the extreme point of which is flattened and hammered out into a triangular blade. It is used for digging up plants in transplanting &c.

"Gháí ramba" is the broad rambá or khúrpa with short curved handle used by grass-cutters in scraping up grass, and by a gardener as a trowel, also as a hand hoe for weeding.

Sickle, as before described.

Cháku, grafting knife.

To prepare large beds, they use a rake or jandar like the agricultural one; only the better taught mâlis in European gardens use the rake, Dutch-hoe, shears, &c., &c.

CLASS XXX.

Not represented.

CLASS XXXI.

DIVISION I.

BUILDING CONTRIVANCES.

There is absolutely nothing in this class to enumerate as in the former classes, but it seems to afford a suitable opportunity for a few remarks on the style of building at present seen in various parts of the Punjab. To this I shall add a note upon native bridges and method of building wells.

I must omit all mention of the more ancient buildings. Of the early Mahomedan style of 12th to 14th century we have some fine specimens at Delhi. These are nearly all constructed of the fine red sandstone brought from Jaipúr and Central India, while for the coarser work (as in the fort of Toghlakábád) the hard gritty stone found in the vicinity of Delhi is employed.

White marble from Jaipúr is also used; very little cement appears, but all the stones are beautifully fitted and joined, and occasionally metal clamps are employed.

The buildings of the later Mogul empire of the 16th and 17th centuries are, many of them, constructed of the same stone, which must have been imported at a vast expense. But among these buildings appear numerous structures made of small but beautifully burnt bricks; they are not above 6 to 8 inches long and 1½ inch thick; they are mostly burnt through like chert-stone. Vast mounds are still to be seen in the vicinity of Lahore and other towns, which are the debris of the gigantic kilns in which these bricks were burnt.

Vast thickness and solidity characterize the brick structures, and the abundant use of a most solid and tenacious mortar, which so cakes the bricks together that when it has been desired to remove a fallen mass of such masonry, the workman's iron pick has proved unequal to the task of separating the materials and the mass has had to be blasted with powder like a rock. Such cement was made by obtaining the best lime free of all ash and impurity. Our Engineers wish now that they could obtain such.

The houses of the poorer class of agriculturists all over the plains require no special description; they are invariably made either of sun-dried bricks smeared over with a mixture of mud and cow-dung, or more often the wall is built up somewhat irregularly by plastering cake over cake of mud, the outer coating being mixed with chopped straw (bhúsa) and cow-dung to make it bind. Small low hovels, with a couple of rudely made wooden flaps for a door, and perhaps a window with a wooden shutter are thus built;

they are roofed with poles either chíl (pine) "balis" where procurable, or stems of small sized mulberry, kíkar, and shísham trees; over these tiles are laid, or "sírki" (a sort of thatch of the múnj grass) and then mud is plastered on outside. The roof is made strong enough to bear a few people on it, and has a raised edge all round, with a wooden gutter pipe to draw off water. In the hot weather the people sleep on the roof. In a wealthy village, houses constructed of burnt bricks are more frequent, and are then built with two stories. A kachá (cutcha) house consists of a sort of verandah in front and one or more little dark rooms behind; they have no fire-places, and not even a hole for smoke, as the people generally light a fire outside and only use a chafing dish of hot embers inside.

Where the house has to accommodate several members of a family, the rooms and the verandah are ranged round the side of a small court-yard or "sahn," which is approached by one door in common to the whole.

The only attempt I have seen to improve the style of the ordinary peasant's hut is in a model sent to the Central Museum by the Reverend Mr. Golaknáth, Missionary at Jálandhar. He has merely improved upon the ordinary design so as to afford more privacy and security to each house. There is the usual court-yard or "sahn"; at the front is a sort of covered entrance or "deora"; alongside, a shed for horses or cattle, and at the opposite end of the yard are the dwelling rooms in two stories; a staircase outside leads to the upper story, both stories having the "dálán" or verandah outside, and the "kothri" or rooms within. The plan of arrangement is this—

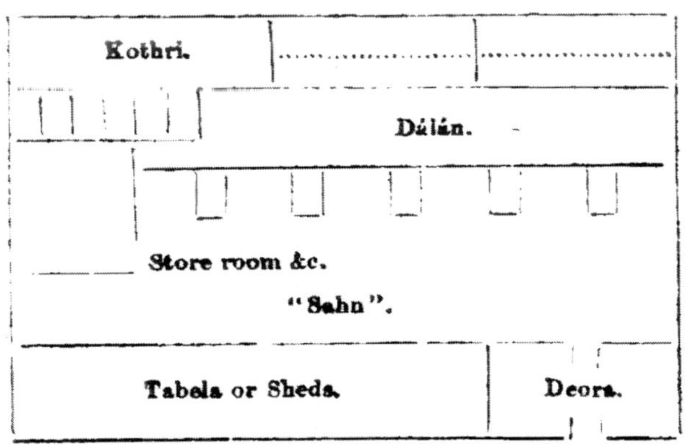

An ordinary house is known by the name of "ghar or "makán", a large mansion is called "haveli." This generally has an entrance gate, at each end of which are rooms in which porters or servants can live; over this is the entrance called "deora," and inside the sahn, round which are the rooms of the family and the ladies' apartments: every house has a good roof space with access by stairs; the roof adjoining the women's apartments is protected at the edge by a high screen made of perforated stone-work, or slabs of tiling perforated in imitation of stone.

On the roofs of large houses various small and often oddly shaped rooms are constructed, looking like towers and turrets from below. These are constructed for coolness, and to enable the inmates to enjoy the evening or the morning breeze. The shape of houses is often strangely irregular, and the building looks as if it had been added to piece by piece without reference to any general design. A house intended for business or for the temporary residence of men, is constructed perhaps with a few rooms or open shops on the ground floor and a large room above opening on to the street and separated from it only by a low balustrade and certain wooden lattices which can be closed up with shutters. Such a building is called " baitak."

A square court-yard furnished with a separate gate and fitted with stalls for horses and cattle, and rooms for servants and " syces " or grooms, is called " tabela." One is always either attached to a large house or built separately for the use of the house.

I have now to add a few extracts taken from various sources, describing the ordinary dwelling houses of the mass of the population in various districts in the plains, and afterwards, of the hills. From Mr. Prinsep's Settlement Report of Sealkot the following is extracted, and is applicable to the houses of the entire agricultural population of the plain districts of the Punjab as far as Amballa :—

" There are only two kinds of houses in ordinary use, and these are made of mud or built of baked bricks. They are huddled together, a congeries of flat roofed huts, separated by narrow alleys, and plastered over with a primitive mixture of the earth, chopped straw, and cow dung, and surrounded outside by rows of cow-dung, (used in these parts for fuel) by stacks of straw, sheds for weavers, goat pens, places for meetings, and temples for worship. All the available space is filled up with heaps of village refuse required for manure. In the larger villages where the residents may have amassed wealth, may be seen a few " hawellees " or houses of ' pukka " masonry. Each family lives in a separate court-yard, and this is all the privacy which exists. Cattle and their owner consort together I have seen them living in the same apartment. In the arrangement of houses or enclosures there seems to be little attempt at order or cleanliness. It is no wonder then that much sickness or liability to epidemic should result in certain seasons."

In the Jach Doab, the following detailed account from the Settlement Report of the Shahpur District by Major Davies must be quoted :—

" The dwellings of the common people, throughout the district consist of one or more rooms called " kothas," with a court-yard in front. This court-yard, named " verhá " is often common to several houses. These rooms are built ordinarily of clay, gradually piled up in successive layers and then plastered. The roofs are invariably flat, and are used as sleeping places during the hot weather. In the court-yard is generally seen a manger (" kúrlí "), and a house in which the cattle are sheltered from the cold in the winter months, which structures (called " sath " in the ' Bar,' where they are very capacious) consist generally of four walls covered with a thatch. The only exceptions to the above general description, are the habitations of the people in the ' Thal,' and in the hills. The former are often composed of nothing but wood and grass, and the latter are built entirely of boulders cemented together with clay ; as however walls of this kind have little or no power of resisting rain, the roof is always supported on strong posts driven into the ground, the walls acting merely as a defence against the weather. As a rule the houses of the zemindars are built for them by the village carpenter (" Tarkhán ") or potter (" Kumhár "), who receive their food while the work is going on, and a present of clothes or money when it is finished ; payment for work at a fixed rate is only made by Khatrís and other non-proprietors. The timber used for roofing is usually " kíkar " or "ber" in the plains, and "kao" (wild olive) in the hills, the first two being usually the produce of the zemindars' own fields; beams of deodar or shísham are only to be seen in the houses of the rich.

"The requirements of a population low in the scale of civilization are few, and we see this exemplified in the furniture of their houses, which consists almost entirely of necessaries. It would be tedious, though not perhaps devoid of use, to give a complete description of all the articles in every day use in a household of this part of India, I shall therefore only enumerate the more important. First, there are the receptacles for storing grain, of various sizes, from the dimensions of a small room to those of a beer barrel. These are made by the women of the house, of fine clay mixed with chopped straw. The larger kind called "sakár." are square, and hold from forty to fifty maunds; the smaller description. "kalhoti," are cylindrical in form, and hold but a few maunds. Next are to be seen some spinning wheels, (as many as there are women), an apparatus for churning milk, an instrument for cleaning cotton ("belna"), a number of circular baskets, with and without lids, made of reeds ("khári," "taung" &c.), in which are kept articles of clothing and odds and ends; trays of reeds ("chhaj," "chhakor") used in cleaning grain; a goat-skin water bag ("kúní"), used on journeys, or when employed in the fields at a distance from home; a set of wooden measures for grain ("topa," "paropi" &c.); a leather bag ("khallar") for carrying flour when away from home; a variety of cooking vessels, some of iron, and others of a composition resembling bell-metal; a number of earthen pots and pans, in which are stored grain, condiments and other articles of food; a coarse iron sieve ("parún"); a pestle and mortar ("daurí"), in which to pound spices and condiments. These, with a few stools ("pírá," "pírí"), and cots, complete the list of the fittings up of an interior here; and the same, with a few minor changes, would probably answer as a description of the furniture of a peasant's house in any part of the Punjab. It must not be supposed that all these things are disposed without order: space has to be economized, and everything, not in use. is therefore carefully arranged on shelves resting on pegs driven into the walls round the rooms."

As a sample of the house building farther 'down country,' but still showing how much alike the system of building everywhere is, I will give an extract from the Amballa Settlement Report:—

"The houses are for the most part what is called *kotha*. The walls are made of mud, or clods of dry earth, taken out of the tanks when they are dried up, or from the dried up and cracked rice fields. The roof of the kotha is also of mud; the beams which support it, and which are principally made of sál wood,* rest partly on the mud walls and partly on upright beams, of drek or bukain,† about six feet high. Across these beams are placed smaller ones, of the bukain, or mulberry tree; over this, grass, and over the grass about three inches of earth is laid. Some of the houses possess a chimney. or rather a hole in the roof, to let the smoke escape. It is always made in the middle of the room, and covered up, when it rains, with a gharra. Every house has a "kotha," a large chest made of earth, about five feet square, outside, and four feet square inside, with a door in the middle on hinges. In this. grains, and the cooking utensils, are placed. The kotahs are more or less ornamented, according to the taste

* *Shorea robusta.* This wood is not to be had up country.

† *Melia sempervirens.*

and wealth of the owners. The rest of the furniture of their houses consists of a 'land,' or shelf in a corner, and "alla" a cupboard in the corner, or in the wall; the door of this, and of the kota, are made of mangoe or jámun. There is a 'manja,' or chárpái, a bed for sitting and sleeping on; this, however, is only used in warm weather, and then out in the open air, by the men. In the cold weather, they make a bed on the ground of sugar-cane leaves, and straw, for the sake of warmth. Two or three gharras for water, a charkha, or spindle for the women, who all occupy themselves in spinning; a "chakkí," hand mill for grinding grain, which also falls to the lot of the female members of the family; "batta," a round stone (pestle) with which they bruise and pound the spices on "sil," a flat stone which they use as a mortar; katorah, a wooden bowl-like dish, used as a kneading trough; "baili," a small brass drinking pot; katorah, one of a larger size; "lunda," or karcha, a large iron pot used for cooking; "chenka," a swing table, hanging from the roof; "chalni," sieve for the atta, and "dor," the wooden spoon. The doors are all fastened from the outside, with an iron chain, and lock at the bottom; and in the inside, by a chain over a staple.

"No light is procurable but through the door. The women sit outside to spin. Spinning, grinding the corn, destroying the vermin in the heads of their children or friends, and nursing, are the only occupations of the women, except of the Jatni, and low caste women, who work in the field also.

"The villages are generally compactly built, on ground a little raised, with one or two principal lanes, about eight or ten feet wide, running through them; from these lanes other blind paths branch off to the different "hawelies" or houses. In the khádar, (low land) between the Jamna and the canal, the houses are generally on high ground to avoid inundations. To the west of the canal, they are built on the "dhang" or high precipitous bank of the old Jamna; by this plan the people are near the water, and generally conveniently situated for their bángar, as well as their khadar lands.

"The houses are generally smeared with mud once a year, after the rains, which gives them a tidy appearance. Thatched houses (chappar) are cheaper than *kothas*, but they are colder in the winter, and generally inhabited by the lower castes, Gujars, Chúras, Chumárs, &c. I consider it is a sign of an inferior village to have more chappars than kothas. The Rajputs, both Hindus and Mussulmans, the Jats, Kimbohs and Brahmins, are all comfortable about their houses."

Houses in the Hills.

I have now to describe the houses in the hill districts. They exhibit more variety than those in the plains, and they have also to stand harder usage. There is often heavy rain, and every winter snow many feet in thickness. The consequence is that substantial walls, and pent roofs far projecting over the edge of the house, are the features of most districts; but flat roofs are not uncommon, even in districts where snow falls.

Stone is invariably used by itself or with mud, or where there is a timber frame work stones are filled in between.

Wood being generally abundant and hitherto obtained and used free of cost, and without the least regard to economy, a great portion of the front of every house, including the upper verandah, is made of wood work.

Chamba, Pangi &c.—In Chamba city the houses are built of wooden frames filled with slabs of the schistose slaty stone that abounds, in that particular style of masonry called "tattar chúl." The buildings are made up of layers of stones and beams of wood, and at the corners there is a sort of frame work of wood, one beam being furnished with a tenon and the other with a mortise (chúl) to receive it. The centre part of the wall has many beams of wood occasionally introduced between the layers of stone: this kind of building, which has been incorrectly stated to be peculiar to Kulu, is to be found all over the hills. The Chamba houses are built up with stones at the sides to the top, and are two stories or even three high; the front is generally made of wood: the beams on the first floor project and form a support for a sort of verandah, which invariably fronts each floor and makes the whole house look as if made of wood: the first floor of the ground has generally the best apartments, and the pillars and railings are sometimes prettily though rudely carved. The roof is pent shaped, with projecting curves and covered with large irregular and thick slates held by wooden pegs, but oftener by shingles or slabs of pine-wood not sawn but split.

In the villages of Chamba, the houses are smaller, built up with mud and stones, having only one story above the ground floor. The upper one has a wooden verandah or open front with pillars, which can be boarded up in the cold season. In the "Chauráh" district flat roofs are common, and mud and stones plastered over smooth and afterwards colored with whitewash or some colored earth work, are generally adopted. In the higher hill districts flat roofs are not so common, and pent roofs predominate. In Pangí the houses of the few wealthy or inhabitants of the "kotis" or official houses of the Chumba State, are built of stone and timber in the "tattar chúl" style; they have two or three stories, sometimes furnished with open verandahs, but always on the side facing the inner enclosure; on the outside they present a plain fort-like appearance, with windows higher up furnished with sun-shades or small hanging balconies prettily carved. They have sloping roofs, slated or shingled.

The poor people's houses in Pangi are the most wretched dens imaginable; such is the collection of filth both inside and outside that it is quite necessary in travelling to make a circuit and keep as far from a house as circumstances will permit.

The houses are small as a rule, having one ground floor, the rooms of which are dark and low; this is built of stones and mud, or rarely stones and timber, and has a door and windows: over this is a second storey, a room built entirely of wood; in fact it is rather a sort of open "baitak" or sitting place, consisting of wooden posts all round, which are only partly boarded in, except during the winter, when every part of the house is closely boarded over, leaving only the tiniest exits, for no one goes out except when it is impossible to help so doing.

All the winter the people crouch in their houses: they rarely if ever use fire, and get warm only by contiguity: they never change their thick and usually filthy woollen garments, so that the odour of a house may be imagined; to add to this, the poorer people have to store up in summer their whole winter supply of food. A portion of this consists of butter, which is kept in jars, and certainly does keep wonderfully; for drinking they collect quantities of sour milk, which is deposited in a large earthen pan or receptacle sunk in the ground of the lower story: the milk is kept for months, till covered with green mildew and frequently full of maggots: the stench of it is indescribable. Fire is often dispensed with for cooking, and a mess is made up of maize-meal moistened with water, and with this "lassí" or sour milk, and flavoured with "chukri," which is a powder made by collecting young rhubarb stalks in the spring, drying and then crushing them up for use. A few of the upper rooms in houses—generally very old houses—exhibit curious carving. I annex a sketch of the peculiar way in which a room I saw was roofed, and how the centre of the ceiling was carved; the roof was supported by pillars composed of oblong bricks of deodar wood placed across and across. The wood was black and hard with age; the front of the room had an open veranda, and the other sides all wood; it was approached by a rude flight of stone steps.

Kúlu, Plach &c.—The houses in Kúlú are not unlike those in Chamba, but in no part of the valley are they like the Pangí houses: the climate is however nothing like so rigorous, nor is the gently sloping and fertile valley of Kúlú—I speak of the populous parts—in any degree like the remote and secluded Pangí, with its steep precipices and huge crags inaccessible save over lofty passes—a prey to avalanches and to bitter winds.

The Kúlú houses have generally only one story above the ground floor, built much as before described, but there are houses with two stories. As I am writing I have a sketch of the Munáli village before me. The houses are several of them two-storied: the lower story is built of stones carefully plastered over and whitewashed; it is approached and also lighted by a single door set in a heavy wooden frame with some carving on it; the ends of the rafters forming the first floor above this project a good way out, forming a verandah roof to the lower floor. The second floor projects above the ground floor, inasmuch as the front, composed wholly of pine planks, is brought up to the extreme edge of the aforesaid rafters; two large square apertures are cut in this boarded front; the rafters forming the roof of this story again project, and on it is built a second but very low garret story, also of wood: the two *ends* of the house are of stone and plaster up to the top. The roof is pent and projects a very long way over the building all round, giving a peculiarly picturesque appearance. It is composed of shingles of wood: a beam at the top of the roof serves as the means of fixing on the shingles on one side, which have their ends projecting *above* it; the shingles on the other side have their ends *under* it.

A beautiful specimen of an old Kúlú house may be seen in the Munáli (Dúngri) forest: it is attached to the temple there, which is ancient and covered with curious carving, I cannot here describe it as I should be trespassing on antiquities, which are not within the scope of my book. The house is built in an oblong, with one wing at right angles. It has only one story above the low ground floor, and the usual pent roof; the rafters supporting the floor of the first story project I should think seven feet at the ends and sides of the house, and a series of pillars or uprights extend from the outer edge to the roof, which covers over all. All round the edge is a balustrade, which is covered with devices of serpents, birds, and fancy patterns; above the balustrade the spaces between the pillars and the roof are generally filled in with planks, except at the ends of the verandah and at certain intervals where there are sort of windows; the verandah is approached from outside by a stout plank or slab with steps notched or cut into it. At the top of the steps there is a sort of passage running through the house, and supported by black wooden pillars carved.

Pillar

Enlarged pattern

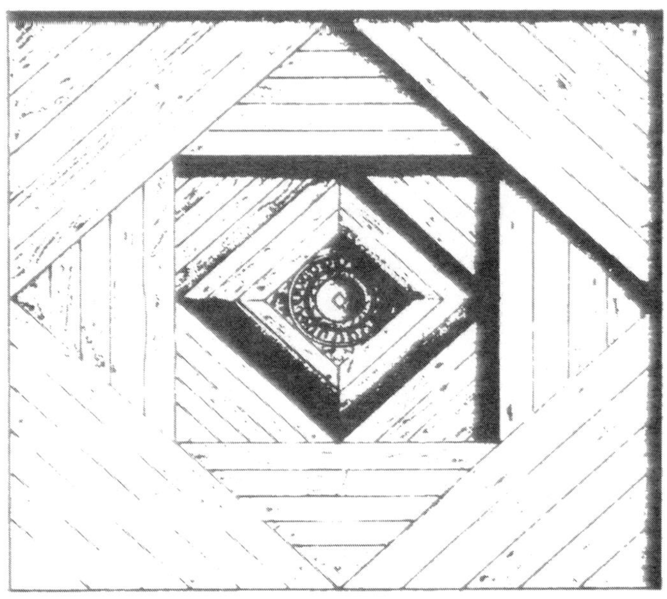

Diagram shewing arrangement of roof beams

S. Sedgfield Lith: Calcutta

Carved ceiling-Pangi.

Towards Plách, and in the neighbourhood of the Mandi State, the character of the houses alters, and bears witness probably to bygone days of insecurity. Every house is tall, square, broad based, and slightly smaller at the top than at the base; it has a pent roof, or rarely a flat one, and looks like a fort; the lower story consists of bare walls of stone plastered over and colored with white yellow or grey earth; no entrance is to be had, and no window seen, but habitation appears to commence about 9 or 10 feet above, where the rafters of the second floor project all round and forms the floor of the verandah which surrounds the room inside: this verandah floor has no balustrade and rarely any pillars attaching it to the roof or to the verandah above (unless there is a second story) and it is perfectly frightful to see the reckless way in which little children are left to loll about on this insecure and aerial boarding; the wonder is they do not always fall over—but then they are accustomed to it; a notched pole or set of moveable steps gives access to the habitable rooms above; if this is withdrawn the proverbial castellate character of one's house is realized.

The only use which the outside of the ground floor is put to is to hold against its outer walls a sort of rude rack work in which the dry fodder destined for the winter's supply is stored, consisting of dry stalks of the amaranth and "batúa" crops, (*Chenopodiaceous* plants) or of hay and straw. I have seen separate buildings. or rather sheds, consisting entirely of such rack work stored with fodder, each tier of rack work being approached by a rude ladder. Women may be seen climbing about among the rafters gathering down or storing up the fodder as the case may be. In these parts women do nearly everything, field work included; actually driving the plough is the only thing they do not habitually do. They by no means realize the poetic ideal that "men must work and women must weep," but rather that men must smoke and women must work!

To pursue our way further, we approach the Tibetan or semi-Tibetan hill districts, and for a description of their houses I shall have recourse to the travellers who have specially noticed them. In Cunningham's Ladakh, the following description of the houses is given:—

"The generality of the houses throughout Ladak are so much alike that a description of one will serve for all. The houses usually consist of two or three stories and sometimes of four. The foundations and lower parts of the walls are built of stone, the upper walls of large sun-dried bricks, 20 × 10 × 16 inches. In the better houses some of the rooms are of considerable size, twenty-five feet long and eighteen broad; but they are always very low, the highest not exceeding seven and a half or eight feet. The roofs of these large rooms are always supported by plain wooden pillars. The roof is formed of poplar spars five or six inches in diameter, peeled white. and laid only one to one and a half feet apart. The beams are covered with small straight pieces of poplar branches about one inch in diameter peeled white and placed touching each other. Generally they are laid straight across the beams; but sometimes at different angles, in the alternate intervals so as to form a pattern like herring bone. The whole is then covered with a layer of leaves and a thick coat of well beaten clay. The floors are generally of earth, but the better sort are paved with small slit pebbles about the size of turkey's eggs, set in clay with the flat surfaces upwards. They form a clean, hard, smooth and lasting floor. The principal room generally has a balcony towards either the south or the west, from ten to twenty feet in length, and usually about two feet and a half in width, where the family sit to enjoy the sun in the winter season. The doors are mere rough planks of wood, joined together by wooden tenons, and sometimes strengthened by cross bars fastened with wooden pieces. Purdahs or wadded curtains are also used as an additional means of excluding the cold wind; but when the doors are shut, there is only a dim light admitted into these apartments through one or two loopholes, which are closed with small shutters at night. If supplied with glass windows and fire places, many of these houses would form very comfortable residences; but at present they must be wretched habitations for the winter.

The houses of the poorer classes are generally of two stories: the lower storey being appropriated to their cattle. The roofs are much more coarsely made, and the rooms are small and very low, being sometimes under six feet in height. In Ladakh, the upper storey is usually reached by a flight of earthen steps; but in Lahúl, by the sloping trunk of a tree notched into steps.

The royal palace at Lé is a large fine looking building, that towers in lofty pre-eminence over the whole city. It is 250 feet in length and seven stories in height. The outer walls have a considerable slope, as their thickness diminishes rapidly their increase of height. The upper stories are furnished with long open balconies to the south, and the walls are pierced with a considerable number of windows. The beams of the roof are supported on carved wooden pillars, and covered with planks pointed in various patterns on the outside. The building is substantial and plain; but its size and height give it a very imposing appearance.

In the remote district of Spiti the houses exhibit a new peculiarity. I quote from Mr. P. Egerton's "Tour in Spiti." *

"The houses in Spiti are comfortably built, and strangely enough, though stone and slate abound as they do, they are built of sun-dried bricks, and have flat roofs made of earth laid on rafters and twigs. The usual form of building is an oblong square. The lower storey is used for cattle pens, and the upper storey is built on three sides only, with parapet walls on the fourth side, so that the centre forms a kind of open court."

The houses are high solid fort like looking buildings outside. The upper part being plastered with a wash of some white or colored clay.

The windows appear to be all on the upper storey, which increases their fort like appearance.

Houses of Simla States, Kanawar and Basahir.

Beyond Simla the houses are all built of flat stones which are interspersed with bars of wood, which cross at the corners of the house, lying one on the other, but are not fitted in with tenon and mortise as in the "tattar-chul" building: sometimes the house is plastered.

The beams which form the roof of the basement room project beyond the wall and form the foundation of a balcony, which, however, has no railing or pillars, and is merely sheltered by the roof, which has an additional flap or fly, so to speak, for the purpose.

* Page 18.

In many cases the lower room has a single small door and no window ; and the room is often so low that a good sized man could not stand outside on the ground under the balcony without knocking his head against the beams. Occasionally the balcony is boarded in up to the roof.

The windows are extremely small, and consist of plank within plank, like this—

leaving only a small aperture in the middle.

The balcony runs round three sides of the house. Large houses are built in the same way, but with two tiers of rooms and balconies outside, being in fact continuations of such rooms. Access is gained from the ground floor to the upper rooms, not by a ladder outside, but by a notched pole inside the lower room, fitted to an open trap or hole in the floor.

This style of house is observed all up the valley of the Sutlej; in places where there are large buildings for temples or residences of idols, the regular building of wood and stone may be observed to good effect. These large fort-like structures have generally only balconies of carved wood above, and below a good space of masonry. The building is quite regular and true, and consists of alternate layers of the tabular schistose gneiss stone which abounds, and straight, neatly dressed, beams of deodar (cedar); they are not joined at the corners, but merely lie across, the stones being adjusted accordingly. The effect of the grey stone contrasted with bands of the deep brown which the cedar acquires in time, is picturesque Sometimes, as at the Rogi temple, the beams are carved all over.

Higher up in Kanáwar, which is a district of the territories under the Raja of Basahir, the pent roof disappears. The best examples of the next style appear at Chíní and the village of Pangí. a few miles further on. The houses still have the basement of stone and wood in layers, and an upper verandah or balcony of wood generally boarded in all round; but the roof is always flat to avoid the effects of the furious wind. The roof is made of poles spread over with birch bark and then plastered with mud ; every flat roof has a rim or low balustrade, like the edge of a tray, consisting of boards nailed round. Attached to a large house, numerous smaller ones, entirely of wood, may be seen ; often one or more of these little houses, no bigger than a large chest, may be seen resting on the roof of a larger house, and supported only on a few slabs of stone.

Lastly, turning to the Kashmir State, Lieutenant Lowther thus describes the houses at Srinagar : *

" Deodar and pine timber are very much employed in building both houses and boats ; nearly all the buildings (even the *palace*) are wooden : in some of them we occasionally find noble specimens of imperishable deodar. The " great mosque," nearly 400 years old, contains some fine straight pieces, used as pillars to support the roof: they are set up in basements of black marble, which durable material they are fast resembling

* Transactions A. H S., p. VIII.

in hardness and color. There are seven principal bridges (over the main stream) many of them having shops and stalls of wares set out upon them: two or three are strikingly aerial creations, which our tornadoes of Hindoostan would soon blow to 'Jericho,' but here the only damage to be apprehended is during an unusually high flood. Such I was informed had occurred some years back, when these, and countless other houses were swept away, to be shortly re-built in the ancient style. The only stone or brick structures I could find were pier heads of bridges, occasional mosques and temples, and a fort: wood from its being plentiful, portable, and cheaply put together, is the material in general use. Most of the dwellings have two, and even three stories, and these are very hastily made by driving timbers into the ground perpendicularly, at the different angles of the intended rooms. Across these, beams are nailed horizontally at intervals, and then a light flooring of poplar, or willow planks, is laid across longitudinally for a flooring. The walls are framed by nailing thin boards of fir over the exterior frame work, and plastering them with compost: light and air being admitted through carved trellises, which open and shut like sash windows. The roof is almost always gable, of thick planks, thatched with many layers of the waterproof birch bark; and the hollow portion of it is used as a loft for storing fire-wood, kitchen stuff, lumber, &c. Some of the more wealthy Pandits and merchants have small gardens overhanging the quays in front of their residences: these seldom contain anything very tasteful, or ornamental: occasionally indeed a trellis may be met with covered with a flourishing vine, or a rambling gourd, evidently cultivated for *shade:* sometimes a gay patch of double hollyhocks, or a solitary rose bush, relieved the dingy approaches; but generally speaking the open plats are filled with graves, and weeds, or offensive rot heaps. In some of the more ruinous suburbs, I noticed highly cultivated fields of tobacco, growing down to the brink of the water, and the markets were well stored with the dried leaf, which is an article of general consumption."

It is not, however, to be supposed that all houses in Kashmir are built of wood. Around Srinagar itself many houses are built up of stones with pent roofs. And in the other valleys, as for instance that of the Kishngunga, which I visited in 1867, there are houses very like those in Kulu, with projecting eaves, wooden verandahs and stone foundations.

Among the poorer classes, however, log huts are not uncommon, and on the right bank of the Kishngunga there is a small village called "Atai Makám Ghází Abdulla," the resting place of some Mohamadan Saint; it is entirely of wood. The houses are in fact log huts, the walls of split poles rudely joined, and projecting one over the other at the corners; the pent roof is always made of loose and irregularly shaped pine shingles, half nailed or rather pegged on to a central beam: what happens when rain falls on to such a roof may be better imagined than described.

DIVISION II.

OF BRIDGES.

I cannot here speak of the remains of Muhamadan and Sikh bridges. There are in Kashmir and Delhi, and elsewhere, bridges of the time of the Mogul Emperors and earlier. which exhibit the style employed.

There is the usual pointed Muhamadan arch; great strength of masonry, and rarely if ever have they more than a small span of arch. Sikh bridges were built exactly like them, and all the bridges we have in the plain districts are now of European design.

In the hill districts however, and in Kashmir, there are certain primitive kinds of bridges which deserve notice.

The first and most satisfactory is called 'sanga' or 'sangla.' The large bridge at Chamba is the best specimen of this bridge: two piers of wood and stone work ('tatar-chûl' work already described) are erected, and at the proper height above the highest flood mark a first tier or row of stout beams is built; the beams slant upwards, and project a little way over the stream. Across the ends a stout square beam is impinged by large wooden pegs, then out of the pier another row of stout beams project at an angle such that they rest on the cross beam just described and project beyond it again. On this second tier another cross beam is placed, and if now the second tier projecting partly across the stream from either pier leaves the intervening space of such a width that beams can be laid across, the said beams are placed in position; if not, other tiers of projecting beams are added till the space between the ends for either pier is so diminished that long beams can be laid across and so complete the connection. The bridge is then finished by a paving of transverse shingles pegged down with wooden pegs, and in very good bridges a hand rail is added.

The arrangement is easily understood from the diagram.

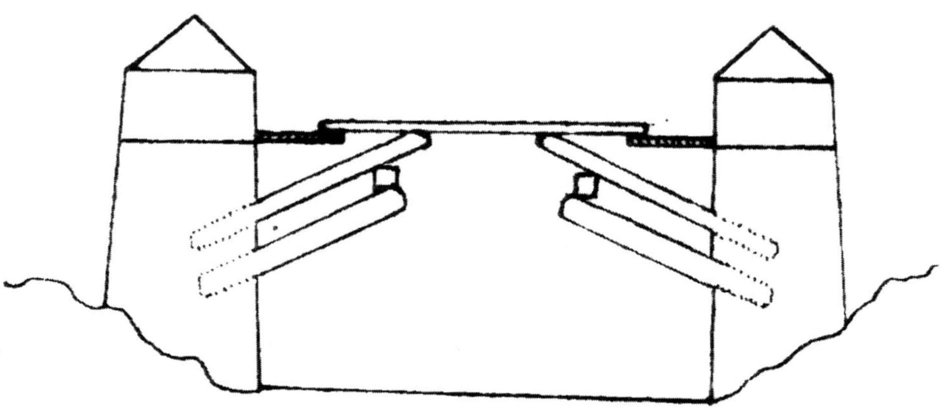

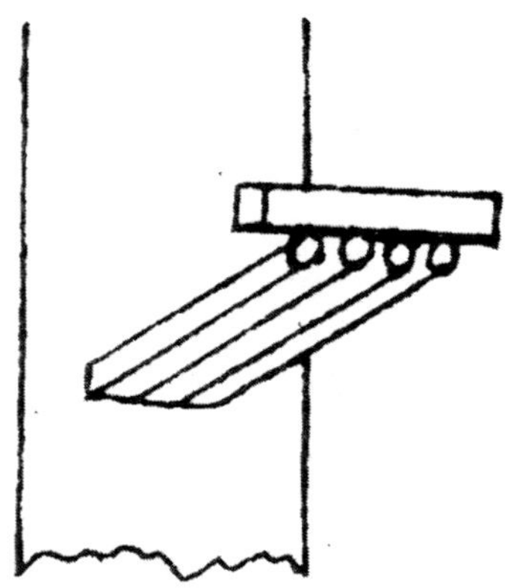

When a sanga is not well made, the cross pieces or footway are either only held down by large stones at the edges or else left loose. In this case the traveller must take care to walk just in the middle, otherwise a piece might tip up and a fall would be the result. Small bridges of this kind are often fitted with mere hurdles, which tip over in this way, and to get across one is rather an acrobatic feat.

The next sort of bridge is a jhúla or rope bridge. Usually it consists of a series of roughly twisted strands made of boughs of the *Parrotia Jacquemontiana* (syn. *Fothergilla involucrata*) which English travellers often mistake for the hazel : there is a resemblance however. Four or five strands thrown across form the footway, they are secured at either end by a series of stakes driven into a pile of stones for a rude pier, or are attached to branches of trees when such grow conveniently. Two other ropes are now suspended, one on either side, as handropes or rails : and the passenger has to cross grasping a rope on either side. In order to keep these three ropes in their relative positions as far as possible, side-stays called 'lingrú' (Chamba territory) are added thus:

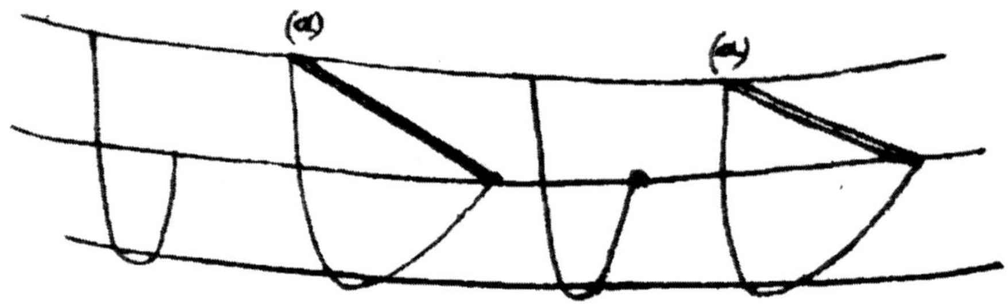

and further to prevent the whole collapsing and the side ropes closing in, spits or cross-bars of stick are placed at intervals as at (*a*) (*a*).

When it is recollected that these bridges swing about in the wind, and with the vibration caused by the motion of the passenger, and that further if they are not more than eight feet over the stream, the motion of the water makes the bridge seem to be going away from under the feet, the process of crossing such bridges is not, to all persons at any rate, a pleasant one.

The cross sticks (*a*) (*a*) are however an unnecessary difficulty. On the Kishnganga and Jhflam they are not used, but the ropes are kept apart by making the side-stays every here and there of wood, either by tying two sticks together in the shape of a letter V and fixing the ropes to the respective points, or using a naturally forked branch of a tree for the purpose.

At Muzaffarabad on the Kishnganga, there is a "jhúla" (below the region of Parrotia trees) made of single strands of twisted hide!—one for the feet and one on each side for the hand rail. These bridges common on the Ravi, Chenab and Jhelum and on the Beas tributaries are not used on the Sutlej.

Leaving these unpleasant bridges, there is yet another kind of bridge, or rather method of crossing streams, called on the Ravi, "garorú" or "karoru," and I believe elsewhere "jhúla." It consists merely of several strands of rope usually of the *baggar* grass *(Andropogon involutum)* slung from a stout post on one side to a stout post on the other. A hooked piece of alder wood hangs over this, and to it is attached two ropes leading one to one side and the other to the other of the stream ; the ropes in question being kept attached to the main strands by running loops. From the alder hook an arrangement of ropes depends : the passenger thrusts either leg through a loop of rope and holds on to the centre rope generally allowing himself to be secured by a blanket or scarf passed round his body.

As the central strands have a natural curve, the hook being let go descends rapidly enough to the centre of the stream, and men on the other side then begin gradually pulling it up the opposite incline till the further bank is reached.

Hutton, quoted by Dr. Stewart,* mentions one in Kanáwar (Upper Sutlej) made of yak's hair rope.

I should mention that when a jhúla or one of these swing bridges or karorus has to be put up, the first difficulty is to get a single strand across the stream: and it is generally effected only by effecting a crossing somewhere else, and laboriously carrying the rope to the desired spot by parties simultaneously working on the opposite bank, but as such bridges are often put up for forest purposes, it is now easy to fit it one by shooting from a gun a weight carrying a string, by which first a thin rope and ultimately a thick one can be pulled across.

Lastly, I have to notice a kind of pile bridge, which is quite peculiar to Kashmir. All the other bridges may be seen anywhere. The bridges consist of piles of logs of deodar timber laid crosswise one over the other at requisite distances, and then planking and a roadway over the top.

I extract Lieutenant Lowther's description from the 7th Vol. of the Trans. A. H. S.:—

"The bridges are wonderful erections of their kind; their visible substance certainly does not inspire confidence in the beholder, but yet theory has given way to practice, and many of them, after *five hundred years*, uphold the gothic style of engineering. Two main points there are which have vastly favored them:—1*st.*—There is not a white ant, or any subaqueous insect to devour their material; the melted snow and icy season together keeping off this description of vermin. 2*nd.*—Cold itself is a most effectual preservative, and constant immersion in a temperature, never even warm, must vastly contribute to prevent fungi or structural decomposition. Occasionally the winds and waves may dislodge a plank, or capsize a supporting beam, but their very simplicity conduces to the rapidity and solidity of their renovation. The principle that yields moderately to the united force of the all-powerful elements, wind and water, evidently surpasses that which endeavours to combat them by artifice. Many a massive rampart and lordly buttress has been levelled to the earth by tides, flood, and air, to which these Kashmerian structures have remained scatheless for centuries; for be it known that one night from a sudden thaw the frigid Jhelum often rises *twenty feet*, driving the inhabitants of the lower districts to their rude craft on its bosom; and often does the hurricane without sign or warning sweep down with mad violence (especially around the Wúlar Lake) without shaking these (apparently) *shaky* communications from their antique foundations. They appear to be built in the following primitive manner:—The number of arches according to the breadth of the stream, having been decided upon in its lowest state, (which is often such as to present nearly half of the dry bed) substantial piles are sunk, or buried at those points, and well covered with layers of stones and shingle; a projecting break-water, at an acute angle, being often constructed to turn the velocity of the current: (this appears very effective in its application). Upon this basis rests the stack, or pile of wood, forming the square compartment, (which from its shape can hardly

* Punjab Plants, p. III.

be called arch, though it answers that purpose effectually): these huge logs are all heaped in tiers crossways, and are usually carried up to 30 feet, or more, so as to be far above the highest watermark: fine sound pine timbers are then laid longitudinally, so as to have their ends meeting on the centre of these heaps; smaller pieces cross them again, and to these are nailed with wooden pegs all the planks which constitute the flooring, (generally fir for lightness.) Through this apparently crazy invention the wind whistles, and the water hisses in wild harmony, but, as I said before, this very plan of ingress and egress to their united forces is the safety of the whole."

DIVISION III.

WELLS.

It would not be proper to close this Chapter without a notice of *well sinking*. It is performed in the Panjab by a class of men known as "Tobá."

A great portion of our cultivation is dependent upon well irrigation, and the apparatus used for raising and distributing the water has already been described partly in this volume and partly in Vol. I.

Every one acquainted with the Panjab alluvial plains knows that they are divided by the great rivers into tracts of country called "Doábs"—a tract between 'two waters.' In the lands near the river, termed 'sailába,' the moisture is so great that wells sunk reach abundant water at 10 to 15 feet, and the ground is moist by constant percolation upwards. And this seems to be *the* feature that characterises "sailába." The word indeed literally means land that is liable to be flooded (sailáb), but much land that is not actually flooded is called sailába, while as far as I am aware no land that has not the abundant upward percolation alluded to, ever is. Wells sunk in the sailába are often 'kacha,' *i. e.* mere pits, without brickwork; or if brickwork is used, it only descends to a short depth, and a well is consequently sunk at a comparatively small cost. Further inland and away from the river the water level recedes, and water is had at the depth of 30, 40, 50, 60 and 80 feet; the cost of sinking wells constantly increases, and beyond this limit wells are not made as a rule. In the Mukatsar pargana of Firozpúr district there are wells 150 feet deep, but rarely used for agricultural purposes; and when they are, the water has to be lifted by the 'charsa' or leather bag and rope—for the weight of the water pots and ropes of a Persian wheel at such a depth would be too great for cattle power to move. Proceeding inland again, the land rises to the 'bár' and 'thal' or desert portions: here the cost of wells would be so great that well cultivation ceases, and scanty crops are given by the annual rain-fall, and the rest of the land is left to the often dense but stunted thickets of jhand, karíl, and other trees that form the staple produce of the fuel reserve lands, or to vast grazing grounds, over which herds of cattle roam during the grazing season.

Passing the "bár," the same order of things in encountered, but in reversed order; till we reach again the 'sailába' of the other river of the Doáb.

In order to sink a well, a hole is first dug one two or three feet greater in diameter than the intended shaft of the well: the digging is continued till the sand and water level is reached. This done, a circular wooden basis or foundation has to be laid down, composed of curved pieces of broad flat wood termed "nímchak." They are in fact segments of a circular ring or rim of wood, which forms the basis of the whole. Nímchaks are in the Panjab generally made of kíkar or bér wood, towards Sind they use tamarisk wood (which is remarkable as kíkar is abundant) considering that it behaves better under water. On this nímchak the circular masonry lining of the well is built up like a tower with bricks and mud for mortar, but sometimes lime. If lime mortar is used the masonry is allowed a long time to dry before the sinking is commenced, and two methods are adopted: either the whole masonry is built up at once, which I understand is the method followed in the south, or else the masonry is built up only to the edge of the soil, and the upper portion not added to the cylinder until the portion first built has all been sunk below the water. In the Panjab the portion under the water is called "kothi," and when the upper portion is added it is built projecting about 3 inches beyond the kothi and is called "tarági." When the well is made in this latter method, the lower part of the masonry is bound round with strong bands of twisted múnj grass, which compacts it together while sinking. On the top of the masonry edge a platform of planks is erected, but resting on the *ground* not on the masonry, which has to sink gradually without interfering with the platform. Where the whole cylinder is built up at once, it is raised first to the level of the soil; and then as many feet *above* the soil—10 to 18 feet—as it is afterwards intended to sink *below* the water level; for, as just stated, the nímchak is only put down when the water level is reached. In the latter method the platform has to be erected in a different manner. On the top of the masonry well stout poles are arranged so as to leave a good space open in the centre, but so to project over the outer edges of the masonry that a broad platform of planks or 'pilchi' or basket work can be erected and which projects all round far beyond the masonry. Over the central aperture a common windlass is now fixed, and the well sinker or toba descends by a rope usually worked by bullocks; at first there is but little water at the bottom: he descends armed with a huge iron shovel, called in the Panjab 'chhám,' and towards Sind "bel;" it is merely like a very large 'phaura' or shovel, but has a short wooden handle about 15 inches long, inclined very much towards the blade.

A stout rope is attached to it and the "tobá" descending guides the chhám as well as he can, throwing his weight on it so as to cause it to strike into the sand and water and bring up a load of sand. This sand, being hauled up, is immediately thrown upon the broad platform just described; and by continually doing this a great weight is placed on the top of the masonry, which causes it to sink rather rapidly. The tobás tell me that the art of throwing the chhám is considerably difficult: at first of course there is a mere slush of sand and water, but gradually the "tobá" has to make his way by diving down through several feet of water. Also the placing of the ballast on the platform requires attention, for if the brickwork were badly loaded it would sink crooked and bulge and break up. When the whole of the masonry has sunk down to the level of the soil, the outer hole being larger than the shaft, earth has to be carefully filled in and stamped down. And then the edge of well can be finished off by a broad masonry edge or "chabutra" or by a place for the Persian wheel, as may be required.

The "Tobá's" tools are :—

The "Chhám," already described.

"Teshi," a small adze for shaping bricks,

"Kandi," a trowel.

Baskets, rope &c. &c.,

A 'cutcha' (kachá) well or well without masonry cylinder is called "kharŏri," and lasts only about a year unless indeed very little water is required from it: it does not cost more than 40 to 50 rupees to sink a well 'kacha,' but a kacha well cannot be sunk over 15 feet. In 'Clarke's Agriculture of the Rechna Doab,' an estimate is given of the cost of digging and lining a pucka well, which I here copy. I doubt whether at the present rates of bricks, labor &c. it could be done so cheap, but the list is interesting as exhibiting the sort of reward giving to the well makers, and the custom of giving the goat, and the turban &c. is universal.

"The average diameter of wells is five and three quarter haths (twenty-two inches to a háth) *i. e.*, 10 feet 6½ inches, estimated cost 162 rupees.

"Sinking a shaft, ten rupees, *i. e.*, one and a quarter mani of wheat.

	Rs.	As.
A goat to workmen, ...	1	0
Masons, @ 1 hath per, ...	27	0
Food for Masons, ...	7	0
Laborers, ...	15	0
Tobá or well-sinker, ...	8	0
Food for three tobás, ...	4	8
Lúngí and turban to tobás on completion, ...	4	0
Blanket to ditto, ...	1	0
1,10,000 bricks, ...	60	0
Carriage of ditto, ...	11	0
Munj, } material used in the band, ...	2	0
Kána, }	1	4
Baskets, ...	0	4
Spade, ...	1	0
Chak of 'Bér' wood, ...	6	0
Making the same,...	2	0
Nails, ...	1	0
TOTAL,	162	0

In sailába land a well costs less; the water being much nearer, less masonry is required.

"It is reckoned unlucky to choose the fractional measure of three quarters for other things, but for a well the reverse of this, perhaps because there is some verbal relation between "páwan" and "páni," water. The wells in this district generally take about nine score of tinds or water-pots. "Chuks" are often contracted for at the rate of one rupee per hath of the well's diameter: thus for seven rupees a man will give a chuk, and bed it in its place in the shaft; for a well of 7 haths diameter."

As this table was drawn up some years ago, I subjoin another which shews the cost of well sinking in different soils, also the difference caused by having the diameter so large as to admit of a *double* Persian wheel apparatus.

The names of soils require a note. Sailába has been before explained. The **Mánjhá Mítha** or "sweet upland" refers to that soil midway between the bar and the sailába where water is at a moderate depth and the soil is sweet or unimpregnated with salts of soda. The "**Khárá Mánjhá**" is 'salt highland' where the soil is hard and salt, and water at a great depth.

Description of Soil.	Depth before reaching water.	PAKKA WELL.				KACHA WELL. (*Single wheel only employed.*)	
		Single Wheel.		*Double Wheel.*		Diameter.	Cost.
		Diameter in feet.	Cost.	Diameter in feet.	Cost.		
			Rs.		Rs.		
Sailába, ...	10 feet.	10	190	13	275	10 feet.	40
Do., ...	15 „	10	225	13	320	10 „	55
						Cannot be sunk.	
Mánjhá Mítha, ...	30 „	10	380	13	550		
Do., ...	50 „	10	670	13	900		
Mánjha Khárá, ...	80 „	10	1,100	13	1,600		

SECTION D.

FINE ARTS.

INTRODUCTION.

It is peculiarly difficult in a work of this kind to write a fitting introduction to a section devoted to the enumeration of specimens of fine art in the Punjab.

It would be inconsistent with the obvious purpose of a work intended for the office table and for work-day reference to enter even into the borders of the land of metaphysical speculation, and yet I feel that even a brief introductory note on the subject must necessarily touch upon such borders.

To understand a series of manufacturing processes, and afterwards to describe them, is merely a work of careful observation and of detailed writing: to understand the art of a country is another matter. Both it is true have two producing causes in common—Nature and Society. Manufactures are merely the offspring of the wants of the body—of the body in its struggle with Nature, its cold, its heat, its sensations, and its diseases; or in the relations of Society, its government, its ceremonies, and its quarrels. Fine art, on the other hand, is the offspring of the mind—of the mind in its perceptions of beauty, grandeur, power, harmony, and repose, in Nature; and in its sympathies and emotions resulting from the contact with others, in Society.

Fine art and manufacture often combine together; but the art alone is what this section is concerned with, and that in its present form, arises from the native mind; and before we can understand the art, we must to some extent understand the mind.

To examine this subject minutely, interesting though it would be, is, as I before said, manifestly impossible in a book like this. I must be content to take the results without speculating on the causes, and if in so doing I lose a definite sequence or order in my remarks, and note, as I fear I shall have to, somewhat discursively, such peculiarities in native art as strike the examiner of a collection, I can only crave the indulgence of my readers.

There is one preliminary difficulty with regard to Art expression which is recognized more perhaps in a collection of works of native art than in such a collection in Europe—I mean the mere mechanical power of expression.

The actual work of drawing, the perspective, the method of delineation, and the style of producing 'effect,' are as a rule inferior; and this will surely be admitted when we have once reflected that the mere minuteness and delicacy of handling which many native works exhibit, and which occur in rendering the separate hairs of a beard, or the pearls on a tiny necklace, are a species of mechanical power intrinsically of a low order.

In the present state of native art, we at once observe, as in any other very early art, an extreme conventionality of treatment;—the adoption of certain forms, which may or not be satisfactory representations of certain objects or phenomena, to do duty always for all subjects or phenomena of that class. All native pictures have the skies painted exactly alike; if clouds are introduced they are so in a conventional form, and of an invariable tint. If trees are introduced, their color and treatment is always the same. It is not that a particular tree cannot be imitated: if the artist is bent for the purpose of his subject, on drawing an orange or a mango tree, he will render separately, and with accuracy, the orange leaf and the golden fruit, but it always is stiff, intractable, and regular;—conventional in its individuality.

To express any effect of light and shade; to paint a storm cloud, to catch the gleam of the sun-light playing on wind-waved branches or rippling wheat fields;—all these things are as impossible to the skill of the native artist as they are foreign to his idea of painting.

Some few native artists copy Nature, but very few. They learn by mere routine when young, and execute copies of works that have been done in the same faulty and conventional style as they themselves ultimately, and as a matter of course, attain to.

There were two native artists whose works in the collection showed a real endeavour to draw things as they are: their names are Kishndás of Kapúrthala, and Bishndás of Amritsar. Many of the best works of the former were in simple pencil outline, with very little shading. The Maharaja of Patiala's artist is also better than most.

I do not know that the imitative faculty is very strong among native artists; but I have occasionally seen studies of figures, representing different castes and tribes, which have caught expressions of face and other peculiarities very faithfully: still the force of conventionality is such that it is traceable in every work, and is like a blight upon every promise of higher purpose and better execution.

It is only another phase, after all, of that great curse of India—CUSTOM. What has been, is, and shall be, seems to be the determination of the mind of the masses; and son follows father in the same trade and with the same implements, from generation to generation. Improvement must come from without, or not at all; and it may be predicated for a certainty, that without the establishment of schools of design in this country, art will never make any material progress.

A number of the Dutch paintings which are admired by a certain class of minds, and please to some extent all minds,—because the mere success of imitation is instinctively pleasing,—owe their entire merits to their excellence in imitation.

The order of merit is not a high one: the mere accuracy of representation of a number of tin cans, a few carrots, a cabbage, a cut lemon, or a wine glass, is not anything very great or very noble; but it is true imitation. Lights on the glass, with all the innumerable reflections and counter-reflections, are really reproduced; the texture and crispness of the leaves, the metallic surface of the vessels, are all truly expressed;

but such is the baneful effect of conventionality in native art, that however correctly an artist could give the exterior form, he would shade his glass purely according to his idea of 'how shading ought to be done.'

No native artist has any idea of using his eyes. This is to a certain extent true of any person before he has any teaching in art. We have to learn to see things before we draw them. But with a native artist this is more than usually the case. I cannot help writing down an instance that occurred to me a short time ago. A youth who had already made fair progress in the copying of flowers and other objects, asked for some lessons in drawing and perspective. Anxious to see what he could do, I took a rose, half opened, with one bud and just two leaves, and laid it on a thick book, so as to raise it to a convenient height for seeing it. The rose and the bud were fairly drawn, and one leaf hanging over the edge of the book, but the other leaf lying on the book was hidden partly by the flower which was in front of it. The draughtsman immediately drew the whole leaf, but standing straight up behind the rose. I pointed out that it was not sticking up like that. The leaf was rubbed out and drawn, but this time below the surface of the book, as if the latter were a hollow glass box full of water. I drew the leaf for him, and he immediately objected to the result, 'because the whole of it' was not shown. At last it dawned upon him, that as he could only *see* part of the leaf he was only to draw what he could see. He afterwards made rapid progress, soon perceived the effects of foreshortening and distance diminution, and readily enough acquired the rules of simple perspective; but he had learnt so far to *see*, and that was the starting point.

Native artists are quite wanting in any sympathy with Nature, or love of beauty for its own sake. The English word 'picturesque' could not be represented in the language; there is no trace of such an idea in their books.

Take Walter Scott's description of Edinburgh in Marmion.* I quote this as every one knows it: the passage which commences—

> "The wandering eye could o'er it go,
> And mark the distant city glow
> With gloomy splendour red;" &c.

* Canto IV. XXX.

And compare it with any descriptions in the Anwar-i-Suhaili, or in any other Persian or Indian book of modern or comparatively modern time, and notice the picturesqueness of the one and the materiality, however prettily expressed, of the other.*

Perhaps this defect the oriental writers have in common with all early poets and authors. It is said that Virgil is never picturesque; with him a grove is always thick, shady or black, or impenetrable; the sun is bright, shining or burning—mere enumerations of material qualities. More rarely, the sea and rocks, and so forth, being associated with danger, are distinguished by epithets more or less abusive.

One reason why there is so little landscape drawing among natives is this want of perception. They have no admiration of form, and no capacity of receiving ideas of grandeur, harmony, or repose. I have never met a native in this country who *seemed* at any rate to enjoy a beautiful view.

Natives, however, excel in two branches of art, which gives them great power in certain classes of manufacture. Unable to design a good *form* or outline of a solid, they will design a piece of tracery, arabesque or flat pattern, with surprising skill; hence the beauty of their embroidery, their chasing in metal work, their illumination of manuscripts, and their surface wood-carving.

The other branch of art is coloring. Natives seem to have quite an instinct for color, without the faintest idea of the theory of light and its composition, or the rules about complementary colors; they have seized the results empirically, and in nearly all their works exhibit a perfect knowledge of contrast and combination.

In painting, the use of European water-colors is becoming more common, but hitherto there has been a considerable mechanical difficulty in colors: they were nearly all body or opaque colors, ground up in river

---

* I do not speak of the older writers. I should be afraid to say that some of the Sanskrit writers are not picturesque—Kalidásá in the Sakuntala, for instance.

Oriental writers are abundantly fanciful in metaphor and simile in their descriptions, but that is not picturesqueness.

mussel shells. Brushes were made of the fine soft hair of the squirrel ("guleri,"). They are very small in size, and fine in point, bound by thread to a stick, without the use of quill or metal as with us; they are however well adapted to the usual style of painting with painful finish, minute touches, and endless stippling.

The reader will now be prepared for the list of specimens, which follow.

CLASS XXXII.

Unrepresented.

CLASS XXXIII.

SPECIMENS OF WRITTEN CHARACTERS.

The principal place in which manuscripts are now copied is Kashmir, where excellent paper is made.

Formerly the art of writing, "khúshnavísí," was in great repute. It was quite a fine art. The writer would prepare his ink and his pens with great science, and then patiently elaborate every letter with the greatest care, and finally put in the diacritical points of the letters, not always in relation to the letter they designated, but, like figures in a landscape piece, for effect and adornment.

The Nastálik, or plain flowing Persian hand, is now the only one that is written well by any considerable number of people. The art of fine writing like many others of a useless character is dying out before the wants of a more practical age. Plain neat writing for the lithographic press is more in demand.

Besides the writers in Kashmir, and His Highness the Maharaja of Patyála's State penman, and Imam Wairdi* (a real artist) at Lahore, there are hardly any Khúshnavíses of repute in the Punjab. Whenever they do write it is in the Nastálik style; the Nashk, or Arabic style is very rare, and still more so the ornamented Arabic or Suls. Natives have an intense dislike to our printed "nashk," which they can with difficulty read, and prefer a lithographed "tálik."

One kind of writing deserves to be noticed: the nail writing. It consists simply in embossing with the end of the thumb-nail, letters, flowers and other forms on the paper For this purpose the thumb-nail is allowed to grow to a great length and cut into a point. By the adroit rubbing first with one side, then with the other, the letter is raised up, and the field or surface below rubbed down evenly: sometimes color is introduced, the field decorated with branching flower-work and the surface of the raised letter gilded. I have a picture of a stag and of a bird raised and gilt in this way.

Imám Wairdi at Lahore is the best artist I have seen, but one or two other men do the work also.

Of other fantasies in fine writing, those in which the collection of 1864 most abounded, were,—writing inside a bottle, writing on glass and then silvering it over behind; and, lastly, writing letters in either Nastálik, or in peculiar form (suls and togra-suls) combined and twisted together so as to form a tiger, a group of birds, a flower, or a vase of flowers. I have one of the latter before me at this moment done at Lahore. It is on glass, and consists merely of the letters of the alphabet (Persian) combined to form a group of three flowers coming out of a vase.

* He is a Persian.

The letters appear silvered as ordinary looking glass, the ground is mottled, made by rubbing on gold paint (gold leaf ground fine) mixed with ink.

Some of the most beautiful writing is to be seen on seals. But at Delhi only is this well done, and even there the work is far surpassed by the Kashmir artists. The seal engraver's art has been described already.

Besides these ornamental writings, for common correspondence the running or Shikasta' Persian is used.

Hindu shopkeepers, and Musalmans also in villages, keep their accounts in what is called 'landa', a rude and very clumsy degradation of the Devanágri. This style of writing varies so, that a Lahore shopkeeper could not read the 'landa' of the villages in other pergunnas of the same district, nor could a Jalandhar 'banya' read the writing of his brothers in Sealkot.

The bankers and larger merchants generally, whether Hindu or Muhamedan, keep account books in a very regular and neat looking hand (also a corruption of Nágri) called "Mahájani" or Saráfi ;" and of course there are special characters used by Naurya merchants and Parsees.

In Kashmir, "Shástri " (or Nágri) is used in the corrupted forms, as Shárda and Dogra. The Catalogue also mentions a specimen of the "Bhot" writing, which I presume to be Tibetan used by the Buddhists.

In the Chamba districts a rather peculiar corruption of Nágri is used called Chambiálí, and on the Sutlej another variety is in use in Basáhir.

The following list gives an idea of the articles exhibited in 1864 :—

Ludhiana.

929.—[10827]. Writing by the nail (Asghar Husain).

930.—[10831]. Writing cut out with scissors.

Amritsar.

931.—[10840]. Poetry &c., in illuminated characters.

932.—[10838]. Lines containing date and praise of the Punjab Exhibition, &c.

Sealkot.

933.—[10842]. Grain of rice with writing on it (Muhammad Ramzan).

Lahore.

934.—[10844]. Specimens of hand-writing on frames.

935.—[10849]. A series of "firmáns," of the Emperors Shah Jahán, Alamgír, Mohamad Shah, Ahmad Shah Dúraní, Taimúr Shah ; and a "nikanámah," marriage deed, of the time of Mohamad Shah, (Pandit Manphul).

936.—[ ]. Copy of 'Yusaf and Zulaika,' by the celebrated writer Mír Ali Katib (Delhi.)

937.—[10859]. "Adh-Granth." The earlier of the sacred book of the Sikhs compiled under the orders of Arjan, fifth Guru.

938.—[10860]. Janm Sákhi.—The life of Bábá Nának. A M.S. written in Kashmir about 25 years ago. Title page beautifully illuminated.

939.—[10847]. 'Joshan' or Kurán in the "Khat-i-raihán" a style of writing.

940.—[10861]. Volume of poetry written with the nail and illuminated by Imám Wairdi of Lahore.

941.—[10863]. Arabesques in nail work (Khat-i-nákhún) Lahore, by Ghulam Mustafa.

MONTGOMERY.

942.—[10870]. Specimens of writing from Pákpattan.

PESHAWAR.

943.—[10877-8]. Specimens of both Persian and Hindi writing.

KASHMIR.

944.—[10883]. Persian plain writing, "Khat sha'áí sáda."

945.—[10884]. Twisted or combined letters, "Suls Pechán."

Specimens of the other characters before alluded to were sent.

PATYALA.

946.—[10890]. 13 copies of hand-writing of different kinds used in the country.

CLASS XXXIV.

PAINTINGS AND DRAWINGS.

Delhi.

The best paintings are the miniatures executed on ivory at Delhi. They are usually of an oval size, but occasionally oblong with the edges rounded. Ivory is sawn up into very thin plates, which are most carefully seasoned and pressed that they may not curve, and are finely polished. The painting when finished is protected by a very thick but clear glass, smoothed off at the edges like a pebble.

The glass is made at Aleppo, and is polished with 'burbura,' corundum and oil, at Delhi.

The paintings consist either of portraits or of landscape subjects, the latter being almost entirely confined to ruins and ancient buildings at Delhi or at Agra.

As regards portraits, the most usual are pictures of kings and of the beauties of the courts of the Mogul Emperors: modern portraits are however copied from photographs, often with surprising fidelity. Even by transmitting an uncolored photograph, accompanied by a sufficiently careful description, a miniature may be obtained in about a month's time. A single figure is usually charged at 50 Rs.

The work is always executed either in color, which is generally soft, rich, and effective, or else in Indian ink—mere light and shade. These latter are often pleasing, especially in the landscape subjects, for then the very conventional treatment of the trees and sky becomes less prominent than in the colored ones. They use gilding freely along with color. The earlier paintings of interiors and buildings, minutely finished as they were, had generally such impossible perspective that the whole effect was destroyed. This has been to a great extent remedied by the introduction of photography. As all these miniatures are copied from photographs of the buildings, the right perspective is copied undesignedly and without knowledge.

These works exhibit absolutely no originality, nor can any improvement, other than what the introduction of photography just alluded to and the supply of better colors from Europe account for, be traced.

The best painters at Delhi at the time I am writing, are Ismail Khan and Ghulam Hosain.

The pictures are executed in all sizes, from a tiny miniature, to be set in a stud, button or bracelet, to the larger size which is occasionally seen set in silver and mounted on a casket of carved ebony or sandal-wood. A few of the paintings may be enumerated.

947.—[10899]. &c. Pictures of the Táj Mahal, at Agra, the Fort at Delhi, the Badsháhi Mosque, the Kashmir Gate of the City, the Diwán Khás of the Palace Delhi, the Kutab Minár, the Tomb of Humáyun, &c.—ISMAIL KHAN.

948.—[10906]. Small sketches for setting in bracelets.

949.—[10908]. 12 studs and sleeve links.

950.—[10918]. Picture of the Tomb at Mecca.—NAZR ALI KHAN.

951.—[10929] Portraits of Emperor Akbar, Aurangzeb, Nádir Shah, Jahángír, Alamgír, Humáyun; also of the wife of Shahjahán, the favorite wife of Jahángír—Núr Mahal &c., &c.—ISMAIL KHAN AND GHULAM HUSAIN KHAN.

952.—[10954]. A large picture executed on paper representing the Nawáb of Jhajjar on a hunting expedition.—GHULAM HUSAIN KHAN.

KANGRA DISTRICT.

953.—[10964]. Picture of the tea plant, by ATTARA of Kangra.

This is a rather faithful drawing of the tea plant, about one-fourth the natural size.

954.—[10967]. Picture of Gaddis (or hill shepherds). This picture, which is ethnographically interesting, is now in the Lahore Central Museum. It is drawn on English foolscap paper, in outline with a pen, and a very slight shading of color.

The proportions and perspective are extraordinary, but the dress and habits of the Gaddis are portrayed to the life. The dull-grey full bosomed flannel coat, inside which several little lambs and kids are stowed to keep them warm, and are seen in the picture peeping out, drolly enough,—the flint and steel, the knife, and the ladies always carrying the heaviest loads;—all these are excellent.

AMRITSAR.

955.—[10975]. Book of colored portraits of castes and tribes, by SANI.

956.—[10976]. Series illustrating the Shawl trade, by BISHN SINGH of Amritsar.

The shawl weaver.
,, cleaner.
,, darner and piece joiner.
,, presser.
,, wool washer.
,, ,, dyer.

957.—[10981]. Picture of an Ekka.

958.—[10982]. The Darbár or Court of Ranjít Singh.

959.—[10985]. The Municipal Committee of Amritsar in session.

All these are by BISHN SINGH.

LAHORE.

960.—[11016]. Illustrations of the work "Amír hat."

961.—[11017]. Do. of the Sudama Charitra.

962.—[11018]. Do. of the Ramáyan, (Artist unknown).

Two ancient drawings, one representing in outline, quaint but true, a gentleman reflecting previous to swallowing a glass of physic which he holds in his hands, and which, to judge by his expression, must be eminently disagreeable: the other a winged angel riding on a horse, which on closer examination is found to be the form of a horse made up by a combination of snakes, tigers, birds, antelopes and fishes. These were exhibited and afterwards presented to the Museum by Pandit Rada Kishn of Lahore. There are one or two native artists at Lahore, but their works are not of sufficient merit to be described.

Oval pictures of Sikh Chiefs and ladies on ivory are executed by these people, but so inferior to the Delhi work as to merit no place in the collection.

Peshawar.

963.—[11034]. Portrait of Khwája Muhamad Khan.

964.—[11035]. Portrait of Yusufzai woman. Muhamad ji, of Peshawur.

Kapurthala.

965.—[11036]. Album of outline drawings—of birds, figures, plants, &c., Kishn Singh. These show greater promise of improvement in native art than almost anything in the collection.

966.—[11039]. Study of an agriculturist with his wife followed by a beggar. The figures in this were admirable.

967.—[11037]. Portrait of Amir Dost Muhammad Khan on glass.

Kashmir.

968.—[11043]. Portrait of His Highness the Maharaja Ranbír Singh of Jamu and Kashmir, G. C. S. I.

This is a faithful likeness, but stiffly drawn.

Faridkot.

969.—[11044]. Picture of a rich Hindu beauty (on ivory). This is well finished and colored, but the feet are drawn out of perspective: the figure could not stand at all in reality with the feet in such a position.

970.—[11044]. A most wonderful drawing—perspective apart—showing the lamentable results of drinking "post" or decoction of poppies. The expressions of the persons in various stages of incipient or advanced stupefaction are given with painful accuracy. The above are by Gopal Singh of Faridkot.

Patyala.

By the State artist (his name is not given.)

971.—[11045]. Portrait of Maharaja Karm Singh.

972.—[11046]. Portrait of Maharaja Narendar Singh, the late ruler of Patyala.

973.—[11047]. Portrait of Maharaja Mahendar Singh, the present Maharaja.

974.—[11051]. Drawings of animals.

975.—[11050]. Album of pictures.

All these are most excellent, the coloring and finish is good, and the expression of the faces really true to life. The portrait of the late Maharaja Narendar Singh is in the Museum at Lahore.

CLASS XXXV.

MODELS.

The collection in the Exhibition of 1864 was principally rendered interesting by the number of models of European design, which could find no place in this book at all, were it not for the circumstance that they were made by native hands. The Jury's Report is given as it is issued, and sufficiently notices these articles.

White box wood and the wood of Karíl *(Capparis aphylla)* seem to be the materials preferred for modelling. The models consisted of the following groups :—

Mr. J. Gordon's models of buildings at Amritsar.

Models of canal falls, and other canal-engineering contrivances.

Models of churches.

Eliminating these, the purely native models were very few.

976.—[11012]. Model of the Taj at Agra in soapstone, belonging to the Central Museum Lahore: it is doubtfully of Punjab workmanship.

977.—[ ]. Model of the Tomb of Hazrat Salím Chístí, at Fattihpúr Síkrí, exhibited by Rai Kanaya Lal, Executive Engineer.

978.—[10997]. Model of the great 'Darbár' or Sikh temple at Amritsar. Exhibited by Sirdár Bhagwán Singh.

This was made at Amritsar, and is elaborately finished, colored and gilt to represent the original. It takes to pieces and exhibits the interior decorated with the embroidered canopies, the copy of the "Granth" &c., &c., in minute *fac simile* of the original.

979.—[10957]. Model of the Kutab Mínár near Delhi, carved in ivory by Jitu of Delhi.

980.—[11022]. Model of Jahángir's Tomb at Shádara near Lahore, by Iláhi baksh, a Lahore workman,—made of ivory colored.

Great ingenuity and delicacy of work is displayed by these models. The best model of all, that of a Railway carriage, executed at Lahore, has been already noticed.

981.—[11042]. Model of the "Sangla" or wooden bridge over the Raví at Chamba.

(*Vide* the note on these bridges under Section C. page 333.)

Lastly, there was in the Exhibition of 1864 a small mechanical model of a singing bird, made by a workman at Nábha. This article I did not see, but the Jury described it as follows :—

"No. 11,100 is a musical toy sent by the Rája of Nábha. On winding up the box the lid opens and discloses a small bird, which flutters its wings and sings in an extremely discordant manner, until the machinery and the listener is exhausted. The workmanship is rough, and the toy is of course copied from a Parisian model, but considerable ingenuity has been displayed in the imitation."

JURY REPORT ON THE FINE ART SPECIMENS.

Jurors :—

Major General A. A. Cunynghame, C. B. E. A. Raikes, Esqr., H. M. 93rd Highlanders.

Lieut-Col. R. Maclagan, R. E., Ghulam Mahbúb Subhaní.

Baden Powell, Esquire. Lepel Griffin, Esqr., B. C. S., *Reporter.*

In scarcely any part of India are the fine arts in so low a condition as in the Panjab. In Delhi, indeed, which is politically included in the province, the art of painting on ivory has for long been cultivated with great success, but in the Panjab proper there is, at present, little in painting, sculpture, or architecture, worthy of notice. The reasons for this state of things are simple, and it is so desirable that they should be fully appreciated, that a few words in explanation of them may not be considered out of place in this report.

During the rule of the Muhammadan emperors, in the days of their strength and still more in the days of their weakness and decline, the Panjab was the battle field of India. Army after army of invaders poured down upon its plains from the north-west frontier, sometimes successful in reaching Delhi—the object of their ambition—sometimes driven back by the Imperial forces, but always a curse and a scourge to the Panjab, destroying its harvests and decimating its population.

There was no cultivation of the fine arts at that time, for the people were poor and it was all they could do to support and defend their families.

When the Moghal empire fell, the prospects of the fine arts did not improve. The condition of the Panjab between 1760 and 1810 resembled that of England during the reign of King John. In every direction rose forts of brick or mud, the homes of petty chiefs and barons, who with two or three hundred horsemen behind them ravaged the surrounding country and carried off the plunder to their strongholds. Those of the Sikh chiefs who were the most powerful, were only the most successful robbers : any differences between them were only differences of degree.

At length Ranjít Singh rose to power on the ruins of the Sikh confederacies. But he had won his kingdom by the sword, and had no reverence for the brush or the chisel. His life was passed in incessant war to extend and consolidate his empire, and he had no time to devote to the fine arts. Like most of his nobles he was grossly illiterate, and could neither read nor write, and in his Court, in its most brilliant days, there were but three men who could be truly called educated.

The ten years succeeding the death of Ranjit Singh were years of anarchy and revolution, and the Panjab first found rest when, in 1849, it was annexed to the British Empire.

It will not then be considered strange that the fine arts have not flourished in this province. They are the result of peace and civilization, and it was not to be expected that they should arise in the midst of war and barbarism ; but for the future there is good hope. No one who has carefully examined the articles exhibited, not only in the Department of Fine Arts, but also in that devoted to Manufactures, can fail to have been struck with the promise of future excellence which they display. The native of the Panjab possesses many of the qualities which ensure success in art. In common with the inhabitants of lower India he has an instinctive appreciation of color, and though without any knowledge of the principles which should regulate its use, is often more happy in his combinations than the educated workman of Europe. His color is often exaggerated but it is always warm, and rich and fearless. The native artist is also patient: for weeks and months he will work at his design, painfully elaborating the most minute details; no time is considered too long, no labor too intense to secure perfection in imitation or delicacy in execution. The greatest failing in native artists is their ignorance of perspective and drawing, and it is fortunate that this want is the most easy to supply. Nothing is required but schools of design and judicious instruction to effect a great change both in the fine arts themselves, and in art manufactures in the Panjab.

The Government has at present under consideration a scheme for the establishment of a school of design at Lahore, and although the difficulties at first may be great, there can be no doubt of the benefits that will evenually result from it.

Class XXXIII may be divided into two divisions, one including drawings and paintings, the other models. It is proposed to notice these division separately.

Among the paintings most worthy of notice is a collection by Pundit Manphúl. Many in this collection are of considerable antiquity, and it is interesting to note the changes in the art during the last three hundred years. Painting has undoubtedly declined in the Panjab, and the reasons for its decline are noticed at the beginning of this report. There is a delicacy of treatment about the old paintings which is almost entirely wanting in the works of the present day.

The collection commences at No. 11,015, with an interesting series of 15 of the Emperors of Delhi. Most of these were painted by Purkhu, an artist in the service of Raja Sansár Chand of Katoch, who was a great patron of art, and prepared a fine collection of paintings. There is a remarkable clearness of tone and delicacy of handling in most of Purkhu's works, but he was not so great a master of color as many other artists inferior to him in other respects. His son Ramdyal, who is still living, inherits much of his father's talent. Number 76 is a clever portrait of Maharaja Gulab Singh, said to be one of the best likeness ever taken of that prince. The next painting to it 77, is an interesting portrait of Raja Sansár Chand by Purkhu. The series of Muhamadan Saints, Nos. 88—100, are very interesting. The paintings are by different artists, whose names are unknown, and some of them are very old. The most noticeable among them are Baháuddín Zakaria, who died at Multan, A. H. 666; Syad Julál Bokhári of Uch, A. H. 686; and Dáta Ganj Baksh, whose tomb is at Lahore, A. H. 465. An unnumbered portrait of Maharaja Ranjit Singh, said to be an admirable likeness, was hung at the entrance of the Court; there are very few really good likenesses of this monarch. The best was taken at Rupar in 1831 by Jíún Rám, a painter of Meerut, in the suite of Lord William Bentinck. The Pattiala paintings, 11045—11049, are well executed, especially the portrait of Maharaja Karam Singh.

But the most clever and truthful paintings in this class, are the work of Bishan Singh of Amritsar. This artist has exhibited no less than ten paintings, three of them of considerable size. These latter 10,983—10,985, represent the Durbars of Maharaja Ranjit Singh and Maharaja Sher Singh, and the Municipal Committee of Amritsar, and are of great merit. The perspective of the buildings is incorrect, but the figure drawing is admirable. The color is tasteful and rich, the likeness are good, and the expression of the faces is varied and truthful. A series of six pictures, Nos. 10,976—10,981 of smaller size, illustrating the processes of the shawl manufacture, is equally good. The best of the series are Nos. 10,979 and 10,980, shawl pressing and cleaning. In these the detail is most carefully worked out, yet is not allowed to interfere with the unity of the design, and the coloring is especially good.

No. 10,964 is a very curious work illustrating, in different compartments, the trades carried on in the Kangra hills. As a painting, however, it has no artistic merit.

No. 10,975, a book of water color drawings of different tribes in the Panjab, by Sani of Rawalpindi, possesses considerable merit; also some outline drawings, (unnumbered) by Kishen Singh, a Kupurthalla artist. The Delhi paintings on ivory have been treated of elsewhere. The only Delhi paintings in Class XXXIII are two, representing the Nawab of Jhajjar hunting the boar and the leopard. These are animated, clever works, and the grouping of the figures is good, but the color is poor, and the drawing most indifferent.

The majority of the models exhibited have been, as might be supposed, prepared under European superintendence.

The most noticeable are a series of four, executed from the designs of Mr. John Gordon, Executive Engineer of Amritsar. The workmanship and carving of all these are extremely careful and good. The first, No. 10,991, is a model of the Town Hall and Municipal buildings now in course of erection at Amritsar, at an estimated cost of 1,25,000 rupees. This, when completed, will be one of the finest buildings of the kind in India. It has a frontage of 280 feet, and, with its quadrangle, covers an acre of ground. The second, No. 10,990, represents the Amritsar Government College, lately finished; it adjoins the Town Hall, and is similar to it in style. The third, No. 10,993, is the Clock Tower at Amritsar now in course of erection, at an estimated cost of 23,000 rupees; the style adopted in this building is the decorated Gothic. The ornamentation, though simple, is very effective, and the proportions are singularly graceful. It is proposed to place in it a clock with illuminated dials, and as it is situated on the highest ground in Amritsar, and is itself 145 feet in height, it will be a very prominent object in the city. The fourth model sent by Mr. Gordon, No. 10,992, is of an ornamental gate for the new public gardens at Amritsar. The detail of this work is very rich. The wings and piers are to be constructed of plastered brick, the gate itself is wrought iron; the estimated cost is 1,000 rupees.

The Barí Doab Canal Workshops at Madhopur exhibit some well executed models—Nos. 11,001 to 11,004. The most noticeable of these represents two of the nine bays of the Dumrai fall, in the 1st Division of the Bari Doab Canal. This fall, which has been found to answer better than any other, is the invention of Captain Dyas, R. E., Director of Canals, Panjab. It is as great an improvement on the simple perpendicular fall, as that is on the Ogee, which has been found so disastrous in its action on the Ganges Canal. In Captain Dyas' system the water, falling from the higher level, passes through a wooden grating, which diminishes the velocity of the water at the crest of the fall, and distributes it over a much larger area than would in any other plan be the case, rendering the flow of water from the cistern gentle and equable, and preventing the destruction of the bed of the canal. This very interesting model has been more particularly noticed here, as it was observed that many visitors to the Exhibition mistook it for a cotton gin. Lieut. Garstin, Bari Doab Canal, exhibited several well executed models connected with the canal works—Nos. 10,986—10,989.

Nos. 11,025 and 11,033 were models of the Churches at Gujrat and Derah Ghází Khán, in wood. The workmanship of these was good.

Two models of bridges were specially worthy of attention. The first (unnumbered) was exhibited by the late Mr. Byrne, Executive Engineer, and represents the bridge lately built over the Gaj, near Dharmsálá. The design is clever and bold, and being a laminated wooden arch, is well adopted for hill torrents. The second (unnumbered) shows five arches of the masonry bridge in course of construction over the Markunda torrent near Amballa. This model is most beautifully executed.

Sirdar Baghwán Singh exhibits a complete model of the Darbár Sahib, the great Sikh Temple, in Amritsar: great care and labour has been expended on this work. The elaborate ornamentation of the temple has been perfectly reproduced, and the whole model takes to pieces, showing the interior, which is as highly finished as the exterior.

Two models in soap-stone are worthy of notice for the delicacy of their workmanship, one representing the Juma Masjid at Delhi; and the other, exhibited by Kanheya Lal, Assistant Engineer, the tomb of Salím Chístí at Fatahpúr. A work of equally minute and careful detail, is 10,975 by Jítú, the Kutb Minar at Delhi, executed in ivory.

One of the best models in the Department is that of a first class Railway carriage, (unnumbered). This was entirely made by natives, and is a most creditable production. Although on a very small scale, the detail is given well and carefully, and the workmanship is admirable.

A thermantidote (unnumbered) is also worthy of attention. The machine is worked by treddles, and by the same action the water is raised by a force pump to the top of the tatties, the surplus returning to the reservoir.

The last model to be noticed here, is the wooden bridge over the Ravi at Chumba. This is a curious and picturesque structure. It was built in its present form about forty years ago by Raja Charrat Singh. The model contributed by the present Raja gives a very exact representation of it.

PRIZES.

Models.

		Rs.
1.	Mr. John Gordon's models.—The Amritsar Town Hall, College, Clock Tower, and the Ornamental Gate of the Rámbágh, ...	70
2.	Model of Railway Carriage, ...	50
3.	Sirdar Baghwán Singh's model of the Darbár Sahib at Amritsar, ...	50 with Medal.

Paintings.

4.	Bishen Singh, Amritsar, ...	50
5.	Pattiala State, ...	30
6.	Sani, book of paintings, ...	25
7.	Kishen Singh of Kapurthalla, a book of paintings, ...	30

MEDALS AND CERTIFICATES.

8.	Model of the Kutb at Delhi, ...	Certificate.
9.	Model of Thermantidote, ...	Do.
10.	The Madhopur models, ...	Do.
11-12.	The Gujrat and Dera Ghazi Khan Churches, ...	Do.
13.	Model of Bridge over the Ravi, ...	Medal.

ENGLISH INDEX.

P.

Q.

R.

S.

T.

VERNACULAR INDEX AND GLOSSARY.

The name of a district placed after a word indicates that the term is locally used.
" Pji." = Panjábí; " P." = Persian; " H." = Hindí; " A." = Arabic; S. = Sanskrit.

C.

D.

H.

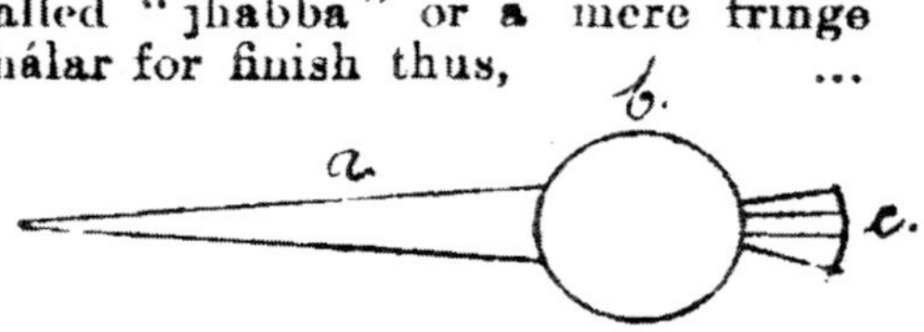
a
b.
c.

HAND-BOOK

OF THE

MANUFACTURES AND ARTS

OF THE

PUNJAB

CLASS XII. METAL MANUFACTURES.

WHITE GOODS.—*Continued.*

From Rádhá Nagar.

Dopatta (scarf).
Dhotí máre dár (waistcloth worn by Hindús).
Doryá, (striped muslin all white.)
Chárkhána, (check).

From Banáras.

White dopatta or scarf.
Dhotí, waistcloth worn by Hindús.

From Farkhábád.

Abra liháf, (calico print for bed covers, &c.).
Chít, (chintz or print).
Jájam (floor cloth) a kind of coarse red cloth used for flooring, and is generally stamped with a pattern in black on the red ground.
Saláthi.

From Agra.

Darí (" Durrees," cotton carpets.)
Shatranjí, (carpets).
Kálín sútí (pile carpets in cotton).

(*The following have been nearly all described in the text, hence no explanation is added.*)

From Delhi.

Malmal pagrí, (muslin turban).
Dosútí, tinsútí, chaustúí, &c., &c., (p. 7.)
Gambroon, (p. 9.)
Síri sáf (a kind of muslin).
Gárhá, (thin cloth, p. 8.)

From various places, Lahore, &c.

Plain or sádá báfi.

Adhotar (coarse muslin).
Khadar (coarse thin cloth.)
Chaunsí, painsí, áthsí, chísí, &c. } *All very much alike in quality.*
Hazárí (broad white cloth). } *All very much alike in quality.*
Gazzí (thin cloth). } *All very much alike in quality.*
Dhotí, a cloth woven of a size for wear round the loins.
Ghátí, (stiff glazed white cloth, p. 6.)
Doryá, muslin striped with two lines together, all white.
Silaí Khatá, plain striped muslin (stripes close together.)
Chárkhána, check muslin.
Táftá, a fabric of 'tafta' (twisted thread, made both in silk and cotton.
Mahmúdí, (a fabric which used to be made as long cloth, but is superseded by imported 'lathá ;' it was made of cotton and also of silk.

Khes báft.

Dotáhí, (pages 5, 6.)
Chautáhí.
Palang posh.
Khes.
Lungí, (p. 3.)

COLORED GOODS.

Khes báft.

Khes sádá, (p. 5.)
Khes dabba (check large).
Khes tukrídár showing pieces of different colours joined together.
Khes dorukha (different coloured plaid on either side).
Khes Jat ká, (jat or villager's khes).

Súsí sádí, (page 6.)
Do. dokanní.
Do. chaukanní.

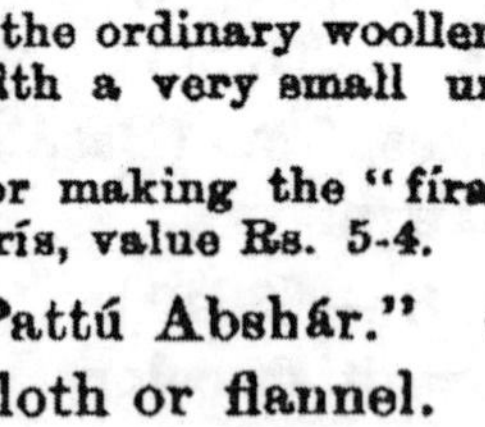

THE SHAWL-LOOM.

BAHAWALPÚR SILKS.

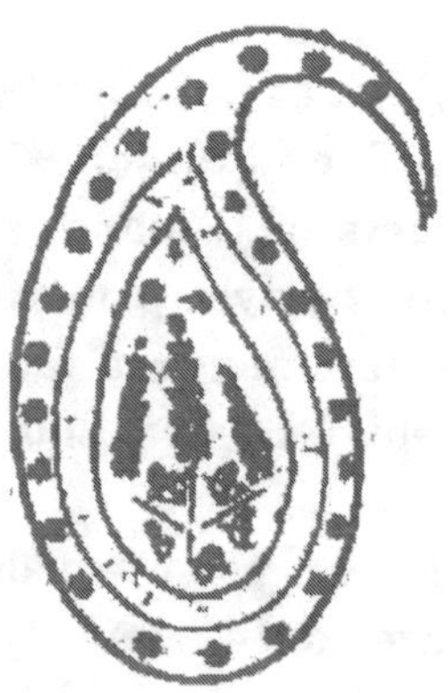

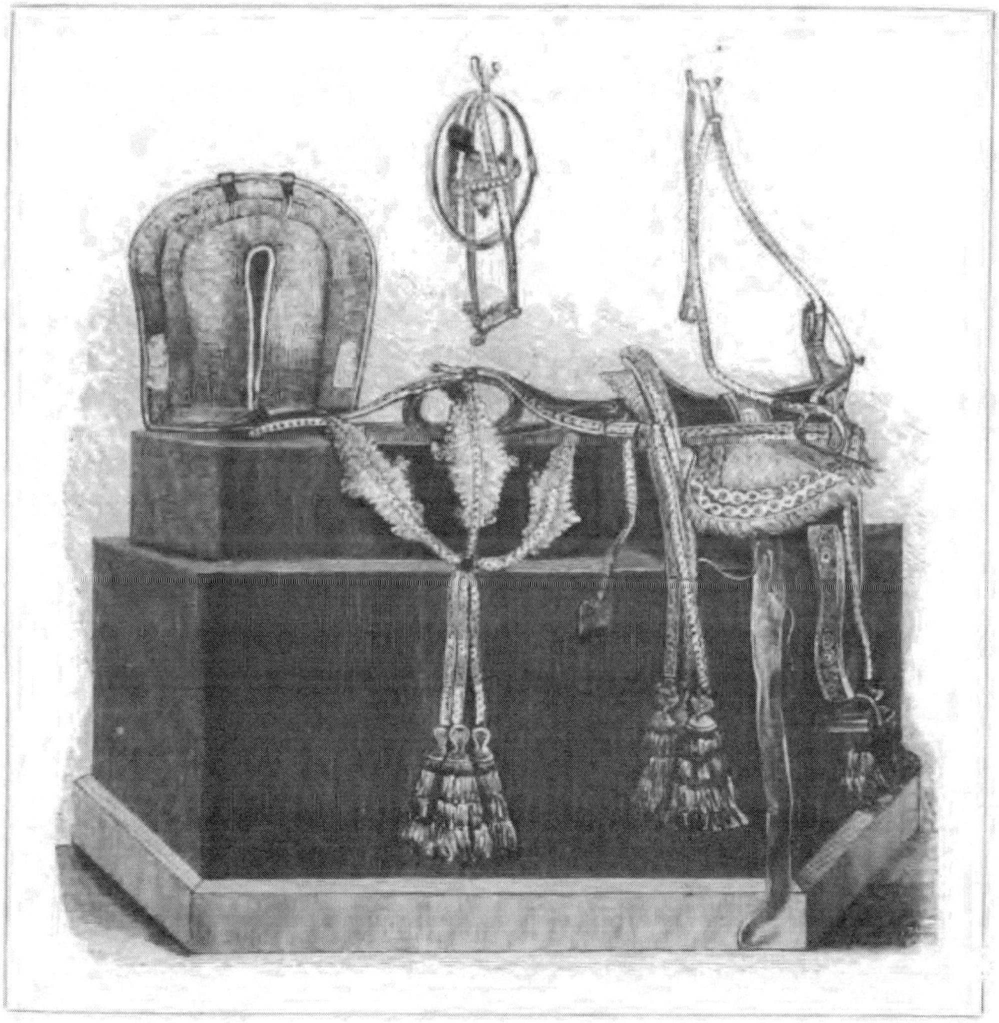

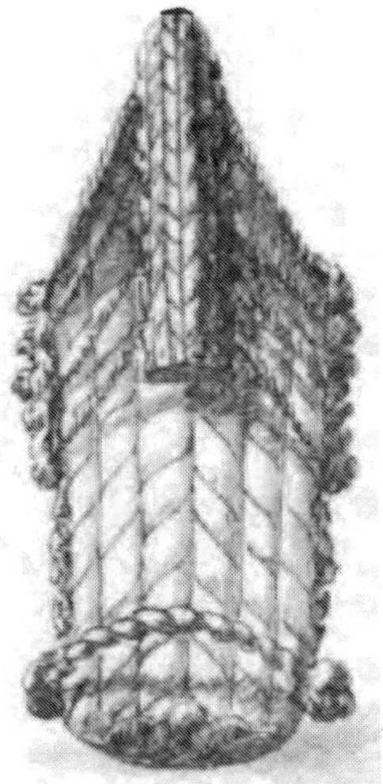

Straw shoes (Himalayan)

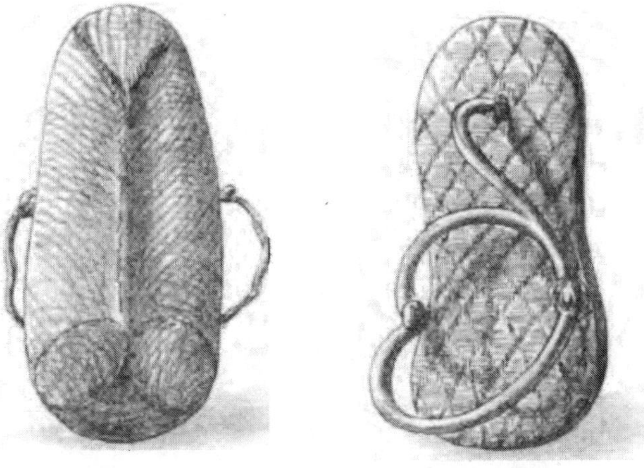

Deraját grass, & leather sandals

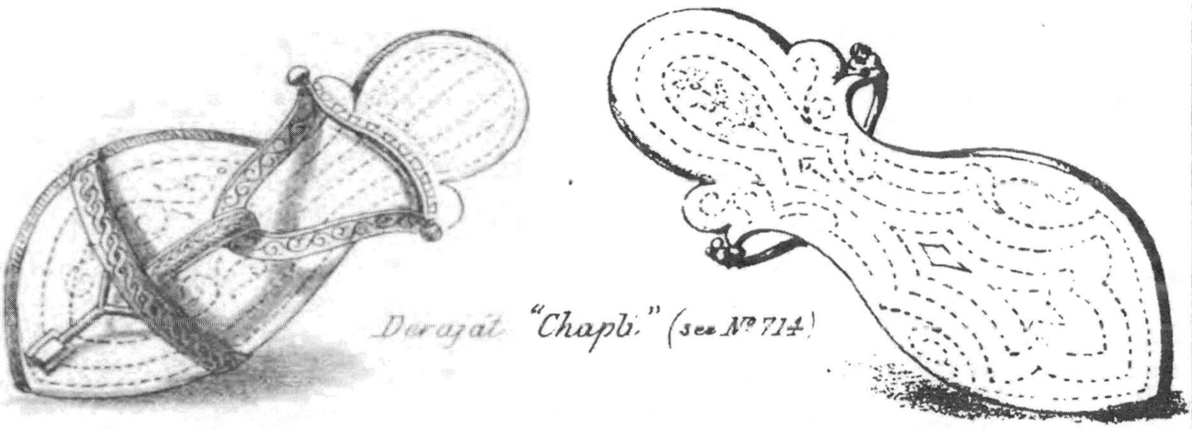

Derajat "Chapli." (see No 714)

(Fig 2) Bakmála shoe

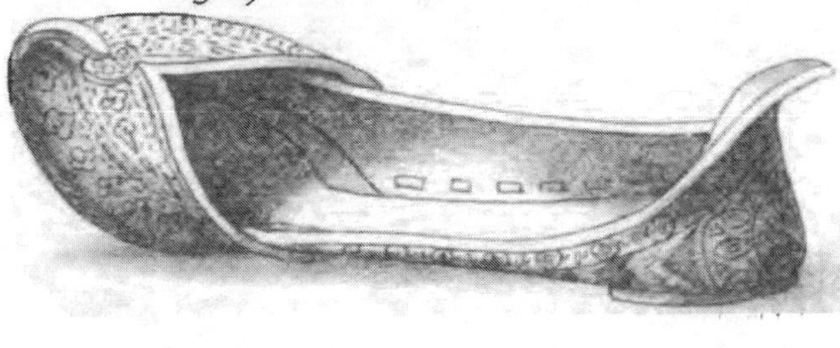

Fig. 3

S. Sedgfield Lith: Calcutta

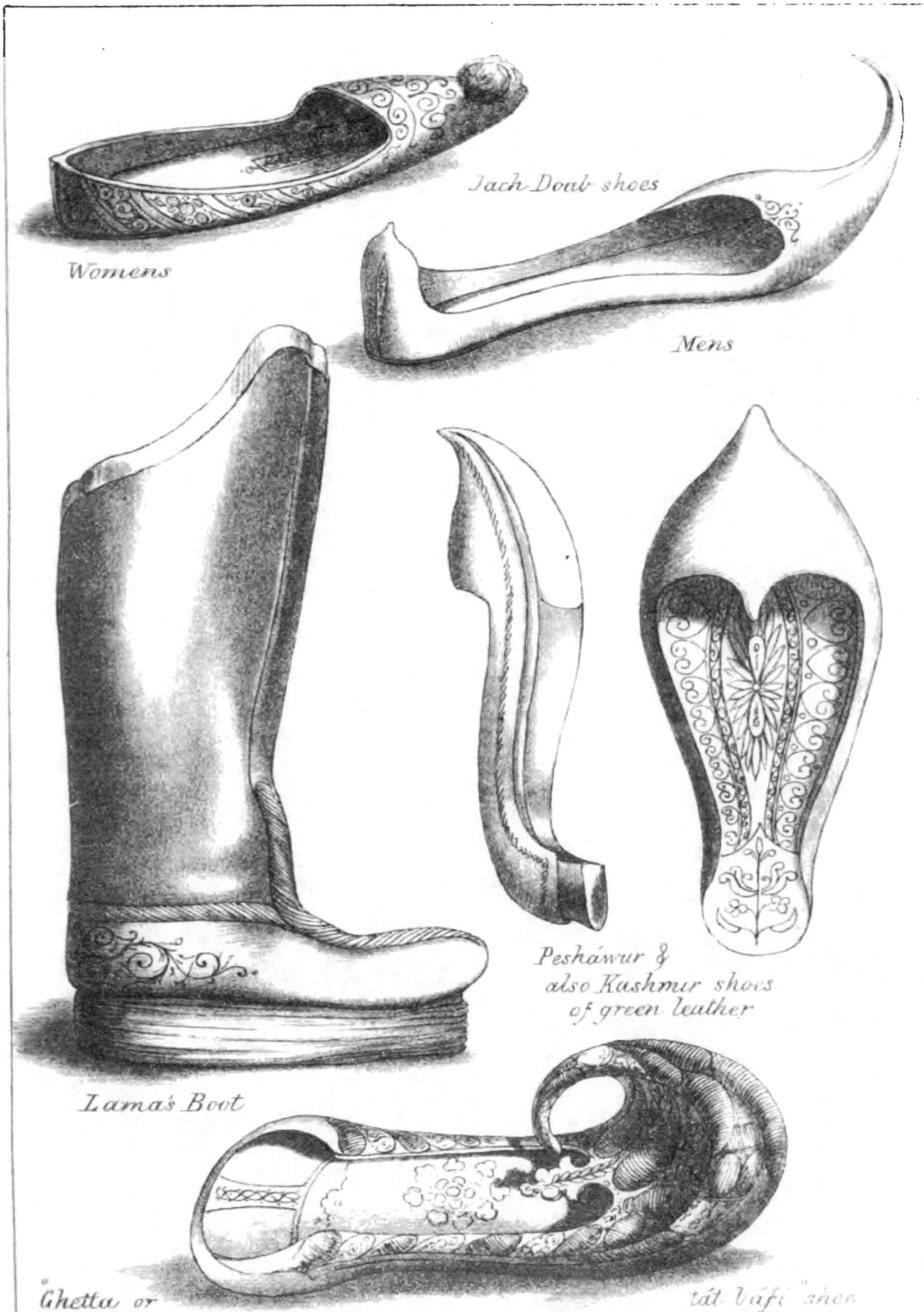

S. Sedgefield

Fig. 1.

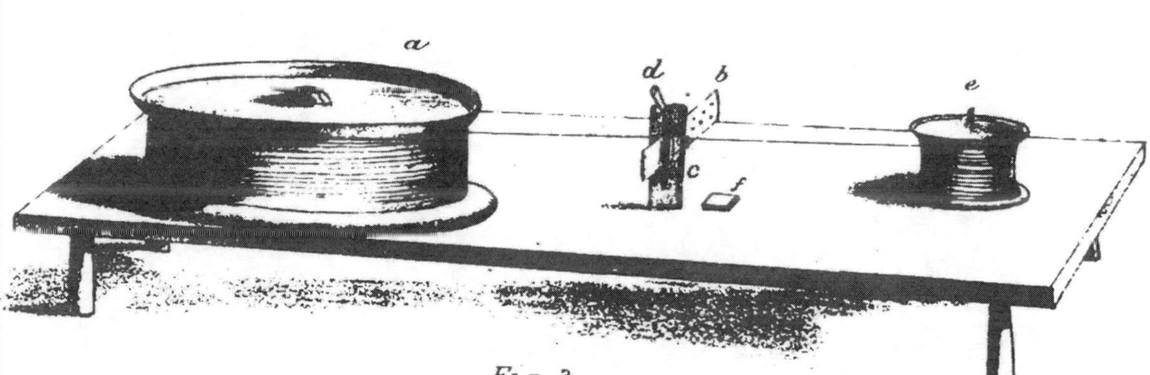

Fig. 2.

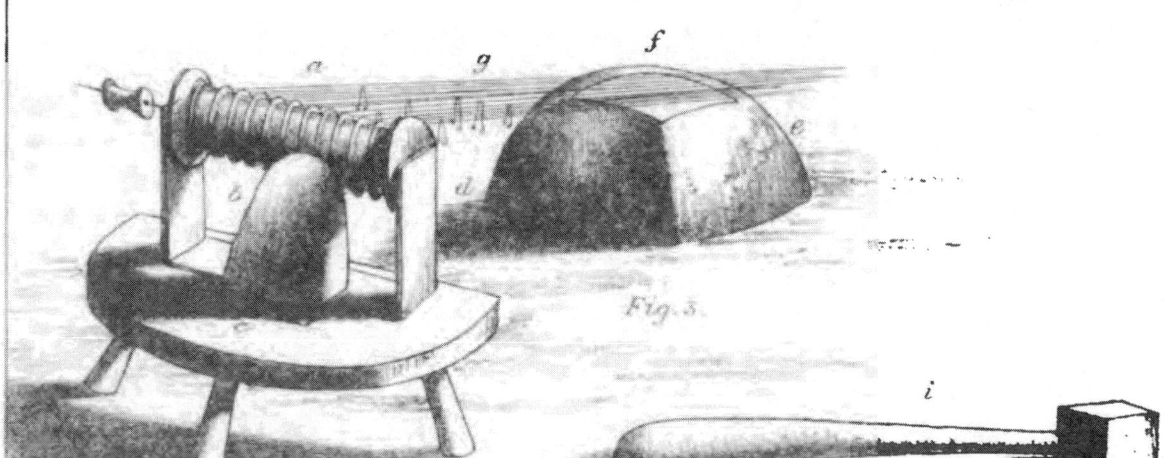

Fig. 3.

Fig 4

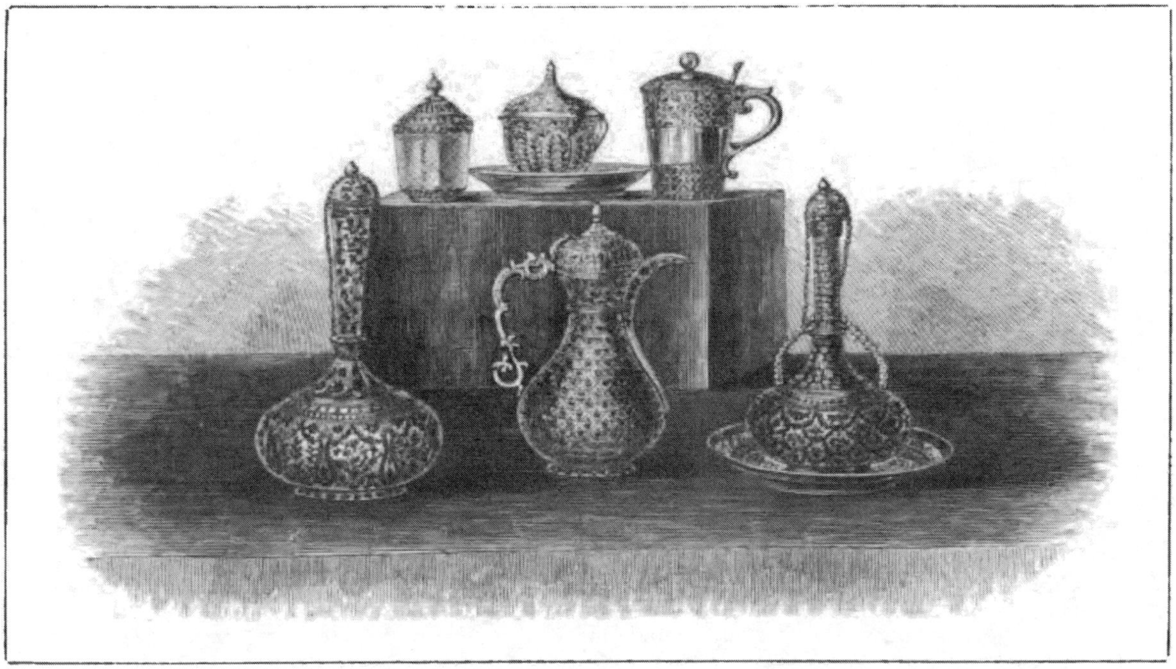

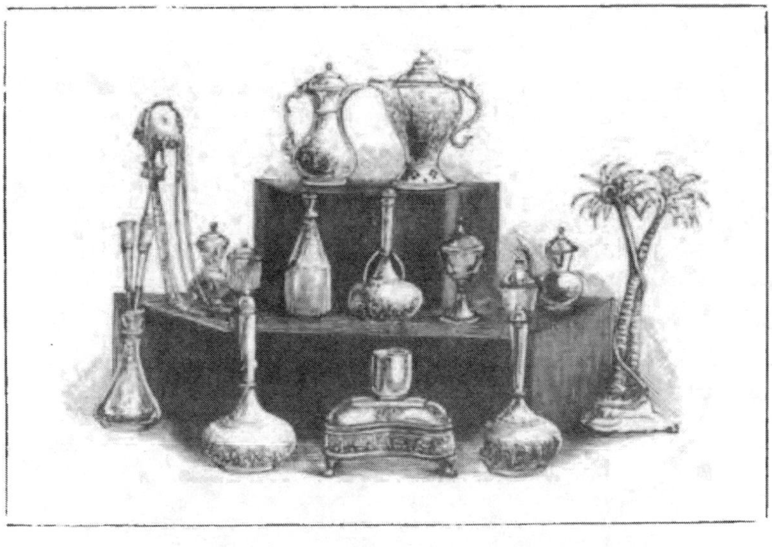

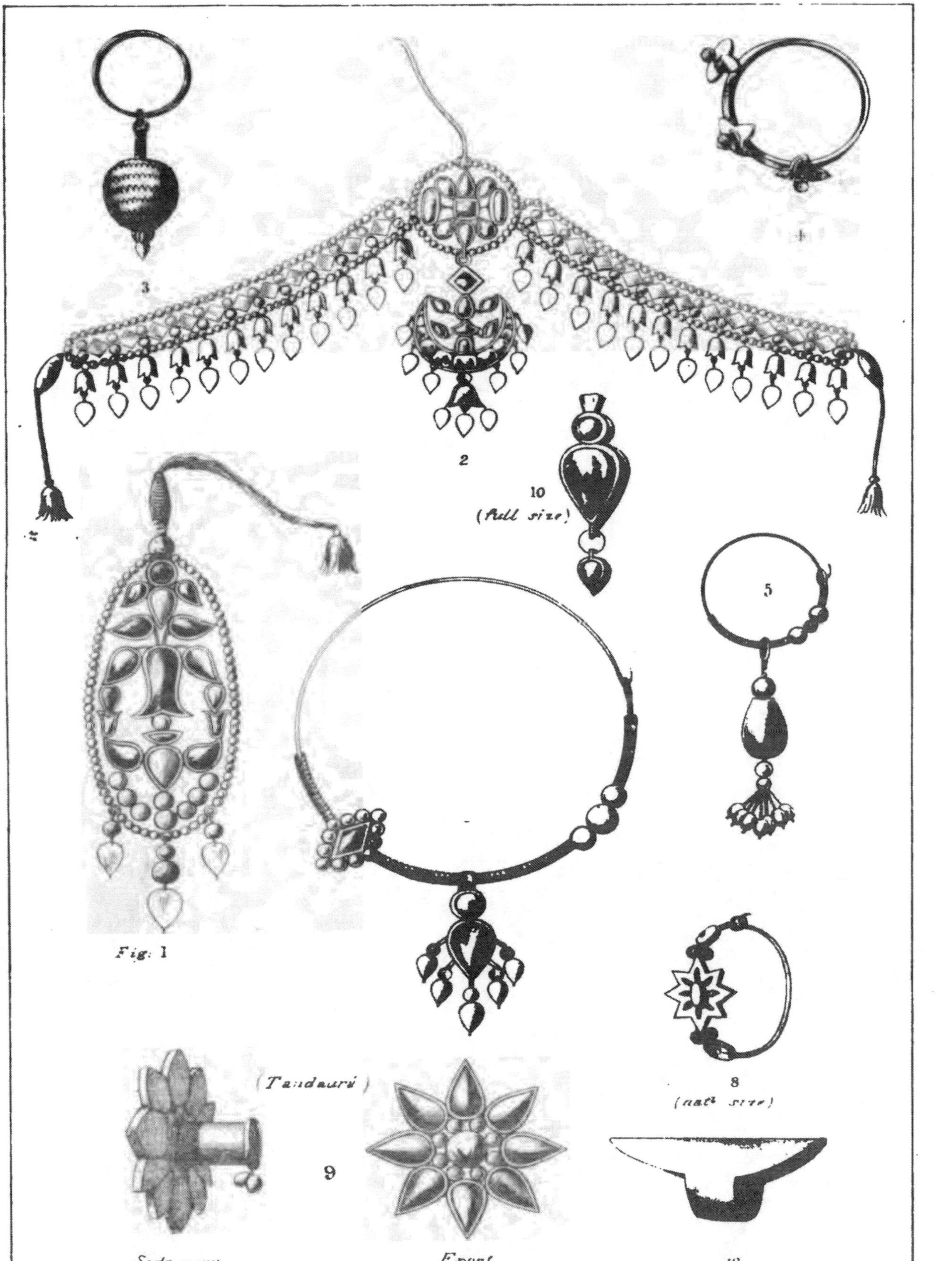

S. Seeg... Lith. Calcutta

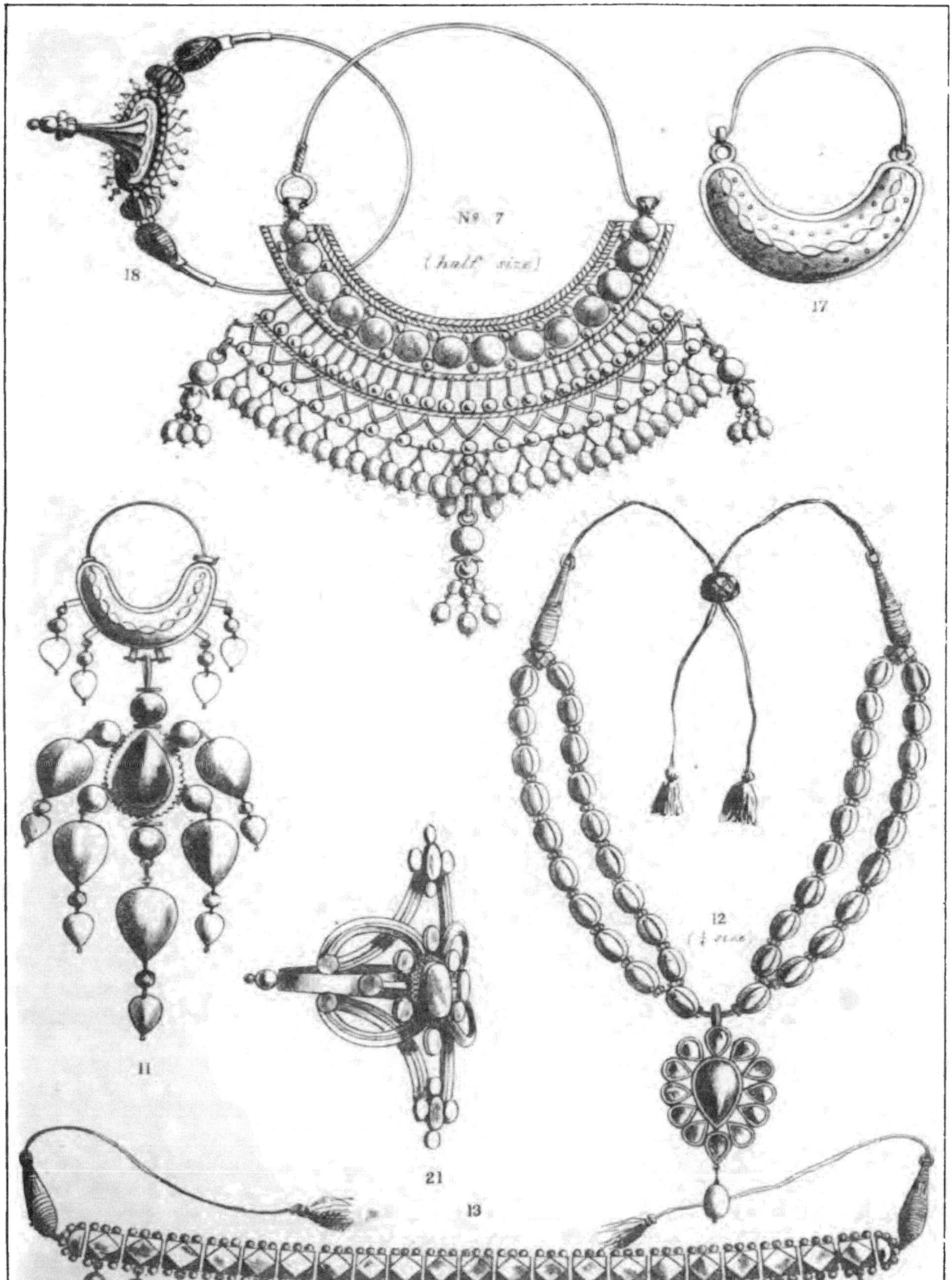

Nº 14 “Khandi”

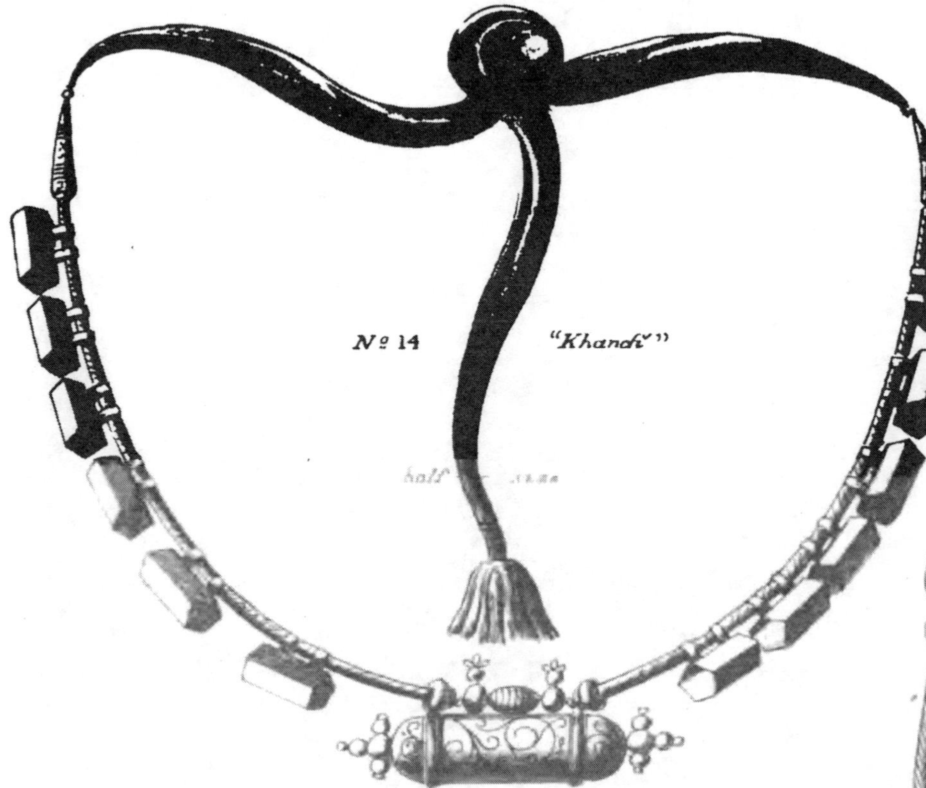

half size

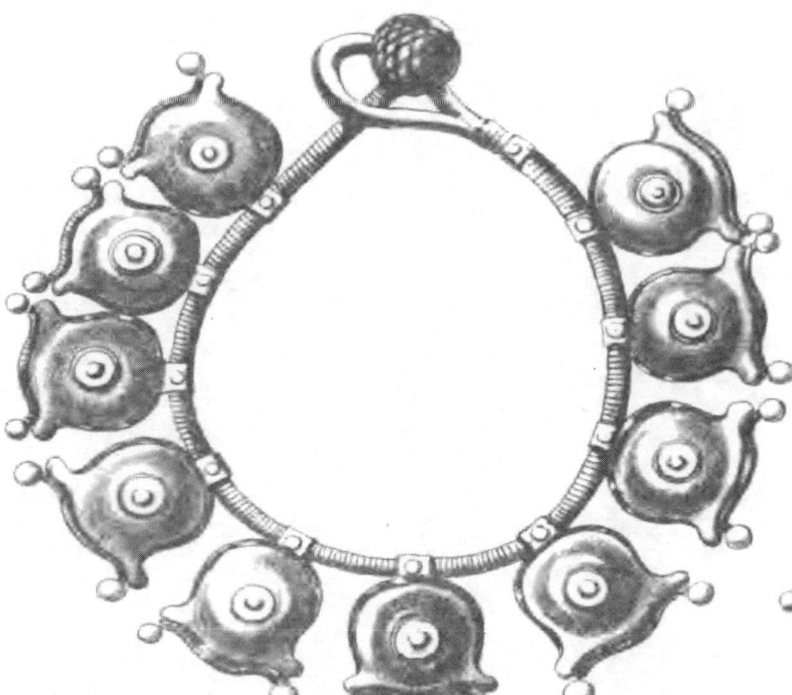

Póntha or Gungrú worn on the ankle.
nearly full size

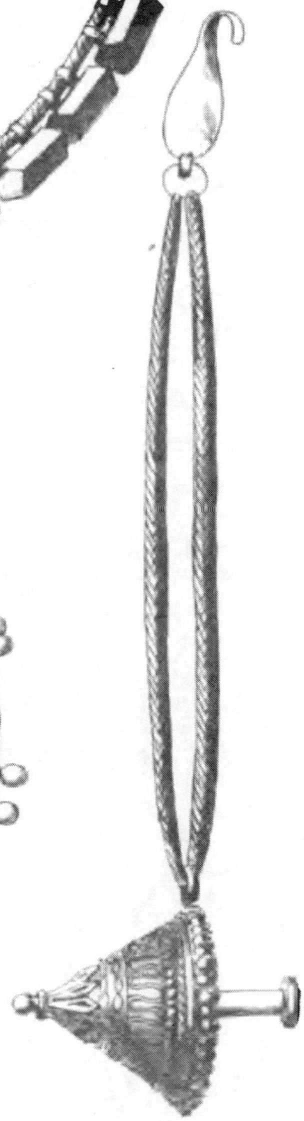

Ear-stud with
Suspender
(Kilil)

S. Sedgfield. Lith:

S. Seigfield Lith.

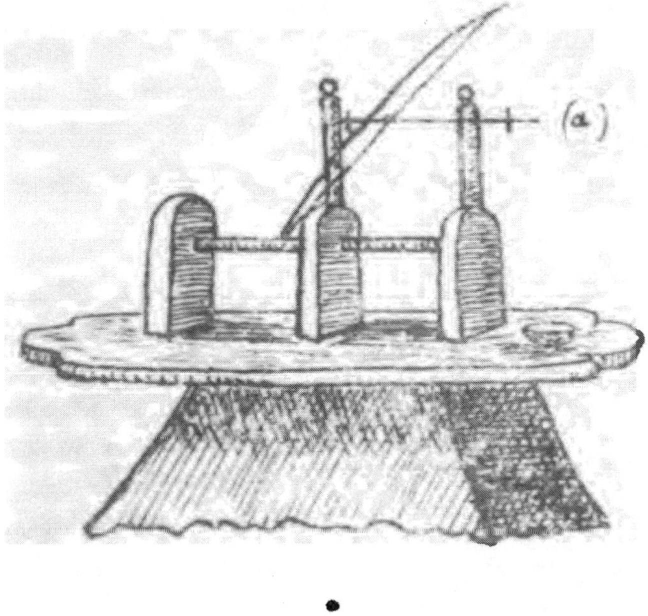

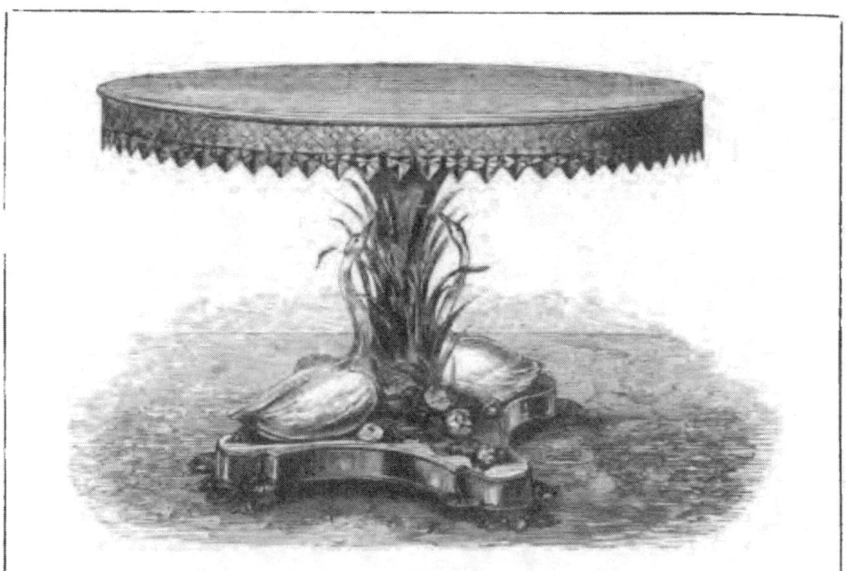

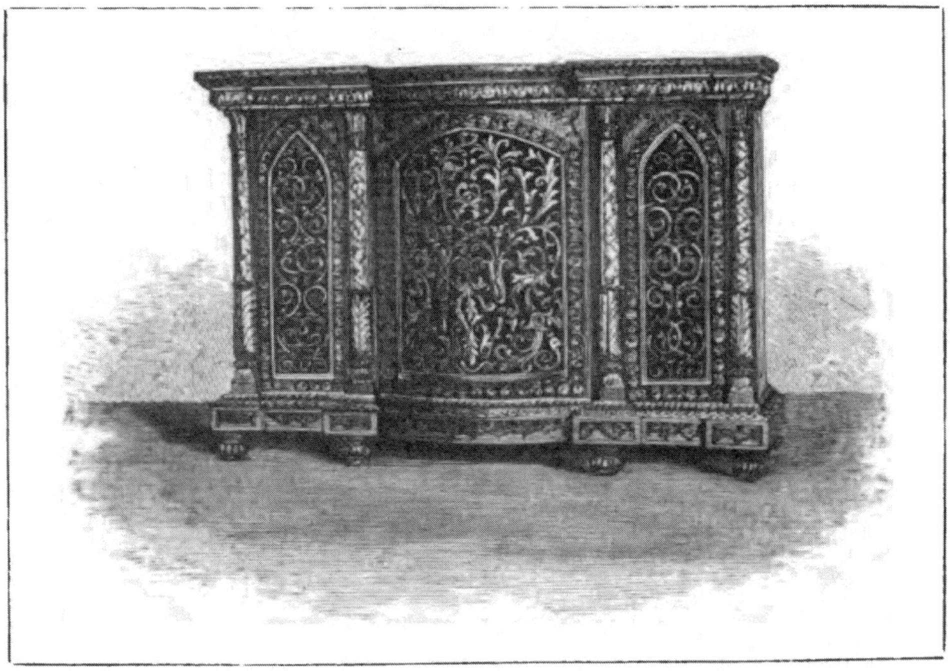

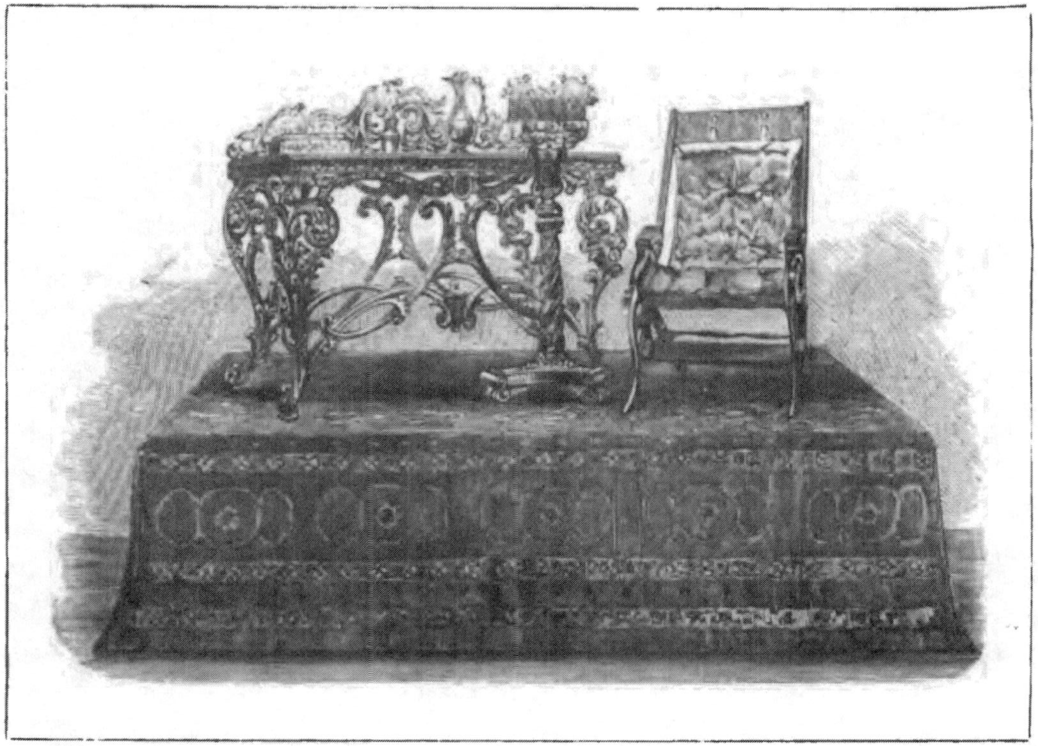

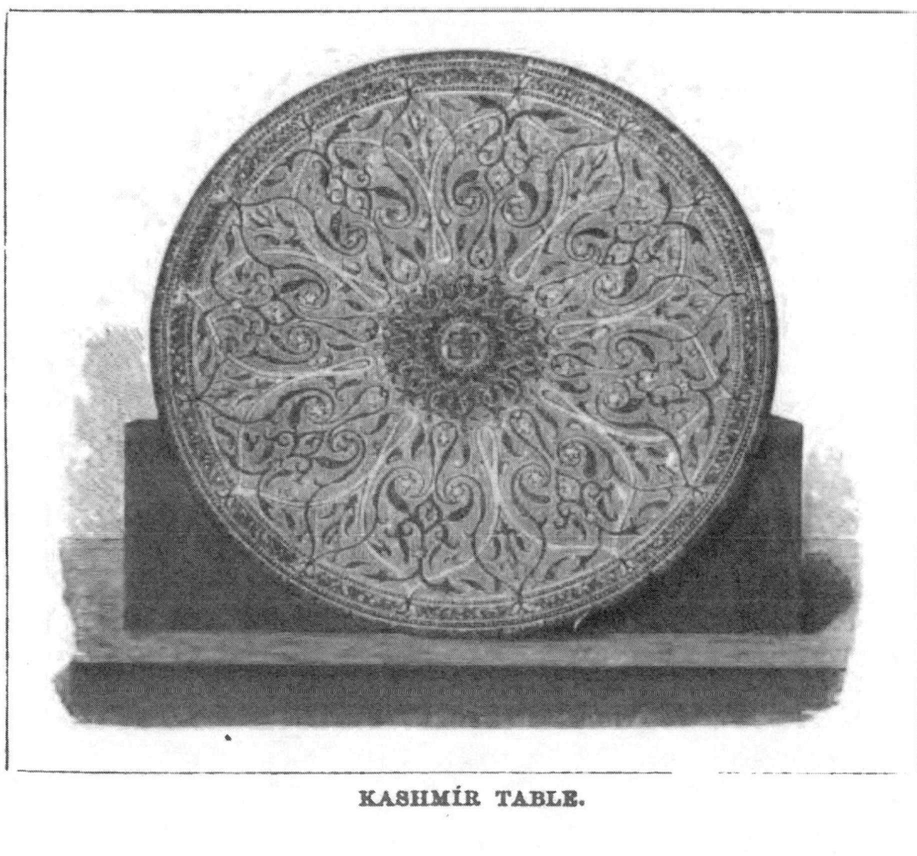

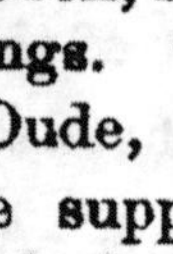

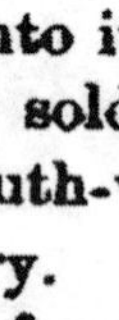

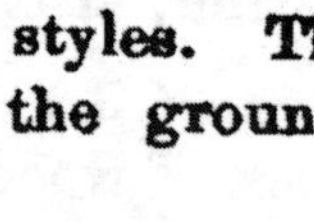

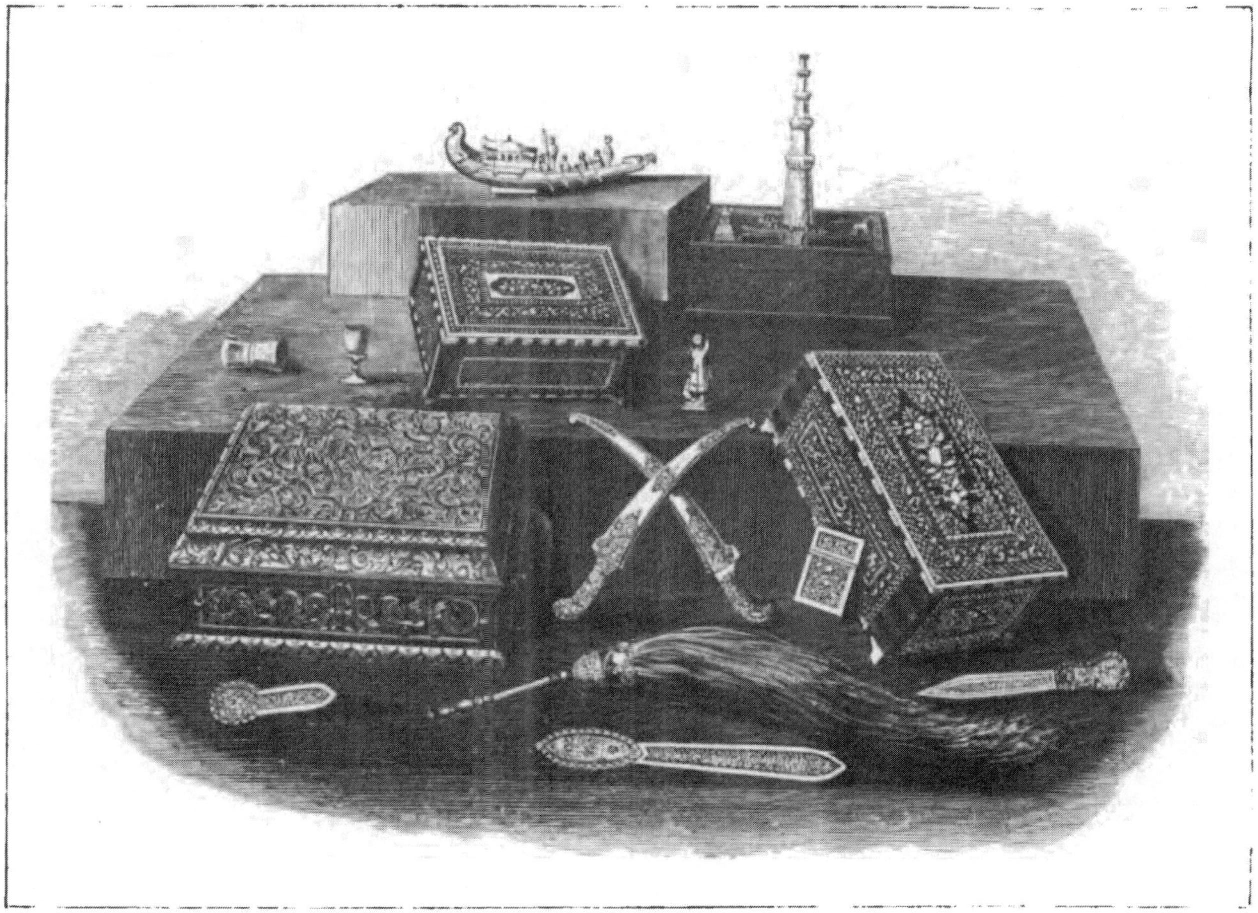

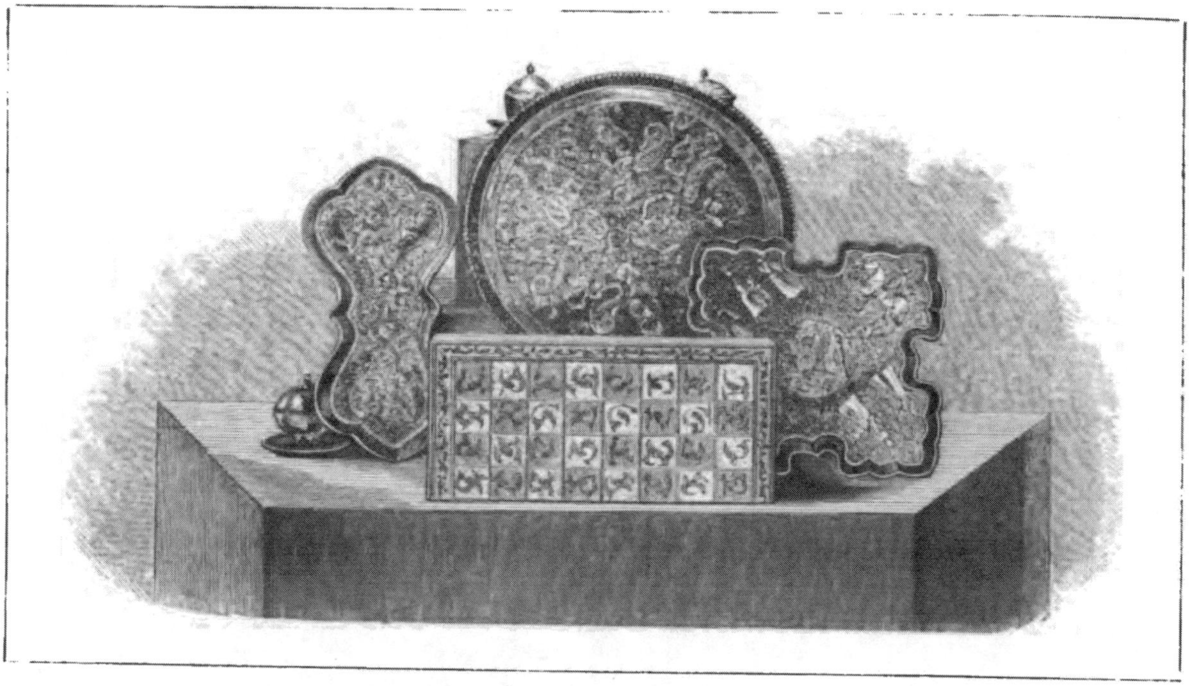

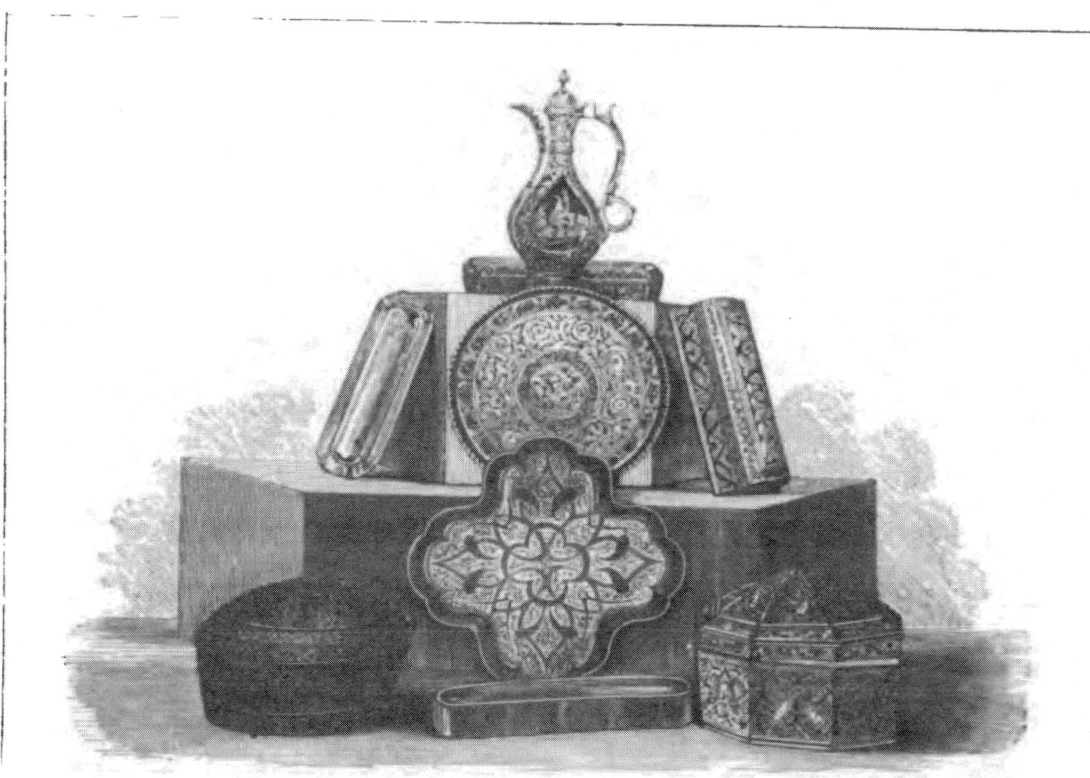

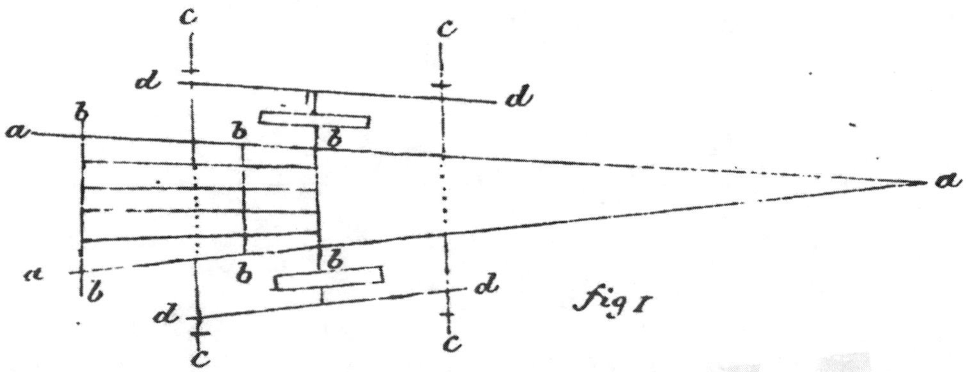

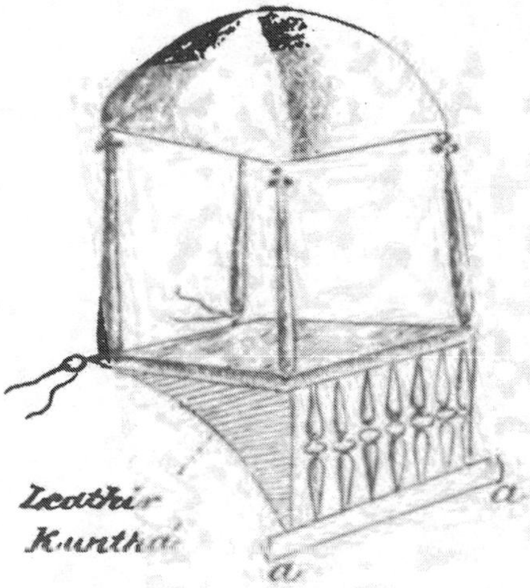

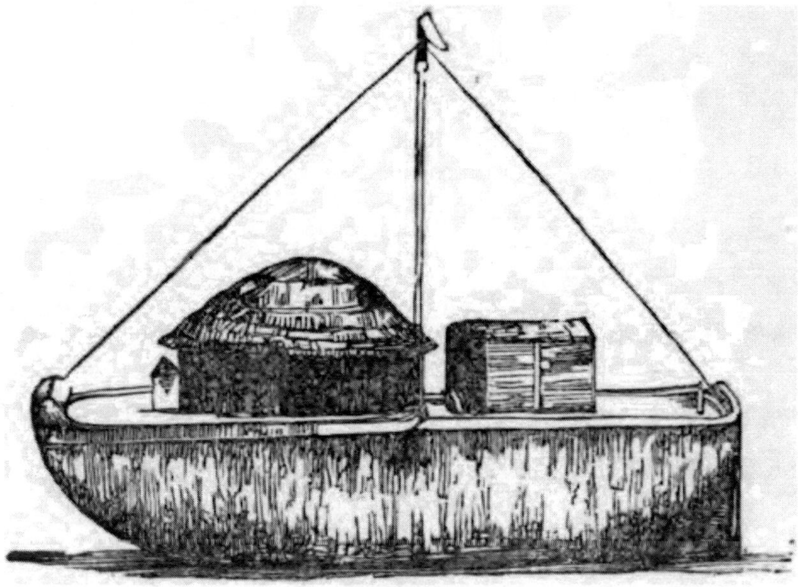

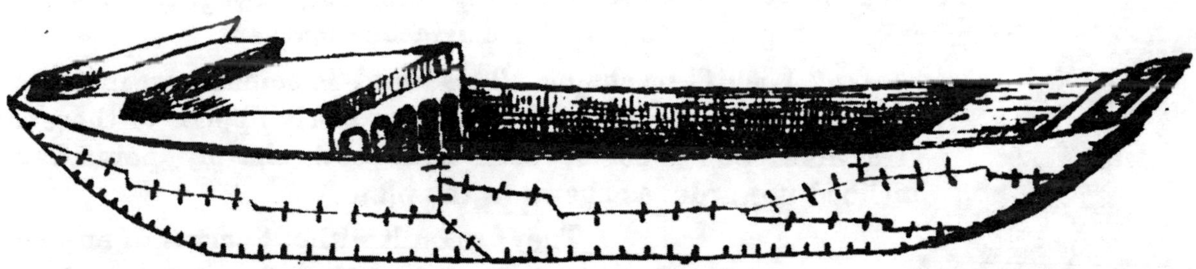

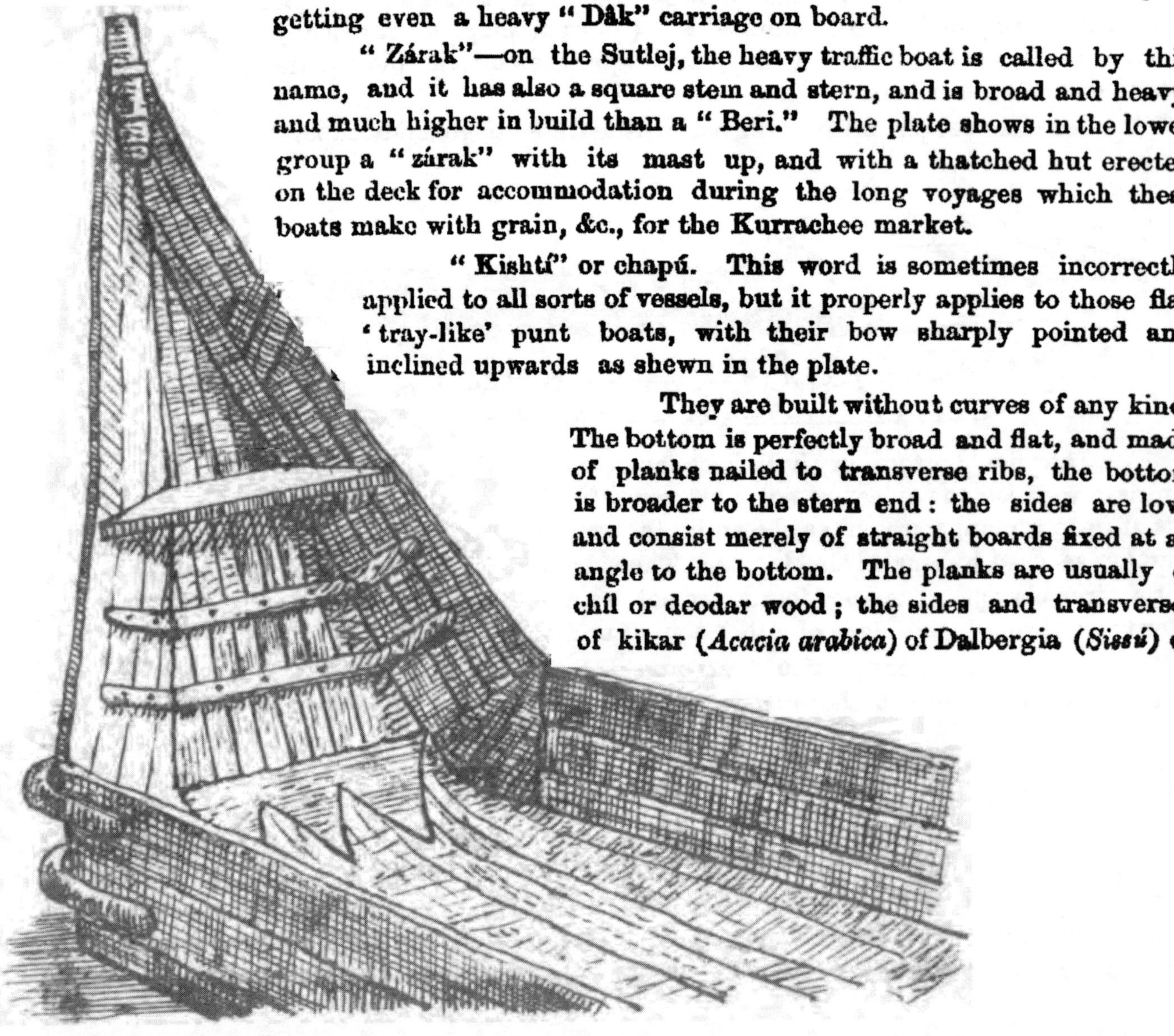

ASTROLABE.

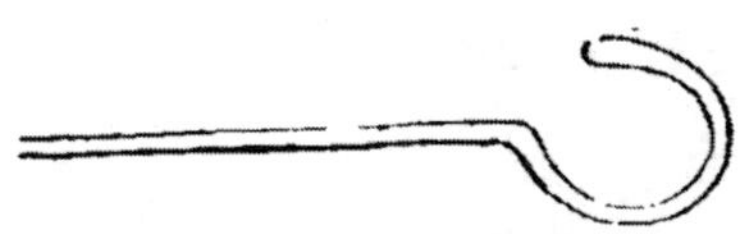

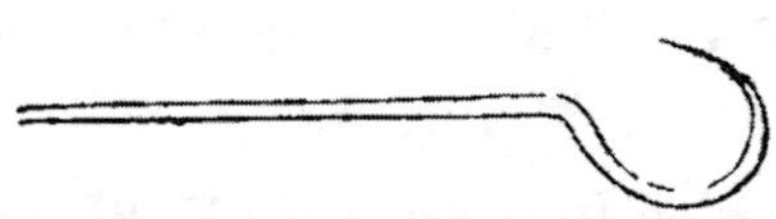

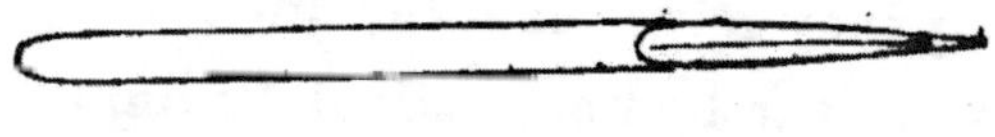

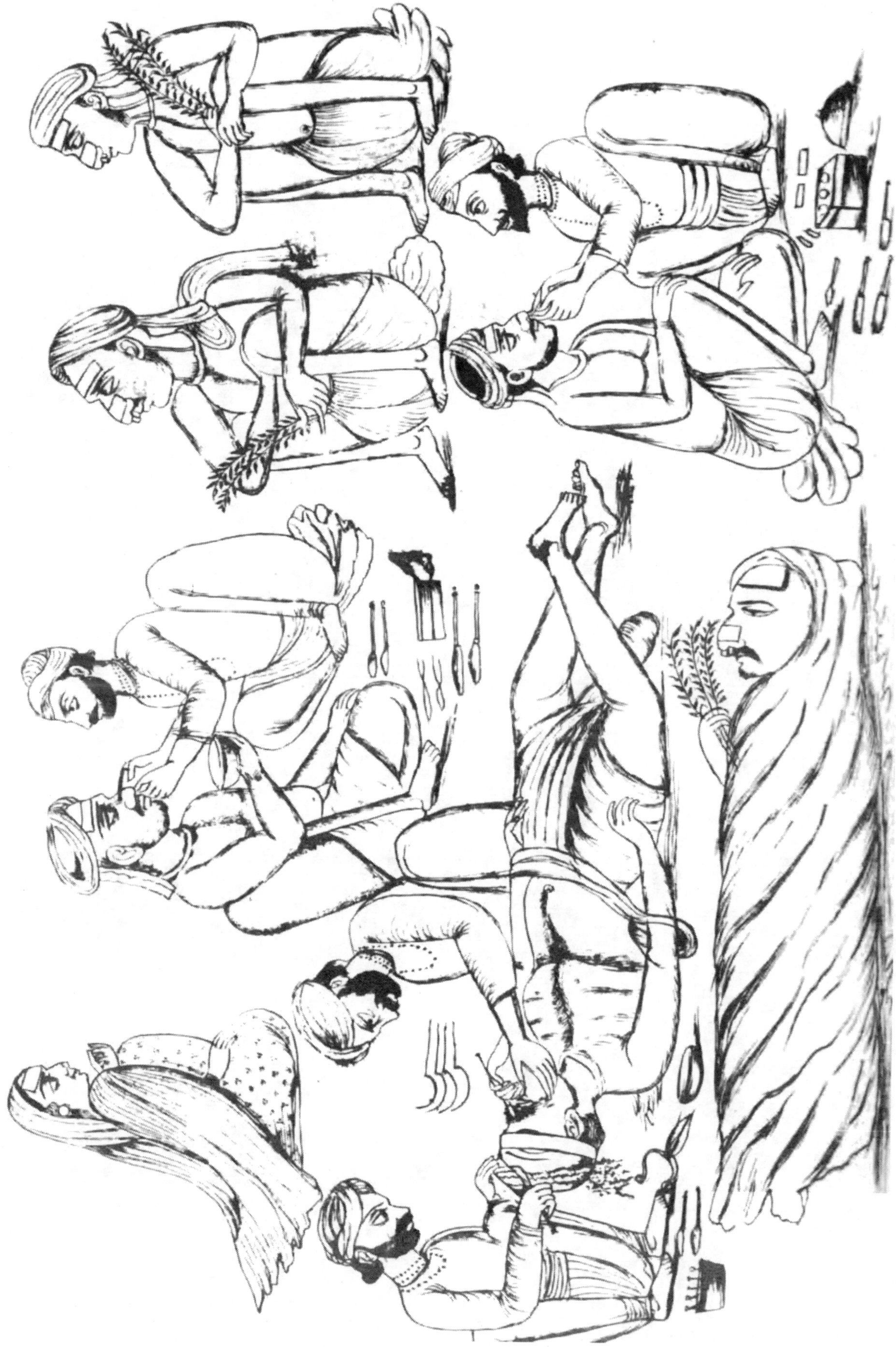

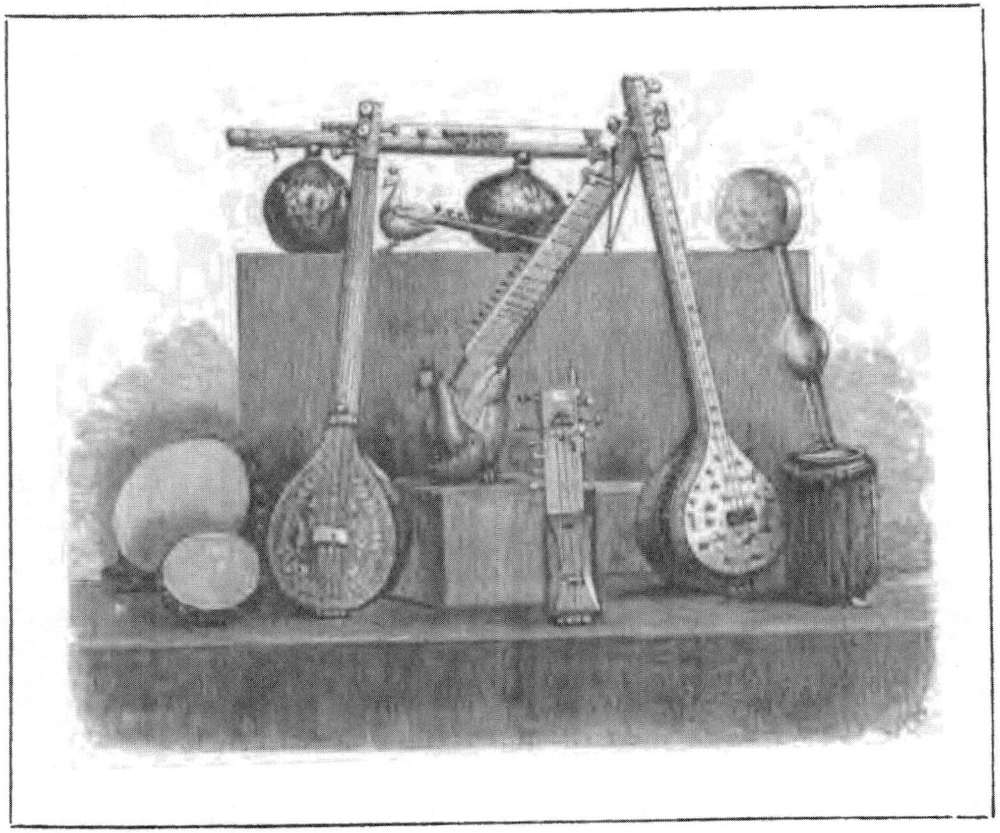

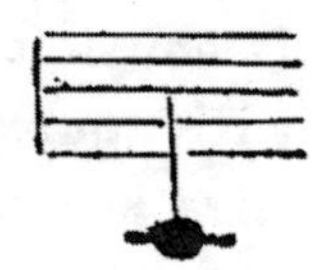

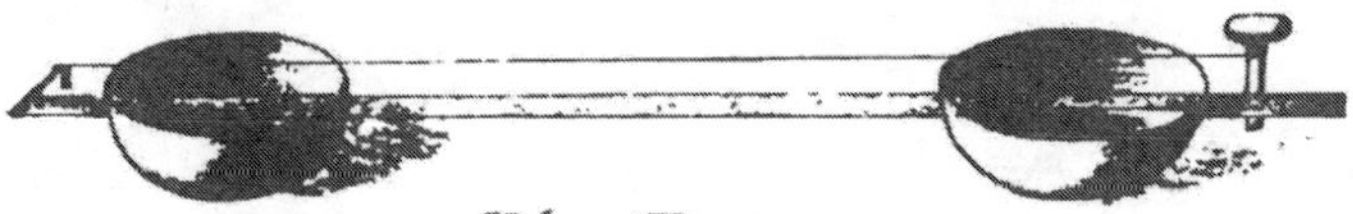

Kíng (Fig:1.)

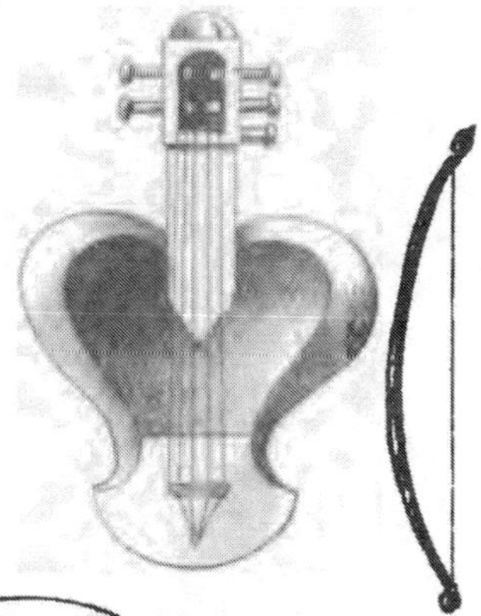

Sdranda

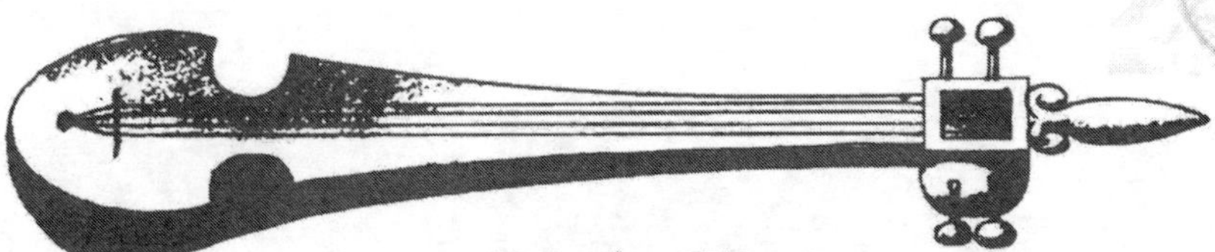

Chártára (Fig:2)

Kamánch (Fig:3.)

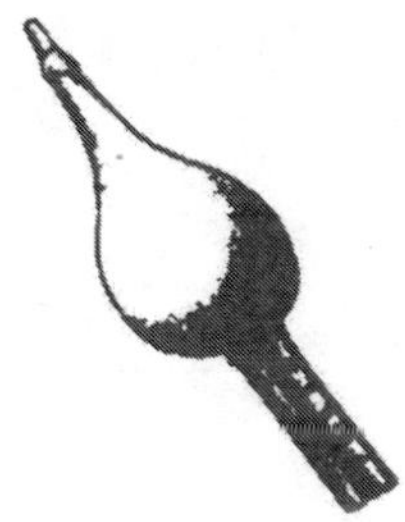

Bín Jogí

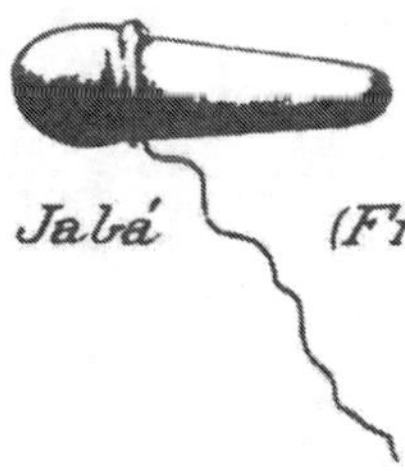

Jabá (Fig:4.)

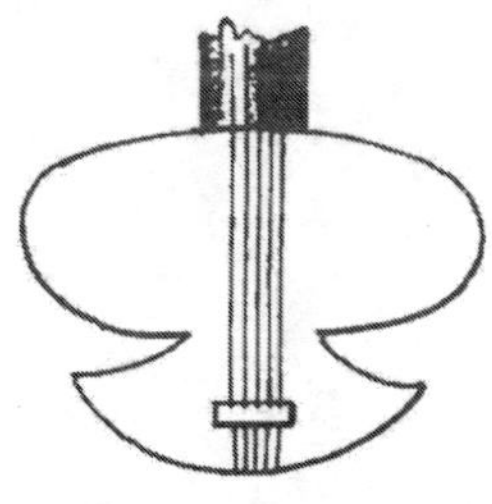

Cháng (Fig:7.)

Mizráb (Fig: 5.)

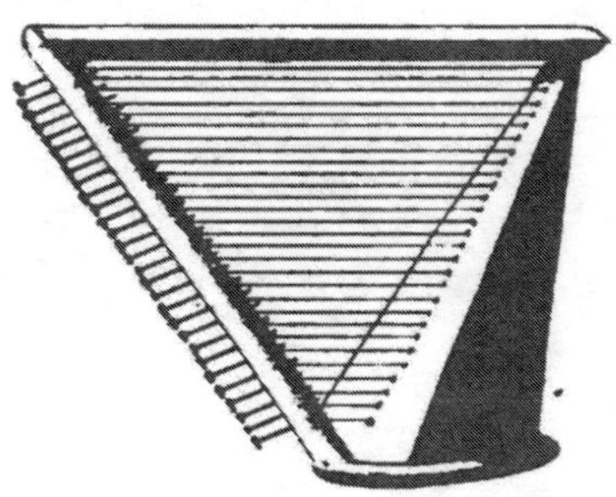

Kánún (Fig:6)

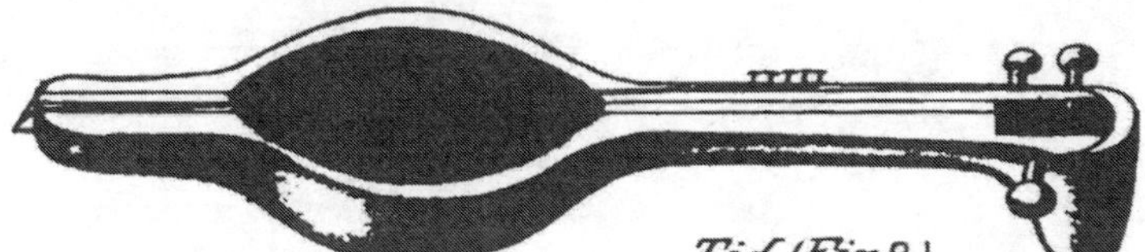

Tid (Fig:8.)

Chikára (Fig:9.)

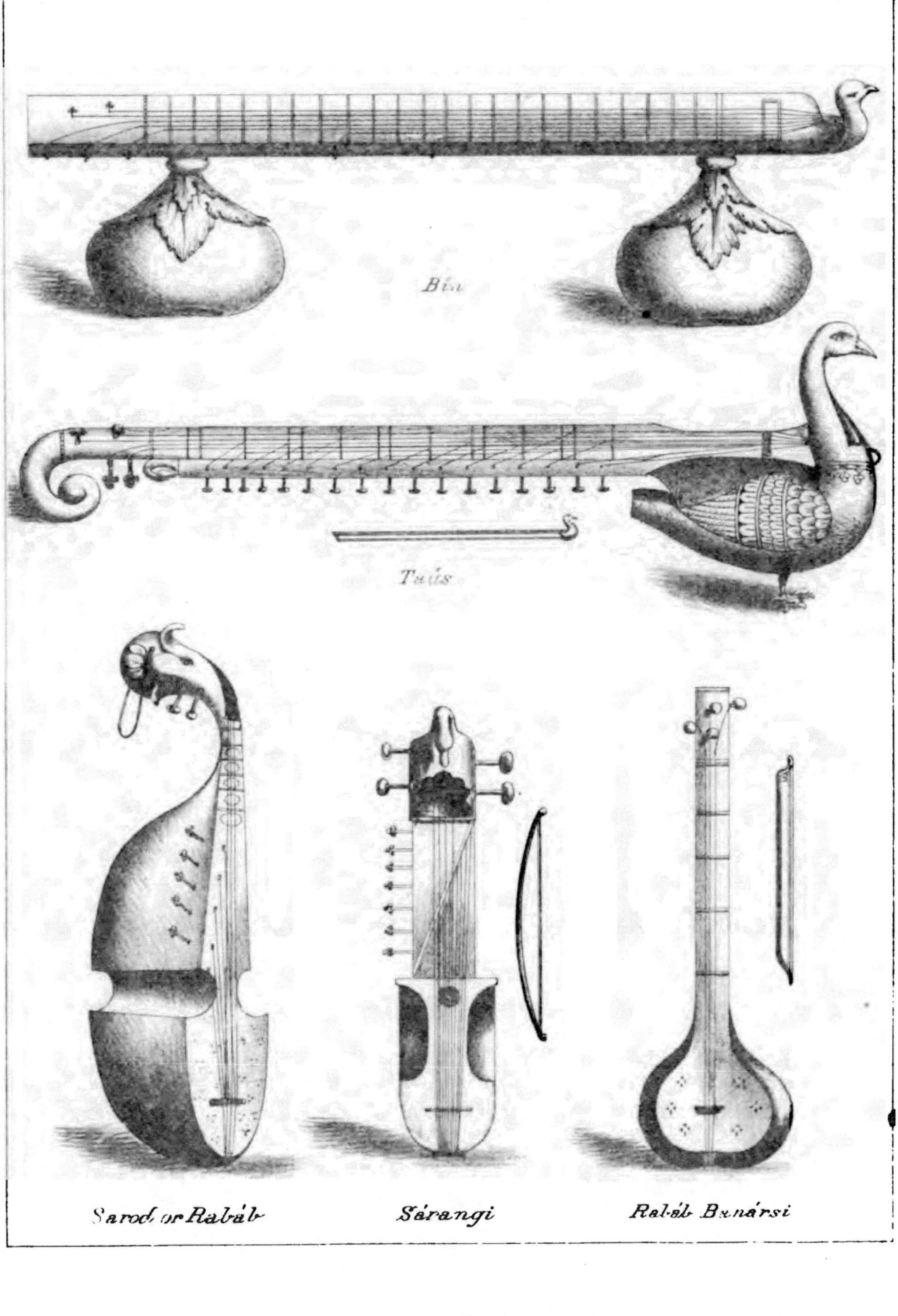
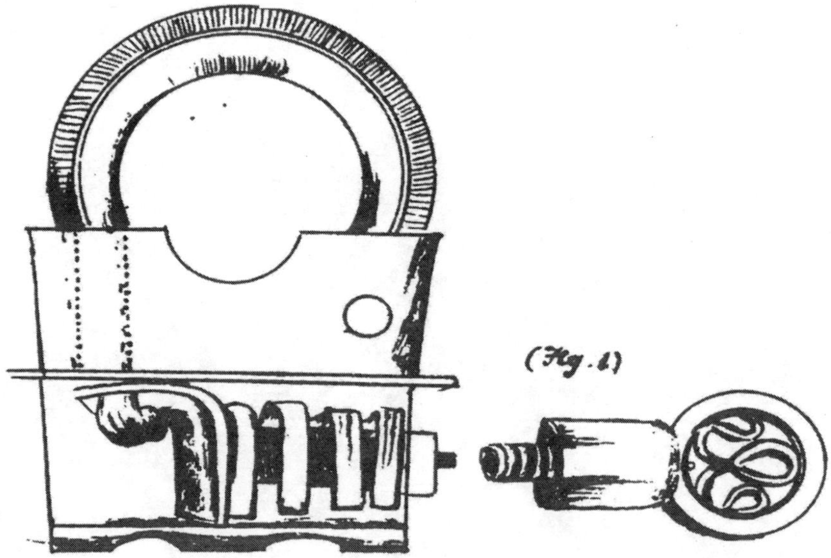

Key (half size)

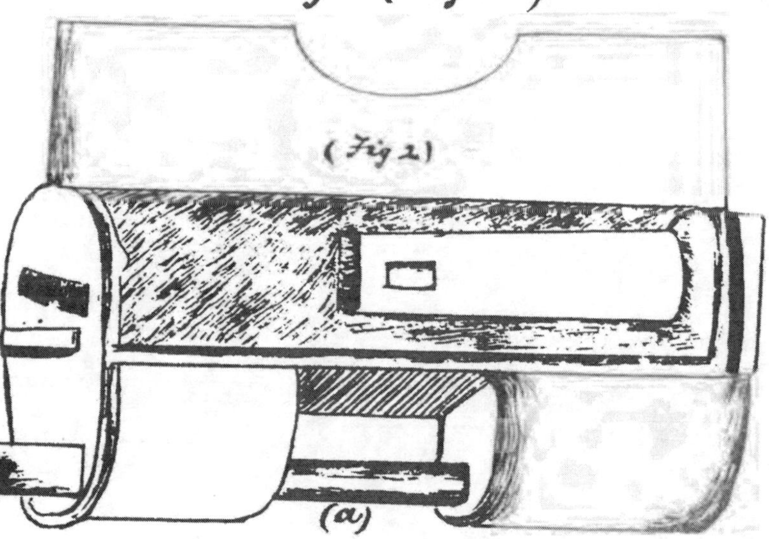

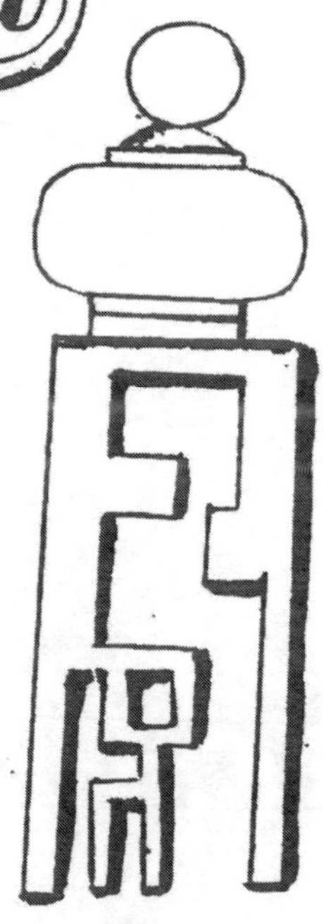

Fig 3

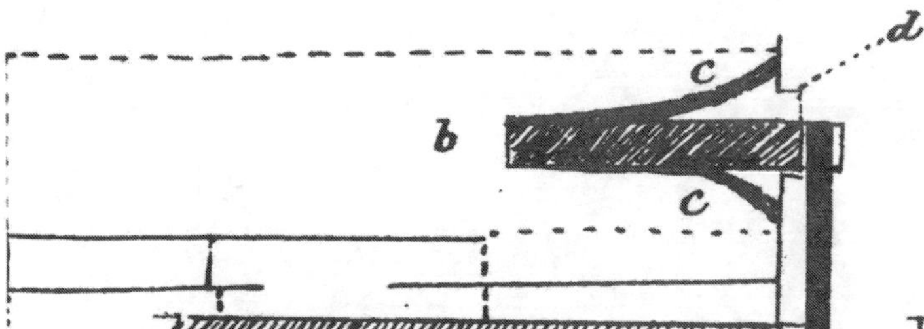

Shut.

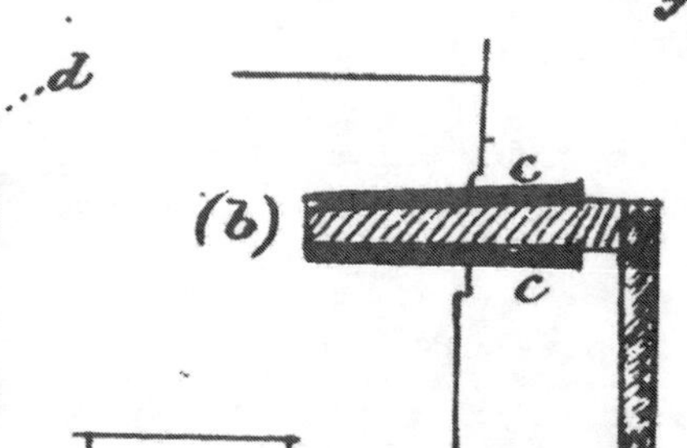

Open

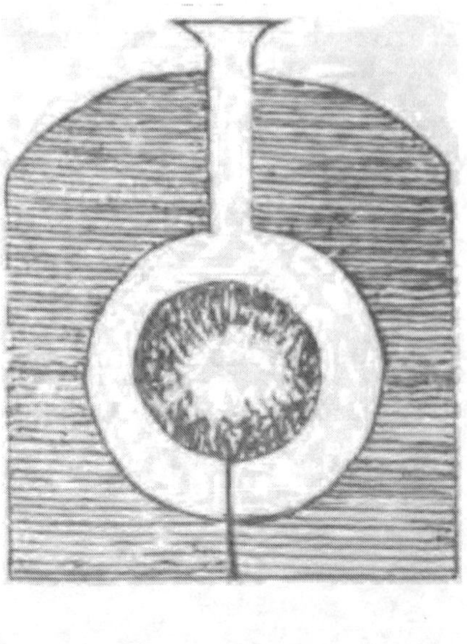

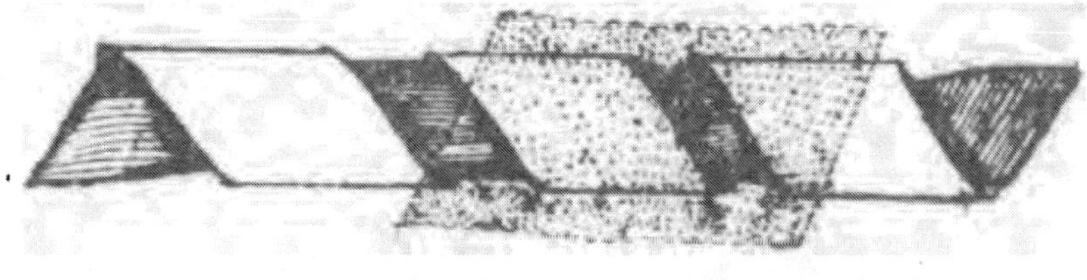

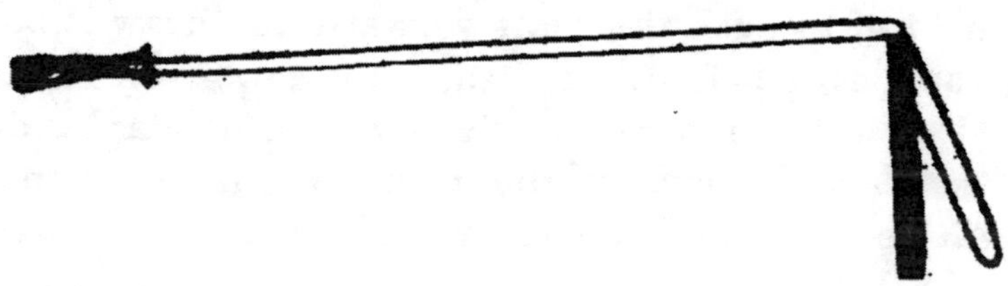

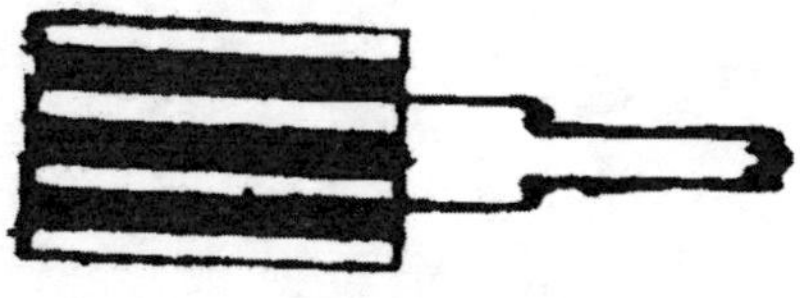

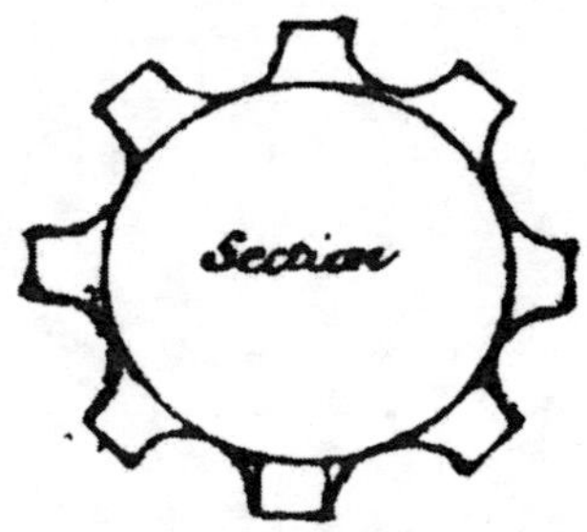

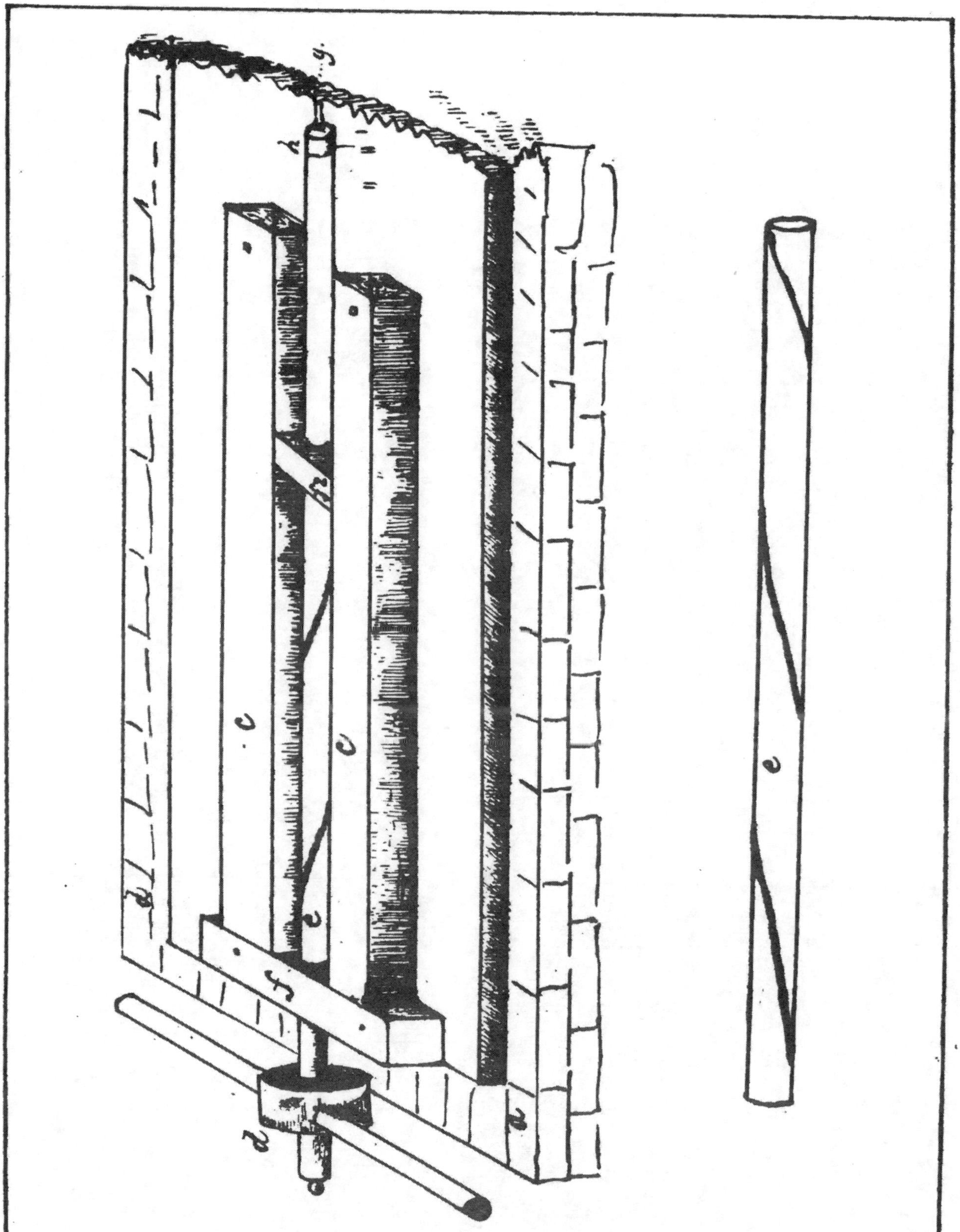

to illustrate rifle boring

(p. 380)

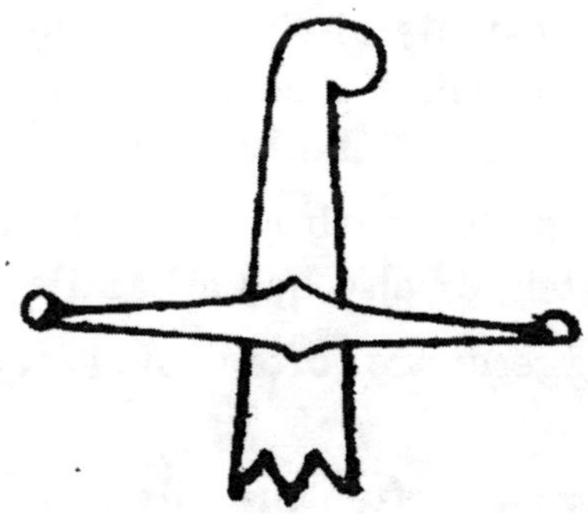

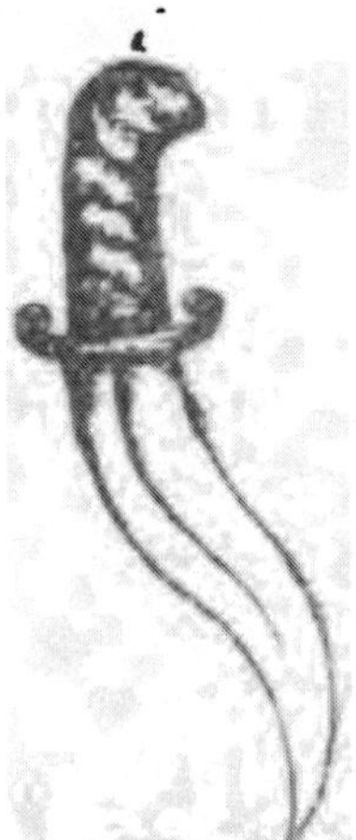

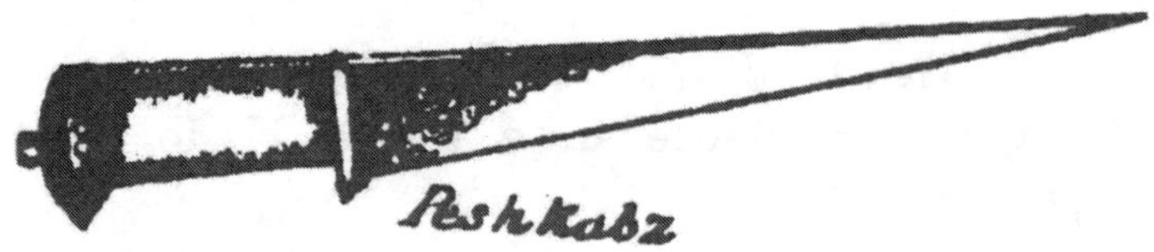

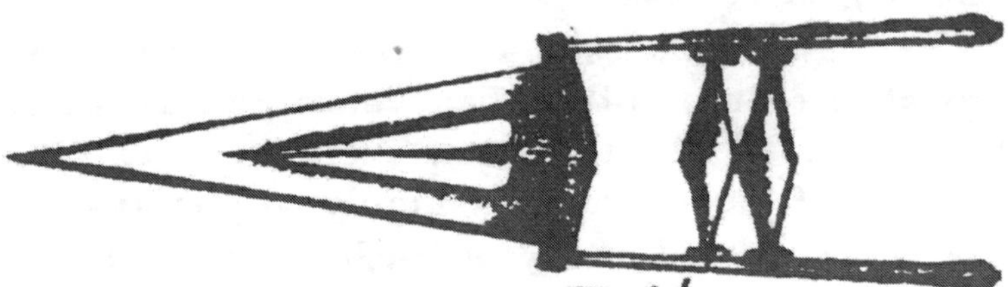

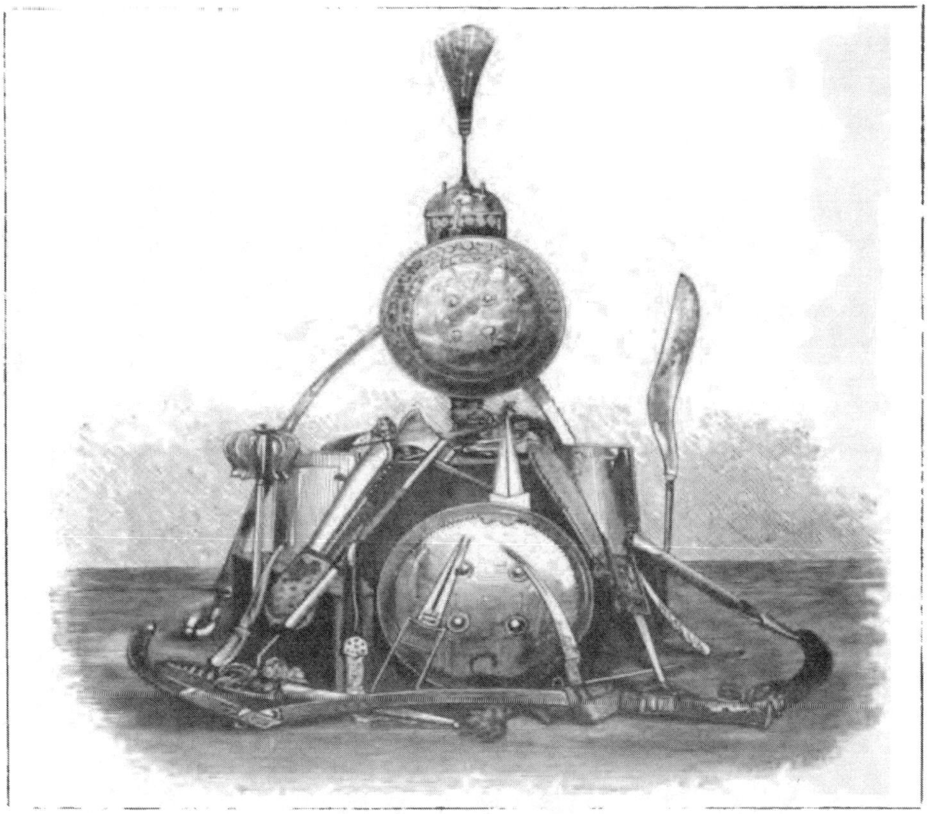

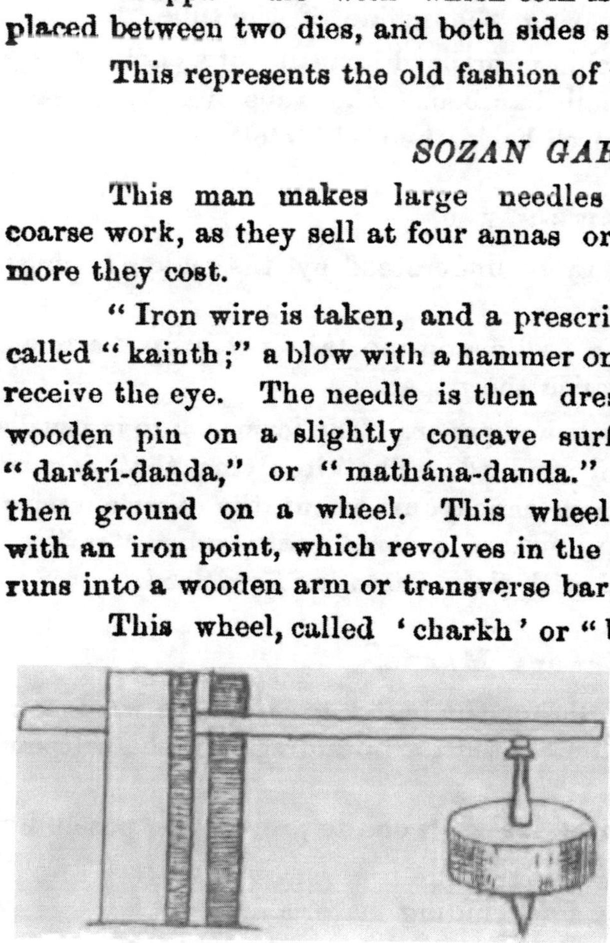

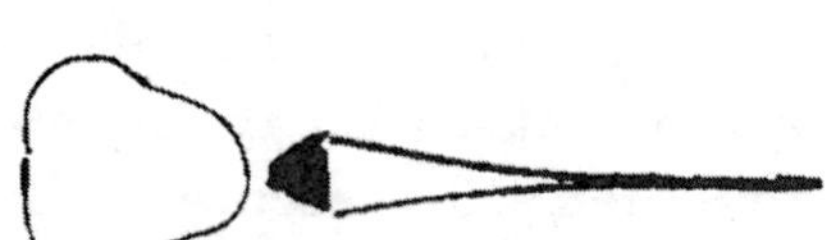

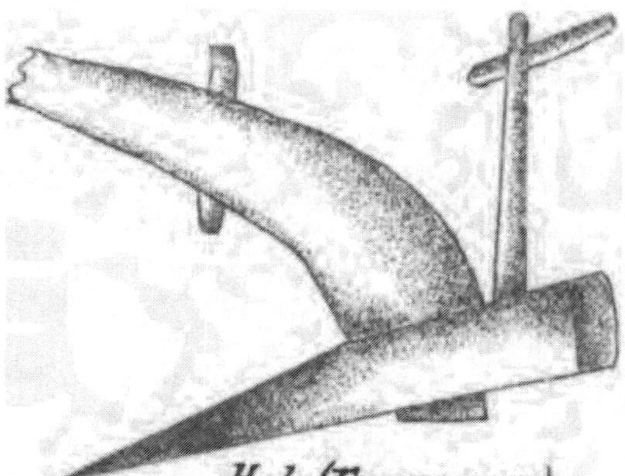

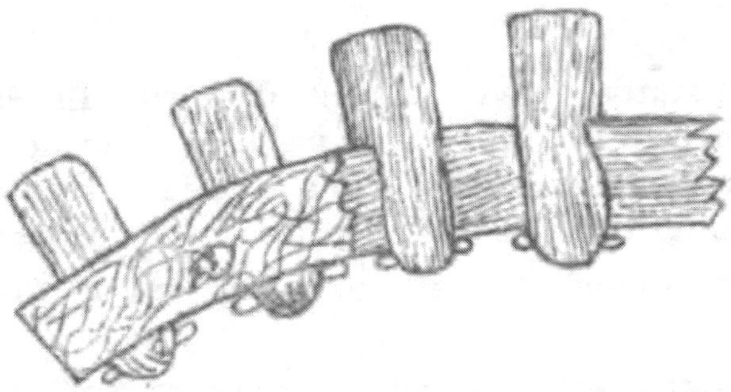

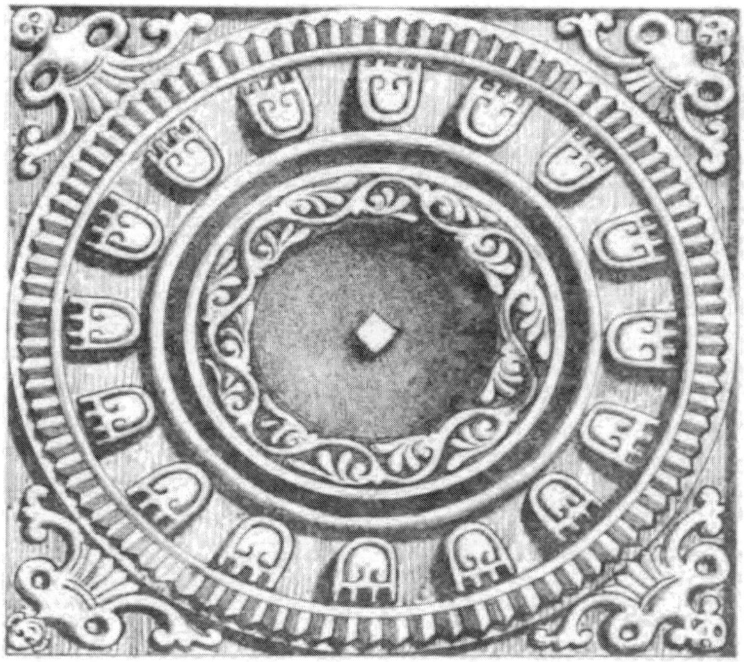

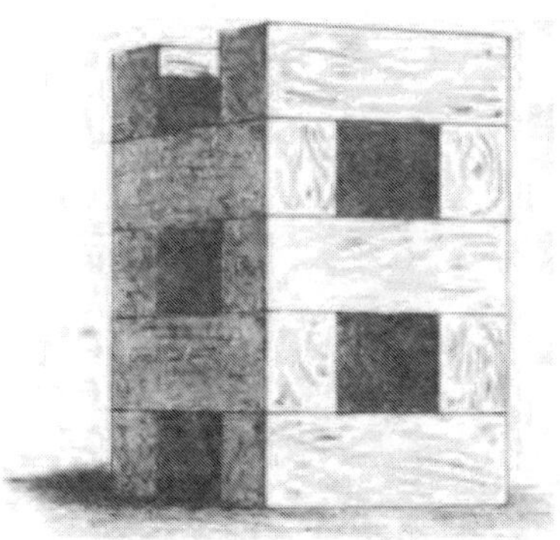

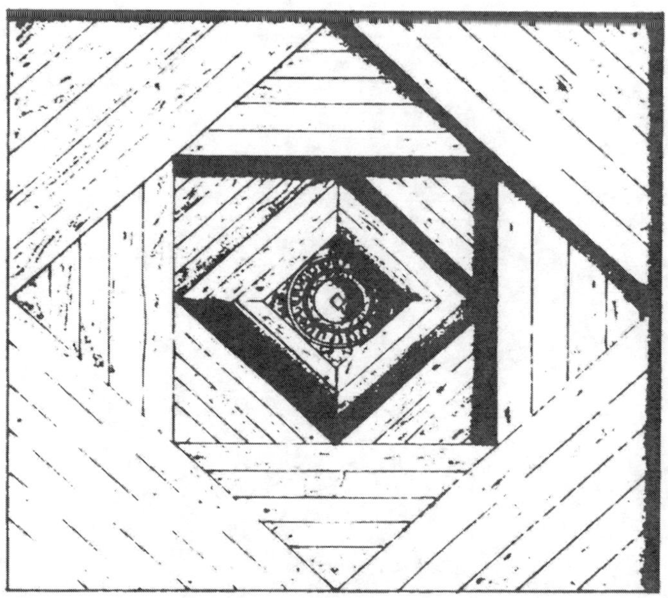

ENGLISH INDEX.

A.

B.

C.

G.

H.

I.

J.

H.

M.